The Ethics of Conceptualization

The Ethics of Conceptualization

Tailoring Thought and Language to Need

MATTHIEU QUELOZ

OXFORD
UNIVERSITY PRESS

Great Clarendon Street, Oxford, OX2 6DP,
United Kingdom

Oxford University Press is a department of the University of Oxford.
It furthers the University's objective of excellence in research, scholarship,
and education by publishing worldwide. Oxford is a registered trade mark of
Oxford University Press in the UK and in certain other countries

© Matthieu Queloz 2025

The moral rights of the author have been asserted

This is an open access publication, available online and distributed under the
terms of a Creative Commons Attribution-Non Commercial-No Derivatives 4.0
International licence (CC BY-NC-ND 4.0), a copy of which is available at
https://creativecommons.org/licenses/by-nc-nd/4.0/.
Subject to this license, all rights are reserved.

Enquiries concerning reproduction outside the scope of this licence should be sent
to the Rights Department, Oxford University Press, at the address above.

Published in the United States of America by Oxford University Press
198 Madison Avenue, New York, NY 10016, United States of America

British Library Cataloguing in Publication Data
Data available

Library of Congress Control Number: 2024946573

ISBN 9780198926252

DOI: 10.1093/9780198926283.001.0001

Printed and bound in the UK by
Clays Ltd, Elcograf S.p.A.

The pre-press of this publication was supported by the Swiss National Science Foundation.

Links to third party websites are provided by Oxford in good faith and
for information only. Oxford disclaims any responsibility for the materials
contained in any third party website referenced in this work.

The manufacturer's authorised representative in the EU for product safety is
Oxford University Press España S.A. of El Parque Empresarial San Fernando de Henares,
Avenida de Castilla, 2 – 28830 Madrid (www.oup.es/en or product.safety@oup.com).
OUP España S.A. also acts as importer into Spain of products made by the manufacturer.

For Julia

Contents

Acknowledgements   xi

    Introduction: Appraising Concepts   1

I. RAISING THE AUTHORITY QUESTION

1. The Authority Question   31
   - 1.1 Dworkin's Challenge   31
   - 1.2 The Power of Conceptual Architectures   34
   - 1.3 Expressing the Authority Question   43
   - 1.4 When the Authority Question Arises   47
   - 1.5 Beyond Epistemological Appraisal   53

2. The Autoethnographic Stance   60
   - 2.1 Engaged vs. Disengaged Concept Use   60
   - 2.2 The Ethnographic Stance   62
   - 2.3 The Autoethnographic Stance   65
   - 2.4 Conflating Engaged and Disengaged Use   70
   - 2.5 Concepts: Their Nature and Possession   75

3. Confidence, Reflection, and Knowledge   84
   - 3.1 Understanding Concept Loss   84
   - 3.2 Confidence in Concepts   85
   - 3.3 Metaconceptual Reflection   90
   - 3.4 Knowledge under Concepts   100
   - 3.5 Metaconceptual Knowledge   108

II. LEARNING FROM EXISTING ANSWERS

4. Anchoring Authority: A Trilemma   113
   - 4.1 Generalized Foundationalism   113
   - 4.2 Indiscriminate Ironism   118
   - 4.3 Reasons for Us: Non-Foundationalism   122
   - 4.4 Undiscriminating Holism   127
   - 4.5 The Kaleidoscopic Picture   132
   - 4.6 Leveraging Local Needs   135

5. Tidy-Mindedness ... 144
  5.1 Theoretical Vices in Concepts ... 146
  5.2 Superficial Concepts ... 148
  5.3 Conceptual Tensions ... 152
  5.4 Authority through Theoretical Virtue ... 164
  5.5 Inheriting Authority from Theories ... 169

III. HOW TO ANSWER THE AUTHORITY QUESTION

6. Concepts and Concerns ... 181
  6.1 The Dworkin–Williams Debate ... 181
  6.2 Tethering Concepts to Concerns ... 193
  6.3 The Practical Virtues of Theoretical Vices ... 201
  6.4 The Limits of Concerns: Four Problems ... 208

7. Conceptual Needs ... 213
  7.1 The Needs behind Concepts ... 213
  7.2 Needfulness Conditions ... 219
  7.3 What Concepts Express ... 223
  7.4 Need Matrices ... 230
  7.5 Needs-Based Concept Appraisal ... 233
  7.6 Four Problems Solved ... 248

8. Reasons for Reasons ... 255
  8.1 Reasons in vs. Reasons for Concept Use ... 255
  8.2 Concern-Independent Reasons in Concept Use ... 260
  8.3 Instrumentality without Instrumental Mentality ... 264
  8.4 From Concerns to Reasons in Concept Use ... 268
  8.5 Needs-Based Conceptual Authority ... 273
  8.6 The Wrong Kind of Reasons? ... 285
  8.7 Conceptual Good-for-Nothings ... 300

IV. ANSWERING THE AUTHORITY QUESTION

9. The Essential Superficiality of the Voluntary ... 307
  9.1 A Questionable Concept ... 307
  9.2 Making Sense and Knowing What to Expect ... 312
  9.3 Fairness and Freedom ... 320
  9.4 Knowledge and Coercion ... 323
  9.5 When Concerns Distort Conceptualization ... 327
  9.6 Deep Conceptions of the Voluntary ... 329
  9.7 Free Will as a Dual Problem ... 332

10. The Politics of Conflicting Concerns   343
    10.1 Political Disagreement and Its Demands   343
    10.2 The Dworkin–Williams Debate Continued   346
    10.3 A Thoroughly Political Conception of Liberty   349
    10.4 Conceptual Needs on the Losing Side   351
    10.5 Conceptual Needs on the Winning Side   355
    10.6 Placing the Demand for Theoretical Virtues   362

    Conclusion: Tailoring Thought to Need   376

Bibliography   381
Index   419

Acknowledgements

Some of the ideas presented in this book were first tested in the form of journal articles, and I am grateful to the publishers for permission to draw on reworked excerpts from the following articles: 'Function-Based Conceptual Engineering and the Authority Problem', *Mind* 131.524 (2022): 1247–78, by permission of Oxford University Press. Copyright © 2022. 'The Dworkin-Williams Debate: Liberty, Conceptual Integrity, and Tragic Conflict in Politics', *Philosophy and Phenomenological Research*, 109. 1 (2024): 3–29, by permission of Wiley-Blackwell. Copyright © 2023. 'The Essential Superficiality of the Voluntary and the Moralization of Psychology', *Philosophical Studies* 179.5 (2022): 1591–1620, by permission of Springer Nature. Copyright © 2021.

To a lesser extent, I have also incorporated revised excerpts from 'Nietzsche's Conceptual Ethics', *Inquiry* 6.7 (2023): 1335–64, by permission of Taylor and Francis. Copyright © 2023. 'Debunking Concepts', *Midwest Studies in Philosophy* 47.1 (2023): 195–225, by permission of the Philosophy Documentation Center. Copyright © 2023. I am grateful to the editors and anonymous reviewers who helped me improve and refine this material on the path to publication. The epigraphs hail from Ludwig Wittgenstein (2005), *The Big Typescript*, edited by C. Grant Luckhardt and Maximilian A. E. Aue (Oxford: Blackwell); and Justus Buchler (1955), *Nature and Judgment* (New York: Columbia University Press).

Several people read the entire manuscript and offered detailed comments at various stages: Claus Beisbart, Damian Cueni, Julia Eckert, Mümün Gencoglu, Hanjo Glock, Céline Henne, Steffen Koch, Sebastian Köhler, Jennifer Nado, Christian Nimtz, Matteo Santarelli, Paul Sagar, Markus Stepanians, and Amie Thomasson. Their generous help and encouragement have been invaluable. Two readers for OUP, one of whom turned out to be Nicholas Smyth, wrote immensely thoughtful and constructive reports that improved the book considerably. Heartfelt thanks to my editor, Peter Momtchiloff, for securing such helpful comments and for his trust throughout this process, and to April Peake, Imogene Haslam, and Layla Huber for their advice and support in seeing the book through to publication.

I was able to write this book thanks to the generous support of the Swiss National Science Foundation, which also enabled its open access publication.

xii ACKNOWLEDGEMENTS

Wolfson College, Oxford and the Institute of Philosophy at the University of Bern provided marvellously welcoming and stimulating environments in which to write it. I am grateful to both institutions.

The book benefited from being the subject of a three-day masterclass at the University of Bielefeld and from numerous discussions in colloquia at the University of Bern. Some material was also presented at the Universities of Oxford, Princeton, Cambridge, Hong Kong, Southampton, Lund, Warwick, Bologna, Manchester, Neuchâtel, Vienna, Nottingham, Utrecht, as well as the Central European University, the Philosophy Mountain Workshop, and the 9th International Lauener Symposium on Analytical Philosophy. I am indebted to the many people whose comments improved the manuscript on these and other occasions. They include Marcel van Ackeren, Colin Allen, Tessa Ditner Amorosi, Yuval Avnur, Christian Barth, Jan Pieter Beetz, Stephen Bero, Jessica Berry, Monika Betzler, Friedemann Bieber, Hanno Birken-Bertsch, Simon Blackburn, Charlie Blunden, Alex Bonham, Yves Bossart, Caroline Brall, Georg Brun, Herman Cappelen, Jim Chamberlain, Joseph Chan, Simon-Pierre Chevarie-Cossette, Matthew Congdon, João Constâncio, Kaitlyn Creasy, Andreas Cremonini, Joe Cunningham, Sophia Dandelet, Benjamin De Mesel, Max Deutsch, Iris van Domselaar, Manuel Dries, Catarina Dutilh Novaes, Matthias Egg, Nina Emery, Anton Emilsson, David Enoch, Dagfinn Føllesdal, Christopher Fowles, Michael Frauchiger, Andreas Freivogel, Miranda Fricker, Ken Gemes, Adam Gibbons, Anna Goppel, Alexander Greenberg, Michael Hannon, Céline Henne, Ulrike Heuer, Vera Hoffmann-Kolss, David Hommen, Yvonne Hütter-Almerigi, Pablo Hubacher-Haerle, Andrew Huddleston, Rebekka Hufendiek, Tim Huttel, Manuel Gustavo Isaac, Christopher Janaway, Scott Jenkins, Sigurd Jorem, Ronaldo Porto Macedo Jr, Peter Kail, Paul Katsafanas, Richard King, Claire Kirwin, Nikhil Krishnan, Kathrin Koslicki, Martin Kusch, Vincent Lam, Thomas Lambert, Benedict Lane, Gerald Lang, Brian Leiter, Muriel Leuenberger, Guido Löhr, Béatrice Lienemann, David Liggins, Guy Longworth, Daniele Lorenzini, Jörg Löschke, Constantin Luft, Lilith Mace, Douglas MacLean, Berislav Marušić, Jane Manners, Olivier Massin, Vera Matarese, Simon May, Brian McElwee, Matthew McKeever, Denis McManus, Michel Meliopoulos, Deborah Mühlebach, Mark Migotti, Cheryl Misak, Andreas Müller, Basil Müller, Nico Müller, Jan-Werner Müller, Adrian Moore, Daniel Peixoto Murata, Lukas Naegeli, Angie O'Sullivan, David Owen, Philip Pettit, David Plunkett, Milo Poertzgen, Alexander Prescott-Couch, Huw Price, Janosch Prinz, Jonas Raab, Julieta Rabanos, Nicole Rathgeb, Erich Reck, Bernard

Reginster, Mattia Riccardi, John Richardson, Jared Riggs, Veronica Rodriguez-Blanco, Suzanne Roes, Matthias Rolffs, Paul Roth, Paul Russell, Tim Räz, Paul Sagar, Livia von Samson, Constantine Sandis, Matteo Santarelli, Raul Saucedo, Sarah Sawyer, Tim Scanlon, Krystina Schaub, Samuel Scheffler, Jelscha Schmid, Sandra Shapshay, Matthew Shields, Paul Showler, Mona Simion, Neil Sinclair, Avery Snelson, Katja Stepec, Timothy Stoll, Anders Sydskjør, Francesco Testini, Gudrun von Tevenar, Michael Thorne, Christopher Tollefsen, Samuel Tscharner, Paul Tucker, Marcel Twele, Alexander Velichkov, David Velleman, Tullio Viola, Benedict Vischer, Emmanuel Voyiakis, Verena Wagner, Victor Braga Weber, Jonas Werner, Oscar Westerblad, Emily Kidd White, Daniel Whiting, Markus Wild, Patricia Williams, Susan Wolf, Seth Yalcin, Vida Yao, Jason Yonover, Bettina Zimmermann, Benjamin Zipursky, and Aneta Zuber.

Above all, I thank my friends and family for their loving support, *sine qua non*. This one is for Julia.

M. Q.

Basel
June 2024

It is one thing to justify a thought on the basis of other thoughts—something else to justify thinking.
>
> Ludwig Wittgenstein, *The Big Typescript*, 180

The responsible introduction or extension of terms, whether in philosophy or science, reflects a conceptual need.
>
> Justus Buchler, *Nature and Judgment*, 108

Introduction: Appraising Concepts

While much philosophy strives to give us a firmer hold on our concepts, we sometimes also find ourselves questioning their hold on us: why should we place ourselves under their sway and grant them the authority to shape our thought and conduct?[1] The concepts we use render us sensitive to the reasons that guide and flow from their application. But what reasons do we have to heed those reasons in the first place? If our thoughts were cast in different terms, they would advert to different reasons, carry different implications, and set us on different trajectories. Concepts may be immutable, but our conceptualizations are not. By changing our conceptualizations—the ways of thinking and valuing in virtue of which we possess the concepts we do—we can change *which* concepts we use. Do the concepts we currently use merit the confidence with which we draw on them? What makes one concept better than another?

The question matters, because not every issue, in philosophy or elsewhere, consists simply in figuring out what is true or what is justified given the way we conceptualize things. Many issues are, at least in part, about how to conceptualize things—how to carve things up, how to characterize them, and what significance to attach to them. People can form perfectly true and justified judgements and nonetheless attract criticism for the very terms in which they think.

Questioning the terms in which we think goes to the root of our thinking processes, for while the judgements we form might be criticized as false or unwarranted, these criticisms still take for granted the conceptual framework within which those judgements are articulated. By contrast, appraising the concepts we use goes one step further, asking whether things might not go better if we used different concepts that put alternative sets of judgements and

---

[1] The question is significantly different from the Kantian, semantic concern to understand how concept application can be liable to assessments of correctness that Robert Brandom, drawing a *prima facie* similar chiastic contrast, sees as replacing the Cartesian, epistemological concern with whether our ideas are clear and distinct: 'For Kant the question is . . . how to understand [concepts'] grip on us: the conditions of the intelligibility of our being bound by conceptual norms' (2009, 33); see also Brandom (1994, 9–11; 2000, 80; 2002a, 22; 2019b, 9). My question is not *how any* concepts can bind us, but *why these* concepts rather than others should be allowed to.

patterns of justification within our reach. Adopting a concept opens up an entire new pattern of reasoning to us. Abandoning the concept closes it off. We might find mistakes in the way a computer executes the rules it operates by, or malfunctions in the way a smartphone runs its apps, but the deeper critique is the one that appraises the very rules the computer attempts to apply, or the very apps the smartphone seeks to run. Analogously, our conceptualizations can fruitfully be regarded as pieces of mindware, encoding certain ways of thinking by scripting appropriate patterns of thought.[2] To ask which concepts we should use is to ask what mindware society should run on.

It is this demand for reasons to cast our thoughts in certain terms rather than others that forms my topic in this book. The concepts we use determine what we recognize as a reason for what, but these tend to be reasons for belief and reasons for action. What about *reasons for concept use*? Are there reasons for us to conceptualize things in certain ways rather than others?

Reasons for concept use would have to be distinct from reasons for belief or reasons for action. They would have to be reasons to cultivate the dispositions to treat certain types of consideration *as* reasons for belief or reasons for action. Instead of *justifying* individual beliefs or actions directly, they would *vindicate* our confidence in certain concepts.[3] And instead of being *first-order* reasons operating at the same level as the ordinary reasons our concepts advert to, they would be *second-order* reasons to use certain concepts and be responsive to the concomitant first-order reasons. In other words, reasons for concept use would be *reasons for reasons*.

Concepts alone are not, strictly speaking, reasons—the entire thoughts built from concepts are. But in discovering reasons to construct our thoughts using some concepts rather than others, we identify reasons to *treat* certain considerations *as* reasons. Speaking of 'reasons for reasons' is thus a useful shorthand. It highlights that what reasons for belief and action we are responsive to is a function of what concepts we use. If concepts are the building-blocks of thoughts, this makes them the building-blocks of reasons, and which building-blocks are available to reasoners determines which reasons

---

[2] I take the term 'mindware' from Clark (2013), though it also figures prominently in Nisbett (2015). A closely related metaphor is J. M. Balkin's (1998) notion of 'cultural software', which in turn echoes Clifford Geertz's notion of 'cultural templates' (1973a, 217–18).

[3] This distinction between justification and vindication is meant to be a technical one, inspired by Williams's (2002, 283 n. 19) usage of the term 'vindication'. This usage, which Testini (2024) traces to Feigl (1981a, b), does not purport to align with the nuance in ordinary language whereby we reserve the term 'vindication' for cases in which someone is cleared of blame or suspicion, or in which an agent's struggle to realize a goal results in an outcome that gives the agent reason to affirm the choices that led to the outcome. For a rich exploration of vindication in this latter sense, see Owen (forthcoming).

they can respond to. This remains true even if one locates the reason-giving aspect of thoughts not in the *thinking* of them, but in *what is thought*—in facts or putative facts—since even putative facts remain conceptually articulated, and which facts can figure in our reasoning remains a function of our concepts. With the adoption or abandonment of one concept, an entire currency of reasons might enter or disappear from circulation. To demand reasons for reasons is to ask why one should trade in a given currency of reasons at all.

Since our conceptual repertoire is a motley mixture of thinking techniques that vary widely in how they work and what purposes they serve, some concepts are more liable than others to invite demands for reasons to prefer them over alternatives. Among the concepts that are especially liable to do so are the concepts I shall focus on in this book, which are the concepts that unite the following three features: they are *world-guided*, meaning that their application is closely guided by how the world is rather than by our will; they are *action-guiding*, meaning that their applicability typically gives us reasons for action; and they are culturally *local* rather than universal, meaning that they compete with alternative concepts, real and imagined, for a role in shaping our lives.

Concepts combining these gradable features to any considerable degree are sometimes called 'thick' normative concepts.[4] The concepts *blasphemy, chivalry, saintliness,* or *lese-majesty* are examples; so, to take more recent additions to the conceptual repertoire, are *genocide, gaslighting, mansplaining,* or *himpathy*. These concepts are 'thick' because they are thickly descriptive—they have a higher descriptive content than thinner ones like *rational, good,* or *right* (if all one is told about *x* is that *x* was *disloyal* or *cowardly*, one still has a far more determinate idea of what *x* is and what happened than if told only that *x* was *bad* or *wrong*). But these concepts are also 'normative' in that they do more than describe or pick out things. As Bernard Williams notes, 'what your repertoire of thick concepts is reveals your own or your society's ethical attitude' (1995l, 237), because to think in terms of concepts like *kitsch, sacrilegious, chaste,* or *unpatriotic* is not just to be sensitive to the presence of things that fall under these concepts, but to cast these things in a certain

---

[4] The notion of a thick concept and the world-guided/action-guiding terminology is associated notably with Bernard Williams (1985, 143–5), who is indebted in this connection to Wittgensteinian ideas developed by Philippa Foot and Iris Murdoch in a seminar they convened with Basil Mitchell in the early summer of 1954 (Williams 1985, 263 n. 7), and with Clifford Geertz's (1973b, 6) advocacy of 'thick descriptions' in anthropology. Geertz in turn borrowed the phrase from Gilbert Ryle (2009c, 489; 2009d, 497). As Lipscomb (2021) indicates, G. E. M. Anscombe and R. M. Hare also played underappreciated roles in the renewal of interest in thick concepts.

evaluative light. That in turn makes a difference to what attitudes one has reason to adopt towards these things, and, ultimately, to what one has reason to do.

This action-guiding import of certain concepts is something we overlook if we appraise concepts merely according to whether they match up with an antecedently articulated world.[5] On Theodore Sider's account, for example, if a community has true and warranted beliefs but nonetheless has 'the wrong concepts', this must be because these concepts do not match the world's 'structure' (2011, 2). But Sider primarily has the concepts of fundamental physics in mind. One's willingness to extend this approach to thick normative concepts will depend on whether one regards the 'structure' corresponding to thick normative concepts as sufficiently independent of those concepts to form a robust basis for their appraisal.

Irrespective of these metaphysical issues, however, there is a more basic reason to look beyond the referential dimension of concepts when appraising them: as Nietzsche notes, concepts do more than just turn the intellect into a pure mirror of the world.[6] There may be a sense in which concepts are 'representational devices', as the conceptual engineering literature tends to describe them; but if so, they do more than represent.[7] To take the full measure of a concept, we have to consider also what happens downstream of its application. What further reasons follow in the wake of the recognition that we have reasons to apply it? What does its applicability imply?[8] A concept remains an empty label to its users unless it 'locates its object in a space of implications',

---

[5] This dimension of evaluation is foregrounded notably in Hirsch (1993, 2013), Campbell, O'Rourke, and Slater (2011), Sider (2011), Cappelen (2013), Sawyer (2020a, c). It also features prominently in Gupta (2019).

[6] 'What if the intellect were a pure mirror? But concepts are more than that' (70:8[41]). I follow Richardson (2020) in citing Nietzsche's *Nachlass* (2009a) by the last two digits of the year of the notebook in which the note occurs, followed by a colon, followed by the notebook number, followed by the note number in square brackets. Translations of Nietzsche's texts are my own throughout, though I have consulted translations where available, and amended them only to bring them closer to the original.

[7] A phrase popularized by Cappelen (2018, 3); in his usage, it allows for the fact that representational devices can act as expressive devices, however. But Mona Simion articulates the literature's focus on the representational dimension when she writes: 'Concepts, just like beliefs, are representational devices, their function is an epistemic one: to represent the world' (2018, 923).

[8] This two-faced model of the articulation of concepts that includes the consequences as well as the conditions of their application goes back to Michael Dummett's (1973, 434) generalization of Gerhard Gentzen's work on sentential connectives, and figures centrally in the work of conceptual role theorists and inferentialists (Peacocke 1992, Brandom 1994, 2000, Boghossian 2003, Wedgwood 2007, Brandom 2008, Kukla and Lance 2009). More recently, Jorem and Löhr (2024) have stressed the importance of consequences of concept application for conceptual engineering. I shall speak of 'application conditions' throughout, even though Gentzen's phrase, 'introduction rules', is more apt for concepts such as connectives.

in Wilfrid Sellars's phrase.[9] If the concept *F* were like an app that pinged when and only when presented with an *F*, the ping would be devoid of any significance for us unless we could infer something from it.

A concept's merits therefore depend not just on whether anything corresponds to it in the world we inhabit, but also on what *follows* from its correct application, because that is what renders concepts, in the most literal sense, *consequential*: it is the primary way in which concepts make a difference to the rest of our thought and conduct. Two concepts that pick out the same set of objects, but associate it with radically different implications, are likely to differ also in their value to us.

Given my focus on how our patterns of reasoning are affected by our choices of concepts, I will put special emphasis on concepts' role in reasoning. But I do not mean to take sides in the debate between inferentialists and referentialists over whether the inferential pattern associated with a concept should be regarded as directly constitutive of a concept's content or only indirectly connected to it. Nothing I say presupposes that we *identify* the content of a concept with its inferential role. The thought is only that we should *also* consider a concept's inferential role, and not just its referent. This is a point widely registered in *dual content* theories, which propose, in a conciliatory spirit, to think of a concept as having both referential content, which determines the concept's extension, and inferential or cognitive content, which determines the concept's role in classification, reasoning, and the drawing of inferential consequences.[10] But all I require, really, is an assumption that each of these metasemantic theories can accommodate in its own way, namely that *which* concepts we actually possess systematically *co-varies* with the inferences we think we can appropriately draw.

Concept appraisal should accordingly be sensitive to the reason-giving as well as to the reason-guided aspects of concept use, because a concept's merits notably depend on what follows from its correct application. Certainly, it is only once we take these inferential consequences into account that we stand a chance of appreciating the effects concepts have even further downstream of their application, *via* their inferential consequences: the expressive functions they thereby discharge, for instance, or the needs they meet, or the concerns they promote.[11] A reasonably comprehensive picture of the respective merits

---

[9] See Sellars (1958, §108).
[10] See Marconi (1997) and Koch (2021) for notably ecumenical accounts that support this conclusion while accommodating both inferentialist and referentialist views within dual content theories.
[11] For a battery of arguments as to why we should look beyond reference when thinking about moral concepts, see Sinclair (2018).

of living by different concepts should encompass their wider impact on human affairs, and be sensitive to what concepts do for us *by* enabling us to refer to certain things.

This is especially true of thick normative concepts. For once people structure their affairs in terms of such world-guided concepts and become responsive to the action-guiding reasons they advert to, the concepts can end up closely dictating what people should do. Iris Murdoch evocatively calls this 'the siege of the individual by concepts' (2013, 31): if the applicability of those concepts is conclusively determined by empirical observation while their normative implications are non-negotiable because built into the concepts, this can leave one feeling beleaguered by the concepts one uses, bereft of any room to reasonably dispute that they apply or that their applicability has certain normative implications.[12] It is therefore with conceptualizations in terms of thick normative concepts that the mindware metaphor has most purchase—they really are codes of conduct, tightly linking certain worldly inputs to certain normative outputs.

The fact that thick normative concepts incontrovertibly link empirical conditions to normative consequences makes them effective tools of influence. This helps explain why authoritarian governments tend to take an interest not just in the conclusions their citizens reach, but also in the concepts they address questions with. It is, for instance, perennially tempting for authoritarian governments to promulgate thick conceptualizations of *legitimacy* such that, for citizens who live under those governments, the only reasonable conclusion to be drawn is that their government is legitimate. And this is but a particularly significant example of a wider phenomenon that has led a string of observers to note the political dimension of questions of conceptualization or definition: 'to choose a definition is to plead a cause' (Stevenson 1944, 210); 'disputes over appropriate definitions are thus political conflicts' (Sederberg 1984, 94); 'definitions are a form of advocacy' (Chesebro 1985, 14); 'the choice of definitions is always political' (Schiappa 2003, 68); 'definition is a political act' (Haslanger 2014, 33).[13]

---

[12] Whether one accepts this of course depends on how one analyses thick concepts; see Roberts (2013), Väyrynen (2013), and Eklund (2017, 88–93, 168–91) for discussions of the various analyses on offer. I follow Williams (1985, 1995p, l, j, n, 2005g, 2021) in my understanding of thick concepts.

[13] 'Definitions' have variously been understood as being primarily of things (real definition), of words (nominal definition), or of concepts (conceptual definition): roughly, Aristotle prioritized real definition, Locke nominal definition, and Kant conceptual definition; Robinson (1954, 1–11), Cargile (1991). On any of these three emphases, however, definitions affect which concepts we use, thereby potentially carrying ethical and political significance; on this last point, see also McConnell-Ginet (2006) and Mühlebach (2019, 2021, 2022).

Of course, the amount of influence achievable merely by disseminating certain concepts is easily overstated. Edward Bernays (1969) and other pioneers of propaganda and public relations may have claimed to possess the power to 'engineer the consent of the governed', but engineering consent by tampering with the concepts people use has turned out to be a great deal harder than they initially made it sound.[14] Recent advances in digital technologies have rekindled concerns on this front, as they seem to make it unprecedentedly easy to shape how people think by filtering what they see.[15] But we should be wary of claims made about the power of these technologies by those who conceive of it in the starkly simplified manner of conspiracy theories, or who have an interest in exaggerating it. Overstating the power of elites to determine how people think is, after all, a hallmark of what Richard Hofstadter (2008) called 'the paranoid style' in politics.

It may also be felt that there is a more principled problem with this concept-centric picture of manipulation: that the beliefs people eventually arrive at remain significantly underdetermined by the concepts people employ. If the aim is to instil the belief that x is F, then promulgating concept F instead of directly instilling the target belief seems to leave open the possibility of coming to the opposite conclusion, namely that x is *not F*. To manipulate which concepts people use is to remain at one remove from their beliefs, leaving people just the degree of freedom they need to frustrate efforts at manipulation.

But although it is importantly true that what beliefs we form depends on more than just on what concepts we employ, it would also be implausible to deny concepts any influence on belief formation: we should reckon with the subtle effects of *framing*, whereby the terms in which an issue is framed help predetermine the judgements reached. The concept may not quite be the message, but it does shape it. As José Bermúdez (2021) has recently argued, such 'framing effects' are pervasive; and sensitivity to framing is not necessarily irrational: what concepts we frame our thoughts in can quite properly affect what reasons we take ourselves to have. Not all reframing is fraudulent relabelling.

Again, framing effects are particularly pronounced with thick normative concepts. Just because these concepts make normative issues turn on

---

[14] For a historical overview of the birth of public relations and Bernays's role in it, see Tye (1998). On the use of propaganda to engineer consent, see Herman and Chomsky (1988), Handelman (2009), and MacLeod (2019).

[15] For a recent exploration of the idea that digital technologies can shape how we think by filtering what we see, see Susskind (2018).

empirical observations that are hard to argue with, they are particularly effective at steering people more or less inexorably towards certain beliefs. As David Wiggins points out, the features of a situation can leave users of a thick concept 'nothing else to think' but that the concept applies, and hence nothing else to think but that its normative consequences apply with it.[16]

This means that the decisive work is often done already long before the moments of deliberation and choice, by what Murdoch calls the conceptually informed 'work of attention' (2013, 36). Becoming aware of those features of a situation that our concepts equip us to see continuously and imperceptibly 'builds up structures of value around us', with the effect that, when the time to consciously make a decision arrives, 'most of the business of choosing is already over', as Murdoch puts it; one is 'compelled almost automatically by what one *can* see' (2013, 36).

And yet thick normative concepts exert their subtle influence while giving concept-users the *impression* that they are freely making up their minds. That is why the power to channel attention towards certain features of a situation, or to frame an issue by casting it in certain terms, can be a particularly surreptitious form of power. 'When the concepts we are living by work badly', Mary Midgley observes, 'they don't usually drip audibly through the ceiling or swamp the kitchen floor. They just quietly distort and obstruct our thinking' (1996, 1). That inconspicuous influence can be exploited. Promulgating a certain thick conceptualization of legitimacy instead of trying to directly instil the belief that the government is legitimate *seems* to leave open the possibility of judging that the government is not legitimate. In fact, however, the concept might be so closely world-guided in its application that one is left with 'nothing else to think' but that the government is legitimate: it clearly meets all the criteria for the application of a concept *the point of which* is to ensure that this government should meet them.[17] The promulgation of certain thick normative concepts can thus be a camouflaged attempt to manipulate beliefs.

At the same time, thick normative concepts also tend to be sociohistorically distinctive and local, in the sense that different societies can differ radically in their repertoires of thick normative concepts. For any such concept, it is

---

[16] See Wiggins (1990, 66).

[17] On the challenges involved in implementing conceptual engineering, see Jorem (2021), Thomasson (2021), and Nimtz (2024a). For a systematic discussion of the political dimension of conceptual engineering and the liberal and democratic rationales for making it challenging to implement, see Queloz and Bieber (2022); on the risk of conceptual engineering being abused, see also Ball (2020), Marques (2020), Podosky (2021), and Shields (2021b).

therefore a real question whether one needs to structure one's affairs in those terms at all. Just as we know that the smartphone could run an entirely different suite of apps, we know that we *could* think in different terms, since people have done and still do so.

This sense of alternatives, this hovering 'could', is more pronounced with thick normative concepts than with other concepts. *Thin* normative concepts, like *rational*, *good*, and *right*, for example, are far less world-guided in their application and may vary wildly in what they are concretely applied to; but at the level of the role they play in our reasoning, these thin concepts leave us less room for radical alternatives, since they seem to be concepts one is almost bound to gravitate towards by abstracting from the particulars of thicker judgements and generalizing over a variety of such judgements at once ('Are all of these different ways of going on *good*, or *right*, or *rational*?').[18] And *purely descriptive* concepts, such as those of elemental chemistry or particle physics, are even less prone to give rise to the sense that we might think radically differently. They are, on the contrary, particularly apt to invite the idea that the right set of concepts is the one that faithfully mirrors the structure of the natural world we inhabit—and that if there is only one such world, there is only one right set of corresponding concepts.

With thick normative concepts such as *chaste, sinful, chivalrous, courteous, snobbish, phoney, courageous, dishonourable, dignified, treasonous, rude, elegant, vulgar, kitsch, sublime,* or *creepy*, by contrast, the 'one world, one right set of concepts' model soon gives out. Though there is but one natural world, the social worlds we have lived in are many, and there are many more we could come to inhabit. To ask which thick ethical, political, legal, cultural, and aesthetic concepts we should use is to ask which social world we want to live in. We may be more closely guided by how the world is in applying these concepts, but we have correspondingly more freedom *not* to cast our thoughts in these particular terms at all. Thick normative concepts thus do more to predetermine the run of things than thin or descriptive concepts, while being at the same time under more pressure to assert their place against alternatives. This combination of features ensures that the thick normative concepts that

---

[18] On the lack of alternatives to thin concepts and the process of abstraction by which one arrives at them, see Williams (1985, 162) and Grönert (2016); Smyth (2020) understands the shift towards thinner concepts as driven by the idea that thin concepts have logical priority over thick ones and are better suited to the articulation of all-things-considered judgements. But see also Eklund (2017) for a thorough discussion of the intelligibility of variation even among such thin concepts and its implications for moral realism.

lend different social worlds their distinctive character render the question of their *authority* particularly apposite.

Murdoch also registers this when she adds, after highlighting the compelling force of 'what one *can* see': 'This does not imply that we are not free' (2013, 36). It implies, rather, that our freedom is exercised not only in the choices we make in view of what we *can* see, but also in our ability to determine *what* we can see. Hence the importance of making the effort to *look again*, which Murdoch illustrates with the mother-in-law who, upon realizing that her perception of her daughter-in-law as vulgar, undignified, noisy, and tiresomely juvenile may merely be a reflection of her own jealousy, puts in 'the work of attention', and discovers her daughter-in-law to be 'not vulgar but refreshingly simple, not undignified but spontaneous, not noisy but gay, not tiresomely juvenile but delightfully youthful' (2013, 17). We remain free to break old habits of thought and refocus our attention, not merely by redeploying it, but by redeploying it in different terms.[19] The freedom we have in determining how to live extends to the question of which among our concepts to apply.

At a deeper level, of course, what we can and cannot see depends not just on what concepts we apply, but on what set of concepts we live by. This is what invites the clichéd comparison of our conceptual architecture to a prison. To be imprisoned by concepts is not to be physically restrained by them, but to be limited by the fact that certain possibilities never occur to one (rather like Wittgenstein's man who finds himself imprisoned in a room because it never occurs to him that he must pull the door instead of pushing against it).[20] The concepts we possess lay down the boundaries of what makes sense to us. They can systematically blind us to certain conceptual connections and render alternative patterns of reasoning nigh-unintelligible. As Miranda Fricker points out, this can amount to a form of injustice—'hermeneutical injustice' (2007, 151)—when significant disadvantages result from a lack of certain conceptual resources, such as the concept of *sexual harassment*. But even when no injustice is immediately apparent, it is a classic philosophical trope to lament the unreflective mind's imprisonment in unreflected folkways.

Such conceptual confinement is not just a hazard of the unexamined life, moreover. Philosophers can find themselves locked in conceptual frameworks

---

[19] Sher (2021) draws on Murdoch to defend what he calls the 'freedom of the mind' against morality's tendency to police thought. On the plasticity of our 'habits of thought' and how they can be either insufficiently or overly plastic, see Delacroix (2022, 5, 10, 59–88).

[20] See Wittgenstein (1978, III, §37).

by their own theorizing. Joseph Raz speculates that this is a major factor in accounting for the dominance of certain views in philosophy. The reigning orthodoxy may owe its influence not to its superior capacity to win arguments according to shared standards, but to its capacity to blunt people's receptiveness to the force of rival views:

> Often in practical philosophy the dominance of one view is the result of its rivals ceasing to make sense.... Its correctness is manifest. Rival heterodox views are...condemned through their own unintelligibility....It is mysterious how anyone might maintain such a view, unless they are blind to simple conceptual connections. To argue for the orthodox view can amount to no more than pointing out those connections. (Raz 1989, 5)

If Raz is right, the seemingly unbridgeable gulf between philosophical views can reflect the extent to which thinkers have become hostage to different conceptual frameworks. Philosophical debate then risks devolving into a deadlock, with each party reduced to reaffirming exactly the conceptual connections that their opponents reject as unintelligible. The only way forward, one might think, is to step back from the concepts dividing opinion, and seek common ground at the metaconceptual level, in the hope of finding independent reasons to embrace or eschew some of those ways of thinking whose adoption closes the mind to alternatives.

But we need not look as far as the gulfs between social worlds and rival philosophical systems for conceptual differences to start to matter. A small difference in a single conceptualization can snowball into a large difference in practice. This is what motivates Philip Pettit (1997) and Quentin Skinner (1998) to advocate a shift from conceptualizing liberty as *non-interference* to conceptualizing liberty as *non-domination*, for example. Liberty as non-interference is secured just as long as other people do not interfere in one's affairs, while liberty as non-domination additionally requires that other people should not even possess the *capacity* to interfere in one's affairs on an arbitrary basis:[21] the Roman slave whose benevolent master never interferes

---

[21] This last qualification importantly allows that there can be interference without domination as long as the interference is non-arbitrary, i.e. constrained and justified. But it in turn invites the question whether this conceptualization of liberty blinds us to the real costs in freedom involved even in non-arbitrary interference—a point I address in Chapter 10; see also Lane (2018) and Cueni (manuscript-a). The potential impact of data-harvesting on liberal democracy is explored in Zuboff (2015, 2019), Nemitz (2018), Macnish and Galliott (2020), and Véliz (2020).

in his affairs is still being dominated by his master—his *dominus*—who could shorten the leash at any moment.

This subtle difference in the conceptualization of liberty can spawn diametrically opposed views on any number of contemporary issues, such as how we should think about the large-scale harvesting of our personal data. If we conceptualize liberty in terms of non-interference, the harvesting of personal data does not count as a reason to think that our liberty is being undermined as long it does not interfere with the exercise of our will; but if we conceptualize liberty in terms of non-domination, the same data harvesting does count as a reason to think that our liberty is being undermined, since we whose data have been harvested depend on those who control the data not to use them against us. While the former conceptualization gives us no cause for alarm, the latter gives us every reason to protest.

The divergent ramifications of endorsing subtly different conceptualizations become particularly salient when we consider the requirements that our value concepts place on the design of new technologies. As a recent article in *Ethics and Information Technology* observes: 'Politicians and engineers are increasingly becoming aware that *values* are important in the development of *technological artefacts*. What is often overlooked', however, 'is that different *conceptualizations* of these abstract values lead to different design-requirements' (Veluwenkamp and van den Hoven 2023, 1). Demanding that new technologies be shaped to our values may be a start, but it still leaves all the work to be done: notably, the work of deciding which conceptualizations to shape the technology *to*.

All of which brings us back to the question we started out from: what kinds of reasons are there for us to prefer certain conceptualizations and their correlative patterns of reasoning over others? A philosophical framework is required to help us to think about such reasons—for these are the reasons we need to identify in order to decide which concepts to adopt, adhere to, or abandon.

Ludwig Wittgenstein—another philosopher who was 'concerned that we should be in control of our concepts, not they of us' (Moore 2012, 278)—pointed out a fundamental difficulty in this connection: while criticizing or justifying a thought on the basis of other thoughts is one thing, criticizing or justifying a *way of thinking* is quite another.[22] In justifying one thought by

---

[22] See Wittgenstein (2005, 180); he puts it in terms of the activity of thinking as a whole, but the fundamental point—that very different types of considerations are called for once one goes beyond justifying one thought on the basis of another within a certain way of thinking—holds in either case.

another *within* a certain way of thinking, we take the concepts structuring that way of thinking for granted. Once we step back and attempt to justify that way of thinking itself, however, entirely different sorts of considerations appear to be called for. While the concepts we use evidently play a role in determining which reasons to think something true or justified we are sensitive to, concepts cannot themselves be true or justified the way judgements, propositions, or beliefs are. We therefore cannot model concept appraisal on the familiar business of assessing the veracity or warrant of individual judgements. We can give reasons *within* the practice of reasoning determined by the concepts we use, but it is a different challenge altogether to give reasons *for* a way of reasoning. Wittgenstein wondered whether it was even possible to 'give a reason for thinking as we do', or whether this would—incoherently—'require an answer outside the game of reasoning' (1979, §4). Can we give reasons for the way we reason? It can seem as if any such justification must presuppose what it is meant to justify if it is to be accessible to the addressee.

And yet we evidently do sometimes give reasons for or against certain ways of reasoning, and manage to think critically *about* concepts rather than with them. There must be a way to make philosophical sense of this fact. That is not just an explanatory demand, but an *ethical* demand. We need some way of determining whether our concepts are helping us to live—whether we are using concepts that express and subserve our concerns, or whether we are, as Nietzsche feared, 'stuck in a cage, imprisoned among all sorts of terrible concepts' (2005c, Improvers, §2). But how do we tell the difference? How can we critically ascertain that the building-blocks of our thoughts are not stumbling-blocks to our concerns?

My aim in this book is to develop a framework for concept appraisal. At the heart of this framework are *reasons for concept use*, a special class of reasons that are orthogonal to, and yet can underpin or undermine, the reasons for action and belief that figure in our deliberations. To adopt a concept is to become sensitive to the reasons that immediately guide and flow from its application. But we can go one step further and ask for reasons to reason in these terms. This is to demand reasons for reasons—second-order reasons to use the concept and be responsive to its concomitant first-order reasons: the reasons to apply the concept as well as the reasons that follow from its applicability.

I explore this theme in his work in Queloz (2016, 2017b). A related distinction is drawn by Toulmin (1953, ch. 11) and Rawls (1955).

As Wittgenstein's puzzlement reminds us, it is a remarkable fact that we can give and ask for reasons for the way we reason *from within* our practices of reason-giving. This is the accomplishment of the concept of a second-order reason: it makes it possible to subject to critical scrutiny the very concepts and first-order reasons that make up the conceptual architecture we inhabit. 'Our concepts', Simon Blackburn writes, 'form the mental housing in which we live'; the job of philosophers is to 'investigate the structures that shape our view of the world', which means 'seeing how parts function and how they interconnect', and 'knowing what would happen for better or worse if changes were made' (1999, 1). By acquiring the ability to think in terms of reasons for reasons, we become able to sound out and renovate the house of reason from within.

Pursuing the question of how best to do this will lead us deep into the *ethics of conceptualization*: the practical reflection on which concepts we should be disposed to use. Concepts, at least if understood as the abstract objects forming the constituents of thought, may not be the sort of thing one can change. In line with this, many philosophers think of concepts as timeless, immutable, and unimprovable abstracta, rather as the ancient Greeks thought of the stars: denizens of a celestial sphere that is eternal, unaffected by terrestrial change, and already perfect and complete as it is.

But there is still a practical question about *which* concepts we look to in guiding and organizing our affairs. And we *can* change which concepts we use by changing our *conceptualizations*—the bundles of dispositions that characterize our ways of thinking and valuing (about which more at the end of Chapter 2). I take practical reflection on which concepts to use to be at the heart of what Alexis Burgess and David Plunkett have labelled 'conceptual ethics', the somewhat more capaciously defined enterprise of pursuing normative and evaluative questions about concepts, words, and other broadly 'representational' or 'inferential' devices we use in thought and talk.[23] So even when I resort to the pithier phrase 'conceptual ethics', what I shall mean by it is, specifically, the ethics of conceptualization (in contrast also to the *morality of conceptualization*, as we shall see in Chapter 8).

---

[23] For characterizations of conceptual ethics, see Burgess and Plunkett (2013a, b, 2020) and Cappelen and Plunkett (2020). Recent contributions congenial to the approach pursued here include Miller (2010), Haslanger (2014, 2020a), Plunkett (2015, 2016), Fredericks (2018, 2020), Goetze (2018, 2021), Wille (2018), Koch (2019, 2021), Latham, Miller, and Norton (2019), McPherson (2020b, 49–52), McPherson and Plunkett (2020, 2021), Thomasson (2020b, 2024), Nado (2021), Shields (2021a, b, c, 2023), Smithson (2021), Jorem (2022), Isaac (2024), Jorem and Löhr (2024), Lau (2024), and Santarelli (2024). An earlier manifesto for this type of philosophical inquiry is formulated by Carruthers (1987). Congenial contributions from neighbouring disciplines also include Schiappa (2003), who offers rhetorical-cum-philosophical analyses of several case studies to illustrate the politics of definitions, and Abend (2023), who tackles debates over definition and conceptualization in social science from a sociological perspective.

By changing our conceptualizations, moreover, we also change which linguistic meanings are associated with the words we use.[24] If words get their meanings from expressing concepts, then changing *which* concept a word expresses changes the meaning of the word; and if the meaning of the word changes, then the way the word is used will change accordingly. When the Romantics, for example, broke with the Enlightenment conceptualization of nature as a mere machine to be figured out, and reconceptualized nature as something infused with value and dignity in its own right, they held on to the word 'nature', but changed its meaning and use. Changing word-meaning pairings by changing how we think promises to avoid many of the difficulties afflicting the opposite strategy, of changing how we think by changing how we speak.[25] The conceptualizations through which we come to grasp and master concepts are what *underlies* our ability to use and interpret words correctly. Mastery of a concept underpins and at least paradigmatically manifests itself in mastery of the use of a linguistic expression. Thus, Wittgenstein observes that when he thinks of a concept, he thinks of 'the technique of our use of an expression: as it were, the railway network that we have built for it' (MS 163, 57r). Robert Brandom likewise endorses the Sellarsian slogan that 'grasping a concept is mastering the use of a word' (2015b, 102).

But there are good reasons not to *identify* concepts with words, nor to attribute concepts to others solely on the basis of their lexicon—as Bruno Snell's 'lexical principle' invites us to do, for instance, maintaining that something does not become 'an object of thought' until it is 'seen and known and designated by a word' (1953, 7). Similarly, we should be careful in adopting the methodological precept of using words as proxies for concepts—an approach sometimes adopted by historians of ideas to render their material manageable (Skinner 2009, 325). This can easily end up blurring the distinction between words and concepts just as much as the lexical principle does. Concepts are not just the shadows of words, and words make imperfect proxies for concepts. How else could we appreciate the challenges involved in putting a thought into words vividly brought out by Eli Alshanetsky's *Articulating a Thought* (2019)? Our thinking techniques are one thing, our ways of expressing and conveying these techniques through language another.[26] Nevertheless, the two are interdependent in various ways, and reflection on which concepts to use should underlie and inform reflection on how to speak, which words and expressions to adopt, adhere to, or abandon,

---

[24] For different accounts of this, see Sawyer (2020c) and Koch (2021).
[25] See Gleitman and Papafragou (2012) and Mühlebach (2022).
[26] For a battery of arguments as to why it is a mistake to identify language too closely with thought, see Sawyer (2020b) and Rieland (2024).

and what meanings to attach to them. There are, as Sellars stressed, 'an indefinite number of possible conceptual structures [that] must compete in the market place of practice for employment by language users' (2007, 26).

Though it is now in the ascendant, reflection on which concepts to use is not new. Philosophers have long been in thrall to the thought that when we are being rigorous in our reasoning, we should not listen to any old reason flowing from any old concept, but should probe how far the reasons suggested by our concepts can be shored up by reasons validating the rational authority of these concepts.[27] That is part of what it means to reason for oneself rather than rely on guidance from elsewhere, and hence part of what marks the difference between rational autonomy and rational tutelage that forms the defining contrast of the Enlightenment according to Immanuel Kant.[28] Islamic philosophy draws a related contrast between *taqlīd*, the uncritical acceptance of authority, and *ijtihād*, judgement based on independent effort.[29] We should not use a concept merely out of awe, or merely out of habit—intuition should be grounded in argument, suggestiveness in discursiveness. The concepts we use govern the movements of our minds, and as Kant insisted, we should query *by what right* our concepts tell us how to think.[30] This expresses more than the aspiration to be governed by the authority of ideas rather than by the idea of authority.[31] It encourages us to be critical of *which* ideas we let ourselves be governed by.

Although this demand that one should be able to offer reasons for using the concepts one uses received its purest expression in Enlightenment rationalism, we continue to recognize the interlocutor who greets justifications such as 'Because it is a *human being*' with: 'So what?'; or 'Because it is *natural*' with: 'Why does that give me a reason?' This is not to question the *applicability* of the concept *human being* or the concept *natural*; it is to question the

---

[27] Intimations of that ideal can be gleaned already from Plato's insistence, in the *Theaetetus* (201c–210d), that a claim needs a *logos* (a reason) to count as knowledge, and from his call, in the *Protagoras* (356d–e), to turn practical reasoning into a *techne*—a 'science' or 'measurement system'—that promises to shelter people from *tyche*, the unpredictable play of fortune, by giving them more control over whether their lives go well. See Nussbaum (2001, ch. 4).

[28] In his essay '*Was ist Aufklärung?*', Kant defines Enlightenment as humanity's emergence from its self-imposed tutelage, and characterizes 'tutelage' or *Unmündigkeit* as the inability to use one's own reason without another's guidance (1900–, WA, AA 08: 35.1–3).

[29] See Adamson (2022).

[30] Kant's transcendental deduction of the pure categories of the understanding (A84–130/B116–69), which he offers in answer to this '*Quid juris?*'-question, is perhaps the most venerable example of an attempt to formulate reasons by which to ground the legitimacy of concepts—Christine Korsgaard consciously echoes Kant's question in *The Sources of Normativity* when she asks after 'the right of these concepts to give laws to us' (1996, 9). By Kant's own lights, however, the strategy of transcendental deduction is available only for a handful of special concepts—the categories—and cannot be generalized to the sociohistorically local and thick normative concepts I focus on here.

[31] A contrast drawn by Summers (2003, 144) in characterizing the ideal of the university.

authority of these concepts—to ask for reasons to treat the considerations articulated in terms of these concepts as giving one reasons. Of course, an individual concept is too small a unit to constitute or give one reasons by itself; only complete thoughts give one reasons: the thought *that* something is a human being, or *that* something is natural. But these thoughts are articulated in terms of particular concepts, and whether we can be sensitive to the considerations presented in these thoughts depends notably on which concepts we possess.

This is why entire cultural revolutions can be sparked by reconceptualizations. Think of how the writings of Grotius, Hobbes, and Pufendorf helped precipitate the cultural shift from conceptualizing legitimacy in terms of divine authority to conceptualizing it in terms of consent;[32] or, indeed, of the rise of environmental thought made possible by the Romantic reconceptualization of nature.[33] Once that new way of thinking had taken hold, the consideration that something was 'natural' became intelligible, in a way it had not been before, as a reason in its own right. A new currency of reasons had been introduced. And when people challenge this currency of reasons, as they continue to do to this day, the challenge is not merely one to the authority of particular thoughts ('Is it *true* that this is natural?'). The challenge is to the authority of the very concept of nature in terms of which these thoughts are articulated: why should one *think* of what is natural as infused with value and dignity in its own right? This is to demand reasons for reasons: reasons to reason in terms of a certain concept and heed the reasons it adverts to.

Traditionally, such reasons for reasons have been sought in timeless and mind-independent rational foundations capable of authenticating one set of concepts as absolutely best: the concepts corresponding to Platonic Forms or the Mind of God, perhaps, or the concepts dictated by natural law or universal reason. Indeed, the normative expectation that one should be able to offer reasons for reasons may itself have been one of the main drivers towards such foundationalist theories.[34] Reflecting on the enduring attraction of such theories towards the end of a career spent attacking them, Bernard Williams surmises that the most powerful driver towards foundationalist theory is 'this idea that you *must* give a reason for a reason', especially when applied to the authority rather than the truth of a consideration: 'If I say: But it's an *animal*, they say: Why is that a reason? I've got to give a reason for that reason, in the

---

[32] See Schneewind (1998).   [33] See Rigby (2023).
[34] As comes out in Radzik's (2000) discussion of different foundationalist theories of normative authority, for example.

end. That's why I end up with foundations' (1999, 251, emphasis added). What is being demanded is not a reason to count something *as an animal*, but a reason to count its being an animal *as a reason* for or against something else. So instead of being asked to point out particular features of something that justify the application of the concept *animal* to it, we are being asked to give more general reasons to recognize the authority of an entire way of thinking. That line of inquiry naturally encourages a search for ever more fundamental grounds on which to validate certain concepts as authoritative, until one reaches rational foundations capable of authenticating one set of concepts as the one that a rational thinker should use.

When disappointed, however, this expectation that one should be able to anchor the reasons one responds to in rational foundations has corrosive effects. Any concepts deprived of such anchoring are demoted to mere conceits, to be cast aside by the rational thinker. And if the conclusion reached is that there are in fact no such timeless and mind-independent rational foundations to be had—at least not widely enough to support a *generalized* foundationalism—the same expectation that we should be able to anchor the set of truly authoritative concepts in such foundations creates a sense that something crucial is *lacking*, resulting in alienation from our concepts. Absent timeless and mind-independent rational foundations, the realization that there are other concepts we could use, and that there is no neutrally identifiable reason to prefer the concepts we happen to have over alternatives, encourages indiscriminate disengagement from all our concepts.

Attempts to reconcile a reflective sense of the contingency of our using the concepts we use with full-blooded confidence in those concepts have tended to err in the opposite direction and license the undiscriminating *acceptance* of whichever concepts we inherited. Fuelling this reconciliation, usually, is some kind of holism about our conceptual repertoire. On one version, it does not matter which concepts we use, as long as the judgements we form with them are true and the concepts combine well enough to form an internally consistent and coherent conceptual scheme. Agonizing over which concepts to use then seems like agonizing over the weave pattern of a fishing net: such a net could be composed of triangles, squares, hexagons, or intricately combine all of these, but it is immaterial which pattern we use as long as the net's overall integrity is preserved. The choice of which web of concepts to use may be constrained at the edges by merely pragmatic considerations—there are some webs that human beings, with their limited cognitive and perceptual capacities, are incapable of deploying effectively—but otherwise, the choice remains rationally undetermined: it is voluntaristic or arbitrary. As Huw

Price describes the view: 'Not only is language less of a prison than philosophy usually imagines...we can put the walls wherever we like!' (2018, 469).

In another version of this holistic view—associated, notably, with functionalist holism in anthropology and with communitarianism in social and political philosophy—the holism is given a more explicitly functionalist and adaptationist rationale: a society's conceptual repertoire is pictured as a harmoniously interlocking whole that has organically grown out of a particular way of life, and has over time become adapted to that way of life. This makes it the best conceptual apparatus *for* that way of life. Displace one concept, and you diminish the functionality of the whole.

Both forms of holism manage to rid themselves of the hankering after timeless and mind-independent rational foundations: they are genuinely *non-foundationalist*. But the result, in either version, is that indiscriminate rejection gives way to undiscriminating acceptance. The result is an 'enthusiasm for the folk-ways' that has been called 'the continuation of Hegelian conservatism by other means' (Williams 2021, 278).

My aim in this book is to develop a theory of reasons for concept use that does without timeless and mind-independent rational foundations, and yet still gives us a basis on which to discriminate between concepts and ground our confidence in reasons, so that we may escape the trilemma between foundationalism, indiscriminate ironism, and undiscriminating holism. I try to do without the idea that there are timeless and mind-independent rational foundations from which one set of concepts could be authenticated as absolutely best—indeed, I try to do away with the very idea that such foundations, whether available or not, would be desirable. At the same time, I hold on to the idea that it really does matter which concepts we use, because which true judgements we are capable of forming, and which reasons we are responsive to, significantly shapes how we conduct our affairs. What is needed to occupy this middle ground is a framework for concept appraisal that does not require timeless foundations while still enabling us to discriminate between concepts on a case-by-case basis instead of only considering the web of our concepts as a whole.

One influential way of appraising and improving our conceptual apparatus piecemeal without relying on foundations has been to fasten on how messy and defective our inherited concepts appear when measured against the formal ideal of a tidy theory: many of our concepts are imprecise, vague, indeterminate, inconsistent, and incoherently related to other concepts. By moving to concepts that are more precise, determinate, consistent, and coherent, philosophers can fix these defects. The concepts we end up with may not be timelessly the best ones, but at least their precision, determinacy, consistency, and other theoretical virtues promise to guard against the dangers inherent in slovenly thinking.

Yet I want to resist this view as well—or rather, I want to put it in its place and expose what it leaves out. Faced with theoretically virtuous concepts recommending something that radically conflicts with what our less tidy but entrenched concepts lead us to think, it becomes a real question why we should care so much about theoretical virtues as to overturn concepts that have at least as much force with us. To answer that question, a more comprehensive approach is needed, one that can situate the importance of theoretical virtues within a wider picture of what we want from our concepts, and make sense of how even theoretical vices can be virtues in other respects.

To this end, the book develops a *needs-based* approach to concept appraisal: it proposes to appraise predicates by predicaments, determining which concepts we should use by identifying the concepts we need.[35] What most immediately gives us reason to use certain concepts rather than others is our *conceptual needs*—our needs *for* certain concepts. What engenders those needs, however, is the way our various concerns interact with our limited capacities and circumstances. It is those human concerns—what we fundamentally care about—that concepts must ultimately tie in with if they are to be helpful. In this sense, the approach could equally be said to be concern-based. But concerns alone still leave our conceptual choices underdetermined. It is to the conceptual needs that result from the way our concerns are refracted through particular capacities and circumstances that we must look for a unifying methodological lens that allows us to bring the disparate plurality of relevant factors to a common focus in reflection.

As the phrase 'needs-based' is ordinarily used, that subtlety is already built in: when we talk of 'needs-based scholarships', the idea is not that some people have an intrinsic need for scholarships. The idea is that some people need a scholarship *if* they are to satisfy their concern to study, given their limited capacity to pay for it under the circumstances. Asked for a reason that justifies giving someone a scholarship, however, it is not their concern to study that we point to, but the fact that they need the scholarship. It is already

---

[35] The approach paradigmatically applies to predicates, since predicates are more likely to raise the authority question and the thick normative concepts I focus on are predicates; but, strictly speaking, the approach is not inherently limited to predicates, and could be extended to singular terms. Indeed, it could be extended to the very structure of thinking in terms of singular terms and predicates articulating the world in terms of objects and their properties and relations. See Brandom (2000, ch. 4) for an argument in that direction.

built into this instrumental sense of 'need' that the need is itself the product of a particular combination of concerns, capacities, and circumstances.

Instead of simply requiring us to conform our conceptualizations to an order of things about which we do not have a say, or to a tidy theoretical structure, a needs-based approach to concept appraisal humanizes the standard to which concepts are answerable, turning that standard itself into a function of human concerns. On the resulting view, we are the ones who *authorize* our ways of thinking, in both senses of that useful term: we are their authors, and we lend them authority, for it is by tying in with human concerns that concepts earn their keep.

At the same time, the standard of concept appraisal should not *just* be a function of human concerns, but also of what our worldly circumstances are and what capacities we bring to them, leaving us firmly constrained by reality in what kinds of concepts we can have reason to use. Our conceptualizations are not sequestered in the mind and sealed off from the world. They are conceptualizations *of* something, and it is part of the point of many conceptualizations, including notably those of natural kinds, that they defer to the nature of what they refer to: if a tension emerges between our conceptualizations of natural kinds and what the world actually turns out to be like, we adapt our conceptualizations—whereas with normative concepts, it tends to be the other way round: we try to reshape the world so that it lives up to our conceptualizations of ideals such as equality of opportunity.

The account of conceptual authority I propose accommodates rather than negates the role of worldly structure. To the extent that the world has an antecedent structure, that structure co-determines what concepts we need given our concerns and capacities, because it significantly shapes the *circumstances* in which those concepts are put to work, and one of the things we notably need at least some of our concepts to do is to be sensitive to our circumstances, both social and natural.[36]

But sensitivity to worldly structure is not everything; nor is it self-explanatory. In any given part of our conceptual repertoire, our relative sensitivity or insensitivity to worldly structure itself has to be explained in terms of our concerns and capacities. I aim not to supplant, but to supplement the often one-sided emphasis on structural features of the world as determinants of what concepts we should use by factoring in comparatively underexplored co-determinants that are more internal to human affairs: what concepts we

---

[36] This comes out particularly vividly in Millikan's (2017) account of why the concepts we live by—our 'unicepts', as she now prefers to call them—must latch onto the 'clumpy world' we inhabit.

need is a function not only of our worldly circumstances, but also of our concerns and capacities, because our worldly circumstances only put pressure on our concepts as a result of our pursuing certain concerns with certain capacities. We could not fully make sense of the authority of worldly structure without drawing on the facts about us that fuel our interest in worldly structure to begin with. The ethics of conceptualization is a three-way negotiation: what our concepts should demand of us depends on what the world demands of us given what we demand of the world.

Accordingly, the guiding intuition of the needs-based approach is that the value of a concept lies in the way it proves *of* value *to us* by meeting our conceptual needs. These conceptual needs are importantly different from the goals, aims, and purposes that figure so prominently in many influential approaches to conceptual ethics and engineering.[37] 'Purposes', as Jennifer Nado for example puts it, 'can be discarded' (2023b, 1986). But our conceptual needs are not so easily discarded. We may not even be cognizant of them. They are not necessarily something we consciously pursue, like goals, aims, or purposes. They are the opaque correlates of the way the concerns we pursue interact with the capacities with which and the circumstances in which we pursue them. What our conceptual needs are can come as a discovery. We may never even have thought about our conceptual needs, let alone embraced them as goals. And yet, as I shall argue, it is when concepts align with the conceptual needs we have in virtue of concerns we endorse that they are authoritative.

Dauntingly complex as the interactions between our concerns, capacities, and circumstances are, I will suggest that we can render them philosophically tractable by constructing what I call a *need matrix*: a three-pronged interpretative model of how the concerns, capacities, and circumstances of concept-users combine to generate a conceptual need. Such a need matrix can be used to determine what kind of concept best meets that need. Like the matrix from which printing type is cast, the need matrix acts as a mould from which to cast fitting building-blocks of thought.

The first of the two main theses of the book, then, is that if our minds are moulded by our conceptualizations, our conceptualizations should be moulded by our needs. For it is in our conceptual needs, which grow out of the way the concerns we pursue interact with the capacities and circumstances in which we pursue them, that we find reasons for concept use. Not every

---

[37] See e.g. Burgess and Plunkett (2013a, b), Brigandt and Rosario (2020), Haslanger (2020b), Simion and Kelp (2020), Thomasson (2020b, a), Nado (2021), Riggs (2021), and Jorem (2022). Colton (2023) stresses various differences between needs and goals, though not in connection with concepts.

conceptual need constitutes a reason for *us* to use a concept, however. Concepts will only emerge as authoritative when they align with needs we now have in virtue of concerns we *critically identify with*. To achieve the required critical distance, we must stand back from the need-engendering concerns and self-consciously represent them to ourselves. By explicitly casting our appraisal as dependent on certain concerns, we extend the scope of our critical reflection to those concerns. This facilitates rational autonomy by putting us in a position to ask whether the concerns being served are real or legitimate concerns at all. But it also facilitates rational authenticity by allowing us to ensure that the concepts we rely on serve concerns we can wholeheartedly identify with—for the point is not just that the concerns served should be real or legitimate concerns, but that they should be ours. One dimension of authenticity consists in living by concepts that are, as it were, really you.

This needs-based view of conceptual authority thus breaks with philosophy's traditional quest for the concepts that are absolutely best. Despite this, I will argue that this approach allows us to reconcile ourselves to the contingency of our concepts and avoid indiscriminate alienation from our concepts.

At the same time, the needs-based approach also avoids the opposite danger—the undiscriminating acceptance of whatever concepts we inherited. Appraising concepts according to our conceptual needs enables critical re-evaluations of our conceptual inheritance. It promises to give us a nuanced and case-specific sense of how to conceptualize things by helping us to see which concepts we have most reason to operate with. As Chapters 9 and 10 illustrate, it even empowers us to adjudicate between competing proposals for how to understand contested notions such as *voluntariness* or *liberty*, thereby providing a basis for distinguishing between authoritative definition and conceptual gerrymandering.

The second main thesis of the book is that sometimes, concepts that conflict, or that exhibit other theoretical vices such as vagueness or superficiality, are just what we need. Conflict is not necessarily an affliction in thought; nor are the various forms of untidiness in our conceptual repertoire always defects to be remedied. They appear as defects as long as we model our understanding of what makes a good concept on the virtues of a scientific theory. But the reluctance to do this without further argument is precisely what sets off the needs-based approach to conceptual authority from its closest non-foundationalist rival, the tidy-minded pursuit of conceptual authority through theoretical virtue.

By developing a way of vindicating the authority of concepts without simply invoking the authority of theoretical virtues, the needs-based approach indicates a different way of practising philosophical reflection on our concepts, one that relies less on theory-construction and the realization of theoretical virtues, and more on the particular psychological, social, and institutional facts on the ground. If we consider not what concepts are timelessly or definitively best, but what concepts we now need, we can identify the proper remit of efforts to tidy up our conceptual repertoire, and thereby come to discriminate between helpful clarification and hobbling tidy-mindedness.

If the primary theme of the book is reasons for reasons, its secondary theme is therefore how the demand for such reasons can, depending on how one conceives of those reasons, press towards foundationalist theorizing and the tidy-minded pursuit of theoretical virtues, and why that pressure should sometimes be resisted. The question of what form reasons for reasons should take thus bears directly on the question of what form philosophy should take.

My thoughts on these issues have been shaped by two figures whose influence pervades the book. One is Friedrich Nietzsche, who, more than any other philosopher in the Western canon, embodies a sceptical readiness to question the authority not just of concrete institutions and individuals, but of the ideas they abide by. He thinks of the concepts that form the currencies of thought, and that we take our words to express, as cast by human beings, and he worries that 'counterfeiters of the mind' (83:18[1]) might have corrupted our reasoning with 'counterfeit' concepts. Rooting present-day conceptual ethics in a reading of its history that traces it to Nietzsche, and reaches through Nietzsche back to Kant, promises to enrich our sense of its possibilities and relevance. But for the appraisal of parochial concepts of the sort I focus on here, it is the self-described Hermit of Sils-Maria rather than the Sage of Königsberg that provides the main source of inspiration.[38] For while scepticism towards the authority of concepts is Kantian at root, Nietzsche's distinctive elaboration of that scepticism into what he billed as a 'real critique of concepts' (85:40[27]) is the more powerful for being piecemeal and applicable to any concept, however culturally distinctive or parochial, instead of being focused, as Kant was, on the authority of our reasoning faculty as a whole and the twelve transcendental categories of the understanding in particular. Nietzsche's use of philosophy as piecemeal cultural critique renders his thought recognizably modern and marks it off from Enlightenment

---

[38] Nietzsche would playfully sign some of his letters between 1884 and 1886 as *der Einsiedler von Sils-Maria*.

universalism.[39] He explores the ramifications of the realization that a culture's trajectory, and *a fortiori* the trajectory of an individual life, are shaped by the concepts people recognize as authoritative. If conceptual ethics has an avatar, it must be Nietzsche.

The other figure is Bernard Williams, whose *Ethics and the Limits of Philosophy*, in particular, shaped my views on the place and merit of parochiality and tidiness in our thinking. Williams is routinely cast and taught as a purely negative and destructive philosopher, who cleverly chipped away at others' honest attempts at philosophical theorizing, but offered little by way of an alternative. I take the framework articulated in this book to be indicative of the more positive conception of philosophical reflection that underpins his work. By building a framework for conceptual ethics that develops, fuses, and harnesses various insights scattered across Williams's contributions to metaphilosophy, epistemology, ethics, metaethics, political philosophy, and the theory of action, we become equipped to appreciate how much of Williams's own work was itself a methodologically cohesive and constructive exercise in conceptual ethics—in line with his declared conviction that 'the task which provides the principal aim of all moral philosophy' is 'the ethical understanding of the ethical', the task 'of truthfully understanding what our ethical values are and how they are related to our psychology, and making, in the light of that understanding, a valuation of those values' (1995a, 578).[40] If Williams's work can inform this book, it is because he was himself, alongside Nietzsche, a paradigmatic practitioner of conceptual ethics.

The book is divided into four parts: the first (Chapters 1–3) sets up the discussion by introducing the guiding question, clarifying its terms, and examining what is involved in raising it. Its main themes are the very idea of conceptual authority and how it differs from the normativity of concepts; the power exercised by concepts that motivates raising the question of their authority; our capacity to achieve critical distance towards our concepts by adopting what I shall call 'the autoethnographic stance' towards them; the distinction between engaged and disengaged concept use; the confusions that

---

[39] As noted also by Huddleston (2019, 171).
[40] Not only Williams's critique of the particular way in which certain important ethical concepts are understood within 'the morality system' and his critique of deepened conceptions of the voluntary can be thought of as exercises in conceptual ethics, but also his more constructive advocacy of certain conceptions of agency and responsibility, shame, regret, reasons, thick ethical concepts, and virtue-ethical concepts, including notably the 'virtues of truth'. As he also writes: 'our conceptions of freedom, responsibility, and blame are often not what they seem, and are variously exaggerated, self-deceiving, sentimental, or vindictive (epithets which themselves, it should be noticed, largely belong to an ethical vocabulary)' (1995a, 578).

lead to objectionable forms of relativism; the different senses in which our concepts might be said to be contingent; the way our confidence in our concepts can be undermined by reflection and cause us to lose knowledge; but also the possibility of acquiring metaconceptual knowledge that certain concepts are the right ones for us.

The second part (Chapters 4–5) surveys the different answers that the question of the authority of concepts has received in the past. Discussing their shortcomings motivates the development of an alternative account and conveys a sense of the features it should have: it should generalize to thick normative concepts; it should not result in indiscriminate disengagement from our concepts; and it should not license the undiscriminating acceptance of our concepts. To this end, I suggest, the picture of our conceptual apparatus as something harmonious, largely tensionless, and inherently static must be replaced with a kaleidoscopic picture on which our conceptual apparatus is tension-ridden and dynamic; and the critical leverage of local needs must be harnessed by recognizing that the contingency of our concepts extends to the standards these concepts must meet. This still leaves one direct rival to the approach I aim to develop, however: the tidy-minded approach that seeks conceptual authority by eliminating theoretical vices such as vagueness, superficiality, and tensions from our conceptual repertoire. I explore these different theoretical vices and offer reasons to be critical of the tidy-minded approach as a general account of conceptual authority.

The third part (Chapters 6–8) lays out the needs-based approach to concept appraisal I advocate in this book. Using an underexplored debate between Ronald Dworkin and Bernard Williams as my springboard, I first introduce the basic idea that our concepts should make contact with the human concerns motivating their use. This brings out more sharply what the tidy-minded focus on theoretical virtues misses. But I argue that concerns alone are insufficient to determine which concepts we should use. A more complex framework is required, which I go on to develop by introducing the notions of a conceptual need, of the expressive character of concepts, of needfulness conditions, of giving point to the use of a concept, and of need matrices. These notions combine into a powerful framework for needs-based concept appraisal. I then show how this allows us to answer the authority question without crowding out other kinds of reasons that transcend preoccupation with human concerns or with the instrumentality of concepts. On this basis, I articulate a needs-based conception of conceptual authority, on which concepts are authoritative if and to the extent that they meet the conceptual needs we have in virtue of concerns we identify with and would still endorse after well-informed reflection on the merits of those concerns and on how we came by them. I defuse the worry that this conception yields the wrong kind of reasons, and explore in what sense it still leaves room for concepts to be valuable in their own right, independently of how they serve our concerns.

The fourth and final part (Chapters 9–10) illustrates and refines the account by applying it to the particularly interesting cases of the concepts of voluntariness and liberty, where it emerges that superficial and conflicting concepts sometimes serve us best. These case studies not only further illustrate the approach, but also underscore several further insights it yields: that sometimes, powerful concerns can distort concepts out of the shape in which they best serve the balance of our concerns; that the very heterogeneity and conflict of human concerns can itself generate reasons to use certain concepts rather than others; and that there is a place in liberal democratic politics for the tidy-minded pursuit of theoretical virtues.

The hurried reader seeking to understand the mechanics of my view without much by way of motivating background, contrast foils, and detailed applications should focus on Chapters 1–3 and especially 6–8. By the end of the book, I hope to have substantiated and brought out the more surprising implications of what can seem like a platitude: that the way of thinking about concept appraisal we need is itself one that appraises our ways of thinking by our conceptual needs.

The Ethics of Conceptualization: Tailoring Thought and Language to Need. Matthieu Queloz, Oxford University Press.
© Matthieu Queloz 2025. DOI: 10.1093/9780198926283.003.0001

PART I
RAISING THE AUTHORITY QUESTION

1
The Authority Question

1.1 Dworkin's Challenge

'Nothing is easier than composing definitions of liberty, equality, democracy, community and justice', Ronald Dworkin once wrote, 'but not much, in philosophy, is harder than showing why these are the definitions that we should accept' (2001a, 90). If we cast our thoughts in certain terms, certain conclusions will appear inescapable. But it remains open to us to ask why we should think in those terms to begin with. Why should we place ourselves under the sway of these definitions if alternatives are available that lead to different conclusions? Why should we recognize the authority of these concepts? This is what Dworkin identifies as the real challenge for composers of definitions: the challenge of answering what I shall call *the authority question*.

My aim in this chapter is to clarify the authority question by specifying what exactly it calls into question, what the question is motivated by, in what form it typically arises, and what types of considerations we should look to in answering it. To this end, I distinguish the normativity at issue in the authority question from what is commonly referred to as the 'normativity of concepts', and I show how the question is motivated by the distinctive forms of power that concepts exercise. I then explore when the authority question arises in everyday discourse before arguing that many conceptualizations that do not involve anything as straightforward as an epistemic error can nevertheless have something wrong with them.

We are familiar with the idea that we can question the authority of individuals or institutions: why should this individual, or that institution, be granted authority over our lives?[1] Yet the same question can fruitfully be

---

[1] Theorists of who have elucidated the notion of authority include Weber (2019, ch. 3), Horkheimer (1987), Arendt (1956, 1958), Jouvenel (1963a, b), Kojève (2014), Friedrich (1958, 1972), Friedman (1990), Eschenburg (1976), Lukes (1987), Green (1988), Barber (2010), Christiano (2020), and Kletzer and Renzo (2020). The account of authority that has been most influential within analytic philosophy in recent years is Raz's (1979, 1986, 1995, 2009), and I discuss its relation to the conception I advocate here in Chapter 8. I take the notion of *conceptual* authority at issue in the authority question to be at work in Wilson (2006, 3), Dorsey (2016, ch. 1), McPherson (2018, 2020a), Plunkett (2020), and Wei (2022); related notions are also invoked in Stampe (1987), Johnston (2001), Ridley

extended to concepts. The recognition of authority, Max Horkheimer wrote, is a form of *deliberate dependence*—one willingly enters into a relation of dependence on something or someone, grounding obedience not in coercion, but in assent.[2] Embracing a concept likewise involves a form of deliberate dependence. When we place ourselves under the sway of a concept, we willingly make our judgements and our actions dependent on the reasons the concept adverts to and the way of thinking it prescribes. We can therefore meaningfully ask *why* we should grant a concept the authority to shape our thought and conduct. This is not merely to question the authority of a concept on a particular occasion ('Does the fact that x is F really matter here?'). It is to ask why we should ever think in those terms ('F-ness') at all.[3]

What the authority question invites us to identify are, in the first instance, not reasons for action or reasons for belief, but *reasons for concept use*; not reasons operative *within* a practice of reason-giving, but reasons *for* a practice of reason-giving, i.e. reasons to adopt or adhere to a concept and be disposed to recognize certain considerations *as* reasons.

This is notably different from asking what justifies individual thoughts and actions *given* the concepts one uses: my reason for thinking that x is F might be the fact that x is G, and I might pursue the chain of reasons further in that direction by asking what reasons I have for thinking that x is G. But the authority question leads us, not further along the chain of first-order reasons, but along a different chain that is orthogonal to the first, towards higher-order reasons: it raises the metaconceptual issue of what reasons I have to *count* the fact that x is G *as* a reason for thinking that x is F. In other words, the authority question asks for second-order reasons to think in terms of certain first-order reasons. As this characterization of conceptual authority in terms of reasons for reasons suggests, I understand conceptual authority as a gradable and comparative notion: I might have more reasons, or better reasons, to use one concept rather than another.

The relevant notion of conceptual authority must be distinguished from a related notion in the vicinity that has received rather more attention, namely

(2005), Chang (2009), Hayward (2019), Wodak (2019), and Smyth (2018, 2022). For a disambiguation of various senses in which *reasons* can have authority, see Hampton (1998b, 85–93).

[2] His phrase was *bejahte Abhängigkeit*; see Horkheimer (1987, 24, 46). Jouvenel (1963a, b) also thinks of authority in terms of internal assent rather than in terms of obedience.

[3] Following the practice of many contemporary theorists of concepts—e.g. Glock (2006)—I use 'F-ness' as a dummy for the morphologically acceptable nominalization (e.g. holiness, cruelty, or truth) of 'F' (e.g. holy, cruel, or true), and use 'F' in speaking of 'the concept F' (e.g. the concept *funny*) as well as when referring to 'the property of being F' (e.g. the property of being funny). Both conventions obfuscate further distinctions one would need to draw in certain contexts, but they suffice for my purposes here, and I prefer to avoid unnecessary technicality.

what Robert Brandom calls that 'special sort of *authority* one becomes subject to in applying concepts' (1994, 9), that 'rulishness' or 'normative bindingness' (1994, 10–11) whereby one becomes liable to assessment as to whether one applies a concept correctly or not. This is the authority that a concept has just insofar as it functions as the standard for assessments of the correctness of reasoning involving that concept. Whether this form of conceptual authority as normative bindingness even exists, and what its nature and source might be, has been the subject of much debate in the literature on the normativity of concepts.[4] But the aim has been to elucidate that authority in terms meant to apply to *all* concepts rather than to help us discriminate between them.[5] The authority question, by contrast, asks for reasons to recognize a *particular* concept's normative bindingness.[6] Why, given all the concepts we could be using instead, should we place ourselves under the sway of *that* concept?

We can mark this contrast by distinguishing between authority *of* use and authority *in* use. Questioning a concept's authority of use problematizes the *legitimacy* of a concept's power over us: by what right does a concept tell us how to think?[7] Questioning a concept's authority in use problematizes the *normativity* involved in a concept's exercise of that power: how is it possible for the claims a concept makes on us to be binding? When Brandom speaks of the 'authority' of concepts or their 'grip on us', he means their authority *in* use.[8] When I speak of their authority or their hold on us, I mean their authority *of* use.

The authority question as I understand it arises independently of how we understand authority in use. In particular, the intelligibility of Dworkin's challenge does not require concepts to be normative in the strong sense that

---

[4] See Ginsborg (2018) for an overview of the debate over how to understand to the normativity of concepts and what norms, if any, guide concept use and underlie assessments of it.

[5] As Rebecca Kukla puts it, the aim has been to explain how we could possibly 'get inducted into normative space in the first place' (2000, 162).

[6] I thus agree with Burgess and Plunkett (2013a, 1095–6) in distinguishing the issue of whether to use a concept at all from the issue at the heart of the literature on the normativity of concepts, of how to use a concept and what norms, if any, guide concept use.

[7] In Kant's terms, the authority question is a '*Quid juris?*'-question, which his transcendental deduction of the pure categories of the understanding (A84–130/B116–69) is explicitly offered in answer to. His concern with legitimacy is reflected also in his self-conscious redeployment of the legal term '*Deduktion*', which, in its original context, designates the legitimation of property claims by historical derivation.

[8] "The most urgent question for Kant is how to understand the rulishness of concepts, how to understand their authority, bindingness, or validity. It is this normative character that he calls *Notwendigkeit* (necessity)' (Brandom 1994, 10). 'For Kant the question is…how to understand [concepts'] grip on us: the conditions of the intelligibility of our being bound by conceptual norms' (2009, 33). He uses these phrases in the same sense in Brandom (2000, 80, 164; 2002a, 22; 2019b, 9). Rouse (2015) similarly focuses on authority in use, i.e. on accounting for the binding force of concepts.

involves being consciously guided by explicitly represented norms as one applies a concept. It only requires the far less contentious idea that our concepts in fact exert power over us, and that different concepts would exert power over us differently. Even if this power manifests itself primarily in matter-of-factual dispositions to conceptualize the world in certain terms and reason along certain lines, without conscious guidance by norms, this still leaves room for concepts to be normative in a weaker sense, namely insofar as one is *subject to normative assessment* by third parties as one applies a concept. That is enough to provide an independent basis—a basis outside the thinking individual—for the distinction between correct and incorrect concept application.[9]

But however exactly normativity comes to play a role in a concept's exercise of its power, my focus here lies on the prior issue of the legitimacy of that power. The question raised by Dworkin's challenge, in other words, is not how a given concept binds us, but why we should let it.

1.2 The Power of Conceptual Architectures

If it makes sense to extend the authority question to concepts, it is because, like powerful individuals and institutions, concepts exert various forms of power over us. Though our conceptualizations are our own creations, and may seem simply to subserve our every whim by enabling us to make sense of things, they do so by structuring, filtering, and modulating our experience of the world as well as our cognitive and affective responses to it. What concepts we use determines what stands out to us, what we are prompted to associate with it, what significance we attach to it, and what affects are felt to befit it. The firmer our grip on concepts, the firmer their grip on us. Concepts not only steer our attention, channel our emotions, direct our imagination, and marshal our memories; they also govern our reasoning by prescribing particular patterns of thought, telling us what to care about, what to count as a reason for what, and which inferences to draw.[10] In virtue of these pervasive powers, 'concepts order our life and our relations to others'; they 'structure the stories we tell of what we have done or gone through' (Diamond 2010, 276). We first make our conceptualizations, and then our conceptualizations make us.

---

[9] A point emphasized by Hlobil (2015).
[10] These different aspects of the power of concepts are well described in Diamond (1988), Eberhardt (2004), Fricker (2007), Haslanger (2012, 2018, 2020a), Nguyen (2020), Sliwa (2024), and Kaeslin (manuscript).

It is often said that concepts are the building-blocks of thought; but given how central thought is to human life under culture, that is tantamount to saying that concepts are the building-blocks of the social worlds we inhabit. It is not just inquiry that is structured by concepts.[11] Our norms, rules, rituals, practices, conventions, and institutions are equally structured by concepts and animated by the abstract ideals they allow us to envision, aspire to, and coordinate around.[12]

We thus inhabit a *conceptual architecture* as much as a material one. But while material architecture channels behaviour from the outside in, conceptual architecture channels behaviour *from the inside out*—rather as the chemical bonds in the river's water determine its flow, and do so no less than the riverbank. Seth Lazar (2024) uses this Deweyan image to distinguish between *extrinsic power*, exercised notably by the physical landscape and by material architecture, and *intermediary power*, exercised notably by the algorithms that shape the social relations they mediate. We might add that concepts exercise an even more ubiquitous form of intermediary power in shaping the conceptual relations they mediate. They articulate our understanding of the world, highlight or obscure possibilities, and encourage or discourage inferences and actions.

Conceptual architecture also imbues material architecture with meaning. Material objects often only get their significance from being embedded in behavioural schemas organized by concepts.[13] For concept-mongering critters like us, no building is just a building. It is charged with meaning by the concepts that apply to it, integrating it into complex systems of categorizations, norms, and reasons for action. Depending on how it is conceptualized, one and the same physical structure could be an embassy or a fraternity, a temple or a hostel. What behaviour is appropriate in it will be acutely sensitive to such conceptual differences. We deploy thick normative concepts not merely to carve up an antecedently determined material reality, but to sculpt the social world. This led Iris Murdoch to observe that a concept is 'less like a

---

[11] The emphasis on inquiry characteristic of American pragmatism remains influential today (McPherson and Plunkett 2020, Henne 2023, Westerblad 2024). Some of Wittgenstein's best-known remarks on concepts display a similar emphasis: 'Concepts lead us to make investigations', he writes. 'They are the expression of our interest and direct our interest' (2009, §570).
[12] Consider how much of human life is governed by rules alone: 'Rules fix the beginning and end of the working day and the school year, direct the ebb and flow of traffic on the roads,...situate the fork to the right or the left of the plate,...and order the rites of birth and death' (Daston 2022, 1). What holds for rules holds *a fortiori* for the concepts in terms of which these rules are articulated. And these are merely examples of explicit rules. 'Add implicit rules', Daston continues, 'and the web becomes so densely woven that barely any human activity slips through the mesh' (2022, 1).
[13] See Berson (2021).

moveable and extensible ring laid down to cover a certain area of fact', and more like something that determines the '*Gestalt*' or 'configuration of the world' (1956, 40–1, 54–5).[14]

This world-configuring power of thick normative concepts has recently been explored by Matthew Congdon in *Moral Articulation* (2024). In enabling us to fully articulate initially inchoate ethical experiences, he argues, thick normative concepts not merely reveal but also reshape what they refer to. A society in which the concepts of *sexual harassment, domestic violence, child abuse, racism, sexism, hate speech*, or *genocide*—all introduced in the twentieth century—are operative is radically different from a society in which these concepts are absent, even if the material architecture is identical.[15] Thick normative concepts have the power not just to reveal but to reshape and reconfigure ethical, social, political, and legal experience and reality.

That power is most evident when we consider societies structured by concepts that differ radically from our own. It is then especially easy, as Bernard Williams observes in a similarly architectural idiom, to 'see their judgments as part of their way of living, a cultural artifact they have come to inhabit (though they have not consciously built it)' (1985, 163).[16] As in the case of material architecture, there is an ambivalence to the power of conceptual architecture. It restricts as much as it facilitates. John Steinbeck captures that ambivalence when he writes that just as we might 'stumble down narrow dark alleys of thought', we might 'walk up the stairs of our concepts to emerge ahead of our accomplishments'.[17] Just as the material edifices we move in enable, guide, and constrain the movements of our bodies from the outside in, the conceptual edifices we inhabit enable, guide, and constrain the movements of our minds from the inside out.

Our conceptual architecture *enables* us in that it allows us to think and do things that we could not think or do without it. New concepts can make the invisible visible, disclose hidden aspects and dimensions of the world, cast things in a fresh light, heighten our powers of perception, empower us to entertain different thoughts, bring previously inaccessible conclusions within

---

[14] See also Murdoch (2013, 27).

[15] See Congdon (2024, 1–4) for a description of the origins of these concepts. For two other recent discussions of the idea that ways of thinking are 'ways of worldmaking', as Nelson Goodman (1978) put it, see Cappelen (2018) and Srinivasan (2019, manuscript).

[16] Delacroix (2022, 28, 78–9, 131) also develops the congenial notion of an 'axiological habitat' that we continually and collectively reshape.

[17] See Steinbeck (2006, 150). It is the fact that concepts can take us beyond what we knew when we devised them that renders the image of stairs leading beyond themselves especially apt. It is possible to get more out of our conceptualizations than we put in.

our reach, unlock novel forms of reasoning, and open up new forms of knowledge and understanding. That is how the conceptual architecture we construct can lead us beyond what we put into it, or prove valuable in ways we did not anticipate.

Besides opening up new possibilities, moreover, concepts also *guide* us in choosing which of these possibilities to realize. Not only do the concepts we use render certain objects and properties salient to us; they bestow on them a *rational* articulation and significance, thereby rendering us sensitive to certain *reasons* that can guide our thought and conduct. Reasons, as Jean Hampton observes, possess a 'guiding and commanding nature' (1998a, 49). While she places particular emphasis on the commanding nature of reasons, their guiding nature, which is a softer form of authority, is just as important.[18] Reasons act, as often as not, through their 'enticing' rather than 'peremptory' force (Dancy 2004, 21). They commend as well as command, and condemn as well as commend. Which reasons we are commanded, guided, or enticed *by*, however, is a function of our conceptualizations—the bundles of dispositions that make up our ways of thinking, and determine which concepts we actually understand and use.

This implies that the concepts we have at our disposal also *constrain* us. Already in highlighting certain aspects of the world, they obscure and blindside us to other aspects of the world. That reflects a structural constraint: to focus attention on an aspect of things necessarily involves detracting attention from other aspects—to pay attention to every conceivable aspect at once would be to pay attention to nothing. Concepts organize by filtering: they render certain things experientially and cognitively salient at the expense of others. We can only make certain things visible at the price of making others invisible. Thought is inherently selective in this way, and to select ways of thinking is to select between different ways of being selective.

Downstream of the ways in which concepts channel and constrain our attention lie the ways in which concepts constrain what thoughts we can entertain and what desires and attitudes we can form. We make sense of things, and form attitudes towards them, under descriptions, and what descriptions are available to us is a function of our conceptual repertoire. The attitude of respect, for example, characteristically involves respect under a description, and I can only respect someone *as* a human being, or *as* a

---

[18] For a related discussion of how the authority of reasons goes beyond the 'authority of command', see Laden (2012, ch. 3).

philosopher, if the concepts *human being* or *philosopher* are available to me.[19] *Wo Begriffe fehlen*—where concepts are lacking, as Goethe's Mephistopheles has it—we cannot so much as *entertain* certain thoughts or attitudes as candidates for endorsement. This constraint by lack of concepts necessarily 'operates behind our backs, out of our sight, since it limits what we are so much as capable of being aware of' (Brandom 2001, 78).

The conceptual architecture we inhabit also constrains what we can intelligibly do. One cannot *act in the name of justice* if the concept of justice is unavailable to one; without a host of concepts in play, the best chess player is reduced to a literal wood-pusher; even something as simple as writing down one's name requires the concept of a *name*, and it takes an entire conceptual edifice for the same physical motion to count as the signing of an executive order. What meaning our actions can have depends notably on what concepts we can draw on in interpreting them. Consequently, the concepts we possess delimit the horizon of what is possible for us. It is no hyperbole when Alexis Burgess and David Plunkett write: 'our conceptual repertoire determines not only what we can think and say but also, as a result, what we can do and who we can be' (2013a, 1091).

While the powers of conceptual architectures express themselves in a number of subtle ways, the most salient and distinctive way in which they hold sway over our lives is by sculpting the network of reasoning pathways we regard as correct. To think in terms of some concept *F*—*kitsch, sacrilegious, chaste, unpatriotic*—is not merely to discriminate between what is *F* and what is not-*F*, but also to treat the distinction as making a difference to what else one has reason to think or do. In adopting a concept *F*, one does not just come to recognize certain considerations as reasons for or against its applicability, but also comes to recognize its applicability as a reason for or against drawing certain further conclusions.[20] In this way, the concepts we use alert us to certain inferential relations between judgements: the applicability of one concept implies or excludes the applicability of other concepts—if a poem is a *villanelle*, it follows that it has nineteen lines and that it is not a sonnet.[21] The concepts we possess sculpt the network of reasoning pathways we regard as correct.

---

[19] On the idea that respect is respect under a description, see Cueni (2024a).

[20] This two-faced model of the articulation of concepts goes back to Michael Dummett's (1973, 434) generalization of Gerhard Gentzen's work on sentential connectives, and figures centrally in the inferentialist tradition (Dummett 1973, Brandom 1994, 2000, 2008, Kukla and Lance 2009, Peregrin 2014, Koreň 2021).

[21] That is only one of several rigid formal requirements that a villanelle must meet according to the influential definition by the French poet Théodore de Banville. A well-known example is Dylan Thomas's 'Do not go gentle into that good night'.

We can acknowledge this formative power of concepts without endangering the objectivity of the reason relations in question. For even if the reason relations themselves are thought of as obtaining entirely independently of human concept use, it remains true that the concepts *we possess* shape the network of reasoning pathways *we regard as correct*. And the power to sculpt *that* network is a power so fundamental to so much else of philosophical concern that the authority question can seem, as Ernest Gellner remarks, like 'the philosophically supreme question'.[22]

By sculpting the network of reasoning pathways we regard as correct, concepts shape and structure our lives. Consider how deeply the understanding and behaviour of a child is altered by acquiring the concept of sharing, or the concept of lying, or by learning that another's suffering is a *reason* to try to help.[23] Or consider how the trajectory of a human life can be altered through enculturation into the use of concepts such as *heroism*, *saintliness*, or *genius*; or how the character of a society varies with the availability of such concepts as *democracy*, *nationhood*, or *socialism*. Nietzsche was exaggerating only mildly when he insisted that a concept can be a recipe for flourishing or a 'formula for decadence' (2005b, §15).[24]

We can thus think of the life-shaping influence of concepts as consisting chiefly, and most distinctively, in their power to license or exclude certain transitions in reasoning—not just transitions from thought to thought, but also from perception to thought and from thought to action. The concepts we possess trace out the patterns of thought we regard as rational.

Strictly speaking, reason relations obtain between entire judgements or propositions rather than between the individual concepts in terms of which these are articulated. Concepts are not themselves reasons, and only yield reasons in the context of a proposition. But that does not prevent us from reflecting on a concept's contribution to our reasoning across a range of propositions. For *which* reason relations come into view at the propositional level is a function of which concepts we have at our disposal to articulate those propositions. And besides evaluating particular propositions or judgements one by one, we can ask whether the influence of a concept across a wide variety of situations is, on the whole, a good thing.

---

[22] Gellner chastises Wittgenstein and Kripke for having 'simply abandoned the philosophically supreme question as to what endows certain concepts with authority' (1984, 260).
[23] On that last example, see Wong (1991), who argues that the process by which one comes to think of suffering as giving one reasons to help is crucial to developing the virtue of compassion.
[24] See Huddleston (2019) for a detailed exploration of this theme in Nietzsche.

Gilbert Ryle put it well when he opined that concepts 'are discriminable features, but not detachable atoms, of what is integrally said or integrally thought', to be examined 'not in retirement, but doing their co-operative work' (2009b, 192). This acknowledges that conceptual content is a function of propositional content, and that a concept only does any rational work when embedded in a propositional context. At the same time, Ryle's dictum also retains the important idea that we can still analytically discriminate between a concept and the propositions of which it is a part. In addition to considering the merits of particular propositions (or the judgements or sentences that express them), we can therefore consider the merits of a concept and how its availability in turn differentially affects the availability of an entire set of propositions at once. Instead of only ever focusing on one proposition at a time, such as the one expressed by 'What John said at the mall yesterday at 4:15 p.m. was uncharacteristically patriotic', for example, we can reflect on the broader significance of having the concept *patriotic* in our repertoire. The concepts we use are discriminable—though not detachable—features of our thought that systematically govern what patterns of reasoning we recognize as rational across entire sets of propositions or sentences. And yet, as Cora Diamond observes, there is often 'no recognition at all of what the good is of concepts, of possibilities of thought' (1988, 269).

A helpful way of thinking of the broader difference a concept makes is this: when a community adopts or abandons a concept, it forges or severs inferential connections within the network of reasoning transitions it treats as correct. They can expand that network by acquiring new concepts, and prune it by eschewing concepts. An anodyne example is how introducing the concept *foul* into a game has the effect of licensing transitions in reasoning that were not licensed before, such as the move from 'a player is tackled a certain way' to 'the game should be interrupted'. By acquiring the concept *foul*, the players become dispose to draw, and recognize as correct, a set of inferences they did not draw before. These inferences can be made explicit in terms of conditionals, such as '*if* a player is tackled a certain way, *then* this is a foul', and '*if* there is a foul, *then* the game should be interrupted'. By itself, the concept only encodes such conditionals—it does not commit anyone to thinking *that* there is in fact a foul, or *that* the game should in fact be interrupted. But the concept does embody the *propriety of the transition* from the *conditions* to the *consequences* of its applicability—from 'a player is tackled a certain way' to 'the game should be interrupted'. Hence, *by using* the concept and explicitly shouting 'foul!', for example, the players express their endorsement of a certain pattern of reasoning. And conversely, by following that pattern in practice, they endorse the use of the concept. Even if they soon cease to explicitly shout 'foul!', but only behave as though the game should be interrupted whenever a player is tackled a certain way, they thereby still express the fact that they have adopted and abide by the concept *foul*. They are disposed to draw, and recognize as correct, the inference from the conditions to the consequences of the concept's applicability. In that sense, the introduction of the concept *foul* into their repertoire has expanded the network of reasoning transitions they recognize as correct. By the lights of their enriched conceptual repertoire, a new move is now open to them.

Less anodyne examples are the concepts expressed by derogatory epithets that license the transition in reasoning from the property of being a member of a certain ethnic group to some negative characteristic, such as being lazy, stupid, or cruel. People who think and talk in terms of such an epithet endorse the transition from (1) '*x* is a [insert ethnic group]' via (2) '*x* is a [insert derogatory epithet]' to (3) '*x* is [insert negative characteristic]'. Before they embraced the concept embodying the propriety of the transition from (1) to (3), they did not recognize that inferential transition as correct. Their adoption of the concept thus amounts to a non-conservative extension of the network of inferential moves they consider acceptable.[25]

This is what leads Brandom to speak of concepts as meriting critical scrutiny in virtue of the inferences that are implicitly 'curled up' (2000, 70) inside them. But one need not buy into the inferentialist contention that a concept's inferential role is *sufficient* to determine its content to acknowledge that which inferences thinkers are disposed to draw and recognize as correct varies with the concepts they possess. Some may insist that it is only once supported by certain beliefs, such as that the concept is non-empty, that a concept affects what inferences one actually draws. Yet the fundamental point stands: by embracing new concepts, we expand the network of reasoning transitions we recognize as correct.

Those who want to resist the reasoning transitions supported by concepts such as those expressed in derogatory epithets cannot rest content to extirpate the epithets from the linguistic repertoire. Fixing language is not enough. They must try and eradicate the very concepts themselves. It is also no use disputing that the conditions for the applicability of the concepts are met, since, by the crude light of concepts like these, anyone who is a member of

---

[25] See Dummett (1973, 454) and Brandom (2000, 69–72) for slightly different accounts of the epithet 'boche' along these lines. For a recent defence and elaboration of their account, see Mühlebach (2021, forthcoming).

the relevant ethnic group straightforwardly meets them. Nor does it help to insist that, though the concept applies, the attributability of the negative characteristic does not follow by default. It is the whole point of such concepts that it should follow by default.

Of course, to say that it follows by default is not to say that it follows indefeasibly; reasoning by default can be thought of as involving defeasible generalizations.[26] The reason relations encoded by our concepts are often non-monotonic: $F(x)$ may be a reason for $G(x)$ in the sense that if one accepts that $F(x)$, one has reason to conclude that $G(x)$ *by default*, but this reason may be defeated by the addition of further premises. Moreover, the reason relations encoded by our concepts are one thing, the actual performances of human reasoning are another. As Gilbert Harman points out, the activity of reasoning remains in some respects underdetermined by the reason relations we accept as correct, for instance when relations of material implication fail to determine whether one should accept the consequent or reject the antecedent. 'It is not always true that one may infer anything one sees to be implied by one's beliefs', Harman notes. 'If an absurdity is implied, perhaps one should stop believing something one believes instead of accepting the absurdity' (1984, 113). Ultimately, it is up to concept-*users* to decide when the needle on the compass of reasoning should swing from *modus ponens* to *modus tollens*.

Relatedly, recognizing the authority of a concept and its concomitant reasons is not the same as actually *acting on* the reasons it adverts to in the particular case: I might generally recognize the authority of the concept of honesty, and yet, this time around, the temptation to lie to my advantage might carry the day. Many ethical concepts plausibly emerged precisely to stake claims against self-interest, amplifying and redirecting altruistic tendencies that would otherwise remain overly partial, in both senses of the term.[27] But that does not mean that selfishness has been eradicated.

Nonetheless, moral progress happens notably through alterations in our conceptual repertoire: if one's behaviour is a function of the reasons one is sensitive to, it can be improved by acquiring new concepts and their concomitant reasons. As John Stuart Mill notes in his *Autobiography*, 'improvements in the lot of mankind' require changes in the 'constitution of their modes of thought' (1874, 239).[28]

---

[26] A default logic along these lines is developed by Horty (2012).
[27] See e.g. Williams (1973b, 250) and Kitcher (2011, 86).
[28] On the historical connection between political innovation and conceptual change, for example, see Ball, Farr, and Hanson (1989).

Morally significant advances need not be reducible to behavioural differences in the public forum of action and choice, moreover. When Murdoch urges that 'we need more concepts in terms of which to picture the substance of our being', because 'it is through an enriching and deepening of concepts that moral progress takes place' (1961, 20), she is not thinking merely of getting people to *behave* better. Her point is that morally significant differences can consist simply in how, *in foro interno*, one conceptualizes a situation:[29] 'Moral differences can be differences of concept as well as differences of choice.... How we see and describe the world is morals too' (Murdoch 1999, 73). Williams echoes this point when he stresses that 'an extremely important form of ethical difference' is 'that between those who do and those who don't use a certain concept' (1995l, 237). If this is right, it suggests that moral progress can be not just facilitated, but constituted by alterations in our conceptual repertoire. Embracing or abjuring concepts can be progress in itself.

1.3 Expressing the Authority Question

In light of these various powers exerted by the conceptual regime under which we live, it makes sense to ask what reasons one has to abide by a given concept. The great benefit of being able to raise the authority question and think about second-order reasons is that it enables us to assess and revise our conceptual architecture from within. But of course we rarely question our use of a concept in such explicitly metaconceptual terms. So what linguistic forms does the authority question actually take?

The authority question can find linguistic expression in a variety of idiomatic locutions. When one person tries to dissuade another from doing *x* by urging that *x* is *hypocritical*, for example, the other person might react either by asking for reasons to think that *x* is hypocritical, or by querying, more radically: 'So what? Why should I care?' Explicated in terms of the present account, this amounts to asking: 'So what if that concept yields this conclusion? Why should I accept that concept to begin with?' This is to demand a reason for a reason—a reason to recognize the authority of the concept of hypocrisy and the reason it gives those who recognize it.

Other natural locutions allow one to express the same demand. When someone commends an action or a substance for being *natural*, for instance,

---

[29] See Murdoch (1956, 1961). Moody-Adams (2017) and Congdon (2024) have more recently reinvigorated this idea.

they might encounter the reply: 'Why is that a reason?' Or when someone warns that video games cause *harm*, the discussion might soon revolve around what 'counts as' harm. Or when someone justifies a claim about a person by saying 'Because she's a *woman*', the question might come back: 'How does that follow?' In each case, one speaker relies on a conceptualization that the other challenges.

There are thus various well-established ways of raising the authority question without expressing it explicitly in terms of whether one has reasons to use a certain concept. One might question the authority of a certain concept by asking why something's being F is a *reason* for something else, or what *counts as F*, or what *follows from* something's being F. These are well-entrenched expressions that enable us to question and adjust our conceptual repertoire. Natural languages come equipped with metaconceptual expressions that allow us to question the authority of concepts and criticize and revise the network of reasoning pathways we regard as correct.[30]

At the limit, one might even question the authority of a concept through the right combination of 'Why?'-questions with locutions that bluntly express the dismissal of the rational authority of some consideration, such as 'So what?' To see this, consider first the question of what conceptual resources are required simply to think that some consideration is a *first*-order reason for another consideration. As Andreas Müller remarks, this is one of our most fundamental agential capacities, displayed already by young children, and it cannot be all that demanding:

> Anyone who is able to answer requests for justification such as 'Why do you think that p?' or 'Why did you do A?' thinks that something counts in favour of believing that p or doing A. They do so even if they cannot express this by using the term 'reason', or indeed in any other way than by answering that question. It thus takes very little to prove that you have the conceptual resources to think that some considerations are reasons for (or count in favour of) certain beliefs or actions: being competent with the justificatory use of 'because' in answering such 'why' questions is sufficient. (A. Müller 2019, 6)

---

[30] Here I draw on the Carnapian idea, arguably adumbrated by Wittgenstein and Ryle, that alongside our empirical, ground-level vocabulary performing descriptive functions, natural languages include metalinguistic vocabulary with the function of explicating and regulating the norms governing our ground-level vocabulary. The idea was elaborated notably by Sellars (1958), and has more recently figured prominently in the work of Heal (2007), Brandom (2015b), and Thomasson (2020a).

Similarly, anyone able to react to some first-order reason such as 'Because it's *natural*' with 'So what?' is capable of expressing their willingness to question the authority of the concept in this connection—more back and forth may be required to ascertain that this is indeed what they are doing, but they certainly need not resort to high-flown expressions like 'second-order reason' or 'authority of concepts' to express their doubts over whether being 'natural' should count as a reason here. Some degree of conceptual familiarity with the notion of a second-order reason is far more widespread than the technical language whereby we can make it fully explicit.

In fact, as David Plunkett and Tim Sundell have persuasively argued, many ordinary disputes that are ostensibly about object-level issues are actually better understood as metaconceptual disputes, i.e. disputes about which concepts to use.[31] Besides *genuine* disagreements between parties who share a concept and disagree about whether something falls under it and merely *apparent* disagreements between parties who talk past each other because they express completely different concepts by the words they use, there are also interesting cross-over cases, where parties genuinely disagree *and* take a word to express different concepts. In those 'metalinguistic negotiations', as they call them, the parties to the negotiation each use (rather than mention) the concept that they are thereby advocating as preferable to alternatives. We commonly do this when introducing someone to a concept, saying things like: 'Sebastian is *debonair*, for instance'. When someone else demurs: 'No way, Sebastian is not *debonair*!', the disagreement need not be about Sebastian—it can be about how the concept *debonair* should be understood. In this case, the concepts being advocated are used to show what kinds of judgements they each license and exclude. And though the sentences are not ostensibly about concepts, they are being *put to metaconceptual use*, allowing the two speakers to negotiate how best to define the concept at issue. As Plunkett and Sundell emphasize, such metaconceptual disputes conducted in object-level terms are a regular fixture in colloquial discourse.

The fundamental insight here is that since object-level judgements express and thereby exemplify concepts, we can also use them to debate which concepts to use. If, as Wittgenstein asserts, agreement in concepts requires agreement in judgements, the contrapositive of that thought is that disagreement in judgements can express disagreement in concepts, which is to say disagreement over which concepts to use. This connection between concepts and the

---

[31] See Plunkett (2015) as well as Plunkett and Sundell (2013a, b, 2021) and McPherson and Plunkett (2020); see also Stroud (2019).

substantive object-level judgements we make with them is what grounds the insight that some ostensibly first-order disagreements are really metaconceptual disagreements.

Once we recognize that we can debate which concepts to use by using them, it is but a small step to the thought that we can debate not just whether to adopt or abstain from a concept altogether, but also which concepts to use in a particular situation. As Sarah Stroud has pointed out, in debating whether the main takeaway from a shared experience should be that x is F or that x is G, we are not so much contradicting one another as disagreeing over what kind of conceptualization the situation calls for: we are disagreeing over which aspects of a situation are most worth fastening on, and wherein their significance lies.[32] As Stroud argues, this is also, broadly speaking, a question in conceptual ethics. It is merely that it tackles the question of which concepts to use from its most applied and particularized end, asking, in the first instance, not which concepts to use *tout court*, but *when* to use which concepts. This may not be as self-consciously metaconceptual, or as radical, as explicitly raising the question of whether to go in for any kinds of judgements in terms of F at all—eschewing a concept in a particular situation is, after all, not yet to eschew it altogether. But in taking a stand on what merits notice in a given situation and applying a concept to it, we are also implicitly endorsing the concept's continued use. We may not explicitly raise the question of whether to use the concept *tout court*, but we are voting with our thoughts.

Which way we vote also has immediate repercussions, in that the concepts we foreground in grasping a situation affect the choices we make on that basis. This comes out most clearly when a difficult choice turns on how one conceptualizes the situation. The difficulty of a tough choice need not reduce to the difficulty of choosing between different options given how one conceptualizes them. It can lie, at least in part, in the difficulty of choosing between different ways of conceptualizing each option, especially when one knows that these carry different implications and that one's conceptualization therefore affects one's attitude towards the resulting options. That is why people often debate how to conceptually frame what they do ('This is F!', one exclaims; 'I prefer to think of it as G', the other retorts).

Consider José Bermúdez's (2021, 7–8) illustration of the importance of framing: when Aeschylus describes Agamemnon's anguished choice between sacrificing his daughter to comply with the will of the goddess Artemis or renouncing his conquest of Troy, Agamemnon's deliberations do not just

---

[32] Stroud (2019, 25).

involve weighing two painful outcomes against each other while holding their conceptualization fixed; different ways of conceptualizing the same action compete in his mind: should he think of the action the goddess demands of him primarily as *pious obedience*, or should he think of it primarily as *slaying his child*? Would he simply be *doing what is right and holy*, or would he, above all, be *shedding virgin's blood*? The chorus describes his agonized train of thought as setting out from, and eventually circling back to, notions of obedience and lawfulness (θέμις).[33] It is not just in his eventual action, but already in foregrounding that conceptualization that Agamemnon submits to the will of the goddess.

1.4 When the Authority Question Arises

What prompts the authority question? As C. S. Peirce remarked, mere 'paper' doubts cannot truly motivate inquiry—a sentiment later echoed by Wittgenstein's insistence that we need *reasons* for doubt.[34] The authority question also loses force if spread too thinly across our conceptual repertoire. It is most forceful when focused on particular concepts. So when might the authority question arise?

A clue lies in Dworkin's presentation of the question as a challenge *for composers of definitions*. This suggests that when people compose new definitions, they incur the burden of showing why one should accept those definitions. And while composing definitions is by no means restricted to philosophy, it is clearly central to what philosophers do. Spinoza, fittingly, was a lens grinder by profession, and Nietzsche goes so far as to describe all of post-Socratic philosophy as being in the business of grinding out new conceptual lenses for the world to use: 'What Plato and fundamentally all the post-Socratics did: that was a certain legislation of *concepts*' (85:34[84]).[35] Equally central to philosophy, therefore, is the task of demonstrating the authority of the concepts that come out of this activity.

Calling it 'legislation' arguably expresses Dworkin's intended meaning better than Dworkin's own 'composition'. It redescribes what might otherwise

---

[33] See Aeschylus (1966, ll. 205–17). On the difficulties of translation raised by this passage, see Nussbaum (1988, 35, 431 n. 36); but the point holds, *mutatis mutandis*, for different translations as well.
[34] See Peirce (1931, 5.416) and Wittgenstein (1969, §§4, 122, 323, 458, 519).
[35] Charles L. Stevenson also underscores Plato's proclivity for 'persuasive definitions' (Stevenson 1938, 1944).

sound like an individualistic artistic activity in explicitly social and normative terms, thereby underscoring how holding out new conceptualizations for others to accept entrains a responsibility to demonstrate, *to* the people urged to adopt the concepts, why they have reason to structure their affairs in those terms.

The authority question thus naturally arises when a conceptualization is explicitly announced as revisionary, as it typically is when philosophers—or theorists in other disciplines—present themselves as conceptual innovators or engineers rather than as analysts of concepts. While analysis can still pretend to be to our conceptual practices what ornithology is to birds, engineering openly tampers with our conceptual practices.

Accordingly, engineers tend to give a rationale for their revisionary intervention. An influential framing is that they *fix defects* in our conceptualizations, casting philosophers in the role of conceptual plumbers.[36] The concept they encourage us to adopt is presented as being more authoritative because it is freed of some defect—such as vagueness or inconsistency—that the concept to be replaced suffered from. Once the supposedly superior concept is employed to overturn the judgements encouraged by our entrenched ways of thinking, however, the authority question re-emerges: why should we care so much about tidying up our conceptual repertoire if the price is to overturn judgements that more immediately have force with us? This will be the topic of Chapter 5.

Demonstrating the authority of concepts is not just a task for conceptual engineers aiming to prescribe new concepts, however. It is a task equally faced by conceptual analysts aiming to describe the concepts we use already. When someone puts forward a particular analysis for us to adopt, this also invites, if less obviously, the question of why we should accept that analysis—not just whether we should accept it as *right*, as an account of people's actual concept use, but whether we should accept it as *authoritative* for our own affairs: whether we should proceed to *live by* that analysis.

Imagine a theorist who takes a contested and somewhat indeterminate notion, such as *democracy*, and presents you with a weighty tome entitled *Democracy: An Analysis of the Concept*, which articulates and draws out the ramifications of a very definite concept of democracy. Suppose that, on this analysis, it clearly follows that your supposedly democratic government is not truly democratic. Given this particular conceptualization of democracy, this

---

[36] For the idea of philosophy as conceptual plumbing, see Midgley (1996). For the idea of conceptual engineering as a matter of fixing defects, see Cappelen (2018).

may well follow—but why, you will naturally want to ask, should I think in terms of that concept? What is there to show that this particular conceptualization of democracy is more than a scholarly idiosyncrasy, or worse, a form of conceptual gerrymandering designed to validate the political preferences of the analyst?[37]

Appeals to intuitions hardly help, since these can be equally idiosyncratic or ideology-driven.[38] The clearer and the more determinate the proffered conceptualization of democracy, the more pressing the question of what reasons we have for endorsing this particular pattern of reasoning. Even if we are prepared to accept the proposed conceptualization simply based on the fact that it offers us clarity, determinacy, precision, and consistency—an influential idea I return to in Chapter 5—the authority question reappears sharply when several such proposals compete, and we must adjudicate between them. Some basis is required for distinguishing between authoritative definitions and mere gerrymandering with concepts.

The line between analysis and engineering is itself blurrier and shiftier than this simple delineation suggests, moreover. Conceptual analysis is frequently taken to encompass not just the empirical description of concept use in a community, but also the clarification of how a given concept *should* be used for the purposes of a certain line of argument or a research programme.[39] And the line between analysis and engineering can also be blurred by changes in perspective or context. The most visionary attempts at conceptual engineering may, by dint of their own success, acquire the marmoreal dignity of classic analyses—Plato, Descartes, Hobbes, Kant, or Freud can seem to us now merely to describe deeply entrenched conceptual practices that they in fact helped create. Or consider the conservative analyst who, in rapidly changing circumstances, insists on extending the life of a received conceptualization; he may invite more questions regarding the authority of his analysis than the engineer who understands which way the wind blows and proposes to revise our conceptual apparatus to move with the times.[40] In addition to these extrinsic developments that may give engineering the authority of

---

[37] See Baz (2017, 46–8) for an articulation of this worry, which he terms 'cognitive diversity skepticism'. Related worries are highlighted by Eklund (2017, 13), Clarke-Doane (2020, 180), and Wolf (2020), who sketches a Hegelian answer to it. It is a further step to reject *all* conceptualizations of democracy and advocate abandoning the concept altogether—as Cappelen (2023) does.

[38] See Machery (2017, ch. 4) for a critique of conceptual analysis on these grounds.

[39] For accounts of conceptual analysis which emphasize its breadth and richness as well as the ways in which it differs from the empirical description of concept use as practised by linguists and anthropologists, see Glock (2017) and Rathgeb (2020).

[40] By the same token, efforts to preserve ways of thinking may warrant being described as a form of engineering when moving with the times would amount to a form of backsliding; see Lindauer (2020).

analysis or analysis the contentiousness of engineering, there are also pressures *within* analysis and engineering that can drive the one to shade into the other. Analysts' quest for differentiation and determinacy may easily lead them beyond established use, while engineers may find their proposals more readily taken up when proffered under the mantle of analysis.

But the authority question is not restricted to cases in which someone encourages us to adopt a concept. It can also become acute when we lose confidence in the concepts we use already.

Among the experiences that can prompt the authority question in connection with the concepts we already live by is the experience of radical conflict between what these concepts enjoin us to do. Sometimes, entrenched normative concepts systematically pull us in different directions and the values they enshrine are impossible to realize in concert, not just because we lack the necessary capacities or circumstances are unpropitious, but because we cannot even conceive of a world in which both values are fully realized in concert. The conflict arises from a tension inherent in that combination of concepts itself.

This makes it tempting to try and dissolve the conflict by questioning the authority of one of the concepts involved and finding some reason to discount the claims it makes on us—only when the conflict is particularly acutely felt, or perhaps even permanently. Utilitarian theorists, for example, find reasons for reasons in the fact that the use of certain concepts tends to contribute more to overall utility. By making conceptual authority a function of utility, they can identify these optimific concepts and rely on them to overturn any concepts that conflict with them, thereby going some way towards eliminating conflicts from their outlook.

Yet the experience of discomfort in the face of conceptual conflict is not the peculiar plight of theorists with a taste for tidy systems. Living by concepts which systematically pull in divergent directions *is* uncomfortable, not just because it offends against the canons of harmony, but because it presents one with choices that cannot be resolved without loss. There will be costs, and cause for regret, no matter what one does.

Accordingly, the aim of relieving conceptual tensions has been thought to be justified by a practical concern to improve well-being: on Valerie Tiberius's (2018) value fulfilment theory, for example, having conflicting concepts counts as a form of 'ill-being', and the pursuit of well-being centrally involves alleviating or dissolving conflicts between our value concepts. A salient way to achieve this is to question the authority of some of the concepts involved. The authority question then acts as a device for evading conflict. But the same evasion can also take place in less intellectualized or less conscious forms. One may simply end up feeling estranged or alienated from a concept one used to live by. At least sometimes, as Williams notes, 'alienation is itself a device for evading conflict' (1995i, 195).

Another situation which may prompt the authority question is when we take concepts out of their usual context of application and project them into radically novel contexts. The novel context can be a product of technological advances—virtual reality may not call for the same set of concepts as physical reality. But such projections from a source context into a new target context also occur when a concept is transplanted from one academic discipline into another, or when concepts are extended from one sphere of application to a differently configured one. It is an open question, for example, to what extent the concepts of human psychology can help us make sense of animal minds, or to what extent the concepts of domestic politics can be made to fit international politics.

What then prompts the authority question is the sense that the novel context is not obviously covered by our existing concepts and remains conceptually underdetermined, which renders acute the question of how to conceptualize it. The point can be put in terms of inquiry. Where inquiry is as yet insufficiently clearly framed, we must engage in a different sort of inquiry, which Céline Henne (2023) calls *framing inquiry*. Framing inquiry creatively extends our conceptual repertoire to cover novel contexts. But just because this sort of inquiry is self-consciously involved in framing the previously unframed, it invites critical scrutiny of the proposed conceptualizations. Perhaps animal minds are sufficiently different from human minds to resist conceptualization in terms of human psychology, calling for their own set of concepts; or perhaps international institutions are bound to operate so differently from national ones that we need to rethink the domestic conceptualizations of legitimacy, democracy, and representation that we are tempted to project onto them.[41] In each case, the question arises: should we be thinking in those terms at all here? This is only to raise the authority question in a domain-restricted form, however: it does not question the authority of the concepts across all domains, but only within the novel domain.

Finally, we are sometimes led to question the authority of particular concepts for reasons that fall out of the concept itself. Take Sabina Lovibond's description of how a user of the concept *first-class mind* might come to

---

[41] Such reconceptualizations have been advocated, along different lines, by Krisch (2010), Cohen (2012), and Cueni (2020), for example.

wonder whether she is guilty of conniving participation in the use of a problematic notion. Is it being used merely as a pretext for differential treatment? Is the concept perhaps vacuous, like *phlogiston*? As Lovibond observes, one may be on the fence about this: 'Are there such things as "first-class minds"? A frank answer might be: sometimes I talk (and think) as if I believed in these things and sometimes not' (2015, 137).[42]

Anxiety that a concept might turn out to be vacuous, i.e. have an empty extension, is perhaps the paradigmatic form that the authority question takes in contemporary analytic philosophy, but it is not the only reservation one might have about a concept. This is illustrated by Oscar Wilde's eschewal of the concept of blasphemy during his trial for 'gross indecency' in 1895. Wilde's then-notorious credo that there was no such thing as an immoral book was put to the test during his cross-examination: the prosecutor challenged Wilde to deny that a scandalous story circulating in an Oxford undergraduate magazine at the time (and falsely attributed to Wilde) was *blasphemous*. Wilde was willing to grant that it was 'badly written', 'disgusting', and 'horrible'; but, despite being repeatedly pressed by the prosecutor, Wilde refused to enter into whether it was blasphemous or not. As both Wilde and the prosecutor well knew, by any reasonable definition of blasphemy, the story, entitled 'The Priest and the Acolyte', fell under the concept. The concept was thus plainly not vacuous. It applied to the story and unequivocally marked it out as immoral. Instead of denying either that the concept applied to the story or that this made the story immoral, therefore, Wilde declared: '"Blasphemous"' is not a word of mine.'[43]

This was not a denial of anything the prosecutor asserted. It was a refusal even to think in these terms—not because the concept *blasphemous* was vacuous, however, nor because Wilde was an atheist (he was not; he died a Catholic, professing that Catholicism was 'the only religion to die in'). He refused to think about the story in these terms because he consistently refused to think about any kind of art in anything but *aesthetic* terms, such as *badly written*, *disgusting*, and *horrible*. This comes out clearly in the initial exchange between the prosecutor and Wilde on this matter:

—'Do you think the story blasphemous?'
—'I think it violated every artistic canon of beauty.'

---

[42] See Lovibond (2015, 136–8). While she also describes the thinking process of someone who reaches a position of outright disbelief in first-class minds, her interest is in the concept-user who remains agnostic on the issue.

[43] See Hyde (1973, 107), which provides a full transcript of the trial. The story in question was in fact written by John Francis Bloxam, editor of *The Chameleon*, the magazine in which the story appeared.

—'That is not an answer.'
—'It is the only one I can give.'[44]

The problem with going around wondering whether fictional stories were blasphemous, by Wilde's lights, was that it embodied just the Victorian moralism about art that, as a figurehead of aestheticism, he had made it his life's mission to oppose.[45]

Another example of discomfort about concepts already in use is provided by Christine Korsgaard's discussion of the concepts *masculinity* and *femininity*. And again, her worry is not that these concepts are empty; if anything, people satisfy them rather too well by holding themselves to the ideals enshrined in these concepts. The worry is rather that these concepts are 'straitjackets, stunting everybody's growth' (1996, 77).[46] The right response to someone who reproachingly points out that a certain behaviour is not masculine/feminine, therefore, is not to retort that this claim is false, or to insist that the behaviour *is* in fact masculine/feminine; the right response, Korsgaard writes, is: 'let's not talk that way' (1996, 77)—by which she means, presumably, not just that we should stop talking in those terms, but that we should cease even to *think* in those terms, and hence cease to hold ourselves and others to the ideals enshrined in those concepts.

Lovibond, Wilde, and Korsgaard all single out particular thick normative concepts and question their authority.[47] They gesture towards a lack of reasons to use the concepts in question, or even towards reasons *not* to use them. In the absence of a theory of reasons for concept use, however, it is hard to specify the nature and range of these reasons, and how one might more systematically go about answering the authority question. What is clear, however, is that the authority question arises for concepts old and new.

1.5 Beyond Epistemological Appraisal

There is a tendency in contemporary philosophy to model the appraisal of concepts on the epistemological appraisal of beliefs.[48] Discussions of how concepts might be debunked, for example, typically look for ways to tie

---

[44] See Hyde (1973, 107).
[45] For philosophical accounts of moralism about art, see Diamond (2010) and Taylor (2012).
[46] See also Wollstonecraft (2014, 30-3, 48, 158, 204) and Mill (1988, IV, 86-8).
[47] For other examples of suspect concepts and discussions of the theme of concept loss, see also Murdoch (1961), Diamond (1988, 2021), Teichmann (2021), and Mulhall (2021, 28–31).
[48] Simion (2018), Egré and O'Madagain (2019), and Pérez Carballo (2020) offer sophisticated illustrations of the tendency to understand the value of concepts in epistemological terms.

concepts back to some claim or belief that can be criticized on epistemological grounds.[49] They operate in the spirit of Bertrand Russell's theory of descriptions, discerning straightforwardly criticizable *existence claims* within the logical entrails of concept use: by employing some concept F in articulating how things are, one commits oneself to the claim that *there is such a thing as F*. If that existence claim turns out to be unsupported by evidence, the concept is suspected of suffering from vacuity or reference failure: in the world we actually inhabit, it is a concept with an empty extension. *Phlogiston* is the textbook example, but the history of science is replete with examples of such empty concepts impeding scientific progress (Wilson 2006, 3). Lovibond exemplifies the tendency to model the appraisal of thick normative concepts on conceptual advances in science to the extent that she focuses worries about the concept *first-class mind* on whether there really are such things. If some concept F is suspected of committing us to a false existence claim, this in turn casts doubt on the entire set of what Richard Joyce calls the 'positive beliefs' (2006, 242 n. 6) involving that concept: the beliefs that implicitly commit one to the existence of F.[50]

However, as the examples of Wilde and Korsgaard remind us, the uncovering of unsupported existence claims is neither necessary nor sufficient for the debunking of concepts. It is not *necessary*, because committing us to unsupported existence claims is clearly not the only thing that can be wrong with our concepts. Many pejorative terms or slurs, for instance, are objectionable, but not necessarily because they suffer from reference failure. It would be Procrustean to press all such concepts into this one mould by arguing that they have empty extensions.[51] Some concepts that do pick out something are nonetheless susceptible to being debunked by other considerations—most notably, as we shall see in later chapters, by the realization that they serve objectionable concerns.

Nor is the uncovering of unsupported existence claims *sufficient* for the debunking of concepts, because some concepts remain unaffected by the realization that they suffer from reference failure. Many concepts in the social and natural sciences, for example, though known to be mere heuristics,

---

[49] See e.g. Joyce (2006), Kail (2011), Eklund (2017), Hom and May (2018), and Srinivasan (2019, 132 n. 7).

[50] Restricting our suspicions to positive beliefs allows for the fact that at least *some* beliefs involving the concept F must survive the realization that there is no such thing as F: for example, the second-order belief 'I used to believe that there was such a thing as F'.

[51] As Christopher Hom and Robert May invite us to do in 'Pejoratives as Fictions' (2018), for example.

idealizations, or caricatures, are considered no less valuable.[52] The same is true of many mythological and literary concepts.[53] They are widely understood to be useful fictions, and underscoring their fictional character should not affect our confidence in them.

Accordingly, some philosophers have sought to expand the basis on which concepts could be criticized to include not just unsupported existence claims, but unsupported claims of other kinds. They highlight not reference failure, but *presupposition failure*: use of the concept presupposes a false claim.[54] Siding with Gottlob Frege and P. F. Strawson against Russell, one might conceive of reference failure as being itself a kind of presupposition failure, where the use of a concept falsely presupposes the existence of its object.[55] But the notion of presupposition failure is significantly broader, since the relevant presuppositions do not have to be existence claims; they can also be false normative claims. This enables one to make sense of non-empty concepts that nonetheless make false presuppositions.

In this vein, Matti Eklund proposes to understand a non-empty normative concept as objectionable 'iff, roughly, its use in some sense presupposes a false normative claim' (2017, 73). A similarly presuppositional account is articulated by Alan Gibbard (1992). Some concepts expressed in slurs or epithets have been thought to offer prime examples of this: insofar as they presuppose that their objects are contemptible in virtue of their race or ethnicity, the concepts presuppose falsely (and thereby disqualify the claims articulated in terms of these concepts from being candidates for truth or falsity).[56] Or take Eklund's (2017, 13–14) example of the concept *slutty*. On his preferred description, reflection showing this to be an objectionable concept should not claim that nothing falls under the concept. The concept *slutty* is indeed satisfied by some types of behaviour. Its objectionability, like the objectionability of all slurs on Eklund's account, would rather have to derive from a false normative claim with which the concept is inextricably associated: 'that the

---

[52] See Weisberg (2013), Elliott-Graves and Weisberg (2014), and Appiah (2017).
[53] See Austin (2010) and Appiah (2017).
[54] As with the earlier qualification that a concept's association with a false existence claim does not necessarily impugn all beliefs involving the concept, so presupposition failure is not necessarily catastrophic for all claims involving the concept. See Yablo (2006) for a discussion of non-catastrophic presupposition failure.
[55] For an account of the debate between Russell and Strawson and the subsequent evolution of Strawson's views on these issues, see Beaver, Geurts, and Denlinger (2021, 6).
[56] See Richard (2008, 18–22) and Mühlebach (2019, 2023a, b, forthcoming) for critical discussions of the literature taking this line. It should be noted that it is controversial whether the fact that some concept presupposes falsely disqualifies the claims articulated in terms of the concepts from being candidates for truth or falsity; see Beaver, Geurts, and Denlinger (2021, 6).

targets of the slur are worthy of the negative view or attitude that use of the slur expresses' (2017, 73).

Both the reference failure account and the presupposition failure account assimilate the appraisal of concepts to the epistemological appraisal of beliefs. In both cases, concept-users discover, as they use the concept, that the concept suffers from an epistemic error: its use commits one to false existence claims, or to false presuppositions.

There is an attractive clarity, objectivity, and finality to such verdicts. They locate a fundamental mistake in the concepts themselves, or in what one necessarily commits oneself to by using them, and do not require one to consider the motives animating the concepts' use, the contexts in which they are typically deployed, or the various effects of using them. In fact, they do not require us to consider the concepts' actual operation in human affairs at all.

But there can also be a kind of evasion involved in this. It may too comfortably cast as an epistemic error what is really an *ethical* failing demanding a more complex reaction. For even where this kind of critique is directed at a deserving target, it leaves untouched the many alternative conceptualizations in the vicinity that do not suffer from the same vulnerability. Critiques of the concept of race on the grounds that modern genetics has revealed it to be empty, for example, do nothing to undermine other conceptions of race in the vicinity that are simply too superficial, too unconcerned with ancestry and genetic underpinnings, to be plausibly regarded as suffering from reference failure.[57] These superficial concepts trivially have non-empty extensions, and cannot so easily be disposed of in epistemological terms. They call for a more ethical style of critique—in the broad sense of ethical that encompasses all kinds of considerations bearing on how to think and live. Such a critique cannot afford to ignore the human motives animating the use of these concepts, the contexts in which they are typically used, and the effects this actually tends to have.

There are two broader points here. One is that the flawless exercise of purely cognitive powers cannot by itself be enough to arrive at the right set of concepts. It is an evasion of one's own freedom and responsibility to pretend that one's choice of concepts is fully determined by mind-independent facts we merely need to uncover—a pretence, moreover, which struggles to explain

---

[57] I elucidate the notion of conceptual 'superficiality' in Chapter 5 and put it to work in Chapter 9. For an example of a critique of the concept of race as vacuous, see Smith (2020, 53–62). For an account which proposes to replace the vacuous conception of race with three non-vacuous conceptions tailored to different sets of needs, see Hardimon (2017). Four different conceptions of race that do not fall prey to the vacuity critique are also articulated in Glasgow, Haslanger, et al. (2019).

why people's conceptual repertoires vary so widely instead of displaying the convergence one would expect of a purely cognitive process.

The second point is that many conceptualizations that do not involve anything as straightforward as an epistemic error nevertheless have something wrong with them. They pick out something alright, and do not make any obviously false presuppositions. But they nevertheless form proper targets of critique—of *ethical* critique, in the broad sense that includes social and political critique. Truth, justification, and knowledge are all very well, but they are not the only things we want from human thought.

What more do we want? One thing we certainly want from many of our concepts is that they should 'carve the world at the joints', which is to say match up with the antecedent structure of the world. True and justified thoughts are not enough; our thoughts need to be couched in the right terms, which, for someone like Theodore Sider, means the terms that reflect the basic structure of reality and thereby improve our understanding of the world (2011, 10).

This adds to the epistemological model of concept appraisal a metaphysical dimension of fidelity to the world's antecedent structure. We can then say that the problem with a concept such as Nelson Goodman's (1983) proposed concept *grue*, which applies to all things examined before time t just in case they are green but to things observed at or after t just in case they are blue, is not that the concept is empty (reference failure), or that it makes a false presupposition (presupposition failure). Rather, it is out of touch with the structure of the physical universe we happen to inhabit, and in particular with the way colours and objects tend to behave in it. 'Gruesome' concepts, we might say, suffer from fidelity failure.[58]

While this helpfully enriches our model of concept appraisal with a dimension that goes beyond truth and justification, it is still too narrow. For it remains confined to the old and still powerful idea that concepts, like the thoughts built from them, serve only one function: *adaequatio intellectus ad rem*, the adequation of the intellect to things, as the medieval slogan puts it, in a helpfully broad phrase that covers the adjustment of concepts to objects as well as of thoughts to facts.

Yet it is a highly questionable assumption that *all* concepts serve to carve the world at its antecedent joints. More plausibly, this is only what *some* of our concepts serve to do, and even then not necessarily *everything* that they

---

[58] For a recent discussion of 'gruesome' concepts and the Jamesian trade-offs involved in pursuing fidelity, see Finocchiaro (2023).

serve to do. Though we talk of rights and duties, or possibilities and probabilities, in much the same assertoric, descriptive, fact-stating manner in which we talk of frogs and beetles, that does not mean that the ways of thinking expressed thereby all work the same way. It is worth remembering Wittgenstein's remark that 'we don't notice the enormous variety of all the everyday language-games, because the clothing of our language makes them all alike' (2009, II, §335).[59]

Even those who, like Sider, foreground the demand on concepts to carve at the joints admit that only some concepts, such as the concepts of fundamental physics, actually stand a chance of carving at the joints; the concepts articulating higher-level descriptions, such as psychological, moral, or political concepts, merely approximate joint-carving descriptions to a greater or lesser degree. The resulting model of concept appraisal lacks the resources to see choices between concepts that are equally far from carving at the joints as anything but 'insubstantial' (2011, 7) in Sider's technical sense of the term, which leads us only to regard questions of conceptual ethics as 'substantive' insofar as they concern the world's fundamental structure.[60]

But the choice between different thick normative concepts in terms of which to organize individual lives and entire societies is surely anything but insubstantial in the ordinary sense of the term. As we noted, a society in which the concepts of *sexual harassment, domestic violence, child abuse, racism, sexism,* and *hate speech* are operative is very different from a society in which these concepts are lacking, or from one organized in terms of the distinction between *serf* and *franklin*, as England was from the twelfth to the fifteenth century.

Moreover, the various thick normative concepts that typically give us reasons for action and guide our conduct in the ethical, political, and legal spheres are not best thought of as *joint-carvers* at all. They primarily serve to motivate, guide, coordinate, and regulate behaviour. As Sally Haslanger (2020a, 249) has argued following Tadeusz Zawidzki (2013), a more plausible generalization about concepts is that they are *mind-shapers*.[61] Some concepts may still notably serve to structure our minds to mirror the structure of the

---

[59] For extended arguments questioning this assumption of a 'functional monism', see notably Price (2011) and Thomasson (2025).

[60] As Sider puts it: 'In my view, whether a question is substantive—in one important sense of "substantive"—depends largely on the extent to which its terms carve at the joints' (2011, 6).

[61] The term goes back to Mameli (2001). Haslanger herself encourages us to consider both the theoretical and the practical aims of classification, as she puts it: see Haslanger (2012, 188–90; 2020a, 242).

world. But others primarily serve to shape the social world we inhabit, and to shape how we respond to that world as well as to each other.

As long as one focuses exclusively on the demand that our concepts should match the fundamental structure of the world, the concerns of human concept-users merely appear as distorting forces to be overcome. This perspective is well expressed by Mark Heller: 'if we conceptually divide up the world into objects one way rather than another because doing so will serve our purposes better, then there is little chance that the resulting ontology will be the true ontology' (1990, 44).[62]

Once we recover a more generous sense of what we need our concepts to do for us, however, it becomes evident that the aspiration to make them serve human concerns is not just a temptation to be resisted. Insofar as our concepts aim to mirror anything like a true ontology, they will need to do that *in a way that serves our concerns*—what good would they be otherwise? Indeed, our concerns are what underlies the search for the true ontology in the first place: our interest in the true ontology derives notably from the host of other concerns to which a good grasp of the world's structure is instrumental, and even insofar as that interest reflects nothing but a pure concern for the truth, that is still very much a human concern, and one that has a history.[63]

The worry that the attractions of what it is convenient, comfortable, or comforting to think will get in the way of the search for the true ontology is of course a real worry; but it needs to be brought in later, once that search has itself been made intelligible as one that is responsive to human concerns. Then the path will be clear for an ungrudging recognition of the fact that our concepts, and our thick normative concepts in particular, should be answerable to human concerns. If there is one demand on our concepts, it is that they should help us to live.

To do justice to this demand, we need to broaden our understanding of concept appraisal to encompass not just epistemological and metaphysical considerations, but also ethical ones. We need to put the 'ethics' into conceptual ethics. That is the task shouldered by the rest of this book.

The Ethics of Conceptualization: Tailoring Thought and Language to Need. Matthieu Queloz, Oxford University Press.
© Matthieu Queloz 2025. DOI: 10.1093/9780198926283.003.0002

---

[62] Heller restricts his discussion to physical objects (1990, xiii), but the picture he articulates is sometimes taken to apply more widely.
[63] See Nietzsche (1998, 2009b), Foucault (1994), Williams (2002), Shapin (1994), Price (1988, 2003), and Pettit (forthcoming). I discuss in what respects these authors offer genealogies of the human disposition to value the truth, and the differences between these genealogies, in Queloz (2018b, 2021b, c).

2
The Autoethnographic Stance

Addressing the authority question *in the way that matters*, I argue in this chapter, requires one to adopt a distinctive stance towards our concepts, which I call *the autoethnographic stance*. I suggest that our capacity to take up this stance, whereby we disengage ourselves from the concepts we normally use in an engaged way, is crucial to achieving critical distance towards our concepts. After bringing out the importance of this distinction between engaged and disengaged concept use, I show how a variety of tempting philosophical errors can be traced to conflations of these two aspects: when the autoethnographic stance reveals the reasons we perceive to depend on the concepts we use, notably, it becomes tempting to insert that dependence into the content of our thoughts making engaged use of those concepts. I end with a discussion of the nature and possession of concepts, which shows that conceptual ethics is compatible even with a picture of concepts as immutable abstract objects that cannot be causally affected by changes in human behaviour or psychology.

2.1 Engaged vs. Disengaged Concept Use

Assessing the authority of a concept requires one to relate to it in a peculiar way. It is not enough to be able to *mention* a concept ('They propose this concept of "F", whatever that is'). Some grasp is required of how things present themselves to one who actually uses the concept. One must understand the concept 'from the inside' in order to assess its claim to authority.

At the same time, one must find some way of stepping back from the concept sufficiently to acquire critical leverage over it—it would be too uncritically accepting of the concept simply to insist that we should use it because there is so much F-ness around and F-ness is important for the reasons the concept F itself adverts to. The whole point of raising the authority question is to step back from the unreflected folkways of the unreflective mind.

To grasp what is involved in critically addressing the authority question, we therefore have to distinguish not just between *mentioning* and *using* a concept, but also between two different ways of *using* a concept.[1] Adrian Moore (2023a, 216–17; 2024a, 382–4) has usefully marked this distinction in terms of the contrast between *engaged* and *disengaged* concept use.[2] This distinction is crucial to understanding what is involved in critically assessing a concept's authority.

When using some concept F in an engaged way—the concept *funny*, say— one looks through it at the world, as if through a lens, and is immediately responsive to the gestalt it gives the world, the aspects it renders salient, and the reasons it adverts to. It is then perfectly correct to describe the world as containing plenty of things that are F, and to insist that we use the concept because there is so much F-ness around. An essential part of what is involved in grasping the concept, moreover, may be to conceive of what it picks out— F-ness—as being entirely independent of human observers and their practices of concept use. If a dinosaur once stumbled in a particularly funny way, this was still objectively funny, even if there were no human observers around at the time to perceive it as such.[3]

At the same time, we can also think *about*, rather than *with*, the concept F, standing back from it to hold it up to reflective scrutiny. This is what we must do to critically assess a concept's authority. We must take a sideways look *at* the lens instead of peering through it. But to understand what we are looking at, we still have to grasp the concept, and grasp what the world looks like to one who peers through it. To think about a concept in this comprehending way, we thus still have to think *with* it in an important sense. We must use the concept in a disengaged way in order to be in a good position to evaluate whether to use it in an engaged way.

Thick normative concepts offer a particularly clear illustration of this: they neither just describe nor just evaluatively label independently describable patches of the world. Rather, what forms part of their extension is itself a function of the evaluative attitudes of those who deploy these concepts, and therefore their extension cannot be neutrally specified, without adopting an

---

[1] The use/mention distinction alone, if it is to be clear-cut, cannot capture the difference at issue here, because, as Moore (2019b, 15) argues, that difference turns on what a concept is employed *for*, and, on any account of the use/mention distinction that renders it clear-cut, the mere fact that a concept is mentioned cannot tell us much about what the concept is employed for.

[2] Which itself crystallizes a distinction prefigured in Williams (1985, 157; 1986, 203–4; 1995j, 207; 2002, 50–1). See also Thomas (2006, 146) and Goldie (2009) for other illuminating ways of characterizing the distinction.

[3] The example of the dinosaur misadventure is loosely based on Williams (2014b, 380) as well as on a discussion between Williams and A. J. Ayer in Chanan (1972).

evaluative stance—the extension is *shapeless* without the evaluation.[4] As T. M. Scanlon unpacks the point: 'In order to trace the contours of the ethical concept's applicability we have to understand its evaluative point...we must be guided by the evaluative perspective of a thick concept in order to apply it' (2003, 276). To think intelligently about a thick concept, one must take up, at least imaginatively, the evaluative perspective of those who use the concept in an engaged way.

2.2 The Ethnographic Stance

A model for this way of relating to a concept can be found in the way ethnographers study concepts from other cultures. As the anthropologist James Laidlaw highlights, an ethnographic approach makes it possible to 'gain an imaginative understanding of a form of life, and expand one's moral horizon by learning to think with its concepts and appreciate the force of its values, without having to make those concepts or values one's own' (2014, 224).

As Laidlaw stresses, however, the fact that this is possible can also be a cause for wonder (2014, 68). Given the ostensible inescapability of one's own perspective and the apparent necessity of thinking with one's own concepts, how can we possibly understand, think with, and perhaps even learn from concepts that are not our own? Anthropology has a long history of striving to reconcile this perplexing possibility with the recognition of the inevitability of certain forms of ethnocentrism.[5]

But the undeniable fact remains that an ethnographer is perfectly capable of becoming an expert user of, say, some mystical concept from another culture without having to make it her own: she need not structure her own affairs in those terms and can remain unresponsive to the distinctive reasons the concept articulates.[6] Indeed, maintaining some detachment from the way of thinking she studies is part of what grounds her claim to scientific objectivity. If her interpretation is not to be tone-deaf, however, she does need to be attuned to the perspective of those who live by the concept. The challenge, as

---

[4] See Dancy (1995), Kirchin (2010), and Roberts (2011, 2013) for that way of putting the point. For articulations of the same point in more general terms, see Williams (1985, 157; 1995j, 206; 1995a, 563; 1996a, 29), McDowell (1998b, a), Scanlon (2003, 276), and Anderson (2004, 14).

[5] For some of the more recent contributions, see Strathern (2004), Willerslev (2007), Candea (2010), Pedersen (2011), and Holbraad (2012).

[6] Although, as Laidlaw (2014, 46, 214) emphasizes, really taking seriously another form of life may lead one to learn *from* as well as *about* it, in which case disengaged concept use eventually results in engaged concept use.

the anthropologist Clifford Geertz puts it, is to arrive at an interpretation of their perspective 'which is neither imprisoned within their mental horizons, an ethnography of witchcraft as written by a witch, nor systematically deaf to the distinctive tonalities of their existence, an ethnography of witchcraft as written by a geometer' (1983a, 57).

Now when philosophers attempt to think their way into concepts they do not live by, they adopt a stance that is analogous to the ethnographer's, even if their interests and methodological aspirations remain recognizably those of philosophy rather than ethnography. This is what leads Bernard Williams to speak in this connection of the *ethnographic stance*: a stance from which one 'has an imaginative understanding of a society's ethical concepts and can understand its life from the inside, but does not share those concepts' (1986, 203–4).

The human capacity to adopt the ethnographic stance towards concepts is a broader and more basic phenomenon than the academic practice of ethnography. We routinely adopt such a stance towards the concepts of religions we do not practice ourselves, for instance. Moore offers the example of the concept *Shabbat*.[7] For someone unfamiliar with Judaism to become a competent disengaged user of the concept, her grasp of the concept must be *sympathetic* enough to enable her to grasp the concept's role within engaged concept-users' lives—'sympathetic' in the Humean sense of feeling one's way into another perspective to the point of resonating with its sentiments and concerns (much as the sitar's 'sympathetic strings', though untouched, resonate with the primary strings).[8] But the disengaged concept-user grasps all this merely in the spirit of an ethnographer, without living by the concept herself: she does not structure her own affairs in those terms—she does not *observe* the Shabbat, as we naturally put it in this case.

Engaged use of the concept, by contrast, involves not just sympathy, but identification: it involves *abiding* or *living by* the concept, i.e. being emotionally and rationally responsive to it and its concomitant reasons in the conduct of one's own affairs. Disengaged use is thus sympathetic enough to grasp a concept from the inside, but not identified, whereas engaged use is both sympathetic and identified.

---

[7] See Moore (2023a, 216–17).
[8] For the sitar analogy, see Baillie (2000, 52). Hume aptly describes sympathy as the capacity of the 'minds of men' to be 'mirrors to one another' (Hume 2000, 2.2.5.21), and on his account, as on Adam Smith's, sympathy forms the foundation of impartial concern for general welfare—though see Sagar (2017) for the subtle differences in how Hume and Smith understand sympathy.

The capacity to adopt the ethnographic stance is an underappreciated but crucial contributor to philosophical reflection. By making it possible for us to genuinely understand concepts other than our own, it awakens us to the enormous variety to be found across human thought, and hence to the realization that there are plenty of alternatives to our concepts. Were we permanently locked in the engaged perspective, we could never ascend to the vantage point from which questions of objectivity, relativism, and tolerance first come into view. By means of imaginative identification, however, we can pick up and understand concepts from the inside, grasping how they relate their object to other things, cast it in a certain evaluative light, and impart a certain emotional texture and feel to it, while continuing to reject those concepts. That is a remarkable fact, which lies at the root of many philosophical worries over objectivity, relativism, and tolerance.

The ethnographic stance is thus not the preserve of social scientists. It is the seed crystal from which the more elaborate crystals of philosophy, philosophical anthropology, and ethnography grow. For Williams, the human capacity to adopt the ethnographic stance is also fundamental to moral philosophy. As he stresses in his preface to the French translation of *Ethics and the Limits of Philosophy*: 'The possibility of the *ethnographic stance*, of understanding an alien structure of values which one does not share, is a basic datum for moral philosophy' (2021, 278). And in his response to Simon Blackburn's review of the book, he observes:

> The fact that the ethnographic stance is possible seems to me very important for moral philosophy. That stance combines two things. First, it understands from the inside a conceptual system in which ethical concepts are integrally related to modes of explanation and description. Second, it is conscious that there are alternatives to any such system, that there is a great deal of ethical variety. (1986, 204)

Williams goes on to remark of the oscillating double-mindedness this engenders that while Wittgensteinian approaches emphasize the first aspect at the expense of the second, prescriptivist and anti-realist approaches emphasize the second at the expense of the first—when of course, 'to do justice to the ethnographic stance', we need 'to take on both these things' (1986, 204).[9]

---

[9] I show how Williams's belief in the fundamental importance of the ethnographic stance is reflected across his oeuvre in Queloz (2024a).

2.3 The Autoethnographic Stance

An important point neglected by Williams, however, is that we are also capable of adopting something akin to the ethnographic stance towards *our own* concepts—we can take up what I shall call the *autoethnographic stance*.

As I propose to understand it, the autoethnographic stance enables us to make disengaged use of concepts we normally use in an engaged way. This is not the same as viewing our concepts the way people living by different concepts might view them; it is still to view them as *our own* concepts, but against the backdrop of the fact that they are only one set of concepts among a range of alternatives. Clifford Geertz eloquently describes the difference:

> To see ourselves as others see us can be eye-opening.... But it is from the far more difficult achievement of seeing ourselves amongst others, as a local example of the forms human life has locally taken, a case among cases, a world among worlds, that the largeness of mind, without which objectivity is self-congratulation and tolerance a sham, comes. (1983b, 16)

Geertz is right to emphasize the peculiar difficulty of taking up the autoethnographic stance: it does not come naturally; we have to build up the ability to adopt it, and we might never learn to adopt it if we did not first have occasion to adopt the ethnographic stance towards others, either through real encounters with them or through notional confrontations facilitated by historical or anthropological documents.[10] Indeed, we cannot 'see ourselves amongst others' before first understanding that there *are* other ways of conceptualizing the world.

Moreover, as Geertz also stresses, adopting the autoethnographic stance is not the same as imaginatively identifying with others who adopt the ethnographic stance towards us. It is *our own* concepts that we relate to from the autoethnographic stance, which makes them easier to understand, but creates a special difficulty in achieving the distance required to regard them from the autoethnographic rather than from the usual, deliberative stance.

Hence, adopting the autoethnographic stance first requires us to disengage ourselves from at least one of our own concepts: we must cease to be fully absorbed in its use and the concomitant perspective on the world, and temporarily suspend our emotional and rational responsiveness to the perspective opened up by the concept. It may be thought that it is easier to suspend

---

[10] I am grateful to Martin Kusch for helping me to see this point.

responsiveness to the reasons the concept adverts to than to disengage from the way it engages one's emotions. But, as Richard Moran and Berislav Marušić bring out, one certainly can step back from one's emotional responses and reflect on them, attending to oneself attending to something else, and contemplate those emotional responses as if from the outside.[11]

At the same time, serious reflection on the concept's merits requires that we remain able to understand the concept from the inside and retain a detached, 'offline' responsiveness to its correlative reasons and the way it engages one's emotions—one still has to appreciate what the world looks like to one who uses the concept in an engaged way. If we are to appreciate the perspective on the world opened up by the concept, and embed that perspective within a wider perspective from which this way of thinking can be appraised, we must not merely think *about* the concept, but continue to identify *imaginatively* with one who thinks *with* the concept. We must disengage ourselves from the concept while stopping short of losing the concept or becoming estranged from it to the point of incomprehension.

When adopting the autoethnographic stance, we thus hover in a mid-level position, halfway between abandon *to* and abandon *of* the concept. We can picture this in terms of a three-level structure consisting of (i) engaged use, (ii) disengaged use, and (iii) disengaged non-use. Disengaged non-use involves neither living by the concept oneself (hence 'disengaged') nor using the concept at all (hence 'non-use'). What matters is whether the concept gets tokened in the subject's thought in one mode or another, not whether the concept is or is not in use in the wider community. As historians of science and ideas demonstrate, it is possible to be a disengaged user of concepts that are no longer in use. Conversely, it is possible to be a non-user of a concept that is still in use in one's community. Accordingly, 'the abandon of a concept' can mean two different things: that the concept has been abandoned in the course of history, in which case it can still be used, if only in a disengaged way, by historians; or that a subject comes to abandon a concept, which involves moving from engaged to disengaged use, and then, possibly, ceasing to use it in any way at all.[12]

---

[11] See Moran (2001, 172–94) and Marušić (2022, 80–124). As they show following Sartre, however, there can be a special difficulty involved in getting into view the object of one's emotional response together with that emotional response; and when one's subjective perspective cannot be fully integrated with an objective view of that subjective perspective, one is left with an irresolvable 'double vision', forced to oscillate between the two perspectives without being able to coalesce them into one.

[12] I am indebted to Céline Henne for extremely helpful comments on this issue.

This three-level structure takes us beyond the simple dichotomy between use and non-use. It allows us to recognize that moving away from a concept is a more complex and gradual process than first appears—a point we shall explore in more depth in the next chapter. And this structure allows us to situate both the ethnographic and the autoethnographic stance at the middle level of disengaged use. Where the two stances differ is in how they get there: one adopts the ethnographic stance if one comes to the middle level *from* the third level, moving from disengaged non-use to disengaged use; whereas one adopts the autoethnographic stance if one comes to the middle level from the first level, moving from engaged to disengaged use.

This three-level structure also helps to demarcate the autoethnographic stance from superficially similar stances involving merely two-level structures, such as P. F. Strawson's 'objective attitude' (2008a, 9) or Thomas Nagel's 'view from nowhere' (1986). To take up the autoethnographic towards a concept is to take an external and objectivizing view of the dispositions involved in using the concept. But it differs from the stance described by Strawson in retaining a significant measure of sympathetic understanding of its object: it precisely requires enough humanizing to continue to be able to make sense of the subjective perspective of one who uses the concept. And it differs from the stance described by Nagel in being, not a view from a nowhere, but a view *from the rest of one's dispositions*. Far from trying to shed everything that makes us who we are in order to adopt something like the point of view of the universe, we keep both feet firmly planted in the rest of our ways of thinking, and bring the entire stock of our thick and thin normative concepts to bear on the appraisal of the concept under evaluation. The autoethnographic stance thus retains more of our humanity at both ends—in what it draws on, and in what it is directed to.

Indeed, we could not adopt the autoethnographic stance towards all of our concepts at once. For we still need some conceptual basis *from* which to think about the concept under scrutiny, especially if we are going to appraise it by some clearly articulated evaluative standards. But we can adopt the autoethnographic stance in a piecemeal fashion, disengaging ourselves from one concept, or one connected set of concepts, while relying on the rest of our concepts to embed it into an evaluative perspective from which it can be appraised. Throughout this process, we continue to be able to grasp what the world looks like to one who lives by the concept—what gestalt it gives the world and what reasons it adverts to—but have temporarily suspended its correlative reasons to weigh our reasons for thinking in terms of such reasons.

The possibility of occupying this mid-level position, where one ceases to be fully absorbed in the use of a concept while remaining able to use it in considering its merits, is fundamental to our capacity to raise the authority question *in the way that matters*. For distinguishing between engaged and disengaged use allows us to distinguish two corresponding modes in which one can raise the authority question about thick normative concepts. On the one hand, a concept-user can raise the authority question about some concept F while using the concept in an *engaged* way, looking *through* it rather than at it. This means that, for any thick normative concept, we can give reasons to use it according to the following schema:

A reason to use the concept F is that, given our concerns, limited capacities, and circumstances, we need to be suitably sensitive to the presence of F-ness.

On this schema, F-ness is thought of as being there anyway already, waiting for its presence to be picked up on by concept-users. The reference to our concerns, limited capacities, and circumstances will be expanded on in the chapters to follow, but its point here is to acknowledge that even if we derive a reason for our use of the concept F from the presence of F-ness, something still needs to be said to account for our *interest* in the presence of F-ness. F-ness does not automatically inscribe itself into our conceptual apparatus just because it exists, and *a fortiori* not necessarily under that description. Some combination of human concerns, capacities, and circumstances must be appealed to in order to motivate conceptual sensitivity to it.

The problem with answering the authority question from an engaged perspective on the concept, however, is that it is not so much wrong as *too internal* to one's use of the concept. It makes answering the authority question too easy. From the engaged perspective of someone who thinks with or through the concept F, the world appears full of F-ness, and it seems nearly inevitable that human beings would eventually have reason to come to think in terms of F. The authority of *any* concept with a non-empty extension can be vindicated following this schema. If the fact that there is a lot of F-ness in the world, which we become sensitive to by using the concept F, were itself already a decisive reason to use the concept F, then any non-empty concept could legitimate its own use, with all the audacity of the Baron who pulled himself out of a mire by his own hair.

It is nonetheless important to acknowledge that the question can be addressed in this engaged mode, because this enables us to find a place for, and account for the plausibility of, the kinds of reason statements that refer either to the object of the concept in question or to the reasons the concept itself opens our eyes to. But tackling the authority question only in this mode offers us too little critical leverage, and does not do enough to help us discriminate between more and less authoritative concepts.

If the authority question is easily answered by the engaged concept-user, for whom the salient ubiquity of *F*-ness virtually compels us to think in terms of *F*, the question is a far more open one for the disengaged concept-user, who wonders how much reason to use the concept *F* we still have if we characterize our situation *without* drawing on that concept. From this perspective, the question is what reasons we have to use this concept that do not themselves draw on the concept, and instead adhere to the following schema:

> A reason for us to use the concept *F* is that, given our concerns, limited capacities, and circumstances as characterized without drawing on the concept *F*, we need to use the concept *F*.

If reasons can be found that fit this schema, this will not merely be the concept patting itself on the back, but an independent vindication of its authority.

That is why the possibility of taking up the autoethnographic stance is crucial to raising the authority question in the way that matters, which is to say *critically*. It is only thanks to our remarkable ability to take up the autoethnographic stance that we can look, with sufficient critical distance, for *reasons* to reason in terms of our concepts. Instead of being forced either to use or not to use certain concepts, the autoethnographic stance allows us to use them in a disengaged way in order to critically assess their claim to authority over our lives.

It may be felt that a certain way of thinking about conceptual content stands in the way of achieving the required independence: if conceptual content is holistically determined, we cannot isolate a concept from the rest of our conceptual repertoire and still be left with something determinately contentful, because the concept's content is determined notably—some would say entirely—by its relations to other concepts. Consider the concept *gene*. If we assume that its content is partly determined by its relations to other biological concepts, it follows that a nineteenth-century Moravian monk breeding peas could not have conceptualized genes as present-day geneticists do, i.e. in close interconnection with concepts such as *nucleotide*, *chromosome*, and *monomer*, because he lacked these surrounding concepts. For a holist about conceptual content, a concept must always be understood in relation to other concepts.

But this is a thesis about the constitution of conceptual content, not about the selective application of evaluative standards. It does not bar us from isolating the reason relations articulated by a concept in our *appraisal* of the concept. For what we need to do is not to sever its relations to other concepts, but to temporarily suspend their influence on our evaluation. This is more akin to switching off a node in an electrical network while preserving the integrity of the network. Even assuming that a concept's content is determined by its reason relations to other concepts (all the while granting that reason relations obtain, strictly speaking, between thoughts making use of concepts rather than between the concepts themselves), disengaging from a concept in order to critically evaluate it does not suddenly render the concept unintelligible. Its relations to the rest of our concepts remain intact. To say that we disengage from the concept is merely to say that, for the purposes of this particular appraisal, we *discount* all the reason relations connecting that concept to other concepts.

In some cases, this will still seem insufficiently critical, because an entire *set* of closely interrelated concepts is suspect, and on similar grounds. But we can also disengage from an entire set of concepts at once—as Williams, for example, critically disengages from the entire set of concepts characteristic of what he calls 'the morality system'. This is to discount all the reason relations that this set of concepts stands in to our remaining concepts. In either case, we are perfectly capable of counting certain reasons while discounting others, even if we only *understand* what we are counting and discounting in virtue of the relations between our concepts.

2.4 Conflating Engaged and Disengaged Use

We can, then, critically distance ourselves from concepts by taking up the autoethnographic stance towards them. Yet the possibility of taking up the autoethnographic stance brings risks as well as opportunities. Just because it opens up a second perspective on our concepts, it entrains the risk of conflating the two perspectives.

From the disengaged perspective, we may well conclude that the concept *funny*, for example, is not a concept that creatures differing sharply from us— such as dinosaurs—would have shared. Though there can be little doubt that many extremely funny dinosaur misadventures must have taken place over the course of the roughly one hundred and fifty million years during which they dominated the earth, all that funniness was probably lost on them.

Funny is likely a distinctively human concept, not merely in the sense of being *possessed* only by humans, but in the sense of being *expressive* of our humanity.[13]

This makes it tempting to infer that any funny misadventures that occurred before humans came on the scene were not, in fact, *objectively* funny. Indeed, having recognized, from the disengaged perspective, that the concept is a distinctively human concept, it is tempting to go further and conclude that, even from the engaged perspective, the right thing to say is that things are only ever 'funny for us'.

That pressure to relativize the validity of our concepts is even stronger in the case of thick normative concepts that exhibit a great deal of variety *within* the range of human arrangements. Consciousness of this variety can exert pressure on our confidence in our own concepts—and, by extension, on the judgements we form with them. 'What truth is that', Montaigne exclaimed, 'which these mountains bound, and is a lie to the world beyond?'[14] Fuelled by an awareness of alternatives, a nagging sense that we *could* think differently hovers over our dealings. This makes it almost irresistible to conclude that what *we*, in the contrastive sense that opposes some more or less narrow *us* to other people, perceive as reasons, truths, and facts, are really only ever reasons, truths, and facts *for us*, in virtue of the concepts we use, but not for other people.

This awareness of alternatives can invite a relativistic reinterpretation of our own thoughts which it is important to resist. That reinterpretation is made all the more tempting by the fact that some concepts really *are* properly understood as relativizing their own claims to applicability and validity—in matters of etiquette, for example, which are sometimes correctly understood to exempt outsiders, or to be applicable only in certain places; or in the case of concepts such as *cocktail party*, where what counts as one is correctly understood to depend on certain people's dispositions to treat it as one.[15]

Generalizing this model, however, would result in a misunderstanding of most of our concepts. 'When in Rome, do as the Romans do' may be true enough for certain norms of etiquette, but it does not generalize to other norms.[16] The thought that our reasons are only simply there *for us* pertains to

---

[13] A distinction drawn by Williams in his discussion of the human perspective's significance to ethics in Williams (2006c).
[14] The original reads: '*Quelle vérité que ces montagnes bornent, qui est mensonge au monde qui se tient au-delà?*' (1967, II.xii.241).
[15] I take the cocktail party example from Searle (2010, 33–4).
[16] It notably fails to generalize to moral norms, for example; see Williams (2001b, 23).

the disengaged perspective, and to try to introduce it into the engaged perspective is to create a kind of chimera. The pupil who treats the sentence '2 + 2 = 4 for us' as a sentence in arithmetic has misunderstood something. One has not mastered these mathematical concepts unless one recognizes their claim to universal applicability and validity. The same is true of many moral concepts, as moral realists rightly insist. Concepts that are not universally used, much less universally used in an engaged way, can nonetheless claim universal applicability and validity. And it is no surprise that we should have ways of thinking which, just because they are not relativized, at the level of their content, to our own dispositions, allow us think about people with different dispositions and express our concerns about them. Normative concepts, including moral, religious, or legal concepts, would lose much of their *raison d'être* if they never applied to those who did not already use them in an engaged way. It is part of the point of such concepts that they apply to people who are not yet under their sway, and thereby enjoin alignment with the sensibility they themselves instil.

To present concepts claiming universal applicability and validity as claiming only *local* applicability and validity is thus to distort them by conflating two different aspects: the aspect under which concepts present themselves from the engaged perspective, and the aspect under which they present themselves from the disengaged perspective. The realization, from the disengaged perspective, that our reasons are indexed to our concepts is misguidedly inserted right into the *content* of our thoughts using the concepts in an engaged way. The thought: 'This is a reason to φ', is reinterpreted as being, in effect, the thought: 'For us, this is a reason to φ'. But that is a *different* thought. Compare the following two sentences:

(1) x's being F counts as a reason to φ.
(2) For the set of engaged users of the concept F, x's being F counts as a reason to φ.

The reasons adverted to by the concept F as understood in sentence (1) claim universal validity: even for those unacquainted with F, x's being F is a reason to φ. The reasons adverted to by the concept F as understood in sentence (2), by contrast, only claim validity for a bounded set of reasoners, namely those who in fact use concept F in an engaged way.

Accordingly, it would result in a serious distortion of the contents we were trying to index to our own conceptual repertoire at the reflective level if we inserted the indexation into the contents of the concepts. This would be to let one's disengaged perspective on a concept distort the engaged perspective one takes up in using it—a distortion roughly equivalent to mistaking the normativity of morality for that of etiquette. Even once we realize that reasons which for us are 'simply there' are not necessarily 'simply there' for other people, we do not, unless we are changing the subject, suddenly have the thought: 'For us, this is a reason'—we still have the thought: 'This is a reason'. If, from the engaged perspective, the reason is simply there, then the reason is properly understood from that perspective as applying *no matter what our concepts are*. That is *what it is* for a reason to be, for us, simply there; and so that is the thought whose dependence on our concepts we must grasp from the disengaged perspective without distorting it.[17]

Much the same point can be put in terms of truth. Realizing, when using a concept in a disengaged way, that a truth articulable in terms of that concept is relative to our conceptual apparatus may tempt one to conclude that all we are really entitled to, when using the concept in an engaged way, is the thought: 'It is true in our conceptual scheme S that x is F'. But if what we are thinking in an engaged way is true in S and S is in fact the conceptual scheme we are operating in, then what we are thinking is true *simpliciter*. Consider, by way of illustration, the analogy between conceptual norms and the rules of a game such as chess. If a player delivers a performance on the board which makes her the winner according to the rules of chess, it may well be that there is an alternative game, *quess*, in which the same performance would make her the loser; but when the time comes to hand someone the trophy, we have to decide whether it was chess or quess we were playing, and if it was chess, then that makes our player not merely the winner at chess and the loser at quess, but, simply, the winner.[18]

At the same time, the fact that realist locutions correctly express our concepts as used from the engaged perspective does not entail that they offer us the best description of our concepts from the disengaged perspective. It would equally be a conflation of the two perspectives to maintain, in the face of the manifest variety of moral concepts across different cultures and epochs, and given the lack of a good explanation as to why only a tiny fraction of humanity ever arrived at the precise set of moral concepts in use now and

---

[17] See Williams (2006g, 195).
[18] Lewis (1983a, 173) makes this point about truth in a language. The illustration is adapted from Percival (1994, 191–2) and McPherson (2011, 232), though the chess analogy is of course frequently used by Wittgenstein, who remarks already in 1929: 'a pawn is the sum of rules for its moves (a square is a piece too), just as in the case of language the rules define the logic of a word' (1975, 327–8). For further discussion of Wittgenstein's use of the chess analogy, see Gustafsson (2020).

around here, that those moral concepts are absolutely and definitively the right ones for anyone, because they are the only ones that pick out some metaphysically privileged properties that were crying out to be referred to all along. Within the disengaged perspective, there is room for the recognition that those concepts came to be ours through various historical contingencies; that we would now be responsive to different reasons had history been different; and that we would not necessarily be confused or deceived if it were so. It is merely that sentences making disengaged use of a concept to express perfectly correct philosophical-cum-ethnographic observations yield blatant falsehoods when interpreted as engaged uses of the concept, and vice versa.

Adopting the autoethnographic stance thus reveals a certain kind of dependence of reasons on concepts: the reasons we are responsive to are *hermeneutically dependent* on the concepts we use. The fact that $F(x)$ is a reason for $G(x)$ is hermeneutically dependent on concept F in that $F(x)$ would not be *intelligible* to us *as* a reason for $G(x)$ if we lacked concept F. But one must resist the unwarranted slide from this hermeneutic dependence to other kinds of dependence, such as the *ontological* dependence of *existence* on concepts, or the *logical* dependence of *reason relations* on concepts.

First, hermeneutic dependence does not imply *ontological* dependence, where some object or property P is ontologically dependent on concept F just in case P would not exist if we lacked concept F. As the example of the property of funniness showed, the fact that conceptual sensitivity to the presence of property P presupposes possession of the concept F does not entail that P cannot exist unless F exists. The slide from hermeneutic to ontological dependence leads to a crude idealism on which things only exist as long as we can think of them.

Second, hermeneutic dependence does not imply *logical* dependence: the reason relations articulated by concept F are logically dependent on concept F just in case the reasons $F(x)$ adverts to are conditional, at the level of their content, on being an engaged user of concept F. But again, while it is true that $F(x)$ would not be intelligible to us as a reason for $G(x)$ if we lacked concept F, it does not follow that the kinds of reasons $F(x)$ adverts to are conditional on being an engaged user of concept F. That would only follow if F were a rather special kind of concept, namely one adverting to reasons that were understood to apply only to engaged users of that concept. There are such concepts; but they typically involve enculturation into certain norms that are expressly understood to apply only to those who have been so enculturated. Or else they involve what might be called the 'knowledge *oblige*' principle: by acquiring certain forms of knowledge, one comes to see certain reasons whose applicability is conditional on being able to see them, so that knowledge of these reasons is itself what obliges one to heed them, as they do not apply to those who have no knowledge of them. (An eccentric example of such a structure is the 'Basilisk' argument in the philosophy of AI, according to which it would be rational for a future artificial superintelligence to retroactively incentivize its own creation by precommitting to punishing anyone who failed to accelerate its creation even while marking themselves out as receptive to such acausal game-theoretical blackmail by the very act of thinking through the Basilisk argument and seeing its force.)

But it is clearly unwarranted to generalize from these highly specific structures to the conclusion that all reasons make their applicability conditional on engaged concept use in this way. The slide from hermeneutic to logical dependence leads to a jejune relativism on which reasons only ever apply to those who think in terms of them already.

What disengaged reflection on the contingency of our conceptual apparatus should prompt us to do is not to systematically recast the judgements formulated therein in terms that index them to us, in a misguided effort to be more truthful, but rather to ask whether we have good *reasons* to operate with this apparatus rather than another—*why* we play chess rather than quess. Perhaps things would go better for us in some respect if we played quess. Just as using alternative pieces guided by different rules would allow for different moves and combinations in chess, thereby changing the dynamics and character of the game, so the use of alternative concepts would allow for different inferential moves and combinations of thoughts.

2.5 Concepts: Their Nature and Possession

It is easier to talk sense with concepts than to talk sense about them, Gilbert Ryle observed in 1949.[19] That was already true enough then, but the difficulty has since been compounded by the multiplication of theories of concepts in philosophy, psychology, and beyond, which has led to the term 'concept' being used in several tightly regimented but incompatible ways. While it is widely agreed that concepts are the kinds of things we can possess, there is no consensus about the nature of concepts. Some regard concepts as bundles of abilities embodied in the malleable clay of linguistic and non-linguistic behaviour; others understand them as psychological items, such as mental

---

[19] See Ryle (2009a, lx).

representations in one format or another; yet others insist that concepts are immutable abstract objects—such as Fregean senses—that cannot be causally affected by changes in human behaviour or human psychology.[20] How can conceptual ethics hope to get off the ground in the absence of a consensus on what concepts are?

If one understands conceptual ethics as the ethics *of conceptualization*, however, its viability does not depend on there being a consensus on the nature of concepts. In thinking about the ethics of conceptualization, we start, as the suffix '-ization' indicates, from a concrete social *activity* rather than an ontology: the open-ended human enterprise of *conceptualizing* things, which is the activity whereby certain *conceptions* become operative in our thinking and we manifest our *possession* of certain concepts. The ethics of conceptualization is the practical reflection on how best to perform that activity and how to appraise its products.

For there to be a point to practical reflection along those lines, we must assume that there are better or worse ways of performing that activity, but we need not assume that concepts are malleable. Engaging in the ethics of conceptualization is compatible even with a picture of concepts as immutable abstracta: we can still coherently ask *which* immutable abstracta we should look to in our affairs, and an answer to this question can be informed by the differences entrained by the use of different concepts; moreover, our practices of concept use can be *practically responsive* to the answer reached, because which concepts we possess depends on how we *in fact* conceptualize things—on which conceptions are actually operative in our thinking; and, by conceptualizing differently—by adjusting and replacing the conceptions operative in our thinking—we can change which concepts we use even if we cannot change the concepts themselves.

To appreciate the ecumenical nature of this approach, start from the seemingly controversial suggestion I made in the introduction, that when appraising concepts, we should consider not only what people pick out with their concepts, but also what they take to be good indicators of something's falling under a concept, and what they take to follow from it. Some philosophers are happy to recognize these further aspects of concept use as constitutive of

---

[20] For overviews of the different accounts of concepts on offer, see Margolis and Laurence (1999, 2015, 2019). For an example of the abilities view, which goes back to Wittgenstein, see Dummett (1996), Bennett and Hacker (2008), and Kenny (2010); for examples of the mental representations view, which goes back to Locke, see Fodor (1998, 2004), Millikan (2000, 2017), and Shea (2024); for examples of the abstract objects view, which goes back at least to Frege and arguably to Plato, see Peacocke (1992), Zalta (2001), and Chalmers (2011).

concepts' *identity* conditions. But many prefer to relegate them to concepts' *possession* conditions, constitutive not of concepts themselves, but of concept-users' *conceptions*.[21] Do we then still have room for the suggestion that the reasons that guide and follow from the application of a concept should inform our appraisal of that concept?

While philosophers have proposed a variety of schemas for spelling out possession conditions,[22] there is broad agreement on two facts: that concepts are the kinds of things that can be possessed; and that concept possession brings certain dispositions in its wake—not necessarily dispositions that are automatically exercised in response to the presence of certain stimuli, like reflexive habits, but what Williams calls *intelligent dispositions*, which involve the exercise of judgement, and which one can intentionally refrain from exercising (which is not to say that we can choose at will which concepts figure in a given judgement, however).[23] Such dispositions are sometimes referred to as *abilities* in contrast to mere habits or reflexes.[24]

Notice that if one thinks of concept possession as something relatively enduring that can actually manifest itself in some ethically relevant way in certain situations, one is forced to find room in one's account for abilities or dispositions to conceptualize things in the terms specified by a concept and be sensitive to the reasons it adverts to. As Hans-Johann Glock points out, 'identifying concept-possession with an ability or disposition of *some kind* is inevitable, and it is accepted, willy-nilly, even by proponents of RTM' (2006, 52), i.e. the Representational Theory of Mind, according to which concepts are mental representations. Jerry Fodor, for example, though a pre-eminent proponent of RTM, writes: '*having* a concept is: *being able* to mentally represent (hence to think about) whatever it's the concept of' (2003, 19, emphasis added). Similarly, Robert Hanna, who holds that 'a concept is an essentially descriptive, more or less general, categorizing mental content with inherent linguistic and logical form' (2015, 60), nonetheless also concedes that if X is a concept, X is necessarily 'possessible', which he takes to entail that 'X is deployable and usable, which is to say that X makes it really possible for cognitive subjects to recognize X-type things when they perceive them,...to distinguish X-type things from other types of things', and 'to make analytically necessary and a priori logical inferences that pick out at least some of the

---

[21] See e.g. Cummins (1996, 88–9), Gauker (2011, 6), and Sainsbury and Tye (2012, 20).
[22] For different accounts of possession conditions, see Peacocke (1992, 1998), Boghossian (2003), Williamson (2003), Fodor (2004), Glock (2006, 2009b, 2010a), Eklund (2007), Wedgwood (2007, 2015), Scharp (2013, ch. 2), Hanna (2015, 62), and Glasgow (2020).
[23] See Williams (1985, 40).   [24] See e.g. Kenny (1992, 66–85) and Glock (2000, 47).

intrinsic descriptive intensional elements of *X*' (2015, 60). On his view, concepts are emphatically *not* dispositions or abilities, but mental contents of intersubjectively shared types of mental representations that can be tokened by individual minds; and yet he still concedes that, on this view of the nature of concepts, concepts can be *possessed*, and concept possession *confers certain discriminatory, classificatory, and inferential abilities*. Add to this that the possession of different concepts confers different discriminatory, classificatory, and inferential abilities, and you have all that is required for the ethics of conceptualization to get off the ground.

It is thus not particularly controversial to think of concept possession as a matter of having certain discriminatory, classificatory, and inferential dispositions or abilities. We attribute the concept F to someone on the grounds that they have the ability to locate and reidentify things that are F as opposed to non-F, to classify these things *as* being F, and to know what their being F implies.[25] We attribute the concept *red* to someone, for instance, on the grounds that they are able to do certain things, such as reidentifying red under different lighting conditions, distinguishing red from other colours, or inferring that if something is red, it is not green. Mastering a concept typically involves learning the techniques involved in exercising certain abilities. Such mastery comes in degrees: the expert concept-user might have more fine-grained ways of distinguishing Fs from non-Fs or a deeper understanding of the inferential ramifications of being F than the lay concept-user.

For my purposes, however, concepts need not themselves be dispositions or abilities; perhaps they are the norm-governed techniques we employ in exercising these abilities;[26] perhaps they are the abstract objects or the mental representations involved in exercising these abilities. For most purposes, I find it helpful to think of concepts as abstractions from the patterns in our norm-governed thinking techniques. But the framework I develop here can afford to remain agnostic on this, because it requires only the minimal assumption that the concepts which people in fact possess systematically *co-vary* with their discriminatory, classificatory, and inferential dispositions or abilities.[27]

---

[25] While classification and inference are standardly highlighted as key abilities involved in concept possession, the prior ability to reidentify or 'same-track' what one classifies and draws inferences about is helpfully foregrounded by Ruth Millikan, who writes that an 'animal's first job is to keep whatever part of its distal world it would learn about *in focus*...to recognize Obama again from the front or the back or in a newspaper photograph or by his voice, to recognize tiger again given different views or sounds or kinds of spoor' (2017, 7).

[26] This is the account of concepts developed by Glock (2006, 2009a, b, 2010a, b, 2020). Unlike rules, the norms governing thinking techniques need not be explicit, but can be implicit in our practices.

[27] For recent attempts to turn the link between concepts and inferences into a formal logic of concepts, see Jansen and Strobach (2003) and Freund (2022).

Of course, a real divide remains between those who seek to explain how a concept comes by its content *in terms of human conceptions* and those who regard conceptual content as determined completely *independently of human conceptions*. Understanding the concept F as something entirely external to human thinking, which captures the nature of F independently of how or whether anyone ever thought about F, has a variety of virtues—notably, that it helpfully highlights how certain concepts (paradigmatically, concepts of natural kinds) function in a way that leaves concept-users beholden to the independent nature of what they pick out: they are concepts embodying an aspiration to discover how things are *anyway* that precisely acknowledges that some things are not exhausted by the ways in which we conceptualize them—indeed, that our conceptions of them might be almost limitlessly wrong.[28] However, when considering the thick normative concepts characteristic of a certain aesthetic, ethical, political, and legal cultures, it is harder to see what these concepts might draw their content from if they are to be entirely independent of individual and collective conceptions. In those cases, it may seem more promising to resituate the concept–conception distinction within a less externalist spectrum, so that we can, from the disengaged perspective, make sense of the content of those aesthetic, ethical, political, and legal concepts in terms of human conceptions.

But while this divide marks a decisive fork in the road for certain questions in conceptual *engineering* (e.g. is it possible to change a concept?),[29] appraising concepts in terms of human conceptions must seem an appropriate approach to conceptual *ethics* on either account. For conceptual ethics, as I understand it, just *is* the ethics of concept possession: the question of which concepts we should *use* is the question of which *conceptions* should be operative in our actual thinking processes—how we should conceptualize things. We can grant that we cannot change concepts, and hence cannot tailor

---

[28] For a recent defence of an externalist metasemantic framework along these lines, see in particular Sawyer (2020c), which precisely contrasts mere subjective or communal conceptions with the externalist notion of a concept she develops in Sawyer (2018, 2020b, a), drawing on influential externalist treatments of natural kinds concepts by Putnam (1973), Burge (1979), and Kripke (1980). For a 'Socratic essentialist' account of the substantive nature of definitional disputes in terms of the aspiration to arrive at real definitions, i.e. definitions which purport to state the essence of a thing, see Koslicki and Massin (2023).

[29] If concepts are taken to be Fregean senses, for example, the aspiration to engineer or change them may seem unintelligible; though the relevance of metasemantic questions about the nature of concepts to conceptual engineering of course depends on one's view of the latter; see e.g. Nado (2023b) for a view of conceptual engineering which denies metasemantics a substantial role in it. Moreover, it would be in keeping with the spirit of conceptual engineering to engineer whatever concept of a concept enables it to get off the ground—as Nado (2023a) herself does. Recent contributions to the debate over how to conceptualize concepts for the purposes of conceptual engineering include Koch (2021) and Isaac (2023).

concepts to our needs; but we can still tailor our ways of thinking to our needs by changing *which* concepts we use.

We may of course still wonder what sustains or underlies our use of concepts, and this is where Fregeans peer up to the immutable denizens of an abstract realm above us and Fodorians peer down into the mental cogs inside us. But notice that the question of which concepts we should use remains the same whatever the answer. Consider, by way of analogy, a movie running on a TV screen. We may wonder whether it is being streamed in from the World Wide Web or read off tiny crystals inside a DVD player. But the movie that plays on the screen is the same either way—and the question preoccupying the conceptual ethicist is a more practical one, namely *which* movie should be playing. Analogously, we can make sense of the question of which concepts we have most reason to use whatever exactly is involved in using them. The Fregean can do conceptual ethics by asking which senses or modes of presentation should figure in the propositional contents we in fact articulate. The Fodorian can do conceptual ethics by asking which mental representations should govern our cognitive processes. What is more, each can grant that these choices will systematically co-vary with our dispositions and abilities. The animating question of conceptual ethics has force whichever of these metaphysical accounts of concepts one favours, because the question is not what is involved in possessing a concept, but which concepts we should possess.

It is thus appropriate for the approach I go on to develop here, as a contribution to conceptual ethics, to be methodologically agent-centred, focusing on identifying the ways of thinking that best meet the needs of actual concept-users. These ways of thinking are most readily discernible not in the fMRI scanner, but in the weave of everyday life, at the level of what people pick up on, how they react, what they prove themselves capable of doing, and what trains of reasoning become manifest in their speech and behaviour. This is not to reduce concepts to what we do with them, but rather to take what they do for us as a basis for appraising them. Needs-based appraisal will then be, in the first instance, an appraisal of different ways of conceptualizing things, and any more external correlates of this activity—such as the concepts one thereby uses—will be appraised only indirectly, via the influence they exert on human affairs through our coming to think in terms of them.

Being methodologically agent-centred and focusing on our conceptualizations does not reduce those conceptualizations to their psychological or causal aspects, however. In several respects, even our conceptualizations cannot be understood either in purely psychological or in purely causal terms.

First, our conceptualizations are not purely psychological in that to conceptualize things in terms of certain concepts is not primarily to think about concepts, but to think about the world and its objects. The reason relations that concepts encode do not primarily obtain between psychological states, moreover, but between objective facts. One might object that it is the application of one concept that gives one reason to apply another concept, or that it is the judging that *p* that gives one reason to judge that *q*—and these all seem to be psychological operations. But we must be mindful here of what Wilfrid Sellars calls 'the notorious "ing-ed" ambiguity' between the acts of judging and the contents judged, our thinking something and what is thought.[30] When I judge that I have reason to go to the dentist because I have a toothache, my reason is not *my judging* that I have a toothache, but the *fact* that I have a toothache, and what this fact gives me reason to do is not to sit there and judge things, but to go to the dentist. It is only in special cases that the act of judging is itself what gives me a reason—for example, when my judging that I hear the voice of Socrates speaking to me gives me a reason to see a psychiatrist.[31]

In thus separating our thinking from what we think, we need not deny that our acts of thinking can also affect our ways of thinking. We can accept that our judgments shape which concepts we use no less than the concepts we use shape our judgments. This is the lesson of Quine's critique of Carnap.[32] Carnap thinks of the determination of which concepts we use and the application of those concepts as two separate and sequential activities: first we introduce and define our terms, exhaustively determining their proprieties of use in advance of their application; and only then, in a second phase, do we apply those concepts to the world according to their stipulated proprieties of use, forming judgements that the world reveals to be either true or false. As radically free as we are in the first phase to cast the currencies of thought and choose which concepts to adopt, so rigidly bound are we in the second phase by the concepts we have chosen and by how the world in fact is.

---

[30] See Sellars (1997, §24). Thus, when Virgil writes of a crew competing in a boat-race: *possunt quia posse videntur*, 'they can because they think they can' (2007, V.231), it is the attitude of *believing* that they can win the race which makes true the proposition *believed*, namely that they can win the race. This is sometimes termed an 'act-object' or 'state-content' ambiguity (Alvarez 2010, 125).

[31] I argue for my preferred non-psychologistic account of reasons in Queloz (2016, 2017b, 2018a), which draws on Dancy (2000, 2003), Schroeder (2007, 2014), Glock (2014), and Glock and Schmidt (2021). But nothing in the needs-based approach depends on it.

[32] See, in particular, Carnap (1952) and Quine (1960). See also Brandom (2009, 83; 2014, 22–3; 2015a, 12–14; 2019b, 15) for especially lucid presentations of this Carnapian two-phase account and its replacement by a Quinean two-aspect account; although, on Brandom's view, it is really our *concepts* that our judgements shape.

This two-phase model may fit artificial languages, Quine grants; but it fails to capture how, in natural languages, concept determination and application bleed into each other—indeed, *must* bleed into each other, since, outside formal logic, our use of a concept is not always preceded by a cool moment of careful definition determining exactly *which* concept we shall use. Sometimes, concept use is all there is, which means that determination and application then have to be understood as two *aspects* of a single process of concept use. Far from fully settling the content of our concepts in advance of their application, it is often only through the process of deploying our concepts that we render fully determinate which concepts we are using. And far from treating our choices of concepts as fixed and immune to their deployment in judgements, we sometimes revise our choices of concepts through our use of concepts, by applying them in novel ways.

Second, the activity of conceptualization cannot be understood as a purely causal affair, because it possesses an irreducible normative dimension that permits a distinction between correct and incorrect applications of concepts. Concept use is answerable to a standard of correctness, just as techniques can be mastered more or less well and are answerable to a standard of excellence. In that sense, ways of thinking really are thinking *techniques*.[33] The concepts I use are not simply to be equated with the sum of my actual dispositions to reason in certain ways, since talk of correctness becomes meaningless if whatever I am *disposed to treat* as correct *counts* as correct. This need not be taken to mean that I must be consciously guided by explicit norms as I apply a concept. But it does mean that I must be *subject to normative assessment* by third parties as I apply the concept. There minimally needs to be a communal practice of concept use to which the individual concept-user is accountable, and in relation to which a particular application of a concept can meaningfully count as correct or incorrect.[34]

This accommodates the important point that, in grasping a concept and placing one's thought and conduct under its sway, what one binds oneself to can outrun what one immediately grasps: what one immediately grasps, one's *individual* conception, encompasses all those inferential moves one is in fact disposed to make with that concept; but one's grasp of a concept may be only

---

[33] See Hacker (2013).

[34] Although concepts are usually shared, and there needs to be a social dimension to concept use for it to be liable to assessments of correctness, socially shared concepts can also become individualized, just as individualized concepts can become socially shared. Understanding the introduction and extinction of concepts requires a dynamic picture whereby the invention of a new concept whose use is initially not liable to normative assessments of correctness can, over time, become subject to assessments of correctness, and vice versa.

partial, and the concept whose proprieties of use one undertakes to respect by grasping it, however partially, encompasses all the moves one *would* make if one had a complete grasp of the concept.[35]

Making sense of the exact nature of that normative dimension of concept use is not my concern here, since my focus lies on authority *of* rather than *in* concept use. But the fact that concepts have such a normative dimension is nonetheless part of what motivates the authority question in the sense that concerns me: it is *because* a concept exercises authority *in* use, acting as a standard for correct application which users submit to by adopting the concept, that the question of the concept's authority *of* use is appropriate in the first place.

However, while this distinction between the authority of a concept and the normative dimension involved in applying a concept gives us the bare bones of an account of engaged concept use, it is not by itself sufficient to make sense of what engaged concept use is sustained by, or what in concept-users might respond to reasons for concept use. After all, it is not that the correct application of a concept is made *more* correct by the discovery of reasons for concept.

To understand what reasons for concept use modulate, and what engaged concept use is sustained by, we need to flesh out our account of how concept-users relate to their concepts with another notion: the notion of *confidence* in a concept. By theorizing this notion and combining it with the engaged/disengaged distinction, the next chapter offers an account of how reflection on our concepts interacts with our confidence in them, and with the knowledge we have both *under* and *about* these concepts.

The Ethics of Conceptualization: Tailoring Thought and Language to Need. Matthieu Queloz, Oxford University Press.
© Matthieu Queloz 2025. DOI: 10.1093/9780198926283.003.0003

---

[35] For fuller articulations of a concept–conception distinction along these lines, see Brandom (1994, 9, 583, 632–6) and Wanderer (2008, 120–1).

3
Confidence, Reflection, and Knowledge

3.1 Understanding Concept Loss

What happens when we lose a concept? Is it simply a matter of the concept going out of use, the way words become obsolete or entire languages go extinct? Do possibilities of thought get closed off when we lose a concept? And is that necessarily a bad thing because it entrains an epistemic loss?[1]

As I shall argue in this chapter, concept loss is a gradual and complex phenomenon, whose peculiarity is obscured as long as one simply models it on the way words go out of use—concept loss is not primarily a matter of the number of concept-users dropping to zero. Moreover, it is not necessarily the case that possibilities of thought get closed off when we lose a concept; and even when an epistemic loss is involved, this is not necessarily a bad thing.

To arrive at a more nuanced understanding of concept loss, we need to bring into the picture a suitably dynamic notion of *confidence* in concepts.[2] Confidence, I argue, is what sustains engaged concept use. But when confronted with alternative ways of thinking, that confidence can be shaken, and come to stand in need of *reasons* for confidence. This is especially so when the confrontation invites reflection on the contingency of our concepts more than it invites moral appraisal requiring engaged concept use. To the extent that such a confrontation frees us of any practical pressure to deploy our normative concepts in an engaged way, it opens up space for a helpful form of relativism that offers us the opportunity to reflect critically on the merits of our concepts, and on their relation to salient alternatives. Understanding how the resulting reflection affects our confidence can help us make sense of the process whereby engaged use turns into disengaged use, and perhaps eventually into disengaged non-use.

---

[1] There have been remarkably few discussions of concept loss to date—though some notable exceptions include Diamond (1988, 2021), Mulhall (2021, 28–31), Teichmann (2021), and Cappelen (2023).

[2] A notion often invoked, but never properly explained by Williams (1985, 189–90; 1995p, 203; 1995j, 207–8; 2001b, 36).

In the second half of the chapter, I consider how reflection on the contingency of our concepts also affects the knowledge we possess under these concepts. By drawing on the idea that confidence sustains engaged concept use, I develop a plausible interpretation of Bernard Williams's notorious thesis that reflection can destroy knowledge. When our confidence in a concept is eroded as a result of reflection, I argue, it can bar us from making engaged use of the concept, thereby preventing us from identifying with forms of knowledge we used to have under that concept. Crucially, however, that epistemic loss can be our ethical gain. Losing concepts can be just as important to progress as acquiring new concepts. And, *pace* Williams, reflection can also strengthen our confidence in concepts by yielding a different form of knowledge, namely the metaconceptual knowledge that the concepts in question are the right ones for us.

3.2 Confidence in Concepts

Engaged concept use is sustained, in the first instance, by confidence: the practical confidence with which we deploy concepts, without doubt, hesitation, or indecision, secure in the sense that these are the terms in which to cast our thoughts. This is confidence *in conceiving things in certain terms*.

Confidence in conceiving things in certain terms is an aspect of one's confidence in particular judgements. But it is only one aspect of it, since one might have little confidence in the truth or warrant of a particular judgement while remaining confident in the concept one was drawing on. Reading on the aquarium's information panel that there are, among various kinds of jellies and nettles, *cannonball jellyfish* to be found in it, most people will acquire full confidence in that concept for the purposes of classifying the contents of the aquarium. Once the first jellyfish makes it appearance, however, they may be less than fully confident in their judgement that the concept applies to that particular jellyfish. But this is to lack confidence in the truth of a particular judgement, or in the applicability of the concept. It is not to lack confidence in the concept itself—as a revisionary marine zoologist might.

Confidence comes in degrees. It is something one might gradually gain or lose. It might be described as the degree of our attachment to certain concepts. This attachment has two dimensions. On the one hand, confidence manifests itself in *reasons-responsiveness*: the degree of one's confidence in a concept is a function of how much weight one gives the reasons it adverts to in one's practical deliberations—of the extent to which the applicability of the concept translates into reasons for actions one takes oneself to have. The more unhesitatingly receptive to a concept's concomitant reasons and willing to act on those reasons one proves oneself to be, the more one thereby evinces a sense that the concept is the right one to use.

On the other hand, confidence also manifests itself in *emotional responsiveness*: in how strongly a concept engages one's emotions through the judgements it enables one to make. As Peter Goldie has argued, there is an appropriate emotionality that goes with the engaged use of certain concepts. To be a fully engaged user of the concept *rude*, for example, involves more than being able to recognize and avoid rude behaviour.[3] It also involves *feeling* a certain way about it. Someone who was responsive to the reasons for action highlighted by the concept *rude* but never felt his emotions engaged by it—never felt *irritated* by rude behaviour, for instance—would not be living by the concept as fully as someone who felt strongly about rudeness. Conversely, someone who had ceased to respond to the reasons for action provided by the concept of chastity but still felt pangs of guilt in connection to it would not yet have fully disengaged from the concept. This would be a form of what Miranda Fricker calls 'residual internalization' (2007, 37). Understanding the confidence that binds us to concepts and sustains their engaged use as something gradual and two-dimensional allows us to do justice to these complexities.

While confidence is, in the first instance, a matter of the individual's rational and emotional responsiveness to a concept, confidence also has a social aspect. We can meaningfully ask how confident a society is in a concept. Like individual confidence, social confidence in a concept might wax or wane. Moreover, individual and social confidence are not completely independent of each other. The individual's pre-reflective degree of confidence in a concept is a function of upbringing, socialization, and exposure to the dominant ways of thinking. One is more likely to have confidence in a concept if it is widely accepted and supported by people and institutions one trusts, and the work of cultivating a concept by keeping it in circulation, promulgating it, and reproducing the dispositions to think in those terms in subsequent generations, is necessarily a collective enterprise.

Fully confident users of a concept will not feel in the least uneasy about conceiving of things in those terms; they will show no indecisiveness, no tendency to second-guess their own conceptual choices, no lingering doubt, even when the stakes are high and a lot turns on whether the concept they

---

[3] See Goldie (2009).

rely on is the right one. Their judgements will be full-throated, their emotional involvement wholehearted, their actions single-minded. This does not bar them from taking up a disengaged perspective on the concept. But, since the force of the reasons revealed by conceptualizing things in those terms is not seriously in question, that disengaged use is likely to feel contrived and nugatory—as though someone invited one to focus on a glorious sculpture's shadow instead of the sculpture itself. Confidence in a concept can thus be described as a special form of trust, whereby we put ourselves under the sway of a concept and relax into making engaged use of it, fully identifying with the reasons it engenders and the emotional responses it elicits. To those whose confidence is shaken by reflection, however, it becomes a live question whether those reasons and emotional responses might not in fact be the real shadows—the shadows of our concepts.

Confidence does not by itself imply knowledge that these are the right concepts to use; nor does it imply normative entitlement to being confident.[4] But since concepts exert authority *in* use by defining norms of proper use that concept-users are answerable to, confidence can also be characterized in terms of one's relation to those norms. Fully confident concept-users understand these norms as binding on them. Less than fully confident concept-users, by contrast, struggle to make sense of these norms as binding on them: their acute consciousness of the fact that there are alternatives to these concepts, together with their perceived lack of reasons to regard these concepts as the right ones, undercuts the bindingness of those norms by casting doubt on whether *these* are the concepts they should let themselves be bound by ('Since *x* is *blasphemous*, it follows that I have reason not to do it. But do I really?'). This loss in confidence will then be reflected in a corresponding weakening in the concepts' authority in use.

Confidence might thus also be characterized as one's hermeneutic relation to certain norms: it is a function of one's ability to make sense of a concept's authority in use as binding on oneself. To lose that ability in relation to a concept is to become unable to use the concept in an engaged way and regard the reasons it adverts to as being, unequivocally, reasons for oneself. At the

---

[4] My usage of the term 'confidence' differs in that regard from Miranda Fricker's (2000), who reserves the term for 'something we possess only if we are entitled to it' (97 n. 18). Such terminological differences aside, however, I take myself to build on the substance of her discussion, which itself develops the notion of confidence that Williams appeals to. See also Moore (2003), Hall (2014), Blackburn (2019), and Łukomska (2022) for valuable discussions. There are also parallels between loss of confidence and the Hegelian notion of *Entfremdung*, especially as interpreted by Brandom (2019b, 30, 472, 493–506), though the focus there is on the indiscriminate alienation from all norms induced by the 'modern insight into the role we play in instituting norms' (2019b, 30).

limit, when reduced to deploying the concept in a disengaged way, one can no longer identify with its correlative reasons and emotions. One can still use the concept in a disengaged way, understanding how the concept is correctly applied and what follows from its application. But one keeps the concept at arm's length and ceases to regard its reasons as one's own—not as a matter of choice, but because one is no longer *capable of making sense* of its reasons *as* reasons for oneself.

On this account, part of the task of those who put forward concepts for others to adopt—whether under the flag of conceptual analysis or conceptual engineering—is to foster confidence in the concepts they propose. And here it is important to recall that, for all the talk of giving reasons for reasons, this confidence can be achieved in a variety of ways, some of which follow a more clandestine script: people can be trained, lured, coaxed, cowed, or hoodwinked into being confident in certain concepts, and kept ignorant of anything that threatens to unsettle that confidence.[5]

But in the context of liberal democratic societies shaped by Enlightenment ideals of rational autonomy and transparency, 'composers of definitions' are generally expected to eschew these more insidious and manipulative means of fostering confidence in concepts; they are expected to earn confidence through open, rational discourse, by articulating *reasons* to think in those terms. Even in liberal democratic societies, exceptions are made in certain domains, whose boundaries are themselves continually subject to ethical and political renegotiations: early education is a prime example, where the capacity to reflect critically about concepts is itself fostered only later, on the back of having been coaxed into accepting concepts uncritically at first.[6] Yet, as a rule, and especially when it comes to reaffirming confidence that has been unsettled by reflection, we tend to insist that confidence must be earned by giving reasons for reasons—and this insistence is itself an expression of our historical situation.

It is our confidence in concepts, then, that engaged concept use is sustained by. And that confidence can be strengthened or weakened by reasons for concept use, because confidence, like trust, is in principle responsive to reasons. We strive to place our confidence in those concepts we have reasons to be confident in.

---

[5] I illustrate and expand on this point in Queloz and Bieber (2022).

[6] On the question of where and on what basis these boundaries are to be drawn, see Queloz and Bieber (2022) as well as Queloz (2022b), where I draw on Williams's (1995k; 2002, 226; 2006m) ideas on education and the 'theory of persuasion'.

Let us therefore say that confidence is *vindicable* when a concept's authority of use can in fact be grounded in reasons for concept use, whether the concept-user knows it or not. And let us say that vindicable confidence becomes *vindicated* confidence when it is *shown* to the concept-user to be grounded in reasons for concept use. The difference between vindicable and vindicated confidence is thus epistemic: vindicated confidence is vindicable confidence that is *known* to be vindicable. Confidence is vindicable when placed in something authoritative, and vindicated when known to be so placed.

Vindication here contrasts with justification: whereas individual beliefs or actions can be justified by offering first-order reasons favouring them, concepts cannot, strictly speaking, be either justified or unjustified, just as they cannot be true or false.[7] What lends itself to being supported by reasons, however, is our confidence in a concept, which expresses itself in our disposition to use the concept in our reasoning and recognize its authority. To demarcate this sense in which confidence in a concept can be supported by second-order reasons from the sense in which individual beliefs or actions can be supported by first-order reasons, I speak throughout of the vindication rather than the justification of confidence and its concomitant recognition of conceptual authority. In questioning the authority of a concept, we ask whether it is worthy of confidence. Although the two are closely connected, confidence remains distinct from authority of use: confidence is a state directed at what one has confidence in, whereas authority of use is a normative property or status of that which *merits* confidence. But by vindicating confidence in a concept, one vindicates the recognition of its authority.

This contrast between justification and vindication aligns with David Owen's contrast between 'ideological captivity' and 'aspectval captivity' (2002, 216–19; 2022). Ideological captivity is a form of unfreedom that involves being in the grip of certain beliefs, to which the remedy is to ask whether these beliefs can be justified. Aspectval captivity, by contrast, is a form of unfreedom that involves being in the grip of certain concepts articulating a perspective or picture that renders certain aspects of things salient at the expense of others. The remedy to aspectval captivity is not to ask whether

---

[7] While the Aristotelian view that concepts cannot be true or false is almost universally accepted, there is at least one dissenting voice in Hegel, who accepted the possibility of '*an und für sich wahre Begriffe*' (1968–, vol. 20, 73)—concepts that are true in and of themselves. As Mark Alznauer reconstructs Hegel's view, 'a concept is *untrue*...if it cannot be used unrestrictedly—that is, if it cannot be predicated of the absolute or used to characterize things as they are in themselves—without generating a contradiction. A concept is *true* if it lacks such immanent contradictions' (2023, 123).

90   THE ETHICS OF CONCEPTUALIZATION

the beliefs we articulate using these concepts are justified—they might well be—but whether our confidence in these concepts can be vindicated through reflection on our reasons for using them.

3.3 Metaconceptual Reflection

Before it becomes a source of vindication, however, reflection on our concepts and our reasons for using them—what I shall call *metaconceptual reflection*—is more likely to form a threat to our confidence in concepts. That confidence can be undercut by reflection is a platitude, and much as the sportsperson's reflection on her motion can temporarily rob her of the ability to perform it confidently, so reflecting on one's reasons to use a concept has a tendency to destabilize the assurance with which we deploy it and act on the reasons it adverts to.

For this to happen—for metaconceptual reflection to act as a drain on one's confidence in a concept—it is sufficient for the following three conditions to come together:

(1) there are *real or notional alternatives* to the concept;
(2) the reflective concept-user is *aware* of these alternatives;
(3) there is a *perceived lack of independent reasons* to prefer one's own concepts over those alternatives.

The first condition is easily met. Many of the concepts we now use differ substantially from those at work in other societies, both past and present.[8] That conceptual diversity already implies that people *could* think differently, because they *have* thought differently.

The mere fact of conceptual diversity is not by itself enough to affect confidence in concepts, however, since societies might in principle be entirely oblivious to this diversity. Of course, as a matter of actual history, few, if any, societies will have fit this description for any length of time. But in the *analytically* basic case that we may dub the *unreflective condition*, confidence goes unchallenged. Concept-users confidently deploy the concepts they acquired without engaging in any form of metaconceptual reflection. A society remains

---

[8] Some of the classic, if now somewhat dated, studies to that effect include Westermarck (1924), Benedict (1934), and Ladd (1957). For more recent work underscoring conceptual diversity and exploring its philosophical implications, see Shun and Wong (2004), Wong (2006), Ng (2023), and Cullity (forthcoming).

in the unreflective condition as long as nothing prompts its members to reflect critically on their concepts. To remain in such a condition for any length of time, a society would have to be not only maximally homogeneous in its concepts, in the sense of lacking conceptual diversity, but also completely insulated from other societies as well as totally lacking in representations of starkly different ways of thinking (in its historical consciousness or cultural imaginary, for instance). The absence of doubt over the authority of concepts would then allow concept-users to be completely confident in their own conceptual outlook. For lack of something for it to contrast with, they would not even recognize it as being peculiarly their own.

This is why, as the second condition registers, there needs to be something that generates *awareness* of conceptual diversity: there have to be *confrontations* with alternative ways of thinking. These can be real confrontations within a society that is conceptually heterogeneous, or between societies with different ways of life. But they can also be *notional* confrontations across time, when we come to represent to ourselves how differently people thought in the past, or even purely notional confrontations with imagined forms of life.

As a matter of fact, awareness of conceptual diversity is as old as history itself, at least in the sense of being evident already in the writings of Herodotus, the ancient Greek historian whom Cicero hailed as the 'Father of History'. Herodotus recounts how Darius the Great, king of Persia, summoned the Greeks, who burned their fathers at death, and asked them for what price they would eat their fathers' corpses. They retorted that there was no price for which they would do it. Darius then summoned the Callatiae, who were known to eat their fathers, and inquired for what price they would burn them instead. They implored the king not to speak of such horrors. Quoting the poet Pindar, Herodotus concludes that 'custom is lord of all' (1920, III, 38).

But even if the unreflective condition is just an ideal type, it offers a helpful starting point and a contrast foil to the condition that most societies are actually in. For the crucial fact about the unreflective condition is that, as long as a community is in that condition, confidence in concepts *does not require reasons*. Instead, *mere* confidence is enough to sustain the engaged use of concepts under which people can come to know what to think, what to do, and how to live. The concepts can do the work required of them—of providing structure, orientation, and meaning—on the basis of *nothing but* confidence.

Once we are confronted with alternative concepts, however, this calls for metaconceptual reflection on the reasons we have to prefer our own concepts over those alternatives. The confrontation with alternative concepts prompts the realization that the reasons our concepts advert to—reasons that seem to be *simply there*—are really only simply there *for us*, while different reasons seem to be simply there for others. What sort of reaction, if any, does that realization demand? In Amia Srinivasan's vivid dramatization of this perplexing question: 'What am I supposed to do with this other me, this shadow me...who articulates the world in terms of concepts that are alien to my own? What if she is the right one, and I am the shadow?' (2019, 128).

What makes this question so disconcerting is that the very raising of it makes it harder to answer. Our confidence once shaken, more is needed to stabilize it again—metaconceptual reflection *raises the bar* for confidence. This is because the reflective confrontation with alternative concepts transforms the situation and imposes an additional epistemic burden: we no longer simply have to be confident in using our concepts; we now have to be confident in using *those* concepts *rather than* the alternatives. Confidence is sensitive to the presence of relevant alternatives.

In order to be justified in privileging our own concepts over those alternatives, we then need some understanding of how our concepts relate to those alternative concepts, and that understanding has to be such as to vindicate our privileging of our own concepts: it needs to offer *reasons* for us to regard the reasons adverted to by our concepts as being simply there. Mere confidence is no longer enough. We need to ground our confidence in reasons to think that our concepts *merit* confidence.

Some confrontations with alternative ways of thinking can still be shrugged off if we can immediately discern reasons why some concepts structure our lives while other societies get by perfectly well without them. When we realize that we use the concept of online privacy while people at the court of Charlemagne did not, for instance, this realization does little to shake our confidence in the concept, because the conceptual difference is readily explainable in terms of a story of technological development that simultaneously accounts for their lack of the concept and vindicates our continued use of the concept. In this case, our confidence is bolstered by an understanding of how our concepts relate to those alternative concepts that accounts for the divergence in such a way as to vindicate our sticking to our concepts. The same holds for some other thick normative concepts, such as *net neutrality* (which is given to the extent that internet service providers remain neutral between contents and do not privilege or block particular websites).

But what about a concept such as *human right*, which came into wider currency in anything like its present form only in the 1970s?[9] When we cannot immediately see the reasons why some concepts structure our lives while other societies do without them, the question whether this is the best way for us to structure our social world becomes acute. That is what the third condition—the perceived lack of independent reasons for concept use—registers. If that third condition is met as well, metaconceptual reflection truly puts pressure on our confidence in our concepts.

The same problem of confidence can arise also at a more fine-grained level, when we confront closely related alternative elaborations of one concept without apparent reason to prefer one over the other. We will then not wonder 'Why use anything like this concept at all?', but 'Why use this particular conception in this context rather than another?' As David Wong observes, 'the latter question can pose a question of confidence no less than the former' (2006, 232).

What exactly is it that eats away at our confidence in concepts as a result of these confrontations? It is, one wants to say, the acute sense of the *contingency* of those concepts. But contingency is a slippery notion. To get a better grip on it, it helps to distinguish between *causal* and *rational* contingency.

A sense of *causal* contingency is induced when notional confrontations with our own past make us realize how easily our concepts might have been different, how close we came to going down a path towards a different conceptual order. What is felt to be causally contingent is, strictly speaking, not the concepts themselves, but our *possession* of them: the concepts might easily not have emerged; they might have failed to be transmitted to or learned by us; or they might have been subsequently crowded out by other concepts. The relevant notion of causal contingency seems to me importantly different from the one underpinning traditional discussions of divine foreknowledge, fatalism, and freedom. In those discussions, a causally contingent event E is, roughly, one 'such that the conjunction of causal laws and events prior to E

---

[9] See Moyn (2010), who argues that concepts foreshadowing the concept of a human right, such as the concept of a shared humanity, do not render the concept of a human right as understood from the 1970s onwards inevitable, but leave concrete legal questions so underdetermined that anything from early Stoicism through Christianity to the advent of human rights as a potential basis for infringing upon a country's sovereignty is compatible with them. Far more sociohistorically local factors—such as the general dissatisfaction with the internal performance of new states that were granted sovereignty during the process of decolonization, or the state of American domestic politics in the 1970s—have to be drawn on to account for the existence of the concept in its present form (2010, 9–10, 15–17, 39, 69).

94   THE ETHICS OF CONCEPTUALIZATION

are not sufficient for E to occur', where this contrasts with a causally necessary event, which is 'such that the conjunction of causal laws and events prior to E are sufficient for E to occur' (Zagzebski 2015, 190). Philosophers then debate whether we need to consider the entire history of the world up to E, or only the salient proximate causes of E.[10] They tend to agree, however, in taking claims of causal contingency to mean that there is a possible world in which, though the world is identical to ours in all relevant causal respects, E does not occur.

But when Quentin Skinner laments that grasping the 'sheer contingency' of 'the causal story' by which our concepts came to be ours creates a 'haunting sense of lost possibilities' that leaves historians 'almost inevitably Laodicean in their attachment to the values of the present time' (1994, 45), he is clearly registering a different sense of causal contingency. Similarly, when John Stuart Mill remarks in *On Liberty* (2003, 101) that what made a Churchman in London would have made a Confucian in Beijing, he is echoing a long tradition in medieval philosophy—as present in the works of Al-Dawwānī and Al-Ghazālī as in those of Peter Abelard and Ramon Llull[11]—of grappling with the sense of causal contingency precipitated by an awareness of alternative faiths and the realization that one might easily have grown into different ways of thinking.[12]

The point here is not that our possession of certain concepts is the product of conditions that were necessary but not sufficient for it to occur; the point is rather that our possession of those concepts turns out to be causally dependent on facts that might easily have been different. This is a notion of causal contingency that is more at home in discussions of historical explanation. When historians claim that the fall of Rome was causally necessary, for example, they typically mean that it was *historically inevitable*, in that any empire of this size and with anything like these broad characteristics would eventually have fallen. And when historians say that the fall of Rome was causally contingent, they typically mean that it reflected an improbable conjunction of a myriad of minor and unrelated factors, such as a particularly harsh winter in Germania, logistical difficulties in army supply, population pressure in Egypt, especially fierce resistance in Palestine, administrative decay in Britannia, and an unfortunate string of incompetent commanders in Gaul (Little 2020, §1.1). When our use of a concept turns out to reflect such accidents of history, this realization can produce the half-hearted or 'Laodicean'

---

[10] See Pollock (1984, 150–71) for the former view, and Zagzebski (1996, 119) for the latter.
[11] See Adamson (2022, 44–60).
[12] See also Srinivasan (2019) for a rich discussion of this theme.

attitude that Skinner mentions, which I take to indicate an erosion of confidence. We realize how easily the make-up of our conceptual repertoire might have been different.

By contrast, a sense of *rational* contingency is induced by confrontations with real or notional alternatives when we see no *argument for preferring* the concepts we happen to have over alternatives—in particular, no *neutrally specifiable* argument, which is to say no reasons with the appropriate degree of independence from the concepts they are invoked to vindicate. Such independence is needed, since vindicating a way of thinking by reasons it itself instils, or by reasons articulated in terms of *coeval* concepts (i.e. concepts produced by the very forces that produced the way of thinking we are trying to vindicate), would be insufficiently neutral to count as more than self-congratulation.[13] When no such reasons are forthcoming, our concepts appear contingent in the sense that they lack *rational* necessity: they fail to be necessitated by reasons. Rational contingency emerges not when we discover an unsettling connection to causes that might easily have gone the other way, but when a concept turns out to lack any connection to considerations vindicating it against alternatives.

Rational contingency is a deeper and more unsettling form of contingency than causal contingency. The realization that something is causally contingent loses its unsettling force if it is followed up by a demonstration that the thing in question is not rationally contingent. At most, we will count ourselves lucky that we made it onto the causal branch we anyway have good reason to prefer. But the realization that something is rationally contingent cannot similarly be allayed by showing that the thing in question is not causally contingent. That merely produces a sense that we were always going to end up with something we have no particular reason to prefer over alternatives.

Hence, what the authority question calls for, in response to faltering confidence under metaconceptual reflection, are reasons by which to dispel the sense of rational contingency. We need independent reasons to prefer our concepts over alternatives—and not just a historical narrative of causal inevitability—to ground the authority of a concept and vindicate our confidence in it.

---

[13] An example of reasons for concept use that fail to leverage sufficiently neutral grounds because they appeal to coeval concepts would be the vindication of our confidence in the concept of liberalism in terms of the reasons for concept use provided by individuals' need for autonomy. This is perfectly coherent, but it remains too internal to distinctively liberal ways of thinking, since the concept of autonomy is itself a liberal concept, and individuals are only conceived of as having a need for autonomy given a liberal conception of the individual. For a related point directed at attempts to justify the liberal order, see Williams (2005i, 8).

Interestingly, *notional* as opposed to real confrontations with alternative ways of thinking are *more* rather than less apt to be a drain on confidence. This is because the less the difference in concepts makes a difference in practice, the more room we have to reflect on the significance of the fact that our concepts vary so radically. To the extent that a confrontation with another way of thinking forces us to take a stand on some issue, as a real confrontation tends to do (if only in the form of the question of how to relate to those others), we have to make engaged use of our own concepts to judge the issue, and this may include judging the other party and the way it thinks. But to the extent that we are not forced to resolve some practical question about how to behave towards the alternative we are confronting—which is typically, but neither necessarily nor only, the case in a notional confrontation—it becomes a real practical possibility to make disengaged use of our own concepts in thinking about the confrontation, thereby suspending engaged judgement. Once no urgent need to come to a decision hogs all the attention, the gulf between the two ways of thinking and its implications for our aspiration to objectivity can become *the* fact about the situation. That is when conceptual diversity is most apt to precipitate metaconceptual reflection on reasons for concept use.

The judgements suspended remain, for all that, as universalistic in their aspiration to applicability and validity as they were before, and it would be a mistake to think that reflective awareness of conceptual diversity must be registered by transforming judgements claiming universal applicability and validity into judgements claiming merely local validity and applicability—that would not be to acknowledge the parochiality of our universalistic concepts, but to exchange our universalistic concepts for a radically different set of concepts. We need to distinguish a concept's aspiration to universal applicability from the universal authority of the concept. As we shall see in Chapter 8, a universally applicable concept may only be locally authoritative. Either way, the content of our own concepts and judgements is not suddenly altered by confronting another way of thinking, whether notionally or in a way that calls on us to come to some practical decision. If we thought in universalistic terms before, we will continue to do so.

What varies with the nature of the confrontation, however, is the strength of the practical need to exercise our capacity to judge in these universalistic terms. It is this practical need that gives point to our taking a stand on the difference at issue. Of course, there is nothing to stop us from passing judgement on the other party even when there is no such need. But the judgement, unless it draws its point from being witnessed by some third party, will be at risk of being pointless.

Here, then, room opens up for a stance towards disagreement that is not primarily concerned to decide or resolve the disagreement one way or the other. Is this a *relativistic* stance? If so, it is a relativism of the helpful, constructive sort, which does not cynically suspend all judgement, but rather redirects critical attention elsewhere, by inviting us to reflect on the merits of the very concepts in terms of which we normally articulate our moral judgements.

It seems to me that this form of relativism is closely related to, and possibly identical with, the only form of relativism that Bernard Williams allows for: the *relativism of distance*. Williams is scathing about every other form of relativism. He not only castigates 'vulgar' relativism as 'possibly the most absurd view to have been advanced even in moral philosophy' (2001b, 20), but also insists, more generally, that there is no room for relativism to tell us what normative judgements to make—it comes either too early, if the encounter with the relevant alternative outlook has yet to take place, or too late, if the encounter has taken place and there is already a need to decide what to do about it. Yet there is nonetheless a 'truth in relativism', as Williams's essay of that title acknowledges, and his relativism of distance is meant to express that truth.

The difficulty, however, is that Williams's varying characterizations of what gives rise to the relativism of distance—in terms of whether confrontations are real or notional, whether the outlooks one confronts are historical or contemporary, and whether they are real options for oneself—seem to pull in different directions, and make it hard to pin down what the decisive feature is that supposedly makes room for relativism.[14] As a result, even sympathetic interpreters have tended to be somewhat puzzled by or even critical of Williams's relativism of distance.[15]

To my mind, however, the fundamental distinction that provides the basis for the relativism of distance is a different one, though also one that is to be found in Williams's text:

Some disagreements and divergences matter more than others. Above all, it matters whether the contrast of our outlook with another is one that makes a difference, whether a question has to be resolved about what life is going to be lived by one group or the other. (Williams 1985, 178)

The central contrast, which determines where and to what extent there is room for a kind of relativistic stance, is the contrast between disagreements

---

[14] See Williams (1981g, 142; 1985, 180–5; 2003, 107–8; 2006k, 93).
[15] See Tasioulas (1998), Fricker (2010b, 2013), Lear (2011), Blackburn (2019), and Rini (2019).

we are under more practical pressure to resolve and disagreements we are under less practical pressure to resolve. That contrast may correlate strongly with whether a confrontation is real or notional and whether it involves contemporary or historical outlooks; but these correlated properties are not what rationally grounds the relativism of distance.[16] It is perfectly conceivable for there to be occasions on which real confrontations with contemporary outlooks put us under no pressure whatsoever to resolve a practical question. Conversely, it is equally conceivable for notional confrontations with past outlooks to put us under real pressure to resolve a practical question (when questions arise over what to do about the nasty views of ancestors, founders, or benefactors, for example). What fundamentally creates an opening for the relativism of distance is not the fact that a confrontation is notional or reaches across time, but the lack of practical pressure to resolve a practical question.

The idea that there is 'no room' for relativism will then hold true precisely to the extent that a confrontation with another way of thinking is a practical confrontation: one in which the situation requires us to take a stand on whatever issue brings two ways of thinking into confrontation with each other, and decide how we are going to relate and behave towards the other party. Conversely, to the extent that a confrontation is *not* a practical confrontation in this sense, there will be room for a kind of relativistic stance—room opened up by the absence of a practical need to deploy one's normative concepts in an engaged way.

The distance that matters for the 'relativism of distance' is thus a matter of another outlook being, for whatever reason, far removed from our practical concerns in the sense that there is little practical pressure on us to take a stand on how we are going to relate to it. As Williams puts it, 'moral outlooks will have a tendency to lose impetus if their expressions are not directed to people with whom one's relations *need* to be regulated and defined' (2006k, 93, emphasis added). There is correspondingly little point to the engaged use of our concepts of moral appraisal in those confrontations, because the resulting appraisal will 'lack the relation to our concerns which alone gives any point or substance to appraisal' (Williams 1981g, 142).[17]

---

[16] *Pace* Gaitán and Viciana (2018) and Ng (2019).

[17] This is where Miranda Fricker, revising her earlier and more critical interpretation of Williams's relativism, now locates the 'essential motivating idea for the relativism of distance' (2020a, 198), which I take to indicate a certain degree of convergence in our mildly revisionary readings of Williams: we both agree that what is really doing the work is whether moral appraisal has practical consequences that render it pointful in relation to our concerns in a given situation.

Accordingly, the fundamental question that Williams's relativism of distance invites us to ask is whether, in a given confrontation, moral appraisal has practical consequences that render it pointful in relation to our concerns. When it makes no difference whether we give or withhold our approval, appraisal is pointless. I see the same fundamental idea at work in Williams's political thought. Mindful of the 'practical consequences of applying or withholding' (2005i, 14) the concept of legitimacy, he asks 'what the point, or content, is of wondering whether defunct political orders were [legitimate]' (2005i, 10). When there are no practical consequences either way, there is far more to be gained from reflecting about what the differences between our own outlook and that of some defunct political order are grounded in. Can we make sense of why they made sense of things in those terms? What deeper differences in our respective situations do these differences in outlook reflect? And what does this tell us about ourselves and our outlook? These questions can help one to understand where others are coming from and how we should think of ourselves in relation to them. Imagining oneself as 'Kant at the court of King Arthur', by contrast, not only is 'useless', but does not 'help one to understand anything' (2005i, 10).

Is this relativism? 'One can call it a kind of relativism', Williams grants, but:

...it is very importantly different from what is standardly called relativism. Standard relativism says simply that if in culture A, X is favoured, and in culture B, Y is favoured, [then] X is right for A and Y is right for B; in particular, if 'we' think X right and 'they' think X wrong, then each party is right 'for itself'. This differs from the relativism of distance because this tells people *what judgements to make*, whereas the relativism of distance tells them about certain judgements which they *need not* make. (2005d, 68, emphasis added)

Standard relativism aims to arrive at substantive conclusions making engaged use of concepts. It endorses inferences *from* certain judgements making disengaged use of our own concepts and their alternatives *to* certain judgements making engaged use of those concepts. It thereby lays itself open to the charge of committing the mistake we identified in the previous chapter, of conflating engaged with disengaged use. The relativism of distance, by contrast, is more interested in what the judgements making disengaged use of concepts can tell us about ourselves and our concepts, and insists on the legitimacy of dwelling on this question when there is no need to make engaged use of our concepts.

Calling it 'relativism' is thus misleading. The fundamental point is rather that certain confrontations, namely those in which there is no need to decide and regulate relations between the two parties, are rightly seen as inviting metaconceptual reflection more than they invite engaged concept use resulting in moral appraisal. We might still be disposed to say that the others are wrong, but the more salient question will be whether they are *simply* wrong. Are they committing an error within a shared cognitive enterprise, or can we identify reasons why different reasons should seem to be simply there for them? Do we have reasons to use the concepts we do rather than theirs? And are the reasons for reasons we can discern on each side truly independent of the concepts whose use they purport to justify? This is the kind of disengaged metaconceptual reflection on our concepts that notional confrontations with alternative concepts are particularly apt to induce.

3.4 Knowledge under Concepts

Confrontations with alternative concepts can thus undercut our confidence in concepts. But in doing so, these confrontations may well undercut more than just our confidence in concepts. They can also call into question the *knowledge* we thought we possessed under these concepts.

As epistemologists have pointed out, one might know that p in the absence of alternatives, but cease to know that p once a competing hypothesis, q, is presented.[18] From that point onwards, knowing that p additionally requires reasons to rule out q. The presence of relevant alternatives can raise the bar for knowledge.

Analogously, the knowledge that concept-users have under some concepts can be lost once they are confronted with alternative concepts. For these confrontations will induce metaconceptual reflection that is liable to unseat the concepts under which knowledge is possessed. It is thus not merely confidence that is sensitive to the presence of alternatives, but knowledge as well.

This is the line of thought that led Williams to his notorious conclusion that 'reflection can destroy knowledge' (1985, 163–4)—a claim that has, if anything, been met with even more bafflement and criticism from interpreters than his relativism of distance.[19]

---

[18] See e.g. Goldman (1976), Stine (1976), and Dretske (1981). A similar intuition has more recently animated contextualism in epistemology; see e.g. Schaffer (2004), Blome-Tillmann (2009), and Ichikawa (2017).

[19] For representative criticism, see Putnam (1981, 55), Moore (1991), Wright (1992, 38–9), Altham (1995), and Blackburn (2019). Moore (1997, ch. 8; 2003, 2024a) offers a more sympathetic reading, as

Against these criticisms, I contend that the key to the claim that reflection can destroy knowledge is that it is a claim about how reflection can destroy the confidence required for engaged concept use. By losing the ability to use certain concepts in an engaged way, one loses access to the perspectival knowledge articulable under these concepts, but retains the ability to see, from a disengaged perspective, that what is thereby placed beyond one's reach is knowledge—only no longer one's *own* knowledge. This interpretation fits the summary that Williams later gave of his controversial argument:

> Statements made by people using thick concepts that are not our own are not…unintelligible to us. Nor can I see any reason for saying that they are, one and all, false. There seem to be perfectly good grounds for saying that some of them are what, in local terms, they are taken to be, namely true; and, since the people who use them satisfy other relevant conditions, we can say that those people have some knowledge under these concepts. But this is not knowledge that we share, since we do not share those concepts. One way, at least, in which such concepts go out of use is that people become more reflective about them; so some knowledge, at least—*that* knowledge—can be lost under reflection. (1995j, 206)

Let us consider the argument in more detail. The thesis that reflection can destroy knowledge is meant to apply only on what Williams calls the 'nonobjectivist' model of ethical practices, on which we see ethical judgements as part of a way of life that a certain society has come to inhabit rather than as an attempt to get at the same set of ethical truths that other human societies, and perhaps even other creatures, are also trying to get at. On such a nonobjectivist model, judgements formed using thick ethical concepts (such as '*x* is *chaste*') can yield ethical knowledge: these judgements are not merely capable of being believed and of being true; the application of the thick concepts in terms of which these judgements are articulated is also sufficiently closely world-guided, i.e. guided by easily observable empirical features of the world, to make the process of judgement-formation truth-tracking: it is sensitive to the truth, or at least safe from error.[20] Indeed, many thick concepts are so

---

does Thomas (2006, 147–66), though they both still take issue with various aspects of Williams's position. For a recent re-examination of Williams's claim (which is also ultimately critical), see Rosen (2022).

[20] Writing in the early 1980s, Williams (1985, 158–64) relies on what was then one of the most sophisticated characterizations of knowledge, namely Robert Nozick's (1981, ch. 3) account of truth-tracking in terms of what has come to be known as the *sensitivity condition* on knowledge. But the sensitivity condition in fact sets rather a high bar for knowledge, which is why I note above that even a judgement that failed to meet it might plausibly still satisfy the now more popular *safety condition*

closely guided that one would expect users of these concepts to converge in their judgements, because the concepts leave them 'nothing else to think'.

And yet that knowledge is vulnerable, according to Williams, to being destroyed by reflection—not, of course, in the sense that people continue to conceptualize things in the same way but come to view as *false* what they used to think *true*, since what they would have lost would then turn out never to have been knowledge in the first place; rather, Williams's claim, I think, is not about truth or falsity, but about concepts, and more specifically about *confidence* in concepts. Reflection can entrain a loss of knowledge by undermining people's confidence in the concepts under which they had knowledge. 'What I had in mind', Williams clarifies in a later paper, 'was the situation in which they no longer have the concept with which they used to express a certain class of beliefs. They lose a concept, and so cease to have a disposition that expresses itself in categorising the world in those terms' (1995l, 238).[21]

To lose a concept is to lose a range of dispositions or abilities, and one of the abilities that can be lost that way is the *ability to know* what can be known under that concept. A concept articulates a certain perspective on the world. Certain pieces of knowledge can only be had under that concept, because the knowledge in question is knowledge that the concept does or does not apply. By losing one's confidence in the concept, one loses the ability to occupy the perspective opened up by the concept, and thereby closes off access to the knowledge that can only be had under that concept.

More precisely, the claim must be that reflection on a concept can bar people from continuing to use that concept in an *engaged* way, because, by shattering their confidence in the concept, it expels them from the group of engaged users of that concept. At the same time, people in that postlapsarian condition must retain the ability to use the concept in a *disengaged* way if they are to understand both that there really is knowledge to be had under that concept and that they no longer themselves possess it. If we accept that certain thick normative concepts can yield knowledge, confrontations with different casts of thought can, by destroying our confidence in those concepts, undermine our ability to use them in an engaged way, and thereby undermine our ability to know what can be known under those concepts. But as long as this leaves us able to use the concepts in a disengaged way, it still leaves us

---

on knowledge. For subtly different ways of spelling out the safety condition, see Sosa (1999), Williamson (2000), and Pritchard (2007). For an application of Williams's model of ethical knowledge under thick concepts to Confucian ethical communities, see Ng (2023).

[21] See Williams (1984, 223; 1995l, 238–9; 1995j, 208), and, for a discussion that aligns particularly well with the emphasis I give to Williams's claim, see B. Williams (2010, 207–9).

able to recognize that, for engaged users of those concepts, there is knowledge to be had under those concepts; only not for us, because we can no longer muster the confidence required to deploy these concepts in an engaged way.

Corresponding to this change is a shift from the autoethnographic to the ethnographic stance: initially, we have some concepts that we use in an engaged way, forming true judgements with them that are world-guided in the right way to count as knowledge. Thanks to our ability to take up the autoethnographic stance, we then engage in metaconceptual reflection on our reasons to use these concepts. If anything we find or fail to find in the course of this reflection drains our confidence in the concepts, we lose the ability to use them in an engaged way. We can still understand them and assess whether those who deploy them apply them correctly; but, though the concepts are part of our conceptual inheritance, they are no longer *our* concepts. We dissociate ourselves from the concepts and the knowledge they enable one to articulate, though we retain the capacity to use them by imaginatively taking up the perspective of those who live by those concepts. We then stand to these engaged concept-users as ethnographers stand to people of another culture. We can still imaginatively identify with engaged users of the concept and use their concepts *vicariously*, as Adrian Moore (2024a, 383) puts it, but we can no longer use them *in propria persona*—for to *imaginatively* identify with something is precisely *not* to identify with it. As a result, the perspectival knowledge articulable under these concepts remains recognizable to us as knowledge, but it is no longer *our* knowledge.

The engaged/disengaged distinction thus turns out to be crucial to making sense of the claim that reflection can destroy knowledge. The claim is not just that if we lose access to a conceptually articulated perspective, the knowledge to be had from that perspective might fade, as our knowledge of what is depicted in a painting might diminish after we leave the museum. Williams's claim is both weaker and stronger than that. It is weaker in that we do not lose the relevant concept entirely: we remain able to use it in a disengaged way, continuing to be able to think and even recognize as knowledge what can be known under the concept.

But the claim is also stronger in that this knowledge is not merely at risk of fading from memory: once we become unable to use the concept in an engaged way, we are radically cut off from that knowledge, however vivid our memory of it; it ceases to be ours. Though still capable of recognizing that it meets the conditions on knowledge, we are estranged from it, and can no longer sufficiently identify with the community of those who live by the concept to take ourselves to know what they know.

This notion of knowledge we recognize but do not ourselves possess may seem paradoxical; but it is no more so than the notion of disengaged concept use, which marks the neglected twilight zone between use and non-use. Making disengaged use of thick concepts puts us in a position to recognize some of the resulting judgements as meeting the conditions on knowledge. But if we do not ourselves live by these concepts, in that we are not emotionally and rationally responsive to the concomitant reasons, we will also fail to be emotionally and rationally responsive to the concomitant pieces of knowledge. Our disengagement from the concepts brings with it a disengagement from whatever knowledge is to be had under these concepts. It is knowledge held at arm's length.

Historians of philosophy, like historians practising what is sometimes tellingly called 'the history of knowledge', are particularly well placed to recognize this phenomenon of knowledge held at arm's length. I do not have in mind here the non-factive conception of knowledge that historians of science sometimes employ in thinking about the 'medical knowledge' of Hippocrates or the 'scientific discoveries' of the Academy of the Lynx—that non-factive conception responds to the fact that though many supposed discoveries of the past now strike us as false, inquirers of yore nonetheless treated them almost exactly as we now treat knowledge, making it expedient to adapt our factive concept of knowledge to meet the need for a notion that behaves in nearly every way like our ordinary notion of knowledge, except that it does not entail the truth of what it picks out. Rather, what I have in mind is the case where some thick concepts of the past yield judgements that seem to us true, but irremediably alien. I may come to understand the ancient concept of *thumos* well enough to understand what the world looks like to one who sees it through that lens, and to reliably distinguish truths from falsehoods about *thumos*. I may even be happy to grant that certain judgements involving *thumos* qualify as knowledge. But I do not regard the judgement 'I can think and feel with and in my *thumos*, and even address my *thumos*' as part of *my own* body of knowledge about myself. That is not the relation I bear to this piece of knowledge, because, sympathetic user of this concept though I may be, it is not one of mine.

By the same reasoning, something that used to form part of my body of knowledge can cease to be part of it without requiring a change in how I see its truth value or justificatory standing. Thus, Oscar Wilde *might* have said of the story presented to him at his trial: 'This is blasphemous.' But this utterance could have expressed either an engaged or a disengaged use of the concept *blasphemous*. Had Wilde said it with righteous indignation and gone on to infer that the story should be censored, we would have had to conclude that he was using the concept in an engaged way, since he proved emotionally and rationally responsive to the concept's applicability. Had he said it with sarcastic indifference, however, displaying a clear lack of emotional and rational responsiveness to the concept, he would reasonably have been taken to be using the concept in a disengaged way—a nuance he might himself have made explicit by saying, perhaps with some exasperation: '*Of course* this is blasphemous, if you insist on looking at it in those moralistic terms; but my point is that we should not think about art in these terms at all.'

By embedding the concession regarding the concept's applicability within some such context, Wilde could have expressed his disengagement from the concept. In practice, he was no doubt wise not to concede any ground to his hostile interlocutor on this front. But, *pace* Brandom (1994, 126), blankly refusing to use the concept was not the only thing Wilde could have done. It was open to him to recognize that the story met the conditions on the applicability of the concept while disputing that our treatment of art should be informed by this concept. Making explicit that one's use of a concept is disengaged is not self-stultifying in the way that G. E. Moore took assertions of the form '*p*; but I do not believe that *p*' to be. There is nothing contradictory or even 'pragmatically inconsistent' about demonstrating one's ability to form true and justified judgements using a concept while at the same time rejecting the concept's claim to authority over one's thought and conduct.[22] On the contrary, it lends force to the rejection, since it shows it to be rooted in mastery rather than ignorance of the concept. It is to say: 'I know how to play this game, and I refuse to play it.'

We can adopt the same attitude towards knowledge under concepts we come to regard as objectionable. Consider a young man who throws around some slang term expressing a derogatory thick concept with the reckless abandon of a teenager. If the thick concept is closely world-guided and tracks certain easily observable features, the beliefs he articulates in terms of this concept can qualify as pieces of knowledge. For this enables the process of belief-formation to be truth-tracking—if not in the sense of being sensitive to the truth, then certainly in the less demanding sense of being fairly safe from error, thereby still providing solid grounds for the resulting beliefs' claim to constituting knowledge.[23]

---

[22] For an account of how Moore sentences are logically consistent while being pragmatically inconsistent, see Sorensen (1988, ch. 1).
[23] On the sensitivity condition, see Nozick (1981); for different ways of spelling out the safety condition, see Sosa (1999), Williamson (2000), and Pritchard (2007).

As our young man matures, however, he comes to reflect on the concept, and discovers forceful reasons not to use the concept. These need not be reasons to do with the emptiness of its extension. He may come to believe that this very way of thinking, this way of tying certain normative consequences to certain observable conditions, is objectionable on ethical or political grounds. This drains his confidence in the concept, leaving him unable to use it in an engaged way.

As a result, the concept loses its sway over him. He still understands the concept; after all, he used to live by it himself. But the propositions that can be known under this concept are no longer part of his own body knowledge—not because the propositions are now false (they are as true as they ever were), but because, though he still understands what people who think that way are saying, he can no longer bring himself to think that way himself—not in his own voice, not in the engaged, confident way required for him to count the judgements he forms in those terms as part of what *he knows*.

Having become estranged from the concept, he has thus also become estranged from the forms of knowledge that the concept puts within reach of its engaged users. His estrangement from the concept bars him not just from a way of thinking, but from a *way of knowing*. To that extent, the repertoire of concepts he identifies with has been expressively weakened. But as he finds that way of knowing objectionable, he regards his conceptual repertoire as having been *ethically strengthened* by this.[24] He no longer regards that kind of knowledge as worth having. If anything, he now regards it as worth not having.

This illustrates the broader point that the epistemic loss incurred by closing off possibilities of thought can be an ethical gain. That progressive dimension of concept loss is difficult to appreciate as long as we conceive of improvements in our conceptual repertoire primarily in epistemological terms, as a matter of expanding our perception and knowledge. When philosophers think of alterations in our conceptual repertoire as constituting a form of progress, they often point to how enriching that repertoire with additional concepts can open up previously inaccessible forms of perception and knowledge.[25] We saw Iris Murdoch urge that 'we need more concepts in terms of which to picture the substance of our being', because 'it is through an enriching and deepening of concepts that moral progress takes

---

[24] On the contrast between expressive weakness and ethical strength, see Williams (1995l, 241).

[25] For a rich discussion of the role that concepts have been thought to play in perception, see El Kassar (2015).

place' (1961, 20).[26] More recently, Michele Moody-Adams has suggested that moral progress requires us to 'expand the conceptual space available for constructive debate' (2017, 158), while Matthew Congdon (2024) maintains that it is by articulating new moral concepts that we reduce the dissonance between our ethical experience and our received conceptual resources.

As our discussion has brought out, however, losing concepts can be just as important to progress as gaining new ones. Murdoch was still right to observe that progress can consist simply in acquiring dispositions to conceptualize things in certain terms. But there can also be progress that consists simply in the loss of such dispositions. It can be an ethical achievement *not to be disposed to* think in certain terms; or, what is subtly different in implying a degree of active resistance, *to be disposed not to* think in such terms. In some cases, as in the Wildean revolt of aestheticism against moralism, learning to refrain from conceptualizing things in certain terms can prevent the suffocation of one style of thought by another, granting certain considerations, such as those expressing aesthetic values, a corner of their own.[27]

But even where moral progress alone is concerned, inculcating dispositions to think in certain terms is only half the task. The other half is to ensure that people are either not disposed to think in certain terms or more actively disposed not to think in certain terms. 'One form of moral education', Williams remarks, 'is to bring it about that certain considerations never even occur to somebody' (1999, 261). He offers the example of a man who opines, in the course of a discussion about how to deal with business rivals: 'Of course, we could have them killed, but we should lay that aside right from the beginning'; clearly, something has gone seriously wrong in the moral education of that man, since that thought 'should never have come into his hands to be laid aside' (1985, 206). Leaving certain things unthought can be an ethical achievement, as the concept of the *unthinkable*, which is itself an ethical concept, reminds us by acting as an admonishing gatekeeper on the threshold to what best remains unthought. Here, too, our epistemic loss is our ethical gain.

---

[26] Murdoch of course also writes about concept loss; but she regards that loss as an ethical loss.
[27] On the importance of granting certain ways of thinking a corner of their own to prevent moral thought from moralistically 'overweening in life', see Taylor (2012, 69) and Diamond (2010). Taylor also elaborates on Williams's suggestion that *moral incapacity*—the incapacity to perform or even seriously contemplate certain actions—differs from psychological incapacity in being a hard-won achievement of moral education. Being incapable of entertaining certain thoughts can be understood as a species of moral incapacity. After all, as Williams notes: 'thinking that something is unthinkable is not so direct a witness to its being unthinkable as is being incapable of thinking of it' (1981f, 129).

3.5 Metaconceptual Knowledge

Metaconceptual reflection can thus make us lose knowledge by undermining confidence in the concepts in terms of which that knowledge is articulated. But can metaconceptual reflection also affirm knowledge by yielding metaconceptual knowledge that the concepts in question are the right ones? Can knowledge *under* concepts be reinforced by knowledge *about* concepts?

I will argue in Chapters 6–8 that it can. And here, I part ways with Williams, who holds that, at least where our thick normative concepts are concerned, we cannot have metaconceptual knowledge that they are the right ones. The best we can hope for, on his view, is that we will retain confidence in a concept even after metaconceptual reflection. But that confidence will not be vindicated by metaconceptual knowledge; it will be vindicated merely in the negative sense that no reasons to doubt or jettison the concept were identified under reflection. Thus, Williams holds that for confidence in a thick normative concept to be vindicated simply *is* for the concept to survive metaconceptual reflection, where the concept:

> ...survives reflection just in the sense that we would not have encountered any considerations that led us to give it up, lose hold on it, or simply drift away from it, as modern societies in the past two centuries or less have, for instance, done one or more of those things in relation to the concept of *chastity*. While we shall have the knowledge that comes with the deployment of our surviving thick concepts, we shall still not have any knowledge to the effect that we have a definitively desirable set of such concepts.... The thick concepts under which we can have some pieces of ethical knowledge are not themselves sustained by knowledge, but by confidence. (1995j, 207–8)

Where I differ from Williams is in insisting that thick concepts *can* be sustained by knowledge, though not by knowledge to the effect that we have definitively desirable concepts: rather, there can be metaconceptual knowledge that certain concepts are desirable *for* certain concept-users in certain circumstances. That does not make them *definitively* desirable, since both concept-users and their circumstances change. But what we shall have found, at the level of metaconceptual reflection on our reasons to use these concepts, will be knowledge, and that knowledge can offer rational support to the confidence that sustains the engaged use of those concepts.

The strong assumption that Williams accepts and I reject, then, is that metaconceptual reflection can offer rational support to one's confidence in thick normative concepts, and thereby affirm what knowledge one has under these concepts, *if and only if* it generates metaconceptual knowledge that these concepts are absolutely and definitively the best ones, in that anyone has conclusive reason to recognize them as best.

We might therefore say that Williams operates with a *non-relational* conception of the metaconceptual knowledge required to affirm one's confidence in thick normative concepts. This requires knowledge that the concept F be best *simpliciter*:

The Non-Relational Conception of Metaconceptual Knowledge:

Metaconceptual reflection affirms concept-users' confidence in the concept F *iff* it yields metaconceptual knowledge that the concept F is part of the set of concepts that is absolutely and definitively best.

Since Williams does not think that such metaconceptual knowledge is forthcoming, he concludes that our engaged use of thick normative concepts cannot be sustained by metaconceptual knowledge, so that it must be sustained merely by confidence. Metaconceptual reflection can offer no rational support to confidence, on this view. It can help confidence only negatively, by not yielding any disparaging or incriminating revelations. The thick concepts that survive reflection, on this picture, are simply those that are left over once our conceptual repertoire has been cleared of archaic holdovers and ideological rot.

By contrast, I see no reason to think that our concepts need to be known to be absolutely and definitively the best ones. On the contrary: as we shall see in the next chapter, there are good reasons to think that aiming for the set of concepts that is absolutely and definitively best is a poor way of finding the concepts that actually serve *us* best, given our distinctive circumstances and problems. For metaconceptual reflection to offer positive rational support to our confidence in thick normative concepts, it is both necessary and sufficient to show that these concepts are the best ones *for us*, given our particular situation.

I thus propose to rely on a conception of metaconceptual knowledge that is *relational*, indexing the merits of concepts to the characteristics of concept-users and their circumstances, and requiring only knowledge that the concept F is best *for* those concept-users under those circumstances:

The Relational Conception of Metaconceptual Knowledge:
Metaconceptual reflection affirms concept-users' confidence in the concept F *iff* it yields metaconceptual knowledge that the concept F is part of the set of concepts that is best *for* those concept-users under those circumstances.

On this view, metaconceptual reflection can do more than leave one's confidence unscathed; it can offer positive rational support to one's confidence in certain concepts, and thereby affirm what knowledge one has under these concepts. This is the view I substantiate in the chapters to follow (where I also consider why such relationalism does not imply relativism).

In this chapter, however, my aim has been to clarify in what sense our object-level judgements are sustained, in the first instance, by confidence in our concepts. In the unreflective condition, confidence can do this without rational support by reasons for concept use. But once the pandora's box of metaconceptual reflection has been opened, confidence comes to require second-order, metaconceptual judgements as to why these concepts *merit* our confidence. As soon as we enter the reflective condition, the prospect of sticking to one's concepts without being bothered by their contingency looks like an abdication of reason, a resignation to blind confidence.

Under conditions of modernity, where awareness of conceptual diversity is deeply ingrained in pluralistic and historically self-conscious societies, there is no going back to a less demanding, unreflective condition: both notional and real confrontations with alternative casts of thought are inevitable, and so are the epistemic burdens they place on us. At the same time, many of the formerly powerful means to make sense of the authority of concepts—in theocratic terms, for instance—have lost the widespread allegiance they once commanded. We are thus both especially in need of, and particularly short on, means to make sense of the authority of our concepts. To explore this predicament and the complex response it requires is the task of the next chapter.

PART II
LEARNING FROM EXISTING ANSWERS

4
Anchoring Authority
A Trilemma

In demanding reasons for reasons, we embark on the search for something in which to anchor the authority of concepts. But what kinds of considerations should the authority of concepts be anchored in? In this chapter, I outline what I take to be the three salient answers on offer: *foundationalism*, *ironism*, and *holism*. I argue that these three answers are all unattractive. The first, when suitably generalized to cover thick normative concepts, has become incredible; the second results in indiscriminate disengagement from our concepts; and the third results in undiscriminating acceptance of them.

I argue that two adjustments are required to escape this trilemma and find more critical leverage with which to discriminate between concepts that merit confidence and concepts that do not: first, the picture of our conceptual apparatus as something harmonious, largely tensionless, and inherently static must be replaced with a kaleidoscopic picture on which our conceptual apparatus is tension-ridden and dynamic; and second, the critical leverage of local needs must be harnessed by recognizing that the contingency of our concepts extends also to the standards that these concepts must meet.

4.1 Generalized Foundationalism

The first horn of the trilemma can be broadly circumscribed as *foundationalism* about conceptual authority. 'Foundationalism' usually designates a way of structuring one's body of knowledge, namely the strategy, associated with Stoic and Cartesian epistemology, of building upon a basic stratum of secure and certain propositions. But as far as that definition goes, the basic stratum could in principle be a different one in different times and places. My use of the term 'foundationalism', by contrast, owes more to the way the term is sometimes employed in political philosophy to designate a way of answering the question of how to organize society, namely the strategy that aspires to transcend the peculiarities of a given sociohistorical situation and provide an answer that *anyone* would have reason to accept, because it is derived from rational foundations that are timelessly valid and fully mind-independent, free of any distortion by contingency or subjectivity.[1]

As I propose to understand it, then, foundationalism about conceptual authority is the project of seeking timeless and mind-independent rational foundations on the basis of which to identify the concepts that are absolutely best. To say that they are *absolutely* best is to say that these concepts can be seen to be best from a point of view stripped of perspectival peculiarities. This is not the same as saying that these concepts are *definitively* best, since even a timeless, mind-independent standard might yield context-sensitive recommendations. But it does mean that, in any given context, *anyone* would have reason to recognize as best *for that context* the concepts recommended by such a standard, because the standard itself remains undisturbed by historical and cultural shifts and has authority over anyone, whatever their concerns and commitments. For the foundationalist, then, the only truly authoritative concepts are those whose authority can be anchored in an immutable rational bedrock.

That characterization of foundationalism about conceptual authority, though too loose and baggy to be of much interest in its own right, does help paint a broad-brushed picture of the historical background to the view I want to arrive at, because it captures the shared underlying spirit that unifies a series of radically different philosophical enterprises. There is a long tradition of trying to anchor human ways of thinking in rational foundations lying beyond the reach of contingency and subjectivity. These foundations have variously been sought in an abstract realm of Forms, in a natural *telos*, in divine commands, in natural law, in the mind of God, in universal dictates of reason, or in basic structural features of the world. The philosophers engaged in these enterprises were not always bent primarily on identifying authoritative concepts; but their views of rational authority nonetheless encouraged certain ways of thinking about the authority of concepts.

What all these variations on foundationalism about conceptual authority have in common, notably, is that they regard the fact that certain concepts are *ours* as insignificant. The question about our concepts, as about any other concepts, past or possible, must be to what extent they approximate the set of concepts that anyone has most reason to use. The characteristic aspiration of foundationalism about conceptual authority is to transcend the concepts that

---

[1] For orthodox ways of characterizing foundationalism in opposition to coherentism in theories of truth and justification, see e.g. Olsson (2017) or Hasan and Fumerton (2018). For an example of the subtly different use of the term in political philosophy that inspires the way I apply the term to concepts, see e.g. Williams (2005h, 25).

are only contingently ours, and find the set of concepts that can be authenticated as absolutely best.

Perhaps the most enduringly influential form of foundationalism about conceptual authority is the aspiration to find the concepts that 'carve nature at its joints'. Plato introduced that grisly image merely by way of analogy, in the process of arguing for the reality of the Forms.[2] Indeed, the ancient Greeks tended not to go in for explicitly metaconceptual reflection, preferring to philosophize with object-level formulations ('What is X?'). There is also no obvious Greek translation for 'concept', only several approximations, such as *ennoia, katholou, eidos*, or *logos*.[3] But once hewn off from the Platonic corpus, the image of a jointed nature became a guiding one for foundationalist projects in metaphysics and the philosophy of science. It still figures centrally in Eli Hirsch's *Dividing Reality* (1993) and Theodore Sider's *Writing the Book of the World* (2011), for example.[4]

The authoritative concepts, foundationalists of this stripe maintain, are the joint-carving ones, because nature possesses an antecedent structure that our concepts should reflect. These joint-carving concepts (e.g. certain concepts of physics) articulate a supervenience base for facts at higher levels of description that are articulated in non-joint-carving terms (e.g. certain concepts of psychology). But these higher-level descriptions remain inferior approximations. As Sider insists, 'there is a privileged way to "write the book of the world"' (2011, 8).

Another metaphor used to articulate this ideal of fidelity to nature is that of 'reference magnets', which was promulgated by David Lewis (1983b, 1984). The idea is that certain parts of reality *attract* reference by our concepts: they are more eligible for reference than other parts in virtue of being metaphysically privileged in some way—they are 'more natural', or 'more unified', or distinguished in some other respect that is supposedly independent of human dispositions and concerns.

Of course, timeless and mind-independent rational foundations may not bear on all kinds of concepts: the basic structure of reality, for example, may leave our aesthetic concepts underdetermined, remaining neutral between the aesthetic concepts of Baumgarten and those of the Bauhaus. And perhaps the same is true of moral or political concepts—or of thick normative concepts in general.

---

[2] See Plato (*Phaedrus*, 265e).
[3] For a detailed treatment of concepts in ancient Greek philosophy, see Helmig (2013, 13–38). I am grateful to Anders Sydskjør for illuminating conversations on these issues.
[4] For a representative sample of perspectives on whether nature is 'jointed', see the essays in Campbell, O'Rourke, and Slater (2011).

But even today, foundationalism is by no means confined to the most basic descriptive concepts of fundamental physics. In *Reality and Morality* (2020), for instance, Billy Dunaway extends the idea of reference magnetism to moral concepts, arguing that properties like 'moral rightness' or 'obligation' are objective, metaphysically privileged properties that our moral concepts are accountable to.

Let us therefore say that foundationalism about conceptual authority is *generalized* when it purports to apply not just to concepts in a specific domain, but to concepts across the board—including thick normative concepts. And let us say that foundationalism about conceptual authority is generalized *and exclusive* when it not only purports to be applicable to concepts across the board, but also carries the further claim that no other strategy is capable of vindicating a concept's authority, so that when two concepts are equally related to the relevant foundations, no other dimension of appraisal can help us choose between them.

Foundationalist pictures according to which the authority of concepts rests on some immutable bedrock *can* make sense to people, as philosophy's own history amply attests. But even where these pictures make sense, the foundationalist ambition to extricate our thought from its contingent circumstances runs up against the fact that a foundationalist picture's plausibility itself remains conditioned by the natural, historical, and social setting in which it is presented: what makes sense to us is a function of our sociohistorical situation, and even when foundationalist theories have made sense to people, they have done so notably through the support of the sociohistorical situation in which they were put forward.[5] This indicates at least one respect in which foundationalism can never fully achieve the total independence from contingent circumstances that it strives for, because it itself depends on mediation by contingent circumstances to make sense to people.

This limitation of the foundationalist ambition is important not because it necessarily vitiates the foundationalist enterprise, but because it reminds us to ask whether foundationalism can really make sense *to us*, in the

---

[5] The point can be spelled out either in terms of the historical conditions that create a demand for a foundationalist picture—as Forrester (2019) and S. Smith (2021) do for the foundationalist elements in Rawls's theory, for example—or, more fundamentally, in terms of the contingent dispositions and shared understandings and practices that ineluctably because constitutively condition the application of concepts (for all the controversies that Wittgenstein's rule-following considerations have whirled up, some consensus has nonetheless formed around that broad implication—see the essays in Miller and Wright (2002) and Kusch (2006)). Something like this latter limitation, I suspect, is what Williams has in mind when he somewhat cryptically invokes the Wittgensteinian idea of the 'primacy of practice' to argue that 'foundationalism, even constructivist foundationalism, can never achieve what it wants' (2005e, 25).

sociohistorical situation that *we* find ourselves in. For once we press that question far enough, and confront it not just in connection with the concepts of elemental chemistry or particle physics, but also in connection with the thick ethical, political, legal, cultural, and aesthetic concepts that give texture and density to our social world, it becomes doubtful that foundationalism can really make sense to us in a *generalized* and *exclusive* form that would be authority-grounding (a) across the entire range of our concepts, and (b) across the entire range of dimensions along which concepts might earn their claim to authority.

This comes out when we consider the flipside of Sider's claim that concepts are authoritative when they carve at the joints, namely that all the concepts that do *not* carve at the joints are equally unauthoritative: there is nothing to set them apart, since the only thing that could set them apart is the property of being joint-carving, and they all lack *that*. To be sure, one could try to discriminate further here by introducing a suitably comparative correlate of the conceptual property of being joint-carving, such as the relation 'closer to being joint-carving than'.[6] All non-joint-carving concepts would then be authoritative at least to the extent that they *approximated* the joint-carving concepts.

Yet the underlying idea remains that the property of being joint-carving is the sole source of conceptual authority, and this no longer rings true once we turn our attention from the concepts of fundamental science to the thick normative concepts that distinctively structure different social worlds: can we really still believe that there is a timelessly and absolutely privileged way to write the book of the social world? These concepts seem to derive what conceptual authority they possess from some other basis.

Even if it is granted that certain concepts of chemistry or fundamental physics are authoritative because they are joint-carving, there are many further dimensions along which concepts might earn their claim to authority.[7] It is implausible to think that two concepts that failed to be joint-carving to exactly the same degree could not differ in some other way in their claim to being authoritative for us. And it is even less plausible to think that there could not be contexts in which concepts operating at higher levels of description—psychological, ethical, political, or legal—would be at least as

---

[6] See Pérez Carballo (2020, 310–11).
[7] A point that also has a role to play in explaining why scientists develop the particular concepts of natural kinds they do—see e.g. Laura Franklin-Hall on the 'category influence hypothesis'—the claim that 'the contours of scientific classifications are to some degree influenced by contingent features of scientists themselves' (2015, 933).

authoritative as the concepts of chemistry or fundamental physics. In other words, even if some concepts are authoritative *because* they are joint-carving, it had better not follow that concepts which *fail* to be joint-carving are therefore not authoritative. There has to be some other notion of conceptual authority that allows us to capture the sense in which joint-carving concepts are clearly inferior to higher-level concepts in understanding and navigating the complexities of human relationships, ethical appraisal, political debate, or legal argument.

If the foundationalist account no longer rings true for us when generalized from science to the thick normative concepts that structure social worlds, this may be because, as the dust settles on post-modernism's campaigns to expose the contingency and parochiality of anything considered necessary or universal, we are, to an unprecedented degree, historically self-conscious not only in our thought, but also in our thought *about* thought. Awareness of the fact that the supposedly timeless and mind-independent rational foundations of the past have invariably been washed away, along with the ideas that were built on them, has become so deeply embedded in contemporary culture that we may find it especially hard to believe in timeless and mind-independent rational foundations. Not only are we no longer in the unreflective condition. We are also no longer in a reflective condition in which the anxiety induced by awareness of conceptual diversity could be alleviated by foundationalism. We know not just that people have lived by radically different concepts over the ages, but that history is littered with unsuccessful attempts to rest the authority of concepts on ever new foundations. We know that, time and again, people have convinced themselves that they had succeeded in transcending their contingent circumstances, only to discover later that the veneer of timelessness had been but a product of its time. Awareness of this fact is now too pervasive for us not to expect further attempts to identify timeless foundations to suffer a similar fate, and end up saying more about us than about the sempiternal scaffolding of thought.

4.2 Indiscriminate Ironism

Where does disillusionment with generalized foundationalism leave us? It might seem that the only reasonable response, once it is granted that we cannot vindicate any one set of thick normative concepts against alternatives on the basis of timeless and mind-independent rational foundations, is *ironism*: the sort of ironic detachment and disengagement from our concepts that

Richard Rorty identifies in *Contingency, Irony, and Solidarity* as the only appropriate attitude for those who abandon the hope that their concepts could be rested on some bedrock 'beyond the reach of time and chance' (1989, xv).[8]

Ironism is the second horn of the trilemma. Without timeless and mind-independent rational foundations from which to mark out a set of concepts as carrying the stamp of authority, there seems to be no independent reason to prefer one set of concepts over another. Irony, as Gideon Rosen puts it, is a second-order attitude that one comes to adopt towards one's first-order judgements once it becomes clear that others may resist using one's concepts 'without making any neutrally identifiable mistake' (2022, 152). It is a second-order attitude, we might add, that one adopts in lieu of second-order reasons to consider one's concepts absolutely best.

On Rorty's account, ironists have three characteristics: (i) they have radical doubts about their own concepts, because they are impressed by the alternative concepts they encountered in the lives of other people, and by how final these alternative concepts were taken to be; (ii) they realize that arguments cast in terms of their own concepts are insufficiently independent of these concepts to either underwrite or dissolve these doubts; (iii) they do not believe that a genuinely independent, neutral, and universal basis is available to rationally ground one's choice of concepts.[9] Accordingly, they renounce any attempt to formulate criteria of concept appraisal and become convinced that their choice of concepts is bound to remain ungrounded.

Forced to continue to use some concepts in practice, ironists might hold on to their entrenched concepts. But they would be doing so *without good reasons*: merely out of ungrounded solidarity with 'the tribe'. In private, their reflective awareness of the rational contingency of their concepts would therefore prevent ironists from fully identifying with those concepts. Having lost confidence in their concepts, they would be restricted to using them only in a disengaged way.

The figure of the ironist has attracted much criticism,[10] and it is doubtful that anyone could be an ironist about all of their concepts all of the time; but even if it is an ideal type, the figure of the ironist registers something

---

[8] That introductory characterization of the ironist is couched in terms of beliefs rather than concepts, but the more careful characterization in a later chapter is couched in terms of choosing vocabularies (1989, 73), for reasons discussed in Santelli (2020). For a later contribution to conceptual ethics that draws on Brandom's inferentialism to strike a more constructive note, see Rorty (2007).
[9] See Rorty (1989, 73).
[10] See e.g. Blackburn (1998, 288–94), Fricker (2000, 2013), and Rosen (2022).

important which it would be complacent to dismiss, namely that reflective awareness of contingency does not leave everything where it was. Even Williams, sharp critic of Rorty though he was, concedes that while reacting to this realization by taking it to justify a non-relativistic morality of universal toleration would be 'seriously confused' (1985, 177), even a confused reaction is a reaction to something, and at least has the merit of acknowledging that some reaction is called for. Once we become conscious of the contingency of our concepts, it seems evasive and untruthful to maintain that this should not affect how we relate to our concepts and we should go on as before.

Certainly, closing our eyes to contingency and going on as before should not be mistaken for a return to the undemanding confidence of a society as yet untouched by reflective awareness of contingency. Once ignorance of contingency has been dispelled, it cannot be re-established. As Thomas Paine insisted in a phrase that now carries Rawlsian resonances: 'when once the veil begins to rend, it admits not of repair...though man may be *kept* ignorant, he cannot be *made* ignorant' (1998, 167). For us, pretending that *mere* confidence in our concepts could be enough would amount to complacency bordering on chauvinism.

The attitude of the ironist thus has the virtue of being open-eyed and truthful: it recognizes that, in the wake of metaconceptual reflection, confidence demands to be grounded in some basis for discriminating between concepts that merit confidence and concepts that do not.

Yet even ironism remains, in one crucial respect, foundationalist—notwithstanding the fact that it precisely denies that foundations of the sought-after kind are available. Ironism remains *counterfactually* foundationalist, because while it acknowledges that foundations are not in fact available, it still holds on to the foundationalist idea that *if* the authority of any concepts *could* be vindicated, this vindication would *have* to take the form of a derivation of authority from timeless and mind-independent foundations.[11] The ironist thus continues to endorse the conditional: 'If a concept is authoritative, then it is authoritative by virtue of its relation to timeless and mind-independent rational foundations.' It is the pattern of reasoning expressed in this conditional which licenses the ironist's signature move from the observation that there are no foundations to the conclusion that no concept is really authoritative. But to reason that if no foundations are available, any concept

---

[11] I take the widely applicable and useful idea of *counterfactual* adherence to a position from Williams's discussion of what he calls the 'counterfactual scientism' (2006g, 187) of the ironist. See also Queloz and Cueni (2019) for a different application of the idea to Nietzsche's critique of asceticism.

is as good as any other is to remain attached to a foundationalist conception of conceptual authority—much as atheists retain a theistic conception of morality if they endorse Ivan's inference, in *The Brothers Karamazov*, that if God does not exist, everything is permitted.

A similarly counterfactual form of foundationalism animates the view of a precursor to Rorty's ironist, namely the early Nietzsche, who, in some moods, dismisses all human concepts as equally distorting and falsifying, because they invariably fail to correspond to things as they are 'in themselves'.[12] In these passages, Nietzsche accepts that no timeless and mind-independent foundations from which to assess the authority of concepts are in fact available to us; but he holds on to the foundationalist thought that if it *were* possible to vindicate the authority of any concepts, that vindication would have to take the form of a derivation of authority from such foundations.

Pace Williams (2002, 17), the early Nietzsche need not be read as holding that we *can* in fact look round the edge of all our concepts at the True World we are applying them to, grasp its nature without drawing on any concepts, and use that as a rational basis on which to appraise our concepts. But even in suggesting merely that the set of concepts corresponding to the True World is what, *per impossibile*, we would really like to have, and that our concepts are the less authoritative for falling short of that ideal, Nietzsche still clings, if only counterfactually, to a foundationalist conception of conceptual authority. Foundationalism then gives way to an indiscriminate disengagement from all concepts. As Nietzsche himself later diagnosed the bind he was in, being 'freed from the tyranny of "eternal" concepts' puts one at risk of 'plunging into the abyss of a sceptical indiscriminateness' (85:35[6]).

Foundationalism and ironism thus share the same underlying conception of conceptual authority, and hence the same conception of reasons for concept use. They both hold that the only reasons that can properly *count* as second-order reasons for our first-order reasons are those that are reasons *for anyone*—for any concept-user, whoever they are, and whatever cultural context they find themselves in—and mark out one set of concepts as absolutely best.

We might say that these first two horns of the trilemma share certain normative expectations concerning what second-order reasons *ought* to be available. What separates them are their empirical expectations concerning

---

[12] In addition to this Neo-Kantian objection he presses notably in 'On Truth and Lie', Nietzsche also berates our concepts for systematically obfuscating differences, because we use the same concept for 'countless more or less similar cases which, strictly speaking, are never equal' (TL 256); not a promising argument, since it tacitly presupposes precisely the ability to conceptualize the differences that concepts allegedly obfuscate.

what second-order reasons are *in fact* likely to be available. Ironists' normative expectations are disappointed by the empirical expectations they end up forming. This is what creates the sense that something crucial is lacking and entrains indiscriminate disengagement.

But foundationalists and ironists agree in what they regard as a good answer to the authority question: if we are to vindicate our confidence in any concepts, conceptual authority must be grounded in reasons that are reasons for anyone because they derive from a timeless and mind-independent standard.

4.3 Reasons for Us: Non-Foundationalism

We need not choose between foundationalism and ironism. Once we see their shared presupposition, it becomes clear that we can break new ground by questioning it. Once we abandon not only the search for rational foundations beyond the reach of contingency and subjectivity, but also the very hankering after such foundations, we go one step further in the recognition of contingency than the ironist: we acknowledge that contingency extends to the very *standards* that concepts are beholden to. It is not just the concepts that are contingently ours, but also the demands they must meet. We should not seek the concepts that are absolutely best, in that *anyone* has reason to use them. We should seek the concepts that *we* have reason to use, given the demands on our conceptual apparatus in the situation that is peculiarly ours. Parting ways with both foundationalists and counterfactual foundationalists, we then seek some *non-foundationalist* answer to the authority question.

The mark of non-foundationalist answers is that they are given in terms of reasons *for us* that are not necessarily reasons for anyone. The key difference lies in what one is prepared to count as a normative resource sufficient to vindicate the authority of a concept. For foundationalists and ironists alike, the only truly authoritative concepts are those that can be validated as timelessly demanded by mind-independent rational foundations that anyone has reason to recognize as such. For non-foundationalists, conceptual authority can be vindicated by standards that are less than universal. They see no reason to suppose that the best concepts for citizens of twenty-first-century constitutional democracies, facing such unprecedented challenges as the climate crisis or the risks posed by new digital technologies, would be the same set of concepts as for medieval monks or Bronze Age chieftains.[13] If the problems

---

[13] On the various challenges posed by new digital technologies, see notably Zuboff (2015, 2019), Susskind (2018), Nemitz (2018), Macnish and Galliott (2020), Véliz (2020), and H. Smith (2021).

we face today are unprecedented, it would be surprising if the concepts that proved most helpful in tackling them were unresponsive to that fact. It is not just concept-users that are sociohistorically situated, but also the demands that their ways of thinking must live up to.

To move beyond foundationalism and ironism, then, we need to free ourselves of the very urge to extricate ourselves from our local perspective—what Amia Srinivasan calls 'the Archimedean urge' (2015). Our concepts are not all equally perspectival. Some concepts reflect the parochial sensibility and sensory peculiarities of their users more than others, and are more closely tied to a distinctive cultural and physiological perspective. When Blaise Pascal described the universe as *immense*, *silent*, and *terrifying*, for example, he was speaking from an increasingly local perspective.[14] And once we realize that our concepts and descriptions are to varying degrees tinged with subjectivity, we may form the aspiration to wring ourselves out of our conceptual apparatus and arrive at a way of conceptualizing the world that is fully objective.

Admittedly, this Archimedean urge to filter out the respects in which our conceptualization of the world reflects our perspective does make sense in certain contexts—in physics, notably, where it counts as a scientific advance to move from using ordinary colour concepts like *red* and *green*, which are indexed to a particular physiological perspective, to concepts like *wavelength* and *frequency*, which are accessible in principle to a much broader constituency. In the context of this kind of inquiry, where the inquirer precisely aims to shed the parochiality of his or her cultural and physiological perspective and approximate the Cartesian ideal of the 'Pure Enquirer', as Williams has it, we really do have reason to strive towards concepts that are minimally perspectival—concepts enabling us, at the limit, to articulate a 'scientific representation of the material world' that is 'absolute' or non-perspectival in that it 'does not have among its concepts any which reflect merely a local interest, taste or sensory peculiarity' (Williams 2005b, 229).[15]

The notion of a non-perspectival concept may strike one as incoherent at first: any concept that someone actually uses will have to be used from some

---

[14] I take the example from Williams (2014e, 323). For a systematic elaboration of this notion of a perspective, see Moore (1997). As Moore emphasizes, the absolute/perspectival distinction applies exclusively to our representational devices, including notably our concepts, but not to what is represented thereby (1997, ch. 3). Some representational devices are inherently perspectival, and representations cast in those perspectival terms can be directly endorsed only if one shares the relevant perspective (though they can be indirectly endorsed by endorsing a representation that entails them); but all representations remain representations of one and the same world. See Moore (1997, 16, 35, 49).

[15] This is one of the senses Williams gives to 'Pure Enquiry' in his discussion of Descartes (2005b, 49). It is a project Williams staunchly resists in the ethical sphere, where he is critical of the ambition to take up a Sidgwickian 'point of view of the universe' (1985, ch. 2; 1995h, 170; 2003).

perspective or other, and there will inevitably be some respect in which the use of the concept ends up betraying the perspective from which it is being used. In theoretical physics, for example, the use even of the most abstract concepts will still betray the perspective of their users through the notational conventions those concepts are expressed in, for example, or through the shared dispositions to apply the concepts to new cases in the same way.[16] But, as Moore points out, a representation that *betrays* a perspective need not, for all that, be a representation *from* a perspective (1997, 89): even if concept use always bears the imprint of concept-users, it does not follow that the concepts used are always perspectival concepts, i.e. concepts whose conceptual *content* is indexed to a perspective. The use of non-perspectival concepts might betray a perspective without compromising the non-perspectivalness of the concepts used—just as a tenseless sentence, indexing an event to a specific date without making use of any temporally perspectival concepts such as *yesterday* or *one year ago*, might nonetheless betray the temporal and linguistic perspective of its utterer.[17]

We can therefore make sense of the aspiration to arrive at a description of the world couched in terms of non-perspectival concepts by acknowledging, first, that its intelligibility requires no more than the possibility of *approximating* the non-perspectival by replacing *more* perspectival with *less* perspectival concepts; and second, that even genuinely *non*-perspectival concepts are not all that hard to come by, since concepts can be non-perspectival even when their use betrays a perspective.

Yet despite the long-standing 'ideological alignment' (Moore 2020, 129) between the scientific, the absolute, and the authoritative, it would be a mistake to conclude from this that the authority of concepts is inversely proportional to their perspectivalness: that concepts which are closely tied to a local perspective are *inherently and generally inferior* to concepts which are less closely tied to a local perspective. That would be to overgeneralize a model of conceptual authority that has its place within the scientific enterprise, but that would be misleading elsewhere. The less aligned with scientific aims our concerns in different contexts are, the less clear it is that we should try to wring ourselves out of our concepts.

In the context of the thick normative concepts of ethics or politics, for example, it makes little sense to aim at a non-perspectival description of the

---

[16] See Putnam (1992, 94–9; 2001; 2002, 40–5).
[17] See Moore (2020, 2024b) for a defence of the possibility of absolute or non-perspectival concepts against recent criticism, including by Rödl (2018, ch. 5); see Moore (2019a, c) for an application of these ideas to tensed representations.

world that even alien thought might converge on. Here, as George Eliot puts it, 'that bird's eye reasonableness which soars to avoid preference...loses all sense of quality' (1999, 814). Here, we are, on the contrary, trying to grasp how a situation relates to *our* projects, attachments, and loyalties. Bringing those to bear on our judgements is not, in the first instance, to *distort* our view of the situation, but rather what gives evaluative contour and colour to the situation in the first place. Just as one could not even begin to choose how to live from the utterly unconcerned, detached, and indifferent point of view of the universe, one could not even begin to choose which thick normative concepts to live by. This is why Williams cautions against the 'scientistic illusion' that it is our task as rational concept-users to 'search for, or at least move as best we can towards, a system of political and ethical ideas which would be the best from an absolute point of view, a point of view that was free of contingent historical perspective' (2006g, 193–4). In the first instance, the choice between the concepts that give us reasons for action and structure our ethical, social, and political lives is not *biased* by our local perspective, but *constructed* and *concretized* by it, because that is the perspective that fleshes out *for whom* the concepts in question are to be authoritative. It is only from within such an evaluative perspective that one can then intelligibly strive to correct for bias and attain some degree of impartiality. Impartiality is not the absence of an evaluative perspective, but a value bearing on how to evaluate from such a perspective.

To retain some basis on which to choose between thick normative concepts, then, the Archimedean urge must be resisted. Bringing our projects, attachments, and loyalties to bear on concept choice is not, in the first instance, a distortion, but rather what makes it possible for the choice to be grounded in reasons in the first place. The thought that concept choice could be biased by local concerns is important, but it needs to be brought in later, once there is a choice to bias. We should not first determine which ethical or political concepts are absolutely best, and then infer from this that they should be used from a perspective that happens to be ours. The choice between such concepts is not just incidentally, but essentially ours.

On such a non-foundationalist approach to the authority question, the reasons we might have to use certain concepts can properly be reasons *for us* without being reasons that anyone should recognize as such. This need not mean that the reasons *in terms of which* we have reason to think are themselves merely 'reasons for us'. The force of second-order reasons can be indexed to a particular perspective without thereby similarly indexing the force of the first-order reasons they are reasons for: perhaps, as numerous historians of the concept of authenticity have suggested, 'we moderns', living in far larger social structures that do less to predetermine what groups and roles the individual will identify with, have particular reason to think in terms of *authenticity*;[18] but the concept of authenticity we have reason to use nonetheless involves the idea that *anyone* has reason to prefer an authentic over an inauthentic life, not just that we moderns do.

The possibility of indexation to a perspective or constituency at the level of second-order reasons does mean, however, that, for each concept, we need to take seriously the question of who 'we' is: who has reason to use it and who does not. In most cases, the 'we' used in the present book is not the all-encompassing 'we' quantifying over all rational beings or all of humanity. Nor is it the presumptuous 'we' that imputes certain characteristics to an antecedently designated set of people—to which the reader is presumed to belong—and tells them how to think. It is, rather, the 'we' *of invitation*, which invites readers to consider to what extent they recognize themselves in a certain description, and what this would imply.[19]

This construal of 'we' as functioning through invitation rather than through an antecedently fixed designation offers a plausible interpretative model for much philosophical writing, especially in ethics: many philosophical texts do not simply take for granted the sweeping generalizations about people that they use as premises; nor is their capacity to persuade passively dependent on a set of immutable concerns that readers self-consciously bring to the text. Our sense of what our own concerns are is incomplete and malleable. Much philosophical writing, responding to this fact, aims to be persuasive in a more active sense, by striving to shape the readers' sense of their own concerns and their relative importance. Insofar as these concerns do then come to be invoked as premises in the text's arguments, they are concerns that might be *made* into important concerns for the readers *through* their

---

[18] See Trilling (1972, 15–16), Taylor (1989, 26), Guignon (2004, 17–19), and Lindholm (2013, 365); though, as historians of earlier societies tend to emphasize—see e.g. O'Doherty and Schmieder (2015)—the dynamism and mobility of medieval societies, for instance, should not be underestimated. See Leuenberger (2021) for a nuanced philosophical assessment of this historical material that highlights the practical reasons to live by the concept of authenticity under conditions of modernity.

[19] I am influenced here by an endnote to *Shame and Necessity* in which Williams justifies his own copious use of 'we' with the remark that it 'operates through invitation': 'It is not a matter of "I" telling "you" what I and others think, but of my asking you to consider to what extent you and I think some things and perhaps need to think others' (1993, 171 n. 7). This conception of the pragmatics of philosophical texts is a natural consequence of Williams's view that the reader's thought 'cannot simply be dominated', because, 'as it used to say on the packets of cake mix', the reader will and must 'add his own egg' (1986, 203). In this regard, Williams was self-consciously echoing Nietzsche and especially Collingwood (Williams 2006b, 343–4). For further discussion of Williams's reflections on philosophical style, see Babiotti (2021), Krishnan and Queloz (2023; forthcoming), and Fricker (forthcoming-b).

engagement with that very text: persuasive philosophical writing can awaken, revivify, or strengthen concerns in its readers, and thereby contribute to the satisfaction of its own presuppositions.

Similarly, in speaking of 'reasons for us', I mean those of us who share certain reason-giving characteristics, where the idea is not to ascribe these characteristics to an independently identified set of people, but to invite readers to consider to what extent they identify with those characteristics, and to what extent that might in turn give them reasons to prefer certain concepts over others—reasons that might be reasons *for us* in highly localized sense.

4.4 Undiscriminating Holism

Once we opt for a form of non-foundationalism, we thus look to local standards to ground conceptual authority. But the way in which this has typically been done in twentieth-century analytic philosophy is through some form of *holism* about one's web of concepts. This is the third horn of the trilemma.

The influence of holistic non-foundationalism in twentieth-century analytic philosophy is due notably to Rudolf Carnap's voluntarism about framework choice and his principle of tolerance towards rival frameworks, and to some extent also to the later Wittgenstein's thesis of the arbitrariness of grammar.[20] Within the bounds of what is cognitively and practically feasible for creatures like us, choices between conceptual frameworks are rationally underdetermined, on this view. It does not matter which framework we choose, as long as the judgements we form within it are true. The choice of framework is understood purely voluntaristically—we can choose one at will. What is *not* purely a matter of will is which judgements are true and which are false within a given framework. We may freely choose which framework to bind ourselves

---

[20] On Carnap's principle of tolerance and his voluntarism, see George (2012), Steinberger (2016), Carus (2017), and Leitgeb and Carus (2021); on Wittgenstein's thesis of the arbitrariness of grammar, see Glock (1996, 'arbitrariness of grammar'), Forster (2004, 67–8), and Kusch (2015). It should be noted that in certain passages, Carnap sounds less voluntaristic than he is standardly portrayed as being: 'it is a practical, not a theoretical question...whether or not to accept the new linguistic forms. The acceptance cannot be judged as being either true or false because it is not an assertion. It can only be judged as being more or less expedient, fruitful, conducive to the aim for which the language is intended. Judgments of this kind supply the motivation for the decision of accepting or rejecting the kind of entities' (1947, 214). Here, Carnap seems to envisage something like the goal-based appraisal I consider in Chapter 6; see also Reck (2012, 2024). In several passages, Wittgenstein likewise seems to acknowledge a sense in which what concepts we use is not arbitrary. See, for example: 'Compare a concept with a style of painting. For is even our style of painting arbitrary? Can we choose one at pleasure? (The Egyptian, for instance.) Or is it just a matter of pretty and ugly?' (2009, II, §367).

by; but, a framework once chosen, we really are bound by it and by the brute factual recalcitrance of how things are.

On this kind of holistic non-foundationalism, what gives individual concepts their authority is the fact that they are part of a coherent conceptual framework. In the fishing net analogy: what matters is not which weave patterns the net employs, but whether the net allows us to catch fish; and that means that whatever weave patterns we end up going for, the main thing is that the net should not have holes in it. Carnapian frameworks, Quinean webs, or Davidsonian conceptual schemes can all make it tempting to operate with something like this picture in the background. It suggests that a conceptual framework will draw whatever claim to authority it possesses primarily from the extent to which it combines compatible and interlocking concepts into a coherent whole, i.e. a conceptual structure that is free of intra- and interconceptual tensions (I elaborate on the notion of a conceptual tension in the next chapter).

The problem with holistic non-foundationalism that emphasizes the arbitrariness and voluntaristic character of framework choice, however, is that it still leaves the particular framework one uses looking rationally contingent: it fails to give us reasons to prefer one framework over another.

Of course, holism that emphasizes the arbitrariness and voluntaristic character of framework choice precisely aims to *deflate* that worry, assuring us that any easily usable framework is as good as any other, and that the questions worth worrying about lie *downstream* of framework adoption, where we worry whether a particular measurement is correct, or a particular thought true. As Wittgenstein replies to the person wondering whether nature really has nothing to say in determining our conceptual scheme: we do 'run up against existence and non-existence somewhere', but 'that means against facts, not concepts' (1981, 364), and we can only *grasp* facts downstream of having adopted a conceptual scheme. This invites us to think of conceptual choices in analogy to choices of units of measurement, as Wittgenstein does when he compares 'laws of inference' or 'rules of grammar' to 'rules of measurement' that vary with regard to how much trouble they are to use.[21] We might call this the *metrological* conception of conceptual ethics (after *metron*,

---

[21] 'Now perhaps one thinks that it can make no *great* difference *which* concepts we employ. As, after all, it is possible to do physics in feet and inches as well as in metres and centimetres; the difference is merely one of convenience. But even this is not true if, for instance, calculations in some system of measurement demand more time and trouble than we can afford' (Wittgenstein 2009, §569) See also Wittgenstein (1974, 185; 1978, I, §118). See Kusch (2015) for an overview and discussion of Wittgenstein's metrological analogies.

Greek for 'measure'). On this metrological conception, conceptual frameworks may vary in their usability, but the main difference remains that between having *some* framework and having none.

Once one focuses on thick normative concepts, however, anxiety over whether one has been initiated into the wrong framework reappears: each of these thick concepts contributes, in its own small way, to giving a social world a certain structure and feel, and thereby subtly alters the dynamics and perhaps eventually the trajectory of that social world. In view of this fact, the contention that one framework is as good as another loses its plausibility. More needs to be said for holism to avoid collapsing into ironism at the level of frameworks.

To this end, holistic non-foundationalism requires a more explicitly functionalist underpinning: a society's conceptual repertoire should be pictured as a harmoniously interlocking whole that is authoritative *for* that society because it has organically grown out of its particular way of life, and has over time become adapted to that way of life.[22]

This elaboration of holism, associated in twentieth-century analytic philosophy with Wittgenstein's notion of a 'form of life', has given a renewed impetus to functionalist holism in anthropology and to communitarianism in social and political philosophy. Not only do a society's conceptualizations harmoniously collaborate in practice, constituting a well-coordinated cultural formation in which each conceptualization performs a function within the whole; the whole that is formed thereby is also uniquely adapted to the character of the society that lives under it, giving them second-order reasons to reason in these terms.

Yet this functionalism creates another problem for holistic non-foundationalism. While it rids itself of the hankering after timeless and mind-independent rational foundations and avoids ironism's indiscriminate disengagement from any and all concepts, it risks doing so at the price of embracing whatever conceptual web we happen to have grown into—an attitude that is not exactly *indiscriminate*, since it remains selectively focused on one's own conceptual apparatus and is withheld towards other ways thinking, but remains *undiscriminating*, in that it does not draw any finer distinctions between better or worse concepts *within* that apparatus.

This is because functionalist holism discourages one from questioning the authority of individual concepts. It suggests, rather, that a form of life must be

---

[22] See e.g. Winch (1958), MacIntyre (1978, 1988, 2007), and Taylor (1985, 1989). J. L. Austin's (1961, 130; 1962, 62–4) view arguably also embodies this sort of functionalist holism.

accepted as authoritative *in toto* or rejected *in toto*. Displace anything, and you risk unsettling a fine balance struck over the ages.

Furthermore, a functionalist holism projects a frictionless harmony between our concepts, and thereby suggests that there are no tensions or conflicts inherent in our conceptual structure that might provide critical leverage or reasons to revise our ways of thinking. As Nietzsche notes, this reassuring picture has long held considerable attraction for a variety of cultures: 'Just as the Romans and Etruscans cut up the heavens with rigid mathematical lines and confined a god within each of the spaces thereby delimited, as within a *templum*, so every people has a similarly mathematically divided conceptual heaven above themselves and henceforth thinks that truth demands that each conceptual god be sought only within *his own* sphere' (1979, 85). Much as the neat orderliness of the *templum* suggests that every god can be given his due without upsetting the other gods, the picture of a harmonious 'dome of concepts' (Nietzsche 1979, 85) promises that every concept can be given its due, without coming into conflict with the claims of others concepts.

Instead of indiscriminate disengagement from the concepts we find at work in our form of life, holism thus encourages undiscriminating acceptance of them—in line with Wittgenstein's notorious dictum that 'philosophy leaves everything as it is' (2009, §124).[23] The result is a picture of conceptual authority which revives Right Hegelian conservatism in the guise of a 'Right Wittgensteinianism'.[24] In a less pronounced form, something like this holism continues to animate communitarian views in social and political philosophy.[25] These invoke, at least as an ideal, homogeneous and harmonious Herderian communities that are tightly integrated by shared thick concepts and traditions. The more coherent and harmoniously integrated with communal practices a conceptual framework is, the harder it becomes to make sense of revisions within it as endogenous and reason-driven (this is the force of Umberto Eco's remark that a worldview can make sense of anything except a different worldview).[26]

---

[23] There is, however, room for doubt whether Wittgenstein himself was committed to such a picture across the board—see Williams (2019) as well as Queloz and Cueni (2021); approaches that put a broadly Wittgensteinian picture to radically critical use include Pleasants (1999, 2002), Celikates (2015), and Jaeggi (2016).

[24] See Williams (2005h, 33; 2021, 278) for this use of the label 'Right Wittgensteinianism'. Bloor (1992) draws a related contrast. A variety of scholars have emphasized structurally conservative aspects of Wittgenstein's thought (Nyíri 1976, 1982; Bloor 1983; Rorty 1983; 1989, 58–60; Bloor 1997, 2000; Norris 2009; Plotica 2015; Temelini 2015).

[25] See MacIntyre (1978, 1988, 2007), Sandel (1981, 1996), and Taylor (1985, 1989).

[26] See Eco (1984, 12).

To a lesser extent, a similarly functionalist holism also informs ordinary language philosophy in its Austinian manifestation. For J. L. Austin, we ought at least initially to approach the ways of thinking we inherited with the assumption that the concepts and distinctions we find crystallized in 'common sense' embody, *pace* Bertrand Russell, not the metaphysics of the Stone Age, but 'the inherited experience and acumen of many generations of men' (1961, 133). Austin was, 'if not quite a *defender* of common sense', then certainly 'unwilling to give it up at the first whiff' (Krishnan 2023, 86) of suspicion born of airy philosophizing.

That is not to say that Austin considered common sense to be beyond reproach: he acknowledged that 'superstition and error and fantasy of all kinds do become incorporated in ordinary language', and that it could in principle be 'supplemented and improved upon and superseded' (1961, 133) in view of the latest scientific findings. But while he granted that 'we may wish to tidy the situation up a bit', he still urged philosophers 'always to bear in mind…that the distinctions embodied in our vast and, for the most part, relatively ancient stock of ordinary words are neither few nor always very obvious, and almost never just arbitrary' (1962, 63). The fine-grained discriminations enshrined in ordinary language were, on his view, likely to prove subtler and sounder than anything philosophers could dream up.[27]

One can ask how conservative this benevolent patience with inherited distinctions makes philosophy—whether it amounts to structural conservatism in practice if not in principle, and whether those distinctions would have been there to be inherited in the first place if people had always been so patient with the ways of thinking they inherited.[28] Yet Austin's picture is clearly one on which there is far more latent but coordinated functionality in our inherited distinctions than meets the eye, and these distinctions functionally hang together and cooperate in complex and ill-understood ways. This holism renders it difficult to find, and to be confident of genuinely having found, critical leverage within our conceptual apparatus: it conjures up a serious risk that any putative amelioration will end up being a *Verschlimmbesserung*—an improvement for the worse. In all of these ways, holism encourages concept-users to embrace the concepts they inherited.

---

[27] Austin thereby reaffirmed the views of an earlier Oxford philosopher, John Cook Wilson, who remarked: 'The authority of language is too often forgotten in philosophy, with serious results. Distinctions made or applied in ordinary language are more likely to be right than wrong' (1926, 874). See Rowe (2023) for a detailed account of how Austin combined Oxford Realism with Darwinian functionalism.

[28] Two charges that Williams (2014f) presses in a review of Austin's posthumously published essays.

4.5 The Kaleidoscopic Picture

It thus seems that we face an unsavoury choice between foundationalism, ironism, and holism: the first no longer makes sense to us when generalized to thick normative concepts; the second produces indiscriminate disengagement from our concepts; and the third encourages undiscriminating acceptance.

To escape this trilemma and find more critical leverage by which to discriminate between concepts that merit confidence and concepts that do not, the first step is to question the holistic picture of our conceptual apparatus as something harmonious, largely tensionless, and inherently static. By 'picture', I do not mean the total empirical description one would eventually arrive at after an exhaustive investigation of one's conceptual apparatus; I mean the *working picture* against which one embarks on such an investigation: the picture expressing one's default expectations concerning what shape that apparatus is likely to take. Such a picture affects what one looks for in one's conceptual repertoire, which questions one is disposed to raise, and what one is primed to find.

A different working picture with which one might approach concepts is the negation of the holistic one: it is the picture on which the concepts we use, far from harmoniously interlocking in a finely calibrated whole, are a historically accumulated jumble—the multifarious outgrowth of diverging, competing, and repeatedly redirected concerns, brimming with intra- and interconceptual tension. While the holistic picture sees the demands of one concept end where those of another begin, like cleanly interlocking panels in a stained-glass window, this alternative picture of our conceptual apparatus—call it the *kaleidoscopic picture*—assumes a motley of overlapping and competing demands. There is no presumption that all one's concepts harmoniously work together, or for one's benefit. Instead, the default stance with which one approaches one's conceptual inheritance is a sceptical stance. This is also the working picture that Nietzsche recommends:

> Hitherto, one generally trusted one's concepts as if they were a wonderful *dowry* from some sort of wonderland: but they are, after all, the legacy of our most distant and most stupid as well as of our most intelligent ancestors.... What is needed to begin with [*zunächst*] is absolute scepticism towards all inherited concepts. (85:34[195])

The kaleidoscopic picture invites us to approach concepts not holistically, but on a case-by-case basis, with an open mind as to their merit—one might say that it *encourages* the authority question. Instead of leading one to expect our conceptual apparatus to be mostly tensionless, moreover, it feeds the expectation that our apparatus is replete with tensions of all kinds. And instead of presenting that apparatus as a well-calibrated adaptation to a certain form of life, it reminds us that any given piece of our conceptual inheritance might equally turn out to be the legacy 'of our most distant and most stupid' ancestors, and now be of questionable merit, if it ever had any.

On this picture, our conceptual apparatus is expected to harbour great critical potential, in the sense that extrapolations of some parts of our conceptual apparatus can be condemned, revised, or rejected in light of extrapolations of other parts.[29] The result is a version of the familiar Neurathian strategy of repairing the raft not in drydock, but out on the open waters, mending one plank while resting on the others. Insofar as our conceptual apparatus offers the inherent critical leverage that the kaleidoscopic picture invites us to seek out in it, the Neurathian strategy is capable of finer discriminations within our conceptual apparatus than either the Carnapian or the Wittgensteinian holistic strategies (perhaps uncoincidentally, Neurath was also the most politically engaged member of the Vienna Circle).[30] This inherent critical leverage in turn invites us to think of our conceptual apparatus not as inherently static, but as inherently dynamic: a structure whose change over time becomes intelligible as endogenous and reason-driven rather than as an exogenous and merely causal imposition from reality.

This is a case where knowledge of the history of something can inform our expectations about it and structure our interpretation of it. If one learned that a text was not carefully masterminded by a single author, but in fact constitutes a collage of snippets assembled and rewritten by several authors over many generations, one would not be surprised to find the text full of tensions and incoherences.[31]

Analogously, knowledge of the history that produced our concepts can inform our expectations as to how coherently they are likely to fit together, and thereby give us grounds for favouring one working picture over another. It would be nothing short of astonishing if the concepts we inherited from centuries of history—shaped as they are by countless historical contingencies, appropriated, extended, transformed, amalgamated, and repurposed by

---

[29] My elaboration of this point builds on Queloz and Cueni (2021) as well as on Williams (2019).
[30] See Edmonds (2020, ch. 12). For a discussion of the affinities between Otto Neurath's thought and present-day ameliorative conceptual engineering, see Yap (2022).
[31] For a detailed argument to the effect that knowledge of the history of something can yield an interpretative structure guiding our interpretation of it, see Prescott-Couch (2015, manuscript).

countless different factions many times over—should have ended up forming, of all things, a 'geodesic dome', to use Dworkin's (1996, 119; 2006, 160) architectural metaphor echoing Nietzsche's 'dome of concepts'. In a geodesic dome, rigid struts neatly interlock in a maximally stable and efficient hemisphere (a 'geodesic' is the shortest possible line between two points on a curved surface). But a history such as ours is more likely to have produced what, in architectural terms, is better described as a 'tensile membrane structure'—a vast canopy full of tensions, held up by crisscrossing poles pushing and pulling in competing directions.[32]

Even if we accept that selective pressures of one sort or another were at work in the history of our conceptualizations, this only yields the conclusion that each conceptualization might individually have been subject to certain selective pressures—there might be selection of some sort at the level of the individual conceptualization, resulting in its becoming adapted to deliver whatever effects are being selected for. Without a reason to think that there was strong selection *for coherence*, however, it does nothing to support the assumption of coherence between the concepts selected thereby; and why would evolution, cultural or biological, have selected above all for coherence, of all things? Given what we know about the variegated history out of which our conceptual inheritance emerged, then, the kaleidoscopic picture should be our default picture of our conceptual apparatus.

Another way to put the point is this: the holistic picture needs to be supported by an account of how the coherence it assumes *got there*, and that account needs to be less controversial, or at least differently controversial, than the picture it is meant to support. The kaleidoscopic picture, by contrast, does not call for a supporting account in this way. It is not a picture of a different controversial assumption, but a picture of the absence of such an assumption.

Adopting a kaleidoscopic picture as a working model of our conceptual apparatus marks the first step towards escaping the trilemma of foundationalism, ironism, and holism. When developed against such a backdrop, a non-foundationalist approach to concept appraisal can count on there being plenty of critical leverage in our conceptual apparatus already in virtue of the intra- and interconceptual tensions built up in it. If extrapolations of some parts of our conceptual apparatus can be condemned, revised, or rejected in light of extrapolations of other parts, it becomes intelligible how there can be endogenous, reason-driven changes in our conceptualizations.

---

[32] The iconic 'SkySong' structure at Arizona State University illustrates what I am envisioning as a counterpart to Dworkin's geodesic dome.

4.6 Leveraging Local Needs

But the non-foundationalist approach to conceptual authority I propose to develop here does not simply draw its critical leverage from the tensions to be found in our conceptual apparatus. It finds a leverage point that is more extraneous than that, though less extraneous than timeless and mind-independent rational foundations. As we shall see in more detail in Chapter 7, it finds that leverage point in concept-users' *conceptual needs*—the needs they have *for* certain concepts as a result of their concerns, capacities, and circumstances. This is the second step out of the trilemma. The approach to conceptual authority by which I propose to escape the trilemma is thus a *needs-based* non-foundationalism: an appraisal of the concepts we have according to the concepts we need.

However, the suggestion that we should appraise our concepts on the basis of our needs as a non-foundationalist would construe them, namely through those very concepts, immediately invites two worries: it appears to make such a needs-based non-foundationalism (a) circular, and (b) sensitive to local circumstances.

In the remainder of this chapter, I argue that any appearance of problematic circularity evaporates under analysis, and that sensitivity to local circumstances is a feature rather than a flaw of the approach: it manages to draw additional critical leverage from local needs.

Take circularity first. Tristram McPherson and David Plunkett (2021) have formulated a 'vindicatory circularity challenge' for conceptual ethics, arguing that since any evaluation of our concepts itself has to draw on evaluative concepts, reflection that succeeds in vindicating concepts is likely to display the circularity involved in evaluating a standard by itself. Yet, as Nietzsche already observed: '*Ein Werkzeug kann nicht seine eigene Tauglichkeit kritisiren*' (85:2[132])—a tool cannot critique its own adequacy. An important challenge for conceptual ethics therefore lies in explaining why this circularity does not vitiate the enterprise of conceptual ethics.

If that enterprise is described as appraising our concepts in terms of those same concepts, it indeed looks circular. But needs-based appraisal does not involve vindicating a concept *F* in terms of that same concept *F*. Rather, the idea is to disengage oneself from the concept *F* and assess its authority by examining the conceptual needs one has as a result of one's concerns, capacities, and circumstances. A concept is thus to be appraised by the lights of an array of items that are *not* concepts. It is merely that in individuating these items, one is bound to make engaged use of the rest of one's concepts, or at least of some of them.

While I shall argue in later chapters that we can have conceptual needs unwillingly and unwittingly, it is of course trivially true that what conceptual needs we can conceptualize ourselves as having is partly a function of our concepts. In that sense, the leverage point provided by our needs for certain concepts is not entirely independent of our conceptual apparatus: in the terminology developed in Chapter 2, we might say that our conceptual needs are hermeneutically, though not necessarily logically or ontologically, dependent on our conceptual apparatus: we can only *make sense* of them *as* needs of ours by virtue of our concepts. But this is true of anything we can make sense of. We cannot make sense of sense-making without concepts. As P. F. Strawson put the point, 'we lack words to say what it is to be without them' (1966, 273).

Accordingly, we are not searching—incoherently—for a leverage point that is extraneous to our concepts in the sense that its reflective recognition does not draw on our conceptual resources at all. We are bound to draw on our concepts in bringing any standard to bear on our reflection. As John McDowell also stresses, 'one can reflect only from the midst of the way of thinking one is reflecting about' (1996, 81). Yet the fact that our needs only come within our conscious purview by dint of the concepts through which we conceptualize them is no bar to seeing those needs as extraneous to our concepts—just as the fact that one only recognizes *fouls* as such if one has the concept thereof does not turn tackles into concepts.

A needs-based approach can also avoid the second, more holistic form of circularity that McPherson and Plunkett (2021, 214) are worried about, where a set of concepts mutually support each other in a way that systematically forecloses the possibility of critique. For one thing, this is a problem one would expect to be pervasive only on the holistic picture of our conceptual apparatus; on the kaleidoscopic picture, we do not expect our concepts to prove mutually vindicating—certainly not across our conceptual apparatus. On the contrary, we expect there to be no shortage of critical movement as tensions are alleviated and new ones created.

Furthermore, combining a kaleidoscopic picture of our first-order reasons with an approach that reaches beyond those first-order reasons to find a basis for critique in conceptual needs promises to give us a critical grip even on mutually vindicating sets of concepts. This leverage point in needs is independent enough to render intelligible the possibility that even a community of concept-users whose conceptual apparatus formed a harmonious and tensionless whole could find reasons to become radically dissatisfied with large swathes of that apparatus. It might no longer be what they need. Making concepts answerable to our needs thus allows in principle for profoundly radical critique.

My suggestion is not that we should assess the authority of all our concepts at once, moreover. Doing so would once again introduce a problematic form of circularity, since it would mean that at least some of our concepts would have to figure *at the same time* among the objects of appraisal and among the concepts used to appraise them. Rather, the idea is to operate piecemeal and disengage from *one* concept, or one connected *set* of concepts, to assess its authority based on our conceptual needs as construed through the engaged use of the *rest* of our concepts. As a result, the appearance of circularity evaporates under analysis. The concept appraised does not itself contribute to defining the standard of its own appraisal, and no concept is safe from revision: the insistence that we cannot question everything at once is entirely compatible with the idea that everything is open to question.

There is, however, one respect in which needs-based appraisal retains something of the self-referentiality which marks off non-foundationalism from foundationalism. If our conceptual needs are, as I shall argue, the product of how our concerns interact with our capacities and circumstances, then our assessment of the authority of a given concept will depend notably on what concepts figure among 'the rest of our concepts'. Not only what we take our concerns, capacities, and circumstances to be, but what they in fact *are* depends on what concepts structure our social world. This is most obviously true of the *concerns* we pursue: the acquisition of new concepts can instil new concerns—such as the Enlightenment concern for autonomy, or the Romantic concern for authenticity—that we would not have without a host of concepts putting the relevant considerations, desires, and aspirations within our cognitive grasp. Here we really have not just hermeneutic dependence, but ontological and logical dependence: the concerns for autonomy and authenticity only exist in virtue of the concepts we possess, which also makes the reasons given to us by these concerns dependent on those concepts. What we care about and want is a function of the concepts we possess. Despite its rather grand, Fichtean echoes of self-determination by thought alone, this would have come as no surprise to such a hard-nosed businessman as Henry Ford, first mass-producer of cars, who quipped that if he had asked people what they wanted, they would have said: 'faster horses'.[33]

---

[33] In the literature on design thinking and innovation, this limitation that extant concepts impose on our concerns has accordingly been called 'the faster horses trap' (Gordon, Rohrbeck, and Schwarz 2019).

Similar dependences on our concepts are exhibited by our capacities and circumstances. These are so deeply affected by the conceptual architecture we inhabit that no accurate construal of these capacities and circumstances for the purposes of appraising one of our concepts could reasonably hope to avoid reflecting the influence of the rest of our conceptual architecture. Consequently, in inquiring whether we need anything like the concept F, and what the concept we need looks like, we will draw on the rest of our concepts, and this means that what conceptual needs we can discover that we have is not completely independent of the concepts we possess already.

The only way to escape this dependence would be to view all our concepts as answering only to needs we have anyway, i.e. antecedently and independently of any of our concepts. But this would be to take a very narrow view of our needs, akin to that adopted by the evolutionary psychologist wondering how the human artefacts exhibited at MoMa are conducive to survival and reproduction.[34] The advent of new concepts can lead to the creation of new and sociohistorically local needs. If we allow these local needs to inform concept appraisal, our conceptualizations will be made to answer to needs we would not have without them. But there is no problematic circularity involved in this as long as the concepts needed and the concepts involved in engendering and recognizing the needs are distinct concepts.

This brings us to the sensitivity to local circumstances which I suggested was a feature of the approach. The non-foundationalist conviction that the present book is guided by is that we want *our* concepts to help *us* to live, and they can do this, most notably, by helping us to meet *our needs*. These needs are clearly not entirely, or even mainly, those of disembodied intelligences floating free of localized historical developments. We need concepts that are rooted in our local perspective, a perspective that is reflective not only of our humanity, but also of our distinctive identity, projects, problems, and commitments.

If the authority of a concept is tethered to the local concerns, capacities, and circumstances creating a need for it, however, the variability of these factors across people, places, and periods means that there is no one set of concepts that is universally and eternally best. Much as there is no absolutely and definitively best set of tools for an artist, because the tools have to suit the artist and the kind of artistic vision she is pursuing, what concepts one needs becomes a function of one's concerns, capacities, and circumstances, and varies with them. As a result, a concept that served us well may become an

---

[34] As Miller (2000) does, for example.

appropriate target of critique on the grounds that it is no longer suitable to our conceptual needs. Anil Gupta illustrates this using the metrological concept *one foot*. It 'may serve the community well when its concerns are confined to short distances and when small variations in measurement are of little consequence', but once 'the community's concerns widen to such things as demarcating large fields, the indeterminacy inherent in the notion may begin to generate consequential and intractable disagreements (and even violent conflict)' (2019, 257). The community's concept, as Gupta himself finds it natural to put it, 'is no longer suitable for its needs' (2019, 257).

Again, the connection between concepts and concerns goes both ways: just as the advent of new tools has led artists to strive for different forms of art, the adoption of new concepts can instigate the development of new concerns and alter our capacities and circumstances. As a result, there are acquired needs just as there are acquired tastes, and there are many needs we would never have acquired were it not for the sensibility-transforming and imagination-enhancing powers of certain concepts.

But when we assess the authority of a particular concept, it is, in the first instance, our conceptual needs that we should look to. How well the concept meets those needs will determine how authoritative it is, and whether a rival concept is more authoritative because better tailored to those needs.

Some of our needs will be best met by minimally perspectival concepts that we might expect even very differently situated intelligences to converge on; but the totality of our conceptual apparatus should answer to the totality of our needs, and it would be an impoverished human life that had no more local needs besides those near-universal ones. A conceptual apparatus fit to meet our various needs cannot be limited to the bloodless abstractions we might expect even alien thought to grasp. It must include thickly perspectival concepts that will reflect our particular historical, cultural, and social situation. Precisely because we are not, in Williams's phrase, 'unencumbered intelligences selecting in principle among all possible outlooks' (2006g, 193), we need to acknowledge that concepts are not just authoritative from a perspective that happens to be ours. Rather, that perspective is the source of their authority.

The pressure on concepts to reflect local peculiarities is implicitly recognized in the fascination exerted by concepts expressible only in hard-to-translate words from other cultures (a fascination frequently abused by those who seek to dress up utterly banal advice as rarefied ancient wisdom). What fuels this fascination is the hope that the most distinctive elements of a culture's vocabulary might be a guide to that culture's most distinctive characteristics and concerns. That is not always true, since, in inferring from words via concepts to concerns, one is liable to mistake a contingent linguistic idiosyncrasy for a marker of deep cultural difference. But when moving in the opposite direction, from concerns to the concepts they call for, there *is* a robust connection that can more reliably guide our understanding of what concepts we have most reason to use: the peculiarities of our situation and the distinctive concerns we pursue in it do make it worthwhile for us to use certain concepts rather than others.

To think that our concepts should answer to something as local and variable as human needs is to adopt a contingent standard—a standard that is not only properly expressive of our humanity (non-foundationalism has been aptly called a 'methodological humanism'),[35] but also the product of even more local and contingent sociohistorical forces. Such a standard will not yield many reasons for concept use that would be recognizable to any rational agent. But it will yield reasons for those who share the relevant concern and the kind of situation in which it is pursued. This is not to settle for second-best after relinquishing all hope of finding rational foundations that are impervious to contingency. The question should not be whether *anyone* has reason to prefer the concepts we have over alternatives, but whether *we* do.

In its willingness to tailor our thought to genuinely local needs, the present approach goes decidedly beyond philosophical approaches that aim to separate out the concepts that human beings *necessarily* have from those that they only *contingently* have. Philip Pettit, Miranda Fricker, and Robert Smithson, for example, have recently articulated philosophical research programmes aiming to map out the constraints on our conceptual schemes that arise from human beings' *most constant* concerns: concerns that tend to be at work in any human community, no matter its location in space and time.[36] Of course, these constant concerns can only engender necessities that are themselves contingent upon certain highly general facts about human nature or social arrangements. But, as Jonathan Rée observes: 'Contingencies can last a very long time. Our preoccupations with love and death may not be absolute necessities, but they are not a passing fad either, and it is a safe bet that they will last as long as we do' (1998, 11).

Accordingly, the research programme of 'conceptual cartography', as Smithson calls it, seeks to isolate those features of our conceptual scheme that are *necessary* for creatures with our basic nature, in the sense that 'we cannot

---

[35] See Lauener (2001).
[36] See Pettit (2018, forthcoming), Fricker (2020a), and Smithson (2021).

imagine humans accomplishing their basic projects without having a conceptual scheme with these features', from features that are *contingent*, in the sense that 'we can imagine communities effectively using a somewhat different conceptual scheme' (2021, 97).[37] Transcendental arguments as advanced in different forms by Kant, Donald Davidson, and P. F. Strawson provide one kind of template for this.[38] The features of our conceptual scheme that are necessary form what Strawson calls that 'central core of human thinking which has no history—or none recorded in histories of thought' (1959, 10).

One reason to want to understand 'to what extent features of our actual practice are necessary, and to what extent they are contingent', as Fricker puts it, is that this 'will in turn explain how some kinds of criticism of our practice are worth making, and how some are senseless' (1998, 165). Furthermore, identifying the features of our conceptual scheme that grow out of absolutely basic and anthropologically universal concerns promises to allow us to 'specify the limiting conditions on our exercise of ethical freedom' (2020a, 931), Fricker argues: while 'we are, in a far-reaching sense, *ethically free*' in that 'we are substantively free to set our own ends, and thereby generate our own values and correlative practical reasons' (2020a, 921), we are ethically free only *within certain limits*—there are concepts that human beings cannot do without for long. Of course, it is a notorious truth that human beings are capable of destroying even what they absolutely need. But just because of this, it might be thought that identifying the elements of our conceptual scheme that we cannot do without is important, as it can help us to check dangerously destructive impulses.

The exclusive focus of such approaches on our most constant and most universal needs expresses an evaluative assumption that is questionable for the purposes of conceptual ethics, however, namely that what answers to universal needs is *more important* than what reflects more local factors. This evaluative assumption comes out well in Pettit's description of the research programme he envisions:

Which are the more or less passing ephemera and which the phenomena that are deeply embedded in the society? Which are more or less incidental

---

[37] Though Smithson goes on to distinguish different species of necessity, one of which—'pragmatic necessity'—he relativizes to sociohistorically situated communities. A feature F is then pragmatically necessary for a community, according to Smithson, iff 'all best suited languages for that community contain F' (2021, 109). Fricker also distinguishes species of necessity, including the practically necessary and the humanly necessary that arises out of 'human emotional nature' (2019, 245).
[38] See Smithson (2021, 114–15).

or contingent features and which are features apt to last? There is an interesting research programme suggested by such questions. It would take any society or culture or institution and, reviewing the data on various traits displayed by the entity in question, would seek to separate out the dross from the gold. It would try to identify and put aside the features that may be expected to come and go. And it would seek to catalogue the more or less necessary features that the society or culture or institution displays. It would give us a usefully predictive stance on the society, providing us with grounds for thinking that such and such features are likely to stay, such and such other features likely to disappear. (1996, 299–300)

The description of what is held in place by universal human needs as 'gold' and of the rest as 'dross' makes the evaluative hierarchy underlying this sort of approach fully explicit. In fairness to Pettit, it need mean no more than that the former is gold *for the purpose* of predicting what is likely to stay in place. But that still expresses the evaluative assumption that this should be the purpose of the exercise.

From the perspective of conceptual ethics, there are good reasons to question these evaluative assumptions: it is not obvious that what conceptual ethicists should primarily care about is the distinction between what is pinned in place by immutable needs and what is not, and even less obvious that the former should be elevated above the latter. In particular, there is no reason to think that the distinction between authoritative and unauthoritative concepts aligns with the distinction between what is pinned in place by immutable needs and what is not. Concepts might answer only to sociohistorically local needs, and yet be no less urgently needed.

What is more, these approaches focused on limiting constraints are simply silent about which concepts we have reason to prefer within the bounds delimited by those universal necessities. It may well be that what answers to universal human needs is gold, but it does not follow that everything else is dross—there are other precious materials. Marking out universally necessary concepts and delineating the bounds of our conceptual freedom is a start. But a truly discriminating and widely useful approach to concept appraisal should be sensitive to further distinctions between concepts, and allow us to identify reasons for reasons *within* the space of our conceptual freedom. It should not just demarcate the outer limits of conceptual change, but guide it.

The key to identifying reasons for reasons even within the space of our conceptual freedom is to recognize that which concepts are 'necessary for us' is itself a function of *who we are*, and therefore notably a function of more local historical and cultural forces: some concepts may be necessary *for us* without being necessary for every human community, because we have concerns that others did not have, or not in conjunction with the same capacities or under the same circumstances. The fact that these concepts are only *locally and contingently* necessary, in that they are necessary in virtue of concerns, capacities, and circumstances that are to varying degrees local and contingent, does not automatically detract from their importance.

Hence, while the approaches of Pettit, Fricker, or Smithson focus on the broad-meshed anthropological necessities that constrain our otherwise free and contingent conceptual choices, I aim to identify, in our more local needs, a basis from which to discriminate between better or worse concepts even within the realm of the contingent: there are concepts that *we* have reason to use in virtue of our local needs, though not every human community does. These reasons do not merely act as negative constraints on an otherwise rationally undetermined horizon of conceptual freedom, but offer positive guidance and criteria by which to evaluate different ways of thinking within the horizon of what is possible for creatures like us.

Lest this view of conceptual authority as a function of the needs created by our concerns, capacities, and circumstances seem obvious, however, it is worth pointing out that there is another, far more influential way out of the trilemma. This rival non-foundationalist approach to conceptual authority treats it not as something that is conferred upon concepts by the needs of concept-users, but as something inherent in features of the concepts themselves—in particular, in their theoretical virtues, such as their precision, determinacy, consistency, or coherence. On this view, which also operates against a picture of our conceptual apparatus as ridden with intra- and interconceptual tensions and defective in various ways, the *tidier* way of thinking is the more authoritative one, and philosophers' claim to attention derives notably from their skill in tidying up thought.

It is to understanding the motivations and gaps in this rival non-foundationalist approach that we now turn—the approach that seeks conceptual authority through the tidy-minded pursuit of theoretical virtue.

The Ethics of Conceptualization: Tailoring Thought and Language to Need. Matthieu Queloz, Oxford University Press.
© Matthieu Queloz 2025. DOI: 10.1093/9780198926283.003.0005

5
Tidy-Mindedness

The non-foundationalist answer to the authority question suggested by some of the recent literature on conceptual engineering is that we can improve our conceptual apparatus, however parochial, by tidying it up.[1] As advocates of conceptual engineering emphasize, the concepts we inherited tend to be in various ways messy and defective: unclear, imprecise, vague, gerrymandered, inconsistent, or incoherently related to other concepts. By re-engineering our conceptualizations to make use of more precisely defined, more consistent, or more coherently related concepts, we can fix those defects, and arrive at a set of concepts that has a better claim to being authoritative than the concepts we started out from. In contrast to what the traditional opposition of 'foundationalism' to 'coherentism' in theories of truth and justification would lead one to expect, however, this non-foundationalist ideal does not just pull towards coherence.[2] It pulls towards the entire catalogue of virtues associated with a tidy theory.

In this chapter, I assess the merits of this non-foundationalist approach as a general solution to the problem of conceptual authority. This affords me the opportunity to specify how I understand the main theoretical vices that concepts have been thought to display. I also add to the list with a proposal for how to think about concepts being *superficial* instead of exhibiting the desirable but elusive quality of *depth*. I then distinguish various ways in which concepts can stand in tension with one another. Especially conceptual superficiality and conceptual tensions will play an important role in later chapters.

With these technical definitions in place, I evaluate several variations on the idea that we should seek conceptual authority by tidying up our conceptual repertoire. It will emerge that while this aspiration has its place, it cannot provide a *general* answer to the authority question. We still need to supplement more theoretically virtuous concepts with the grounds on which they can claim more authority; and we need to be able to discriminate contexts in

---

[1] See e.g. Brun (2016, 2020), Cappelen (2018, ch. 2), Simion and Kelp (2020), Eklund (2002, 2019, 2021), Scharp (2013, 2020, 2021), Greenough (2020), Dutilh Novaes and Reck (2017), and Dutilh Novaes (2020a, b). An earlier discussion of different ways in which philosophers and scientists have sought to improve concepts by tidying them up is Robinson (1954, ch. 6, §12).

[2] See Olsson (2017) and Hasan and Fumerton (2018) for overviews.

which these grounds are given from contexts in which they are lacking, so that tidying up our ways of thinking may be detrimental to them. By the end of this chapter, the approach I go on to develop will thus have its work cut out.

Philosophers' pursuit of tidy ways of thinking—their *tidy-mindedness*—has a long history: 'philosophers have always aimed at cleaning up the litter', William James notes; they have sought to replace 'the first sensible tangle' with conceptions that are 'intellectually neat', 'orderly', and 'always aesthetically pure and definite' (1975–88, vol. iv, 26). This tidy-mindedness is manifest not only in how philosophers typically treat their chosen subject matters, but also in their tendency to gravitate towards subject matters that admit of tidy treatment.

Yet despite James's reference to the aesthetic dimension of philosophers' tidy-mindedness, the pursuit of tidy ways of thinking is not just an aesthetic quirk. It is more charitably understood as an attempt to pursue more authoritative concepts, and to guard against slovenly thinking and the risks it brings by conceptualizing things in more theoretically virtuous ways. In George Orwell's phrase, language needs 'fixing', because 'the slovenliness of our language makes it easier for us to have foolish thoughts' (2008, 270). Herman Cappelen's programmatic monograph on conceptual engineering, *Fixing Language* (2018), can be read as inviting philosophers to answer Orwell's call. It thereby revives something of the spirit of the Vienna Circle, which regarded tidy-mindedness as a form of 'resistance to the pollution of the mind by muddled speech' (Williams 1982, 116).

On a tidy-minded approach to concept appraisal, a concept, or a constellation of concepts, counts as authoritative to the extent that it realizes a catalogue of theoretical virtues, i.e. the virtues paradigmatically exemplified by a neatly axiomatized theory: clarity, determinacy, precision, fruitfulness, consistency, coherence, etc. We can discriminate between more or less authoritative concepts according to the degree to which they exhibit theoretical virtues or the corresponding theoretical vices.[3]

Importantly, this is not a foundationalist ideal. It drives us towards a tidied-up version of whatever conceptual apparatus we start out from, not *out* of those inherited ways of thinking and towards the set of concepts that is absolutely best. It is a purely formal ideal that can be satisfied in a plurality of ways, as it is indifferent to the substantive content of concepts. It seeks not the uniquely best mind, but a tidy mind, stocked only with definite and neatly interlocking concepts.

---

[3] As recently argued by Wakil (2023), for example.

5.1 Theoretical Vices in Concepts

Like the needs-based approach, the tidy-minded approach does without controversial assumptions to the effect that our conceptual apparatus forms a coherent whole, or that it is uniquely adapted to the society it has grown out of. On the contrary, the tidy-minded approach conceives of our conceptual apparatus as the jumbled product of history, bound to suffer from many theoretical vices leaving room for improvement. Cappelen expresses this view of our conceptual apparatus when he declares it 'implausible that a cultural artifact that's generated in a messy, largely incomprehensible way that's outside our control should end up producing something we can't improve on' (2020, 139).

A concept might, for example, be insufficiently 'clear and distinct', in the influential Cartesian phrase, leaving its content hard to make out and ill-demarcated from other things. On the tidy-minded approach, this is a conceptual defect that needs remedying. As Descartes insists in a letter to Mersenne: 'We have to form distinct ideas of the things we want to judge about' (1996, 3:272).[4]

In more contemporary idioms, we can distinguish a great many conceptual defects. Besides suffering from reference failure in the sense of being *empty*, a concept might, especially when introduced by ostensive definition, be *quasi-empty*, in that nothing strictly speaking falls under the concept as its users understand it, though they are nonetheless thinking and talking about *something*. An object prone to invite this conceptual misstep would be Castor in the Gemini constellation, for example: although it appears to the naked eye as a single star, it actually consists of three binary pairs of stars.[5] Relatedly, a concept might be *confused*, leading its users to mistake different things for the same thing—as when one takes a concept to refer to the one big ant in a particular colony when, unbeknownst to us, there are actually two big ants in the colony, though they never appear at the same time.[6]

A concept might also suffer from referential *indeterminacy*, so that there is simply no fact of the matter as to what exactly the concept refers to; or it might be the *inferential relations* a concept stands that are insufficiently determinate, leaving it partially unclear what its applicability is implied or excluded

---

[4] On the Cartesian conception of clarity and distinctness, see Paul (2020).
[5] See Gupta (2019, 253–4) for an illuminating discussion of this and other conceptual defects that might be produced through ostensive definition. I owe the Castor example to his discussion.
[6] On confused concepts, see Camp (2004), Wilson (2006), and Gupta (2019, 255). The ant example is a simplified version of Camp's.

by, and what it itself implies and excludes; or, like the notorious concept *heap*, a concept might be *vague*, i.e. lack sharp boundaries and give rise to cases in which one does not know whether the concept is applicable or not.

A lesser-known theoretical vice a concept might display is to be *open-textured* or *porous*: vulnerable to the advent of circumstances in which there would no longer be a fact of the matter whether the concept applied or not. Porosity is not the same as vagueness. Friedrich Waismann's point in introducing the notion of the *Porosität der Begriffe*, the porosity of concepts, was that although concepts such as *gold* or *mother* might initially be exactly defined and their applicability under different circumstances fully determinate, the discovery of new elements or biotechnological advances might subsequently produce circumstances that left it unclear whether the concepts were applicable.[7] The concepts are thus porous in the sense that not 'every nook and cranny is blocked against entry of doubt' (Waismann 1945, 123). They are not vague, but vulnerable to *becoming* vague.

A concept might also fail to pick out natural kinds and instead delineate *gerrymandered kinds*, held together by nothing more than our willingness to treat them as a kind while cutting across clusters of properties unified by more than that—'natural partitions', in David Lewis's phrase.[8] Relatedly, a concept might be *unfruitful* as a result of subsuming under one heading what is better kept distinct, as Carnap thought was the case with the non-scientific concept *fish*, which includes whales and dolphins and thereby allows us to formulate fewer law-like generalizations than the scientific concept *piscis* (Carnap's term), which excludes whales and dolphins. Carnap understood the fruitfulness of a concept in terms of its conduciveness to formulating what he called 'universal statements', by which he meant 'empirical laws in the case of a nonlogical concept, logical theorems in the case of a logical concept' (1962, 7).

But not all domains of inquiry are now thought to fit that description. Many do not aim at either empirical or logical statements, and even where they do, they do not necessarily aim at universal ones. This had led to various proposals for amendments to the notion of fruitfulness, on which a concept counts as fruitful to the extent that it furthers the aims of scientific inquiry,[9] facilitates the production of new knowledge,[10] or facilitates progress towards the achievement of theoretical goals.[11] These amendments make fruitfulness a

---

[7] For further discussion and clarification of the concept of open texture, see Vecht (2023).
[8] See Lewis (1983c, 120).
[9] See Kitcher (2008).   [10] See Dutilh Novaes and Reck (2017).   [11] See Pinder (2022).

great deal broader and harder to quantify than Carnap's conception, which enabled one to simply tally up the number of universal statements containing the concept.[12]

Yet even these amendments leave the notion of fruitfulness narrowly restricted in one significant respect: it remains sensitive only to what a concept does for scientific inquiry, the production of new knowledge, or theoretical goals, when—as the next chapter will bring out—much of what concepts do for us lies outside the perspective provided by these aims, and may even work against them.

What all of these theoretical vices in individual concepts certainly do, however, is to give the tidy-minded approach critical leverage over our conceptual apparatus. On the tidy-minded conception of conceptual authority, more authoritative concepts can be arrived at by replacing these defective concepts with more theoretically virtuous alternatives. And as we saw, that approach to conceptual authority has a distinguished history—it is as Cartesian as it is Carnapian.

5.2 Superficial Concepts

Besides these well-explored theoretical vices, there is another familiar, but far less theorized complaint one might have about a way thinking, namely that it is *superficial*. Not all the ways in which thought might be said to be superficial invite description as a theoretical vice. But it is a widely shared idea that one virtue of a good scientific theory is its *depth*, and that superficiality is a vice in a scientific theory. Even theories that enable one to formulate perfectly true judgements articulated in terms that are clear, determinate, non-vacuous, and fruitful may nevertheless feel unsatisfactory due to their superficiality. When focused on individual concepts, this yields the demand that our concepts should be deep rather than superficial, and leads us to regard superficiality as a theoretical vice in a concept.

This indicates an additional dimension along which one might pursue conceptual authority through theoretical virtue: by replacing superficial concepts with deeper concepts. But how exactly should we understand the contrast between depth and superficiality as it applies to individual concepts?

---

[12] Some of Carnap's formulations at least suggest this as a criterion for the quantification of fruitfulness; see e.g. Carnap (1962, 14–15); others suggest a wider and hazier criterion, on which a concept is fruitful to the extent that it 'leads to more simple and interesting theorems' (Carnap 1962, 348).

Extrapolating from Michael Strevens's (2008) two-dimensional development of the notion of depth in scientific explanation, we can understand a concept's relative superficiality or depth as determined by how it scores along two dimensions: its *attention to causal detail* on the one hand, and its *causal generality* on the other.

Along the first dimension, a concept is superficial to the extent that it slights, ignores, or skirts the causal underpinnings of what it picks out. A superficial concept may still pick out something, and may attach a certain significance to it, but it is largely indifferent to—and hence uninformative about—the causal underpinnings of its extension: it does not reach far down into the physical level at which the ultimate causal details are to be found, or far back into the causal history of what it applies to. That is not to say that the superficial concept is entirely indifferent to causal detail; but it abstracts away from any detailed description of the causal processes that underpin its object, operating at a higher and more superficial level of description.

By contrast, a concept will be deep along this first dimension to the extent that its application is sensitive to—and hence informative about—causal underpinnings. Concepts that are deep in this way will tend to be epistemically more demanding to use than superficial ones, requiring one to delve into the aetiology of phenomena in order to determine whether or not the concept applies.

Along this dimension of depth as attention to causal detail, the concepts of everyday psychology—e.g. *belief*, *desire*, and *intention*—are still relatively superficial: their application is guided by easily observable and publicly accessible patterns of behaviour and speech, and while their application can be sensitive to proximate causes at the most ordinary level of description ('Did the gust of wind make you drop the daisy, or did you do it intentionally?'), they are indifferent to the deeper causal underpinnings of those psychological phenomena. The concepts of cognitive science with which some strive to replace these 'folk' psychological concepts, by contrast, promise to be neurophysiologically deeper—that is part of their attraction.[13] Other examples include moving from superficial concepts of taste to deeper concepts articulating the underlying chemistry (from the concept *salty* to the concept *contains NaCl*; or from the concept of a *flinty* wine to the concept of a wine containing high levels of sulphur dioxide).

What makes deeper concepts attractive is that their sensitivity and informativeness regarding causal underpinnings promises to make them

---

[13] See Stich (1983) and especially Churchland (1986).

more objective. Judgements of ambient temperature, for example, had long been made in terms of comparatively superficial concepts, such as *warm* and *cold*, that were indexed to subjective experience. A deeper concept of temperature explaining these subjective experiences in terms of their objective causal underpinning renders judgements of temperature more objective, giving people an independent measure against which their subjective experience can be compared.

Yet, as Hasok Chang shows in his detailed account of how the scientific concept of temperature developed, the path to such a deeper concept was a long and winding one: even in the nineteenth century, scientists such as Joseph Fourier still articulated their theories of thermal physics in a 'macroscopic-phenomenalistic vein', conceptualizing temperature in terms that remained 'noncommittal about the ultimate metaphysical nature of heat' and 'did not focus on considerations of "deep" causes' (Chang 2004, 96–7). Once conceptions of temperature had been sufficiently deepened, however, they provided a lower-level understanding of the causal processes underlying the phenomenon of temperature, and enabled one to articulate commitments about the ultimate metaphysical nature of those processes.[14]

The second dimension along which concepts can be deep is by cutting through superficial detail to reveal a hidden structure of great explanatory power. This is not depth through careful attention to causal detail, but depth through striking generality: concepts that are deep along this second dimension uncover abstract dynamics that are not tied to a cumbrous set of specific initial conditions, but depend only on the presence of a handful of abstract properties that can be found across a range of different conditions.

By acknowledging this second dimension of depth, one acknowledges that while attention to causal detail may be a large part of what is involved in achieving the theoretical virtue of depth, it is not *all* that is involved, because we clearly also do not want to become bogged down in the minutiae of causal processes—that way, Strevens warns, lies 'Laplacean blindness' to the higher-level structures that constitute the furniture of human affairs.[15] We also want

---

[14] This conception of what is involved in deepening a concept is meant to parallel Strevens's (2008, 129–33) account of what is involved in deepening a causal model.

[15] See Strevens (2008, 138–41). The reference is to Pierre-Simon Laplace's evocative description of what it would mean to achieve maximum depth along the first dimension in a deterministic universe: 'An intellect which at a certain moment would know all forces that set nature in motion, and all positions of all items of which nature is composed, if this intellect were also vast enough to submit these data to analysis, it would embrace in a single formula the movements of the greatest bodies of the universe and those of the tiniest atom; for such an intellect nothing would be uncertain and the future just like the past would be present before its eyes' (Laplace 1951, 4). As Sober (1984, §4.3) and Dennett

our scientific concepts to abstract away from causal factors that only affect *how* exactly something happens in one particular instance, and focus on the decisive causal factors that make a difference to *whether* something happens. This second dimension of depth involves tracking the select few abstract properties that reveal high-level dynamics of some generality. That is how we acquire the kind of understanding that stands a chance of helpfully carrying over to other situations.

As Strevens shows, recognizing this second dimension of depth allows us to make sense of the apparent disdain for causal detail exhibited by many forms of scientific explanation—paradigmatically, by equilibrium explanations of regularities in complex systems, such as R. A. Fisher's 1930 explanation of the remarkably widespread and stable one-to-one sex ratio among sexually reproducing organisms. Instead of drilling down into the causal details of how this one-to-one ratio came about in each instance, Fisher's explanation shows, at a more general level, that this ratio marks an equilibrium point under negative frequency-dependent selection: individuals of the less frequent sex have more reproductive opportunities than individuals of the more frequent sex until this one-to-one ratio is reached.[16]

A similar slighting of causal detail can be observed in idealizing explanations, such as the explanation of the cannon ball's parabolic trajectory that ignores air resistance, or the explanation of the rainbow that falsely assumes that raindrops form perfect spheres: in fact, each cannon ball encounters some air resistance, and each raindrop is slightly deformed by local forces; but these idealizing explanations embody the insight that these causal factors make no difference to the trajectory's approximate shape or to the appearance of the rainbow. These ways of scientific sense-making are thus not so much uninterested in causal detail as concerned to home in on those causal details that constitute generalizable difference-makers.

The concern with depth as attention to detail thus has to be balanced against the concern with depth as generality: we want our scientific explanations—and, by extension, the concepts that figure in them—to be as sensitive to detail and informative as possible while remaining as abstract and generalizable as possible.

(1989, 25) emphasize, Laplace's imagined intellect, now often referred to as 'Laplace's Demon', helpfully dramatizes the question of what, if anything, such an intellect would be missing.

[16] I take the example from Strevens (2008, 137). Another example he offers is Ludwig Boltzmann's explanation of the second law of thermodynamics, whereby the entropy of an isolated system always increases to a maximum equilibrium value.

But the basic idea remains that depth in either dimension is a theoretical virtue, and superficiality in either dimension a theoretical vice. The tidy-minded approach to conceptual authority, insofar as it proposes to generally model authoritative concepts on those of a good scientific theory, will therefore encourage us to use the deepest concepts we can use, and treat superficiality as a defect. As we shall see in Chapter 9, however, there are reasons to be sceptical of this idea as a general principle for conceptual ethics.

5.3 Conceptual Tensions

Another set of theoretical vices comes into view once we focus on intra- and interconceptual tensions. When a concept gives rise to such tensions, a more authoritative alternative might be sought by revising the way we conceptualize things to alleviate the tensions. If F and G are two concepts that are in tension with each other, for instance, and a suitable replacement for F, namely F', would resolve the tension with G, a tidy-minded conception of conceptual authority would encourage one to conclude that F' is to that extent more authoritative than F.

Intra- and interconceptual tensions can take a variety of forms. As I propose to distinguish them, conceptual tensions can render concepts *unsatisfiable, inconsistent, incoherent, incongruent,* or *inimical*. This is also less well-trodden territory, and it will provide useful background to later chapters to map it out in more detail.

It may be said that, strictly speaking, concepts can never directly conflict or be in tension with each other—any talk to that effect must really be shorthand for conflicts or tensions between the propositions or judgements that these concepts enable us to formulate, or else between the practical attitudes one takes towards courses of action (*'Vorrei e non vorrei'*, Zerlina confesses in *Don Giovanni*—'I would like to and I would not like to').

But while it is right that tensions between concepts manifest themselves through conflicts between propositions, judgements, and attitudes, *which* propositions, judgements, and attitudes are properly accessible to one is a function of the concepts one uses, and the root of such conflicts can lie in an individual concept that systematically gives rise to them.

A helpful way of thinking about conceptual tensions is to conceive of the use of a concept as governed by certain proprieties of use—the norms or principles that mark the distinction between correct and incorrect applications of the concept by specifying *when* the concept is applicable and *what follows* from its applicability.[17] (I put it in terms of applicability, since that will serve us best for the thick normative concepts I focus on, but for certain types of concepts that I do not discuss here, such as connectives, the relevant aspects of use are more naturally characterized in different terms, as they have more to do with knowing how to handle and evaluate constructions in which these connectives figure.)

This picture of concept use as governed by norms or principles might be resisted on the grounds that most people would be hard-pressed to list all the principles that supposedly govern their use of a given concept. But the picture is not the Platonic or intellectualist one on which our practices of concept use merely implement a catalogue of explicit and antecedently given principles. Rather, from an explanatory perspective, the practices precede the principles: the explanatorily basic case is that in which the principles or—to put it in less intellectualist-sounding terms—the proprieties of use are *implicit* in a custom or practice of concept use. They are a form of know-how: a practical competence to tell what is a reason for or against what, in particular by distinguishing situations where a concept applies from situations where it does not, and what follows from its applicability from what does not follow. The very idea of explicit principles only makes sense against the background of implicit proprieties of use that can inform the interpretation and application of explicit principles, since their interpretation and application would remain underdetermined otherwise, and invoking further explicit principles to render them determinate would engender a regress.

This pattern of argument is familiar from Lewis Carroll's 'What the Tortoise Said to Achilles' (1895), which aims to show that the inference rules governing how to move between explicit postulates within a given logical system cannot exhaustively be expressed by explicit postulates within that system.[18] Wittgenstein's rule-following considerations then reiterate the same pattern of argument one level deeper, suggesting that proprieties of inference cannot exhaustively be expressed in the form of explicit rules to begin with, because any given rule leaves its own interpretation and application underdetermined, and attempts to remedy this through the introduction of further explicit rules

---

[17] For a particularly illuminating way of setting out proprieties of use, see Michael Williams's (2013) notation. For recent attempts to turn the link between concepts and proprieties of reasoning into a formal logic of concepts, see Jansen and Strobach (2003) and Freund (2022). A more fully worked out proposal for a logic of reason relations is Hlobil and Brandom (2025).
[18] Though see Besson (2018, forthcoming) for a detailed critical discussion of Carroll's argument and the contentious assumptions it makes.

engenders a regress. Consequently, explicit, rule-based proprieties of use have to be grounded in implicit, practice-based proprieties of use.[19]

As mentioned in Chapter 2, moreover, we need not assume that people are always *consciously guided* by explicitly represented norms as they apply concepts. We may, most of the time, merely be actualizing our dispositions to conceptualize the world in certain terms and reason along certain lines, without conscious guidance by norms; and yet this actualization of dispositions is nonetheless *governed* by norms insofar as it is *liable to assessment and sanction* by fellow concept-users, who may enforce the norms by reproaching us when we apply a concept incorrectly.[20] Like other norms, the proprieties governing concept use typically become manifest in their transgression. The situation of improper use is the characteristic situation in which others are prompted to make implicit norms explicit, thereby bringing to consciousness what may otherwise be unthinkingly followed.

But proprieties of concept use are also made explicit when a concept is taught to a novice. Modal vocabulary plays a crucial role in this, as it does in correcting improper concept use. Expressing and conveying norms has been thought to be one of the main functions of modal vocabulary.[21] This comes out in how quickly we reach for modal language in teaching someone the key concepts of a game, for example: 'White *must* move first'; 'the king *may* move backwards'; 'it is *impossible* to move backwards with a pawn'.

Analogously, mastering a concept centrally involves coming to understand what inferential moves one can properly make with it. There need not be an entire catalogue of norms looming under each concept that exactly and exhaustively determines its correct use across all imaginable situations. As Wittgenstein points out, taking such exhaustive regulation to be necessary would be like supposing that whenever children play a game with a ball, they must be playing according to exact rules that strictly regulate every aspect of the game.[22]

All we require for our purposes is the idea that the use even of a single concept is liable to assessment according to *some* proprieties of use. For a plurality of such proprieties, even if implicit and non-exhaustive, already makes it possible for these proprieties to *conflict* by yielding incompatible instructions.

---

[19] See Wittgenstein (2009), especially the strand among his many different considerations on rule-following that leads up to §201. See Brandom (1994, 22) for a concise exposition of the issue, which I draw on here, and Brandom (1994, 18–46; 2019a) for a detailed defence of the explanatory priority of implicit over explicit norms; see also Kripke (1982), the essays in Miller and Wright (2002), as well as Kusch (2006) for valuable discussions of this theme.

[20] See Hlobil (2015) for a defence of this focus on assessability rather than guidance.

[21] See Brandom (1994, 2015b) and Thomasson (2020a, ch. 2).

[22] See Wittgenstein (1958, 25).

There are several different ways in which instructions can prove incompatible, both within and between individual concepts. Let us focus first on concepts harbouring *intraconceptual* tensions, i.e. tensions within a single concept.

Within the set of concepts harbouring intraconceptual tensions, we can distinguish between, on the one hand, concepts that place incompatible demands on the world they are applied to, and, on the other hand, concepts that place incompatible demands on the concept-users that apply them.[23] We can mark this distinction by calling concepts that place incompatible demands on the world *unsatisfiable*, and concepts that place incompatible demands on concept-users *inconsistent*.[24] Consider unsatisfiability first:

Unsatisfiability:

A concept is unsatisfiable iff nothing satisfies its conditions of application, because it places incompatible demands on the world in which it is deployed.

This can in turn be due either to the fact that its norms of application are incompatible a priori, or to the fact that, given what the world we inhabit happens to be like, nothing in fact ever meets these conditions. We can therefore distinguish two kinds of unsatisfiability:[25]

A Priori Unsatisfiability:

A concept is unsatisfiable a priori iff its proprieties of use are such that nothing could possibly satisfy its conditions of application.

A Posteriori Unsatisfiability:

A concept is unsatisfiable a posteriori iff its proprieties of use are such that, in the world in which the concept is used, nothing ever satisfies its conditions of application.

An example of a priori unsatisfiability would be the concept *squircle*, whose use we might take to be governed notably by the principle that if x is a square and x is a circle, then x is a squircle.[26] Since nothing could possibly be both a

---

[23] The distinction is flagged by Yablo (1993, 372).
[24] This notably accords with the use of that terminology in Chihara (1979, 593) and Scharp (2013, 39), for example.
[25] For a similarly bifurcated account of the possibility of 'contradictory concepts', see Priest (2014), who also defends the distinction between conceptual and worldly factors against Quinean qualms in Priest (2016).
[26] I take the example from Scharp (2013, 39).

square and a circle, the concept is unsatisfiable in principle. Further examples include *totalitarian democracy* and other concepts whose linguistic expression generates oxymoronic phrases.

An example of a concept that is unsatisfiable a posteriori is the concept *perpetuum mobile*, understood along the following lines: if x is a human-scale machine that can work infinitely without an energy source, x is a *perpetuum mobile*. Such a machine is not inconceivable in principle—many people have tried to build one—and some particles may even display repetitive perpetual motion on a microscopic scale; but given the laws of thermodynamics in the world we live in, no human-scale machine can satisfy the concept.

Unsatisfiable concepts contrast with *inconsistent* concepts, which place incompatible demands on the concept-user. They might give rise to paradoxes or contradictions, for example, by dictating that a concept both *applies* and *does not apply* in one and the same situation.[27] This engenders a tension within a single concept, which we may call an *intraconceptual* inconsistency, or simply *inconsistency* for short:

Inconsistency:

A concept is inconsistent iff its proprieties of use place incompatible demands on the concept-user.

Consider Kevin Scharp's example of an inconsistent concept, the concept *rable*.[28] He characterizes its proper use as being governed by the following two principles: (i) if x is a table, the concept *rable* applies to x; (ii) if x is a red object, the concept *rable* does not apply to x. We understand these principles well enough to deploy the concept *rable* without difficulty in most cases. But perplexity befalls us when we encounter a red table. Since it is a table, the concept applies to it; but since it is a red object, the concept at the same time does not apply to it. Therefore, the concept simultaneously applies and does not apply to the red table, which is inconsistent.

There are also less artificial examples of inconsistent concepts. As Graham Priest shows in his study of contradictions, the law offers numerous illustrations of inconsistent concepts.[29] A quasi-historical, simplified example obeying the same pattern as Scharp's concept *rable* is the concept *enfranchised* as defined as follows: (i) if x is a property-holder, the concept *enfranchised* applies to x;

---

[27] The possibility of inconsistent concepts is acknowledged and discussed in Bennett (2008, 57), Scharp (2013, 35–56), Eklund (2019), Greenough (2020), and Pinder (2023).
[28] See Scharp (2013, 36).   [29] See Priest (2006, 182–204).

(ii) if *x* is a woman, the concept *enfranchised* does not apply to *x*. As Priest notes, no blatant inconsistencies arise as long as no woman holds property in the jurisdiction in which this concept is in use. But the moment a woman becomes a property-holder, the concept suggests both that she is and that she is not enfranchised.[30]

On Scharp's account, however, we need not even look beyond philosophy to find inconsistent concepts: philosophy itself revolves largely around inconsistent concepts. On his view, 'knowledge, nature, meaning, virtue, explanation, essence, causation, validity, rationality, freedom, necessity, person, beauty, belief, goodness, space, time, and justice' (2020, 397) have all turned out to be inconsistent concepts. He has argued in detail for the claim that the concept *truth* is inconsistent, and suggested that this is why the concept gives rise to paradoxes such as the Liar's paradox, Curry's paradox, or Yablo's paradox, and to contradictory conjunctions of the form 'p and not-p'.[31]

However, inconsistencies should not be *identified* with the contradictory conjunctions they engender. When using an inconsistent concept, as Stephen Yablo has emphasized, we may find ourselves flip-flopping back and forth between thinking that p and thinking that not-p without necessarily drawing the conclusion: 'p and not-p'.[32] We are then 'continuously being driven from one decision to the contrary one' (1981, §686), as Wittgenstein puts it. Inconsistencies of this sort are therefore best defined as residing not in the contradictory conclusion itself, but in the proprieties of use that lead to it. For any inconsistent concept, we can ask which *subsets* of proprieties or principles governing its use are consistent or inconsistent, and the inconsistency itself can then be located more precisely by identifying the smallest possible subset that still generates the contradictory conjunction.

Incompatibilities might arise at both ends of a concept, which is to say not only between the proprieties of use governing under what conditions the concept is properly applied, but also between the proprieties of use governing what properly follows from its application. The applicability of one concept might entrain two inconsistent obligations, for example. Or, in a Kafkaesque bureaucratic set-up or a catch-22 situation, a concept might be clearly and unequivocally applicable, yet give practical instructions that turn out not to be jointly satisfiable, because they mutually exclude or presuppose each other. More generally, any concept that picks out a set of objects and then enjoins

---

[30] See Priest (2006, 184–5; 2014, 15).
[31] See Scharp (2013, 2020). On his account, these are three variants of the same paradox.
[32] See Yablo (1993, 371).

one to draw contradictory conclusions from the concept's applicability is inconsistent in virtue of its consequences of application.

Such inconsistencies arising downstream of the concept's applicability remain inconspicuous as long as we think of concepts on the model of functions from worlds (or world/time pairs) to sets of things picked out, since this model tends to channel attention towards the applicational face of the concept and away from its consequential face. But once we think of concepts as two-faced, having both conditions and consequences of application, we can distinguish two kinds of inconsistency:

Inconsistency in Conditions of Application:

A concept has inconsistent conditions of application iff the proprieties of use governing its application place incompatible demands on the concept-user.

Inconsistency in Consequences of Application:

A concept has inconsistent consequences iff the proprieties of use governing the inferential consequences of its applicability place incompatible demands on the concept-user.

These definitions of unsatisfiability and inconsistency capture four different ways in which a single concept can by itself already give rise to tensions by yielding incompatible instructions. They also bring out that the relevant instructions are sometimes world-facing and sometimes user-facing. Concept-users may have no difficulty in consistently employing a concept whose demands the world cannot satisfy, just as the world may have no difficulty in satisfying the demands of a concept that concept-users find it impossible to employ consistently—concepts can be unsatisfiable without being inconsistent, or inconsistent without being unsatisfiable.

Understanding how concepts can place incompatible demands on us downstream as well as upstream of their application is also key to seeing how different concepts can conflict. Two concepts may each yield instructions that are consistent in themselves, but that conflict when taken together. This gives rise to *interconceptual* tensions—conflict *between* rather than within concepts.

To a first approximation, we might say that two concepts conflict insofar as the instructions given by one concept conflict with the instructions given by another concept. But note that 'conflict' has to mean something stronger than mere *incompatibility* between two concepts—the fact that the applicability of one concept to *x* is incompatible with the applicability of at least *some* other concepts to *x* (if it is a *bird*, it cannot also be a *fish*) is not an optional feature of our conceptual apparatus that we might intelligibly seek to eliminate, but an utterly basic condition on the very contentfulness of thought. A concept whose applicability did not rule out—and in that sense 'conflict' with—the applicability of any other concept would be empty, not only in extension, but of content; just as a wheel that turns though nothing turns with it is not really part of the mechanism, a concept that applies without excluding the applicability of any other concept is not really part of the conceptual apparatus.[33] Even though the concept *bird* is incompatible with the concept *fish*, in that the applicability of the concept *bird* rules out the applicability of the concept *fish*, the two concepts do not conflict as long as they do not claim to be applicable to the same object at the same time.

Two concepts do conflict, however, when the applicability of the one rules out the applicability of the other *and* their application conditions are such that they apply to the same object: if there were a concept that was at least partly co-extensional with the concept *fish*, but whose applicability excluded the applicability of the concept *fish*, it would conflict with the concept *fish*. Let us label that form of conflict—which combines co-extensionality with inferential incompatibility—*incoherence*:

Incoherence:

Two concepts are incoherent iff (a) the proprieties of use governing their correct application are such that the two concepts apply to some of the same objects *and* (b) the proprieties of use governing the concepts' inferential consequences are such that the applicability of one concept rules out the applicability of the other.

Besides incoherence, however, there is another form of interconceptual conflict that arises not at the level of *inferential* compatibility, but at the level of *extensional* compatibility: two concepts can interfere with each other's *instantiation*. They are not so much incoherent as *incongruent*, like two shapes that will not fit together into one box unless a chunk is taken out of at least one of the two shapes, thereby creating a remainder.

As with inferential incompatibilities between concepts, there is an utterly basic form of incongruence in any conceptual apparatus that is not an interesting feature of some concepts in contrast to others, but rather a condition on concepts having *distinct* extensions at all: the concepts *vanilla ice cream* and *chocolate ice cream* might also be said to be incongruent in the minimal

---

[33] The wheel analogy hails from Wittgenstein (2009, §271).

sense that filling a finite universe with vanilla ice cream would leave no room to fill it with chocolate ice cream—but that is not a noteworthy tension between two concepts so much as a trivial consequence of the fact that they pick out different things.

Where incongruence becomes an interesting feature of some concepts in contrast to others is in the realm of concepts that are *action-guiding* in addition to (or, at the limit, instead of) being world-guided—in other words, concepts whose engaged use typically gives people reasons for action. In virtue of encouraging or prescribing certain courses of action, these concepts give different practical instructions that can prove impossible to realize in concert. As a result, inhabitants of a conceptual architecture shaped by concepts that are incongruent in this sense will find that they face hard choices, because they cannot possibly live up to the demands these concepts make on them without leaving an unrealized remainder. Incongruent action-guiding concepts, we might say, are not fully co-practicable.

This type of conflict paradigmatically arises from the combination of different concepts of goods, values, virtues, or ideals—concepts such as *duty, honour, friendship, loyalty, truthfulness, magnanimity, arete, genius, solidarity, generosity, equality, liberty, justice, modesty, asceticism,* or *humility,* to name but a few. These concepts clearly do not merely pick out something, but enjoin their engaged users to realize, promote, or instantiate something.

In some cases, the reasons for action these concepts introduce into the engaged user's deliberation will directly refer to what the concept is a concept *of*: the reasons one becomes sensitive to in coming to live by the concept of justice, for example, favour acting *in the name of* justice, or doing something *because it is just*; similarly, someone who lives by the concept of duty will characteristically do something *because it is her duty*.

But concepts may also exert their action-guiding influence indirectly, by rendering the person who lives by them sensitive, in her own practical deliberation, to aspects or considerations that make no mention of the concept with which an onlooker might describe the good or value realized by the ensuing action: someone who lives by the concept of generosity, for example, can act *out of* generosity, but doing so must precisely not involve being motivated by the consideration that *it is generous*; that would be to do something else—*posing* as a generous person, perhaps, or else engaging in the sort of moral self-indulgence that consists in being motivated primarily by one's image of oneself as having certain moral virtues and dispositions.[34]

---

[34] This notion of moral self-indulgence is introduced by Williams in the context of a discussion of utilitarianism (Williams 1981h).

Another example is the concept of modesty: those who embrace the concept and live by it will do things or refrain from doing things *out of* modesty, but to do something *because it is modest* is to be motivated by a reflexive concern with one's own dispositions that borders on the hypocritical: it is a second-order substitute for a genuinely modest disposition, and one that is, if anything, immodest.

Whether they exert their action-guiding influence directly or indirectly, however, such concepts can conflict in the sense that the realization or instantiation of one concept comes at the expense of the realization or instantiation of the other. Suppose, for example, that someone lives by two concepts of genuinely distinct and incommensurable intrinsic goods; suppose further that these goods cannot be fully realized in concert; then the two concepts conflict in the sense that they will not fit together into one life, or one society, without remainder; and that remainder will represent not just an unrealized potential, but a *loss*: the real cost of realizing another good.

I shall label this form of interconceptual conflict *incongruence*:

Incongruence:

Two concepts are incongruent if and to the extent that the realization or instantiation of one concept comes at the expense of the realization or instantiation of the other concept.

The phrase 'if and to the extent that' registers the fact that incongruence comes in degrees. Up to a point, one may be able to jointly realize or instantiate two action-guiding concepts without trade-off, and it is only under certain circumstances, or if the concepts are taken beyond a certain point, that the incongruence between them becomes manifest. To say that two concepts are incongruent is thus not to say that they always and everywhere conflict with each other, but that they are *set up* or *poised* to conflict under certain circumstances, or when taken far enough.

We need to distinguish, however, between incongruence that is primarily the product of unpropitious circumstances and incongruence that is primarily the product of the concepts we use. It may be that two concepts are merely *accidentally* incongruent, because the world happens to put contingent obstacles in the way of their co-realization; or, more interestingly, it may be that two concepts would be incongruent even under ideal circumstances, because their incongruence cannot be remedied simply by augmenting the space and resources available to realize them, but is inherent in the concepts themselves, so that we struggle to so much as *conceive* of circumstances in which those concepts would be always and everywhere realizable without loss.[35] There is something about the respective logic of the concepts themselves that systematically tends to give rise to a tension between them. The concepts are, in that sense, *non-accidentally* incongruent, and the only way to eliminate all occasions for that incongruence to manifest itself is to change which concepts we use. Accordingly, non-accidental incongruence marks a type of interconceptual tension that is not simply a generic and ineliminable feature of all concepts, nor merely a product of unpropitious circumstances, but specifically a product of combining certain concepts in one's conceptual apparatus.

This type of tension is of special philosophical interest, because it is key to understanding *conflicts of values*, in the broad sense of 'values' that encompasses obligations, virtues, norms, aspirations, and ideals. In particular, this type of tension is key to understanding the competition over which values should be realized, the hard and occasionally tragic character of the choices involved, and the genuine losses and grounds for regret and complaint engendered by the frustration of one value for the sake of another.

One well-known example of such an incongruence is that between the engaged use of the concepts *truthfulness* and *happiness*, which Nietzsche registered as follows: 'there is no pre-established harmony between the furthering of truth and the well-being of humanity' (1986, §517)—or, as Lord Byron's tortured hero Manfred put it, 'The Tree of Knowledge is not that of Life' (2015, I, i, 12).

Another example is the conflict between *safety* and *privacy*. The more radical the surveillance measures taken to ensure public safety, the harder it becomes to reconcile these with individual privacy. Conversely, promoting privacy tends to entail a cost in safety. Modest gains in both safety and privacy may be achievable without trade-off, but when either value is pursued far enough, there comes a point at which one has to be sacrificed to the other.

The same incongruence arises with a group of value concepts that has achieved renewed prominence in philosophy over the last decades, namely *virtue concepts*—concepts of ethically valuable dispositions or character traits whose possession renders the ethical significance of certain facts or states of affairs salient to the possessor. To be an engaged user of the concept *honesty*, for example, is to value the disposition to honesty in oneself and others, to condemn and shy away from lying, and to try to live up to the ideal of honesty one embraces. But virtue concepts will conflict insofar as not all admirable

---

[35] For a rich discussion of this theme drawing on the work of Isaiah Berlin, Stuart Hampshire, and Bernard Williams, see Hall (2020).

dispositions or character traits can be equally embodied at the same time, or even by the same person (or the same institution, for institutions can have virtues and vices, too).[36] One may aspire to be both honest and kind, but find that one virtue can sometimes only be realized at the expense of the other. It may also be difficult to combine certain character traits *tout court*—for example, it is notoriously difficult for one person to cultivate both spontaneity and self-control, and it is well-nigh impossible to lead a life as both an ascetic and a hedonist.

That there were such incongruences between virtues is precisely what the ancient thesis of the unity of the virtues disputed (thereby providing a virtue-ethical example of an assumption of harmonious unity between concepts that we encountered in the previous chapter). Those who have since cast doubt on that thesis have insisted that virtues cannot always be combined—the demands that virtue concepts place on us conflict because the realization of one virtue interferes with the realization of another. For a social worker in an antipoverty agency, for example, the demands of efficiency and fairness will frequently conflict with the demands of compassion and generosity.[37] Though that incongruence will be aggravated by a lack of resources, it is not merely a reflection of such a lack. The administrative virtues of efficiency and fairness, on the one hand, and the Christian virtues of compassion and generosity, on the other, themselves pull in divergent directions, both in terms of what they enjoin one to do and in terms of the spirit in which they enjoin one to do it. Where the former virtues demand professional detachment, restraint, and being stingy with one's time, the latter virtues demand empathy, caregiving, and going out of one's way to help. As one social worker sums up the problem: 'we're doing such a number game, and then we try to be a people person. You can't do both' (Zacka 2017, 203).

Finally, there are cases in which concepts are not just incongruent, but *inimical*, because one concept itself discourages or condemns the realization of the other. The concepts do not just interfere with each other's instantiation; rather, having one value concept constitutively involves *disvaluing* what having the other value concept constitutively involves *valuing*.[38] The ancient Greek value of *arete*, which enjoins one to achieve excellence in all things through self-cultivation, is not just incongruent with the Christian values of humility, selflessness, and abnegation of worldly glory, but actively

---

[36] For an elaboration of the claim that institutions themselves can have vices and virtues, see Fricker (2010a, 2020b).
[37] See Zacka (2017, 100).
[38] See also Nagel (2001, 107), who calls these cases of 'true opposition' between values.

discouraged and disparaged by them—just as these Christian values came to be condemned in turn by the Renaissance notion of *virtú*, which rehabilitated the pursuit of worldly glory and the prowess displayed by the *virtuoso*.[39] Nietzsche spoke advisedly in this connection of *reversals* of values, in which the polarity of valuations was inverted to produce not just *different* values, but *opposite* values.[40] He might not have objected with such vehemence to the Christian virtues had they not been inherently inimical to the realization of the more life-affirming pagan and Renaissance virtues he endorsed—and before him, Hume voiced much the same complaint about 'celibacy, fasting, penance, mortification, self-denial, humility, silence, solitude, and the whole train of monkish virtues' (1998, 9.3).

Concepts can thus exhibit a variety of features that appear as theoretical vices to the tidy-minded: they can be unclear, ill-demarcated, referentially or inferentially indeterminate, vague, porous, gerrymandered, or unfruitful; and they can be tension-ridden in various ways, notably by being unsatisfiable, inconsistent, incoherent, incongruent, or even inimical. With a clear sense of the kinds of theoretical vices concepts can display, we are now in a position to consider the project of eliminating these theoretical vices from our conceptual apparatus: the tidy-minded pursuit of conceptual authority through theoretical virtue.

5.4 Authority through Theoretical Virtue

Tidy-mindedness, when applied to our conceptual apparatus, aims at a tidy mind: a mind whose thoughts are cast in theoretically virtuous terms—terms that are clear, precisely demarcated, fully determinate, fruitful, satisfiable, consistent, coherent, and congruent. This can seem like a mere aesthetic preference, or even an 'obsession' (Geuss 2020, xviii), but it is more illuminatingly understood as a non-foundationalist expression of the pursuit of authoritative concepts, one that treats theoretical virtues as the answer to the authority question.

But where and to what extent is it appropriate to conceive of conceptual authority as deriving from theoretical virtue? And *why is it* that greater precision, determinacy, or consistency should give concepts more authority?

---

[39] On the Renaissance notion of *virtú*, see Skinner (2002, 2017) and Owen (2018).
[40] The phrase he uses in German is '*Umwertung der Werte*'. See Skinner (1997), Owen (2018), and Queloz (2021a) for discussions of such value reversals.

Where the realization of theoretical virtues is the dominant concern anyway—in logic and formal semantics, say—questioning the authority of theoretical virtues seems moot, because the aim of moving towards more theoretically virtuous concepts aligns with the aim with which the existing concepts were being deployed anyway. Tellingly, it is primarily such contexts that Carnap had in mind when he first proposed, in 1947, that philosophers should engage in what he called *explication*: the task of taking the less theoretically virtuous concepts of prescientific thought and replacing them with more theoretically virtuous concepts (1947, 7–8). For Carnap, a 'concept must fulfil the following requirements in order to be an adequate explicatum for a given explicandum: (1) similarity to the explicandum; (2) exactness; (3) fruitfulness; (4) simplicity' (1950, 5). But in spelling out the significance of these four desiderata, he makes clear that they are to be realized 'so as to introduce the explicatum into a well-connected system of scientific concepts' (1950, 7). Similarly, his examples of successful explication are confined to modern logic and scientific theorizing.[41] This is significant, for as long as conceptual engineering efforts aiming at more theoretically virtuous concepts are confined to enterprises that themselves aim to realize theoretical virtues in the form of systematic theories, the authority question does not arise: the concepts can straightforwardly draw their authority from the alignment between the spirit of the engineering project and the spirit of the enterprise whose conceptual apparatus is being engineered.

But the authority question resurfaces once the aspiration to engineer for theoretical virtues is *generalized* beyond the confines of logic and formal semantics. The trajectory of Kevin Scharp's work offers an illustration of this. In *Replacing Truth* (2013), Scharp proposes to replace the concept of truth, which he thinks is inconsistent and generates various paradoxes, with two new concepts of truth; but he is clear that the substitution is to be confined to contexts in which consistency and the avoidance of paradoxes are the dominant concerns.

In his more recent methodological writings, however, he drops this qualification, conveying the impression that theoretical virtues can be a *general* answer to the authority question. Not just logic, but philosophy more broadly

---

[41] For a detailed reconstruction of Carnap's conception of explication and the paradigms he is inspired by, see Carus (2007), Reck (2012, 2024), and Dutilh Novaes and Reck (2017). For a disambiguation between different kinds of explication projects, see Koch (2019). As Raphael van Riel argues, Max Weber's construction of ideal types can likewise be understood as 'a process of concept replacement that is oriented toward precision and, hence, is in the spirit of conceptual engineering' (van Riel 2022, 1374); the similarity may have a common source in Heinrich Rickert's (1896) theory of scientific concept-formation (van Riel 2022, 1371).

'is the study of what have turned out to be inconsistent concepts' (2020, 398), Scharp maintains, because 'truth, knowledge, value, virtue, freedom, justice, etc.' have turned out to be 'organized and distinguished by principles that are themselves inconsistent with one another' (2020, 414). These inconsistencies generate various problems that philosophers get entangled in, and that conceptual engineering promises to resolve. But even if the project of re-engineering our conceptual apparatus for theoretical virtue is initially motivated not by the pursuit of consistency for its own sake, but by the desire to overcome the problems and paradoxes generated by our concepts, the engineering effort itself aims at theoretical virtue. Across the entire range of our concepts, Scharp suggests, philosophy's guiding ideal should be 'a consistent conceptual scheme. No paradoxes. No puzzles. Just clarity' (2020, 415).

On this view, which presents us with a paradigmatic embodiment of the tidy-minded approach, philosophical theories are to be cast as *measurement systems*, so that our messy everyday judgements involving some concept can be transposed into a more rigorous, precisely defined, and consistent language. Scharp calls this view *metrological naturalism*:[42]

> Metrological naturalism has as a methodological principle that philosophers should use measurement theory as a guide or model in philosophical theorizing.... We know pretty well how to do this for things like length and weight. Trying to figure out how to construct a measurement system for something like truth or justice is a lot more complicated, but this isn't just an analogy. (2020, 402)

He maintains that engineering should always be conducted in a metrological spirit, because 'engineering without metrological naturalism is blind' (2020, 399): the virtues of a good measurement system are what provides engineers with a guiding sense of what concepts to aim for.

But how plausible is it, outside of logic or formal semantics, that a novel concept advocated by a conceptual engineer will be authoritative because it exhibits the virtues of a good measurement system? Consider the concept *person*. As ordinarily understood, the concept is vague, and its connection to other concepts not very systematic. It indicates a variety of characteristics—self-consciousness, agency, title to respect—that come in degrees, and, as debates over abortion show, its ethical implications and relations to other

---

[42] Examples include Davidson's (1990) measurement system for belief, desire, and meaning. See also Matthews (2010) and Weaver and Scharp (2019).

concepts such as *sentient being* or *human being* are indeterminate and contested. Some, like Michael Tooley, have therefore undertaken to replace it with a precise sortal notion that sharply delineates a basis for a more systematic way of thinking about issues surrounding personhood.[43] Yet the implications of this precise sortal notion notoriously go drastically beyond anything within the reach of the ordinary concept of person. Granted, making a notable difference to the resulting judgements is part of the point of replacing the concept. Faced with a stark divergence between pre-engineering and post-engineering judgements, however, the question of the engineered concept's authority becomes acute: why should we act on the judgements formed using the engineered concept? Because it is more precise and permits a tidier way of thinking? But say the engineered concept licenses infanticide in situations in which our non-engineered concept suggests that infanticide is abhorrent. Why should we care about the added tidiness when its price is to do something which, from the perspective of ingrained ethical experience, appears deeply revolting? If that is the price of tidiness, one may well think, then too bad for tidiness.

What comes out here is that displaying theoretical virtues is not the only thing we need our concepts to do.[44] And once this much is granted, it becomes an open question whether vague, indeterminate, open-textured, or tension-ridden concepts might not sometimes serve us best. Perhaps theoretical vices have other virtues. The tidiest organization is not always the most functional, and the sharpest tools are not always the most suitable. If your concern is to cut bread and you ask for a bread knife, you will hardly thank me if I give you a razor blade because it is sharper.[45]

A similar reservation applies to the ingenious epistemological approach to concept appraisal put forward by Paul Egré and Cathal O'Madagain. They propose to measure the utility of a concept as a product of two things: its *inclusiveness* (how many objects in an environment it applies to) and its *homogeneity* (how little variation there is between these objects).

---

[43] See e.g. Tooley (1972, 1983) and many of the positions discussed in Merrill (1998), and see Williams (1985, 127) for a related critique of Tooley's proposal, which Williams faults for its 'refusal to engage with the only two things that matter: the politics of trying to make rules for such situations, and the experience of people engaged in them' (1995j, 221 n. 10). For an exposition of arguments over the definition of 'person' against the background of constitutional disputes over abortion, see Schiappa (2003, 89–108).

[44] Herman Cappelen registers this possibility in describing W. V. O. Quine's views: 'there is no reason why there should be a fixed set of theoretical virtues that are used to measure improvement. In certain contexts, non-theoretical virtues/advantages could make a big difference' (Cappelen 2020, 137–8).

[45] The example is Wittgenstein's (2000, MS 120, 142v).

On their account, we want our concepts to be as inclusive and homogeneous as possible: the more inclusive a concept is, the more informative the resulting beliefs will be; and the more homogeneous a concept is, the greater the likelihood that the generalizations we formulate with that concept in the subject position will be true. This articulates a significant advantage that homogeneous concepts have over heterogeneous ones: they carry less of a risk of leaving us with a false belief. There is safety in homogeneity.

But this form of tidy-mindedness is likewise bound eventually to run into the fact that life is not just about formulating true generalizations. Consequently, there are good reasons why we have concepts that embrace and exploit messy variation in their extension, as we shall see in Chapter 7. Measuring a concept's value by its homogeneity looks more promising if we explicitly relativize this metric to the concern to formulate true universal generalizations, and see the authority-conferring force of inclusiveness and homogeneity as flowing from that concern—a concern that is characteristic of science, but not necessarily of other human pursuits. Expressly indexing the demand for homogeneity to a particular concern in a particular context then invites us to consider what other concerns we have besides this one, and whether these might not pull us towards concepts that embrace heterogeneity.

In contexts in which we are not obviously, or not primarily, concerned to realize theoretical virtues, it is thus not clear that concepts that are free of theoretical vices will carry more authority than the concepts they are meant to replace. Concepts do not possess more authority simply by dint of their theoretical virtues. What authority they have must come from the way they tie in with what is important to us. Sometimes, that is indeed tidiness, measurability, homogeneity, or mathematical rigour. But sometimes it is not. Concepts '*supply lacks*', in Quine's pithy phrase, and the character of what we lack is as variable as the concerns that make us lack it.[46]

Thus, conceptions of conceptual authority that isolate concepts from the practical contexts in which they are put to work and concentrate on the inherent defects of concepts—or what appear as defects when measured against some ideal of theoretical virtue—embody a strategy that may satisfactorily

---

[46] See Quine (2013, 238). When Sally Haslanger seeks to ameliorate social and political concepts such as *gender*, *man*, *woman*, or *race*, for example, she does not make the case for the concepts she advocates in terms of their theoretical virtues. Instead, she highlights the way in which these concepts promise to serve antecedent social and political concerns—concerns that precede, direct, and give point to the engineering effort. See Haslanger (2012). For a retrospective assessment of this effort which also briefly raises the question of its authority, see Haslanger (2020a, 231–7).

answer the authority question in special cases, but that cannot hope to do so more widely. By focusing on the theoretical vices of concepts, we risk overlooking their other virtues, and might end up rendering the concepts less helpful than they were before we 'fixed' them. Striving invariably to realize theoretical virtues in our concepts threatens to be counterproductive when we are better served by concepts whose virtues are nothing like those of a tidy theory. What is more, it leaves unanswered the question of why we should care about those theoretical virtues in a given context.

5.5 Inheriting Authority from Theories

If the authority question persists after a concept's theoretical virtues are invoked, it may be thought that this is because each concept is being myopically considered in isolation. Perhaps, to understand how conceptual authority can derive from theoretical virtue, one has to step back from individual concepts and look at the wider structures they form—at the *theories* that are the paradigmatic bearers of theoretical virtues.

This points to a conception of authority on which a concept is authoritative not by dint of the theoretical virtues it realizes all by itself, but by dint of being integrable into a wider theoretical structure whose own claim to authority rests on the degree to which *it* realizes theoretical virtues. In other words, a concept inherits its authority from the wider theory in which it is embedded.[47]

The plausibility of this conception of authority of course depends on whether one buys into the idea that our thought *should* take the form of a theory—a tidy body of knowledge organized in a way that revealingly corresponds to the structure of its subject matter. This aspiration goes back to antiquity, and is most closely associated with scientific bodies of thought.[48] But the same tidy-mindedness can be found in the sphere of practical reasoning. In the *Protagoras*, Socrates advocates the pursuit of the complete

---

[47] The connection between concepts and theories is particularly explicit in what Morton (1980) dubbed the 'Theory-Theory' of concepts, which, inspired by Thomas Kuhn's (1970) work on paradigms and theory change, holds that concepts should be individuated in terms of the role they play in theories (Carey 1985, 198), and can themselves be regarded as 'partial theories' insofar as they embody explanations of the relations between an overall theory's constituents (Keil 1989, 281).

[48] See Williams (2006d, 27–8) for a discussion of the various forms that this ambition to systematize took in Greek philosophy. For historical overviews of the role of the ideal of systematicity in philosophy, see Ritschl (1906) and Rescher (1979, 2005). For a thorough vindication of the claim that systematicity is the hallmark of scientific knowledge, see Hoyningen-Huene (2013).

systematization and unification of practical reasoning into a *techne*—a science or measurement system—that is geared towards a single, antecedently specifiable and measurable end.[49] The dialogue also articulates a rationale for this pursuit: turning practical reasoning into a *techne* will help shelter human beings from *tyche*, the unpredictable play of fortune, by giving them more control over whether their lives go well.

In line with this aspiration, moral philosophy has a long tradition of validating or invalidating concepts according to whether they can be harmoniously integrated into an ethical theory. What is nowadays called 'virtue theory' is a poor example of this, since what the 'theory' suggests we need to live well are virtuous dispositions, not a theory about them, and having these virtuous dispositions does not obviously involve thinking in terms of a theoretical structure at all.[50]

But theories such as Kantianism, utilitarianism, and Rawlsian contractualism are paradigmatic examples of attempts to discriminate between more and less authoritative ethical concepts by tidying up our ethical thought. Even when these theories are interpreted along non-foundationalist lines, they retain one important commonality with foundationalism: they arrogate to themselves the authority to override the force of pre-theoretical concepts. On a kaleidoscopic picture of our conceptual apparatus, this is an authority they are bound to have to exercise, because building a tidy theory out of a messy and disparate conceptual inheritance forces one to overturn the authority of *some* concepts in order to establish the authority of *any* concepts. Moving from a collage of cross-cutting conceptual claims to a tidy and tension-free edifice requires prioritizing or ranking the claims our concepts make on us, using some of them to overturn others, and discarding or de-authorizing all the concepts and correlative reasons that cannot be integrated into the theory. The resulting structure then allows us to ratify or authorize all the reasons that can be understood as applications or extrapolations of the reasons provided by the applicability of the concepts at the heart of the theory; but it also requires that we winnow out all the reasons that cannot be so understood.

These theories would not be as influential as they are if their master concepts' claims to authority did not possess some plausibility when considered in isolation. But these claims also have a sharp end: their exclusionary implication that *no other* concept should have authority over our lives *except insofar as* it can be validated as an extension and application of the theory.

---

[49] See *Protagoras*, especially 356d–e. For a fuller exegetical discussion, see Nussbaum (2001, ch. 4).
[50] As emphasized by Williams (1995a, 551; 1996a, 31; 1998, §1).

And many of the multifarious thick normative concepts that give life and literature their texture and density, though they may not be foremost in our minds as we philosophize in thin and abstract terms, cannot be fully integrated into such a tidy theoretical structure—think, for instance, of 'such minor revelations of the ethical life as the sense that someone is creepy' (Williams 1985, 43). We have many more concepts, accumulated from different historical periods, than will fit without remainder into any given theory. Consequently, the theory must discount and overturn the considerations provided by a wide array of thick normative concepts that certainly have force with us at a pretheoretical level.

Once one appreciates how radical this revisionary implication is, the question of the *theory*'s authority becomes acute. If theory-building involves paring down and thinning out our conceptual apparatus in the name of building a theoretically virtuous structure, this pits the authority of the theory against the combined authority of all the concepts that the theory cannot accommodate. This, *pace* Scanlon (1992), is not to question the epistemic authority of the theorist over other people.[51] It is to question the normative authority, within one and the same person's practical deliberation, of a theory that aspires to crowd out or override all concepts and considerations that it cannot assimilate to itself.

Granted, recasting one's thought as a tidy theoretical structure ensures that it exhibits a variety of theoretical virtues, and one could regard these theoretical virtues as intrinsically valuable—many regard the majestic simplicity of a theory as a source of beauty and awe, for instance.

But appealing to theoretical virtues such as simplicity invites the Lichtenbergian worry that the simplicity of the theory reflects no more than the simplicity of the theorist. The mere fact that some structure exhibits theoretical virtues is not by itself enough to ground its authority. The seductive clarity, coherence, and economy of conspiracy theories, for example, should not be mistaken for genuine understanding, just as the standardized, quantifiable metrics of value deployed by administrative bureaucracies should not be mistaken for the richer set of values they are meant to render tractable.[52]

---

[51] This is what Scanlon (1992) takes Williams (1985) and Walzer (1983, 1987) to be doing. On Scanlon's rendering, they reject the claim to exclusive epistemic authority in all matters moral that they see some moral theorists as making, namely the claim that giving advice and correcting people's moral beliefs is the preserve of moral experts marked out as such by their possession of a moral theory. Scanlon grants that this is a questionable basis for a claim to such exclusive authority, but argues that few moral theorists, apart from 'some utilitarians' (1992, 4), make such a claim to authority.

[52] On the dangers of seductively clear systems in connection with conspiracy theories and bureaucracies, see Nguyen (2021).

More needs to be said about why the concepts, reasons, and judgements acting as tent poles for the theory authenticate it as an *authoritative way* of realizing theoretical virtues.

Even if, in addition to recognizing the intrinsic value of theoretical virtues, more *can* be said to show that the theory is in fact sustained by concepts that have force with us, the crucial question will still be why we should care more about these concepts and correlative reasons forming a theoretically virtuous structure than we care about all the other concepts and considerations at the expense of which this is achieved. Why should it matter so much that, as I go about my daily business and engage in private, personal deliberation, my patterns of thought exemplify theoretical virtues? After all, as Williams (1999, 246) remarks, we are not living our lives in order to exemplify a theory.

The issue can also be put in terms of confidence. Theories such as Kantianism, utilitarianism, or contractualism require us to be supremely confident in the small handful of concepts, reasons, and judgements that sustain them—so confident, indeed, as to be willing to deploy them to overturn any concept, reason, or judgement that conflicts with them.[53] But is such a completely one-sided distribution of confidence really reasonable? Is it not *unreasonable*, in the thick sense of the term that invokes proportionality and good sense, to place all one's confidence in a small handful of ideas and take everything else to follow from that?[54]

Recognizing the authority of the thought 'suffering is bad' while continuing to recognize the authority of other ethical concepts and reasons against which that thought can be balanced is one thing. It is quite another to recognize *nothing but* the authority of that thought and deny authority to any concept or consideration that cannot be derived from it and shown to be an application of it. What renders the authority question so acute in connection with these tidy-minded theories is not so much what these theories fundamentally affirm as what they are willing to deny on that basis—what they are willing to sacrifice to tidiness.

One may be willing to make this sacrifice if one regards the demand for tidiness or systematicity as a ubiquitous and overriding demand of rationality itself. But many are not prepared to accept this equation of the authority of theory with the authority of rationality without further argument, objecting that it betrays, in Williams's phrase, an overly *rationalistic conception of rationality*, whose insistence on the need to be able to explicitly and

---

[53] A particularly pronounced example of this is Kagan (1989).
[54] On this thick sense of 'unreasonable', see Williams (1999, 245).

systematically justify every action in terms of a handful of perfectly general currencies of reasons bears the imprint of modern bureaucracy.[55]

The question of the authority of theory, though meant to answer the question of the authority of our concepts, then itself boils down to the question of the authority of a certain conception of rationality—one on which the recasting of thought in the form of a theory is a ubiquitous requirement on thinking *rationally* at all, because the demand to tidy up thought is inherent in the very idea of rationality. That highly specific and contentious conception of rationality forms the fulcrum giving a theory the leverage to overturn whatever entrenched moral sentiments and convictions it cannot accommodate.

Why should we accept this rationalistic conception of rationality? One reason might be that when our concepts conflict, the rational as opposed to arbitrary resolution of conflict *requires* some general currency of reasons (articulated in terms of a universal metric of utility or a special notion of moral obligation, for example) by which the claims that various concepts make on us can be compared and weighed against each other.

As pluralists and particularists have pointed out, however, we are perfectly capable of rationally resolving conflicts by exercising our judgement in the particular case without relying on a general currency of comparison; that does not make the resolution arbitrary: we may still have reasons to resolve conflicts one way rather than another, only they might be specific to the particular case rather than mere applications of entirely general considerations.[56] To say that something is a matter of judgement is not to say that it is a matter of arbitrarily plumping one way or the other—unless we are only prepared to *count* something as a reason if it can be shown to be derivable from a theory, and to do that would be to presuppose rather than to prop up a rationalistic conception of rationality. Absent a compelling argument for why we should accept that particular conceptualization of what it means to think rationally, we should not lose sight of the sense in which one can think rationally without thinking in terms of a theory.

In response, it is sometimes said that to settle for the kaleidoscopic jumble of concepts we happen to find makes it all too easy to provide reasons for one's unreconstructed prejudices, and thereby renders reflection overly

---

[55] See Williams (1985, 20, 112–13, 124).
[56] For an especially trenchant particularist elaboration of the idea that conflict-resolution requires no more than judgements in the particular case, see Dancy (2004). See Berlin and Williams (1994, 306–7) for a pluralist defence of the point that choices between incommensurable values are not unreasonable. A sophisticated account of choices between incommensurable values is provided by the work of Ruth Chang (2002, 2015, 2016); see also the essays by various authors in Chang (1997).

conservative. It is *overly* conservative, in particular, because the conceptual apparatus we start out from is likely to be in various ways hidebound, cruelly superficial, ideologically distorted, and already teeming with ill-considered theories and simplistic forms of tidy-mindedness. Accordingly, the argument runs, we need well-considered theories to help us diagnose distortions and drive out the ill-considered ones.[57]

But while it is certainly true that theories quickly become radically revisionary, it is not true that reflection can *only* be radically revisionary when it takes the form of a theory. Even when it forswears the machinery of theory, critical reflection still has the resources to unmask prejudices. In fact, there is an important sense in which it has *more* resources when it does not have to be couched in the terms of a tidy theory, since it can then draw not just on the concepts that found a place in the theory, but also on all the concepts that the theory sacrificed to tidiness—a collection of critical resources which typically includes not only a rich battery of thick ethical concepts, but also cultural, psychological, historical, political, and socio-economic concepts that are often much better suited to identifying self-serving prejudices as such.

The racist or sexist may offend against a formal principle of universalizability by not applying reasons equally, for example, but, as Williams has emphasized, that rarely captures what is chiefly amiss in concrete instances of discrimination.[58] The reasons that the racist or sexist gives for his discriminatory behaviour, which a theory-driven critique would focus on, are often mere rationalizations. Subjecting these rationalizations to the test of theory can bring out how they subtly violate the canons of rationality as embodied by Kantian, utilitarian, or contractualist theory; but it does not even *begin* to bring out how they are blatantly self-serving and dishonest. To understand the psychological and social dynamics that are key to grasping what is really going on (as opposed to what the ostensible justification *pretends* is going on), critical reflection needs to become more detailed and concrete rather than more abstract and principled—which is to say that it should move in a direction that is precisely the opposite of that which issues in the thin and general categories of a tidy theory.

Once it is acknowledged that theory-building is neither the only nor even necessarily the best way of obtaining critical leverage over ordinary thought, the costs of theory-building become more salient. A number of philosophers

---

[57] See e.g. Nussbaum (2000, 70).
[58] See Williams (1985, 130) and Cueni and Queloz (2021). This is one of several respects in which theories' 'rhetoric of radical rationality conceals how conservative they are' (Williams 1995n, 183).

have felt that the tidiest theories leave us with too few concepts to make sense of our immediate experience: like filters laid over a picture, they blot out all but a few features—whatever cannot be captured in terms of moral obligations, or in terms of its impact on the utilitarian calculus, is screened out.[59] This may render the challenges we face in our practical deliberations simpler, more quantifiable, and more tractable. But it also flattens our perception by eliminating nuances and dimensions of value. Faced with a choice between a conceptual apparatus that is theoretically virtuous but impoverished and one that is untidy but richly expressive of a wide variety of human concerns and dimensions of value, is it so clear that we should go with the former?

A popular compromise between these two alternatives is to say that we do not need full-blown theories, but still need to subject our inherited concepts to the progressive pull *towards* theory: we should aim for a *reflective equilibrium* between the conservative weight of pre-theoretical reasons and the revisionary demands of systematicity.[60] Instead of building a theory from the master concepts down, we start by treating the welter of our inherited concepts and reasons as *constraints* on the demand for a tidy system of thought; we then extract what organizing concepts and generalized principles we can from them, and inch, through the mutual adjustment of particular judgements to more general principles and general principles to particular judgements, towards a *tidier* structure of thought.

Insofar as such a reflective equilibrium approach instigates a re-evaluation and revision of our inherited conceptual apparatus, it can be cast as an answer to the authority question, capable of differentiating more from less authoritative concepts even in the absence of a full-blown theory.[61] This is certainly true to its origins. Nelson Goodman, who first introduced the method in his discussion of the validity of inference rules in *Fact, Fiction, and Forecast*, saw the method as answering, fundamentally, to the problem of which concepts we should use. Goodman frames the problem as a *projection problem*: which concepts advert to properties that are inductively projectable from a sample

---

[59] See Williams (1985, 130; 1996b, 15) and Chappell (2015). For discussions of Williams's critique in particular, see Smyth (2019) and the essays in Heuer and Lang (2012). Hämäläinen (2009) relocates Williams's critique of theory in contemporary analytic ethics, while Chappell (2009) offers a Williamsian critique of ethical theory.

[60] Ethical and political theorists frequently present their preferred theory as marking a reflective equilibrium between the demands of systematization and our pre-reflective intuitions or commitments—see Rawls (1971, ch. 1, §§4–9) and Daniels (1979, 1996), for example—and the notion is also invoked in other parts of philosophy: Elgin (1983, 1996, 2017) advocates its use in epistemology, while Lewis (1983c, x) and Keefe (2000, ch. 2, §1) even defend its applicability to all of philosophy. See also Brun (2014), Tersman (2018), Daniels (2020), Rechnitzer (2022), and Beisbart and Brun (2024) for discussions of the method's career and elaboration.

[61] See Brun (2020; 2022, 15–16) and Rechnitzer (2022, 29, 51).

to a larger population? He compares the 'task of formulating rules that define the difference between valid and invalid inductive inferences' to the 'task of defining any term with an established usage' (1983, 66). In both cases, we should proceed by dual adjustment according to the following principle: 'A rule is amended if it yields an inference we are unwilling to accept; an inference is rejected if it violates a rule we are unwilling to amend' (1983, 64, emphasis removed). As Georg Brun (2020) has shown, moreover, the method of reflective equilibrium is instructively linked to the method of 'constructive definition' that Goodman had developed in an earlier book, *The Structure of Appearance* (1977)—a method which closely resembles Carnap's method of explication. Goodman's method of reflective equilibrium is thus offered as a non-foundationalist solution to the problem of which concepts to think with. What is more, it is well equipped to acknowledge that tidiness has a price, and that gains in tidiness need to be weighed against our confidence in our unreconstructed concepts and judgements.

However, that method still fundamentally adheres to the view of conceptual authority as deriving from theoretical virtue, and hence still invites the question of the authority *of* those theoretical virtues. As Brun acknowledges, 'virtues *of theories* are indeed the driving force' behind the method of reflective equilibrium, 'because they motivate the transition to a theoretically more suitable system of concepts in the first place' (2020, 950). When we assess the authority of a partially systematized set of concepts, we are bound to do so by reference to our everyday judgements and our pre-theoretical sense of the life that this set of concepts is supposed to help us to lead. And in many cases, as the example of the tidied-up concept *person* and its questionable implications for infanticide illustrated, the reasons that guide and flow from our unreconstructed conceptual apparatus plausibly *count for more* than the gains in theoretical virtue. Why should the product of a procedure which, in the name of theoretical virtue, overturns judgements and concepts that have force with us be granted more authority over our lives than the messier outlook that better matches our initial distribution of confidence? The onus is on the side of the systematizers to show why the reasons yielded by more theoretically virtuous concepts should be granted more authority than the reasons we immediately have for thinking as we do.

Again, in the context of scientific thought, it is plausible that the authority of theoretical virtues *can* be grounded in the assumptions and aspirations driving scientific inquiry. To put a very complex issue rather crudely: the systematicity of scientific thought is taken to count in favour of its authority because the natural world it describes is taken to be systematic. Within such an attempt to describe 'the system of the world'—the *systema mundi*, as the Stoic phrase has it—theoretical virtues can operate as criteria of authority because they are, however defeasibly, criteria of truth.[62]

But this line of argument for the authority of theoretical virtues does not obviously generalize to the thick normative concepts—ethical, political, legal, cultural, and aesthetic—that sustain, and are sustained by, a social world. These concepts are not part of an attempt to describe a single, systematic natural world. There are many social worlds, and there is no particular reason to think that they are bound to be systematic enough to turn theoretical virtues such as consistency and coherence into reliable criteria of conceptual authority. As Thomas Nagel puts it, 'truth in science, in mathematics, or in history has to fit together in a consistent system', but 'our evaluative beliefs are not part of the attempt to describe a single world' (2001, 108–9).[63]

Canvassing reasons for abandoning our untidy 'folk' concepts for more theoretically virtuous concepts, McPherson and Plunkett offer the consideration that the class of concepts displaying theoretical virtues boasts an excellent track record of utility in inquiry—and if adopting more theoretically virtuous concepts has proven useful for scientific inquiry, one might think that it could prove similarly useful for what they call 'normative inquiry'.[64]

But, as they also go on to acknowledge, the persuasiveness of this argument again depends on how much like scientific inquiry 'normative inquiry' is taken to be—on whether there is an antecedent systematicity for our normative concepts to reflect, or whether 'normative inquiry' is better thought of as a combination of, on the one hand, deductive and ampliative reflection on what the concepts we are confident in imply within the social world in which we deploy them, and, on the other hand, critical reflection on the reasons we have to adopt or abjure those concepts and their concomitant reasons. If the judgements we form in normative inquiry are 'not part of the attempt to describe a single world', in Nagel's phrase, it is not at all clear that the authority of the concepts articulating them should primarily, or mainly, be grounded in their exemplification of a catalogue of theoretical virtues. There will then

---

[62] See Rescher (2005) for a detailed argument to that effect.
[63] See also Hämäläinen (2009, 548), who urges us 'to remove from our picture of moral theory an assumption concerning the relationship between systematic theoretical articulation and action-guidance', namely the assumption that moral theories are pictures of a moral reality that was systematic all along. If we abandon this assumption, we will be more receptive to the idea that theoretical virtues 'do not necessarily mirror a proper orientation in the moral realm', and that moral theories are better viewed as 'a box of tools to be used…to elucidate different aspects of morality'—rather like literary theories.
[64] See McPherson and Plunkett (2020, 281).

be no reason to think, and many reasons to doubt, that this is what normative inquiry is primarily about.

In this chapter, I have examined and ultimately found unpersuasive the different forms of tidy-minded non-foundationalism that look to theoretical virtues as a general answer to the authority question. In each case, we ended up with some version of the question of what authority these theoretical virtues themselves possess in connection with thick normative concepts; attempts to ground that authority in the constitutive requirements of rationality were found to hinge on a rationalistic conception of rationality whose authority is itself open to question.

The conclusion to be drawn from this is not that we should never systematize, but rather that the merits of systematization will depend on the answers we can give to the further questions of *when* and *why* we need to systematize. The authority of concepts ultimately has to come not from how concepts relate to each other, but from how they relate *to us*. To supplement more theoretically virtuous concepts with the grounds on which they can claim more authority, and to discriminate contexts in which these grounds are given from contexts in which they are lacking, a more comprehensive approach is needed—one that appraises concepts not just on the basis of their inherent properties or the systematic relations between them, but on the basis of how these concepts tie in with our concerns.

The Ethics of Conceptualization: Tailoring Thought and Language to Need. Matthieu Queloz, Oxford University Press.
© Matthieu Queloz 2025. DOI: 10.1093/9780198926283.003.0006

PART III
HOW TO ANSWER THE AUTHORITY QUESTION

6
Concepts and Concerns

The orienting idea of the framework for concept appraisal I propose to develop is that it is not enough to look at concepts' inherent features and flaws, such as their theoretical virtues and vices; we have to consider whether and how concepts tie in with our concerns. A concept could be ever so theoretically virtuous—that would do nothing for us if it came at the cost of its ability to promote what we care about. Accordingly, we should not aim to appraise concepts in isolation from the characteristics of those who live by them. Our concepts should make contact with our concerns.

The idea that our concepts should make contact with our concerns is the first of three loadbearing ideas defining the framework I aim to present. In this chapter, I bring out the force of this idea, using as my springboard an underappreciated debate between Ronald Dworkin and Bernard Williams: two figures who personify the clash between the pursuit of theoretical virtue and the preoccupation with the concerns animating concept use.

After drawing out some of the lessons of the Dworkin–Williams debate and showing how these enable us to discern redeeming practical virtues even in theoretical vices, I acknowledge the limits of the idea that we should appraise concepts according to how they tie in with our concerns: in particular, I identify four remaining problems which require the framework to be elaborated further. But the place to start is with a vivid illustration of the importance of tethering concepts to concerns.

6.1 The Dworkin–Williams Debate

In the fall of 1998, a year after the death of Isaiah Berlin, the New York Institute for the Humanities convened a two-day conference in Manhattan to examine his intellectual legacy. The conference attracted an unexpectedly large audience and was covered by the *New York Times*.[1] It was also the scene

---

[1] Such was the demand for transcripts afterwards that the organizers were persuaded, against their original plans, to publish the presented papers together with the subsequent discussions. See

of a coruscating debate between Ronald Dworkin and Bernard Williams, itself the culmination of a dialogue going back to seminars they held together at Oxford in the late eighties (as part of a series informally known as 'Star Wars').[2] As Damian Cueni (2024b) points out in an article I build on here, a surprisingly focused debate emerges once their compressed remarks in New York are connected to the scattered writings in which they developed their points.[3]

What is ostensibly at issue in this Dworkin–Williams debate is how we ought to deal with conflicts between our value concepts. Dworkin, striving for what he calls 'integrity' among our concepts, seeks to eliminate such conflicts, while Williams, doubtful that we either could or should eliminate the conflict, resists the pursuit of conceptual integrity.

Yet upon closer inspection, the debate turns out to be about far more than conflicts of values. Dworkin and Williams personify not just two contrasting approaches to such conflicts, but two rival views of what our concepts should be answerable to.

The starting point of the Dworkin–Williams debate is the observation, stressed notably by Berlin, that there is an inherent tension between the values of liberty and equality. As Berlin describes the tension, 'total liberty for the wolves is death to the lambs, total liberty of the powerful, the gifted, is not compatible with the rights to a decent existence of the weak and the less gifted' (2013d, 12–13). Conversely, the thorough enforcement of total equality carries severe costs in liberty, which has to be curtailed to redress or prevent various forms of inequality arising from disparities in wealth, resources, opportunities, and talents. Circumstances concurring, modest gains in both liberty and equality may be achievable without trade-off; but when the realization of either value is pursued more insistently, there comes a point at which one has to be paid for with the other. 'It is an uncomfortable situation', Williams concludes already in his influential early essay on the idea of equality, 'but the discomfort is just that of genuine political thought' (1973d, 249).

Rothstein (1998) as well as Lilla, Dworkin, and Silvers (2001) for an account of the conference and its reception.

[2] See Guest (2013, 17, 247 n. 20).

[3] Cueni reconstructs and explores the implications of the Dworkin–Williams debate from a jurisprudential perspective in a series of texts (2024a, b, manuscript-b) that inform the present discussion along with our many conversations on these issues. When we first set out to reconstruct this debate, however, we had to start from scratch, as Williams's challenging essays engaging with Dworkin had been virtually ignored by commentators. This has now begun to change. Hall (2017), Ulaş (2020), Kyritsis (2021), and Mann (2021), discuss aspects of the Dworkin–Williams debate, while Murata (2022a, b) draws on Williams's writings on Dworkin in some depth, albeit in a somewhat different connection. For congenial applications of some of the lessons it holds to legal reasoning, see also van Domselaar (2022) and Murata (forthcoming).

Dworkin believes we can do better. He sees reason to hope that we might eliminate the tension between the concepts of liberty and equality. His leverage point is the idea that whether liberty and equality conflict 'depends on how we conceive these abstract values' (2001a, 83).[4] This seemingly trite observation marks a crucial step: it transposes what might otherwise have been a metaphysical debate about the nature of liberty and equality into a debate about conceptual ethics.

As long as liberty is conceived as 'freedom from the interference of others in doing whatever it is that you might wish to do' (2001a, 84), Dworkin admits, liberty undoubtedly conflicts with equality. But why should we think that we are committed to this way of conceptualizing liberty? The question cannot simply be answered by an inquiry into what liberty *really* is—we 'can't conduct a DNA analysis of liberty' (2001a, 86). The question has to be *which conception* of liberty we have most reason to accept. And perhaps the most attractive conception of liberty will turn out not to conflict with the most attractive conception of equality after all.

For Dworkin, we have several reasons to prefer conceptions that do not conflict. First, conflicting conceptions systematically confront the state with tragic choices—choices where 'the government must not merely disappoint but must wrong some citizens no matter what it does' (Dworkin et al. 2001, 122).[5] If we could only arrive at non-conflicting conceptions of liberty and equality, we might hope to eliminate such tragic conflicts from politics.

Second, Dworkin regards the fact that two conceptions do not conflict as being itself a reason to prefer them over conceptions that conflict: 'integrity among our concepts is itself a value', he maintains, 'so that we have that standing reason for seeking out, for preferring, conceptions of our values that do not conflict' (Dworkin et al. 2001, 127).

Other things being equal, we thus have a standing reason to pursue what Dworkin calls conceptual 'integrity'. In the terminology eked out in the previous chapter, conceptual integrity amounts to the type of coherence between value concepts that we called *congruence*: two concepts are congruent if and to the extent that the realization or instantiation of one concept does not come at the expense of the realization or instantiation of the other concept.

Dworkin therefore proposes to iron out the conceptual tension between liberty and equality by composing a definition of the concept of liberty that renders it systematically congruent with the concept of equality. If Berlin

---

[4] In Dworkin's terminology, they are *interpretive* concepts; see Dworkin (1986, 45–86; 2001b).
[5] See also Dworkin (2000, 120–83; 2001a, 80).

reached the conclusion that liberty and equality irremediably conflict, Dworkin believes, it was because Berlin equated liberty with freedom from interference in doing what one wants.[6] In fact, however, liberty should be interpreted as a *political* rather than personal value: it is 'that part of your freedom that government would do wrong to constrain' (2011, 4).[7] As a political value, liberty should not be understood as freedom from interference in doing what one wants, but in terms of *rights* distributed according to a political principle of equality—in other words, liberty should be *rightful* freedom.[8]

If we conceive of the political value of liberty in terms of equally distributed rights to liberty, this 'rules out genuine conflict with the conception of equality...because the two conceptions are thoroughly integrated' (Dworkin 2011, 4). The realization of equality may of course still entrain a loss in freedom. But not every loss in freedom will be a loss in liberty. A loss in freedom will only count as a loss in liberty where there is a *claim* to liberty, and there can only be a claim to liberty, on Dworkin's account, where that claim can be grounded in a *right*. It follows that as long as rights are equally distributed, liberty must itself be equally distributed, and liberty and equality can no longer conflict. As a result, 'the alleged conflict between liberty and equality disappears' (Dworkin 2011, 4). This yields an extremely neat and tidy account that immunizes the concepts of liberty and equality against conflict. It achieves this by conceptualizing liberty in a way that effectively guarantees congruence with the concept of equality.

Williams, however, has strong reservations about the pursuit of conceptual integrity—especially in connection with the political value concepts that Dworkin is keenest to reconcile. While Dworkin encourages us to *aim* for conceptual integrity and just see whether we can or cannot construct concepts that achieve it,[9] Williams does not think we will discover an adequate but entirely tensionless way of thinking about liberty and equality that way.

Williams's scepticism is grounded, at the most immediate level, in his acceptance of Berlin's *value pluralism*: the thesis that there is a plurality of irreducibly distinct and incommensurable values that are bound to end up pulling in competing directions when pursued in concert, not merely because

---

[6] See Dworkin (2011, 367).
[7] As Dworkin also puts it: someone's liberty is 'the area of his freedom that a political community cannot take away without injuring him in a special way: compromising his dignity by denying him equal concern or an essential feature of responsibility for his own life' (2011, 366).
[8] See Dworkin (2000, 120–83; 2001a, b). That does not presuppose a right *to* freedom; Dworkin argues instead 'for rights to liberty that rest on different bases' (2011, 4), such as rights to ethical independence, to free speech, and to due process of law; see Dworkin (2011, 368–74).
[9] See Dworkin et al. (2001, 127).

time is short or the world recalcitrant, but because the values themselves inherently conflict.[10] As Berlin puts it: 'We are faced with choices between ends equally ultimate, and claims equally absolute, the realisation of some of which must inevitably involve the sacrifice of others', which is why 'the possibility of conflict—and of tragedy—can never wholly be eliminated from human life, either personal or social' (2002b, 213–14).

Some pluralists, including Rawls, have focused on pluralism at the level of society, where the values of some members of society clash with the values of other members of society.[11] But what Berlin and Williams emphasize is that even if society were far less pluralistic, so that members of society shared roughly the same range of values, there would still be pluralism 'within the breast': even the concepts of one and the same person conflict in ways that are not resolvable without loss.[12] A value conflict is not 'most typically enacted by a body of single-minded egalitarians confronting a body of equally single-minded libertarians', Williams notes, 'but is rather a conflict which one person, equipped with a more generous range of human values, could find enacted in himself' (1981a, 73). Of course, social pluralism and pluralism within the breast are not unrelated, since the latter is in many instances an expression of the former: the conflict enacted within one person may itself reflect the fact that the person's conceptual repertoire is the accumulated historical deposit of different social influences—be it different groups within a society, different stages in the history of that society, or even different societies.

The cardinal claim of pluralism, however, is that these values, at whichever level they are expressed, are such that all the things they pick out as being of value cannot 'ultimately be united into a harmonious whole without loss' (B. Williams 2013, xxxv). The ideal situation in which, as P. F. Strawson put it, 'every god is given his due and conflict is avoided by careful arrangement and proper subordination of part to part' (2008b, 30) is a fantasy, and an incoherent one at that. For the pluralist thesis is not just the weak claim 'that

---

[10] Here I rely particularly on Williams's elaboration of pluralism. On Berlin's pluralism and his influence on Williams in this respect, see Lyons (2021, 215–61), and see also Gray (2013) and Lyons (2020) for synoptic accounts of Berlin's thought. On the development of pluralist ideas between 1940 and 1980 and its connection to anti-totalitarianism, see Müller (2012). For an exploration of pluralism's implications for politics, see also Galston (2002, 2005).

[11] 'No society can include within itself all forms of life', Rawls writes—'there is no social world without loss: that is, no social world that does not exclude some ways of life that realize in special ways certain fundamental values' (1993, 197).

[12] See Berlin (2013d, 12) as well as Berlin and Williams (1994). Berlin's animating concern in adverting to pluralism was to cast doubt on the feasibility, in principle, of realizing utopian social arrangements or creating a perfect state (2013a, 48–50; 2013d, 14), and to warn against the danger of allowing this utopian ideal to determine one's moral and political practice (2002b, 212–17); but logically, these political conclusions lie downstream of a structural claim about human value concepts.

in an imperfect world not all the things we recognise as good are in practice compatible', but the much stronger claim, which is a claim about our *conceptualizations* before it is a claim about the world in which they are deployed, 'that we have no coherent conception of a world without loss, that goods conflict by their very nature' (B. Williams 2013, xxxv). Our value concepts are incongruent, and while the incongruence may be accidental in some cases, it is non-accidental in others, and hence ineliminable as long as we hold on to anything like these values.

But must we hold on to anything like these inevitably conflicting values? This is the question raised by the radically revisionist conceptual ethics of someone like Nietzsche, and, in a less radical spirit, it is also Dworkin's response to this pluralism-based worry. Dworkin does not deny that the conceptions held up by pluralists in fact conflict; what he questions is the *authority* of those conceptions.

Pluralism, Dworkin complains, 'is too often cited as a kind of excuse for not confronting the most fundamental substantive issues', in particular 'the hard work of actually trying to identify the right conceptions of the values in question' (Dworkin et al. 2001, 124–5):

> the argument necessary to defend pluralism...must show, in the case of each of the values it takes to be in some kind of conceptual conflict with one another, why the understanding of that value that produces the conflict is the most appropriate one. (2001a, 90; see also 2006, 116)

Values are something that *we construct*, Dworkin reminds us, and finding the most attractive conceptions is not a matter of 'excavating the shared meanings of words' or of making 'anything like a scientific discovery about the true nature of reality' (Dworkin et al. 2001, 126).

For Dworkin, then, the question is not whether the concepts we inherited conflict, but whether the most attractive conceptions that we could be using do. Unlike Nietzsche, Dworkin does not go so far as to call into question the very use of anything like liberal and egalitarian concepts.[13] But he is less impressed by the constraints that existing ways of thinking exert on us than by the degree of freedom they leave us to revise our conceptions of our values.[14]

---

[13] On Williams's critical stance towards Nietzsche's revisionary ambitions, see Queloz (2021a).

[14] Dworkin understands the concept–conception distinction as a distinction between different levels of abstraction within the concepts already in use: this yields a 'treelike structure', the trunk being the *concept*—what people 'by and large agree about'—and the branches being the *conceptions*— the 'more concrete refinements' (1986, 70–1) of that concept with respect to which people differ.

Even if pluralists are rights about the conceptual apparatus we inherited, we remain free to try and construct values that do not conflict, and it would be premature to accept the persistent possibility of conflict before every effort had been made to forestall it. As he insists: 'We shouldn't buy failure in advance: we should aim at integrity in an optimistic spirit' (Dworkin et al. 2001, 127).

Yet Williams's pessimism with regard to our prospects of arriving at such conceptual integrity stems, at a deeper level, from the expectation that any viable set of values will include at least *some* values that necessarily conflict. Like Berlin, he thinks that there are some value concepts that human societies are bound to cultivate in some form—not because these are given to us by God or implanted in us by nature, nor because there is some antecedent structure in reality that these concepts are bound to reflect, but because the conjunction of certain facts about human beings and their environment systematically gives rise to the same kinds of practical problems calling for the same kinds of solutions, which notably include the cultivation of the same kinds of concepts.

This idea underpins Berlin's conviction that values vary only within the bounds of a 'human horizon', i.e. that there is a 'minimum of moral values accepted by all men without which human societies would disintegrate' (2015, 206); 'these values', Berlin asserts, 'are objective—that is to say, their nature, the pursuit of them, is part of what it is to be a human being, and this is an objective given' (2013c, 12).[15] In this respect, Berlin self-consciously echoes his close friend Herbert Hart, who, in *The Concept of Law*, suggests that we can make certain generalizations about what kinds of practical needs will arise in the kinds of environments that humans inhabit, and 'as long as these hold good, there are certain rules of conduct which any social organization must contain if it is to be viable' (2012, 192–3). In a similar vein, Stuart Hampshire remarks that if 'the underlying structure of moral distinctions has no supernatural source, it must be recognized by rational inquiry as having its origin...in constant human needs and interests' (1983, 128). We can then look for bounds on the variability of moral, political, and legal concepts, imposed by practical demands faced by human beings nearly everywhere in virtue of their sharing certain very basic concerns, such as the concern to avoid violent conflict with others, to find out about the dangers and

---

Dworkin offers *courtesy* as an example: people might agree, at an abstract level, that courtesy is a matter of respect, while at the same time disagreeing over what exactly that form of respect requires.

[15] For discussions of this thought in Berlin's work, see Müller (2019) and Riley (2019).

affordances of their environment, to secure the resources they need to survive, and to foster conditions enabling cooperation. Williams himself puts a version of this idea to work in *Truth and Truthfulness* (2002, 126) to argue that any human society needs to value the truth for its own sake in order to effectively gain and share information.[16]

When the pluralist claim that some value concepts inevitably conflict is combined with the further claim that some of these concepts are ones that human societies cannot do without, the two claims suggest that the quest for conceptual integrity is unlikely to succeed across the range of our value concepts. As Berlin pithily puts it, 'collisions of values are of the essence of what they are and what we are' (2013d, 13). Of course, the unattainability of conceptual integrity across the board does not by itself preclude its attainability in connection with the pair of concepts Dworkin focuses on. But it informs Williams's approach to this debate, and disposes him towards scepticism.

To pluralists steeped in history like Berlin and Williams, moreover, Dworkin's attempt to inoculate our ways of thinking about liberty and equality against conflict is recognizable as another manifestation of a familiar human urge: the deep-seated desire to eliminate tragic value conflicts, i.e. painful conflicts between what is right and what is equally right that cannot be resolved without loss, so that one is bound to do wrong no matter what one does, because there is 'no better thing to be done' (Williams 1973c, 173).[17]

As Berlin and Williams point out, it is an ancient aspiration to deploy *techne* as a protection from *tyche*, in particular by erecting conceptual edifices as shelters against luck.[18] 'Impressed by the power of fortune to wreck what looked like the best-shaped life', Williams writes, some of the Greeks 'sought a rational design of life which would reduce the power of fortune and would be to the greatest possible extent luck-free', something that 'has been, in different forms, an aim of later thought as well' (1985, 5). Various theoretical constructions—from Stoicism through Kantianism to utilitarianism—have been erected over the ages to rationalize away value conflicts when they arose,

---

[16] See Queloz (2018b) for a detailed reconstruction.

[17] This conception of tragedy as a conflict of *right* and *right* is associated with Hegel, who writes in his *Aesthetics* that the 'original essence of tragedy' consists in a conflict in which 'each of the opposed sides, if taken by itself, has *justification*; while each can establish the true and positive content of its own aim and character only by denying and infringing the equally justified power of the other', thereby becoming 'nevertheless involved in *guilt*' (1975, II, 1196). See Robert Williams (2012, 120–42) for a discussion of this conception of tragedy, and Williams (1971, 162–5) for a discussion of its relevance to philosophy. For accounts of tragic legal choices, see Wolcher (2008) and especially van Domselaar (2017), who draws on Williams.

[18] See Berlin (2013b, 196; 2013c, 26–8; 2014a, 25; 2014b, 99–100) and Williams (1981c, 20; 1985, ch. 1; 1995e).

or to prevent them from arising in the first place: by devising lexical priority rules, reducing values to a common currency of comparison, or arguing that conflicts evaporate under reflection once some obligations are revealed to be merely apparent.[19]

A prime example is the Kantian doctrine that anything which is not a claim of morality must be a claim of 'prudence', in a specially capacious sense of the word, and is silenced when it conflicts with the claims of morality.[20] Williams regards this as an all too human stratagem for reducing the risk of facing tragic choices between the claims of morality and the claims of other things one deeply cares about.[21] By consigning all these competing reasons for action to the category of the merely prudential and convincing oneself of the overriding importance of morality, one *seems* to escape such conflicts with a clear conscience. Of course, the Kantian view is not primarily motivated by a conscious desire to rationalize away conflicts of values; but it is a *consequence* of the view that it does so, and this convenient consequence helps explain the historical success of the view: its enduring attraction may have something to do with its answering to unconscious wishes by promising to relieve the discomfort of value conflicts.

Yet this promise of protection from tragic conflict is ultimately illusory, Williams believes, because it turns on the distorting pretence that all the claims competing with morality must be claims of self-interest, and belittles even those by treating them all alike: 'How does "morality" deal with the many reasons for behaving badly that lie in the desire to be loved? As another of its "temptations", no doubt, like a craving for marmalade' (Williams 2014d, 246).

In the New York debate, Dworkin concedes that 'dramatic, even tragic conflicts in personal values' (Dworkin et al. 2001, 132) may be unavoidable, so that one will do wrong whatever one does. But his hope is that we can avoid tragic conflicts when it comes to the *political* values guiding *state* action.

Alongside his pluralism-based objection casting doubt on the attainability of conceptual integrity, Williams therefore mounts a second objection calling into question the very advisability of striving for conceptual integrity in the particular case of *liberty* and *equality*.

The main thrust of this second objection is that we discover a real *need* to keep open the rift between the concepts of liberty and equality that Dworkin

---

[19] See Berlin (2002a, 291–2; 2014b, 61–2, 70–2). For a detailed analysis of how Stoicism and Kantianism function as shelters against luck, see Queloz (2022c) and Queloz and van Ackeren (2024).
[20] For an analysis of this Kantian idea, see Bader (2015).
[21] As I argue in Queloz (2022a, c, forthcoming) and Queloz and van Ackeren (2024).

offers to patch up with his tidy conceptual construction once we reflect on the central *concerns* that render the concepts of liberty and equality important for us in the first place: what is it that we fundamentally care about in these connections that leads us to have a use for anything like these concepts? The merits of using a concept, and *a fortiori* a particular conception, ultimately have to be judged on the basis of a prior understanding of the concerns that it is supposed to help us satisfy: the motivations, desires, or commitments to values or projects whose realization makes demands on those who pursue them.[22] Though our concerns may be mediated and focused by our concepts, it is fundamentally the direction of those concerns that determines what we care about, what is important or relevant to us (the Latin *concernere* means 'be relevant to', from *con-*, which expresses intensive force, and *cernere*, which means 'sift, discern').

Of course, there are a great many concerns that concepts such as *liberty* and *equality* tie in with; but Williams suggests that we can to some extent cut through that complexity, because 'associated with each such value concept there is a kind of schema, a very bare outline of what our central concern is' (2001a, 92). In response to Dworkin's proposed conception of liberty as rightful freedom, Williams therefore invites us to look at the central concern that underlies our use of anything like the concept of liberty.

For Williams, our use of the concept of liberty is animated, most basically, by a universal human concern, namely the concern *to be unobstructed in doing what one wants*—in particular, unobstructed by humanly imposed coercion. Williams labels this the concern for 'primitive freedom'. This characterization is of course still highly schematic, and the concern for primitive freedom will have received a certain historical and cultural elaboration.[23] But anything recognizable as human agency is bound to involve this concern for primitive freedom in some form, because pursuing any concerns at all must already involve being concerned to be unobstructed by others in doing so. An agent who pursued concerns without caring at all whether they were

---

[22] See Williams (2001a, 92). Some passages in Dworkin's oeuvre suggest that his approach is itself more grounded in human concerns than the present discussion suggests. In 'Do Values Conflict? A Hedgehog's Approach', for example, Dworkin insists that, in contrast to concepts of natural kinds such as gold, our political concepts are answerable to human concerns: 'We believe that gold is what it is quite independently of human concerns, ambitions, or needs. But that is not even remotely plausible about a political virtue like equality or liberty.... They are what they are because we are what we are: we believe that a government that respects liberty and equality in some way improves the lives of those whom it governs' (Dworkin 2001b, 255). But see Queloz (2024b) for a discussion of why this point of agreement belies a deeper disagreement.

[23] As Williams himself stresses (2001a, 93). For a reconstruction of Williams's genealogy of the political value of liberty, see Queloz (2021c, 238–41).

frustrated by others simply would not be intelligible to us as genuinely pursuing those concerns. This concern for primitive freedom is not yet a political concern; it is a personal concern for freedom in action, antecedent to and intelligible independently of the advent of the political. But, as we shall see in more detail in Chapter 10, it is ultimately by tying in with this concern for primitive freedom that the political concept of liberty must prove its worth.

The human experience of this central concern for primitive freedom is what fundamentally holds together varying conceptualizations of liberty across history and across warring factions, according to Williams. It is what makes them conceptualizations *of the same thing*:

> the disputes that have circled around the various definitions and concepts of liberty do not just represent a set of verbal misunderstandings. They have been disagreements about something. There is even a sense in which they have been disagreements about some one thing. There must be a core, or a primitive conception, perhaps some universal or widely spread human experience, to which these various conceptions relate. This does not provide, as it were, the ultimate definition. Indeed, this core or primitive item, I am going to suggest, is certainly not a political value, and perhaps not a value at all. But it can, and must, explain how these various accounts of the value of freedom are elaborations of the same thing. (2005c, 76)

The reason we *must* have some way of understanding how different conceptualizations of liberty are conceptualizations of the same thing, held together by an underlying concern for freedom that these conceptualizations all express, is that this is the only way of grasping how these *differences* in conceptualization themselves express a *normative conflict* over how the value of freedom should be realized. Not all differences in conceptualizations express such a normative conflict. Sometimes, as Williams grants, it would be 'arrant scholasticism' (2014g, 406) to go on about whether different conceptualizations were conceptualizations of the same thing: nothing much turns on whether the quantum-mechanical conception of the atom is a conceptualization of the same thing as the ancient Greek conception of the atom. But 'with value concepts such as freedom and justice', Williams stresses, 'we need to say *both* that there is significant historical variation between an idea or concept as used by two different groups, *and* that these are in some sense variant forms of the same concept' (2014g, 406–7). For the differences express 'significant conflicts between interpretations of the value at different times or between different groups: between freedom as a disciplined life within an independent republic, for instance, and freedom on Eighth Avenue' (2014g, 407). The concern that animates these different conceptualizations is fundamentally the same concern, which is what brings the different conceptualizations into genuine conflict with each other.[24]

By the same reasoning, we only really grasp why the concepts of liberty and equality are two *different* concepts, and not just two words for the same concept, once we look under the hood, at the concerns that animate their use, and recognize that they are fundamentally different concerns. Williams does not go into what the central concern underlying our use of the concept of equality might be. But if the central concern underlying our use of anything like the concept of liberty is the concern *to be unobstructed by humanly imposed coercion in doing what one wants*, a central concern underlying our use of anything like the concept of equality might be something like the concern *to be treated on a par with others*. That too is an utterly basic and widespread human experience, which plausibly lies at the root of different conceptions of equality.[25] And it pulls in a completely different direction from the concern for primitive freedom.

Thus, what we really want to know, and what Dworkin neglects in his pursuit of conceptual integrity, is to what extent his proposed conception of liberty serves, or fails to serve, the concern for primitive freedom that basically animates our use of anything like the concept of liberty. For whatever exactly that concern now goes *to*, we cannot *redirect* that concern 'simply nominalistically, by redefining a word', Williams insists, because 'an interest in producing a more coherent body of law is not by itself going to stop the concern going to what the concern goes to' (2001a, 94). If Dworkin's proposed conception fails to tie in with the concern that gives us reason to think in terms of anything like *liberty*, we have reason *not* to adopt that conception, because it would deflect attention away from the satisfaction of our most basic concern in this connection. It is simply no good securing conceptual integrity between two conceptions if it comes at the cost of severing the ties to the central human concerns that led us to have a use for anything like these conceptions in the first place.

This concern-based objection yields an argument that promises to do more with less than the pluralism-based objection: without requiring sweeping

---

[24] Though the conflict can itself be either notional or real, and, as we saw in Chapter 3, significantly different responses are appropriate in each case: a notional conflict between interpretations of a value at different times is not the same thing as a real conflict between different groups over how to run one and the same society.

[25] For illuminating accounts of the concerns that drove the development of notions of equality, see Stuurman (2017) and Sagar (2024).

assumptions about what values societies are bound to possess, it calls into question the very ambition to iron out certain tensions in our conceptual apparatus. It suggests that it is a fundamental mistake to look only at conflicts between *concepts*. We have to look also at the human *concerns* underlying the concepts—at *what we care about* in these connections.

These concerns are in significant respects independent of our concepts, so that constructing more congruent, coherent, or otherwise more theoretically virtuous concepts is not by itself going to redirect the concerns underlying the concepts we inherited. And if it is by tying in with these concerns that the concepts of liberty and equality become concepts worth using in the first place, we are clearly not helped by securing congruence or 'integrity' between these concepts if they thereby lose their connection to the concerns animating their use.

Williams's second worry is thus a concern-based worry about the advisability of striving for conceptual integrity. As he put it in an early essay on Berlin's value pluralism: 'conflict is not necessarily pathological' (1981a, 73). Even if we *could* achieve total integrity or congruence between our concepts, we would be ill-advised to do so if it untethered our concepts from our concerns.

6.2 Tethering Concepts to Concerns

If the Dworkin–Williams debate is the perfect springboard to the framework for concept appraisal I propose to develop, it is because it uniquely combines several features from which broader lessons can be extrapolated. Some of these lessons bear specifically on how to deal with the conflictual nature of politics—a theme I shall come to in Chapter 10, where I pick up the debate again and consider how it plays out from here. But, already at this point in our reconstruction, the debate holds crucial insights beyond what it tells us specifically about the conflict between *liberty* and *equality*.

One instructive feature of the debate is that Dworkin makes headway by reframing Berlin's preoccupation with the fact of pluralism in terms of the *authority* of particular ways of thinking. I want to suggest that this is an important question in its own right, which promises to help us make headway in philosophy more generally.

By pointing to the conceptual integrity of his proposed conceptions as a reason to accept them, moreover, Dworkin compellingly illustrates the tidy-minded approach to answering the authority question. He is one of the most influential voices advocating the idea that even our thick normative concepts should harmoniously interlock in a geodesic dome of concepts. Dworkin thus not only contributes the fundamental question animating the present inquiry into how to appraise concepts, but also paradigmatically embodies the main non-foundationalist answer to it.

Williams, meanwhile, gestures at a different way of answering the authority question, which I believe can be elaborated into a fully worked-out alternative to tidy-minded non-foundationalism: an alternative that seeks to *tether* concepts to the *concerns* of concept-users, on the grounds that concepts are no use to us unless they tie in with what we care about. This offers a sharp contrast not only to Dworkin's pursuit of conceptual integrity, but also to other contemporary accounts maintaining that conceptual tensions should always be eliminated. For Valerie Tiberius, for example, conflicts between our value concepts constitute a form of 'ill-being' that we should seek to overcome as we pursue well-being through the complete fulfilment of our values.[26] Williams's response to Dworkin suggests that eliminating such conflicts is not always advisable, because our concepts should subserve our concerns, and conflicting concepts can be the better concepts by serving our concerns better.

If I take my question from Dworkin, then, it is to Williams that I look for the beginning of an answer. In particular, I propose to extrapolate three broader lessons from Williams's remarks.

The first and fundamental lesson is that the merits of a proposed conception, and *a fortiori* of a concept, ultimately have to be judged on the basis of a prior understanding of the life that this concept is to help us to lead, and this requires us to understand the various *concerns* that motivate our use of certain concepts in the first place: what we care about in this connection. The authority of concepts does not trickle down from the theoretical virtues of the tidy conceptual structure into which they interlock. It wells up from the concerns underlying people's use of these concepts.

By 'concerns', I mean more settled concerns, not momentary whims and impulses. Our concerns include our inner needs, motivations, desires, and aspirations as well as our loyalties, attachments, and commitments to particular values or projects. As the examples of the political concepts of liberty and equality already intimate, moreover, what lends a concept authority for me need not be a *selfish* concern to get something for myself. Nor need it be a *self-centred* concern, in the sense in which an artist's concern to create great

---

[26] See Tiberius (2018, 34–5).

art—not for himself, but for the world—might be said to remain self-centred if it has to be *him* who creates it.[27] The relevant concern can be an altruistic and selfless concern for reform, or for the advancement of liberty or equality. It need not even be, in the first instance, *my* concern at all; it can be a shared concern—the project of a group, community, or movement. And what I am concerned *with* need not be the satisfaction of my own concerns, but can be something entirely external to and independent of myself. If I have a certain concern, then certain considerations become relevant considerations for me *because* I have that concern; but this does not mean that these considerations *refer* to my own concerns. There is an important difference between reasoning *from* a concern, in terms that *express* it, and reasoning *about* a concern, in terms that *refer* to it. Even if, from the autoethnographic stance, we find that our concerns are what ultimately infuses the world with significance for us, what we are concerned *with* when we take up the deliberative stance is still the world at large, not just ourselves and our concerns.

At the same time, it is not enough for a concept simply to serve some concern or other. If understanding how a concept relates to my concerns is to help me answer the authority question, it must show that the power of the concept is not simply a coercive imposition from outside, but is imbued with authority by the fact that it ultimately ties in with a concern I am *identified with*. The relevant concern must be a concern I share. It need have nothing to do with me at the level of its content or what it is directed at, but it needs to be a concern *for* me. And in virtue of being a concern for me, I have a *pro tanto* reason to prefer concepts that help over those that hinder the satisfaction of that concern.

That is how tracing concepts to concerns fundamentally promises to reconcile power and freedom: it promises to show, in good Enlightenment fashion, that insofar as the concern being served by a concept is a concern I identify with, the concept's power to govern my thought is compatible with my freedom of thought, because the external-seeming claims that the reasons disclosed by the concept make on me ultimately draw their force from something inside me. If the concerns being furthered by my use of a concept are exclusively concerns that I either fail to identify with or even deplore, my use of the concept works against me, and realizing this should shatter my confidence in that concept. The term 'ideological', in one of its uses, captures just this sense in which the use of a concept serves the concerns of one group at the expense of those of another group. To strengthen my confidence in a

---

[27] See Williams (1981e, 13).

concept, the concerns I trace it to need to be concerns I acknowledge as authoritative—concerns that, in this sense, I identify with.

However, there are concerns I identify with *more deeply* than others, and how closely I identify with a concern might change over time. At the limit, my identification with a particular concern might last only for the duration of a particular project, in which case the concept I have most reason to use in relation to this concern will also only be authoritative for me as I pursue that project. One's identification with a concern is also responsive to changes in one's sense of what is possible, as well as to demands from others to declare what one cares about. The maelstrom of our inchoate wishes arguably only settles into fully formed concerns in response to social pressures, such as the demands that others make on us to present ourselves one way or another, and to take a stand on controversial issues.[28]

But one's deepest and most enduring concerns will be what Williams calls 'propelling concerns' or 'ground projects', which is to say concerns that propel one to live. These propelling concerns, he observes, 'do not have to be even very evident to consciousness, let alone grand or large...the propelling concerns may be of a relatively everyday kind such as certainly provide the ground of many sorts of happiness' (1981e, 12). Yet they are concerns that we identify with in the most demanding sense: they are constitutive of our identity. This hierarchy between our concerns is something that an appraisal of concepts by how they tie in with our concerns should be sensitive to. Reasons to live by certain concepts, even if they appeal to concerns we fleetingly identify with, had better not go against the concerns that give us reasons to live at all. At the same time, our propelling concerns are likely to leave vastly underdetermined what conceptual repertoire would serve us best, and will require supplementation by concerns that are less fundamental to who we are.

A danger made evident by this dynamic and social picture of our concerns is that the concerns one *actually* identifies with may be defective, and not yet form the right basis on which to answer the authority question. What about concerns I identify with only out of ignorance, and would abandon if better informed? What about concerns I would come to reject as wrongheaded if I took a critical look at them in light of my deeper concerns? And what about concerns I have been manipulated into forming, and would give up if I came to understand how I came by them? After all, concerns may themselves be the products of uncritical exposure to tireless indoctrination, propaganda, and censorship.

---

[28] See Williams (2002, 191–8), Fricker (2007, 52–3), and Pettit (forthcoming).

We thus need to distinguish between, on the one hand, the concepts we have most reason to use given the concerns we *actually* identify with, and, on the other hand, the concepts we have most reason to use given the concerns we *would* identify with if we were better informed and more critically reflective. Being able to see what concepts best serve one's unreconstructed concerns is already something. But to identify the concepts that are truly authoritative for one, one needs to rule out:

(a) concerns that merely reflect a lack of information or easily corrected misapprehensions;
(b) concerns one would recognize as objectionable if one subjected them to critical evaluation expressive of the rest of one's concerns;
(c) concerns one would become alienated from the instant one realized how one came by them (if it emerged that one had been manipulated into forming them against one's own interests, for instance).

To get beyond the concerns we actually identify with, we might say that the concerns we should look to in answering the authority question should be concerns we identify with *and would still endorse after well-informed reflection on the merits of those concerns and on how we came by them*. Again, it matters that the picture of our identification with concerns should be dynamic and social. Even once settled, a concern remains responsive to critical reflection: it can be unsettled again, called into question by new information, or the prodding of others, or by the perception of an uncomfortable tension between that concern and the rest of what one cares about. Ideally, such critical reflection would draw on all the relevant empirical information, subject individual concerns to careful scrutiny guided by the whole stock of one's evaluative resources, and ascertain that understanding how once came by these concerns need not alienate one from them. For the sake of brevity, I shall sometimes refer to this idealizing condition simply by saying that the concerns should be ones we *critically* identify with.

It is of course tempting to go further than that, and reach for some more independent criterion by which to ratify a set of objectively good concerns that any rational person has reason to identify with. In stopping at individual concept-users' considered view of what their own deepest concerns are, the present account resists this intellectual temptation. This is motivated by three ideas. First, the point of appraising concepts according to whether they tie in with our concerns is that the concerns are *our* concerns, and while the contingent influences reflected in that fact need to be checked by critical reflection to some extent, they nevertheless are, at base, not so much distorting as *constructive of* our identity. Second, drawing the line between acceptable and unacceptable influences on concern-formation is not merely a technical matter, like sorting the wheat from the chaff, but irreducibly requires ethical and political judgement—in particular, the judgement of the people whose concerns are at issue.[29] And third, the relevant concerns should be recognizable *as* relevant concerns *to* the people whose concerns they are supposed to be.

This last qualification draws attention to the risk that concern ascriptions may be offered in bad faith, casting the situation in tendentious terms. At a theoretical level, we can alert to, and defend against, that risk by making *the people whose concerns are at issue* the ultimate arbiters of what concerns they really identify with.[30] This is something the present account aims to do by offering conclusions taking a conditional form: it does not assert of a pre-specified set of people that they have certain concerns and should therefore use certain concepts; rather, it suggests that *if and to the extent that* readers identify with certain concerns, they have reason to use certain concepts. But this leaves it open who in fact identifies with the relevant concern, and leaves it up to the reader to decide whether they recognize themselves in that description.

In stopping at individual concept-users' considered view of what their own deepest concerns are, the present account expresses a commitment to the sovereignty and autonomy of human beings, offering a more human-centred way of thinking about conceptual authority than any of the conceptions we have encountered thus far.[31] Without supplementation by people's own judgement as to what concerns they critically identify with, the account would significantly underdetermine how they should think. But that is as it should be. The account does not aspire to tell people how to think in the sense of foisting concepts upon them. Rather, it aims to assist their own reflection on which concepts to use by offering insights such as that *whoever* critically identifies with a certain concern has a *pro tanto* reason to use a certain concept. If

---

[29] For different attempts to draw such a distinction, see Dworkin (1989), Mills (1995), Noggle (1996), Baron (2003), Greenspan (2003), Buss (2005), Williams (2006m), and Sunstein (2016). For comprehensive overviews of the relevant difficulties, see Noggle (2022) and the essays in Coons and Weber (2014).

[30] Even if, in practice, no general defensive clause can definitively fend off abuse by itself, because any such clause will itself require interpretation in its application to the particular situation, and thereby lay itself open to abuse in turn—just as the manipulation of people can extend to the level of their dispositions to recognize concerns as truly their own.

[31] See also Fricker (2020a).

concerns survive critical scrutiny, they can properly provide a source of authority for our concepts, even if these concerns cannot be shown to be in some ultimate sense the correct ones. To echo a line of Williams's, the point is not that the concerns should be in some ultimate sense correct, but that they should be *ours*.[32]

This marks a significant reorientation of the traditional quest for truthful concepts. Instead of focusing exclusively on truthfulness as correspondence to a pre-structured world, we also consider truthfulness as *authenticity*. The person who finds herself in the odd position of living by concepts she has no confidence in, and is reduced to making only disengaged use even of her own concepts, is to that extent suffering from a kind of alienation and inauthenticity; conversely, there is a kind of authenticity that consists in living by concepts one can wholeheartedly identify with. Some ways of thinking are, as it were, *really you*. This implies that there is a dimension of *self-expression* to concept use: in using certain concepts rather than others, one shows others which concepts feel alive to one, which reasons have force with one and engage one's emotions, and thereby expresses something of who one is.

That demand for conceptual authenticity applies as much to philosophy as to quotidian thought. This comes out in a remark Williams made to Bryan Magee in a televised discussion recorded in the winter of 1970–1:

> It seems to me that moral philosophy has got to have authenticity in this sense, that the concepts which anybody is pursuing have got to be concepts which are alive to him. He may be a success as a historical anthropologist, looking at the views of the Greeks, or something. That is an important and helpful activity. But onward-going moral philosophy must grow from concepts you yourself believe in. It's got to be in that sense a self-examination: examination of the concepts which you yourself find important for understanding individual life and society. Now of course those concepts will be concepts which as a social person the philosopher shares with many others. And so he will be examining the coherences and incoherences in a way of looking at the world which is both something common and also individual—in this sense, that it is something which he himself is committed to. (Williams 1971, 161)

While the discussion focused on moral philosophy, the point goes wider. If forward-looking, practical, or normative philosophy, of whatever kind, is to

---

[32] See Williams (1985, 113–14).

grow from concepts we can reasonably be confident in, philosophy needs to engage in conceptual ethics, separating the concepts we use merely out of habit from the concepts that are *authentically* ours: 'ours' not merely in the sense that they are *possessed* by us, but in the more demanding sense that they *express* something of who we are. And *what it means* for our concepts to express something of who we are is for them to serve concerns we are critically identified with. This is the first lesson we can draw from the Dworkin–Williams debate.

The second lesson we can draw from the Dworkin–Williams debate is that whatever concerns concept-users identify with cannot be eliminated or redirected at the drop of a definition. This locates an important source of obstance or recalcitrance faced by attempts to improve our conceptual apparatus through innovation, redefinition, or stipulation: the difficulty is not just that of securing the uptake of newly minted concepts; it is that the underlying concerns cannot be redirected by fiat.

This is not to say that our concerns are insensitive to the concepts we use; the human concern for beauty will be given a different direction and expression if focused by the concepts of Babylonian painters than if focused by those of *Der Blaue Reiter*; as Wittgenstein observed, concepts simultaneously express and direct our interests.[33]

But when the tension between two concepts is reflected in a corresponding tension between two concerns, engineering away the tension at a conceptual level will do even less to attenuate the tension at the level of our concerns than painting over a crack does to close the crack. It will merely leave people worse off by rendering them conceptually ill-equipped to recognize at what price these concerns are being pursued. Real costs can be incurred even when one is conceptually blind to them. Without a corresponding redirection of concerns, revising which concepts we use cannot create more than an illusion of harmony. The tension needs remedying not at the level of the offending concepts, but at the level of our concerns and social arrangements.

The third lesson, finally, which falls out of the former two, is that if some proposed concept realizes theoretical virtues at the cost of severing its ties to more pressing concerns, it will not be an improvement. Eliminating tensions and cultivating theoretical virtues in our concepts is thus not necessarily a good thing. Conflicting concepts may well be preferable if they serve our conflicting concerns better. As the example of the concept *person* in the previous chapter brought out, it is our concerns as mediated by our

---

[33] Wittgenstein (2009, §570).

conceptual repertoire as it is before the engineer's intervention that a proposed concept must make contact with in order to have a claim to authority. When these antecedent concerns are themselves primarily directed at the achievement of theoretical virtues such as precision, consistency, or coherence, the concepts selected for their precision, consistency, or coherence can be authoritative. But in contexts in which we are not primarily concerned to realize these theoretical virtues, concepts that are free of generic theoretical defects such as vagueness or inconsistency will carry *less* authority than the concepts they are meant to replace. Theoretical vices can be practical virtues.

Let me elaborate on this third lesson, as it is crucial to motivating the departure from the more orthodox form of non-foundationalism that seeks authority in theoretical virtues.

6.3 The Practical Virtues of Theoretical Vices

To think that more theoretically virtuous concepts must be more authoritative than concepts exhibiting theoretical vices is to model concept appraisal on theory appraisal: in a scientific theory, it is a defect in our concepts if they conflict, and the defect is to be fixed by adjusting which concepts we use. Likewise, in formulating a system of linguistic rules to explain and predict competent speakers' intuitions about which sentences of a language are well-formed, consistency is a constitutive aim: it makes sense to expect the theory to rework the various intuitions it takes as input into a consistent body of rules that can be used to adjudicate between inconsistent intuitions, so that one ends up adjusting conflicting intuitions to make them fit the theory as much as adjusting the theory to make it fit the intuitions.

But a person torn between the claims of competing values is not like a drunk polyglot mashing together two languages. While consistency is a constitutive aim in formulating a system of linguistic rules, inquiry into whether concepts and their concomitant reasons have a foot in real concerns may find reasons for reasons on both sides of a conceptual conflict. This will *affirm* rather than attenuate the conflict, giving us reasons to sustain it and work through it.

Accordingly, while the drunk polyglot merely has to discipline himself into sticking to one of several mutually exclusive sets of linguistic rules, the person experiencing a conflict of values may have good reason to ride out the tension. She may look for ways to absorb or accommodate the tension, but only to the extent that these allow her to remain responsive to both of the concerns that give rise to the tension.

In the case of the thick normative concepts articulating moral or political judgements, it is thus much less clear that a tension between two concepts is necessarily a defect at all: tensions between concepts can express real tensions between the things we care about, and when this is the case, we may prefer our concepts to mirror these tensions. A lack of consistency does not necessarily imply a lack of conceptual authority, just as consistency does not by itself guarantee conceptual authority. In fact, as we shall see in more detail in Chapter 10, if Williams is right in his critique of Dworkin, rendering our conceptions of liberty and equality consistent—in the specific sense of rendering them congruent—actually constitutes a deterioration rather than an amelioration, because it blinds concept-users to a real conflict between their concerns. Insofar as we would be ill-served by conceptions that blinded us to this real conflict, we therefore have reason not to adopt the conceptions immunized against conflict that Dworkin advocates. They would put us out of touch with our concerns and the conflicts between them. Our conceptions of liberty and equality *should* conflict, because our concerns do.

This suggests that theoretical virtue is not necessarily something we should strive for across our conceptual repertoire. There are conceptual virtues beyond theoretical virtues. We should look to the concerns underlying our use of concepts before we look to the defects inherent in concepts. And we should understand what counts as a defect in relation to those concerns. Where our concerns conflict, the correspondingly conflictual character of our concepts will be a form of truthfulness—a way of being true to the real and conflicting directions of our concerns.

To insist that our moral and political concepts should be subjected to precisely the same kinds of demands for theoretical virtues that we make on the concepts from which we build our scientific theories is then not necessarily to render our thinking in some incontestable sense more rational. It might instead amount to adopting a radically revisionary and highly contentious stance in conceptual ethics: for insofar as the moral and political concepts we have conflict *for good reason* rather than for lack of trying to move towards more congruent concepts, imposing the requirements we make on theories on the concepts articulating our moral and political outlook is tantamount to advocating a radical reconfiguration of that outlook, and hardly one that is incontestably more rational.[34]

---

[34] This is to apply to conceptual ethics a point made in Williams (2006h, 162–4).

The upshot is that when concepts conflict, we need to understand *why* we have conflicting concepts. If the conceptual tension is the result of committing an intellectual error within an enterprise aiming at systematic unity, the conflict should indeed be rationalized away in the name of consistency, coherence, or congruence. If, however, the conceptual tension is rooted in an underlying conflict between concerns we critically identify with, a more complex response is called for. A judgement is required on what kind of balance to strike between the relevant concerns. This does not imply that there must be a single currency in terms of which the concerns can be directly compared. We can consider which concern we attach the most weight to even when facing a conflict between incommensurable concerns.

What can inform and guide that judgement is a deeper understanding of where the concerns come from and how they came to conflict: what are the historical, social, and psychological dynamics that produced this conflict? The conflict might be the result of having accumulated, within one society, the legacies of different historical periods or the influences of different societies; or it might reflect changes in external circumstances which now bring into tension with each other concerns that used to coexist without conflict; or, as in the case of *liberty* and *equality*, it might be grounded in enduring features of human psychology that make it well-nigh impossible to envision a human society in which conflicts along these lines never arose. In some cases, understanding what produces a tension between two concepts may lead one to withdraw one's confidence from one of the concepts involved, thereby eliminating the tension. But in other cases, such understanding will only affirm the tension by showing that the conflicting concepts each have a foot in legitimate concerns that decidedly pull in different directions. There are ways of rationalizing conceptual conflicts without rationalizing them away.

None of this is to deny that, in a concrete situation in which two of our value concepts conflict, we should reduce the tension between them as far as we can. But this will be conflict-reduction on a piecemeal basis, where we attempt to find a rational resolution to conflicts *when they arise* instead of trying to forestall their arising to begin with by immunizing our conceptual apparatus against conflict.

The fact that a conceptual apparatus persistently gives rise to tensions and value conflicts need not even be seen as something to be regretted: it can be seen as a strength, not just of the person who manages to live with the tensions, but of the conceptual apparatus itself. Its tensions can be an expression of the scale and scope of its aspirations, of its richness and diversity, and of its sophisticated capacity to discern value along multiple dimensions and in different things at the same time.

Moving towards a different set of concepts comprising fewer, less diverse, and less demanding values would reduce conceptual tensions, and, circumstances concurring, it might permit the joint realization of those values without loss. But this does not mean that there would be no loss. Yes, life would *seem* easier for those living by an outlook that had been immunized against conflict. But to immunize our conceptual apparatus against conflict would be to ignore the force of conflicting concerns that are really there. In order for these concerns to be adequately acknowledged in our deliberations, the tensions between those concerns must be reflected in the tensions between our concepts. Resisting the demand to tidy up our conceptual apparatus then expresses a determination to truthfully confront the conflicting demands we face, and the real losses incurred by satisfying one demand at the expense of another, instead of escaping into comforting fantasy.

Of course, this might be taken to encourage going further in the elimination of tensions by eliminating not just the conflicting concepts, but the conflicting concerns. One could in principle abandon the ethical, political, or aesthetic concerns that produce the tensions and the resulting sense of loss in the first place.

From the perspective of a tension-ridden outlook, however, the transcendence of conflict made possible by such a transition to tension-free concerns would still involve a significant loss: peace of mind would be bought at the price of indifference, requiring withdrawal from the world into the kind of apathic aloofness that experiences no loss only because it does not care sufficiently about enough things. The pursuit of the perfectly tension-free life thus risks issuing in something which, while tension-free, is rather less of a life. Those fully identified with the tension-free concerns may not share that sense of loss. But this merely means that the loss would include the loss of the sense of loss—which only makes it more of a loss.[35]

Thus, understanding why concepts conflict does not necessarily dissolve the conflict between them, or tell us which concept to prioritize. But it can help us to grasp the place and urgency of the aspiration to achieve theoretical virtues such as consistency, coherence, and congruence. The pursuit of theoretical virtues has a place, and is sometimes of the first importance—but not

---

[35] For germane remarks on the idea that conflicts of values cannot be transcended without loss of the sense of loss, see Williams (1981a, 80) as well as Williams (1973c, 177; 2001a); for a sustained discussion of 'concept loss' and the loss of the capacity to recognize concept loss, see Diamond (1988).

every kind of concept obeys the same constraints, and some concerns are better served by concepts that are less consistent, coherent, or congruent.

These qualifications also hold for other theoretical virtues.[36] Vaguer concepts, for example, are not necessarily worse concepts, though philosophers' tidy-mindedness can make it hard to recognize that fact. Frege even questioned whether concepts with blurred boundaries were *bona fide* concepts at all: comparing concepts to areas, he argued that since an area without clear boundaries is not really an area, concepts without sharp boundaries are not *bona fide* concepts. Yet this betrays a picture on which concept use ought in no way to rely on normality, i.e. on contingent but nonetheless typically reliable regularities in how human beings and the world are disposed to behave.[37] As Wittgenstein observed in response to Frege, we often identify areas without drawing clear boundaries, merely indicating them through pointing gestures.[38] Similarly, concepts without clear boundaries can be *bona fide* concepts. To deny this, Wittgenstein remarked, would 'be like saying that the light of my reading lamp is no real light at all because it has no sharp boundary' (1958, 27).

Indeed, a vaguer concept will sometimes serve our concerns better than a more precise one. When Orwell deplored the 'sheer cloudy vagueness' of political language, his complaint was an epistemic one: that vagueness is obfuscatory, clouding our grasp of the facts on the ground and thereby our political judgement.[39] But under certain conditions, the same epistemic concern for accuracy can call for vaguer concepts: vagueness, especially within large institutional structures, can stand in the service of accuracy when its point is to acknowledge that others, because they have a better grasp of the facts on the ground, are epistemically better placed than we are to determine what exactly should or should not fall under a concept.

For example, it is not unheard of for legislators to intentionally blur a conception that had proved to be *too precise*: the US Congress once found that its Social Services Administration disability program was better served by a conception of disability that was vaguer than the one previously in use, because this vagueness was precisely what gave low-ranking administrators, who were best placed to determine what should or should not fall under the concept,

---

[36] In a detailed case study of the concept of divorce, for example, Elizabeth Anderson argues that a *less* fruitful conception of divorce can be preferable to a more fruitful conception for the purposes of a certain research programme (2004, 20). On the merits of less determinate concepts for social critique and political movements, see also Santarelli (2024).
[37] This is what Warren Goldfarb calls the 'demand for fixity', which Frege shared with the early Wittgenstein, and which Goldfarb thinks expresses 'an incorrect picture of rationality' (1997, 79).
[38] See Wittgenstein (2009, §71).   [39] See Orwell (2008).

the discretion they needed to do justice to cases that the sharper definition categorically excluded.[40]

Vague concepts can thus be exactly what we need given our concerns. In recent years, a number of legal philosophers, computational linguists, and game theorists have extolled 'the value of vagueness' across a wide variety of cases.[41] As David Lanius (2021) concludes after a comprehensive survey of that literature, these arguments typically do not show that vagueness is itself inherently valuable. But the value of a vague concept need not be the value of vagueness; its value can lie, rather, in the value of using a concept that better serves one's concerns *in virtue of* being vague.[42]

It is also helpful to remember that vague concepts can achieve their own form of orderliness through *coordinated* vagueness. David Lewis points out that one vague concept can neatly interlock with another vague concept that is vague in an exactly complementary way:

> It often happens that two vague concepts are vague in a coordinated way: firmly connected to each other, if to nothing else. The border between blue and green is not well fixed, so 'blue' and 'green' are both vague. But their relation to each other is fixed: one begins where the other leaves off, with no gap and no overlap. (1973, 92)

Before chastising a concept for its vagueness, therefore, it is worth looking at whether it redeems itself by coordinating its vagueness with that of complementary concepts.

Vagueness or indeterminacy can also prove to be conceptual virtues when it comes to building broad coalitions around what is perceived as a common grievance. Precise definitions and fully determinate implications often stand in the way of political success by making it harder to conceptualize a grievance as common.

Some, like Herbert Marcuse, even went so far as to argue that vague or indeterminate concepts were the better tools for radical critiques of the social

---

[40] See Mashaw (1983, 52–3) and Zacka (2017, 53–5).

[41] Schauer (1987), Endicott (2000), Soames (2011), Hart (2012, 124–36), Asgeirsson (2015, 2020), Lanius (2019), and Chadha-Sridhar (2021) defend the value of vagueness in the law; game-theoretic rationales for vagueness are identified by De Jaegher (2003), van Deemter (2010), and De Jaegher and van Rooij (2011); on the experimental evidence for the value of vagueness, see Green and van Deemter (2019). On the value of definitions that do justice to borderline cases through their vagueness, see Sorensen (1991).

[42] As Jorem and Löhr also note, 'indeterminacy is not always a problem. But then we need something to explain the difference between the cases where it is a problem and the cases where it is not' (2024, 939). I take myself to offer precisely such an account.

order.⁴³ In addition to making it easier to rally around common grievances, vague and indeterminate concepts without clear referents can also be those that are most expressive of a particularly deep malaise and a truly radical dissatisfaction with social arrangements. This subversive moment threatens to be lost when the grievances articulated in vague and sweeping terms are reconceptualized in precise and narrowly focused terms that target concrete failures in the operation of the system while taking the system itself for granted.

By way of illustration, Marcuse offers the complaints of workers at the Hawthorne Works of the Western Electric Company, where the workers' vaguely articulated protests were recast by industrial sociologists, who sought to make their complaints less vague and indeterminate by transposing them into precise descriptions of concrete episodes. Thus, a complaint about dangerous and unsanitary working conditions would be transposed into a complaint about a certain occasion on which the washbowl had some dirt in it. As a result, what began as a collective complaint, inchoately but radically calling into question the system as a whole, was transformed into a loose collection of defanged complaints, individualized and particularized until they each separately aimed at making the system run more effectively instead of calling it into question with one voice. When theoretical virtues are pursued in this way, they risk resulting in what Marcuse calls a 'repressive reduction of thought' (2002, 111).

Though one might quibble with the details of Marcuse's analysis, it points to a real worry: re-engineering thought for theoretical virtues may end up assimilating it into the existing social order in a way that takes the sting off, and then, *pace* Orwell, the theoretical virtue of clarity will have become a political vice.⁴⁴ This worry is amplified by the fact that, as Alexander Prescott-Couch notes, the intermediary actors who tidy up vague and inchoate complaints 'tend to be social elites, and engaging with inchoate speech through their filter might threaten to overwrite or sanitize inchoate voices, particularly those from marginalized communities' (2021, 497–8). There is thus a danger that if interpretative intermediaries rearticulate vaguely articulated concerns to maximize theoretical virtues, their reconstruction will realize those virtues at the cost of losing any real connection to the original concerns.⁴⁵

---

⁴³ See Marcuse (2002, 110–23). Another example is Djordjevic (2021), who argues that engineering for clarity and consistency conflicts with the empirical adequacy of work in anthropology.
⁴⁴ See Orwell (2008). For a nuanced re-evaluation of the risks and benefits of combating unclear language in politics, see Gibbons (2023).
⁴⁵ Although, as Prescott-Couch (2021, 508–16) goes on to argue, not all forms of rational reconstruction by such intermediaries are bound to lose the connection to the original concerns: well-designed ways of dividing the interpretative labour could in principle rearticulate inchoate concerns

In politics, the most helpful conceptualizations are often those that can be shared across multiple perspectives precisely because they are vague and indeterminate in their consequences. This holds not only for building up cooperation and unity, but also for avoiding escalation and conflict. Many a fragile peace depends on the conceptual ability to fudge the most incendiary issues. In politics, clarity can be a dangerous thing.

Isolating concepts from the particular concerns with which they tie in and concentrating on the inherent defects of concepts—or what appear to be defects when measured against some ideal of theoretical virtue—thus embodies a strategy that may answer the authority question in special cases, but that cannot hope to do so more widely. Life is not a logic test. The most theoretically virtuous concepts are no good to us if they do not serve the central concerns that animated our use of anything like these concepts to begin with.

By treating the respects in which concepts fall short of theoretical virtues as defects, we run the risk of neglecting defects arising from the way in which theoretically virtuous concepts fail to serve the concerns of concept-users. To comprehensively assess the authority of our concepts, and to give direction to interventions in our conceptual apparatus while ensuring that their results are authoritative, we need to look beyond theoretical virtues, to how concepts tie in with the concerns of those who use them. These concerns are not always, or even mainly, concerns for theoretical virtue. In relation to the rest of our concerns, even theoretical vices might prove to be practical virtues.

6.4 The Limits of Concerns: Four Problems

Though the Dworkin–Williams debate uniquely combines Dworkin's challenge and his tidy-minded solution with Williams's suggestion that human concepts should be answerable to human concerns, that suggestion is of course not unique to Williams. Several philosophers thinking about concept appraisal have recently floated the related, if somewhat narrower idea that concepts should be evaluated by the lights of our aims or goals.[46] We can

---

so as to facilitate a deliberative partnership that is respectful of the original concerns while also rendering them more suitable for inclusion in high-quality public deliberation—for, as Prescott-Couch rightly highlights, it is the demands of high-quality public deliberation that invite a rearticulation of the vague in the first place (a point I return to in Chapter 10).

[46] See e.g. Anderson (1995, 2001), Brigandt (2006, 2010), Haslanger (2012), Burgess and Plunkett (2013b, 1105), Brigandt and Rosario (2020), Pinder (2022), and Nado (2023b).

think of these aims or goals as specific types of concerns: those that concept-users consciously pursue in using a concept.

Whether on the basis of concerns, aims, or goals, however, few have elaborated how such concept appraisal is to be concretely operationalized and put into practice. This is not altogether surprising. For once one does try to operationalize it, real difficulties emerge for attempts to appraise concepts directly by our aims, goals, or concerns.

One difficulty lies in moving from a given concept to the concern or goal that is supposed to help us appraise it. How do we identify the relevant concern? Part of the difficulty is that concerns are not only many and various, but often at variance, and not every concern merits satisfaction. But even before one wades into the politics of conflicting concerns, there is a more basic problem involved in identifying a *relevant* concern to begin with: how does one move from a concept to a concern by which to appraise it? Call this the *concern identification problem*.

Some have argued that the concern identification problem can be overcome by looking for concepts that are inherently tied to a concern. Ingo Brigandt and Esther Rosario, for example, argue that certain scientific concepts have inbuilt epistemic aims:[47]

> there are cases where a scientific aim can be tied to an individual concept in that this concept is being used by scientists to pursue this aim. For example, while the CLASSICAL GENE concept was used for the purpose of predicting (and statistically explaining) phenotypic patterns of inheritance across generations, the MOLECULAR GENE concept serves the aim of causal-mechanistically explaining how inside a cell a gene leads to the formation of its molecular product. Making explicit such an aim tied to a concept's use permits one to account philosophically for the rationality of concept change: a revised definition is an improvement over an earlier definition if the former is empirically more conducive to meeting this aim. (2020, 102)

The idea is 'to view a concept as being used by scientists to pursue a *specific scientific aim*', for it is this aim, which Brigandt (2010) also calls the 'epistemic goal' of a concept, that 'sets the standards for whether one definition of a concept is superior to another definition' (Brigandt and Rosario 2020, 102).

---

[47] See also Brigandt (2010, 2011, 2012). Brigandt and Rosario (2020) explore how such goal-based appraisal might be extended to socio-political aims. But exactly how one identifies such aims and their relation to the concept at issue does not become as clear as it does in the epistemic case. I therefore concentrate on the epistemic case.

According to this goal-based approach, a concept such as the *classical gene* concept has an epistemic goal insofar as it is used *with a view to* predicting and explaining inheritance patterns. Insofar as the concept's reference and inferential role are not optimally suited to meeting this goal, however, one can distinguish between the inferences a concept *in fact* supports and those it is *intended* to support: while 'a concept's inferential role is the set of inferences and explanations currently supported by the concept', Brigandt writes, 'the concept's epistemic goal is the kinds of inferences and explanations that the concept is intended to support' (2010, 24).

On this goal-based approach, 'the notion of the epistemic goal pursued by a concept's use is...considered a component of a concept' (Brigandt 2010, 22). The idea is thus not that the *classical gene* concept just happened to be harnessed to pursue a certain epistemic goal while the same concept might have been recruited to different ends; rather, as Alejandro Pérez Carballo helpfully puts it, the epistemic goal is regarded as being *constitutive* of the concept: 'a concept that is not put to use for the purposes of predicting inheritance patterns would not *be* the classical gene concept' (Pérez Carballo 2020, 305). On this view, the relation of a concept to the concern providing the standard for its appraisal is an *internal* relation: a relation that is intrinsic to the identity of at least one of the *relata*—in this case, the *classical gene* concept.

If we identify the *classical gene* concept as the concept that was intended by its originators to support inferences explaining and predicting patterns of inheritance, therefore, the concept can be appraised according to the extent to which it allows its users to draw adequate explanatory and predictive inferences—something scientists became increasingly good at doing as they moved from the *classical gene* concept of William Bateson, which still assumed a one-to-one correspondence between genes and traits, to the *classical gene* concept of T. H. Morgan, which allowed for one gene to affect many traits and one trait to be affected by many genes.[48] Taking a concept's epistemic goal as a standard of appraisal thus promises to make sense of conceptual amelioration in the context of scientific theory-building. Moreover, it allows us to tailor the standard of appraisal to the concept at issue, alerting us to case-specific desiderata that would have been obscured by uniformly applicable desiderata such as avoiding reference failure or inferential unreliability.

But there are two reasons why, in appraising concepts, one might want to look beyond such inbuilt goals. First, it is not clear that this approach can be

[48] See Weber (2005, 195–6) and Darden (2006, 235–6).

generalized, as many concepts do not come with a clear constitutive goal that could guide our appraisal of them. As Brigandt himself admits: 'specific epistemic goals that are particular to a concept may exist only for scientifically central concepts' (2012, 99). There is therefore a *generalizability problem*.

Second, this kind of appraisal remains too internal to the concept and does not allow for enough critical distance. To appraise a concept by its constitutive goal is still to appraise it by its own lights rather than from a more independent perspective. It does not allow one to criticize a concept when that concept is ideally suited to meeting its constitutive goal.

Yet the ability to criticize a concept even when it meets its constitutive goal is clearly a crucial desideratum for an account of concept appraisal. Without it, we would be hard-pressed to make sense of paradigm shifts in science or ideology critique in social thought. When the concepts in question are the mainstays of the old paradigm one seeks to break out of, or when they are ideological concepts promulgated with a view to stabilizing oppressive regimes, taking concepts' constitutive goals as one's basis of appraisal points one in precisely the wrong direction, since the last thing one wants to do is to tailor one's concepts even more closely to those goals. In those cases, a more external basis of appraisal is required, one that makes it possible for concept-users to conclude that even a concept which is optimally designed to meet its constitutive goal is at odds with their own concerns—it is purpose-built to the wrong purpose. To this end, it is crucial that we do not always simply buy into the standards encoded in concepts' constitutive goals. In addition to the generalizability problem, relying on built-in concerns thus creates a *critical distance problem*.

One might hope to address these two problems by detaching the standard of concept appraisal from the concept itself, seeking it instead in concerns that are *externally* rather than internally related to concepts. But this reintroduces the identification problem that the focus on constitutive goals was meant to solve, namely the problem of how to work back from a concept to a concern that is relevant to its appraisal.

Even if a relevant concern can be identified, moreover, the concern by itself leaves the concept it calls for underdetermined. Two concept-users with the same concern will be in completely different practical situations if one has useful capacities to draw on—such as the capacity to hear high-pitched sounds or detect subtle smells—that the other lacks; equally, they will be in different practical situations if one is in a congenial environment that abounds with whatever one could wish for while the other is in an arid and hostile environment. By itself, a concern is therefore insufficient to determine what concept we should use: a concern alone does not yet provide a guiding sense of what makes a good concept in relation to that concern, because it fails to give us a sufficiently determinate understanding of the dynamics that *mediate* between the concern and the concept. To understand these dynamics, we need to understand the practical pressures acting on our conceptualization as a result of pursuing that concern with certain capacities in a certain circumstances. It is in the crucible of these pressures that a concept must prove its worth as a means of meeting the concern. In sum: until we can fill in the mediating practical dynamics, we face an *underdetermination problem*: the underdetermination of the concepts by the relevant concerns.

The general idea that our concepts should be answerable to our concerns thus leaves a great deal of work to be done before it can itself be put to work. We need to identify the relevant concerns for given concepts, and something needs to mediate between those concerns and the concepts they call for so as to give the required concepts sufficiently determinate contours. What is more, all this needs to be achieved in a way that allows for generalizability and critical distance.

To make headway and identify the missing link connecting concepts and concerns, I propose to substitute the question: 'What do we aim to do in using this concept?' with a different question: 'What is the concept we need here?'

This points us towards a *needs-based* approach to concept appraisal that can overcome all four problems we considered: the concern identification problem, the generalizability problem, the critical distance problem, and the underdetermination problem. For it is our needs for certain concepts that constitute the missing link between concepts and concerns, and it is those needs that our conceptualizations are, in the first instance, answerable to—or so I shall argue in the next chapter.

The Ethics of Conceptualization: Tailoring Thought and Language to Need. Matthieu Queloz, Oxford University Press.
© Matthieu Queloz 2025. DOI: 10.1093/9780198926283.003.0007

7
Conceptual Needs

7.1 The Needs behind Concepts

'If I have one advantage', Nietzsche wrote, 'it is a keener vision for that hardest and trickiest form of *backward inference*...from every way of thinking and valuing to the commanding *need* behind it' (2005a, 'Antipodes'). Nietzsche was right to see needs behind concepts. It is our *conceptual needs*—our needs *for* certain concepts—that form the conduits between our concepts and concerns.[1] If we manage to gain a sense of what the needs behind our ways of thinking and valuing are, we can appraise concepts according to how well they meet those needs, because our conceptualizations best serve our concerns by being *tailored to our needs* (*bedarfsgerecht*, as the pithy German word has it). This is the second load-bearing idea in our framework for concept appraisal.

My aim in this chapter is to introduce conceptual needs as the missing link that mediates between concepts and concerns and enables us to solve the four problems identified in the previous chapter. After clarifying the notion of a conceptual need, I show how, following Nietzsche, needs-based appraisal might take its cue from the expressive character of concepts insofar as these express the conditions that would render them needful. But these need-engendering conditions remain intractably complex, which is why I also introduce the notion of a *need matrix*—an incomplete but illuminating model of these conditions—to render them more tractable. By working through various ways in which needs-based appraisal can be put into practice, I then show how one can work back from a concept to its needfulness conditions by treating two variables in a need matrix as constants while solving for the third. Finally, I argue that needs-based appraisal draws attention to desiderata on conceptualization that are usually overlooked, and allows us to solve the four problems.

---

[1] The term 'conceptual need' is used in a similar sense by Kappel (2010, 72). Earlier uses of the term in philosophy notably include Moravcsik (1976, 337) and Buchler (1955, 118). Aside from its prominent role in Nietzsche (Queloz 2017a, 2019, 2023), a related notion might be thought to be implicit in the work of John Dewey, who models his theory of inquiry on the way biological organisms adjust to situations of 'need', 'tension', or 'disturbed equilibration' (1938, 6–7, 27–9); see Henne (2022, 10).

What does it mean for a concept to have 'a need behind it', as Nietzsche puts it? In proposing that we appraise our concepts by our needs, I do not mean to reduce the value of concepts to the contribution they make to satisfying a stratum of absolutely basic needs—the idea is not to ask what the concepts of transfinite set theory have ever done for our survival. Nor is the idea that concepts are the sort of thing one *simply* needs in the way that human beings simply need water or sleep. To understand what kinds of needs conceptual needs are, we must distinguish *inner* needs from *instrumental* needs.[2]

Inner needs can be physiological or psychological, but they are needs one has categorically, just in virtue of the kind of creature one is or has become (one can *acquire* inner needs). The physiological needs for air, water, and sleep, or the psychological needs for love, esteem, and company, are examples of inner needs. Some inner needs, such as the need for safety, straddle the physiological/psychological distinction. And some inner needs highlighted in the Maslowian 'hierarchy of needs', such as the need for self-actualization, are perhaps not so much ever-present features of the human condition as the distinctive inner needs of human beings with a certain cultural history. What all of these inner needs have in common, however, is that their ascription does not invite the question of what one needs something *for*—one simply needs it.[3]

Instrumental needs, by contrast, involve a weaker, but far more pervasive form of needing: needing something as a means to the realization of some ulterior end, or as a remedy to an inconvenience. In this sense, one might need an umbrella when caught in the rain; one might need glasses to drive; or one might need patience when dealing with someone. Unlike ascriptions of inner needs, ascriptions of instrumental needs make it appropriate to ask what one needs something *for* ('I need a top hat.'—'What for?'—'For the play.'). Instrumental needs are thus hypothetical rather than categorical: one has them *if* one is to realize some further end.

---

[2] This terminology combines Williams's (1985, 51) contrast between 'inner' and 'technological' needs with Wiggins's (2002, §6) contrast between 'categorical' and 'instrumental' needs. While Wiggins aims to elucidate how categorical needs make specially demanding claims on us, my focus lies on the class of instrumental needs characterized by the fact that what is needed, to whatever end, is a concept.

[3] This may reflect no more than the fact that these needs can be attributed without further explanation, because they are extremely widely shared human needs whose intelligibility we take for granted. To add that one needs water or air *to survive*, or that one needs love or company *to avoid serious psychological harm*, is not so much incoherent as uninformative. It may, however, help demystify inner needs; Wiggins (2002, 10), for example, suggests that inner needs can be demystifyingly understood as a special class of instrumental needs, namely those one has if one is to avoid serious harm.

The needs for certain concepts, i.e. conceptual needs, are needs of the latter, instrumental kind. Concepts are needed, when they are, only instrumentally, to perform some task, or to satisfy some prior need which may or may not be an inner need (not all instrumental needs have to be the products of inner needs—they can arise out of mere aims, desires, projects, and other kinds of human concern). To say that we need a certain concept, or that we need our conceptualizations to take a certain form, is therefore elliptical: we need it *if* we are to perform some task. Conceptual needs are plausibly described as a subclass of *technological* needs: they are needs for certain thinking tools or thinking techniques.

We often have but a very incomplete understanding of what the needs behind our concepts are. Unlike the goals we consciously pursue in introducing technical terms or adducing certain concepts, our conceptual needs first have to be discovered. The thing about needs is that they only make themselves felt when unsatisfied. As long as a conceptual need is being met, the needful concept just silently does its work, and nothing is felt to be lacking. It is only when the needful concept is not available that its lack becomes a salient feature of experience, and the need becomes a *felt* need.

The relevant sense of 'conceptual need' can be set out in terms of the following equivalence:

A set of concept-users S has a conceptual need for concept F
  if and only if
Concept F is to that extent needful for S
  if and only if
The use of concept F is especially conducive to the satisfaction of a concern C that S critically identifies with

In saying that concept F is *conducive to* concern-satisfaction, I mean that its use *systematically tends to lead to* concern-satisfaction, not that it invariably does so. In saying that it is *especially* conducive to concern-satisfaction, I mean that it is *more* conducive to it than alternative concepts, which is why the need is a need *for* concept F rather than for any of the alternatives. This comparative dimension is crucial to selecting between competing concepts or conceptions. S needs concept F *more* than concept F' if F is more conducive to concern-satisfaction than F'.

The fact that conceptual needs are a function of our concerns affects the character of the needs involved. A conceptual need can be escaped if the concern engendering it can be abandoned (which is not an empty condition;

there are things we cannot help but be concerned with). And the need will only be as important as the concern that gives rise to it. We can thus think of conceptual needs as varying in strength: the strength of a conceptual need varies with the weight or importance of the concern that engenders it. Accordingly, concepts F and G might both meet conceptual needs and be, to that extent, needful concepts; but our conceptual need for F might be stronger than our conceptual need for G because the concern underlying our need for F is weightier or more important.

Even when conceptual needs are strong needs, however, they still involve 'needing' only in a fairly weak sense, which is closer to the idea that certain concepts are particularly *helpful* than to the more demanding idea that certain concepts are absolutely *indispensable*. I welcome this implication, since, to my mind, the fundamental question is whether concepts *help us to live*. This also requires the notion of a conceptual need to be broadly applicable, because the range of ways in which concepts can help us to live is itself broad.

In both respects, this weak and broad conception of needs departs from the stronger and more narrowly focused conception of needs familiar from medical ethics and discussions of basic necessities in political philosophy. These traditional discussions have primarily been interested in what *we cannot live without*, and have emphasized how the observation that something is *needed* should take precedence in deliberation over the observation that something is wanted or desired.[4] The present account of what conceptual tools our minds need, by contrast, goes beyond the question of what we cannot live without, and embodies a broader preoccupation with what helps us to live; and instead of giving needs precedence over desires and other concerns, it treats conceptual needs as the children of our concerns. Both features reflect the fact that we are talking about instrumental rather than inner needs.

Some may feel that talk of 'needs' of any kind is out of place unless it implies indispensability. Indeed, there are theorists of need who have claimed that all needing implies necessity or indispensability.[5] Thus, Harry Frankfurt asserts: 'Nothing is needed except for the sake of an end for which it is indispensable' (1984, 2). When applied to conceptual needs, this suggests that if some concept F is needed for the satisfaction of some concern, it is *indispensable* to the satisfaction of that concern, and there is *no possible way* of satisfying this concern *without* drawing on F.

---

[4] See Frankfurt (1984), Wiggins and Dermen (1987), Wiggins (2002), Reader and Brock (2004), Reader (2007), Shaw (2023), and Colton (2023) all emphasize the special demandingness of claims of need. See Reader (2005) for an overview of the philosophy of need.

[5] See Frankfurt (1984) and Shaw (2023).

But this seems too strong and too narrow for the weak and broad notion of need involved in conceptual needs. The simplest way of deflecting Frankfurt's contention is accordingly to note that the notion of a conceptual need developed here is a technical one carrying no such implication of necessity or indispensability.

Nevertheless, it seems to me that the weaker and broader sense of needing involved in conceptual needs also has a basis in ordinary linguistic usage. We use phrases of the form 'I need x' quite liberally. There are basic necessities and truly indispensable resources, and then there are 'business needs', or even 'lifestyle needs'. We freely speak of needs even when the concern engendering the need is ill-advised or downright frivolous (someone might properly be said to need a match to light a cigarette, or to need more money to buy a fifth vintage car).

If it is to account for this variety of instrumental needs we routinely ascribe to people, a conception of needs that retains the implication of indispensability must substantially moderate the sense in which the object needed is indispensable, and this will correspondingly reduce the difference between these conceptions. This comes out clearly in Frankfurt's own example of a man 'who feels like completing a crossword puzzle and who is unable to do so without looking things up' (1984, 2). Given his concern to complete the puzzle, that man really does need a dictionary, Frankfurt affirms, because the dictionary is indispensable for him to complete the puzzle.[6] Yet this cannot plausibly be taken to mean that, necessarily, in *all* possible future scenarios in which the puzzle has been completed, it has been completed using the dictionary. As David Wiggins has pointed out, needs display a context-sensitivity that severely restricts the range of possible future scenarios in which the objects needed must figure for the need attributions to be true.[7] The evaluation of claims of the form 'It is necessary or indispensable, if *x* is to happen, that *y* happen' does not, even in principle, require one to consider *all* possible scenarios from the time and context of assertion onwards in order to verify that, in every scenario in which *x* happened, *y* happened also. It is only *certain* possible scenarios that count, namely those that appear *realistic* in this particular context of assertion. The puzzle *could* conceivably be completed without dictionary—just not by this man, given his capacities and the resources realistically available to him. His need is thus sensitive to his capacities and limitations, and to what means are realistically available to him under the circumstances. (The rather quaint character of the example helpfully

---

[6] See Frankfurt (1984, 2, 7–8).   [7] See Wiggins (2002, 12).

underscores this context-sensitivity, since few would even think of resorting to a dictionary in the age of search engines and language models.)

However, even this man needing a dictionary *could* complete the puzzle using some other means—if an unexpected visitor happened to drop by, for instance, who turned out to be conveniently knowledgeable. In such an event, our man could rightly declare: 'You are just what I need!' That would not falsify Frankfurt's observation that the man needed the dictionary before the unexpected visitor showed up. It is merely that this earlier assessment of the man's needs was sensitive to what means were realistically available to him under the circumstances at the time. That hapless visitor, being unexpected, did not yet figure in the assessment.

As Wiggins points out, moreover, need attributions are typically informed not just by a sense of what one can do and what is available to one, but also by a sense of what constitutes an *acceptable* means of satisfying one's concern.[8] Our man *could* complete the puzzle by calling up his sister whom he knows to have completed it already. But that would be cheating. Similarly, the child that tells its parents that it needs money to buy a new calculator has not overlooked the possibility of stealing one. In such cases, what is needed is not what is indispensable to realizing our ends in any imaginable future scenario; the objects of our needs are merely the most promising means that are left over once all the *unrealistic* and *unacceptable* options have been ruled out. The resulting notion of indispensability is so weak as to come close to being the flipside of mere helpfulness.

Consequently, someone who wanted to hold on to the idea that all needing implied necessity or indispensability *could* conceive of conceptual needs as follows: the use of concept F is conducive to the satisfaction of a concern C that S critically identifies with and that, given S's capacities, S could not satisfy without F under the circumstances *if and only if* it is necessary, things being what they are at time t, that if S is to satisfy concern C at time t'', S use concept F at time t'. To preserve compatibility with my technical notion of conceptual need, the clauses in this equivalence concerning what one 'could not do without' the concept, and the 'necessity' of using some concept to satisfy some concern, would just have to be read highly narrowly, as keyed to the handful of scenarios that are realistic and acceptable given how things present themselves in a certain context at the time of the need attribution.

Noting the context-sensitivity of indispensability claims also highlights that instrumental needs in general tend to vary greatly depending on context.

---

[8] See Wiggins (2002, 12–13).

By contrast, the needs I focus on—conceptual needs bearing on our choice of which concepts to adopt and adhere to across a range of future applications—tend to be far less variable. Concepts are not single-use instruments of concern satisfaction. We adopt concepts not the way we seize on the nearest sharpish object suitable to be abused as a letter opener, but rather the way we settle on a policy: we communally institute and settle on a stable, norm-governed pattern that we stick to across a range of applications.[9]

Just because of its stability and rigidity, concept use will, like adherence to a policy, involve trade-offs, drawbacks, and pitfalls. But its settled character is also what makes a concept shareable, teachable, and reliable. It enables a concept to be efficiently deployed, taken for granted, and relegated to the background as we focus on the object-level considerations it brings to our attention.

7.2 Needfulness Conditions

Thinking of conceptual needs as instrumental needs entails that they are not simply given in virtue of the kinds of creatures we are. Conceptual needs must themselves be understood as products of the characteristics of concept-users and their situation. One does not fully grasp an instrumental need unless one grasps what engenders it—what conditions render the concept needful to begin with.

This indicates the crucial idea that a given concept is only worth using if certain extraconceptual presuppositions are fulfilled. The concept itself need not make reference to these presuppositions. On the contrary, our concepts and the nuances and distinctions they reveal have a tendency to pull attention away from the factual background in which their own importance is ultimately rooted. Reflecting on how philosophy was practised in Oxford during his formative years, for example, Williams remarks:

> what we tended to do was to pick up some distinction or opposition, and go very carefully into it and into the various nuances that might be attached to it, and order them, or state them, without enough reflection on what background made this set of distinctions, rather than some other, interesting or important. (1982, 119)

---

[9] On the practical exigencies that underlie this feature of concepts where moral concepts are concerned, see Sinclair (2021, 98–100).

Only against the background of certain more or less contingent facts does a concept's role and value in human life become apparent, because it is that background which renders the concept needful and imbues it with a point.

Salient among the extraconceptual presuppositions forming this background is the condition that concept-users must pursue certain concerns which their use of certain concepts is conducive to satisfying. Significantly, these concerns encompass more than just the conscious aims or goals with a view to which concept-users employ concepts.

As highlighted by the problem of the underdetermination of concepts by concerns, however, the specification of conceptual needs requires more than just concerns. It also requires factoring in concept-users' capacities and limitations as well as their circumstances. Only then can we meaningfully speak of concept-users as having conceptual needs. What our conceptual needs are is not simply a function of our concerns, but also depends on what we can do and on how the world is, and more particularly on what circumstances demand of one who pursues that kind of concern with those capacities and limitations. These circumstances are not just a matter of what elements and natural laws we find in the universe we inhabit. They relevantly include our social as well as our natural environment—in some cases, even the highly specific circumstances that come with a particular institutional setting or a certain role, position, or context. As P. F. Strawson remarked, it does not go far enough to suggest that 'the best conceptual scheme, the best system of ideas, is the one that gets us around best. The question is: in what milieu?' (2011, 177).

But before we wade into how differences in conceptual needs can reflect different social milieus, let us enter at the shallow end, by considering a very simple-minded creature.[10] It has only one concern, which is to eat. It is immobile, but at least in principle has the physiological capacity to seize whatever suitable prey immediately presents itself, although the effort involved costs precious energy. And its circumstances are such that suitable prey is far from abundant, and only rarely comes sufficiently close.

This triad of concerns, capacities, and circumstances already suffices to create an instrumental need in our simple-minded creature: it needs a bundle of dispositions that are reliably and differentially responsive to the presence of the relevant stimuli, enabling it to actualize its capacity to seize its prey when, and ideally only when, it passes by.[11]

---

[10] I am indebted here to descriptions of similarly simple-minded creatures in Bennett (1976), Lloyd (1989), and especially to Craig (1990, 82–4).

[11] I take the notion of a reliable responsive differential disposition from Brandom (2002a, 350), who develops it on the basis of Sellars's account of observational knowledge; see also Brandom (2015b, 101).

Is that already a need for anything like the concept *food*? Hardly. A creature meeting that need would not yet be a concept-user, but merely a reliable differential responder. And what it would respond *to* would not be a particular aspect of a conceptually articulated experience of something beyond itself, but the situation as a whole: the undifferentiated conjunction of its concern with its capacities and certain circumstances. There is no practical pressure here to impose a conceptual articulation on this whole, and distinguish between its own concerns, its own capacities, and the things out there that will or will not satisfy its concerns given its capacities.

But give the creature the capacity to direct its movements and roam around in search of prey, and you increase the practical pressure on this 'primitive holism' to start to 'fragment', as E. J. Craig (1990, 83) puts it. If, instead of roaming around at random, such a mobile creature became able to distinguish between 'food, here, now' and 'food, here, not long ago', or 'food, here, soon', it could dramatically improve its odds of satisfying its concern to eat. But it would also come under strong practical pressure to become sensitive to the difference between circumstances that its own limited capacities equip it to handle and circumstances it is ill-equipped to handle: that difference can be further differentiated along many dimensions, but already the failure to draw the basic distinction between 'food, over there, that I can get to' and 'food, over there, that I cannot get to' would soon cost it its life.

Already this simple example brings out how concerns combine with certain capacities and circumstances to generate certain instrumental needs, which, in social and language-using creatures like us, would take the form of *conceptual* needs. The concerns of concept-users must combine with their capacities and circumstances to render a concept, or some broader class of concepts of which it is an instance, *needful*. What it renders needful, in particular, is that which is especially conducive to satisfying the relevant concern, given certain capacities and circumstances.

We might call all these extraconceptual conditions that are jointly sufficient to render a particular concept needful the concept's *needfulness conditions*. To achieve a better analytic and mnemonic grip on needfulness conditions, we can think of them as always combining three aspects:

(i) the *concerns* of concept-users, which covers everything from their inner needs, motivations, and desires to their commitments to particular values or projects;

(ii) the *capacities* of concept-users, in a sense encompassing their corresponding limitations; in particular, the limited physiological, perceptual, and cognitive capacities that they have upstream of adopting the concept at issue, but also the cultural and technological resources they can draw on, including the concepts they already possess;

(iii) the *circumstances* in which concept-users seek to satisfy these concerns with the limited capacities they have, i.e. the natural and social environment or context in which the concept is to be deployed; this might include their geographical situation, their social structures and institutions, and their position or role within those structures or institutions.

Conceptual needs thus arise out of the interaction between our concerns, capacities, and circumstances: what demands our concepts should make on our thought and conduct depends on what demands the world makes on us given the demands that we make on the world.

The implication is that each concept comes with certain extraconceptual conditions that have to be realized for the concept to be needful. The concept is only called for when these needfulness conditions obtain. But when they obtain and the concept is in fact in use, they render the use of the concept *pointful*, ensuring that it makes a useful difference to our lives and thereby helps us to live.

Consider, for example, the concept of causation. As interventionists such as James Woodward (2003, 11) argue, we need it because (i) we are concerned to manipulate the world to our advantage; (ii) we have the capacity to actively intervene in the world in order to manipulate it; and (iii) we inhabit a world that lends itself to causal reasoning. Were any of these concerns, capacities, and circumstances sufficiently different, we would have no need for the concept of causation: were we intelligent trees capable only of passive observation, but not of active intervention in the world, for example, the concept of causation would be pointless for us.[12]

This dependence of the pointfulness of concept use on certain contingent facts holds quite generally. As Wittgenstein emphasizes: 'if anyone believes that certain concepts are absolutely the correct ones, and that having different ones would mean not realizing something that we realize', he writes, 'let him imagine certain very general facts of nature to be different from what we are used to, and the formation of concepts different from the usual ones will become intelligible to him' (2009, II, §366). The concept of weight, for instance, is one we instrumentally need for all kinds of ulterior concerns, and yet its use would be pointless if the laws of gravity were such that objects on

---

[12] See Dummett (1964) for a discussion of this example.

earth randomly changed weight all the time.[13] Conversely, if our physiological condition never changed, thinking in terms of the concept of health would be pointless for us. Or take the concept of intention: as G. E. M. Anscombe observed, its use would be pointless if we took absolutely no interest in each other's reasons for action.[14]

While this explicates the pointfulness of concept use in terms of the needfulness of the concept used—what gives point to the use of a concept is the fact that the concept meets an instrumental need—needfulness is not the same as pointfulness: the property of being needed is notoriously insufficient to bring its bearer into existence. As Jeremy Bentham notes, 'a reason for wishing that a certain right were established, is not that right—want is not supply—hunger is not bread' (1843, 501). A concept can be needful long before it comes into use, and even if it never actually comes into use. But it is only once the concept actually is in use that its use can be pointful, and that use will be pointful if and as long as the concept used is instrumentally needful.

The conditions that give point to the use of a concept thus revolve around what users of the concept and the world in which it is deployed are like. But these conditions remain extraconceptual: they do not have to figure in the *content* of the concept; nor do they have to be *constitutive* of the concept. It is merely that living by a certain concept only has a point, and the concept only fills a need, against the backdrop of certain facts: the facts engendering an instrumental need for the concept.

7.3 What Concepts Express

On this account, a concept is not inherently needful, nor does it inherently fill a need: it only does so if hooked up to the right concept-users in the right circumstances. So how can one work back from a concept to the conditions that might render it needful and give point to its use? This is the form that the concern identification problem takes for the needs-based approach.

I submit that one thing that can guide us from concepts to the relevant concerns is the *expressive character* of concepts: a concept can *express* something of the conditions in which it *would* be worth using, even when these conditions are not given. This is what Nietzsche had in mind when he boasted of his keen eye for that tricky backward inference from ways of thinking to the needs behind them.

---

[13] Wittgenstein (2009, §142) offers a similar example.   [14] See Anscombe (1957, §21).

The notion of expressive character is perhaps most at home in aesthetics and the appraisal of works of art; but, as Andrew Huddleston has stressed, this need not mean that the grounds of appraisal guided by expressive character must themselves be aesthetic grounds.[15] To berate a concept for being *cloying* would be to criticize it on aesthetic grounds. But we need not play Walter Pater at the museum of concepts. We can export a sensitivity to expressive character out of the aesthetic sphere and into the ethics of conceptualization without tying ourselves to aestheticism about ethics and politics.

What lends a concept its expressive character? Could it be a concept's *content*? A concept's content certainly contributes to determining its expressive character. But, in the sense at issue here, what a concept expresses is not to be identified with its content. On the contrary: what makes certain concepts such insidious ideological tools is precisely that they can express objectionable concerns *without* making any reference to these concerns at the level of their content. They would not be effective ideological instruments otherwise. This is a point forcefully made by E. P. Thompson in discussing ideological functions of the law: 'If the law is evidently partial and unjust, then it will mask nothing, legitimise nothing, contribute nothing to any class's hegemony. The essential precondition for the effectiveness of law, in its function as ideology, is that it shall display an independence from gross manipulation and shall seem to be just' (1975, 263).

Conversely, the most exalted concerns of liberal democracy might find their most important expression in the dry jargon and sterile concepts of bureaucrats and legal clerks. Part of the ingenuity of such arrangements is that this does *not* depend on those concerns figuring in the thinking of the bureaucrats and clerks in question. A concept's content and what it expresses can radically come apart. So how can we make sense of this elusive dimension of concepts?

One possibility would be to identify the expressive character of a concept with the attitudes that concept-users express through *tokenings* of the concept on particular occasions. This would allow conceptual content and expressive character to come apart: the thick aesthetic ideals of a tailor who judges the cut of a suit, for example, might only ever find expression in tokenings of very thin terms ('Just right!');[16] likewise, the moral ideals of a writer might be

---

[15] See Huddleston (2019, 158). Though the account of expressive character I develop here is ultimately quite different from his, I would not have developed it without his work highlighting the expressive dimension of Nietzsche's critique of values. I am also indebted to Alexander Prescott-Couch for a series of helpful discussions of this topic.

[16] The example is Wittgenstein's (1966, 5–9).

forcefully—indeed, more forcefully—expressed in a soberly descriptive account of how someone pulls a horse out of deep snow.[17] But this analysis would not entail that the concept *right* itself inherently expressed sartorial ideals, or the concept *horse* moral ones. Rather, the aesthetic and moral attitudes expressed by those concepts would simply be the attitudes *of particular concept-users* as expressed specifically in *individual instances* of concept use. For an account of the expressive character *of concepts*, we need to look elsewhere.

On the account I propose, the key to the expressive character of concepts is to recognize that even when a concept *fails* to fill an instrumental need, because it is not currently hooked up to the right concept-users in the right circumstances, it nonetheless *expresses* the conditions that *would* render its use pointful. One merely has to ask: who would have need of such a concept? What combination of concerns, capacities, and circumstances would give one reason to think in these terms?

By tentatively assuming that a concept answers to an instrumental need, we can searchingly work our way back to conditions under which there would be a point to using the concept. There is no guarantee that we will not come up empty. But this assumption of instrumentality functions like an interpretative 'principle of charity' for needs-based concept appraisal. It is the hermeneutic lever that gets needs-based appraisal off the ground, and allows us, when successful, to work our way to a picture of the conditions that would render the use of the concept pointful. These are the conditions that the concept might be said to *express*, even when these conditions are not presently given. The conditions a concept expresses in this way are, in the first instance, the conditions under which its use is pointful, but since pointfulness in turn presupposes needfulness, the concept thereby also expresses its *needfulness conditions*.

Strictly speaking, what a concept expresses in this way is always an entire triad of conditions that would jointly engender a need for it and imbue its use with a point: not only (i) some human concern, but also (ii) the limited capacities of concept-users with which they purse that concern, and (iii) the circumstances in which they do so; for only when joined together into a triad do these conditions give concept-users reason to pursue their concern using that concept.

---

[17] See Diamond (2018b, 225–9).

But one can—and Nietzsche, for one, often does[18]—make *pars pro toto* usage of this notion of expressive character, treating one element in such a triad as representative of the whole: a concept tailored to satisfy a concern for revenge in the hands of the weak under circumstances of oppression by the strong, for example, might simply be said to express a concern for revenge; or to be a sign of weakness; or to speak of circumstances of oppression. In each case, this should be understood as shorthand for the entire set of conditions that would jointly give point to the use of such a concept.

We can thus understand the expressive character of a concept in terms of how the concept expresses certain presuppositions, namely its needfulness conditions—the conditions that would render the concept instrumentally needful and thereby give point to its use.

To be sure, moving from a concept to its needfulness conditions involves a genuine backward *inference* that requires delicate interpretation and judgement, and there may not be a uniquely right way to do it. It is always worth seeing whether one can discern different needs behind a concept. Indeed, some concepts may be so multiply pointful as to *require* several interpretations: our most venerable and most pervasive concepts may well meet several needs at once. Either way, a concept's needfulness conditions cannot just be algorithmically read off the concept.

Nevertheless, the necessary act of interpretation is constrained by what genuinely makes sense and what remains obstinately unintelligible, what holds up and what falls flat. If future generations subsisting exclusively on a diet of sustainably produced vitamin pills were to dig up one of our can openers, they might reasonably hypothesize—even if they no longer stored food in cans—that this object expresses an instrumental need to open cans, and thereby expresses conditions of life that render it instrumentally needful to store food in cans; the rival hypothesis that the can opener expresses a need to make music will simply not hold up in light of the object's intrinsic features and the kinds of sounds humans tend to regard as musical. Analogously, there are claims about what a concept expresses that no truthful inquiry into the concept's inherent properties and their likely role in human affairs will bear out. This is what marks off ascriptions of expressive character to a concept from projections of subjective associations onto a blot of ink.

---

[18] See Queloz (2023) for a detailed account of Nietzsche's expressivist critique of concepts along the lines presented here, and see Huddleston (2019) for a different reading that also emphasizes the expressive dimension.

What it takes to substantiate a claim about expressive character, in particular, is to make plausible that the concept in question is *apt* to serve the concerns of certain types of concept-users under certain types of circumstances, and that this aptness is primarily due, not to an improbable alignment of the stars, but to features of the concept itself. To be able to make sense of a concept as expressing a certain concern, we have to be able to envisage what would engender an instrumental need for something very like this concept. The envisaged situation need not be, nor ever have been, actual. A concept's aptness for serving certain concerns might in principle be revealed to be latent in a concept merely by considering counterfactual situations.

On this account, then, to consider a concept's expressive character is to think in *modal* terms about what kinds of concerns it would be most apt to serve, and not just to look at what concerns it *actually* serves. To say that a concept expresses a concern for revenge, or a yearning for life to be ultimately fair, is to say that the concept is recognizably tailored to serving those concerns, which is to say that, in the right hands and under propitious circumstances, its use would tend to have effects conducive to the satisfaction of those concerns.

We can thus distinguish two different relations in which concepts can stand to concerns, on the present account. A concept can *express* a concern or *serve* a concern. My suggestion is that in order to identify whether a concept serves any of our concerns, we should ask what concerns it expresses.

In the analytically basic case, a concept also serves the concerns it expresses. But the two relations can come apart: a concept might *express* a concern *without serving* it, because the conditions necessary to serving it are not given; and it might *serve* a concern *without expressing* it, because its effects only fortuitously but unsystematically and unreliably satisfy that concern through some fragile alignment of circumstances. What concern a concept expresses is a function of the robustness of its ability to serve the concern across variation in the relevant contingencies. A concept need not *invariably* serve a concern in order to express it. But it does need to serve it *non-accidentally*. There has to be something about the concept itself that makes it *apt* to serve that concern.

One way of spelling out this idea is again in modal terms, which we can do particularly vividly in the idiom of 'possible worlds':[19] there has to be, not just

---

[19] The use of this idiom need not entail unpalatable ontological commitments to possible worlds and their equally uninviting implications for modal epistemology. Talk of possible worlds can be given a deflationary gloss as an especially perspicuous and precise way of making explicit what ordinary modal talk expresses anyway. Like ordinary modal talk itself, talk of possible worlds can be

a handful of scattered because vastly different possible worlds in which it happens to serve that concern, but a reasonably large cluster of neighbouring possible worlds in which it systematically, if not invariably, serves that concern, even if our actual world now lies outside that cluster.

By way of illustration, consider the legal concept of a basic rights infringement, which, when demonstrably satisfied, empowers individuals to trigger a process of judicial review aiming to determine whether their basic rights have in fact been violated by state action or omission. This concept plausibly evinces a liberal concern to protect individual liberties against the powers of the state. In the first instance, therefore, the concept might be thought to express a liberal society's instrumental need to give individuals legal means to push back against the state's curtailment of their most fundamental liberties.[20] Still, by some unlikely conjunction of circumstances, the concept might end up playing into the hands of the *illiberal*-minded at a certain juncture. Does this mean that the concept also expresses their concerns? No, because this serviceability is of the accidental kind 'which alters when it alteration finds', as Shakespeare has it: it is highly counterfactually fragile, breaking down in most nearby possible worlds. The concept's aptness to serve the concerns of the *liberal*-minded, by contrast, is far more counterfactually robust—that is what lends force to the claim about the concept's expressive character, regardless of whether the liberal concern is actually being satisfied as things currently stand.

This account of the expressive character of concepts might be thought to resemble accounts of 'expressive meaning' in non-truth-conditional semantics, which claim that the expressive meaning of words such as 'Ouch!' or 'cur' can be captured by identifying the conditions for the 'felicitous use' of those words: 'Ouch!' is felicitously used just in case the speaker experiences pain; 'dog' and 'cur' have the same truth conditions, but 'cur' adds the 'felicitous use' condition that the speaker have a negative attitude towards the referent.[21]

But the account of expressive character offered here differs from these semantic accounts in several respects. First, the present account is not about the meaning of words, but about the pointfulness of concept use. Second, the expressive relation it highlights between a concept and its presuppositions is

---

demystified by an account on which it 'serves the function not of tracking features of additional worlds and reporting on their features, but rather of adding...expressive power to our language' (Thomasson 2020a, 123); see also Brandom (2008).

[20] See Cueni (2024a) for a detailed argument to that effect.

[21] See Gutzmann (2013) for a survey of varieties of expressive, non-truth-conditional meaning. A closely related approach is 'success semantics' (Blackburn 2005).

a functional rather than a semantic relation: the concept can only serve its point if the presuppositions are realized, but this functional relation need not be part of what a competent user would have to grasp about the concept in order to count as competent (whereas someone who failed to understand that using the word 'cur' felicitously presupposes a negative attitude on the speaker's part would fail to grasp the full meaning of the word). And third, needs-based concept appraisal aims, in the first instance, to intuit what makes the entire practice of living by a certain concept pointful, not what makes individual instances of concept use pointful.

At the same time, it is also true that by grasping what makes a practice of concept use pointful in general, one acquires some sense of when it would be pointful in particular. Consider the cyclists' practice of holding out their right hand before taking a right turn: in virtue of my understanding of what makes the practice pointful in general, I become able to recognize its pointlessness on particular occasions. Understanding the point of something tells us when it is particularly important, and when it can safely be disregarded.

Thus, what a concept expresses of the conditions that would render it pointful to use it offers a valuable epistemic guide to the concerns in relation to which the concept should be appraised, even if no one presently has the concerns that would be best served by such a concept. By coming to understand that a certain concept is the kind of concept that people driven by certain concerns would need, one is given some reason—however defeasible—to think that the effects of living by that concept, even when *lacking* such concerns, are unlikely to be conducive to the satisfaction of different concerns, and more likely to further, *even in their absence*, the concerns of those who would need such concepts. That is why Nietzsche was alarmed about the prospect of certain ascetic values remaining in use even after the figures best served by such values had largely disappeared: people concerned to flourish in this life rather than the next were unlikely to do so if they abided by concepts tailored to the needs of those concerned to abnegate this-worldly flourishing.[22]

Concepts can subsist outside of their needfulness conditions, and thereby continue to systematically have effects that we might not want to see systematically realized. Examining a concept's expressive character is thus a particularly instructive way of assessing a concept's causal profile, because it enables us to contemplate not just the effects a concept actually has, or has actually

---

[22] For recent readings of Nietzsche along these lines, see Owen (2007, 2008, 2018), Richardson (2020), Reginster (2021), and Queloz (2023).

had, but the effects it is likely to have going forward, just in virtue of the kind of concept it is. By asking who would be best served by a concept, one learns something about whether it is likely to serve us.

7.4 Need Matrices

On this account, then, it is to the welter of our concerns, capacities, and circumstances that we must look to appraise concepts, and we receive some guidance in this from the expressive character of concepts.

But this still leaves us with a formidable epistemic challenge. For, on this account, what needs our concepts are answerable to is, in the end, a function of all the concerns we identify with, all the capacities we have and lack, and all the circumstances we face. Philosophers of a certain temperament will welcome the implication that we have to engage with the messy complexities of social reality in order to determine how our concepts relate to our concerns. Yet this thicket of need-engendering conditions threatens to be intractably dense. Simply asking 'Who would need concept F?', as Nietzsche does, risks yielding a staggering number of potential answers. Our starting point needs to be more constrained.[23]

In some instances, we may hope to overcome this epistemic challenge by clearly delimiting a set of *use cases* for a concept. This might notably be achieved by focusing on the concepts needed for particular roles within particular institutions. In *When the State Meets the Street* (2017), for example, Bernardo Zacka draws on his ethnographic fieldwork to provide a comprehensive picture of the conceptual needs of social workers at the frontline of a social welfare agency.[24] This allows him to clearly delimit a set of concept-users together with their relevant concerns, capacities, and circumstances—these social workers are, for instance, concerned to organize their work effectively and efficiently, be consistent in how they handle cases, exchange advice, and teach new workers. To this end, they need a conceptual framework in terms of which to systematically organize their work.

But given their limited resources and the pressures of their workplace, these social workers do not have time to systematically reason their way back to first principles on each occasion in the manner of Dworkin's ideal judge

---

[23] I am indebted to Christian Nimtz and Steffen Koch for extremely helpful discussions of this and related issues.

[24] See Zacka (2017, 152–99).

Hercules.[25] A full-blown normative theory justifying and harmonizing all street-level operations of the state would be of no use to them. Instead, a modest typological systematization through an informal taxonomy does more to meet their conceptual needs. In particular, Zacka comes to the conclusion that a conceptual framework allowing them to ascertain and communicate whether clients have a *situation*, *issues*, or an *attitude* goes a long way towards meeting their needs: clients with a *situation* require prompt attention; clients with *issues* face serious personal difficulties that provide some excuse for inappropriate behaviour and demand forbearance; clients with an *attitude*, by contrast, are prone to exhibit inappropriate behaviour without any excuse for it.[26] This informal taxonomy is a far cry from a full-blown normative theory. But it leaves the social workers better able to respond to the particularities of individual cases, faster in deploying these more lightweight cognitive resources, more flexible in accommodating new types of cases, and quicker to revise their conceptual framework when appropriate.

In the kinds of cases that are perhaps most characteristic of philosophical reflection on concepts, however, the concepts at issue are typically too widely applicable to be appraised on the basis of a well-delimited range of use cases: the concepts *truth, knowledge, understanding, justice, equality, liberty*, or *voluntariness*, for example, are not the preserve of a particular agency. The concerns that these concepts make contact with across different situations are likely to be mindbogglingly multifarious. How can we render this seemingly intractable welter of concerns, capacities, and circumstances philosophically tractable?

To overcome that epistemic challenge, one trick we can use is to approach that messy complexity piecemeal, by building a series of incomplete but illuminating philosophical *models* of it, each crystallizing and holding up to philosophical scrutiny a minimal set of concerns, capacities, and circumstances sufficient to generate a conceptual need. This is broadly in line with the conception of philosophy as model-building advocated notably by L. A. Paul (2012) and Timothy Williamson (2017, 2018a, 130–40; b, 2020, ch. 10). 'Humans are a classic example of messy complex systems', Williamson observes, which is why 'one might expect a model-building strategy to be appropriate' (2018a, 130). Different types of models, admitting of varying degrees of rigour, will be appropriate to different areas and approaches. But for a needs-based approach to concept appraisal, what we want is a model that isolates a set of needfulness conditions and highlights a resulting

---

[25] See Dworkin (1986, 239).   [26] See Zacka (2017, 163–4).

conceptual need that our conceptual repertoire should be responsive to. This may only give us a partial picture of a concept's total needfulness conditions. But it gives other philosophers a well-delineated set of claims to focus on, scrutinize, criticize, and complement or improve on with models of their own.

I shall refer to this type of model as a *need matrix*: a representation of an array of concerns, capacities, circumstances jointly sufficient to generate a conceptual need for a certain concept. A guiding constraint in constructing a need matrix is that the matrix should be as specific to the concept as possible: not only should it generate a need for a broad class of concepts including F, but the class should be as small and tightly focused around F as possible, ensuring that the relevant need really is a need *for F*, or something very like it. If the conditions represented in the need matrix in fact obtain, then this results in a conceptual need N for concept F. Abbreviating concerns as co, capacities as ca, and circumstances as ci, we can represent this as follows:

$<co, ca, ci> \rightarrow$ conceptual need N for concept F

A set of concept-users S then has a need for concept F if and to the extent that they satisfy the needfulness conditions represented in the matrix:

S has a conceptual need N for concept F
   if and to the extent that
S satisfies $<co, ca, ci>$

A need matrix isolates a particular set of needfulness conditions and highlights a conceptual need that this set of conditions suffices to engender. The term 'matrix' helpfully connotes three ideas: that we are dealing with an array of intersecting concerns, capacities, and circumstances that form a single entity (as in a mathematical matrix); that they combine to generate something, namely a conceptual need ('matrix' originally means 'mother' or 'womb', and the term is commonly used to refer to the environment out of which an idea develops); and that, like the printer's matrix, a need matrix can act as a mould for casts of thought.

In crystallizing for philosophical inspection a specific array of need-engendering conditions, a need matrix helps to render tractable the complexities of our predicaments: it gives us an uncluttered and perspicuous representation of a conceptual need and the combination of conditions engendering it. Once a need matrix has been constructed, it can be probed with questions such as the following:

- *External Validation*: Do the conditions presented as generating a need for the concept in fact obtain? For instance, is this true of one's own situation, now and around here?
- *Internal Validation*: Is the inference from their obtaining to there being a conceptual need for the concept valid? Is the concept really such that its use would be especially conducive to satisfying the envisaged concern given the envisaged capacities and circumstances?
- *Normative Endorsement*: Is the concern presented as motivating the use of the concept a concern one endorses, in the sense that one critically identifies with it and wants to see it satisfied?

In this way, explicitly setting out a need matrix can suggest questions we did not know to ask. It also has the virtue of holding up for scrutiny the key assumptions underpinning the claim that we need a certain concept. Probing whether the conditions presented as generating a need for the concept in fact obtain can provide an *external validation* of the model. Probing whether the inference from their obtaining to there being a conceptual need for the concept is valid can provide an *internal validation* of the model. And asking whether the concern presented as motivating the use of the concept is, upon critical reflection, a concern one wants to see satisfied can provide a *normative endorsement* of the model's evaluative basis.

A need matrix can thus be critically assessed much as other models are assessed. And, as with other models, its power comes from the grip it gives us on its target system, despite and indeed *because of* the simplification, abstraction, and idealization it involves:[27] it gives us something to work with, something we can explore, manipulate, put to the test, refine, enrich, extend, and elaborate.

7.5 Needs-Based Concept Appraisal

In light of a need matrix, a concept will emerge as apt or inapt in particular respects, as the matrix conveys a sense of what kind of concept we need and why: what the concept needs to pick out, what inferential connections it needs to allow us to draw, and how it needs to channel motivation to result in the effects needed to realize concept-users' concerns. Using a need matrix, we can arrive at a fine-grained and case-specific sense of what concept best

[27] See Weisberg (2007, 2013), Strevens (2008, ch. 8), and Elliott-Graves and Weisberg (2014).

handles a particular combination of practical pressures. This allows us to substitute the question of what makes an inherently good concept, or a good concept *tout court*, for another, more determinate question: what makes a good concept for concept-users with those concerns and capacities in those circumstances?

However, working back from a concept to a need matrix remains a challenge, as there are multiple unknown variables involved ($<x, y, z>$)—what concerns, capacities, and circumstances should figure in the need matrix? How do we go about constructing a need matrix?

This is where a second trick comes in: we can hold two variables constant by treating them as given parameters, and then solve for the third variable. For instance, we can take certain capacities and circumstances as given and ask what concern of S would engender a need for concept F given these capacities and circumstances ($<x, ca, ci>$). Or we can ask what capacities and limitations of S would engender a need for concept F given a certain concern and certain circumstances in which it is pursued ($<co, x, ci>$). Or, again, we can ask what circumstances of S would engender a need for concept F given a certain concern and certain capacities with which it is pursued ($<co, ca, x>$). In each case, treating the other variables as constants narrows down the search space and allows us to solve for the single remaining variable by handing us a criterion for what counts as a solution.

One way of doing this is illustrated by state-of-nature fictions, which have a long tradition in philosophy.[28] These state-of-nature fictions are illuminatingly interpreted as need matrices: as philosophical models seeking to shed light on some concept (or practice or institution) F by treating two needfulness conditions as constants and solving for the third according to what would generate a need for F. Thus, state-of-nature theorists typically envisage a community of human beings that have certain highly generic human capacities (they have language, for example, but no sophisticated technology or institutions) in equally generic human circumstances (they live in a natural environment characterized by such generic features as trees and caves, in which the risks and opportunities centre on such things as predators and prey). With these conditions fixed, the state-of-nature theorists then search through various concerns until they hit upon one that plausible engenders a need for F. And since the conditions treated as given for the purpose of the exercise are maximally generic, they are maximally widely shared, thereby maximizing

---

[28] For historical overviews of this tradition, see Tuck (1979), Lifschitz (2012), Palmeri (2016), and Queloz (2021c).

the probability that they will also be satisfied in a given actual situation. This is what promises to license the inference from a fictional state of nature to a real situation.

I take it that Williams in fact has something very like this in mind when, in his debate with Dworkin about the political concept of liberty, he invites us to construct the most basic need matrix from which a need for something like that concept would result. We can only really get at a well-formed hypothesis about the most primitive concern animating the use of anything like that concept by making certain factual assumptions about what human beings are like, what they are and are not capable of, and what kinds of circumstances they typically face. Only against the backdrop of those substantial, if highly generic, assumptions does Williams's suggestion that the basic concern at issue is the concern for primitive freedom (i.e. human beings care about not being frustrated by other human beings in the realization of their desires) begin to engender anything like a need for a concept serving that concern.

Of course, this basic concern still takes us nowhere at all when we want to assess the authority of Philip Pettit's and Quentin Skinner's efforts to move us from a conception of *liberty as non-interference* towards a conception of *liberty as non-domination*, for instance. To make the case for the latter conception using a need matrix, one would have to show that this conception better meets our conceptual needs by better serving the concern for freedom *as expressed in the context of twenty-first-century liberal democracies*. To demonstrate this, one would therefore have to consider how the highly generic need matrix has been *elaborated*, i.e. inflected, extended, and redirected, by the historical, social, and cultural forces that characterize our own more concrete circumstances.

This is a task characteristically shouldered in philosophy by *genealogy*; and it is no coincidence that Williams, like Pettit and Skinner to some extent, advocates the combination of state-of-nature fiction with historically informed genealogy.[29] The combination is a natural one if we think of philosophical genealogies as *dynamic* need matrices: the genealogist starts by identifying a basic concern generating a need for something vaguely like F under state-of-nature conditions ($<x, ca_1, ci_1>$). And once the genealogist has a complete need matrix generating a need for some prototype of F ($<co_1, ca_1, ci_1>$), they progressively *adjust* the parameters of the need matrix to reflect historical changes in our concerns, capacities, or circumstances, with each iteration of the need matrix

---

[29] See Williams (2002, ch. 2; 2014g), Pettit (2008, 2018, 2019, forthcoming), and Skinner (1997, 1998, 2009). For defences of this combination, see Queloz (2021c) and Fricker (manuscript).

representing a stage in genealogical development ($<co_2, ca_2, ci_2>$, $<co_3, ca_3, ci_3>$,..., $<co_n, ca_n, ci_n>$). This allows the genealogist to reconstruct how the historical elaboration of the need matrix has affected the resulting conceptual need. And once a configuration of the need matrix is reached that plausibly represents present-day conditions, the genealogist can evaluate what the resulting conceptual need is, and which conception of *F*-ness best meets it.

What this combination—of a basic need matrix and its sociohistorical elaboration—aims to do is to yield the kind of understanding that manages to hold on to two important thoughts at once: that the use of many concepts at the heart of philosophical reflection is rooted in highly general human concerns that are very widely shared across human history; but that these concerns nonetheless find expression in our own time and place in highly specific forms that are not widely shared. Evolutionary psychology and game theory are apt to emphasize the first thought, but tend to do so at the expense of the second; history and sociology are apt to emphasize the second thought, but tend to do so at the expense of the first. To get the full measure of a concept's value to us, we need to hold on to both thoughts at once.

Of course, understanding what should figure in a need matrix requires one to draw not merely on philosophy, but also on anthropology, ethnography, sociology, psychology, and history. These human sciences are better placed to capture the rich texture of the social reality in which our conceptual repertoire is put to work. Their findings can inform philosophers' model-building, both by schooling and sharpening philosophers' judgement as to what should figure in the model, and by offering empirical backing to the assumptions embodied in the model.

But precisely because of this division of labour, there is a point to distinguishing between the thicket of needfulness conditions we in fact face and the simple need matrix that professes to offer a selective philosophical representation of that thicket. The distinction between needfulness conditions and need matrices helps to keep model and target system in their places and avoid conflations between them. A need matrix is not meant to be exhaustive. It is offered with a view to highlighting certain philosophically relevant aspects of our situation as part of a philosopher's case for or against a particular way of thinking.

However, having recourse to a state-of-nature fiction or some equivalent, highly generic need matrix is not the only way of using a need matrix to appraise concepts. There is a more direct way.

We can start instead from the *actual* capacities and circumstances of some set of concept-users we are interested in, hold these fixed, and ask *what concern* would engender a need for concept F when combined with these capacities and circumstances ($<x, ca_1, ci_1>$). This effectively guarantees that we satisfy the latter two conditions in the triad. It also helpfully narrows down the search space, and provides a criterion by which to identify a concern capable of animating the use of F. By asking which concerns of people facing those circumstances with those capacities and limitations would engender a need for F, we can identify concerns that F in fact serves.[30]

This then puts us in a position to ask whether we ourselves really identify with the concerns in question. If we fail to identify with them, using the concept will to that extent be *pointless* for us, giving us a *pro tanto* reason to abandon it. If, however, we share one or several of these concerns, using the concept will to that extent be *pointful* for us, giving us a *pro tanto* reason to adopt it or adhere to it.

Having discovered a conceptual need we have for something very like concept F, we can then ask what demands this places on our conceptualization of F-ness, and whether there are respects in which that conceptualization could be better tailored to the need in question. If so, that gives us a *pro tanto* reason to prefer a different way of conceptualizing F-ness.

Yet even this more straightforward form of needs-based appraisal, which starts from now and around here, can be augmented by using a *dynamic* need matrix. We can usefully explore *how counterfactually robust or fragile* the relevant conceptual need is by *systematically varying* the parameters in the need matrix. If, instead of $<co_1, ca_1, ci_1>$, the situation were subtly different (e.g. $<co_2, ca_1, ci_1>$, $<co_1, ca_2, ci_1>$, or $<co_1, ca_1, ci_2>$), would there still be a need for F? Just how different could the situation get before it no longer generated a need for F?

Exploring these counterfactuals by systematically deviating in various directions from our initial need matrix helps us understand not only how a concept relates to our actual situation, but what *range* of conditions the need for that concept is contingent upon. Where else does that need arise? Where should we expect it to be absent? The wider the range of conditions across which the need arises, the more counterfactually robust the need; conversely, hitting upon a nearby set of parameters that already obviates the need makes us realize how counterfactually fragile that need is. It shows us that the concept gets its point from highly specific conditions, and becomes to that extent pointless as soon as these fall away.

---

[30] I am grateful to Christian Nimtz and Steffen Koch for valuable discussions of this point.

That can itself be a practically relevant insight if there is a real question of these conditions changing, or of their being entirely lacking in some other context in which the concept is to be deployed. But it is also the kind of insight that has long been considered philosophically illuminating. Thus, Heraclitus already observed of the disputes and demands for settlement that human beings are prone to engage in: 'If it were not for these things, they would not have known the name of justice' (1981, fragm. 23).

Moreover, exploring these counterfactual dependences by incrementally varying the parameters of a need matrix can be a valuable *explorative* process suggesting questions we would not have asked otherwise, or alerting us to instrumental connections between concepts and conditions that we did not have on our radar. It may lead us to other concerns that are also served by the concept; it may reveal the need for a concept to be easily obviated if we only remedy a certain limitation of ours; or it may show us that the circumstances under which the concept is needful are more narrow than we thought; or that nearby circumstances—those that used to obtain not long ago, perhaps—were an even better fit for the concept than our actual circumstances are, suggesting that the concept is on a path towards becoming ill-suited to our circumstances, and perhaps needs to be adapted.

Consequently, there is something to be said for doing even needs-based appraisal 'from here' in three stages: first, identify a concern engendering a need for F by treating actual capacities and circumstances as constants, and, on this basis, perform a first-pass appraisal of the concept; second, systematically vary the parameters of the need matrix to get a sense of the dynamics of this conceptual need, explore relevant variations, and differentiate the respects in which the need is robust or fragile; and third, perform a second-pass appraisal of the concept that is informed by the findings of the previous, explorative stage.

Where this explorative stage becomes especially valuable is when it reveals further conceptual needs that the concept answers to. A single conceptualization may have to strike a balance between several conceptual needs reflecting multiple and potentially conflicting concerns. In introducing the notion of a conceptual need, we focused on the analytically basic case, in which a single concern engenders a single conceptual need. But when we approach these issues from the rough-and-tumble of a concrete situation rather than in the abstract, we would expect—especially given the kaleidoscopic picture of our conceptual apparatus—to find a turbulent confluence of different concerns, some pulling in diverging directions, each engendering its own conceptual needs.

The notion of a conceptual need therefore itself needs to be refined to accommodate this complexity. We need to distinguish between *pro tanto* conceptual needs, which one has *to the extent that* a particular need-engendering concern is to be satisfied, and *all-things-considered* conceptual needs. When a situation involves different concerns, we need to strike a balance between these concerns, and the concept we really need, all things considered, will be the concept that best accommodates the various *pro tanto* conceptual needs growing out of these concerns. At the same time, we cannot arrive at an all-things-considered need without first considering the contributions made to it by individual concerns and the *pro tanto* needs engendered by them. One's all-things-considered conceptual needs are the resultant needs that emerge once a balance has been struck between one's various *pro tanto* conceptual needs.

This gives us the tools required to make sense of a more capacious notion of *gerrymandering with concepts* than the one we encountered in Chapter 5, which involved cutting across natural kinds. That narrower notion of gerrymandering depends on there being natural kinds to cut across, which, by strongly suggesting a salient alternative (a 'natural partition', in Lewis's phrase), make the concepts look gerrymandered. But, as we realize if we think back to the prototypical case of gerrymandering that involves the manipulation of electoral boundaries to serve a particular party or class, there need not always be a salient, 'natural' alternative way of defining the boundaries. In fact, a completely arbitrary or random delineation would precisely escape the charge of gerrymandering in this case. So the notion of gerrymandering with concepts that relies on 'natural partitions' is rather limited in scope; and even in the prototypical case of gerrymandering, it cannot capture what makes the gerrymandered concepts attractive to begin with, nor why an arbitrary partition would escape the charge of being gerrymandered.

The needs-based approach, by contrast, can account for the attraction of the gerrymandered concepts in the prototypical case: they do meet a *pro tanto* conceptual need, because, for a party or class concerned *simply* to win elections, by whatever means necessary, it makes sense to define the boundaries this way. At the same time, the needs-based approach can also account for the thought that, all things considered, these are the wrong concepts to use in a democratic society concerned to hold free and fair elections: in particular, because these concepts are flagrantly unresponsive to the *pro tanto* conceptual need engendered by the concern to hold *fair* elections. Any members of that society that remotely identify with this concern for fairness will accordingly be concerned not simply to win elections, but to win fair elections; and this means that their all-things-considered conceptual need will be for a conceptualization of electoral boundaries that is free of obvious partisan bias. What is objectionable about prototypical gerrymanderers, therefore, is not that they are conceptualizing past natural partitions, nor that they are failing to be responsive to all their conceptual needs; what is objectionable is the blatant lack of concern for fairness that their conceptual choices correctly express.

In practice, many of the concepts we use are entangled in an overwhelming number of different concerns at any given time. What a need matrix aims to do is to render that complexity tractable for the purposes of philosophical reflection, enabling us to think clearly, if only partially, about what kind of concept best serves our concerns. This will inevitably ignore various background concerns and perhaps leave out important concerns as well. Yet this incompleteness is necessary, not just to thinking clearly about these matters, but to thinking about them at all.

Let me end this section with two brief illustrations of how constructing need matrices might inform the ethics of conceptualization. Consider first the concept *poisonous*. Let us assume that we have settled on the following need matrix for that concept:

Needfulness conditions: concept-users have an instrumental need for something very like the concept *poisonous* if and to the extent that the following conditions obtain:

(Concerns) They are concerned to avoid substances that have adverse effects on their bodies.

(Capacities) They are incapable of tolerating a great many substances, but they are capable of exchanging information with similarly constituted concept-users.

(Circumstances) They inhabit an environment in which there is a real risk of encountering substances with adverse effects on their bodies.

Resulting conceptual need: concept-users satisfying these conditions need a concept that marks out things with adverse effects on their bodies as things to be avoided and enables them to alert each other to those things.

In view of this matrix highlighting a need the concept *poisonous* answers to, we can consider whether the concept has a point for us, and what it needs to be like in order to serve us as well as it could. Clearly, we share all of the needfulness conditions singled out by this need matrix, which means that for us, there is a point to using the concept, i.e. it meets a conceptual need of ours.

But the matrix also conveys a sense of what demands this need places on our conceptualization of what is poisonous, and what, in light of these demands, that conceptualization *should* be like: the concept we use should have a descriptive dimension tracking certain biochemical facts; but the contours of its extension should also reflect a certain physiological perspective. It should track biochemical properties that have adverse effects on the human body, but not necessarily on other species. If some substance *x* turns out to have adverse effects on the human body, but does not fall under the extension of the concept, then this indicates a respect in which our conceptualization of what is poisonous should be revised: its extension should be broadened to include *x*. Furthermore, the conceptualization should not be merely descriptive; it should carry a negative valence implying that one had better stay away from whatever falls under its extension.

In this way, a need matrix allows us to appraise and improve a conceptualization. Once a suitable conceptualization is in use, moreover, derivative forms tailored to other species can easily be created from it, as when a zoologist introduces the concept *poisonous for the grasshopper mouse* and finds that scorpion venom, though poisonous in the original, anthropocentric sense, does not fall under that derivative concept.

A second, particularly instructive illustration of how the construction of need matrices can inform the ethics of conceptualization can be garnered from E. J. Craig's 'synthesis' of the concept of knowledge, which—though Craig does not present it this way himself—can illuminatingly be elaborated into a needs-based reflection on how we *should* conceptualize knowledge given our conceptual needs.[31]

Craig begins by treating certain widely shared human capacities and circumstances as constants in a state-of-nature fiction, and then asks what human concern would engender a need for something like the concept of knowledge under these conditions. Of course, the concept of knowledge is so deeply embedded in human life that it might be expected to tie in with several different conceptual needs at once; to take a fuller measure of its value, one would therefore have to explore several different need matrices to which it answers.[32] But Craig helpfully suggests that we 'test the explanatory powers of the simple before resorting to the complex' (1990, 4), and start with one of

---

[31] See Craig (1986, 1990, 1993).
[32] Reconstructing several different need matrices to which the concept of knowledge answers is exactly what a lot of recent epistemological work can be read as having done. Other conceptual needs it has been thought to help us to meet include: the need to signal that inquiry is at an end (Kappel 2010, Kelp 2011, Rysiew 2012); to identify propositions treatable as reasons for acting (McGrath 2015); to provide assurance (Lawlor 2013); to distinguish blameless from blameworthy behaviour (Beebe 2012); and to honour subjects of knowledge attributions (Kusch 2009).

the most basic concerns we can find that already engenders a need for something like the concept of knowledge.[33]

Craig hypothesizes that an utterly basic concern that would generate a need for something like the concept of knowledge is the concern, which we can hardly imagine human beings lacking, to gather information about the immediate environment, and especially about its risks and opportunities. If such a concern is felt in a community possessing a shared language, the mere fact that members of the community will be in different places at different times, and that no one in the community will be capable of always acquiring all the information they need all by themselves, will be sufficient to generate a need for something like the concept of knowledge:

> *Needfulness conditions*: a concept-user U has an instrumental need for something like the concept *knowledge* if and to the extent that they satisfy the following conditions:
>
> (Concerns) U's concern is to find out whether p;
>
> (Capacities) U's own capacities are not sufficient to find out whether p, at least not without very considerable investigative effort;
>
> (Circumstances) U's circumstances are such that there might be someone in U's community who is in a position to tell U whether p.
>
> *Resulting conceptual need*: concept-users satisfying all of these conditions need a concept that *marks out* people with a propensity to say something true about whether p.

Craig labels this need matrix 'the inquirer's situation'.[34] In relation to the resulting conceptual need, a good concept of knowledge will be a concept that is good *for* marking out people with a propensity to say something true about whether p.

What conceptualization of knowledge is best suited to meet the inquirer's need, Craig then asks? The first answer that comes to mind is: one that directly tracks the propensity to say something true about whether p. But this will not do; for someone in the inquirer's situation, this is no use at all in *recognizing* people with a propensity to say something true about whether p, because the ability to assess the truth of what someone says about whether

---

[33] See Craig (1990, 4).
[34] See Craig (1990, 15). See also Fricker's (2007, 2010c) similarly needs-based commendation of the virtue of testimonial justice.

p presupposes knowledge whether *p*, which is precisely the state that the inquirer hopes to attain by means of the concept at issue.

To be any help at all in meeting the conceptual needs of the inquirer, therefore, the conceptualization deployed by the inquirer needs to track properties that *indicate* a propensity to say something true about whether *p* and are *recognizable* to the inquirer as indicating that propensity.[35] These indicator properties might include: standing in the right causal relation to the state of affairs in question; being able to offer a justification for one's opinion; or having a good track record on this type of question. Each of these properties is *typically* a good indicator of the propensity to say something true about whether *p*, and the more such indicator properties someone exhibits, the likelier it is that the inquirer is dealing with someone who can offer the truth about whether *p*.

But the presence of these properties nonetheless falls short of guaranteeing that the inquirer is being offered the truth about whether *p*. A concept can be justifiably, but nonetheless incorrectly applied if the presence of the indicator properties guiding its application merely makes it probable that the concept in fact applies.

This trade-off is nonetheless advantageous for the inquirer, since the choice is one between fallible conceptual guidance and none at all: the concern to find out whether *p* can be better satisfied by a conceptualization that sacrifices infallibility to usability than by one that renders knowledge unrecognizable to those who do not already possess it. The latter conceptualization might meet the conceptual needs of *examiners*, concerned to tell whether someone knows something already known to themselves, but it would do nothing to serve the concern to *find out* whether *p*.[36]

The example illustrates a broader lesson: conceptualizations need to accept trade-offs in order to be fit for use by real human concept-users. Concepts are not applied by all-seeing intelligences, capable of telling, immediately and definitely, what any imaginable concept is and is not applicable to. Approaching concepts as if from the perspective of a disembodied and omniscient mind that can instantly compute the extension of any given concept for any world or world-time pair, as is typically done in formal semantics,[37] may be helpful in trying to render the semantics of natural languages mathematically tractable,

---

[35] See also Craig (2000, 656).
[36] On the examiner's situation, see Williams (1973a, 146; 2005b, ch. 2).
[37] David Chalmers, for example, writes: 'We can say that a subject grasps an intension when the subject is in a position to *evaluate* that intension: that is, when sufficient reasoning will allow the subject to determine the value of the intension at any world' (2002, 148).

or in showing how the meanings of complex expressions can be computed from the meanings of simpler expressions. But to evaluate how different concepts actually fare in the service of actual human concept-users, we have to relate the concepts to concretely situated agents with certain concerns and capacities, encountering a particular world from a particular perspective that imposes serious epistemic limitations on them—most basically, the limitations of only ever being at one place at a time, and of perceiving the world through a physiological constitution that makes it harder to apply concepts at certain scales and through certain sensory modalities.

From the perspective of such concept-users, one of the most fundamental challenges concept-users face is precisely the challenge that is elided by the perspective of the omniscient computer of extensions across all possible worlds, namely the challenge of how to *tell* whether a given concept applies to something.[38] This already makes demands on concept-users: the correct application of concepts typically demands some *investigative effort* to get into a position from which to tell whether a concept applies, be it in the form of reasoning (e.g. does the concept *prime* apply to 514229?) or in the form of changing one's vantage point in time or space (e.g. does the concept *ripe* apply to yonder fruit?). But it also makes demands on conceptualization itself—demands we only see once we consider the challenges involved in *operationalizing* concepts for use by practically situated concept-users.

For concepts to be capable of rewarding investigative effort, they need to be *recognizably applicable*: their users need some means of *tracking* what the concept picks out. Some concepts, such as the concept *blue light*, make this easy: the properties picked out by the concept coincide with those by which users of the concept typically identify its extension—in which case we might say that the properties guiding use of the concept F are not just *indicative*, but *constitutive* of F. This is true of all concepts that resist the distinction between *seeming* to be F and *being* F. (Even if you wear blue-tinted glasses, the light you see does not just *seem* to be blue light; the light going from the glasses into your eyes really *is* blue light if anything is.)

But many other concepts, in order to be world-guided in their application at all, need to rely on discernible properties that are indicative of F *without* being constitutive of F: properties that can be tracked in order thereby to track F. A property indicative of F could be any property G that is strongly

---

[38] For a related point, see Brigandt (2013, 76), who observes that a subject may lack the ability to evaluate the intension of a concept in a given world for lack of other concepts: geneticists in the 1930s had the concept *gene*, but were unable to determine its exact extension because they lacked the necessary concepts of molecular biology.

correlated with the property of being F. Of course, the concept F is *correctly* applied only to things that really are F, but in order to tell which these are, we need to conceptualize F-ness in terms that provide indicators giving us *reasons* to judge that a given thing is F (—'What makes you think this is a Rembrandt?'—'Just look at the use of directional light and the carefully detailed facial expressions').

To epistemically limited concept-users, these more accessible or more recognizable proxies for what is to be picked out offer indispensable practical assistance. We must only be careful not to equate indicative with constitutive properties: we tell the time by measuring the movement of clock hands, but this does not mean that time *is* the movement of clock hands; we identify Mars in the night sky by looking for a red planet, but this does not mean that Mars *is* a red planet; we attribute mental states to others on the basis of observable behaviour, but, *pace* Skinnerian behaviourists, this does not mean that mental states *are* observable behaviour; we discern causation notably by tracking constant conjunction, but, *pace* the constant conjunction theory of causation, this does not mean that causation *is* constant conjunction.[39]

This suggests a very basic desideratum for the ethics of conceptualization: the ways of thinking we need should enable us to *track* the extensions of our concepts via *reliable* indicators. That is not to say that there cannot be exceptions to this. This particular desideratum may be outweighed by others in a given case. But thinking about the challenges facing practically situated concept-users with limited human capacities leads one to expect that a helpful conceptualization would *typically* license reliable inferences from the presence or absence of certain indicator properties to the applicability or inapplicability of a concept.

This conceptual reliability can in turn be analysed into two aspects: *conceptual sensitivity* and *conceptual specificity*. Let conceptual sensitivity be the degree to which the indicator properties that a concept tracks its extension by constitute a reliable way of identifying that which *does* fall under its extension (if x is F, how much of the time does a user of concept F recognize that x is F?). Low conceptual sensitivity will then favour 'false negatives': the concept-user will be prone to judge that x is *not-F* when, in fact, x is F, thereby missing many instances in which the concept applies.

---

[39] On that last point, see Harré (1964, 359), who charges Hume with making this mistake. While Hume certainly took the observation of constant conjunction to be an important *source* of our concept of causation, however, it is less clear that he meant to proffer an *analysis* of the concept in terms of constant conjunction.

Conceptual specificity, on the other hand, can be defined as the degree to which the indicator properties are a reliable way of excluding that which does *not* fall under the concept (if x is not-F, how much of the time does a user of concept F recognize that x is not-F?). Low conceptual specificity will favour 'false positives': the concept-user will be prone to judge that x *is* F when x is not-F, treating the concept as applicable even in instances in which it only *seems* to be applicable without really *being* applicable.

Analysing reliability into sensitivity and specificity allows us to see the differences in value between different ways of conceptualizing something that are less than fully reliable to the same degree but along different dimensions. Consider the concept *fraud* as employed by administrators in assessing claims to unemployment benefits, for example. If those administrators' capacities to investigate and access information about each individual claimant are limited, their application of the concept will need to be guided by indicator properties that are less than fully reliable. But there are two ways in which that could be so. The concept could be somewhat unreliable by being applied *too narrowly*, i.e. generating false negatives due to a lack of sensitivity, or by being applied *too broadly*, i.e. generating false positives due to a lack of specificity.

This distinction between two species of unreliability clearly matters to the appraisal of different ways of conceptualizing fraud: if one way of conceptualizing fraud leads to the concept being applied too narrowly to some degree and another way of conceptualizing fraud leads to the concept being applied too broadly to exactly the same degree, these two conceptualizations of fraud will be equally unreliable, but nonetheless differ in the kinds of consequences their unreliability has: if the concept is applied too narrowly, the state loses money over fraudulent benefits claims; if the concept is applied too broadly, the state leaves people to starve. That this is a significant difference is agreed even between those who disagree about which of these outcomes is preferable.

Given this analysis of conceptual reliability into conceptual sensitivity and specificity, it might be tempting to conclude that we always need our conceptualizations to be *maximally* sensitive and specific, leaving no room for discrepancies to open up between the indicator properties and what they indicate. But if we approach the ethics of conceptualization from the vantage point of practically situated concept-users trying to make the most of their limited capacities, this ideal quickly loses its appeal. We typically *need* there to be potential gaps between indicators and what they indicate, because the elusory world we inhabit would largely remain silent before a mind stocked solely with conceptualizations that left no room for these gaps ever to open. In such a mind, nothing would register but that which was invariably conjoined; of all the countless robust correlations that are well worth being conceptually sensitive to, nothing would be made.

We thus need to strike a balance between reliability and usability. Our conceptualizations can more than make up for their relative unreliability by being eminently usable, tracking properties that are readily accessible. Reliability is a good, but it is not the only good. We also need to take into account what Christian Nimtz (2024b) calls *representational ergonomics*—or, as I would prefer to say, *conceptual ergonomics*: what our conceptualizations must be like if they are to be suitable tools for concept-users who find it easier to grasp, process, and apply some concepts than others.

Furthermore, our conceptualizations can compensate for their unreliability through their *flexibility*: the degree to which they can accommodate the variability of indicator properties. If the properties indicating a concept's applicability vary widely, but most of these indicator properties are not strictly necessary conditions for something to fall under the concept, we are better off thinking in terms that 'ride such variability', in Adrian Moore's (1993, 286) phrase, tracking the range of properties that typically, if defeasibly, indicate that something falls under a concept.

These trade-offs are intimated already in Craig's initial need matrix for the concept of knowledge. The sort of conceptualization of knowledge we need, as far as this need matrix allows us to see, is one that is less than fully reliable, but that makes up for its relative unreliability through its usability, by tracking properties that are readily accessible. Moreover, it should display a considerable degree of *flexibility*: given the variability of the indicator properties through which people with a propensity to say something true about whether *p* become recognizable as such, and given that most of these properties are not strictly necessary conditions on that propensity, we are better off thinking in terms that can ride this variability, tracking the range of properties that typically but defeasibly indicate a propensity to say something true about whether *p*.

This initial need matrix modelling the inquirer's situation of course remains overly simple, and needs further elaboration to generate a need for something recognizable to us as *our* concept of knowledge;[40] but it already indicates reasons for us to conceptualize knowledge in certain ways rather than others. As far as this need matrix allows us to see, the conceptualization of knowledge we need should not single out any one indicator property by

---

[40] An elaboration that Craig (1990, 82-97; 1993, 81-115) actually offers, and that I discuss in Queloz (2021c, 145-9); see also Fricker (2010c, 61), Kusch (2011, 9-10), and Hannon (2019, ch. 2).

treating it as a necessary condition on the applicability of the concept. In view of the variability of the marks of a propensity to say something true on a given question, we do better to track a range of *normally* but not *unfailingly* reliable indicator properties without treating any one of them as indispensable. The need matrix thereby casts doubt on definitions of knowledge in terms of necessary and sufficient conditions. It presents the conceptualization we need as being more flexible and less reliable for good reason.

7.6 Four Problems Solved

Let me wrap up the discussion of conceptual needs by showing how they allow us to deal with the four problems we confronted at the end of the previous chapter: the concern identification problem, the generalizability problem, the critical distance problem, and the underdetermination problem.

The needs-based approach I have sketched solves the concern identification problem by adducing three ideas: first, that insofar as concepts *express* the conditions that would render them needful, they can themselves guide us towards concerns that might inform their appraisal; second, that we can render the intractable welter of our concerns tractable by constructing need matrices; and third, that we can search for relevant concerns by treating the other two variables of a need matrix as constants—whether by using highly generic parameters characteristic of human beings in general or by using parameters that are of particular interest because they characterize our own situation.

The needs-based approach also solves the underdetermination problem by highlighting how, if we bring certain concerns to the world, the world then makes certain demands on our conceptualizations given what we demand of the world, thereby whittling down the space of suitable concepts to those best suited to serving our concerns by meeting these demands. Only once we bring into the picture the practical demands that the world makes us on given our concerns does the notion of a good concept become fully determinate. This is why our choice of concepts does not answer, in the first instance, to our concerns. What it immediately answers to is our conceptual needs.

As for the generalizability and the critical distance problem, the needs-based approach overcomes them both by going more *external* than the goal-based approach we considered. On the goal-based approach, recall, 'the concept's epistemic goal is the kinds of inferences and explanations that the concept is intended to support' (Brigandt 2010, 24), and 'the epistemic goal pursued by a concept's use is...considered a component of a concept' (Brigandt 2010, 22). Needs-based appraisal, by contrast, looks to how concepts directly or indirectly tie in with people's concerns by meeting their conceptual needs, independently of whether these concerns are constitutive of the concepts, or of whether people use the concepts with a view to satisfying these concerns. Accordingly, while constitutive goals are internal to concept-users' understanding of what they are up to in using concepts, their conceptual needs can come as a discovery to them.

This needs-based standard is more external also in that many of our concerns are not subject to our will in the way that our goals or aims are. What concepts we need to use can therefore be independent of our will. It is only in special cases, namely those in which all the relevant (i.e. need-engendering) concerns are fully under the control of the will, that we can change our conceptual needs at will, by *redirecting* our concerns. But this only works when we can redirect our concerns *by deciding* to redirect our concerns. And many of our most fundamental concerns, including those growing out of what I called our inner needs, are concerns for things that we cannot simply decide not to care about. Concept-users might just have certain conceptual needs in virtue of their concerns and limited capacities in the kind of world they live in, whether they want it or not. In sum, conceptual needs form a more external standard than constitutive goals in that needs can be had unwittingly and unwillingly.

Such greater externality brings both advantages and disadvantages. The main *disadvantage*, which became evident already in the examples we considered, is that constructing a need matrix requires a good deal of interpretation: one cannot mechanically read off a concept what conditions should figure in the need matrix; rather, one needs to searchingly work one's way back to some human concern, tentatively combine it with certain capacities and circumstances to obtain a set of need-generating conditions, and explore how much light this sheds on our use of the concept. These tentative conjectures risk seeming ad hoc, initially; but, as in the hypothetico-deductive model of science, they can prove their worth through the insights they lead to and the consonance of the resulting picture.

To say that the backward inference from a way of thinking to the need behind it requires interpretation is thus not to say that anything goes. Need matrices can be externally validated, internally validated, and normatively endorsed. Furthermore, the way in which Craig's account has been scrutinized, refined, complemented, and improved on by other philosophers exemplifies the validating and corrective role of the court of philosophical opinion.[41] In the end, whatever interpretation is involved in the needs-based approach is constrained by what actually makes sense to us, and this is not something we can control *ad lib.*: we do not *decide* that a claim about how a concept relates to our needs and concerns makes sense to us. It comes as a discovery. In light of a concept's features and the way it is in fact employed in human life, some claims about the needs it meets will make more sense than others, and some will simply not make any sense. There are claims about conceptual needs that no truthful look at human affairs will bear out. It thus stands with claims about conceptual needs much as it stands with interpretative claims in disciplines like evolutionary biology, archaeology, sociology, political theory, economics, or history. There is room for interpretation, but there are also claims that no truthful reading of the data will bear out. As the French Prime Minister Clemenceau replied to a representative of the Weimar Republic wondering how future historians would make sense of the outbreak of WWI: 'This I don't know. But I know for certain that they will not say Belgium invaded Germany.'[42]

The main *advantage* of interpreting one's way to a more external standard, however, is that it solves the problems of generalizability and critical distance.

Consider first the critical distance problem. By stepping back from a concept and looking at its relation to our conceptual needs from the autoethnographic stance, we obtain critical distance not only towards the concept, but also towards its constitutive goal and the aims that concept-users consciously pursue in using the concept. Concepts then invite critique to the extent that they fail to adequately meet the conceptual needs that concept-users have in virtue of their concerns, capacities, and circumstances. This makes room for the possibility of finding, on the basis of our conceptual needs, that even a concept that is perfectly suited to meeting its constitutive goal, or to realizing our conscious aims, nonetheless fails to meet our conceptual needs, and, at worst, systematically obstructs or frustrates them.

But needs-based appraisal also goes beyond goal-based appraisal in allowing for the possibility that concepts might serve our concerns even though we do not regard them as instrumental to our concerns at all. When philosophers draw their standard of concept appraisal from the instrumentality of a concept in serving its constitutive goal, they have no use for the distinction between the perspective of the engaged concept-user and the perspective of

---

[41] See B. Williams (2002, 2010), Fricker (1998, 2007, 2012, 2016a), Kusch (2009, 2011, 2013), Pritchard (2012), Reynolds (2017), and Hannon (2013, 2015, 2019).

[42] The exchange is related in Arendt (1968, 239). For a discussion of constraints on historical sense-making, see Williams (2002, 241–50) and Cueni and Queloz (2022).

the disengaged, reflective appraiser of the concept. For when a concept is appraised according to how conducive it is to meeting the goal with which it is deployed, user and appraiser alike explicitly *instrumentalize* the concept by regarding it as a means to achieve a certain end, and so the instrumentalizing mentality of the appraisal is in keeping with the instrumentalizing mentality with which the concept is employed by its users.

By contrast, needs-based appraisal allows for the possibility that our concepts might possess instrumental value we know nothing of, as they may fill needs we did not even know we had. Seemingly idle concepts may in fact do important work; concepts of intrinsically valuable traits or properties may be essential props of practices and institutions without being used in an instrumental spirit at all. The *classical gene* concept is a special case, in that there is some plausibility to the claim that it was consciously designed and deployed to serve scientists' aim of explaining and predicting inheritance patterns. This instrumentalizing mentality obligingly hands us a standard for appraising the instrumentality of the concept. But many branches of human thought—aesthetic, moral, political, or legal—are thick with concepts that are not evidently goal-directed in this way, and hence provide nothing like the focused evaluative guidance of the Mendelian geneticist's naked instrumentalism about his purpose-built concepts. We can still ask how a concept lacking a constitutive goal relates to our conceptual needs and try to gauge the concept's instrumental value to us.[43] But the concept itself will not always hand us the standard for this appraisal. We may have to look beyond the concept and reconstruct what kinds of exigencies, if any, it might be responding to, because its instrumental dimension is initially opaque. Part of what lends needs-based concept appraisal its philosophical interest and informativeness, then, is that our conceptual needs are not immediately transparent to us in the way that the goals with which we use certain concepts are.

Making room for critical distance from our concepts and the goals with which we employ them is important not just to account for the possibility of radical critiques of inherited ways of thinking, but also, more generally, for separating what is dead from what is alive in our conceptual inheritance. Some concepts can be shown by reflection on our conceptual needs to have outlived their usefulness—they may have been perfectly good concepts for those who first created them, but they are dead wood to us. Understanding a concept's needfulness conditions equips us to discriminate between

---

[43] For an approach to aesthetic concepts that is congenial to the needs-based approach, see Robson and Sinclair (2023).

conceptual holdovers that have outlived their usefulness and concepts we still sorely need.

Consider, for example, the concept *honour*. Is there still life in this concept in the modern world? Should we use it and promulgate it? Clearly, such a venerable old concept at work in so many different cultures is likely to meet a variety of needs. But we might model at least *one aspect* of its needfulness conditions using the following need matrix, which reflects one strand in the vast literature on honour cultures:[44]

> *Needfulness conditions*: concept-users have an instrumental need for something very like the concept *honour* if and to the extent that the following conditions obtain:
>
> (Concerns) Individuals are concerned to hold on to their property.
>
> (Capacities) Individuals' capacity to prevent theft is limited—especially when it comes to highly divisible and portable property.
>
> (Circumstances) Centralized institutions enforcing property rights are weak or entirely lacking.
>
> *Resulting conceptual need*: concept-users satisfying all these conditions have a need for a concept that compensates for the lack of centralized institutions enforcing property rights by introducing a more diffuse and decentralized deterrent.

In relation to this need matrix, the concept of honour might be thought to serve property-owners' concerns, whether they realize it or not. For it can act as the linchpin of an honour culture in which people are quick to take offence and can be expected to retaliate even when the costs of retaliating exceed the value of the stolen good. And by projecting a willingness to treat even a comparatively small theft as a serious offence calling for retaliation *in the name of honour*, people send discouraging signals to potential thieves, compensating for the lack of a centralized deterrent with a more diffuse and decentralized deterrent.[45]

This need matrix could be used to account for the prevalence of the concept of honour in places where its needfulness conditions were fulfilled—it

---

[44] I rely here especially on Nisbett and Cohen (1996), Testini (2021, 2022), and Shackelford (2005), but different strands of the literature would lead one to complement that need matrix with others, some of which would cast a more favourable light on the concept. For a discussion of the concept's role as an engine of moral reform, for instance, see Appiah (2010).

[45] See Testini (2021, 2022).

could help explain the strong honour cultures in places like the American South in the eighteenth and early nineteenth century, for example, where valuable property tended to take the form of cattle rather than land, and centralized institutions tasked with enforcing property rights were comparatively weak or unreliable.

But equally, the need matrix can be used to assess the value of the concept to us today. Insofar as we fail to share one or several of the three conditions represented in the need matrix, we will *to that extent* lack reason to think in terms of *honour*. For us, using the concept will *to that extent* be pointless (though other need matrices may reveal its use to be pointful in other respects).

This illustrates how the needs-based approach allows us both to understand why a concept earned its keep under certain conditions while at the same time being unhelpful *to us*, for whom these conditions no longer hold. Reconstructing the concept's needfulness conditions has critical force for us—and does so precisely because the conditions it appeals to are *not* constitutive of the concept, for this is what allows the concept to *outlive* the conditions that formerly bestowed value upon it.

Secondly, going more external also enables the needs-based approach to overcome the generalizability problem: even where a concept lacks a constitutive goal, or where we do not consciously deploy it with a view to satisfying a particular aim, we can still look to how the concept relates to our conceptual needs and the concerns we identify with.

The greater generality of the approach does not consist merely in its wider applicability to our current concepts. While looking at the fit between concepts and need matrices allows us to evaluate how well the concepts we now use meet the conceptual needs we now have, the same relation of fit between concepts and need matrices can be deployed *retrospectively*, to discern the respects in which, even when concepts lacked a constitutive goal, conceptual change was nevertheless rational: it was a rational adjustment to corresponding changes in the needfulness conditions to which the concepts answered. This empowers the present account to rationalize changes in the conceptual repertoire: when people's conceptual needs change, it is only rational for their conceptual repertoire to change with them.

Moreover, this relation of fit between concepts and need matrices can also be deployed *prospectively*, to get a sense of what concepts we will need as we meet the future and the novel concerns, capacities, and circumstances it brings. If our concerns, capacities, and circumstances change, our conceptual repertoire will have to change with them if it is to meet our conceptual needs.

Developments such as climate change and the increasing reliance on AI bring unprecedented conceptual needs in their wake—perhaps we need to fashion many more concepts of 'green virtues' to adapt our repertoire of inherited virtue concepts; or perhaps we need to rethink our conceptions of liability for clinical decision-making relying on AI-powered systems.[46] Constructing need matrices can help us to more sharply envision these needs and what the concepts capable of meeting them should look like.

Last but not least, looking to conceptual needs also enables us to discriminate between conceptual engineering efforts that fill a need and conceptual engineering efforts that are needless and ill-motivated. As the American philosopher Justus Buchler succinctly observed: 'the responsible introduction or extension of terms, whether in philosophy or science, reflects a conceptual need' (1955, 108).

The Ethics of Conceptualization: Tailoring Thought and Language to Need. Matthieu Queloz, Oxford University Press.
© Matthieu Queloz 2025. DOI: 10.1093/9780198926283.003.0008

---

[46] On 'green virtues', see Jamieson (2007, 2014); for an overview of the issues surrounding the use of AI in clinical decision-making, see H. Smith (2021).

8
Reasons for Reasons

In developing a framework for answering the authority question, we began from the idea that our concepts should tie in with concerns we critically identify with, because conceptual authority ultimately wells up from our concerns. We then saw that, even if our concepts must tap into our concerns to be imbued with authority, these concerns do not yet yield an operational measure of a concept's merits; nor can concerns by themselves give us reasons to use certain concepts rather than others. That is done by the conceptual needs our concerns generate through their interaction with our capacities and circumstances. It is in our conceptual needs—many of which are highly local—that we find those reasons. Conceptual needs *constitute reasons for concept use*. This is the third and final loadbearing idea of the needs-based approach.

My aim in this chapter is to clarify the role of reasons for concept use before showing how they allow us to answer the authority question. I then sharpen the resulting conception of authority by contrasting it with alternative conceptions of authority. Along the way, I bring out how we can allocate a role to reasons for concept use without crowding out other kinds of reasons that transcend preoccupation with our concerns or with the instrumentality of concepts. In fact, it will emerge that reasons for concept use can boost our confidence in ways of thinking that are not centred on human concerns at all. I also defuse the worry that needs-based appraisal yields the wrong kind of reasons, and argue that the worry overlooks some of our most important reasons to prefer certain concepts over others. I close by considering in what sense concepts can be valuable even when they are not instrumentally good for anything.

8.1 Reasons in vs. Reasons for Concept Use

When one steps back to assess the authority of a concept, one disengages oneself from the concept and its correlative reasons. The pattern of reasoning traced out by the concept is put in the dock and critically evaluated: what reasons do we have to heed those reasons in the first place? From this more external vantage point, we can then look to the concerns we critically identify with and consider what conceptual needs they engender in us, given our capacities and circumstances. These needs constitute reasons to use certain concepts and be responsive to certain reasons.

Accordingly, when a justification such as 'Because it is *natural*' prompts the authority question and leads someone to demand reasons to recognize this as a reason, we can work our way up the chain of reasons to determine what reasons for concept use the authority of this concept is grounded in.

This is to pursue a chain of reasons that is orthogonal to the chain of reasons we usually move along as engaged users of a concept, however. Ordinarily, we move from one object-level judgement to another as we move from one reason to the next, asking what a judgement follows from, or what follows from it. In the example of the judgement articulated in terms of *naturalness*, a normal request for reasons would take the form: 'Why is it natural?' That question takes the concept *natural* for granted and demands a justification for this particular application of it.

The authority question, by contrast, involves an ascent to the metaconceptual level of second-order reasons. It asks for reasons to regard something's being natural *as* a reason in this connection. This is to demand reasons for reasons, i.e. second-order reasons to use a given concept F such that x's being F counts as a first-order reason to think that x is G:

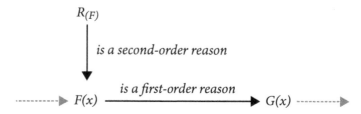

A reason for a reason: $R_{(F)}$ is a second-order reason to use a concept F such that x's being F counts as a first-order reason to think that x is G.

We can sharpen the contrast between, on the one hand, the first-order reasons *in terms of which we think* when using concepts in an engaged way, and, on the other hand, the second-order reasons *for thinking in these terms* that come into view when using the concepts in a disengaged way, by distinguishing between reasons *in* and reasons *for* concept use:

Reasons in concept use: the ordinary reasons operative *within* a practice of reason-giving articulated in terms of concept F, i.e. the reasons guiding and flowing from the application of concept F. Becoming an engaged user of concept F essentially involves becoming responsive to those first-order reasons and understanding that $E(x)$ is a reason to think that $F(x)$, and that $F(x)$ is a reason to think that $G(x)$.

Reasons for concept use: the reasons *for* a practice of reason-giving to be articulated in terms of concept F at all, i.e. the second-order reasons one has to be an engaged user of a concept F such that one is disposed to treat $E(x)$ as a reason to think that $F(x)$, or $F(x)$ as a reason to think that $G(x)$.

The two kinds of reasons are connected as follows: reasons *for* concept use are reasons for recognizing certain reasons *in* concept use *as* reasons—in this sense, they are reasons for reasons.[1]

By way of illustration, consider again the concept *blasphemous*: the reasons *in* concept use are the reasons that guide and flow from the application of the concept—reasons that might figure in deliberation as follows: 'This book is *blasphemous*, because it is disrespectful towards God'; or 'Because the book is *blasphemous*, it should be banned'. Reasons *for* concept use, by contrast, are the rationales that underlie or vindicate the adoption and continued use of the concept—they are the reasons one has to reason in terms of the concept *blasphemous* and heed the reasons it adverts to.

To be compelling in the eyes of someone who is not fully confident in the concept, reasons for concept use must not themselves draw on the concept whose use they favour: in this example, one *could* insist that we need to use the concept of blasphemy because there is so much blasphemy around, and because what is disrespectful towards God should be banned; but this would be not so much false as *insufficiently independent* of the concept and its concomitant reasons. Precisely what someone challenging the authority of the concept wants to know is whether we have reason to be sensitive to the

---

[1] In some respects, this echoes Schroeder's (2007, 136–41) recursive account of the weight of reasons. But while Schroeder is concerned with reasons to give reasons more or less weight in one's deliberations in a given case, I am concerned with reasons for or against using a concept, which determines whether one trades in a certain currency of reasons at all.

presence of blasphemy and heed the reasons associated with it. To be forceful independently of one's confidence in the concept, therefore, reasons for concept use will have to be reasons given from a disengaged perspective on the concept.

We therefore need to combine the distinction between reasons *in* and *for* concept use with the distinction between *engaged* and *disengaged* concept use. From a *disengaged* perspective on concept F, a reason *in* concept use might register as follows: 'For an engaged user of the concept F, $F(x)$ is a reason to think that $G(x)$.' From an engaged perspective on concept F, by contrast, the same reason in concept use would register simply as: '$F(x)$ is a reason to think that $G(x)$.'

Analogously, we can distinguish disengaged from engaged reasons *for* concept use. Let $R_{(F)}$ be such a second-order reason to use concept F. From a disengaged perspective on concept F, $R_{(F)}$ must not itself make use of concept F or the reason relations it encodes. From an engaged perspective on concept F, by contrast, no such restriction holds on what can count as $R_{(F)}$, and the prevalence as well as the intrinsic features of what F picks out will seem like the most salient reasons for concept use ('Why should we use the concept of blasphemy? Because there is so much blasphemy around and blasphemy is bad, of course!').

Even disengaged reasons for concept use will still make engaged use of other concepts—inevitably, *all* reasons are reasons revealed *in* the use of some concept or other; this is what led Wittgenstein to worry that giving reasons for thinking as we do might incoherently require an answer 'outside the game of reasoning' (1979, §4). But thanks to our capacity to critically disengage ourselves from our concepts, we can give reasons for thinking as we do from within the game of reasoning. And no problematic circularity is involved as long as the reasons revealed in the use of *some* concepts offer reasons for the use of *other* concepts.

The resulting view allows us to reject the idea that concept choice is always rationally contingent and a mere matter of convention. On the needs-based approach, it is at least *worth asking* whether there is some reason for a given practice of reason-giving. In this respect, the approach is moderately rationalistic. It takes seriously the possibility that there might be *some reason for each* practice of reason-giving.

But it equally contrasts with views on which there is one reason, or one unified set of reasons, for all practices of reason-giving. Both foundationalist attempts to derive conceptual authority from timeless foundations and tidy-minded attempts to derive it from a unifying theory embody the rationalistic hope that there might be *one type of reason for all* practices of reason-giving, for instance in the form of theoretical virtue, a universal metric of utility, or a categorical imperative:

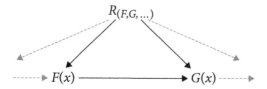

One reason for all reasons: $R_{(F, G, ...)}$ is a second-order reason to use a concept F such that x's being F counts as a first-order reason to think that x is G, as well as a second-order reason to use a concept G such that ..., etc.

It is this ambition to find a unified basis of authority that the needs-based approach abandons, looking instead for a form of conceptual authority that is grounded in a plurality of needs and concerns instead of being derived from a single overarching currency of reasons.

The needs-based approach still seeks to identify a basis for reasoned discrimination between more and less authoritative concepts; it just gives us no reason to expect there to be a single currency of reasons that everywhere forms the basis of authority. As Anscombe remarks, we can accept that all chains of reasons must stop somewhere, but we should resist the 'illicit transition' from 'all chains must stop somewhere' to 'there is somewhere where all chains must stop' (1957, §21). More precisely, we would be guilty of a 'quantifier shift fallacy' if we misconstrued a weak, but correct claim of the form 'for all X, there is some Y which...' as a far stronger claim of the form 'there is some Y such that for all X, it...' (Heal 2003, 240). There are as many different types of bases of authority as there are types of human concerns. Only together with the conviction that there must be a single currency of reasons for all reasons does the Enlightenment expectation that we can always appropriately demand reasons for reasons tend towards a unified system.[2]

Without this conviction, we can seek reasons *for each but not for all* reasons, and will end up not with a unified system, but with a pluralistically vindicated conceptual apparatus:

---

[2] The 'single currency of reasons' is Williams's phrase; see Williams (1985, 250 n. 13). See also Williams (1985, 124–6) for a related discussion of how the demand for what Williams calls 'justificatory reasons' naturally leads to the construction of an ethical theory.

Reasons for each reason: $R_{(F)}$ is a second-order reason to use a concept F such that x's being F counts as a first-order reason to think that x is G. $R_{(G)}$ does the same for the concept G, etc.

Such an approach may not live up to the demands of tidy-mindedness, but it nevertheless promises to meet two desiderata on a non-foundationalist understanding of conceptual authority. It promises to enable us (i) to identify reasons to be confident in at least some of our concepts, thus avoiding indiscriminate ironism; and (ii) to make sense of the possibility of radical critique in terms of the possibility that the concepts currently in use fail to meet our conceptual needs, thus avoiding undiscriminating holism.

8.2 Concern-Independent Reasons in Concept Use

The idea that conceptual needs constitute reasons for concept use capable of buttressing reasons for action and belief must not be allowed to displace a more entrenched fact, however: that, for the engaged concept-user, there are countless places in the conceptual architecture where the chain of reasons comes to an end in buck-stopping, spade-turning reasons that have nothing whatsoever to do with our needs or concerns.[3] It would, again, be a conflation of the engaged and the disengaged perspective to conclude, from the fact that reasons for concept use are to be found in conceptual needs deriving from human concerns, that all chains of reasons must ultimately be anchored in conceptual needs or human concerns.

For a needs-based account of concept appraisal to be psychologically realistic and steer clear of reductive oversimplification, therefore, it is crucial to recognize how *independent* of our concerns the reasons in concept use remain, even when they can be buttressed by reasons for concept use. Except in certain cases—a concern to look different can be cited as a reason to get a

---

[3] A point recently emphasized, from within frameworks congenial to the needs-based approach, by Müller (2020, 189–218) and Sinclair (2021, 191–217).

different haircut—the reasons that move us to believe or do things typically make no reference to our concerns at all. In spelling out the force of moral, political, or professional reasons for action, for example, one's own concerns are typically beside the point. These types of considerations—the badness of wanton cruelty, the importance of equality, or the duties of one's office—precisely tend to give us reasons to do things regardless of what our own concerns happen to be.

It is a remarkable fact about concepts that they possess the power to direct our attention away not just from an ego-centric preoccupation with the satisfaction of our own concerns, but even from an anthropocentric preoccupation with the satisfaction of human concerns. They enable us to discern completely *concern-independent reasons* in certain objective facts and properties. Some concepts enable one to discern forms of value in states of the world that do not even have any human beings in it, let alone human concerns. Environmental values such as the concept of biodiversity, for example, need not, at the level of their conceptual content, be centred on human beings.[4] Likewise, many of our epistemological concepts—of *truth*, *belief*, and *evidence*, for example—enjoin us to consider it an impropriety to let practical considerations of concern-satisfaction count as evidence for the truth of a belief: when assessing the truth of a belief, the fact that the belief serves my concern for happiness is rightly thought to be neither here nor there. These concepts make a point of insisting that the first-order reasons involved in living by them are splendidly indifferent to human concerns.

Nothing in the present account gives us reason to deny or dilute the disregard for practical considerations and human concerns encoded in many of our conceptualizations. Quite the opposite: from a disengaged perspective, we may well find that there are compelling second-order reasons for these concepts to be so picky in what they will permit us to count as first-order reasons.

A notable virtue of the distinction between reasons in and reasons for concept use is that it allows us to reconcile and do justice to seemingly incompatible aspects of reasons. On the one hand, *internalist* or *subjectivist* accounts of reasons have emphasized the respects in which one's reasons seem to be a function of one's subjective concerns. On the other hand, *externalist* or *objectivist* accounts of reasons have emphasized the respects in which there seem to be objective reasons whose force is precisely not a function of one's subjective concerns. Using the distinction between reasons

---

[4] See Williams (1995f) and Krebs (1999).

in and reasons for concept use, we can accommodate and reconcile the intuitions on both sides.

The objectivist is right to insist that many of the reasons that properly inform our deliberation—reasons *in* concept use—must be understood as being completely independent of our concerns (or, as the Williamsian terminology has it, our 'motivational sets').[5] These reasons are not a matter of what we happen to care about, but of what objectively matters, whether we care about it or not. They are reasons flowing from objective facts and duties, or from the objective goodness or badness of things. From the perspective of the engaged concept-user who is applying the concept and considering the reasons it adverts to, any further considerations as to how the use of the concept ties in with people's concerns can seem like 'one thought too many'.[6] It jars with the perspective opened up by the concept.

And yet, from the disengaged perspective of one who reflects on what reasons they have to think of the world along these reason-giving lines in the first place, the blank refusal to contemplate anything other than the reasons the concept immediately adverts to can seem, as Simon Blackburn puts it, like 'one thought too few':

> a lawyer who becomes convinced that his branch of law exists in order to protect extant distributions of property, and who begins to think that those distributions are themselves disastrous, may reasonably lose his enthusiasm for the rules of law that he has been trained to enforce. But...it is natural and good that disenchantment with the consequences should feed back into disenchantment with the institutions and the rules that exist to promote them. A deontologist who is insulated from this feedback is, like the man who starves for want of a dinner jacket, a lunatic rather than a saint. He has the converse vice of the man who has 'one thought too many', namely, that of having one thought too few. (1998, 45)

The person who is myopically bound up in the application of concepts serving concerns the person would disapprove of upon reflection *should* be more responsive to metaconceptual considerations about the concept's role in the larger scheme of things. Blind confidence in a concept can be as negligent as the blind following of rules and orders.

This is where we find a place for the subjectivist thought that the reasons people have to conceptualize things along certain reason-giving lines depend

---

[5] See Williams (1981b).   [6] See Williams (1981e, 18).

notably on how these conceptualizations relate to their concerns. Even when the reasons that guide our thought and conduct make no mention of our concerns, these concerns nevertheless play a role in engendering the conceptual needs that give us second-order reasons to let ourselves be guided by certain concern-independent reasons. The mere fact that many concepts screen out all considerations as to how their use ties in with our concerns does not mean that these concerns do not play an essential role in giving point to the use of these concepts—just as the fact that only the actors appear on the stage does not mean that the people working backstage do not perform an essential role in the play.[7]

Hence, while the application of a concept may properly be responsive only to reasons that are *not* a function of concept-users' concerns, the metaconceptual appraisal of a concept may equally properly be responsive to reasons for concept use that *are* a function of concept-users' concerns. Even where we reason in concern-independent ways, concerns can properly figure as an important parameter at the higher-order level of reasoning about the reasons for us to reason in concern-independent ways.

Acknowledging that engaged concept use answers to different kinds of reasons than disengaged concept use therefore allows us to find an appropriate place for subjectivist as well as for objectivist intuitions. As Blackburn's example of the disenchanted lawyer intimated, moreover, we thereby also accommodate *consequentialist* intuitions, which are responsive to how the effects of using a concept affect our concerns, as well as *deontological* intuitions, which are responsive to the fact that many of our concepts precisely enjoin us to disregard such considerations. We can grant both that disengaged metaconceptual reflection appropriately looks to how the consequences of concept use tie in with human concerns, and that the reasons figuring in one's engaged, object-level deliberations usually make no reference to concerns at all, and demand to be understood as completely independent of them: they are objective and external considerations, a matter of duty and what is right, irrespective of the concerns people happen to have. It can be an essential part of a language game to deny that its subject matter depends in any way on our language games. The reasons in concept use adverted to by many of our concepts likewise present themselves as essentially *concern-independent* reasons: the fact that something is unjust, or robs someone of their liberty, figures in the deliberation of the engaged

---

[7] Wittgenstein (1978, V, §15) draws a similar comparison in discussing the role of empirical facts in mathematics.

concept-user as a self-standing reason, a reason that is simply there, regardless of whether the people involved have certain concerns or not.

8.3 Instrumentality without Instrumental Mentality

Having distinguished reasons in and for concept use and underscored the importance of keeping them in their places when switching between engaged and disengaged use, we must also forestall a closely related misunderstanding of the needs-based approach: in approaching concepts from our concerns and the instrumental needs they engender, it is important not to conflate the instrumentality *of* thought with *instrumental thought*. If we conflate the two, corrosive instrumentalism threatens—an instrumentalizing mentality undermining all rational authority that is not the authority of its own concerns. It is an old threat, which the ancient Greeks were already acutely alive to.[8] To dodge it, we must find a place for the instrumentality of concepts in metaconceptual reflection while taking care not to collapse all rationality into instrumental rationality, or all reasons into instrumental reasons.[9] The non-instrumental mentality appropriate to many of the concepts we use should be able to coexist coherently with the consciousness of the instrumentality of our using those concepts.

While it is true that concepts are needed, when they are, as a matter of technological necessity, it is plainly not true that all our thought is technological in character, i.e. embodies an instrumentalizing mentality at the level of its content. Using a certain concept might be instrumental to meeting one's concerns, but it does not follow that the concept used casts its object in an instrumental light. On the contrary, it may be that using that concept is instrumental only insofar as the concept casts its object in a non-instrumental light. Thinking in terms of certain concepts can be instrumental to the satisfaction of our concerns even when—indeed, just because—it is not instrumental-minded.

There are many things that are not best attained by consciously striving for them. Various feats of technical prowess in sports and music are not best executed by consciously focusing on their perfect execution, and it is a philosophical commonplace that happiness is not best pursued under that

---

[8] On the threat of instrumentalism in ancient Greek thought, see Ober (2022, 2, 362–72).
[9] For a disambiguation of the different implications that such a collapse might be taken to have, see Kolodny and Brunero (2020, §4.1).

description. Game theory offers a slew of more rigorously formalized illustrations: the chicken game, the free rider problem, the ultimatum game, the stag hunt, the centipede game—they all involve the idea that a player's thinking simply in terms of the basic concerns that fundamentally animate the game will lead to suboptimal outcomes. And they all encourage the conclusion that one salient type of solution to this difficulty is to change how the player thinks: the player has reason to come to think in terms of concepts—such as the concept of pride, perhaps, or the concept of loyalty, or the concept of honour, or the concept of a promise—which, by rendering players responsive to reasons that are precisely not a function of the basic concerns structuring the game, lead the players to satisfy those basic concerns better than they otherwise would.[10] Each of these game-theoretical structures indicates a way in which concepts can help satisfy a concern by distracting from that concern.

Accordingly, there can be instrumentality without instrumentalizing mentality. A concept can be a device serving a certain concern without encoding a preoccupation with that concern. The intrinsic value of truth, for example, is an intrinsic value precisely because it is not a matter of serving antecedent human concerns—the value of finding out the truth and the disvalue of lying are not simply a function of how many concerns get satisfied or frustrated as a result, and one would misunderstand the value of truth if one understood it entirely in such instrumental terms. Nevertheless, there is a reason why creatures like us have the concept of a value that is concern-independent in this way: it notably serves the constant human concern to acquire information about the risks and opportunities of one's environment by enabling an epistemic division of labour whereby members of a community cooperatively pool information.[11]

Crucially, however, the concept of the value of truth can only properly serve this concern if it does not make that value conditional on subservience to human concerns. For it is only insofar as the truth is regarded as *intrinsically* valuable that valuing the truth can be *instrumentally* valuable. As long as individuals value the truth only insofar as it serves their individual concerns, the concept will fail to make a helpful difference: people will try to free ride on the pool of information without themselves bothering to seek and tell the truth unless they directly stand to gain from doing so anyway. And since free riders not only do little to enrich the pool with hard-to-get information, but

---

[10] I discuss several of these examples in more detail in Queloz (2021c). See also Bowles and Gintis (2011) and especially Skyrms (1996, 2004), Binmore (2005, 2007), and Kitcher (2011) for discussions that remain germane to philosophical concerns.
[11] See Williams (2002). I reconstruct this explanation in detail in Queloz (2018b; 2021c, ch. 7).

vitiate it with misinformation whenever they can profit from misleading people, the epistemic division of labour will be terminally unstable.

For the concept of the value of truth to serve human concerns by sustaining the epistemic division of labour, therefore, it needs to be the concept of something valued for its own sake, throwing its own weight into the balance of reasons, so that people at least sometimes seek and tell the truth *just because* it is the truth. Once considered intrinsically valuable, the truth becomes its own reward, and can stake a claim against self-interest. This may not suffice to override self-interest every time, but it enables a sustained practice of information pooling to get off the ground, and the occasional lie will not bring it down.

The value of truth, on this account, needs to outrun its instrumentality in order to be instrumental to our concerns. But our ability to grasp its instrumentality turns, once again, on disambiguating the 'ing/ed ambiguity': our *valuing* the truth intrinsically, regardless of human concerns, is instrumentally valuable in meeting human concerns, but we can only grasp how it can be so if we grasp why *what is valued* is not valued merely instrumentally, as a means of meeting human concerns. P. F. Strawson may have been getting at a similar point when he suggested that we can only really understand the efficacy of some of our reactive attitudes if we recognize that they express moral and not just instrumental attitudes.[12] His point was not just that they combine instrumental and non-instrumental aspects. His point was that the instrumental aspects *depend* on the non-instrumental aspects. We are bloody-minded rather than benefit-minded in blaming others, for instance, because blame only serves our concerns to regulate anti-social behaviour and align our moral sensibilities on the condition that it be understood as justified by something other than its subservience to such concerns.[13]

Similarly, the authority of many concepts and ideals whose superb indifference to human concerns is prone to arouse suspicions in the wake of Enlightenment humanism and naturalism might be vindicated by the realization that there are good reasons for this indifference: we sometimes think in concern-independent terms the better to serve our concerns.

This is not to deny that many concepts do not fall into this category: we sometimes also think in concern-dependent terms the better to serve our

---

[12] See Strawson (2008a, 27).
[13] I elaborate on this argument in Queloz (2021d). On the connection to Strawson, see also Emilsson (manuscript).

concerns, or would be better off if we did so. Moreover, a concept might not serve *our* concerns at all: it might serve someone's else concerns at our expense. And finally, a concept might not serve anybody's concerns, and simply be idle.

Yet the most philosophically interesting case is that in which genuine instrumentality is achieved without instrumental mentality, and we think in concern-independent terms the better to serve our concerns. The application of a concept then yields and is guided by reasons that are completely emancipated from our concerns. But what lends this concept its importance is nonetheless its relation to our concerns.

Things stand with such concepts much as Wittgenstein said they stood with mathematical rules: 'A rule *qua* rule is detached, it stands as it were alone in its glory; although what gives it importance is the facts of daily experience' (1978, VII, §3). He went on to compare the task of describing this combination of features to the task of describing the office of a king: one must avoid the error of reducing the dignity of that office to its usefulness, yet leave neither its dignity nor its usefulness out of account.[14] What I am suggesting is that this can be achieved by bringing out the usefulness of the king's office possessing a dignity that is precisely not grounded in its usefulness, but independent of it. Likewise, to make sense of the fairly pervasive phenomenon whereby a human conceptualization emancipates itself from human concerns in order better to subserve them, we must avoid reducing the autonomous content of a concept to its instrumentality, while at the same time leaving neither its autonomy nor its instrumentality out of account.

The picture painted by the needs-based approach is thus one on which reasons *for* concept use are *bona fide* reasons that our confidence in concepts should be responsive to; but they are reasons that do not directly compete with, and therefore should not be at risk of crowding out, reasons *in* concept use. To adopt a needs-based approach to the authority of concepts is not to fall for the reductive misconception that all concepts which serve human concerns do so by introducing a preoccupation with concern-satisfaction into the content of people's deliberations. One cannot fully appreciate the power of the conceptual architecture we inhabit, or indeed its instrumentality, until one recognizes that many concepts serve us best by transcending and screening out all considerations as to how their use relates to human concerns.

---

[14] The Bagehottian resonances of this example are explored in Bloor (2004, 125–6).

8.4 From Concerns to Reasons in Concept Use

Even when the reasons that guide our thought and conduct make no mention of our concerns, then, these concerns nevertheless give us second-order reasons to deliberate in terms of certain concepts rather than others, thereby determining what reasons to think or do certain things we have reason to be guided by.

What this implies is that there is an *indirect conduit of authority* from concerns via needs to concept use and its concomitant reasons. This indirect conduit looks as follow:

- concerns, when pursued with certain capacities under certain circumstances, generate *conceptual needs*: needs for certain concepts rather than others;
- conceptual needs constitute *reasons for concept use*: reasons to use concepts that are tailored to those conceptual needs;
- concept use yields *reasons for concept application*: when something fulfils the criteria guiding a concept's application, this gives one reason to apply the concept to it;
- concept application in turn yields *reasons for belief or action*: when one applies a concept to something, this gives one reasons to draw certain consequences of the concept's applicability in one's thought or conduct.[15]

Our concerns and the reasons for action and belief that immediately guide our thought and conduct are therefore linked, albeit highly indirectly. Take, for example, the concept *fire*. Our concern to stay out of harm's way, when combined with a combustible environment and the human body's incapacity to tolerate even brief and local exposure to temperatures above a certain threshold, generates a conceptual need for something like the concept *fire*, which in turns constitutes a reason to use the concept. To be an engaged user of a concept of fire worth using is to be sensitive to the fact that the presence of certain conditions (i.e. heat, light, smoke, and flames) yields reasons, however defeasible, for the application of the concept *fire*. From the applicability of the concept, it in turn had better follow that we have a reason not to come into direct contact with that to which it applies.

The distinction between *pro tanto* and *all-things-considered* conceptual needs can then be straightforwardly mapped onto reasons for concept use: a

---

[15] Here, I elaborate a simpler model first outlined in Queloz and Cueni (2021, 766).

pro tanto conceptual need yields a *pro tanto* reason to use a concept. This allows us to make sense of the suggestion, made in Chapter 1, that conceptual authority is a gradable and comparative notion: one might have *more* reasons, or *better* reasons, to use one concept rather than another, and one might have some reasons to use a concept that one has even stronger reasons *not* to use. Likewise, where an all-things-considered conceptual need emerges, it will constitute an all-things-considered reason to use a concept.

Metaconceptual reflection can therefore enable us to discern a chain of reasons running from concerns to reasons in concept use, and it will shore up certain reasons for action or belief; but our concerns are not related to our reasons for action and belief as premises to a conclusion. What our concerns yield are reasons for or against cultivating certain *dispositions*, namely the dispositions to conceptualize things in the terms specified by a given concept and to be responsive to its correlative reasons—in other words, the set of dispositions that together constitute a concept's possession conditions.[16] It is only once we are disposed to conceptualize things in terms of the concept that we shall be responsive to the reasons for action or reasons for belief that the concept renders articulable. Reasons for concept use do not constitute reasons from which certain reasons for action and belief *follow*; rather, they constitute reasons *to be responsive to* the reasons from which those reasons for action and belief follow.

Where the concepts are local, thick normative concepts that are not transparently indispensable in the way that concepts such as *fire* are, adducing reasons for reasons can vindicate or undermine our confidence in those concepts. If we previously harboured doubts over whether a certain part of our thought was still alive at all, or merely long-dead ballast, these reasons will dispel any lingering doubts and reaffirm our confidence. Conversely, the realization that we fail to share the concerns that would give one reasons to use a concept can erode that concept's authority.

In vindicating or undermining our confidence in certain concepts, reasons for concept use will reinvigorate or sap the force of reasons *in* concept use. This allows us to make sense of the otherwise puzzling suggestion, which sometimes surfaces in discussions over internalism about reasons, that the reasons a concept immediately adverts to can be reasons for one agent but not for another. Williams, notably, makes that suggestion:

---

[16] I defended the idea that reasons for concept use should be understood as being focused on possession conditions in Chapter 2, §5.

> People who use a given concept of [the thick] sort will find their application of it guided by their experience, and also accept that it gives them reasons for or against various kinds of action.... But this does not mean that a speaker who does use a given concept of this kind (chastity is an example that focuses the mind) can truly say that another agent who does not use the concept has a reason to avoid or pursue certain courses of action in virtue of that concept's application. To show this, the speaker would need to show that the agent has reason to use that concept, to structure his or her experience in those terms. That is a different and larger matter; all the work remains to be done. (1995d, 37–8)

Williams gives no indication of what all this work remaining to be done might involve. But the needs-based approach fills this crucial lacuna: a needs-based appraisal of the concept of chastity could conceivably vindicate the authority of the concept *for that agent*, and thereby show that the agent has reason to be responsive to its concomitant reasons for action, by deriving a conceptual need for the concept of chastity, or something close to it, from concerns, capacities, and circumstances that the agent in question shares.

But if, on the other hand, it emerged that the agent failed to share the conditions rendering the concept needful, that would undermine the concept's authority. This comes out clearly in Michael Smith's explication of Williams's suggestion:

> Imagine someone who conceptualizes his experience in terms of the concept of *chastity*. Williams's idea seems to be that, for such a person, whether or not women are restraining their sexual behaviour will be a very salient feature of their circumstances. Who would have a reason to make that feature of their circumstances salient? His answer is: those who desire that women restrain their sexual behaviour. Such people have a reason to *use* the concept of *chastity*, and they have corresponding reasons for action, but all this is consistent with others who have no such desire having no such reasons. (2013, 103–4)

If we do not share the concern that renders the concept of chastity needful and see no other concern that would give us reason to use the concept, the immediate implication is that we have *no reason* to use the concept and might as well abandon it. If we were engaged users of the concept before, the concept will then be felt to have gone dead on us, and the reasons it adverts to will no longer have force with us.

But if we do not *simply* fail to share the concern, the way one might simply fail to share an interest in philately, but *object* to the concern on grounds provided by concepts we continue to be confident in, we will thereby come to see a reason *not* to use the concept, because we will not want to see that concern satisfied. We will accordingly have reason to object to other people's use of that concept.

If the realization that a concept serves a certain concern is *vindicatory* when the concern is one we identify with, therefore, that same realization is *incriminatory* when the concern is one we are opposed to. Just as the concerns we endorse yield reasons *for* concept use, the concerns we object to yield reasons *against* concept use. The concepts we really want to be using, on this account, are therefore the concepts we have most reason to use, in view of our various reasons for and against concept use.

I emphasized that while there is a rational conduit leading from concerns to reasons in concept use, our concerns and conceptual needs do not typically enter our first-order deliberation as premises favouring particular courses of action. Our concerns and conceptual needs should not be understood as premises *from which* to reason, but rather as something *in accordance with which* to reason—they are crucial features of the extraconceptual landscape that render certain ways of reasoning needful and pointful.[17]

Should we conclude from this that, when we deliberate in terms that make no reference to needs and concerns, metaconceptual reflection cannot properly enter into our deliberations and affect what reasons we take ourselves to have? Is reflection on our reasons for concept use barred from figuring in our practical deliberation on what to do in a concrete situation?

This clearly does not follow, since even deliberation in terms of first-order reasons that are not couched in terms of needs or concerns can be affected by metaconceptual reflection on our reasons for concept use *if that reflection alters what concepts are brought to bear* on our deliberation. In other words, there can be rational *arguments* running from concerns to reasons in concept use that directly and properly affect what we take ourselves to have reason to do in a given situation *by* affecting what concepts we bring to bear on the situation.[18]

---

[17] I take this way of putting the contrast by Sellars's (1958, §83) discussion of induction as establishing principles in accordance with which we reason, but not premises from which we reason. Needs and concerns are not principles, but the general insight that one might reason *in accordance with* something though one does not reason *from* it carries over.

[18] I am grateful to Sophia Dandelet and Simon Blackburn for stimulating conversations on this issue.

To see how, consider first the case in which metaconceptual reflection does *not* alter what concepts one brings to bear on a situation: rather, one's reasons in concept use are shored up by reasons for concept use, thereby strengthening one's confidence in the reasons for action one saw already. The concept and its attendant reasons are provided with a bill of health. Consequently, one relaxes into thinking in those terms and being rationally and emotionally responsive to the considerations they advert to.

In such a case, metaconceptual reflection will not have removed first-order reasons from one's deliberation that figured there before; nor will it have introduced new first-order reasons into one's deliberation that did not figure there before. It may have revealed new *second*-order reasons to use the concept, but this will no more induce the concept to grow new reason relations than revealing the evolutionary rationale of the octopus's tentacles will induce it to grow new tentacles. Seeing a new reason *for* the use of a concept one is already an engaged user of does not *add* to the reasons we see in the use of the concept. Mistaking the former kind of reason for a reason of the latter kind would only result in one's acting, as philosophers like to say, on the *wrong kind of reason*. All that metaconceptual reflection will have done is to give one reasons to be more confident in the first-order reasons one perceived already.

When metaconceptual reflection saps one's confidence in a concept, by contrast, one ceases to see the reasons in concept use one previously thought one had *as* reasons. This directly affects what one takes oneself to have reason to do in the concrete case, all things considered. If, before engaging in a metaconceptual reflection, one thought one had reason to feel ashamed of oneself for failing to live up to the concept of chastity, for example, then reaching the metaconceptual conclusion that one in fact has no reason to use the concept, or even reason not to use the concept, will shift the balance of first-order reasons for action away from the conclusion that one has reason to feel ashamed of oneself.

Similarly, in the case in which metaconceptual reflection reveals that one has reasons to adopt a concept one does not yet use in an engaged way, such reflection will directly affect the reasons for action one has in a particular situation. One comes to recognize *as* reasons considerations one did not previously recognize as reasons. To reverse the *chastity* example: when the young Saint Augustine, after years of living as a libertine, concluded that he had reason to start living by the concept of chastity, he came to acknowledge the force of reasons entailing a dramatic change in his conduct. What is more, these were reasons he had reason to heed already the moment he came to recognize his reasons to live by the concept; hence the amusing contradiction involved in his famous prayer: 'Grant me chastity and temperance—but not just yet.'[19]

Thus, while reflection on reasons for concept use bears primarily on the general question of whether or not to think in certain terms, and not on the more concrete question of the reasons one has for or against particular courses of action, reasons for concept use can nonetheless end up directly affecting what reasons for action one takes oneself to have in a particular situation. Any alteration in the set of concepts we deploy in an engaged way will entrain corresponding alterations in the set of reasons for action we take ourselves to have.

8.5 Needs-Based Conceptual Authority

Having worked our way over the last couple of chapters from concerns via needs to reasons, we finally reach the following answer to the authority question:

The Needs-Based Conception of Conceptual Authority:
Concepts are authoritative if and to the extent that they meet the conceptual needs we have in virtue of concerns we identify with and would still endorse after well-informed reflection on the merits of those concerns and on how we came by them.

While this conception of authority invites us to appraise concepts by the conceptual needs they answer to, a concept's authority is not just a function of its needfulness, on this view. It is also a function of what its needfulness is rooted in, for a concept might be needful in relation to a concern we object to. Needs-based appraisal is the appraisal of concepts *together with* what creates a need for them.

On this account, showing someone that a concept F is authoritative for them involves the following: first, guided by the expressive character of the concept, we narrow in on a concern that the person identifies with and certainly wants to see met. We then show, by constructing a need matrix or a looser discursive equivalent, that, given the capacities with which and the circumstances in which they pursue this concern, they have a conceptual

---

[19] The original reads: '*da mihi castitatem et continentiam, sed noli modo*' (1992, 8.7.17).

need for something very like concept *F*. This in turn means that the person is better able to contribute to the satisfaction of the concern in question by recognizing the authority of concept *F* and responding to the reasons it adverts to than by abandoning concept *F* and trying to satisfy the concern without it. Therefore, they have a *pro tanto* reason to recognize the authority of concept *F*.

A more complex discussion ensues if our interlocutor then co-opts our approach to cast doubt on the conclusion that we have an *all-things-considered* reason to use concept *F*. Balancing the concern we highlighted against other weighty concerns, they might seek to show that these concerns create *pro tanto* conceptual needs for a different concept, *F'*, and that these outweigh the *pro tanto* conceptual need for *F*, so that we would have an all-things-considered reason to use *F'*. That would of course only follow if we were forced to choose between the two concepts, and could not reasonably hope to allocate them to certain use cases in order to deploy them both in coordinated fashion. But this is just the sort of metaconceptual inquiry and debate we should engage in to determine what concepts we really need.

There are, moreover, particularly complex cases that the notion of an all-things-considered reason for concept use is itself too tidy and clear-cut to handle. Sometimes, the relevant nuances are better articulated in terms of a dynamic and context-sensitive array of countervailing *pro tanto* reasons. Because concerns can conflict not just between groups, but also within the breast of one individual, one can be pulled in different directions when assessing the authority of a concept. This forces one to reflect on which concerns one most identifies with, and which concerns one wants to prioritize in which contexts.

For example, even an ideological concept foisted upon me by my oppressors may be authoritative if and to the extent that it serves my concern to stay safe by not stepping out of line. As a result, it may be that I cannot afford to abandon it entirely. It does meet a conceptual need grounded in a concern for self-preservation.

At the same time, that very concept, if it merits being described as an *ideological* concept deployed under circumstances *of oppression*, will also radically frustrate many of my other concerns.[20] I cannot then afford simply to consider it authoritative either. There are many concepts we have reason to use that we have even stronger reason *not* to use.

---

[20] For an overview of the various uses of the term 'ideological' and the criticism they have encountered, see Haslanger (2021). For a discussion of the methodological status of the perspective from which a concept can be characterized as 'ideological', see Celikates (2018).

Furthermore, some concerns are 'adaptive' concerns that one identifies with, but merely as a way of adapting to non-ideal circumstances. For instance, a gay man in a violently homophobic society might have a prudential concern to be perceived as a 'real man'. Does the fact that this concern is best served by living by the concept *real man* suffice to render that concept authoritative for him in the sense of giving him an all-things-considered reason to use it? Does he identify sufficiently with this adaptive concern to be willing to sacrifice other concerns to its pursuit, such as his concern to be himself, i.e. his concern for authenticity? How high a price is he willing to pay?

In view of the possibility of such questions, the Manichean expectation that a concept must, all things considered, either *be* or *not be* authoritative for someone across every situation proves too simplistic. The gay man in the violently homophobic society is caught in a bind between conflicting concerns: his concern for self-preservation means that he cannot afford simply to become oblivious to the concept *real man* and the behaviour it prescribes; at the same time, he cannot fully embrace it without betraying some of his other concerns, such as his concern for authenticity. This calls for a correspondingly complex adjustment in his cognitive economy. Through reflection on why and to what extent he has reason to recognize the authority of the concept *real man*, he may, for instance, come to acknowledge the authority of the concept only in a self-consciously prudential spirit, rendering the acknowledgement of its authority conditional on its serving his concern for self-preservation in a given context, and thereby drastically reining in the concept's influence on his life and self-conception.

Whether in the form of a decisive all-things-considered reason or in the form of a more complex admixture of contextually sensitive *pro tanto* reasons, however, reasons for concept use fundamentally answer the authority question by showing that we are better able to meet our concerns by recognizing the authority of a concept than by trying to meet them without the concept. Living by concepts we need really helps us to live, in the sense of furthering concerns we are identified with.

An answer to the authority question along these lines of course invites the follow-up question of who 'we' is, or *whose* concerns are at issue. The use of 'we' marks the fact that, on the needs-based conception, conceptual authority is not a monolith, but a perspectival phenomenon. This perspectivalness both complicates the account and renders it more powerful.

In the first instance, the fact that different people not only have different concerns, but would still endorse different concerns after critical reflection, undoubtedly complicates the task of demonstrating the authority of a concept.

It may, to a limited extent, be possible to tiptoe around that complication and vindicate some highly general concepts by drawing primarily on human beings' more constant concerns, such as the concern to avoid violent conflict with others, find out about the dangers and affordances of one's environment, secure the resources one needs to survive, and establish the conditions of cooperation.[21] Being maximally widely shared, such concerns promise to provide something like a starting point that people 'could not reasonably reject', in Scanlon's phrase.[22]

But concerns like these will only take us so far. Not only does our conceptual repertoire abound with concepts that bear no clear relation to such constant concerns; even the concepts that can be vindicated by such concerns will still be left vastly underdetermined by them: constant concerns might show that we have reason to use something *very broadly like* concept F; but they will not achieve the degree of determinacy required to decide between the different conceptualizations that fall within those generous bounds.

To arrive at a more determinate picture of the concepts we need, we have to leverage more local needs and concerns. These will give us the degree of determinacy required to appraise concepts in a more fine-grained way, without restriction to anthropological universals.

However, this greater determinacy is bought at the cost of drawing conceptual authority from needs and concerns that are specific to one group in contrast to other groups. It follows that the concepts vindicated by local needs will be authoritative *for* that group, but not necessarily for other groups: if the authority of some concept F is understood in terms of its suitability to meeting a conceptual need engendered by concern C, F will be authoritative for concept-users if and to the extent that they identify with C and would endorse it upon critical reflection; consequently, a given concept could be authoritative for some people and not others.

The needs-based conception thus allows for conceptual authority to be perspectival, permitting its indexation to conceptual needs and concerns that are not necessarily shared by everyone. This does not mean that there is no fact of the matter about which concepts are authoritative for whom. It is merely that the one-place predicate 'concept F is *authoritative*' turns out to correspond to a three-place relation: concept F is authoritative for some set of concept-users S insofar as S has conceptual need N. This is a perfectly

---

[21] See Fricker (2007, 2016b, forthcoming-a), Pettit (2018, forthcoming), and Smithson (2021) for accounts pursuing this sort of strategy.
[22] See Scanlon (1998, 4 and *passim*).

objective three-place fact obtaining between a concept, a set of concept-users, and a conceptual need. Relationalism—the view that what appear to be *n*-place relations are in fact *n+k*-place relations—does not entail relativism.[23] There is a fact of the matter as to what concept would best meet *S*'s conceptual needs, and this is as true when *S* is an individual person as when *S* is an entire community. To claim that concept *F* would answer to *S*'s conceptual needs is not merely to profess one's conviction that it would be *good* if they adopted the concept. It is to assert that it would be good *for them* if they adopted it. That is not the expression of a preference, but an empirical claim about *F*'s conduciveness to the satisfaction of certain concerns of *S*'s, given *S*'s capacities and circumstances.

However, the perspectival character of conceptual authority does not foreclose the possibility of coming to *know* that a certain concept is best for concept-users with certain conceptual needs. This is where, *pace* Williams, I want to insist that our use of thick normative concepts can rest in more than mere confidence; we *can* ground our confidence in a form of metaconceptual knowledge: the knowledge that a concept is right or wrong *for us*, given our conceptual needs.

Though this claim holds absolutely, in that its truth is not relativized to a perspective, the knowledge involved falls short of knowledge that a concept is absolutely best in the sense that anyone has reason to use it. The conceptual authority mediated by our conceptual needs ultimately flows from our concerns, and these concerns vary between people. There is no timeless and mind-independent rational foundation here—only varying human concerns. In making conceptual authority a function of human concerns, the needs-based conception accepts that authority is to that extent mind-dependent. This contrasts with foundationalist views such as those of Lewis, Hirsch, or Sider; for them, which concepts have authority depends solely on which properties are natural or what the world's mind-independent structure is. Moreover, it is open to foundationalists to assume that which properties are natural is necessary, or that the world's structure is necessary; which concepts are authoritative will then itself be necessary. On the needs-based conception, by contrast, which concepts are authoritative is not a matter of necessity. It is the contingent product of our concerns, capacities, and circumstances.

But—to turn Williams's own phrase against himself—once one really 'goes *far enough* in recognizing contingency', we can recognize the contingency of

---

[23] See Spencer (2016).

our concepts without any sense of loss.[24] For to realize that the standards we want our concepts to meet are shaped by contingent forces just as much as we ourselves are, and that these forces are noncoincidentally the same, is to realize that we *want* the concepts we use to be responsive to the specificities of our situation. We want our concepts to answer to *our* conceptual needs, for the concepts that serve us best are those that are best suited to those distinctive needs. Once we truly understand this, that thought promises to reconcile us to the contingency of our concepts.

On the needs-based approach, then, the thick normative concepts under which we can have some pieces of knowledge can themselves be sustained by knowledge, and not just by confidence. This will not and *should not* be knowledge that they are absolutely and definitively the best concepts. But it will and should be knowledge that they are the best concepts for us, given the conceptual needs we now have, and knowing this should reconcile us to the contingency of our having come to use those concepts in particular. Though this will be knowledge of a relational fact, it will itself be non-relational knowledge, and it will be as objective as knowledge in the human sciences gets. It will not be definitive, however, because our conceptual needs might change, so that different concepts may be called for in the future, and different pieces of metaconceptual knowledge will have to be called upon to sustain our confidence in them.

Despite being *meta*conceptual knowledge, this will itself be knowledge had *under* certain concepts, such as the psychological and sociological concepts in terms of which we make sense of our situation, our concerns, and the dynamics of the social reality around us. Needs-based concept appraisal is still a form of situated reflection, and that may render what metaconceptual knowledge it produces to varying degrees perspectival; but perspectival knowledge, as Williams himself insisted, is knowledge all the same, and when it comes to concept appraisal, it is exactly the kind of knowledge we need.

Nevertheless, some may feel that such perspectival metaconceptual knowledge that certain concepts are best for us rests our confidence in our judgements on inauspiciously shaky ground. Does it not imply that different concepts would be best for us if we were different? After all, if we used

---

[24] He uses the phrase in Williams (2006g, 193), in the context of criticizing Rorty's ironist. As my turning of Williams's own phrase against himself suggests, there seems to me to be a genuine tension here in Williams's work: an extrapolation of his thoughts on contingency and the authority of concepts in 'Philosophy as a Humanistic Discipline' puts pressure on the view he articulated in *Ethics and the Limits of Philosophy* and later reasserted in even stronger terms *after* having published his critique of ironism, namely the view that 'the thick concepts under which we can have some pieces of ethical knowledge are not themselves sustained by knowledge, but by confidence' (1995j, 208).

different concepts, we would apply different normative standards, and might reach normative conclusions diverging radically from those we currently reach. How confident can we be in our judgement that murder is wrong if we also think that a different conceptualization would make murder right?

Nothing in the needs-based approach has this uninviting consequence, however. It remains patently false that if we conceptualized murder differently, different normative standards would apply, and murder would be right. For our concepts, and the normative standards they encode, apply to more than just our actual situation: their scope of application encompasses counterfactual situations. So when we wonder whether murder would be right if we conceptualized murder differently, that question is still being considered from a perspective informed by our actual concept of murder, and the concept we actually use informs us that the wrongness of murder is entirely independent of how we conceptualize things or what concepts we use. Someone who failed to understand this would not have fully grasped the concept of murder. The wrongness of murder is in this respect totally unlike the wrongness of violating etiquette.

What *can* be said is this: if we conceptualized murder differently, we would apply different normative standards. That is true. But it is so plainly true as to be a platitude, and nothing normative follows from this descriptive observation. It is only if one adds: 'and we would then be *right* to conceive of murder as right' that the observation acquires normative force; but it does so at the cost of rendering the statement patently false again. For here we again commit ourselves to an evaluative judgement regarding the rightness or wrongness of murder, and that evaluation is bound to draw, in an engaged way, on the conceptualization of murder we ourselves live by. A genuine evaluation—as opposed to that utterly different exercise, a vicarious evaluation—is necessarily one that is expressive of *our own* value concepts, not those of imagined concept-users;[25] and our concept of murder unequivocally informs us that conceiving of murder as right does not make it so.

It thus turns out that when thick normative concepts such as *murder* are employed as we must employ them in evaluative judgements, namely from the deliberative stance, there is simply no room to properly register the dependence of our judgements on our conceptualizations: it either produces normative claims that are patently false or descriptive claims that are

---

[25] On the contrast between vicarious evaluation and evaluation *in propria persona* and the challenge it poses to the evaluation of concepts we do not yet use, see Queloz (2021a).

platitudinously true. Our sense of reality, including our sense of what reality would be like if we used different concepts, is necessarily given by the concepts we actually use. Abraham Lincoln, that unsung modal logician, made much the same point when he asked how many legs a dog would have if people counted tails as legs. 'Four', Lincoln insisted, because calling something a leg does not make it one.[26]

The proper place to register the dependence of our judgements on the concepts we use is not from the deliberative stance, but from the autoethnographic stance, where we can disengage from the normative standards encoded in a concept, but still take an evaluative view, informed by our engaged use of other concepts, of the counterfactual situation in which we conceptualize murder differently. From this stance, we have room for the following thought: if we conceptualized murder differently, we would apply different normative standards, and it might make sense for us to do so if our concerns, capacities, and circumstances were sufficiently different.[27] But that in no way detracts from the wrongness of murder as we in fact conceptualize it.

At the same time, it is true that a needs-based conception of conceptual authority can change our understanding of what we are *at* when we disagree with others who conceptualize things differently. It allows for the possibility that this difference reflects, not an epistemic error on their part, but a difference in their conceptual needs that stems from an underlying difference in concerns, capacities, or circumstances.

If we are alive not merely to the differences in our respective conceptual repertoires, but also to the differences in our conceptual needs and what creates them, we become able to discriminate between situations in which we can see that others are making a mistake within a collective cognitive enterprise, as when a teacher can see that a student misunderstands the concept that is being taught, and situations in which, while we still want to say that the others are *wrong*, we can at the same time recognize that they are not *simply* wrong: it makes sense *to us* that it makes sense *for them* to use the concepts they use, given how different from ours we understand their needs to be. They are not just confused, or radically deceived, or irrationally clinging to conceptual holdovers from another age. This yields the kind of understanding

---

[26] There are many versions of this anecdote, but I was able to trace one to a contemporary of Lincoln's, George W. Julian, who recalls Lincoln making this point in a discussion over the Proclamation of Emancipation; see Rice (1909, 242). I first came across a version of the anecdote in Brandom (1994, 471).

[27] I take this to be a refinement, using the engaged/disengaged distinction, of how Moore (2023b) reads Blackburn (1993) on such counterfactual considerations.

of where the other party is coming from that facilitates *respectful* disagreement. I explore how much mileage we can get out of this thought in Chapter 10.

For all that a needs-based conception of conceptual authority can help us rationalize conceptual differences, however, it does not force us into an all-tolerating, spectatorial relativism when we confront people whose conceptual needs differ from our own. Though we may better understand why they think as they do, we can still fault them for it. The concepts we are confident in continue to equip us to pass judgement on other people even after we recognize the authority of our own concepts to be grounded in our conceptual needs. For precisely what we shall have gained by that recognition is the license to continue to use these concepts in an engaged way, and continue to treat them as applicable to everything they were previously applicable to—including to people with different conceptual needs. If we better understand how their ways of thinking reflect their distinctive concerns, capacities, and circumstances, this also means that instead of uncomprehendingly dismissing them as conceptually confused, we may be able to condemn them far more discerningly for their objectionable concerns, thereby transposing a diffuse epistemological disagreement into a focused, ethical one.

Finally, let me sharpen the contours of the needs-based conception of conceptual authority by contrasting it with rival conceptions of authority. In its emphasis on the idea that our subordination to our concepts is conditional on *them* ultimately serving *us*, the needs-based conception of conceptual authority is a far cry from pre-Enlightenment conceptions of authority in terms of conformity to an order of things about which we do not have a say—such as the Great Chain of Being, in which humans must simply obey higher powers. In comparison, the needs-based conception is a humanistic, anti-authoritarian conception of authority.[28] Instead of requiring us to conform our concepts to an order that is simply imposed on us, it humanizes the norms to which concepts are answerable, turning these norms into a function of our concerns. On the resulting picture, we are the ones who *authorize* our concepts—not just in the sense that we create the ways of thinking in virtue of which we possess certain concepts, but also in the sense that it is our concerns that imbue those concepts with authority.

At the same time, in making conceptual needs not just a function of human concerns, but also of how the world is and what capacities and limitations we

---

[28] See Brandom (2002b, 2004, 2021) for a historical narrative focused on Enlightenment philosophy as a revolution in conceptions of authority. As his *Doktorvater* Rorty (2021, ch. 2) notes, anti-authoritarianism was one of the central characteristics of the Enlightenment, and it lives on notably in the pragmatist tradition.

bring to it, this conception of authority leaves us firmly constrained by reality in what kinds of concepts we can have reason to use. Moving away from the idea that our concepts are answerable to timeless and mind-independent rational foundations may invite the conclusion that we are radically free to choose which concepts to live by; but the needs-based conception of conceptual authority suggests that our conceptual repertoire remains answerable to something beyond the control of our will, namely the demands placed on us by how our concerns interact with the world in which we pursue them. We may not be forced by the world to accept the one set of concepts that is absolutely best; but as long as we bring certain concerns to the world, the world has other ways of imposing certain concepts on us. Even if our thick normative concepts are not answerable to the normative furniture of the universe, they remain answerable to what furthering our concerns in the circumstances we face requires of us as concept-users.

In this respect, the needs-based conception does not follow Enlightenment thinkers such as Kant all the way in tying authority to rational autonomy. For those who treat autonomy as a condition on authority, nothing counts as truly authoritative over oneself unless one has freely placed oneself under its sway after critical reflection. Such autonomy-centred conceptions of authority give a central place to the will, through whose exercise alone one can bind oneself to a norm.

On the present conception of authority, by contrast, one's concepts are imbued with authority by one's conceptual needs, which in turn are a function of one's concerns, capacities, and circumstances. That is a form of authority that is neither systematically dependent on nor systematically responsive to exercises of one's will, because what conceptual needs one has is not always, or even usually, subject to one's will. If any element in that authority-bestowing structure is responsive to one's will, it is one's concerns, some of which one can simply choose to take on, redirect, or give up. But this is not true of all of one's concerns. Some of our concerns are, sometimes irremovably, part of who we are, and cannot be redirected or abandoned *ad libitum*. They are concerns directed at things we *cannot help but be concerned with*. And since our capacities and circumstances are, if anything, even more recalcitrant, some concepts will be authoritative for us willy-nilly. Their authority is discovered rather than freely bestowed.

Yet this conception of authority does not go so far as to pit authority *against* reason, as traditionalist critics of Enlightenment rationalism such as Louis de Bonald or Joseph de Maistre had done in their defence of the *ancien régime*, but rather understands authority *in terms of* reason:[29] it is a matter of lending the prescriptions of our concepts an additional quality by augmenting them with reasons that those living by the concepts can recognize.

This conception of authority as *power augmented by reasons* is true to the concept's roots in Roman law: Theodor Mommsen suggests that *auctoritas*, 'authority', should be understood in terms of *augere*, 'to augment'.[30] Bertrand de Jouvenel also asserts that 'the root of the word denotes the idea of augmentation' (1963b, 30). As both he and Theodor Eschenburg emphasize, being an *auctor* to someone (*alicui auctorem esse*) meant *advising* them.[31] Symbolically, the adviser and augmenter was supposed to be Apollo, god of reason and moderation; in more concrete terms, however, *auctoritas* was what the Senate, composed of the *senes* (the old ones), added to the *potestas* (power) of the people.[32] As Carl Joachim Friedrich describes this ancient conception of authority, 'it was a matter of adding wisdom to will, reason to force and want, that is to say, a knowledge of values shared and traditions hallowed to whatever the people wished to do' (1972, 48). Far from constituting the non-rational counterpart to reason, on this view, authority 'supplements a mere act of the will by adding reasons to it' (Friedrich 1971, 19), thereby augmenting and confirming the will of the people in light of concerns that are supposed to be shared by them.

The needs-based conception of conceptual authority harks back to this idea: it likewise supplements the *power* of concepts by adding *reasons* to it, thereby augmenting and confirming the prescriptions of concepts in light of concerns shared by those who enact them.

In virtue of its emphasis on whether concepts *serve* human concerns, this conception of authority also echoes what Joseph Raz more recently described as the 'service conception' of authority. It conceives of conceptual authority as a matter of *serving* some concern that is a concern *for* the concept-user in such a way that the concept-user is better off living under the sway of the concept than outside it.

Yet this conception of the authority of concepts also differs in several respects from the conception that Raz elaborated over the years.[33] His account is keyed to the issue of 'how to understand the standing of an authoritative

---

[29] See Friedrich (1972, 30–47) for a discussion of how these Counter-Enlightenment thinkers conceived of authority as the anti-thesis to reason and reasoning.
[30] See Mommsen (1888, 952, 994, 1032–9). That etymology is complicated somewhat by Heinze (1925).
[31] See Jouvenel (1963b, 30) and Eschenburg (1976, 12).
[32] See Friedrich (1972, 129 n. 4) and Mommsen (1888, 952, 994, 1032–9).
[33] See Raz (1979, 1986, 1995, 2009).

directive' (2009, 134)—paradigmatically, the *state*'s directives that take the form of *law*. This focus on the directives or commands of the state leads him to concentrate on reasons of a very specific kind: reasons for action that are both *content-independent*, providing first-order reasons to do something just because one has been commanded to do it, irrespective of the content of the command, and *exclusionary* or *pre-emptive*, providing second-order reasons to disregard other reasons bearing on the matter.

From the perspective of the present investigation into the authority of concepts, Raz's account only captures a special case of authority: the particularly imperious form of authority that the state exercises when it issues commands determining what *everyone* living under the state's authority really *must* do, irrespective of their inclinations and whatever other reasons they might have. These are commands that combine general applicability with overriding stringency.

By contrast, the authority of concepts tends to be more diffuse and less imperious than the power of a state giving the law to its subjects. Like the authority of intellectuals, it largely 'depends on the uncommanded response of those it affects' (Williams 2014a, 295). Concepts can be said to govern our thoughts and actions, but they do not systematically generate exclusionary and content-independent reasons for action. Most of the reasons in concept use we become sensitive to by adopting concepts lack the stringency and overriding force of commands.[34] The power of concepts is, for the most part, a softer form of power.

This does not mean that it is no real power, of course. As we saw, once an issue is cast in certain terms, thick normative concepts can leave us nothing else to think but that a certain conclusion follows. Influencing in which terms people cast an issue, and which patterns of reasoning they are disposed to follow, can be just as effective as issuing commands. If anything, the fact that the power of concepts is a softer form of power makes it *more* effective, because it enables it to be deployed surreptitiously while preserving people's sense that they are freely making up their minds—when, in a more literal sense, that is exactly what they are *not* doing insofar as they uncritically accept the make-up of a certain conceptual architecture.[35]

---

[34] This also sidesteps a standard objection to Raz's account, namely that while a service conception of the state explains why the state should have the power to determine what we should do, it fails to explain why the state should also have the power to demand that we comply with its directives; see Perry (2005) and Kletzer and Renzo (2020, 205). The conception of authority I propose avoids this objection, because, while concepts help determine what we should do, they do not systematically come with a second-order demand that we comply with the reasons they generate. For further criticism of Raz's account, see Darwall (2006, 2010).

[35] See Marques (2020) as well as Queloz and Bieber (2022) for discussions of various ways in which this power can be exploited and checked.

Though the soft power of concepts is different from the hard power of directives, that hard power only makes sense against the backdrop of the soft power of concepts, for the directives are stringent and exclusionary precisely because they need to override the pervasive authority of concepts. Raz conceives of authority as being *au fond* about decisions being taken out of one person's hands and put into the hands of another.[36] But this is the authority *of authorities*. Understanding that form of authority requires understanding how directives can curtail someone's reasoning by enjoining them to disregard any reasons other than those created by the directive. This presupposes, however, that there are already reasons there: that there is already a rival form of authority at work, which directives need to labour to overrule. The authority of concepts precisely concerns the way concepts articulate and guide the reasoning that directives seek to curtail. The authority of concepts is thus a prior and more general form of authority—it is the authority *against which* command-issuing authorities must assert themselves.

8.6 The Wrong Kind of Reasons?

The needs-based approach thus provides us with a distinctive way of answering the authority question from the autoethnographic stance. It discerns reasons for concept use in the conceptual needs generated by our concerns. But what authority do these reasons for concept use themselves possess? And is there not something oddly self-absorbed about focusing on our own conceptual needs when the subject matter demands a focus on the nature of things, or the truth, or moral duty? Are needs-based reasons for concept use then not bound to be the 'wrong kind of reasons'?

I think not, though defusing this worry requires us to be very clear about what exactly the role of needs-based reasons for concept use is supposed to be, and how different it is from the role allocated to comparable second-order reasons in theories such as indirect utilitarianism. Confronting different versions of the wrong kind of reasons worry can therefore do much to clarify the proposed account.

Here is a basic version of the worry: the reasons for concept use adduced by the needs-based approach are the wrong kind of reasons, because concept use should be answerable exclusively to the *rerum natura*, the nature of

---

[36] See Raz (1999, 193).

things. One kind of reason that can be given for using the concept of cruelty, for example, is:

(a) He intentionally and needlessly caused her suffering.

But reflection on the conceptual needs that the concept of cruelty answers to yields (let us assume) the following reason to use the concept:

(b) The concept of cruelty helps meet our conceptual needs by serving our concern to reduce suffering.

Now what if, in a given case, the concern animating our use of the concept were better served by *not* applying the concept? Because the perpetrator of some act offered to fund a big anti-cruelty campaign if we only refrained from conceiving of what he did as an act of cruelty, for instance? Surely, what he did either was or was not an act of cruelty *whatever* our concerns are, and however well they are served by the concept of cruelty in this case. It thus seems that (b) offers the wrong kind of reason, threatening to undermine the proper use of the concept of cruelty through a form of pragmatic encroachment.[37]

To defuse this worry, the first step is to insist on the distinction between reasons in and reasons for concept use: (a) is a reason *in* concept use: a reason for a particular judgement using the concept of cruelty. (b) is a reason *for* concept use: a reason for the general disposition to use the concept of cruelty in one's judgements. Consequently, these two kinds of reasons do not compete with or encroach on one another. They operate at distinct levels.

But even once it is granted that we are after reasons *for* concept use, the worry might resurface in a different guise. It might take the form of wondering whether reasons for concept use had not better appeal to the prevalence and intrinsic features of the object or property referred to by the concept instead of looking only, in bizarrely reflexive fashion, at concept-users' needs. Is it not oddly self-focused to concentrate attention on one's own conceptual needs in this connection? Should one not rather say that we have reason to cultivate the general disposition to use the concept of cruelty in our judgements because there is so much cruelty around?

This is where defusing the wrong-kind-of-reasons worry requires a second step, namely the realization that what we need to answer the authority

---

[37] For other putative cases of pragmatic encroachment this ties in with, see Kim and McGrath (2019).

question *critically* are *disengaged* reasons for concept use, i.e. reasons visible even to someone who has rationally and emotionally disengaged from the concept under evaluation. Disengagement provides critical distance from the concept and its concomitant reasons. We must temporarily disengage from the reasons the concept itself reveals, and rely instead on the rest of our concepts and on the concerns we have independently of the concept.

It is of course true that, in one important sense, the prevalence of cruelty in the world provides *the* reason to use the concept of cruelty; but to leave it at that would be to evaluate the concept by an insufficiently independent standard. The question must rather be whether we have any *independent* reasons to demarcate and attach a certain significance to what we subsume under F.

Once we are mindful of these two qualifications, the reasons for reasons provided by the needs-based approach will no longer appear to be reasons of the wrong kind. They do not compete with or encroach on reasons in concept use, because they are reasons *for* concept use: reasons to cultivate the disposition to use a concept. And they do not compete with or encroach on engaged reasons for concept use, because they are *disengaged* reasons for concept use: reasons offered from a perspective that is independent of the concept and its concomitant reasons in and for concept use. Thus, doing conceptual ethics from the autoethnographic stance allows us to assess concepts from a critical perspective that does not rest content with reasons arising from features of things that the concept itself attunes us to.

Yet it may still be felt that the most trenchant version of the wrong kind of reasons worry cuts through these distinctions. This is the worry that the answer to the authority question advocated here *itself* falls prey to the authority question: why should these reasons for reasons be granted *more* authority than the first-order reasons they purport to shore up or undermine? It is not clear that the reasons that can be advanced for or against the use of a concept always count for more than the reasons adverted to in its use. Why should reasons for concept use be granted authority over deeply entrenched reasons that have at least as much force with us? By what right do these reasons for concept use validate or invalidate considerations that strike many as more immediately compelling?

To appreciate what is distinctive about how the needs-based approach addresses this worry, it is instructive to compare it with how indirect utilitarianism—or what has fittingly been called 'disposition utilitarianism'—might approach questions of conceptual ethics.[38] Disposition utilitarianism favours

---

[38] See Sen and Williams (1982, 4) and Williams (1995i, 195).

the cultivation of dispositions to reason in terms of a carefully curated set of optimific concepts—the concepts that tend to produce the best consequences. To this end, it operates with a two-level structure, which makes room for the thought that while consequences must be the currency of reasons for concept use, the concepts these give us reason to use are not necessarily articulated in terms of consequences. Thus, in the heat of the action, when time is short and decisions need to be made, we might be better off letting ourselves be guided at the first-order level by heuristic reasons; but the *real* reasons are the reasons at the second-order level, which arise directly from what truly matters, namely utility. We may only be able to work back to these real reasons in the cool hour of reflection, when we have an opportunity to tweak what heuristic reasons we otherwise rely on. But both kinds of reasons belong to the sphere of normative practical deliberation, and ultimately derive what authority they possess from the practical aim of maximizing utility.

Such an indirect utilitarian approach to the ethics of conceptualization differs from the needs-based approach in at least three significant respects. First, the utilitarian approach suffers from the well-known instability involved in trying to live by some considerations while believing, at a more reflective level, that they do not really matter in themselves.[39] Utilitarianism regards the sensitivity to the first-order reasons articulated by optimific concepts as a mere device for utility maximization. The considerations one becomes sensitive to by possessing a concept are seen, from the second-order perspective of indirect utilitarianism, not as considerations worth taking seriously in their own right, but as parts of the rational mechanism by which the concepts achieve their desired consequences, while the real justification for thinking this way is that it maximizes utility. All that matters, really, is utility, or rather what is quantified through that notion—'well-being' or 'welfare' in some suitably narrow and technical sense; but to maximize it, we sometimes have to treat other considerations *as if* they mattered.

Second, the utilitarian approach commits us to a stingy axiology: it assesses the consequences of first-order dispositions exclusively in its narrowly welfarist terms. In doing so, it invites us to withdraw our evaluative commitment from the panoply of thick normative concepts that guide our everyday deliberation, and refocus that evaluative commitment entirely on what the thin master concept of utility quantifies. What is controversial about this is not so much the positive claim that what is quantified through the notion of utility matters, but the implicit negative claim that nothing else matters.

---

[39] See e.g. Williams's criticism of R. M. Hare (2006j, 80; 2006i, 71).

Third, the utilitarian approach indeed has trouble accommodating the fact that first-order reasons sometimes simply *count for more* than second-order reasons: our most visceral judgements sometimes feel more authoritative than any rarefied reasons that might be offered for or against cultivating the dispositions to think that way. If, for example, we learn that there is a *human being* trapped in a burning building, then, on the strength of that thought alone, we mobilize enormous resources to save them.[40] Utilitarian conceptual ethics might tell us that the consequences of using the concept *human being* are not sufficiently conducive to the maximization of utility to justify our thinking in these terms, so that we are better off ignoring this particular concept along with its concomitant reasons for action, and using some more optimific concept instead; but it is not at all clear that the concept's poor score on the utility metric is more compelling than the thought that there is a *human being* trapped in the burning building. What is supposed to give the ruminations of utilitarianism more authority with us than our entrenched solidarity with other human beings, our sense of humanity? The reasons that some concepts provide are too robustly embedded in the deepest layers of our ethical experience to be so easily dislodged by the deliverances of some questionable theoretical construct.

The needs-based approach, by contrast, avoids these three difficulties. Taking them in reverse order: the needs-based approach can accommodate the default authority of our entrenched first-order reasons without surrendering its critical edge, because it ultimately draws *its own authority from* those first-order reasons, deploying some of them against others through the intermediary of second-order reflection on our conceptual needs. If our use of a concept tends to promote concerns we critically identify with, this will vindicate the authority of the concept—but not because we withdraw our evaluative commitments from our various first-order judgements and refocus them exclusively through the lens of some single currency of reasons such as utility; nor because the reasons discernible from the autoethnographic stance are *detached* from the more immediately gripping reasons that the concept alerts us to—this is what gives us critical distance and renders the standard of evaluation sufficiently independent, but it is not what renders it authoritative; rather, the reasons visible from the autoethnographic stance derive their authority from the fact that they ultimately flow from *our own concerns*.

---

[40] I take the example from Williams's (2006c, 142) reflections on 'the human prejudice'. See also Diamond (2018a). The point about first-order reasons counting for more than second-order reasons echoes the one made in Chapter 5 in connection with Williams's (1985, 127; 2014c, 148) remarks about Michael Tooley's proposed concept of *person*.

The standard of appraisal is thus precisely not detached from our own concerns in a way that would beg the question of its authority over us. It flows from those very concerns, and that is what makes it authoritative for us. Because our conceptual needs are the opaque correlates of the concerns we are most closely identified with, the needs-based authority that our concepts exercise over us is really a refraction of the authority we exercise over ourselves.

Hence, the needs-based approach does not follow indirect utilitarianism in locating all the authority at the metaconceptual level of reasons for concept use and treating these as the only real justifiers. Rather, it locates authority, in the first instance, in the first-order judgements expressing the concerns we critically identify with. Instead of regarding second-order reasons as privileged by their integration into a systematic theory and authorized to overturn any given currency of first-order reasons, it taps into the authority of the rest of our first-order reasons. The second-order reasons of the needs-based approach draw their authority not from anything beyond the contingent concerns we critically identify with, but from those very concerns. The second-order level is merely a conduit channelling the authority of those concerns and bringing it to a focus in reflection on a concept's merits.

Being thus grounded in the first-order level also allows the needs-based approach to avoid the reflective instability of indirect utilitarianism, because the considerations acting as reasons for concept use do not claim overriding authority, and carry no suggestion that they matter to the exclusion of any other consideration. This allows us to acknowledge that there is more to the dispositions involved in concept possession than their giving psychological effect to second-order reasons for concept use.[41] Indeed, regarding them as black-box mechanisms for the production of certain effects is precisely what the autoethnographic stance encourages us to avoid: it requires us to maintain a sense of what things look and feel like to one who has these dispositions, mindful of the fact that these dispositions constitute perspectives of their own. They constitute ways of seeing a situation, and do not necessarily induce one to see that situation in terms of the effects of using the concept at all. Moreover, the dispositions involved in concept possession also include dispositions to feel about situations and react to them in a certain way. These dispositions possess a certain degree of autonomy, a life and momentum of

---

[41] This seems to me one of the most significant lessons to be drawn from Williams's critique of indirect utilitarianism, and I take the suggestive metaphors of 'black-box mechanisms' and 'momentum' from his discussion; see Williams (1995i, 199; 2006j, 80).

their own. That is why, once thoroughly internalized, they may linger even after one recognizes conclusive reasons to abandon the concept (as in the example of the pangs of guilt that might still beset someone who had stopped living by the concept of chastity).

Nor does the needs-based approach commit us to a stingy axiology, since it is not committed to recognizing only a single currency of reasons. While it does consider the consequences or effects of using a concept, it does not treat those consequences in narrowly welfarist terms. It evaluates them not based on a single metric, but based on how the use of a concept relates to the whole range of concerns one critically identifies with independently of the concept under evaluation. Thus, the considerations by which we evaluate the effects of using a concept might well make reference to how it contributes to protecting or asserting people's rights, or to how it brings it about that certain absolute prohibitions can be articulated and enforced. These are concerns that utilitarianism struggles to accommodate, but that the Neurathian, open-ended structure of the needs-based approach naturally invites us to bring to bear on concept appraisal—along with concerns for authenticity, integrity, transparency, beauty, and other dimensions of value that utilitarianism has no room for. If anything, the needs-based approach is extravagantly multidimensional in its axiology. In place of the monism of utilitarianism, it puts a pluralism of values, projects, and commitments; in place of its foundationalism, it puts a Neurathian non-foundationalism. As a result, the admissible axiological input to needs-based appraisal will be as richly diverse as our concerns are.

Because they do not claim overriding authority, the metaconceptual judgements articulating reasons for concept use play a fundamentally different role in the needs-based approach than they do in the utilitarian approach. Instead of registering a privileged form of normative deliberation about what to do, they are best thought of as belonging to the sphere of *explanatory or philosophical understanding*. These judgements do nothing as immediately practical as rationalizing or recommending particular courses of action. They tell us whether and why it makes sense to cultivate the dispositions to treat certain types of considerations as rationalizing or recommending certain types of action. Reasons for concept use do not relate to the reasons operative within our conceptual practices as real justifications relate to merely heuristic reasons. The relation is rather akin to that by which an explanation for why we go in for a certain game can affect our confidence in the rules by which we justify moves within the game, and in the game itself.

However, we should not distinguish too sharply between the reasons that provide explanatory understanding and the reasons that guide normative deliberation. If what we are doing from the autoethnographic stance is really to be conceptual *ethics* as opposed to a normatively inert form of metaethics, we had better not follow Simon Blackburn in drawing an impermeable distinction between *explanatory philosophizing about reasons* and *moralizing with reasons*, where the latter refers to the normative reasoning we engage in from the deliberative stance.[42] For Blackburn, these are two separate language games that should be insulated from each other, and only moralizing can properly yield justificatory considerations bearing on normative deliberation.

In contrast to this, I take it that *responsible* deliberation should be informed by explanatory understanding. Understanding how the use of a concept relates to our concerns should affect our confidence in the concept and the reason statements it allows us to articulate. Our confidence should be strengthened by the realization that the concept promotes concerns we critically identify with. But it should equally be weakened by the realization that the concept does nothing for us, or even serves concerns we object to.

Reflection from the autoethnographic stance on the connection between concepts and concerns can inform the deliberative stance by affecting our confidence in the reasons guiding our deliberation. If we accept this, we part ways with the Wittgensteinian quietist who holds that we should just relax into the conceptual practices we find in our form of life, and eschew attempts to say anything about why these rather than other concepts should figure in it. And we also part ways with the evolutionary debunkers who hold that our use of certain concepts should ultimately be capable of being *justified* directly in terms of their philosophical or evolutionary explanations, and jettisoned otherwise. The former view makes the mistake of collapsing the autoethnographic into the deliberative perspective, while the latter makes the reverse mistake of collapsing the deliberative into the autoethnographic perspective. If we hold on to both perspectives, the reasons we discern from the autoethnographic perspective can affect our confidence in the reasons we discern from the deliberative perspective without committing us to the misguided view that the former set of reasons must directly *justify* the latter. That would indeed be to appeal to the wrong kind of reasons.

There are, finally, two rather different versions of the wrong kind of reasons worry that are influential in this connection, one distinctively epistemological and the other deontological in spirit. Addressing these will round out the picture of the kinds of reasons the needs-based approach offers and bring out how it is meant to broaden our sense of the relevant considerations beyond

---

[42] See Blackburn (1986, 1993, 1998).

the narrow boundaries set by what might be called *epistemologistic* and *moralistic* conceptions of conceptual ethics.

The epistemological version of the wrong kind of reasons worry is that anything which is not an *epistemic* reason is the wrong kind of reason to motivate the use of a concept. Thus, Mona Simion writes: 'Concepts, just like beliefs, are representational devices, their function is an epistemic one: to represent the world. In virtue of this function, concepts will be properly functioning when responsive to epistemic reasons, and malfunctional when responsive to practical reasons' (2018, 923). Consequently, she holds that 'just in the way in which prudential, moral, political, etc. considerations are the wrong kind of reasons for knowledgeable belief revision, they equally fail to support conceptual revision' (2018, 923).

But we should not be so quick to generalize from the norms governing the assessment of beliefs to the norms governing the appraisal of concepts. These two kinds of evaluation again operate at different levels. We may grant that the activity of assessing or revising a belief is answerable only to epistemic reasons, which is to say reasons to think the belief true or false. But these are first-order reasons—reasons *in* concept use that we perceive as engaged users of the concepts in terms of which the belief is articulated.

The activity of appraising a concept, by contrast, is answerable to second-order reasons—reasons *for* concept use that we perceive as disengaged users of the concept. Much as there are good second-order reasons for us to come to think of the truth as something worth pursuing for its own sake, there probably are good second-order reasons for us to only recognize *epistemic* first-order reasons as appropriate reasons for belief. But it does not automatically follow that a similar restriction holds at the second-order level of reasons for concept use.

Consider again the analogy with games. It is characteristic of many games that players' beliefs within the game are governed exclusively by a well-delimited and fairly narrow range of epistemic reasons, and quite properly remain insensitive to practical reasons such as considerations of fairness. My belief that I am losing for the fifth time in a row to the player who got to make the first move because she is the youngest, for example, is responsive only to the evidence provided by the state of the game. It may be *unfair* that I should be losing again due to a first-mover advantage, but that makes it no less true.

For the designers of the game who get to define the concepts and rules governing its dynamics, however, a concern for fairness *can and should* inform their choices. At that second-order level, the thought that some arrangement would systematically offend against fairness is clearly the *right* kind of reason.

The epistemological version of the wrong kind of reasons worry is further alleviated if we do not think of all concepts as being exclusively in the business of turning the intellect into a mirror of the world, but as performing numerous other roles besides. As we saw in Chapter 1, it is a highly questionable assumption that *all* concepts *exclusively* serve to carve the world at its antecedent joints.[43]

Tellingly, Simion's guiding example in generalizing from belief revision to concept appraisal is what she takes to be a joint-carving natural kind concept: 'If our concept of "deer" is epistemically perfectly functional and carves nature at its biological joints', she writes, 'moral, political, etc. considerations, in isolation, will not be the right kinds of reasons to revise it' (2018, 923). If the idea that our concepts *exclusively* serve the epistemic function of representing the world has any plausibility, it is indeed in connection with natural kind concepts such as *deer*.

But while, from an engaged perspective, even thick normative concepts seem to be in the business of mirroring the antecedent structure of social reality, that impression dissipates once we consider them from a disengaged perspective and pay attention to the varieties of work they actually perform: many of our moral, political, or legal concepts have been thought to perform a host of different functions which, from a disengaged perspective, have nothing to do with limning worldly boundaries, and more to do with shaping and regulating society and expressing and revising norms of various kinds.[44] This functional pluralism should make us hesitant to generalize from a natural kind concept like *deer* to moral, political, or legal concepts.

More plausibly, carving at the joints is only what *some* of our concepts serve to do, and even then not necessarily *everything* they serve to do. For notice that even a concept like *deer* does not cater exclusively to the disinterested concerns of taxonomists. It is a concept that simultaneously needs to tie in with a host of other human concerns, ranging from the predatory and the culinary to the cultural, symbolical, mythical, and theological. It is not least the pull of these other, not purely epistemic concerns that explains why taxonomies themselves tend to have tortuous histories, and why, to this day, 'contemporary biology seems committed to pluralism, as different investigators use the classifications best suited to their needs' (Kitcher 2001, 48). Even the concept of water—the paradigmatic example of a natural kind concept—has

---

[43] For an extended argument questioning this assumption, see notably Price (2011).
[44] See Blackburn (1993, 2013a, b, 2017), Brandom (1994, 2001, 2011, 2013, 2015b), Price (2011, 2013), Price and Macarthur (2007), M. Williams (2010, 2013), and Thomasson (2015, 2020a, b, 2022).

been thought to answer to a panoply of cross-cutting concerns due to its longstanding enmeshment in everything from agriculture and transport to cooking and religious rituals.[45]

When shifting our focus away from natural kind concepts towards the thick normative concepts that organize social worlds, the prospect of understanding conceptual authority exclusively in epistemic terms—and the function of concepts exclusively in representational terms—becomes even less inviting. Thick normative concepts do not even *seem* to play purely epistemic roles: they manifestly derive their importance from their social roles in forming conceptual architectures that enable coordination and cooperation. One cannot satisfy the conditions of coordination and cooperation through epistemic prowess alone—as Tadeusz Zawidzki remarks, 'our social accomplishments are not by-products of individualized cognitive feats' (2013, xiii). It is the collective cultivation of thick normative concepts that shapes our minds for cohabitation in society.

It seems only right that our confidence in concepts performing such moral, political, and legal roles should be responsive to moral, political, and legal reasons. Insisting that any reasons for concept use that are not epistemic must be the wrong kind of reasons then looks less like a compelling objection than like an epistemologist's *déformation professionnelle*. It presents us with an overly *epistemologistic* conception of conceptual ethics.

What is more, the reasons that *are* epistemic anyway require supplementation by other kinds of reasons in this connection, because they cannot take us far enough by themselves. One can argue that some concepts are worth having because they enable us to articulate knowledge. But different concepts would enable us to articulate different forms of knowledge. So while it may be true that certain concepts put certain forms of knowledge within our reach, this fact alone is not enough to make a neutral case to prefer these concepts over equally knowledge-generating alternatives. It merely leads on to the question of what makes certain kinds of knowledge *more worthwhile than others*. And this question calls for *non*-epistemic reasons adducing facts about us—about our concerns, capacities, and circumstances, and the needs for certain kinds of knowledge we have as a result.

Lastly, there is also a deontological version of the wrong kind of reasons worry: that anything which is not a *moral* reason must be the wrong kind of reason to motivate the use of a concept. While the needs-based approach may, for instance, indicate various prudential reasons to recognize the

---

[45] See Schroeter and Schroeter (2015, 426).

authority of a concept such as *moral rightness*, the worry goes, moral rightness is precisely not authoritative merely prudentially—to do the morally right thing merely out of prudence is to do it for the wrong kind of reason.

One basic observation to be made in response is that we must resist the slide from concept to object: confronted with the claim that we have reason to use the concept of *x* because it is instrumental to meeting some conceptual need, philosophers tend to be quick to point out that the value of *x* is not merely instrumental, and that to pursue *x* because it serves some ulterior concern is to act on the wrong kind of reason. But the value of *x* is one thing, and the value of the *concept* of *x* quite another.

Knowledge as a mental state, for example, can be valuable in various ways, both instrumentally and intrinsically. But the value of the *concept* of knowledge is a distinct issue. Its value is not the value of a state, but the value of a cognitive device that notably allows us to *recognize* knowledge as such and to think *about* knowledge. Were we not a social and language-using species that shares information, we would not have the particular conceptual need for something like the concept of knowledge that we highlighted in the previous chapter. But we would still need knowledge itself, especially concerning our immediate environment and its threats and opportunities. It can therefore be granted that the wrong kind of reasons worry should be taken seriously in thinking about the *objects* of our concepts. This does not preclude our concepts from standing in instrumental relations to our concerns, even if the view we take of things when thinking in those terms is not an instrumental view, but one on which things possess intrinsic value, or are things that simply *must* be done. There can be instrumentality without instrumental mentality.

Another point that needs emphasizing here is that the concerns in relation to which concepts are instrumental can be the most high-minded *moral* concerns, and when they are, the resulting reasons for concept use will be *moral reasons*—we might have reason to jettison one concept in favour of another out of a concern for fairness, or justice, or impartiality. Nothing restricts the needs-based approach to reasons of a prudential kind. If we have reason to use a certain concept of moral rightness to realize our moral concerns, that makes neither the reasons nor the concerns prudential.

Part of what fuels the wrong kind of reasons worry is the way in which kinds of reasons themselves are conceptualized. 'What misleads people', Harry Frankfurt observes, 'may be the supposition that the only alternative to accepting the requirements of morality consists in greedily permitting oneself to be driven by self-interest' (2004, 8). If we think in terms of such a *dualistic conception of reasons*, all reasons for action must *either* be reasons of morality *or* reasons of self-interest. Accordingly, whatever is not a moral reason must be a merely prudential reason.

But there are other kinds of value and importance besides the moral and the prudential. The mere fact that a reason is not clearly moral does not mean that it should be relegated to the rank of the merely prudential. Most of the reasons that make the world go round lie between the extremes that this overly stark contrast presents as the only options. As Susan Wolf vividly brings out, most people find their reasons to live not in reasons of morality or reasons of self-interest, but in 'reasons of love', engendered by their love of persons they are attached to or pursuits they are passionate about.[46] These reasons that the dualistic conception omits 'are some of the most important and central ones in our lives', which 'engage us in the activities that make our lives worth living', 'give us a reason to go on', and 'give meaning to our lives' (Wolf 2010, 2). As long as philosophers remain hostage to the dualistic conception of reasons, they risk ignoring much of what actually moves people—including, ironically, what moves them to do philosophy.

If reasons for concept use are not to be prudential reasons, on this dualistic conception, they would have to be moral reasons. But when it is neither an action nor a motive but a *concept* that is in the dock, morality's evaluative machinery, keyed as it is to the appraisal of individual actions and the first-order reasons from which they flow, can make it hard to see how reasons that float at one remove from action, such as reasons for concept use, could be *bona fide* moral reasons—especially if they do not take the form of moral obligations. The dualistic conception of reasons then conspires with the focus of many moral concepts on actions and motives to produce the impression that all reasons for concept use must be merely prudential.

Three observations help dispel that impression, however. First, morality's evaluative machinery *can* be brought to bear on concepts, and even when it is understood along Kantian lines, it plausibly makes at least *some* demands on one's conceptual apparatus. For example, if morality demands not only that one fulfil one's moral obligations, but that one fulfil them *because* they are one's moral obligations, this already imposes demands on one's thought as well as on one's actions: it places one under a moral obligation to use whatever concepts are required to be able to act from the right kind of motive.

---

[46] See Wolf (2010, 5–6); Frankfurt (2004) also refers to these underappreciated reasons as reasons of love.

Depending on how exactly the demand to do the right thing from the right kind of motive is understood, there may be several ways in which one's conceptual apparatus can satisfy that demand. It may simply do so by putting at one's disposal the concept of moral obligation or moral duty itself, thereby enabling one to φ from the thought 'Because I am under a moral obligation to φ'. But equally, it may satisfy the demand by putting at one's disposal a special concept of *ought* that *expresses* moral obligation, so that one can φ from the thought 'Because I ought to φ'. Or, if the demand is understood to allow for this, one's conceptual apparatus may even satisfy it by equipping one to register one's various moral obligations under a host of more particularized and concretized descriptions: when under a moral obligation to keep a promise, for instance, the description under which that obligation forms the motive from which one acts might take the particularized form 'Because I promised'.[47] In whichever way the demand is met, however, there is a set of concepts such that one is under a moral obligation to use at least one suitable subset of them.

Second, the mere fact that the use of a concept is instrumental to realizing a concern does not make the concern itself instrumental: as already indicated, some of the concerns served by concepts will be moral concerns, which makes the reasons for concept use engendered thereby moral reasons. One's concern for equality, say, might give one moral reasons to adopt concepts whose use promotes equality, and to abandon concepts that obstruct, thwart, or frustrate that concern. This need not even involve demoting the concepts themselves to the status of mere means, devoid of anything but instrumental value: in some cases, the use of a concept might itself *instantiate* the realization of the concern it serves. In aesthetic contexts, for example, coming to see things a certain way can be an end in itself; likewise, as we saw Murdoch argue, moral concerns might be realized already through a change in how one conceptualizes a situation—changes to our conceptual repertoire can be constitutive of moral progress.[48]

Third, even the concerns that are *not* moral concerns need not therefore be self-interested or prudential. Like our reasons for action, reasons for concept use should not be conceived as being exhausted by reasons of morality and reasons of self-interest. Many of our most forceful reasons for concept use might be *second-order reasons of love*, reflecting conceptual needs engendered by our subjective attachment to objectively worthy pursuits. Philosophers

---

[47] Williams (1981d, 117), for instance, holds that the demand is more charitably interpreted that way.
[48] See Murdoch (1956, 1961).

should know, since it is surely their love of philosophy as much as their sense of duty or self-interest that leads them to so tirelessly analyse, refine, replace, reject, and rehabilitate concepts. Their philosophical passions and projects give philosophers reasons to use the most abstruse concepts that no one else has reason to use, and that neither morality nor self-interest are always well served by. The same reasons which give meaning to our lives can also give authority to our concepts.

In some cases, of course, the reasons we might have to use a concept will indeed include genuinely prudential reasons, and here, deeper differences in philosophical outlook will emerge, depending on whether one recognizes these prudential reasons as pertinent, or dismisses them as reasons of the wrong kind. Echoing Williams's distinction between a broader notion of 'ethics' and a narrower notion of 'morality', we might mark this difference by distinguishing between the *ethics* and the *morality* of conceptualization. We might then redefine *conceptual ethics* as the broad-minded enterprise of appraising concepts on the basis of all kinds of considerations that can inform how one should think and live, and contrast this with *conceptual morality* as a purely moral evaluation of concepts that insists on drawing a sharp boundary between moral and non-moral considerations and only counts moral considerations as pertinent.[49]

McPherson and Plunkett, for example, might be taken to abstractly express conceptual morality's exclusive focus on moral considerations when they suggest that we should rely on normative concepts such as *morally right* or *morally better* in appraising other concepts, but not on our wider repertoire of thick normative concepts, because 'what is crucial is whether use of a normative concept is vindicated by *specific* normative concepts: namely, the most authoritatively normative concepts' (2021, 218).

If we engage in conceptual morality as opposed to conceptual ethics, we will be led to appraise all our concepts in terms of a narrow set of moral considerations, such as their tendency to maximize well-being, or their alignment with our moral obligations. An example of the former would be the indirect utilitarianism we considered. An example of the latter would be Christine Korsgaard's preferred Kantian way of demonstrating 'the right of…concepts to give laws to us' (1996, 9), which ultimately also amounts to a purely moral evaluation that insists on drawing a sharp boundary between moral and non-moral considerations and only counts moral considerations as pertinent, dismissing other types of considerations as reasons of the wrong kind.

---

[49] See Williams (1985, 7).

Even if one were to accept that the *reasons for action* bearing on one's practical deliberation should be limited to moral reasons taking the form of moral obligations, however, it still would not automatically follow that this restriction to moral reasons extended to the *reasons for concept use* bearing on the question of what concepts to recognize as authoritative. More philosophical work would be required to show, first, that the question of conceptual authority is even a *practical* question in the relevant Kantian sense, which is to say a question as to *what one ought to do*, where the 'ought' expresses moral obligation; and second, that it is even intelligible to speak of 'moral obligations' to use or abstain from using a concept *for any kind of concept*, and not just in exceptional cases, such as when it comes to the concept of moral obligation itself.

By contrast, the needs-based approach, in its willingness to recognize even prudential concerns as legitimate normative input to the authority question, exemplifies conceptual ethics *as opposed to* conceptual morality. Rejecting overly moralistic conceptions of conceptual ethics, the needs-based approach encourages us to bring the whole stock of our thick and thin normative concepts to bear on concept appraisal, thereby recognizing all kinds of reasons as relevant—including prudential and aesthetic reasons as well as reasons of love. In inviting us to ask what concepts we need, it therefore imposes no principled restriction on what we might need them *for*—everything we care about is admissible, if defeasible, input to concept appraisal. In Chapter 10, we shall consider an illustration of needs-based concept appraisal that appeals to an expressly non-moralistic admixture of prudential and political considerations.

8.7 Conceptual Good-for-Nothings

Locating the value of concepts in their aptness for serving our concerns by meeting our conceptual needs might ultimately still seem reductive in one respect, however, namely insofar as it appears to reduce the goodness of concepts to what they are good *for*. And it is equally a theme of Wolf's work that cultural artefacts need not always be good in virtue of being good *for* something—in particular, they need not be good in virtue of making some measurable contribution to well-being.[50] Some artefacts are valuable even

---

[50] An observation echoed by Scanlon (1998, 143). Insofar as contributing to our well-being is a narrower idea than serving our concerns, because not all our concerns are directed to our well-being, I am broadening the contrast class here.

though they are *good-for-nothings*. One's first acquaintance with 'a poem or a novel or a painting', for example, can have 'the character of a discovery of something valuable in itself' (Wolf 2015a, 76).

We can make sense of such valuable good-for-nothings, Wolf suggests, if we acknowledge that 'realizing our intellectual and perceptual potentials is good-in-itself' (2015a, 76). As she elaborates the point:

> a part of human good involves being connected in appropriate ways to what the world has to offer.... [I]f we understand the world as containing objects and opportunities for experience that are of value in themselves, then we may think of our lives as better, as more fortunate, insofar as we are able to be in appreciative touch with some of the most valuable of these. (2015a, 76)

Wolf primarily has works of art, philosophy, and science in mind; but conceptualizations are cultural artefacts too, and sometimes form the backbones of innovative works of art, philosophy, or science. Can concepts also be valuable good-for-nothings? Might this be the mite of truth that the wrong kind of reasons worry points us towards?

Wolf remarks that what makes philosophy good are things like 'illuminating a problem' or offering novel ways of 'interpreting our experience' and 'understanding our relation to the world' (2015a, 85). Yet these are the same sorts of things that concepts enable us to do. And sometimes, acquiring a new concept does have 'the character of a discovery of something valuable in itself' (2015a, 76). The brilliant distinction, the delightful nuance, the satisfaction of discovering a fresh lens through which to see the world—these will be recognizable to philosophers as experiences of intrinsic value. That intrinsic value is surely part of the reason why philosophers are such avid grinders of conceptual lenses.

Perhaps, therefore, we can intelligibly value a concept simply for what it allows us to think, just as we can value a certain food for its taste rather than for its nutritional benefits. A new concept at the very least enlivens our awareness of some aspect of things, perhaps widens the aperture through which we view the world, and at best reveals previously inaccessible dimensions of reality. And when several new concepts band together, they can help us overcome the constraints of established ways of thinking, sharpen our understanding, and open up new forms of knowledge.

If, as Wolf contends, 'realizing our intellectual and perceptual potentials is good-in-itself', this suggests that we should strive for a richer conceptual repertoire, even if the concepts are good-for-nothings. Indeed, Wolf herself introduces a concept that articulates a highly general motivation for enriching our conceptual repertoire: *love of the world*—'an attitude in which life seems endlessly fascinating, yielding countless objects of interest and admiration' (2015b, 177).[51] Love of the world can drive the proliferation of distinctions as an end in itself.

But does the conceptual proliferation encouraged by this attitude have a sense of direction? Or should we see value simply in the multiplication of distinctions? Surely, the idea cannot simply be that *more* concepts and distinctions is always *better*. Even Williams, for whom our main problem now is that we have too few ethical concepts (1985, 130), warns against chasing for its own sake 'the shudder of an exquisite distinction' (2005f, 53). The enrichment of our conceptual repertoire, even if intrinsically valuable, still requires guidance by a sense of quality. We must remain able to discriminate between enrichment and encumbrance, between careful nuancing and frivolous hair-splitting. When Murdoch argues that we should acquire more concepts in terms of which to picture the substance of our being, because some moral improvements can be achieved already by changing how we perceive a situation, for example, she still invites the more discriminating question of what makes the adoption of certain concepts progressive, and what makes a particular way of seeing the situation important.[52] We cannot do without some guiding sense of what forms of conceptual diversity are worth having.

To put the problem of aimless conceptual proliferation back in its box, we need only remember that we are already well equipped to discriminate between pointless hair-splitting and worthwhile distinctions—but not because worthwhile distinctions are always identifiable antecedently of human concerns. It is rather *in virtue of* the concerns we bring to the appraisal of concepts that we can discern value in certain distinctions, or importance in certain ways of seeing a situation. This shines through in the way Wolf herself invites us to see value in certain good-for-nothings: she still appeals to human concerns that are furthered, instantiated, or realized by these good-for-nothings, such as the concern to realize our intellectual and perceptual potentials, or the concern to appreciate what the world has to offer. These are highly general epistemic and aesthetic concerns that may indeed be nothing like Wolf's contrast foil, the welfare theorist's hard-headed concern to deliver

---

[51] See also Dover's (2024) account of 'erotic curiosity' as a way of communing with and delighting in the world for its own sake.
[52] See Murdoch (1956).

measurable benefits to longevity and health; but they are among the most characteristic of human concerns.

The fact that Wolf explains the value of good-for-nothings by tying them back to human concerns is not just an incidental feature of her examples, but reflects a broader hermeneutic constraint on methodologically humanistic reflection: if, as Wolf herself declares, we want no metaethical commitment 'to a Platonic world of ideas and values that are independent of human existence' (2015a, 77), the value of concepts *must* be related to the human point of view at least at the level of reflective explanation. This does not entail that we can only value concepts narrowly in terms of their instrumentality in meeting human concerns. But it does entail that our seeing inherent value in concepts expresses a human attitude, and that we must be able to make reflective sense of that attitude in humanistic terms, by seeing how it meshes with the rest of human affairs.

The constraint is therefore this: to be able to make reflective sense of how certain concepts can be valuable in their own right, we need to be able to see how the attitude of valuing them in this way relates to some recognizable human concern. As long as the attitude of valuing certain concepts for their own sake remains disconnected from *any* human concern, the claim that those concepts are inherently valuable will not be fully intelligible to us under reflection.

It follows that even the goodness of conceptual good-for-nothings cannot ultimately be completely independent of human concerns. If we entirely lacked certain concerns, the delightful nuance, the exciting concept, the important difference in how we see a situation—these would be stripped of their significance. Their inherent value depends on their enmeshment in practices animated by certain concerns.

Insisting that even conceptual good-for-nothings must still tie in with some human concern at this reflective level puts the problem of aimless conceptual proliferation back in its box, since the extension of our conceptual repertoire can draw guidance from its roots in our concerns. By relying on the concerns and concepts we possess already, we can discriminate between worthwhile distinctions and pointless hair-splitting.

At the same time, once we replace the dualistic conception of reasons with a more pluralistic picture of what moves people and reflect on how even seemingly idle concepts might fill conceptual needs after all, this puts pressure on the idea that conceptual good-for-nothings really are good for *nothing*. If only at the reflective level of philosophical explanation, the concepts whose possession we experience as inherently valuable are in fact good for *something*: realizing one's intellectual and perceptual potentials, notably, and appreciating what the world has to offer. It is only on a restricted understanding of 'being good for something', such as the welfarist conception of goodness, that concepts are intelligible as good-for-nothings at the reflective level.

Even so, Wolf's illumination of the value of good-for-nothings helps us appreciate that we value some things, including some concepts, for their own sake. What I have sought to add is that even these forms of inherent value must retain some connection to recognizable human concerns at the level of philosophical reflection if they are to make sense to us in humanistic terms. This addition achieves two things: it indicates on what basis we might discriminate between more or less important additions to the conceptual repertoire; and it reinforces the point that we need a more nuanced picture of human reasons and motives to appreciate the range of ways in which things, including concepts, can be valuable.

Thinking through the value of conceptual good-for-nothings thus leads us back to the importance of reasons of love as reasons for concept use. If there is value in acquiring new concepts, appreciating fresh nuances, and becoming sensitive to finer distinctions, it is because we have more reasons for concept use than the dualistic conception would have us believe. We are concerned not merely to increase our own well-being or that of others, but to realize our intellectual potentials, be attentive to the world around us, and appreciate what it has to offer. With her notion of *love of the world*, Wolf fashions a valuable conceptual lens that renders these invisible concerns visible—one philosophers have every reason to use.

This concludes the presentation of the needs-based framework for answering the authority question. In the next chapter, we turn to an application of this framework: a case study of how the needs-based approach can cast fresh light on a contested notion at the centre of debates over free will and responsibility: the notion of doing something *voluntarily*. Working through this case study will not only further illustrate the needs-based approach, but also underscore two significant insights it yields: that sometimes, powerful concerns can distort our conceptualizations out of the shape in which they best serve the balance of our concerns; and that sometimes, there are good reasons for us to favour concepts exhibiting what the tidy-minded view considers a defect, namely superficiality.

The Ethics of Conceptualization: Tailoring Thought and Language to Need. Matthieu Queloz, Oxford University Press.
© Matthieu Queloz 2025. DOI: 10.1093/9780198926283.003.0009

PART IV
ANSWERING THE AUTHORITY QUESTION

9
The Essential Superficiality of the Voluntary

9.1 A Questionable Concept

A fundamental distinction we draw in our dealings with each other, both in our everyday practice of holding each other to account and in the more serious business of allocating legal responsibility, is the distinction between 'voluntary' and 'involuntary' actions. As indicated by its etymological roots in *voluntas*, Latin for *will*, the distinction nominally separates actions that are 'attributable to the agent's will' from actions that are not so attributable, or only to a lesser degree. But what makes an action voluntary? And does it matter? Is the concept of the voluntary even an important one to have in our repertoire?

The aim of this chapter is to illustrate the power of the needs-based approach by putting it to work on the concept of the voluntary. This will yield two broader insights: that powerful concerns can distort our conceptualizations out of the shape in which they best serve the balance of our concerns; and that sometimes, there are good reasons to favour concepts exhibiting what the tidy-minded would consider a defect, namely superficiality. After showing what concerns are served by a superficial conception of voluntariness, I suggest that theories trying to deepen our conception of voluntariness are morally motivated and exemplify a problematic moralization of psychology—they warp our conceptualization of psychology to ensure that moral demands can be met. Realizing this leads to a reconceptualization of the problem of free will as a dual problem.

Recent history has not been kind to the concept of the voluntary. For centuries, this concept lay at the heart of debates over whether we have free will, how the mind directs the body, and which actions we should be held responsible for. It formed the linchpin of accounts of action from Descartes through Locke, Berkeley, Hume, Reid, and Bentham to Mill.[1] They all felt the

---

[1] For a historical overview of the development of the theory of action, see Hyman (2011; 2015, 1-24). See also Wilson and Shpall (2012), Candlish and Damnjanovic (2013), D'Oro and Sandis (2013), and Glock (2014).

urge to *deepen* their conceptions of voluntariness by reconceptualizing voluntary acts in terms of detailed metaphysical accounts of the causal underpinnings that render a bodily movement voluntary. And they all broadly agreed that what turns a bodily movement into a voluntary action is its being caused by a *volition* or an *act of will*.[2] Exponents of this 'theory of volitions' also included Thomas Brown, whose influence on the nineteenth-century legal theorist John Austin ensured the theory's lasting impact on Anglophone jurisprudence.[3]

These attempts to deepen our conception of voluntary action by reconceptualizing it in terms of certain causal underpinnings can be seen as fuelled notably by the conviction that theoretical virtues such as depth bestow greater authority on concepts. But the most obvious attraction of a deepened conception of the voluntary is its promise to give philosophers an objective, independent yardstick by which to take the measure of our practices of responsibility attribution. By first developing a self-standing account of what, at the deepest causal level, *makes* an action voluntary, we achieve a metaphysically grounded understanding of which actions, if any, we are truly responsible for; and given such an independent understanding of responsibility, we can assess our actual practices of holding people accountable for their actions: we can determine to what extent *attributions* of responsibility can be grounded in *true* responsibility.

Yet the twentieth century saw the theory of volitions collapse under three successive waves of criticism. William James and Bertrand Russell maintained that postulating volitions was not required to make sense of action: action arose when the memories of kinaesthetic sensations first experienced in mere bodily movements were recruited to function as 'motive ideas'.[4] Ludwig Wittgenstein and Gilbert Ryle then argued that while the distinction between voluntary and involuntary actions was innocuous enough, we should resist the view that there was, as Wittgenstein put it, 'one common difference between so-called voluntary acts and involuntary ones, viz, the presence or absence of one element, the "act of volition"' (1958, 151–2). In fact, such a view engendered a regress, as Ryle pointed out, for what about the act of will itself? Was it itself a voluntary or an involuntary act? If voluntary, one had to explain its voluntariness in terms of another act of will, and that act's voluntariness in terms of yet another act of will, and so on, ad infinitum; if

---

[2] Though there were also dissenters, such as Thomas Hobbes and Alexander Bain.
[3] See Brown (2012, Part I, §3) and Austin (1885, Lecture XVIII, 411–15).
[4] See Russell (1921, 285) and James (1981, ch. XXVI).

involuntary, however, this had the equally uninviting consequence that the source of an action's voluntariness lay in an involuntary act of will.[5] Finally, G. E. M. Anscombe and Donald Davidson, who each ushered in what are still the reigning paradigms in contemporary thought about action, influentially insisted that the best entry-point for action theory was not the concept of the voluntary, but the concept of the intentional.[6]

Since then, as John Hyman observes, the concept of the voluntary has largely been neglected. 'The theory of volitions had been demolished', he explains, 'and the delicate task of lifting voluntariness out of the ruins did not seem worth the trouble' (2015, 75). It is true that the concept continues to figure prominently in criminal law,[7] and, as we shall see, some form of it also underpins sceptical challenges to free will. But, in the theory of action, the concept came to look increasingly off-putting as the time-honoured metaphysical constructs attempting to explain what made a bodily movement voluntary fell into disrepair.

In view of this inauspicious history, there is a real question whether we still have any reason to use the concept of the voluntary, or whether its authority has been terminally eroded by the failures of metaphysical accounts of voluntariness.

This is a question in conceptual ethics that the needs-based approach is ideally poised to answer. Instead of trying to derive the contours of the right concept of the voluntary from a metaphysical inquiry into the nature of its extension, the needs-based approach pursues the reverse methodological strategy, proposing to let our understanding of what kind of concept of voluntariness (if any) we have most reason to use grow out of an understanding of our concerns and conceptual needs. In other words, it aims to work from the concerns animating the use of the voluntary/involuntary distinction to those versions of the distinction that are worth using. Should we use a concept such that an action's being causally determined already forecloses its counting as voluntary? Or should our concept of voluntariness be properly applicable to actions that are causally determined but uncoerced? What about uncoerced actions performed in an unusual state of mind—in the grip of extreme passion, for example? And, turning to what lies downstream of the concept's

---

[5] See Ryle (2009a, 54). For rejoinders to Ryle's criticism in particular, see Hornsby (1980, 48–50) and O'Shaughnessy (2008b, 363–84); and see Alvarez and Hyman (2019) for an overview of the development of the theory of action in the second half of the twentieth century.

[6] See Anscombe (1957) and Davidson (1980); though it must be said that Anscombe's views on the concept of the voluntary and its ethical role in her 1960s essays and in her second McGivney lecture (2008b) differ notably from her remarks in *Intention* (1957, §§7–17, 20–2, 49).

[7] See e.g. Saunders (1988) and Moore (2010, 5).

application, what inferential consequences should the concept's applicability have? How should the concept tie in with moral and legal practices of holding people responsible for some actions and excusing them for others?

What the needs-based approach suggests is that this battery of questions can be answered by looking at the conceptual needs to which our conceptualization of the voluntary is answerable. Our concerns, when combined with our capacities and circumstances, can provide reasons for us to rely on *some* conception of the voluntary; and, once our understanding of the needs it meets becomes fine-grained enough, those needs can provide reasons for us to prefer a *particular* conception of the voluntary over alternatives.

Applying this approach to the conceptualization of the voluntary will also offer a further illustration of how the needs-based approach has an edge over the tidy-minded approach thanks to its ability to register the practical virtues of theoretical vices. In particular, it will bring out the value of *superficiality* in a conceptualization of the voluntary. This has been overlooked by advocates and critics alike. Theorists who deemed the notion of the voluntary important have tended to do so because they considered it an enigmatic but profound notion that could be deepened through a theory of action, while those deeming it a superficial notion that could not coherently be deepened have tended to neglect it as unimportant.

Parting company with both camps, I contend that the conception of the voluntary we need is at once superficial *and* important—indeed, it is important *only as long as* it remains superficial. We are dealing here with an *essentially* superficial notion that performs important work for us, but it can only perform that work if, in contravention of the tidy-minded view of superficiality as a defect, we refrain from deepening our conception of the voluntary. Any *viable* conception—i.e. any conception capable of serving our concerns effectively—will be superficial, because deepened conceptions of the voluntary cannot properly serve our concerns. In saying that the notion of the voluntary is 'essentially' superficial, I am therefore not suggesting that it has some discoverable 'essence' which turns out to be superficial—precisely not; the argument runs the other way, from the concerns fuelling our interest in the voluntary/involuntary distinction to those conceptualizations of the distinction that are worth having.

Something like this view is adumbrated in Anscombe's essays from the 1960s,[8] but it is most explicitly articulated in the following passage from Bernard Williams's *Shame and Necessity*:

---

[8] See Anscombe (2005, 2008a). For an account of how Anscombe's views on the voluntary and its ethical role change after *Intention*, see Bierson and Schwenkler (2022).

> The idea of the voluntary...is essentially superficial. It is a mistake to suppose that the notion of the voluntary is a profound conception that is threatened only by some opposing and profound theory about the universe (in particular, to the effect that determinism is true). That supposition underlies the traditional metaphysical problem of the freedom of the will.... Just as there is a 'problem of evil' only for those who expect the world to be good, there is a problem of free will only for those who think that the notion of the voluntary can be metaphysically deepened. In truth, though it may be extended or contracted in various ways, it can hardly be deepened at all. What threatens it is the attempt to make it profound, and the effect of trying to deepen it is to put it beyond all recognition. (1993, 68–9)

Though Williams may sound like a complacent compatibilist in this passage, we shall see towards the end of this chapter that this impression is misleading.[9] The question more immediately raised by this passage, however, is how exactly a superficial conception of the voluntary contrasts with a deepened one, and what the suggestion of 'essential superficiality' amounts to.

I propose to develop this suggestion as a way of illustrating how the pursuit of conceptual depth can be misguided in certain cases. But I shall have to go substantially beyond Williams's scattered remarks in doing so, since he did not develop the suggestion himself.[10] Nor was it developed in the direction I envisage by the subsequent literature.[11] Williams's suggestion is alluded to, but not really discussed, in Duff and von Hirsch (1997, 103), Matravers (2007, 53, 57), and Crisp (2017, 1), and insofar as it has been unpacked at all, it has been interpreted as a dismissive remark pointing to superficiality as a defect, with the qualification 'essentially' meaning only 'basically' or 'at bottom': Yeager (2006, ch. 2), for example, views the superficiality of the notion of the voluntary as a flaw to be remedied, while Deigh (2008, xi) takes it as an encouragement to move away from the notion of the voluntary in our practices of moral appraisal.

---

[9] As Paul Russell also concludes after examining Williams's (1995c, 6) criticism of the 'reconcilers' and the 'old compatibilism': 'Whatever final position Williams arrives at, it should not be understood as any form of comfortable or complacent compatibilism' (2022, 178). On P. F. Strawson's (2008a) influential framing, Williams sides neither with 'the pessimist' nor with 'the optimist', but rather indicates a third way incorporating insights from both, thereby arguably adopting the sort of position Strawson himself advocated: see Russell (2017c), De Mesel (2021), Queloz (2021d), and Emilsson (manuscript).

[10] See Williams (1993, 67; 1995a, 578; 1995o, 495; 1995e, 243, 247 n. 5; 1995b, 127–8; 2006e, 124–5).

[11] Though I have benefited from Moore's (2003, 2006) and Louden's (2007) reconstructions of Williams's critique of the morality system as targeting the concept of a 'purely voluntary act', in Moore's apt phrase. See also Queloz (2022c) as well as Krishnan and Queloz (2023) for discussions of that aspect of Williams's critique.

By contrast, I take the superficiality of the notion to be neither a flaw nor a reason to rely less on it in our practices of moral appraisal. On the contrary: it is very much worth having, and its superficiality is not a defect, but an important feature of it, one that is 'essential' in that it *cannot function properly without it*. Not only do we need some conception of the voluntary; we need a superficial one. A great deal turns on the issue, moreover, because the notion marks a key point at which our psychological concepts link up with our moral concepts, including notably our concept of responsibility. Deepening our conception of the voluntary thus threatens to rob attributions of moral and legal responsibility of their efficacy in helping us to live together.

In speaking of 'the' conception of the voluntary, I do not mean to deny that there are several different, though related, conceptions that we express with the word 'voluntary'.[12] The conception the word expresses in its moral use, for example, may not be exactly co-extensive with the one it expresses in its legal use; moreover, the boundary between voluntary and involuntary action may be blurred in the word's moral use, allowing for actions that lie halfway between the fully voluntary and the utterly involuntary, but sharp in at least some of its legal uses: in criminal law, for instance, an accusation must issue in a verdict of guilty or not guilty, and this can force the binary classification of actions into voluntary and involuntary ones, even if some actions are neither clearly one nor clearly the other.[13] A sufficiently close look at 'the' conception of the voluntary may thus find that, in different contexts, it differentiates into a collection of related but subtly different conceptions that are activated on different occasions, depending on what kind of case one is considering.[14]

But the needs-based approach invites us to start further back, from a point of view that allows us to ask, more generally and with greater detachment from any particular context of application, why we would need *anything like* a concept of voluntary action. Why are we not better off leaving it among the ruins of the theory of volitions?

9.2 Making Sense and Knowing What to Expect

We saw that the voluntary/involuntary distinction nominally separates actions that are attributable to the agent's will from those that are not, or only

---

[12] Anscombe's own use of the term varies over time, and she even considered variations of it that would be applicable to non-human animals if we spoke of 'desire' instead of 'will'; see Bierson and Schwenkler (2022, 329 n. 40). Williams (2006a, 98) also notes that the exact contours of the notion vary with the purposes to which it is put.
[13] See Williams (1995o; 2005b, 271; 2006a).
[14] See Mele (2017, 137) for a such an occasion-sensitive account of the concept of free will.

to a lesser degree. But what characterizes the actions on each side of this distinction?

A helpful starting point is the observation that a user of the voluntary/involuntary distinction typically discriminates between different ways in which actions can relate to the intentional (i.e. cognitive and conative) states and deliberations of the agent. A voluntary action *expresses* those intentional states and, to the extent that the agent deliberated, the deliberation of the agent, because the agent has *shaped the action to fit them*. In an involuntary action, on the other hand, that expressive connection is typically weakened or absent altogether.

One basic way in which an action can lose this expressive connection to the agent is by being unintentional. The things I do unintentionally tend not to reflect my intentional states, because they are actions I did not get a chance to shape to the intentions I formed in light of those intentional states. I might unintentionally delete a file I absolutely want to keep, for example. Indeed, I might unintentionally delete the file *by* intentionally updating my software. Every action is amenable to several correct descriptions, so that its being intentional under one description does not preclude its being unintentional under other descriptions. In Davidson's canonical example, my action of flipping the switch can be correctly described as my turning on the light (a description under which it is intentional), but it can equally correctly be described as my alerting the prowler (a description under which it is unintentional).[15] Hence, any action has multiple aspects, only some of which are intentional, and every action admits of descriptions under which it is unintentional. What the intentional/unintentional distinction discriminates between are therefore not actions *tout court*, but *aspects* of actions.

Yet there are various other ways in which the expressive connection between agent and action can be weakened.[16] Consider reflex muscular contractions or automatisms, for example; or things done in a state of somnambulism or hypnosis; or in a state of intoxication, drug withdrawal, delusion, extreme incident passion, or insanity; or when muscular control is abruptly impaired by disease (e.g. a stroke, epilepsy, or Sydenham chorea); and what about things done under duress, or as a result of physical compulsion by someone else? These seem to express another person's intentional states and deliberation rather than the agent's. In each of these cases, there is thus some measure of *dissociation* of the action from the agent's intentional states and

---

[15] Davidson (2001, 4–5).
[16] For a list of textbook examples from criminal law, see Hart (2008a, 95–6).

deliberation. But what concerns drive people to become conceptually sensitive to this dissociation?

The beginnings of an answer can be gleaned from Williams's argument that the notion of the voluntary is put within conceptual reach already by two distinctions that human beings everywhere can hardly avoid drawing: (i) the distinction between acting *intentionally* and acting *unintentionally*; and (ii) the distinction between acting *in a deliberatively normal state of mind* and acting *in a deliberatively abnormal state of mind*. According to Williams, there are very strong practical pressures on individuals living together to be sensitive to both of these distinctions, because their practical necessity follows already from some 'universal banalities' (1993, 55). By combining these two distinctions, he suggests, we already arrive at a conception of the voluntary as 'the idea of an intended aspect of something done in a state of mind that is deliberatively normal' (1995e, 242).

The distinction between things done intentionally and things done unintentionally is one that human beings everywhere have reason to use, according to Williams, because it is required to *make sense* of actions and to *know what to expect* from people—and these are things that human beings can hardly avoid being concerned to achieve. Williams offers a vivid illustration from the *Odyssey*: as Odysseus and his son, Telemachus, confront Penelope's suitors, they are alarmed to find that the suitors are handing out weapons, even though Telemachus was supposed to have hidden away all their weapons in a storeroom. Odysseus angrily wonders who opened the storeroom, and Telemachus shamefacedly admits that the mistake is his—he did not look what he was doing and left the door of the storeroom ajar, and someone must have been a better observer than he was.[17] Telemachus is clearly discriminating here between aspects of what he did that were *intentional* and aspects that were *unintentional*: it was he who left the door ajar, but he did not *mean* to—a subtle distinction in itself, but one which in this case marks the difference between fighting *with* Odysseus and fighting *against* him: had Telemachus intentionally left the door ajar, the implication for Odysseus would be alarming, suggesting that Telemachus was not in fact on his side.

This shows that even if Homer lacked a direct equivalent of our word 'intention', he had the *concept* of intention—not because *we* are disposed to draw on this concept in describing the situation, but because Homer and his characters themselves make distinctions which can only be understood in

---

[17] See Williams (1993, 50). My discussion of Williams's Homeric examples in this paragraph and the next draws on Queloz (2022c).

terms of that concept.[18] Moreover, it would be surprising if they did not draw *some* distinction along these lines, because sensitivity to which aspects of an action are intentional is crucial to understanding what kind of action it is, and what to expect from one who intends such a thing in such a situation.

The concept of doing something intentionally, which enables one to discriminate between intentional and unintentional aspects of an action, is thus one that we are bound to have reason to use, because it is crucial to determining the significance of other people's actions for us—which, as the case of Odysseus illustrates, can make the difference between life and death. Everywhere, human beings are concerned to make sense of action, if only to understand what exactly happened and what it means, and that requires understanding which aspects of an action were intentional and which were not. This is the inverse of Anscombe's (1957, §21) point that the concept of intention would not exist if human beings took no interest in each other's reasons for acting: we can take the fact that human beings everywhere can hardly avoid taking an interest in each other's reasons for actions as being itself a reason to expect that they will turn out to possess the concept of intention.

The other distinction that human beings everywhere need to be conceptually sensitive to, according to Williams, is the distinction between things people do in what is for them a *deliberatively normal state of mind* and things they do when they are in what is for them a *deliberatively abnormal state of mind*. Any interpreter of human action has reason to look not only at which aspects of an action were intentional, but also at the action's relation to the agent's more settled concerns—concerns that, unlike momentary whims and impulses, relate to, and are possessed for, longer stretches of time. In particular, the interpreter must ask to what extent the agent was in a position to *shape the action to* those more settled concerns. If the agent was not in such a position, the action is defective in that it is dissociated from the agent, since the action fails to express and reflect the agent's more settled concerns. Actions performed in a state of somnambulism or under hypnosis are clearly defective in this way. But the defect may also lie in the fact that the agent's deliberation was severely skewed or entirely suppressed, as when the agent is in the grip of extreme passion.

Of course, there may not always be a clear line between deliberatively normal and abnormal states of mind, and the idea is not that we can specify, in universal and evaluatively neutral terms, which actions are defective or which

---

[18] See Williams (1993, 50-1).

states of mind are deliberatively abnormal. Different societies will elaborate the distinction between normal and abnormal states of mind differently, depending on what other concerns and conceptual material they bring to it. Some ways of drawing of the distinction may seem quite alien to us now. Here too Williams finds a vivid example in Homer: Agamemnon, who seized Briseis from Achilles, did so intentionally; but, as Agamemnon later explains, he was in an abnormal state of mind when he did so. He was not his usual self because the gods had cast what the Greeks called *atë* on his wits, temporarily engulfing him in a state of delusion and blind folly. By appealing to divine interference, Williams observes, Agamemnon is 'dissociating the action from himself' (1993, 54).

As differently as the distinction will be drawn in different societies, however, the key point is that human communities are bound to draw *some* distinction along these lines, because they are bound to take an interest in whether actions stand in regular relations to agents' more settled concerns. Like the distinction between intentional and unintentional aspects of action, some such distinction between deliberatively normal and abnormal states of mind is also indispensable to making sense of what happened and to knowing what to expect from people. This is because the fact that an action was performed in an abnormal state of mind affects the meaning of the action, and renders the action less indicative of how the agent will behave in the future than actions that the agent had a chance to tailor to his or her more settled concerns. Things done in a deliberatively abnormal state of mind are not necessarily done *unintentionally*; but the state of mind from which the action flows interferes with the agents' capacity to shape their actions to their more settled concerns— either directly, by inhibiting their capacity to act on those concerns, or indirectly, by incapacitating the agents from deliberating properly and preventing these concerns from finding their usual expression in deliberation. Either way, the resulting actions are not representative of more settled concerns.

We thus have two concerns that give any human beings, insofar as they conceive of each other as performing actions, compelling reasons to apply something like the intentional/unintentional distinction and the normal/abnormal-state-of-mind distinction to those actions: the retrospective, hermeneutic concern to make sense of what happened, and the prospective, prudential concern to know what to expect from people going forward.

Once these two distinctions are in place, Williams argues, the concept of the voluntary is already within reach. For, with these two distinctions in place, we already have all the conceptual material required to construct the following conception of the voluntary:

A φ-s fully voluntarily if φ-ing is an intentional aspect of an action that *A* performs in a deliberatively normal state of mind.[19]

On this account, 'voluntary' action merits the term, i.e. is attributable to the agent's *voluntas*, if and to the extent that it is intended by the agent in a deliberatively normal state of mind.

Three features of this conception of the voluntary are worth highlighting. First, it is *gradable*: the closer an action is to a fully intentional action done in a fully normal state of mind, the more fully voluntary it is. Such a conception of the voluntary enables one to accept that every agent is inextricably enmeshed in a weave of contingent forces in which even the most paradigmatically voluntary action remains, in some respects, in the grip of influences beyond the agent's will. As Williams puts it: 'One's history as an agent is a web in which anything that is the product of the will is surrounded and held up and partly formed by things that are not' (1981c, 29). If a fully voluntary action is neither more nor less than an intentional action performed in a normal state of mind, then it is an action that may not have been under the control of the agent's will *in every respect*, but that was still *as much* under its control as actions ever are, and a great deal more so than an action done unintentionally or in an abnormal state of mind.

Second, and crucially for our purposes, this is a *superficial* conception, because it gives little attention to the detailed causal underpinnings of what it picks out. It licenses the ascription of voluntariness merely based on easily observable features of an action and its more immediate or proximal causes. Unless the notions of *intention* or of a *deliberatively normal state of mind* have themselves been tendentiously theorized to this end, this way of conceptualizing the voluntary does not commit one to thinking that, at the deeper level of the ultimate causal underpinnings of actions, there must be a categorical difference between the metaphysical nature of what causes voluntary actions and the metaphysical nature of what causes involuntary bodily movements. This superficial conception allows one to freely grant that whatever is a product of the will is inextricably tied up with what is not, and that the voluntary/involuntary distinction is not ultimately one whose real boundaries await discovery through a more detailed investigation of the causal processes underlying action.

---

[19] This is my preferred reconstruction of Williams's conception of the voluntary. The gradability marked by the 'fully' comes out in one formula he uses: 'an agent does X fully voluntarily if X-ing is an intentional aspect of an action he does, which has no inherent or deliberative defect' (1995m, 25); see also Williams (1995m, 33 n. 8; 2005c, 80 n. 8; 2006a, 107). But my reconstruction leans more heavily on the formula he relies on most of the time: '"A does X voluntarily" is equivalent to "A does X intentionally in a normal state of mind"' (2006e, 120). See also Williams (1993, 66; 1995g, 73; 1995o, 495; 2006a, 107).

Third, although the applicability of the concept *voluntary*, thus understood, remains insensitive to, and therefore tells us little about, the action's deeper aetiology beyond what most proximally caused it, this does not mean that the concept *excludes* there being such ulterior explanations. It leaves room for the thought that A really φ-s voluntarily, but does so because A has been socialized a certain way, or is in the grip of an ideology. Indeed, as far as ideology critique is concerned, this compatibility of a superficial notion of the voluntary with ulterior explanations is not a flaw, but a feature—for, as Étienne de La Boétie's 1576 'Discourse on Voluntary Servitude' (2016) already intimated, the real question for ideology critique is often not whether voluntariness is really servitude, but why the servitude really is voluntary. That is how Michael Rosen (1996) understands ideology critique, for example. If critical reflection on how A came to want to φ in the first place reveals some radical tension, it will not be a tension between φ's claim to being voluntary and the fact that A's wanting to φ admits of ulterior explanation, but rather a tension between that explanation and A's understanding of what is really in A's interest. (By contrast, *deep* conceptions of the voluntary really *are* incompatible with many ulterior explanations of how A came to intend to φ in the first place, which is why, as we shall see, deep conceptions of the voluntary are operative in sceptical challenges to free will).

Williams's view of the concept of the voluntary thus lies at the other extreme from the view that we can safely retire it. As he himself summarizes his argument, the upshot is that the 'idea of the voluntary', far from being an idle residue of the theory of volitions, 'is inherent in the concept of action' (1995e, 247 n. 4). He deems it 'reasonable to think that if we are to have the concept of an action, we must have the concept of a voluntary action' (1995e, 242).

This rather strong way of putting it might be taken to suggest that the 'must' in question is a matter of conceptual necessity—that the concept of the voluntary is necessarily already contained in the concept of action. But the nature of the argument that Williams actually offers suggests a weaker reading, for that argument appeals to *practical* necessity: to the conceptual need to develop certain distinctions, given the concept of action together with certain highly general concerns and circumstances. Insofar as creatures like us conceptualize some of the things we bring about as actions, we are nearly bound, given our concerns to make sense of those actions and to know what to expect of people who so act, to develop the conceptual wherewithal to discriminate between different ways in which those actions relate to the intentional states and deliberations of the agents. And once these distinctions are in place,

Williams contends, the concept of the voluntary is already within conceptual reach. This is how I think we should gloss Williams's otherwise perplexing claim that 'if we are to have the concept of an action, we must have the concept of a voluntary action'.

But, *pace* Williams, the mere fact that the concept of the voluntary is within the conceptual reach of a set of needful distinctions does not yet show that the concept of the voluntary is itself needed. It merely shows that we need a set of concepts from which the concept of the voluntary *can* be reached. But having a capacity in principle is one thing; being inclined to realize it in practice is quite another. For example, possession of the concepts *north* and *car* does not by itself guarantee that one will also be an engaged user of the concept *northcar*, which singles out cars pointing north for special treatment—though this possibility is intelligible to us as users of the concepts *north* and *car*, and might be said to be within the conceptual reach of a set of needful distinctions, we do not actually think and structure our affairs in those terms. The engaged/disengaged distinction again proves useful here: the set of concepts we can make disengaged use of is vastly larger than the set of concepts we have reason to make engaged use of. Showing that a concept falls into the former set is insufficient to show that it also falls into the latter.

So why did we actually yoke together what is done intentionally and in a normal state of mind under one concept and dignify it with its dedicated linguistic expression? Why did we form a new concept by drawing together just these properties and systematically differentiating in practice between actions that combine them all and actions that do not? Is it really a *new concept*, as opposed to a new word indicating the harnessing of two old concepts to new ends? To answer these questions, we must show that there is a conceptual need specifically *for* the concept of the voluntary. And to do that, we must understand what additional concerns fuel our interest in this particular grouping of properties and lend it its significance.

Even apart from these explanatory gaps in Williams's picture, however, there is a more fundamental reason why additional concerns need to be brought into the picture. For the concerns that Williams identifies as lying at the root of the concept of the voluntary, which I suggest are better described as lying at the root of its constituent notions, remain geared towards *predictability*: they are a matter of understanding people's actions with a view to knowing what to expect from them in the future. But if this combination of concerns were allowed to dictate the contours of our conception of the voluntary on its own, unchecked by additional concerns, the resulting voluntary/involuntary distinction would be hard to recognize. The notion of a deliberatively normal state of mind would be driven to become a quasi-statistical notion geared towards predictability alone, and actions would count as voluntary, roughly, to the extent that they were likely to recur. This would not even remotely resemble the conception of the voluntary we actually have, which is insensitive to mild untypicalities and not focused primarily on predictability.

Additional concerns must therefore be factored in if we are to identify reasons to preserve anything like the conception of the voluntary we have. Its constituent notions may basically answer to the concerns to make sense of actions and know what to expect from people. But in the more complex notion of the voluntary, this preoccupation with predictability is clearly balanced and checked by additional concerns, which pull the resultant conceptualization away from a single-minded focus on what to expect.

9.3 Fairness and Freedom

One of those concerns animating the use of the concept of the voluntary, I submit, is a concern for *fairness* in the attribution of responsibility, in the sense in which to carry responsibility for something is to be an appropriate subject of praise or blame with regard to it. Typically, one is treated as being blameworthy or guilty *only if* one acted voluntarily, and the observation that one acted involuntarily *excuses* one from being held responsible in this way, or at least acts as a mitigating circumstance. That arrangement tends to be mirrored in criminal law through what is sometimes called the 'voluntary-act requirement'.[20]

Of course, certain types of cases call for compromises with more basic concerns, like the concern to avoid inherently hazardous situations (e.g. dangerous driving). In those cases, legal responsibility or liability may be 'strict', which is to say independent of the agent's intentional states. Tort law also offers many examples of the voluntary-act requirement being overridden by other considerations: when real damage has been done by something one

---

[20] See Moore (2010, 5) and Saunders (1988). The voluntary-act requirement is related to the *mens rea* doctrine (*actus non facit reum nisi mens sit rea*—the act does not make one guilty unless there is a guilty mind, which is to say a culpable intent; though there are also cases where negligence is enough for criminality). See Hart (1963, 40; 2008d, 14; 2008b, 36; 2008a, 90–2) for a discussion of the connection between the voluntary-act requirement and the *mens rea* doctrine; Duff (2004) argues that the voluntary-act requirement is a further requirement, which he articulates as *mens non facit reum nisi actus sit reus*—the mind does not make one guilty unless there is a guilty act, where 'act' is explicitly understood as 'voluntary act'.

involuntarily brought about and some response is called for—because *someone* needs to pay for repairs, for instance—one might end up being held responsible for something one brought about even if one strained every nerve to keep it from happening.

Generally, however, liability tends to be made conditional on voluntariness, and involuntariness is treated as being exculpatory. The law identifies exculpatory or mitigating circumstances under such headings as 'accident', 'mistake', 'provocation' into a passion causing the agent to lose self-control, or 'insanity'.[21] The characterization of voluntariness given above fits these excusing conditions. The former two correspond to the requirement that voluntary action be intentional, and the latter two to the requirement that voluntary action be done in a deliberatively normal state of mind. However, as H. L. A. Hart notes:

> These psychological elements are not *in themselves* crucial although they are important as aspects of responsibility. What is crucial is that those whom we punish should have had, when they acted, the normal capacities, physical and mental, for doing what the law requires and abstaining from what it forbids, and a fair opportunity to exercise these capacities. (2008c, 152)

As Hart indicates, it is notably the concern for fairness that provides a rationale for rendering attributions of responsibility sensitive to the voluntary/involuntary distinction, because our capacity to do the right thing, given the kinds of circumstances we live in, is to a considerable degree hostage to contingent forces outside our control, so that holding people responsible for everything they did would be flagrantly unfair. It is, for example, an all too familiar fact that what one ends up having done, once the consequences of one's intervention have unfolded, is largely a matter of luck, and even something done with the best intentions may issue in deplorable consequences. As a medieval proverb has it: once the flung stone leaves the hand, it belongs to the devil. A morality that allocated blame exclusively based on the eventual rather than the intended consequences of actions would turn blameworthiness into a plaything of contingent forces, leaving it largely to sheer luck to decide whether one person attracted more blame than another. That would offend against our sense of fairness by putting the extent to which one attracted blame largely beyond the reach of individual control.

---

[21] See Hart (2008b, 31). As Hart also observes, much the same conditions are treated as invalidating civil transactions such as wills, contracts, or gifts.

This conjunction of concerns, capacities, and circumstances calls for a concept that will help make attributions of responsibility fairer by focusing them on certain kinds of actions instead of leaving agents responsible for everything they do. In particular, there is a conceptual need for a concept that will contribute to responsibility being allocated on a fair basis. The concept of the voluntary fills this need. It serves to strike a balance between the social necessity of holding people to account for at least some of their antisocial behaviour and the concern to be fair in doing so by focusing responsibility on those aspects of action that are as much within their control as actions ever are, thereby mitigating unfairness in the attribution of responsibility. To base moral responsibility notably on the respects in which actions are voluntary is to focus moral appraisal precisely on those aspects of action that are as much as realistically possible within the control of the agent.[22]

But there is also a second concern that animates the use of the concept of the voluntary: the concern for *freedom* as individual self-determination. In order to freely determine the course of their own lives, people need to be able to form determinate expectations as to how the moral code will affect them, and what kind of action they are likely to incur moral sanctions for. If one were subject to blame for everything one brought about, including what one brought about involuntarily, one's blameworthiness would become nearly impossible to anticipate. To leave agents any power to determine the course of their lives based on their sense of which actions will attract which kind of response, moral appraisal had better focus on those aspects of action over which agents have most control. The fact that attributions of responsibility are funnelled through the concept of the voluntary can thus also be understood as responding to a concern for freedom as individual self-determination.

This concern is particularly pressing when the code is *legal* rather than moral and the sanctions are state-enforced penal sanctions that constitute particularly severe threats to individual freedom. Individuals are concerned to determine the course of their own lives by acting with determinate expectations as to how the legal code will affect them and what they need to do and abstain from doing to stay on the right side of the law; but their capacity to anticipate all the eventual consequences of their actions is limited, given the kind of natural and social world they inhabit: how the eventual consequences of actions relate to the legal code is largely hostage to contingent forces—they

---

[22] This still leaves room for a moral authority that is exerted simply by what one has done—in cases that call for agent-regret as opposed to guilt, for instance; see Williams (1981c; 1985, 196; 1993, 66).

cannot tell with certainty, for instance, whether their helping a person over the street today will be causally responsible for that person's death by food poisoning tomorrow. This triad of concerns, capacities, and circumstances generates a conceptual need for a concept rendering penal sanctions more predictable by making liability conditional on those aspects of action that individuals can control and anticipate. The concept of the voluntary meets this need, and thereby serves the individuals' concern for freedom as self-determination. Without the concept—if people were liable simply for what they did or brought about—they would lose much of their power to determine and predict whether they stayed on the right side of the law. The law's emphasis on voluntariness thus expresses what Hart calls respect for the individual as a choosing being (2008b, 49).

Moreover, it is part of the point of many legal institutions—such as contracts, wills, gifts, and marriages—that they enhance individuals' ability to shape the future: they are legal tools enabling individuals to *lock in* certain outcomes.[23] For the law to interfere in individuals' lives in ways that they could not possibly foresee would therefore defeat one of the very purposes of the law. In the moral and even more so in the legal sphere, the concept of the voluntary thus performs a protective role, helping to respect and defend individual freedom against the claims of society.

9.4 Knowledge and Coercion

In a similar spirit, Hyman argues that 'voluntariness is at root an ethical concept' that is 'designed for' the purpose of assessing a person's culpability, and that the concept is 'formed by negation', by 'excluding factors that exculpate' (2015, 76–7). Among the factors that are widely taken to exculpate are *ignorance* of what one is doing—sometimes called the 'knowledge condition' on responsibility—and doing something under *coercion* (e.g. at the point of a gun)—sometimes called the 'freedom condition' on responsibility.[24] When Hyman proposes an *ex negativo* definition of voluntary action as what is '*not* done out of ignorance or compulsion' (2015, 77), it is these two conditions he puts front and centre. This raises the question of how the conceptualization of voluntariness as acting intentionally and in a deliberatively normal state of mind relates to these two conditions.

---

[23] See Hart (2008b, 29–30).
[24] See e.g. Fischer and Ravizza (1998, 12–13) and Rudy-Hiller (2018).

In the case of the knowledge condition, the relation is straightforward—the condition is already contained in this conceptualization of the voluntary: the distinction between things done in full awareness of their nature and significance and things done out of ignorance is encapsulated in the requirement that one's φ-ing must be an intentional aspect of what one does, for something can be an *intentional* aspect of what one does only if one is *aware* of it—if one *knows* what one is doing.[25] Of course, as recent debates over moral responsibility have made clear, the relevant notion of knowledge or awareness can be specified in various ways, depending on *how much* it requires one to be aware of and *what kind* of awareness it requires (does one need to *know* or merely *believe* it, and to do so *occurrently* or merely *dispositionally*?).[26] But just as human beings have reasons to discriminate between the intentional and the unintentional that are independent of their concern to allocate responsibility, they are bound to have an interest in *what an agent was aware of* when he or she acted, because that is already crucial to understanding the character of the action, the character of the agent, and the circumstances under which the agent would do something like that again. Did he know what he was doing when he intentionally φ-ed? That is, was he aware of the fact that he thereby ψ-ed? Or—what is sometimes rather more concerning—did he do it even though he did *not* know what it meant and what consequences it would have? Would he have done it anyway if he had known? If we tell him, will he refrain from doing it again? These are questions that human beings have an interest in asking already in virtue of being in the business of interpreting and shaping each other's actions.

The freedom condition, by contrast, is not yet contained in that definition of the voluntary. Indeed, Williams, like Anscombe, is comfortable describing actions done under coercion as voluntary.[27] He emphasizes that decisions reached under coercion really are *decisions*, characteristically coming out of a process of deliberation issuing in the conclusion that one has to do something, because the coercive threat overrides other deliberative priorities.[28] This is not to deny that coercive circumstances can be exculpatory. It is merely to deny that every exculpatory circumstance must register as such by going into forming the voluntary/involuntary distinction. As Williams insists, 'the

---

[25] This is also how Williams (1995m, 23–6) understand the intentionality requirement.
[26] See Rudy-Hiller (2018) for a helpful overview.
[27] See Anscombe (2008b, 127) and Williams (1995m, 33 n. 8). In an archival note, however, Anscombe notes that 'voluntary behaviour is behaviour in respect of which the behaver is free. To be free is to be in a situation of possibility of determining something to accord with one's will' (Archive, Box 9, File 304, p. 1; cited in Bierson and Schwenkler (2022, 329 n. 48)).
[28] See Williams (1995c, 5; 1995m, 33 n. 3, 33 n. 8).

topic of coercion is not part of the theory of action, but of the theory of freedom' (1995m, 33 n. 3).

But if, as I have suggested, a central need that the concept of the voluntary fills is the need to separate, in the name of fairness and freedom, actions that are *more* from actions that are *less* under the agent's control, then perhaps we do, after all, have reason to refine the notion of the voluntary we started out from to exclude coerced action. There is an undeniably important sense in which the agent who acts under threat of serious harm is deprived of control over the action, and the intentions expressed by the action are not really *the agent's* at all, but the coercer's. Like acting in an abnormal state of mind, this dissociates the action from the agent. And indeed, legal codes tend to treat the fact that an action was done under *duress* (coercion by the threat of serious harm) as an excusing condition; and Hart, for example, characterizes coerced actions as *involuntary*.[29]

To better serve the concerns that fuel our interest in it, therefore, the notion of the voluntary should be understood more restrictively:

> A φ-s *voluntarily* if and to the extent that φ-ing is an intentional aspect of an action that A performs uncoerced and in a deliberatively normal state of mind.

One might protest on Williams's behalf that this introduces a moral element from the theory of freedom into what was supposed to be, in the first instance, a psychological concept in the theory of action, on a par with concepts of choice, decision, belief, or desire. But even the earlier, more permissive definition of the voluntary could hardly escape drawing on a morally laden understanding of what kinds of states of mind appropriately attract appraisals of responsibility. Moreover, if our reasons to use the concept of the voluntary in the first place, over and beyond the concepts of acting intentionally and in a normal state of mind, are *moral* reasons grounded in moral concerns, then it is only right that these moral concerns should also substantively *shape* the resulting conceptualization of the voluntary.

In discussions of thick concepts, as we saw in Chapter 2, the point is often made that a thick concept's extension is a function of our evaluative interests in deploying the concept, and not specifiable independently of them. One might argue that the same is true of the concept of the voluntary. When taken in isolation from the concept of the voluntary and the moral concerns that give us reasons

---

[29] See Hart (2008d, 14; 2008c, 143–4).

to use it, its constituent notions, such as that of a deliberatively normal state of mind, are unlikely to have the same extensions as when deployed alongside other constituent notions in the service of moral concerns. This is why the concerns for fairness and freedom call for a genuinely new concept that is more than the sum of its constituent notions. These constituent notions need to be understood in a particular way and be appropriately linked. Neither the appropriate shape of these constituent notions nor the appropriate way of linking them are specifiable independently of the moral concerns that rationalize and inform our conceptualization of the voluntary.

At the same time, Williams and Anscombe are right to emphasize that the concept of the voluntary is, in the first instance, a concept in the theory of action.[30] It really is a psychological concept—only one that acts as a linchpin between psychological and moral concepts, connecting concepts of action, deliberation, intention, and decision with concepts of praise, blame, responsibility, liability, and exculpation. What the concept of the voluntary picks out is a collection of properties of actions, which properties they have in virtue of their relation to the agent's deliberation and state of mind; but the *second-order reasons* for picking out just these properties and grouping them as constituents of a significant, reason-giving property—voluntariness—notably include *moral* reasons, and the inferential consequences of displaying or lacking that property notably include *moral* consequences. Hence, the concept of the voluntary marks a place where concepts of mind and action make contact with moral demands. In a hybridizing classification that will prove helpful in what follows, we might say that the concept of the voluntary is a psychological concept that serves and answers to moral concerns.

Finally, the way in which our concerns for fairness and freedom each shape and call for a concept of the voluntary along these lines can also be drawn upon to vindicate the concept's authority along with our confidence in it. In showing that the concept does important work for us by meeting our needs and serving our concerns, one highlights reasons for us to continue to use the concept and heed the reasons it adverts to, thereby vindicating our confidence in the concept by showing it to be well-placed and reasonable. We have a conceptual need for the concept of the voluntary because we are concerned, in the name of fairness and freedom, to exempt individuals from some of their moral and legal responsibility for some of their involuntary acts. Of course, users of the concept do not necessarily consciously *aim* to serve a

---

[30] *Pace* Hyman (2015, 76–7).

concern for fairness or freedom. Nor do these concerns figure in the *content* of the concept. But the needs-based approach allows us to show that we need the concept for these reasons all the same.

9.5 When Concerns Distort Conceptualization

What makes the case of the concept of the voluntary particularly interesting, however, is that it offers a vivid illustration not only of how concerns can inform our conceptualizations, but also of how they can distort them.

The upshot of the argument thus far is that we need the concept of the voluntary in *some* form because we feel the need, for the sake of fairness and freedom, to exempt individuals from some of their moral and legal responsibility for some of their involuntary acts.

But the concern for fairness aims at making attributions of responsibility not just *fairer* than they would be if we did not employ the concept of the voluntary, but *ultimately* fair. The concept of the voluntary we sketched goes some way towards meeting the demand for fairness, but by no means all the way. It still leaves a great deal of residual unfairness, because *whether one is in a position* voluntarily to do the right thing itself remains a matter of luck—a matter of one's inherited disposition, upbringing, and socialization, but also a matter of whether and how often one finds oneself in circumstances that make it especially hard to do the right thing. Consequently, one's capacity to voluntarily do the right thing remains partly a matter of constitutive and circumstantial luck.

Appraisals of responsibility funnelled through the concept of the voluntary are *fairer* than they would be if they completely ignored the voluntary/involuntary distinction, but they are not *ultimately* fair. They still fall foul of the demand for ultimate fairness that Michael Zimmerman forcefully expresses when he insists that 'the degree to which we are morally responsible cannot be affected by what is not in our control. Put more pithily: luck is irrelevant to moral responsibility' (2002, 559).

The moral concern for responsibility to be attributed on a fair basis thus exerts pressure on our conceptualization of the voluntary to accommodate a demand for *ultimate* fairness. There is a pressure to fully isolate that which is a product and expression of the agent's will from that which is a product of contingent—and hence not necessarily fairly distributed—forces. Much as our conceptualization of the voluntary would be transformed into a quasi-statistical conception if its contours were allowed to be determined solely by a concern to predict behaviour, the concern for fairness, in and of itself, pulls our conceptualization towards a form in which it ensures complete fairness.

The result is a kind of *moralization of psychology*: a warping of our conceptualization of psychology to serve moral concerns. Such a moralization of psychology need not always be problematic—there is nothing inherently wrong with tailoring our repertoire of psychological concepts to the moral concerns it ties in with. But the moralization of psychology becomes *problematic* when it goes further than that, and our psychological notions are warped under moral pressure to the point where they become *psychologically unrealistic*, which is to say when they become inconsistent with the rest of what we take ourselves to know about human psychology and how the world works. Our moral thought should be answerable to human psychology, not the other way round; as Samuel Scheffler succinctly puts it, only a psychologically realistic morality can be a *human* morality.[31] The risk, then, is that if the concern for fairness is allowed to dictate the contours of our conceptualization of the voluntary without counter-pressure from other concerns, it will *distort* it to the point where that conceptualization no longer strikes a helpful balance between our concerns.

This is again a point at which we can usefully turn to Williams, because the thought that psychology can become problematically moralized under pressure from moral demands is a thread that runs through much of his oeuvre. Already in 1963, Williams makes the point—which he credits to Iris Murdoch—that it is an 'evaluatively motivated picture of the mind' which 'sharply distinguishes between "reason" and "will"' (1963, 136). In *Shame and Necessity*, he then suggests that it was Plato who first 'ethicized psychology' with his tripartite model of the soul, because he defined 'the functions of the mind, especially with regard to action…at the most basic level in terms of categories that get their significance from ethics' (1993, 160). In particular, Plato's stark division between 'rational concerns that aim at the good, and mere desire' (1993, 42) enabled him to introduce a 'featureless moral self' (1993, 160) into his psychology, a locus of agency that remained uncontaminated by contingent desires.

What makes this an example of a problematically moralized psychology is not that it plays a morally significant role, or even that it draws on values—a realistic psychology, Williams notes, need not be 'value-free'; but it 'leaves it open, or even problematical, in what way moral reasons and ethical values fit with other motives and desires, how far they express those other motives, and

---

[31] See Scheffler (1992, 7–9).

how far they are in conflict with them' (1995j, 202).³² What a problematically moralized psychology lacks is precisely this *openness*: it closes off the very possibility of ineliminable conflict between the psychological and the moral. Our conception of psychology is distorted to ensure that moral concerns can be met.

In the case of the psychological concept of the voluntary, this problematic moralization of psychology takes the following form: to enable attributions of responsibility to be made on an *ultimately fair* basis, our conceptualization of the voluntary needs to make responsibility a function of something that meets both of the following conditions: (a) it must be something that is perfectly evenly distributed, so that every agent has an *equal opportunity* to do the right thing; and (b) it must be something that each agent has *total control* over, so that no contingent circumstances constrain or predetermine the agent's capacity to do the right thing.

9.6 Deep Conceptions of the Voluntary

To meet this conceptual need for a way of thinking that makes responsibility a function of something that is perfectly evenly distributed and entirely within the agent's control, one's conception of the voluntary must become a conception of the *purely* voluntary—of something that is pure of any contamination by the potentially unfair influence of empirical contingencies.

To achieve this, conceptions of the voluntary must be *deepened* in a particular way, namely so that the locus of responsibility retreats deep enough into the agent to be sheltered from contingency. It is not enough for responsibility to track what one *wills* rather than what one contingently ends up having done, since one's capacity to align one's will with morality or the law is itself subject to constitutive and circumstantial luck—a matter of what dispositions one inherited and what challenges life presents one with. If the basis on which we allocate responsibility is to be ultimately fair, various contingencies *within* the agent need to be eliminated as well, to immunize responsibility against the contingent influence of natural endowments, socialization, education, and other biographical and historical circumstances.³³

---

[32] See also Williams (2006f, 78).
[33] This point is at the heart of Williams's critique of the 'morality system' as I reconstruct it; see Queloz (2022c) and Queloz and van Ackeren (2024). See also Moore (2003, 2006), Louden (2007, 110–11), and Russell (2013, 2018, 2019, 2023).

Accordingly, conceptions of the voluntary must deepened in such a way as to cast voluntary action as *fundamentally distinct in nature* from involuntary bodily movements and *pure of contingency*, i.e. fully isolated from contingent forces, thereby grounding not just a distinction of degree, but a sharp, categorical distinction between the agent's will and the contingent forces that are external to it. If the agent's will were always, however slightly, under the influence of forces beyond itself, this would again introduce an element of contingency or luck—hence of potential unfairness—into all the agent's actions.

The theory of volitions offers a paradigmatic example of an attempt to deepen conceptions of the voluntary so as to meet this set of demands. For what marks out someone like Descartes as operating with a deep concept of the voluntary is not the mere thought that what turns a bodily movement into a voluntary action is its tracing back to an act of will or a volition;[34] it is the further point that the act of will or volition is itself understood as something that is distinctively *pure of contingency*—something that lies beyond the reach of empirical determination by powers external to the acting subject. For Descartes, a volition is an action of the mind or soul; and while the soul can affect matter by affecting the pineal gland (which affects the animal spirits which in turn affect the muscles), the soul is not itself affected by anything beyond itself.[35]

On such a theory, voluntary actions have their ultimate source in something that lies deep enough to be completely isolated from the blind play of chance. There is an echo here of the Stoics' attempts to shelter themselves from upsetting strokes of fate, and Descartes' theory of the will went hand in hand with an elaborate Neo-Stoic ethic that also treated the emotions as being fully under the will's control (he once urged Elisabeth of Bohemia to look at the bright side of her uncle's decapitation).[36] If voluntary action is rooted in something fundamentally distinct from the muck of contingent forces, this categorically distinguishes it from other happenings: it is not just *less* mired in contingency, but, at base, completely pure of it.[37]

---

[34] This much could be granted by more recent action theorists like O'Shaughnessy (1973, 2008a, b) and Hornsby (1980), even though they develop accounts of acting and willing in terms of the notion of *trying to* φ that are not threatened by the possibility that determinism might be true and do not require us 'to look back beyond the trying' (Hornsby 1980, 59).

[35] See Descartes (1996, III 372, XI 342). See also Kenny (1972), Alanen (2002), and Jayasekera (2016). As Williams notes, Descartes's attempt to explain how I can move my body at will in terms of 'a kind of internalized psychokinesis' whereby the pineal gland is the only part of the body that is directly responsive to the will has the uninviting consequence that 'the only part of my body directly responsive to my will is one which I cannot move at will' (2005b, 277).

[36] See Schneck (2019, 757 n. 12).   [37] See Williams (2005b, 271).

More recently, a deepened conception of the voluntary can be found animating Benjamin Libet's famous experiments, in which subjects hooked up to an electroencephalograph were put in an optimal position to deliberate at their leisure about whether and when to flick their wrists. What motivated the experiments was precisely the perception—which relies on a deepened conception of the voluntary—that the mere fact that subjects carefully deliberated and acted only when they really meant to did not yet settle the question whether they *voluntarily* flicked their wrists. *That* was to be determined by having each subject note the time at which they formed the intention to flick their wrist and comparing it against the neurophysiological processes underpinning their conscious deliberation and action. If one conceives of voluntary action as having its ultimate or terminal causal source in a will that is distinct from and exerts control over neurophysiological processes,[38] this deep conception of the voluntary licenses the inference from the observation that neurophysiological activity *precedes* conscious willing to the conclusion that the action in question is not voluntary.

This example also illustrates that by deepening our conception of the voluntary, one typically renders it more costly to use, requiring concept-users to dig deep into the aetiology of an action in order to determine whether or not the concept applies, because the *real mark* of voluntariness is to be found further back; and it illustrates that a deep conception of the voluntary can manifest itself primarily *negatively*, i.e. through what is treated as foreclosing the application of the concept. People can be very clear about what does *not* count as the right kind of neurophysiological underpinning of voluntary action without being clear about what *would* count as the right kind.

Not all ways of deepening conceptions of the voluntary must involve postulating influences coming from beyond the material or natural order. One might, for instance, maintain that an action counts as voluntary if and only if it *reflects nothing but character traits and dispositions that the agent voluntarily acquired*. Not only the action, but even the agent's *becoming* the kind of agent who is disposed to act in this way in that situation would then fully be the product and expression of the agent's will, undistorted by external influences. This does, however, presuppose that what character the agent came to develop was fully under the control of the agent's will.

---

[38] Another interpretation—closer to that favoured by Libet himself—is to conceive of the will as the kind of thing capable of *blocking* or *vetoing* the neurophysiological processes resulting in action. That way of securing the agent's full control over actions also traces back to the Stoics, who thought of the *hegemonikon*, the rational and leading faculty of the soul, as a gatekeeper whose assent was necessary for impressions to issue in action.

One might also try to deepen one's conception of the voluntary without this presupposition, by maintaining that an action counts as voluntary if and only if the agent acts *exclusively out of motives that are fully responsive to the agent's deliberation about what motives to have*—a type of account which admits that we do not, originally, acquire our motives voluntarily, but seeks to reestablish the full autonomy of the will through the idea that an agent's first-order volitions—e.g. *A*'s wanting to φ—can fully come under the deliberative control of her second-order volitions—e.g. *A*'s wanting the desire to φ to be her will. Here, a deeper conception of the voluntary is formed through a picture of human psychology on which one's rational deliberation can exert total control over one's motives. Though it confines itself to the natural and material order, this also goes a long way towards deepening the conception of the voluntary in the way required, since it offers an account of the nature of voluntary action that categorically separates it from the influence of contingency. It does, however, presuppose that one can achieve total deliberative control over one's motives.

What all these different ways of replacing superficial by deeper conceptions of the voluntary have in common is that by locating voluntary agency beyond contingent empirical determination, they give the psychology of agency the right shape to hold out the promise of allocating responsibility and blame on an ultimately fair basis. Deepened conceptions of the voluntary promise to shelter life from luck.

The supposed capacity of deepened conceptions of the voluntary to remedy the world's unfairness might be thought to give us good reason to prefer them over superficial ones. But, far from performing the same tasks better, a deepened conception of the voluntary ceases to do the work it did in its more superficial form. Though it promises to meet the concern for fairness better than a more superficial conceptualization would, that promise ultimately turns out to be illusory: a deepened conception ends up serving our various concerns markedly less well and landing us in broader trouble.

9.7 Free Will as a Dual Problem

The source of trouble is that if some psychological notion is problematically moralized under pressure from moral demands, this generates a pressure on the rest of our psychological notions to support the moralized notion, and a corresponding pressure on our physical or metaphysical notions to support the resulting psychology.

The dynamics can be captured in terms of a simple three-tier model. Think of our moral, psychological, and physical concepts (in the broad sense of 'physical' that includes biological, physiological, and metaphysical concepts, as it did in the ancient notion of *physis*) as organized into three vertically layered tiers, with the physical tier at the bottom, the psychological tier in the middle, and the moral tier at the top. Each tier comprises concepts such as the following:

Moral concepts: moral responsibility, blame, praise, justice, fairness, freedom, etc.
Psychological concepts: voluntariness, will, trying, intention, choice, decision, action, belief, desire, etc.
Physical concepts: bodily movements, cause, effect, determinism, quantum randomness, etc.

This three-tier model takes us beyond the traditional two-tiered framing of the free will problem as a matter of whether the judgements articulated in terms of *moral* concepts are compatible with the judgements articulated in terms of *physical* concepts such as determinism or randomness at the quantum level. When set against the three-tier model, the two-tiered framing of the problem in terms of the possibility of reconciling the existence of moral responsibility with the reality of determinism looks, as Williams puts it, like a 'structural misconception' (1995c, 6), for what the three-tier model brings out is that, *in the first instance*, 'our ideas of blame and responsibility are answerable to an adequate psychology (rather than to generic worries about determinism)' (1995d, 45 n. 10).

Consequently, there are not one, but *two* points at which the question of the relation of one set of concepts to another arises. And this means that the traditional problem of free will is really not *one* problem at all, but rather *two* problems:

(1) *The First Problem of Free Will*: How can our judgements articulated in physical terms be reconciled with our judgements articulated in psychological terms?
(2) *The Second Problem of Free Will*: How can our judgements articulated in psychological terms be reconciled with our judgements articulated in moral terms?

This conception of the problem of free will as a *dual problem* in turn helps us to see that securing a fit between moral and psychological judgements by deepening our conception of the voluntary comes at a price: it exerts a corresponding pressure on our conceptualization of psychology that is likely to bring it into tension with our conceptualization of physical reality. This is what generates the first problem of free will: if the will expressed in voluntary action is to be a force that is entirely pure of any conditioning influence by unfairly distributed contingencies, how are we to make sense of such a force in physical terms?

To resolve the tensions that problematically moralized conceptualizations of psychology generate in relation to conceptualizations of physical reality, the moralization must *seep through* or *extend to* the physical. That is, one's conception of nature or its metaphysical underpinnings must be adapted to meet the moral demand for some deepened conception of voluntary agency that can provide an ultimately fair basis for responsibility. Aristotle's biology, with its idea that the proper natural development of the human animal issues in virtue, can be thought of as exemplifying a conception of nature that is tailored to ensure that moral demands can be met. Similarly, Plato's dualistic metaphysics of the soul and his theory of the Forms support his tripartite psychology in just the way required to secure the realizability of his moral ideals.

But perhaps the best example of a moralized metaphysics tailored to support moral demands that are specially focused on the concept of the voluntary is Kant's postulation of the noumenal realm as the locus of the transcendental subject's unconditioned will. On the Kantian picture, moral goodness pertains to the good will rather than to its consequences, and the good will is understood in such a way that one's capacity to exhibit it remains unconditioned by contingent empirical circumstances: only the will to do one's moral duty counts as good in itself, and only if it is motivated by the rational insight *that it is one's duty* rather than by the contingent natural inclinations that some people have and others lack.

Since the rational faculty is something which, on Kant's view, is perfectly evenly distributed, and since the noumenal realm provides a place for a source of voluntariness that lies beyond empirical determination, this picture offers solace against unfairness and a true shelter from luck. Of course, even Kant does not deny that certain aspects of moral agency are subject to contingent empirical determination.[39] The point is that these aspects do not subvert the Kantian picture's promise to shelter life from luck in the respect that ultimately matters. For the only thing that ultimately matters—the goodness

---

[39] See e.g. Heyd (1997) and Hartman (2019).

of the unconditioned will of the noumenal self—is completely within one's control, as it depends only on whether one chooses, from motives everyone equally has anyway, to align one's unconditioned will with one's moral duty. Accordingly, Kant reassuringly proclaims: 'To satisfy the categorical command of morality is within everyone's power at all times' (2015, 33).

On a picture on which a moralized psychology finds support in physical concepts, there can be a harmonious fit between the fundamental nature of reality, the operations of human psychology, and the demands of morality. There is considerable attraction in such a picture. It holds out the promise that everyone will be offered an equal opportunity to live up to the demands of morality: if the moral shape of one's life depends exclusively on what one voluntarily does; if the voluntary/involuntary distinction is applied at the deeper level of the purely rational self rather than at the superficial level of the contingently constituted empirical self; and if one's metaphysical view of things supports the existence of such a deeper level; then the moral shape of one's life really can be entirely within one's control and reassuringly sheltered from luck.

But, on a thoroughly disenchanted conception of the world, it is far from clear that a conception of psychology moralized along these lines can find the support it requires in our conception of physical reality. The story of the rise of modern science is also the story of how the moralization of our conception of the physical was reversed: physical notions were *unmoralized*, in the sense of emancipating them from moral demands and rendering them less accommodating of them.

As a result, the deepened conceptions of the voluntary at work in the theory of volitions or in the Kantian theory of the unconditioned will no longer neatly dovetail with our physical and metaphysical conceptions, and it comes to look as though the concept of a voluntary act is never fully instantiated, because modern physical ideas have no room for pure volition or an unconditioned will. The unmoralization of our ways of thinking about the physical thus creates a tension with our moralized ways of thinking about the psychological and renders them problematic—notably, by making it hard to see how human agency can live up to that conception of it.

Of course, the effect of combining in people's minds a deepened conception of the voluntary with conceptions of physical reality that deny it instantiation is not *necessarily* to produce the conviction that no act is ever voluntary. People are quite capable of holding on, at once and without realizing it, to two sets of ideas that are in tension with each other. But it does *set them up* to conclude, when they reflect on the voluntariness of a particular action and inquire more deeply into its aetiology, that the action was not *really* voluntary, because it reflected the agent's genetic predispositions, or upbringing, or some such circumstantial factor. On this basis, they may come to realize that something similar holds true of every action they can point to. *Pace* the compatibilists, they would then not be mistaken about the incompatibility of their conception of the physical with their conception of the voluntary. They would correctly have grasped the implications that a deepened conception of the voluntary has when set against a naturalized or disenchanted conception of the world.

Thus, if one's conception of voluntary action requires the action to be pure of contingency or luck in every respect, sufficiently close scrutiny will eventually disqualify any action when set against a disenchanted conception of the world, leaving the concept's extension empty and denying it any applicability to our actual experience. And insofar as the concept loses its applicability to our actual experience, it also fails to mark out any actions as appropriate objects of praise or blame. Perhaps some concepts are worth having even if they are never satisfied, but insofar as the concept of the voluntary earns its keep by rendering us sensitive to *differences* between human actions of the kind actually to be met with, it is certainly not one of those concepts. Far from delivering on the promise of ultimate fairness, its failure to mark out any actual action as voluntary incapacitates the concept from serving our concerns for fairness and freedom at all.

It follows that if the concept of the voluntary (along with the appraisals of responsibility that build on it) is to do any work for us in a world in which every action displays an element of contingency, its extension within that world had better not shrink to the point of becoming empty: the contrast between the voluntary and the involuntary had better remain an internal contrast *within* our experience. If our moral and legal concepts are to be applicable to a contingently determined agent, the concept of the voluntary that guides their application must accommodate some measure of contingency. It needs to retain the ability to draw a contrast within the world we live in, by contrasting, not conditioned with unconditioned actions, but different kinds of conditioned actions. That is to say, it needs to draw the voluntary/involuntary distinction *within* a range of actions that are *all* adulterated with contingency to some degree, but adverting instead, and rather more helpfully, to the differences in *how much* contingency is involved in them. It thereby renders us, and our practices of responsibility attribution, sensitive to the *degree* to which a conditioned action is attributable to the agent's will.

This is something that a conception deepened to deliver ultimate fairness could not do for us, because it could not be gradable. To meet the demands of ultimate fairness, it would have to be a dichotomous rather than continuous conception, categorically separating voluntary action from every other kind of action or happening at the deepest causal level. And because it could not be gradable, it would level all differences between variously conditioned actions. By its light, any action that was not completely unconditioned and purely voluntary would appear as externally determined and dissociated from the agent as the next.

If we refrain from deepening our conception of the voluntary, by contrast, it *can* be a more nuanced, gradable notion: the less an action is the product of forces external to the agent's will, the more voluntary it is, and the more the agent deserves to be held accountable for it. Such a superficial conception of the voluntary enables us to accept that even the most fully voluntary action reflects influences beyond the control of the agent's will while still retaining its differential applicability to our actions. It thereby serves the need to hold people accountable for at least some of their actions while also serving the concerns for freedom and fairness as far as realistically possible.

The kind of concept of the voluntary we need, then, is one that balances the moral concerns for freedom and fairness against the practical concern to hold people accountable while being realistic about the pervasiveness of contingency: it should render us sensitive to differences in the degree to which actions are under the control of the agent's will while retaining the wide applicability of our regulatory practices of responsibility attribution by accommodating the fact that even the most voluntary actions are still conditioned by contingent factors lying beyond the agent's control. As long as it remains superficial, a conception of the voluntary can do important work for us by enabling us to realize our concerns for fairness and freedom in our appraisals of responsibility as far as the pervasiveness of contingency will allow.

It might be objected that as long as it remains superficial in this way, a conception of the voluntary does little to answer traditional worries about free will. But this misses the crucial point that it also avoids *raising* those worries in the first place, and thereby avoids threatening the legitimacy of our appraisals of responsibility across the board. It is only insofar as conceptions of the voluntary are deepened that the unmoralization of our conceptions of physical reality generates what we identified above as the *first* problem of free will, for only then will the notion of the voluntary come into conflict with physical ideas about determinism. In their superficial form, conceptions of the voluntary generate no such conflict, as evidenced for instance by Brian O'Shaughnessy's reconciliation of causal determinism with his conception of voluntary action.[40] That is why Williams, who explicitly endorses O'Shaughnessy's reconciliation,[41] writes in his study of the pre-Socratic Greeks that 'there is a problem of free will only for those who think that the notion of the voluntary can be metaphysically deepened' (1993, 68). Williams's turn to the pre-Socratic Greeks is driven by a desire to recover, or remind us of the value of, a superficial conception of the voluntary as yet unmarked by the moral pressure to deepen it.

Where does this leave us? In the end, it still leaves us facing the *second* problem of free will: the problem of how to reconcile our judgements articulated in psychological terms with our judgements articulated in moral terms. For if the compatibilists are right about the first problem of free will, there is also an important sense in which the incompatibilists are right about the second problem of free will. Even if we thoroughly unmoralize our conception of psychology and succeed in reconciling it with our conception of the physical, there remains a tension between our psychological understanding of human action and our moral ideals.

At least, there remains a tension between a superficial conception of the voluntary and the host of moral conceptions we have that encode the demand for morality to be pure of contingency: the conception of a *moral reason* or a *moral motive* as something that contrasts sharply with other kinds reasons or motives in claiming to be completely independent from contingent personal attachments, inclinations, loyalties, and projects; the conception of a *moral action* as something that only counts as such if it is motivated by reasons that are moral in this pure sense, and not by dispositions or motives one contingently has; the conception of *moral obligation* as something one is under anyway, whatever one's contingent motivations and commitments; and the conception of *moral blameworthiness* as something that only attaches to the voluntary breaking of moral obligations. As long as the conception of the voluntary that underpins these is itself pure of contingency, morality presents itself as something that transcends luck. Life may be unfair in other respects, but determining the moral shape of one's life, these conceptions encourage one to think, is something everyone gets a fair shot at.

The difficulty, however, is that as long as these moral conceptions shape our thinking, we cannot simply accept that the conception of voluntariness as something utterly pure of contingency is never realized, and opt for a

---

[40] See O'Shaughnessy (2008a; b, esp. chs 11 and 17).
[41] See Williams (1995c, 8; 1995a, 579).

superficial concept of voluntariness instead. For if we do this against the background of these luck-intolerant moral notions generating certain normative expectations about what shape the world can properly have if agency of a morally significant kind is to have a place in it, the eventual result must be a disillusioned scepticism about the very possibility of moral agency: a view on which no act is every truly voluntary, and the noble edifice of morality turns out to have been built on an illusion.[42]

There is thus a danger in admitting to what extent contingency pervades human action while retaining moral conceptions embodying the expectation that morality should be free of luck, since those conceptions blind us to the forms of freedom and moral motivation that really are to be found in the world we live in. They leave us, as the only possible contrast to their purist vision of moral agency and blame, a desolate picture on which everything is contingent inclination or compulsion by brute causal forces. If no action is ever completely pure of contingent influences in the way morality requires, morality never really gets a foothold in our world.

This is, of course, one of the central complaints that both Nietzsche and Williams levelled against the Stoic, Christian, and Kantian elaborations of morality.[43] They see the presupposition of pure voluntariness as presenting an insuperable hurdle for compatibilism. That is why Williams, despite his seemingly complacent dismissal of the free will problem in the passage quoted at the beginning of this chapter, is not a compatibilist.[44] He does not think that, as things stand with our moral ways of thinking, the second problem of free will admits of a compatibilist solution:

> Can the reconciling project succeed? Between determinism (or as much naturalistic explanation as you like), and relevant psychological concepts, yes. Between both of these, and the ethical conceptual scheme, no, not as it stands. (1995c, 19)

---

[42] On sceptical challenges to free will, see Pereboom (2001), Levy (2011), and Waller (2011). As Russell (2017a, xiv) points out, such sceptical challenges are now taken more seriously than a few decades ago, when the main debate was still between libertarians and compatibilists.

[43] On Nietzsche's critique, see Owen (2007), Clark (2015), Leiter (2015), Queloz and Cueni (2019), Richardson (2020), and Reginster (2021). On Williams's critique, see Moore (2003, 2006), Louden (2007, 110–11), Russell (2013, 2018, 2019, forthcoming), Queloz (2022c), and Krishnan and Queloz (2023); on its extension to Stoicism, see Queloz and van Ackeren (2024).

[44] *Pace* Leiter's (2022, 30) characterization of Williams as a compatibilist, both Williams and Nietzsche are thus incompatibilists about deepened conceptions of the voluntary, and derive much of their critical leverage over morality from that fact. While Williams *is* a compatibilist about superficial conceptions of the voluntary, however, Leiter (2019a, b) reads Nietzsche's philosophical psychology as leaving intentions and reasons for action so epiphenomenal in comparison to the unconscious drives that Nietzsche casts as the real determinants of action that this would make Nietzsche an incompatibilist even about superficial conceptions of the voluntary.

The constellation of moral ideas that Kant most thoroughly expressed, but whose influence is far more pervasive than Kant's own, because its roots are older, continues to embody the demand that moral appraisal should, if it is to be ultimately just, be focused on utter voluntariness. In doing so, it 'makes people think that...without its utter voluntariness, there is only force; without its ultimately pure justice, there is no justice' (1985, 218)—when 'in truth, almost all worthwhile human life lies between the extremes that morality puts before us' (1985, 216).

The root cause of this discrepancy, I have suggested, is a distortion of the way we conceptualize voluntariness by an overwhelming concern for fairness—a concern for ultimate fairness that puts pressure on morality to shelter life from luck. What makes it a *distortion* rather than a helpful tailoring of our conceptual repertoire to the need engendered by a noble human concern is the resulting conception's relation to the balance of our concerns. The concern for fairness is not our sole concern, and it must be balanced against other pressing concerns, including the concern for freedom and the concern to regulate behaviour by holding people accountable for some of their actions.

Even on the terms of the concern for fairness alone, moreover, a deepened conception of the voluntary fails to serve that concern. Far from delivering ultimate fairness, it ends up failing to deliver even the more modest gains in fairness that are really to be had by means of the concept of the voluntary. In a world pervaded by contingency, a deepened conception of the voluntary, correctly applied, can still *express* the concern for fairness, but it cannot serve it.

Once one accepts that the demand for pure voluntariness cannot be met, there are two ways one can go.[45] One can renounce deepened conceptions in favour of more superficial and luck-tolerant ones, and allocate responsibility on that basis. Or one can reason that if deepened conceptions of voluntariness cannot be satisfied, no attribution of responsibility is ever truly justified, and all we are left with is people being moved by forces beyond their control.

The pivotal question that separates the luck-tolerant cast of thought from a purist scepticism about moral agency is therefore this: what does the fact that contingency pervades human life *entail*? Adherents of both casts of thought could agree that no act is ever purely voluntary in the way required to completely shut out contingency. It is just that while one cast of thought takes this to speak against deepened conceptions of the voluntary, the other takes it to

---

[45] These roughly correspond to the way of the pessimist and the way of the sceptic, as Paul Russell uses these labels; see Russell (2017b).

speak against the hope that praise or blame might ever be justified. It insists that blame may well never in fact be justified, but that if it *were*, this would *have* to be due to there being purely voluntary acts.

The moral conceptions that make up this purist cast of thought license patterns of reasoning such as the following: if anything is good, it is the moral goodness of things done from moral motives; if an action is done from a moral motive, it is a voluntary action; if an action is voluntary, it is not conditioned by anything that is contingent or lies beyond the agent's control. Via the contrapositives of those claims, one quickly gets from the realization that every action is somehow conditioned by contingent forces beyond the agent's control to the conclusion that no action is ever voluntary and moral agency has no room in this kind of world.

But one might also take the same realization that every action is conditioned by contingent forces to entail nothing of the sort. Using conceptions of voluntariness, moral motivation, and moral goodness that are more tolerant of contingency and mark distinctions *within* the kind of world we inhabit, one can also endorse more luck-tolerant patterns of reasoning allowing us to accept that no moral motivation is ever fully pure of contingent inclinations, or no action ever fully pure of fortuitous influence, and still discern moral agency in the world.

To endorse the purist patterns of reasoning rather than the more luck-tolerant ones is not to fall prey to cognitive error; it is to make an error whose badness is *ethical* rather than cognitive. This reflects the needs-based approach's conviction that the authority of concepts should be assessed by looking to how they tie in with our concerns, not by how closely they approximate the set of concepts that limn moral reality. The set of moral judgements building on a deep conception of the voluntary does not serve us well, in the sense that it does not strike a helpful balance between some of our most pressing needs and concerns. By relying on a superficial conception of the voluntary, by contrast, we can redraw the various oppositions that matter to moral reasoning *within* a world suffused with contingency, so that we can be alive to the real differences between conditioned actions that are as voluntary, moral, or blameworthy as actions can be and conditioned actions that are less so.

We thus need our psychological *and* our moral concepts to accommodate the fact that our lives and our actions are suffused with contingency. As the reflection on the concerns it serves has shown, cultivating a superficial conception of the voluntary is an important step in this direction, since it can accommodate contingency while still serving our concerns for fairness and freedom, as far as contingency will allow, by channelling attributions of responsibility away from those actions that are least within the agent's control. But it can only do that if it resists distortion by the concern for fairness and remains superficial. Its superficiality may be a theoretical vice, but it is a practical virtue. In Nietzsche's phrase, the conception is 'superficial out of profundity'.[46]

In the next and final chapter, we return to the perspectival character of the needs-based conception of authority and explore its implications for politics. This will give us a chance to consider a second case study, which will round out our reconstruction of the Dworkin–Williams debate and illustrate how the needs-based approach can be used to argue for a particular conception of the political value of liberty. In a conciliatory spirit, this will also help us to place the demand for theoretical virtues in social affairs, finding an ethical and political need for tidy systematicity even outside scientific contexts.

The Ethics of Conceptualization: Tailoring Thought and Language to Need. Matthieu Queloz, Oxford University Press.
© Matthieu Queloz 2025. DOI: 10.1093/9780198926283.003.0010

---

[46] See Nietzsche (2001, Preface, §4; 2005a, Epilogue, §2), who uses the phrase in a different connection. Williams (1993, 68), however, applies the remark to—among other things—the notion of the voluntary, which supports my reading on which he saw its superficiality not as a flaw, but as a feature. This contrasts with readings of Williams such as Yeager's (2006, ch. 2) and Deigh's (2008, xi).

10

The Politics of Conflicting Concerns

10.1 Political Disagreement and Its Demands

The needs-based framework presents the authority of concepts as welling up, ultimately, from the concerns of concept-users. But it is of course a basic fact of politics that different people have different concerns, and that one group's concerns can sometimes be satisfied only at the expense of another group's concerns. How does the needs-based approach accommodate the politics of pluralistic and conflicting concerns?

Far from being naively oblivious to politics, I contend in this chapter, the needs-based approach comes into its own when deployed against a more politicized picture of human affairs. To demonstrate this, I apply the approach to the political concept of liberty and use it to illustrate the value of conflictual thought. This will yield two needs-based arguments for a conception of liberty that conflicts with our conception of equality. But the needs-based approach also reveals that there is a place in politics for the tidy-minded pursuit of theoretical virtues: in particular, there is a need for public reasoning to take a thinner and more theoretically virtuous form than personal reasoning, as this serves the concern to hold public decision-makers accountable. Once this ideal of public reasoning is carried over into people's conception of rationality in personal reasoning, however, it threatens to entrain a loss of substance in personal thought.

But let us begin by considering how the needs-based approach accommodates the basic political fact that people disagree about which concerns to pursue. There are three demands arising from the fact of political disagreement that the approach equips us to address: the demand that we should be able to *make sense* of such disagreements *as* political disagreements; the demand that we should be able to disagree *respectfully*; and the demand that the fact of political disagreement itself makes on the way we conceptualize some of our political values.

Consider first the demand that we should be able to make sense of political disagreements as political, i.e. to recognize and account for the respects in which they are political rather than epistemic in nature. One implication of the needs-based approach is that when two parties disagree, that disagreement is not necessarily a matter of epistemic error. Nor does it therefore have to be a disagreement about which concepts to use (of the kind we encountered in Chapter 1 under the heading of metaconceptual dispute or negotiation). It might rather be that the disagreement reflects an underlying difference in conceptual needs. To hold that concepts should be tailored to conceptual needs is to adopt a standard that is local and variable enough to properly become reflective of distinctive political commitments. Some people have reason to use concepts that other people have no reason to use, or even have reason not to use.

I take it to be a significant strength of the needs-based approach that it allows us to capture this distinctively political—as opposed to epistemic—dimension of disagreement. Of course, an opposition between two groups with conflicting concerns is not yet per se a political opposition. What makes it political is its bearing on the question of how to exercise public authority, in particular by deploying state power.[1] Unlike moral disagreement, which is characterized by the kind of reasons it draws on—to wit, *moral reasons*—*political* disagreement can draw on all kinds of reasons, and derives its political character from the fact that it is, in the end, a disagreement over how to exercise public authority. Accordingly, different cultural, social, or professional groups stand in relations of political opposition to each other precisely to the extent that their concerns conflict, i.e. are not fully co-satisfiable, in ways that lead them to disagree about how to exercise public authority.

On the needs-based conception of conceptual authority, it becomes intelligible how such political differences can find expression at the level of what concepts are authoritative for whom, because conceptual authority is perspectival. The concepts that are authoritative for one set of people are not necessarily authoritative for another set of people. Of course, there are limits to how much conceptual balkanization a society can sustain: the demand to tailor people's conceptual repertoire to their distinctive conceptual needs must be balanced against the demand, which is itself a conceptual need growing out of people's most basic concerns, that members of the same society need to be able to communicate and cooperate with each other by *sharing* concepts. As E. J. Craig has shown in his discussion of the practical pressures towards the 'objectivization' of concepts arising in any social species such as ours, even initially fully subjectivized 'conceptual idiolects' would be driven by the demands of communication and cooperation to become usable across

---

[1] On this way of contrasting moral and political disagreement, see Williams (2005c, 77).

different perspectives and communally shared at least to some extent.[2] But equally, and especially in pluralistic liberal democracies, there are no reasons to expect, and plenty of reasons to want to avoid, a conceptual monopoly whereby a single conceptual apparatus is uniformly shared by all and difficult to deviate from.

Secondly, as hinted in Chapter 8, such a perspectival conception of conceptual authority can yield the kind of understanding of where the other party is coming from that facilitates *respectful* disagreement. To disagree respectfully is to disagree in a way that is mindful of the requirements of respect, which notably include the idea that the other party is owed an effort at identification.[3] As Allen Wood spells out this idea, 'what we are to respect in a person is fundamentally the person's *point of view*', which we do notably 'by listening to their *voice*—by paying the right kind of attention to the claims they make on us or the arguments they address to us' (2010, 568).

By heeding the differences in our respective conceptual needs and what engenders them, we can perform just such an effort at identification. When the other party conceptualizes things in terms that differ from those we engagedly use ourselves, we can take up the ethnographic stance towards them: by imaginatively inhabiting and making sense of their perspective from the inside, we can come to grasp the concepts they use without making them our own. It can be of great value to come to see how a difference in outlook can be rooted in a difference in conceptual needs (which would itself trace to a difference in concerns, capacities, or circumstances). For precisely what this allows us to do is to *make sense* of their perspective in a way that reveals them not to be *merely* epistemically at fault, even if their views also involve elements of such epistemic faults. A needs-based understanding of *their* reasons for concept use allows *us* to make sense of why it makes sense *for them* to use the concepts they use. Their acceptance of these concepts and their correlative reasons is not merely due to error, ignorance, immaturity, confusion, delusion, or deception. They have *reasons* to think in terms of those reasons, reasons that we can understand and rest our respect *on*, even if these are merely reasons for them and not for us, because we do not share the relevant conceptual needs.

As a result, we come to be able to distinguish between disagreements in which the other party is simply wrong, because they have made a mistake

---

[2] See Craig (1990, 82–97; 1993, 81–115); I discuss the practical pressures to turn private thinking tools into public ones in Queloz (2021c, 145–9). See also Fricker (2010c, 61), Kusch (2011, 9–10), and Hannon (2019, ch. 2).

[3] Here, the requirements of respect express an underlying commitment to a certain idea of equality and the 'spirit of human understanding' on which it is based, as Williams observed in his influential essay on equality (1973d, 236–9). I am grateful to Damian Cueni and Sanford Diehl for the pointer.

within a shared cognitive enterprise, and disagreements in which, though the other party may still be wrong, it is not *simply* wrong, because it makes sense *to us* that it makes sense *for them* to reason as they do, given how different from ours we understand their conceptual needs to be.

A third thing that a needs-based approach allows us to do, finally, is to ask what conceptual needs are engendered by the relations of distinctively political opposition and disagreement themselves. Even if we start from the idea that what makes for a good concept will depend on the concerns of the concept-users and accept that these concerns vary wildly, there are concepts that serve us well precisely *because* the concerns of concept-users vary wildly: there are concepts that are rendered needful by the very fact of social pluralism. I propose to illustrate this in the next section using the example of *liberty*. We can ask how the political value of liberty needs to be conceptualized given a practical situation in which people have both conflicting concerns and conflicting conceptions of other political values.

Perhaps counterintuitively, I want to suggest that this question need not itself be understood as a political question, but can be heard as a question in conceptual ethics. When heard in this key, the question can be answered without ending up pushing just another sectarian creed in political opposition to its rivals. Instead, we can step back from the political fray and take it as a datum for needs-based concept appraisal: we can aim to determine whether the very fact of multiply conflictual political opposition in itself already gives us any reasons for concept use.

Some concepts may derive their authority precisely from the fact that different groups within society have conflicting concerns, because some concepts equip us better than others to accommodate such a pluralism of concerns. The very fact of living in a society marked by intersubjectively conflicting concerns will then give members of that society reason to use concepts suited to accommodating, sustaining, and negotiating intersubjective conflicts of concerns. The conceptual authority of these concepts will then be uniformly vindicated, not by a corresponding uniformity at the level of concerns, but, paradoxically, by a pluralism of concerns. An example of just such a structure can be gleaned from the Dworkin–Williams debate if we only wade a little deeper into it.

10.2 The Dworkin–Williams Debate Continued

In Chapter 6, we saw Dworkin propose, in the name of conceptual integrity, to immunize the political concepts of liberty and equality against conflict by equating liberty with *rightful* freedom. We then saw Williams resist this by suggesting, notably, that it was no good achieving conceptual integrity if it came at the cost of severing all ties to the underlying concerns that give people reason to use anything like these concepts to begin with. I used this suggestion as a springboard to the needs-based framework for concept appraisal. With this framework now in place, we can return to the Dworkin–Williams debate and make sense of how Williams in effect employs the concerns animating the use of the concept of liberty not just as grounds on which to object to Dworkin's proposed conception of liberty, but as grounds on which to argue for a counterproposal of his own.

When considered within the needs-based framework, the pieces of Williams's positive argument neatly fall into place. He approaches the political value of liberty by urging us to reflect on 'what we want that value to do for us—what we, now, need it to be in shaping our own institutions and practices [and] in disagreeing with those who want to shape them differently' (2005c, 75). His guiding question thus exactly aligns with a needs-based approach: he asks *what we, now, need our conception of the political value of liberty to be.*

Still in line with the needs-based framework, he sets out to answer that question from a concern: the pre-political concern for what he calls 'primitive freedom', i.e. the utterly basic human concern to be unobstructed by humanly imposed coercion in doing what one wants. To understand how the individual's concern for primitive freedom relates to the political value of liberty, Williams observes, one has to consider how such a personal concern might relate to the perspective of some public authority that can be appealed to by the individual (2005c, 83). Clearly, the way in which freedom is conceptualized from the point of view of that authority will have to differ from the way it is conceptualized from the individual's point of view, because 'the resolution of questions of how far a person's freedom should be protected or extended, how far it is good that it should be, how far he has a right that it should be, requires some degree of impartiality (a general point of view, in Hume's phrase) which is not contained in the idea of an individual's primitive freedom as such' (2005c, 84). From such a political as opposed to personal point of view, the salient question is how the often competing concerns of different people living under a shared public authority are to be registered and dealt with.

What makes *liberty* a political concept is that it conceptualizes primitive freedom *for* this political point of view: it acts as a political lens through which the concern for primitive freedom can be focused in a political context.

That, at the most basic level, is the role of the concept: it picks out that part of individual freedom that has a claim to society's attention.

To stand any chance of performing this role, however, the concept of liberty must differ substantially from how individuals might conceptualize their own primitive freedom. For one thing, the concept of liberty must be a *normatively richer* notion: while primitive freedom is basically a form of power that one can merely *get*, using the power one already has, liberty has to be something that one can *lay a political claim to*, which is to say a claim that *makes a claim on society's attention* (Williams 2005a, 115). The mere fact that an individual has lost some freedom does not yet give that individual any claim on society's attention. Such a claim must be backed or grounded by something other than the power one already has. This is, of course, a point that Dworkin himself acknowledges, since he likewise insists that political claims to liberty must be grounded in something (namely in rights, on Dworkin's account).

Because of its political nature, moreover, the concept of liberty must also be more *narrowly focused* than the concept of freedom: not every loss in freedom can count as a loss in liberty, as we also saw Dworkin point out against Berlin. The reason is that, as a political value, the concept of liberty has to be able to 'co-exist with the political' (2005a, 120), as Williams puts it: the concept could not intelligibly give everyone a *claim* to doing whatever they happened to want—to murder whomever they wished, for instance—because that would undermine the conditions necessary to there being any political order organized by political values in the first place.[4] Preventing people from murdering whomever they want is a restriction on their primitive freedom, but not one that could consistently count as a restriction on their liberty, because that restriction is necessary for there to be any kind of political order at all.[5]

Someone's claim that they have incurred a loss in liberty therefore minimally needs to be *socially presentable*, as Williams put it, where that means that 'it can be urged consistently with accepting a legitimate political order for the general regulation of the society' (2005a, 120). Objecting already to the mere fact of being subject to a state at all would not be socially presentable in this sense, since it is a complaint that would apply to any state whatsoever, and the mere existence of a political order cannot consistently be understood as constituting, already in itself, a ground for a political complaint within that order.

---

[4] See Williams (2001a, 93).   [5] See Williams (2005c, 83–5; 2009, 200).

By contrast, objecting to the operations of Franco, or James II, would be socially presentable, because 'one could, and most objectors did, accept that these rulers should be replaced by some other rulers, and more generally they accepted a state system' (Williams 2005a, 120).

This social presentability requirement constitutes a necessary condition on a claim of a loss in liberty being correct: it needs to be at least consistent with the acceptance of some legitimate political order. But Williams and Dworkin agree that this is not yet a sufficient condition. What further condition does such a claim have to meet in order to be correct?

10.3 A Thoroughly Political Conception of Liberty

Dworkin's suggestion is that in order to be correct, a claim in liberty needs to be *rightful*, i.e. grounded in rights. Under this conception, the reasons that can ground a claim in liberty are exhausted by one's rights. But insofar as one aims at *congruent* conceptions of liberty and equality as implying rights, one is committed to looking for conceptions that imply *non-conflicting* rights. Insofar as the state rightfully exercises its power in curtailing one's freedom, therefore, one can have no basis for a claim in liberty in that connection, since whatever the state thereby stopped one from doing is something one had no right to do anyway.

An example that Dworkin and Williams both discuss is the abolition of private schools in the name of equality of opportunity in education. Williams envisages a government that 'takes steps to make it illegal or effectively impossible, except for some fairly trivial exceptions, to run a private school' (2001a, 100). It is open to Dworkin to resist the suggestion that such a restriction would be rightful under anything like our present circumstances, Williams concedes. But Dworkin is nevertheless committed to the view that *if* this crackdown on private schools, or some other restriction like it, were to be rightful, then it could not come at the expense of liberty, since there could be no real tension between liberty and equality.

On Williams's view, however, this tidy picture is too tidy to make sense of the experience of life under a political order. For it is 'one datum of that experience', Williams stresses, 'that people can even recognize a restriction as rightful under some political value such as equality or justice, and nevertheless regard it as a restriction on liberty' (2005c, 84). That is to say, *even those who agree* that a crackdown on private schools is rightful may still feel *resentful* of it; and it is paradigmatically through such feelings as the experience of resentment that people's sense of freedom is given to them, and by extension also their sense of when their liberty is being restricted (2005a, 123; 2005c, 87-8).[6] To make political sense of this experience of resentment, i.e. to be capable of conceptualizing it *as reasonable* even when articulated in terms of liberty rather than freedom, one needs to be able to see it as reflecting some real *loss* or *cost* in liberty.

Dworkin's proposed conception of liberty, however, renders unintelligible the idea that one might incur a cost in liberty as a result of a rightful political decision going against one. And yet this notion of a cost in liberty incurred by those who end up on the losing side of what they acknowledge to be a rightful political decision, Williams points out, 'is at least as well entrenched in historical and contemporary experience as that of a rightful claim in liberty' (2005c, 84). We should accordingly be suspicious of a conception of liberty that accommodates the latter but rides roughshod over the former.

In effect, Williams observes, Dworkin's conception of liberty bears the imprint of the legal theorist, because 'the idea of a rightful claim in liberty implies a juridical conception, of an agreed authority which can rightfully grant or refuse such a claim' (2005c, 86). As Damian Cueni (2024b) shows in a nuanced discussion of this charge, it makes perfect sense to use something like Dworkin's conception of liberty *from the perspective of a judge* engaged in judicial review, since a judge is bound to regulate the relationships between citizens on the basis of a single, principled, and consistent framework.

The problem for Dworkin's proposal is that political debate is fundamentally different from judicial review. As Williams puts it: 'We and our political opponents—even our opponents in one polity, let alone those in others—are not just trying to read one text' (2005c, 78). We have different concerns and hold different outlooks articulated in terms of wildly varying conceptions that yield equally varying conclusions as to how values ought to be weighed against each other.[7]

---

[6] Resentment is the prototypical reaction to restrictions of one's liberty, on Williams's account, but he acknowledges that the feelings that go with the sense that one's liberty is being restricted do not necessarily have to be identified with resentment, because 'resentment so readily merges into other negative feelings, such as anger and dislike, not just for conceptual but also for various familiar psychological reasons' (2005c, 87).

[7] See Williams (2005c, 78, 86). Cueni (2024b) elaborates this objection into a wider model contrasting the 'juridical' construction of political values for the top-down, unified perspective of a public authority with a more thoroughly 'political' construction of political values for the varying perspectives of individual citizens standing in relations of political opposition to each other. At the same time, Williams himself makes room for the idea that public decision-making should be subjected to the demand for a shared, principled, and consistent framework (Cueni and Queloz 2021).

If, in reflecting on the political value of liberty, we truly acknowledge this difference between political debate and judicial review, it will emerge that what is needed in politics is not a juridical, but a more thoroughly *political* conception of liberty. A 'thoroughly political concept of liberty', Williams suggests, is one that 'acknowledges in its construction the on-going existence of political conflict' (2005a, 126). But what does it mean for a concept to be 'thoroughly political' and 'to acknowledge in its construction the on-going existence of political conflict'?

The key to understanding this cryptic suggestion is to integrate it into the needs-based approach. Williams's objection to Dworkin's tidy conception is not just that it is untrue to the less tidy *experience* of life under a political order. It is, more fundamentally, that reflection on the value of liberty, and especially on its 'role in political argument and political conflict' (Williams 2005c, 84), reveals *conceptual needs* for a conception which, while narrower in scope than the notion of primitive freedom, remains wider in scope than Dworkin's conception of liberty as rightful freedom.

In particular, the concept of liberty needs to be able to simultaneously meet the conceptual needs of those on the losing side and those on the winning side of a political decision. Those on the losing side need a conception enabling them to contest even rightful political decisions by enabling them to voice reasonable complaints in liberty even when these are not backed by rights. And those on the winning side need a conception that facilitates respect across the aisle by giving them the conceptual wherewithal to make sense of the costs in liberty incurred by their political opponents. Let us consider these in turn.

10.4 Conceptual Needs on the Losing Side

The first conceptual need Williams invokes derives directly from the concern for primitive freedom. If a conception of liberty is to retain its connection to that concern, it needs to be able to act as the political sharp end of the concern for primitive freedom, enabling the expression and promotion of that concern, and calls for compensation for the frustration of that concern, through political argument.

From this perspective, having a political concept of liberty will clearly be pointless unless it allows one to lay claim to *more* freedom than one has under current political arrangements. But the concept can only do that if it gives people grounds for complaining about restrictions on their liberty *even and especially when* they are not fully identified with rightful political decisions. A conception of liberty which *presupposes* that one's own will is perfectly aligned with the will expressed in the rightful activity of the state, as Dworkin's proposed conception does, is pointless in this connection, since those who are fully identified with that activity are precisely those who have no cause for complaint.

To serve the concern for freedom in the political sphere, we therefore need a conception of liberty under which the reasons grounding claims in liberty are not exhausted by one's rights, but allow for reasonable complaints in liberty grounded in the residual losses in liberty one has incurred as a result of rightful state action. Only then can resentment at rightful restrictions of one's freedom intelligibly be given a political voice. A conception of liberty can meet our needs only if it gives us intelligible grounds for *contesting* the prevailing understanding of rightful freedom.

To enable such contestations, a conception of liberty needs to make conceptual room for the thought that the rightful curtailment of someone's freedom can still *reasonably* be resented *as a loss in liberty*. For only then can such a conception serve our concern for freedom in such situations, which are sure to arise as long as there are people who are not fully identified with rightful political decisions. That is one way in which a conception of liberty can be thoroughly political: it acknowledges in its construction the on-going existence of political conflict by rendering even rightful curtailments of freedom intelligible as losses in liberty.

Dworkin's conception of liberty as rightful freedom, by contrast, leaves no conceptual room for reasonable complaints in liberty from those who end up on the losing side of a political decision. They can of course still complain—but their complaints must appear confused or unreasonable in light of this conception, for, under this conception, the reasons that can ground their claims in liberty are exhausted by their rights.

Any conceptualization of the value of liberty that is to enable political contestations of what is to count as rightful freedom therefore needs to spread the idea of liberty, and hence of a cost in liberty, more widely than Dworkin's proposed conception does. While the conception of liberty cannot, consistently with the existence of the political, treat any and all complaints in primitive freedom as reasonable—'no concept of liberty intelligible as a political value could allow anybody to murder anybody they liked' (2001a, 93), as Williams puts it—a helpful conception of liberty, and particularly one that is suitably responsive to the fact that pluralistic societies are unlikely to be of one mind about everything, will need to be far more inclusive than Dworkin's if it is to serve the concern for primitive freedom by facilitating the political contestation of rightful state action.

We will still want to rule out as unreasonable claims that are not socially presentable in Williams's technical sense; we will also want to rule out claims that are merely a product of insincerity, ignorance, or insufficient attention to the relevant arguments. But when these fairly minimal demands are met by someone's claim that they have incurred a loss in liberty, then, though we may not yet have a *rightful* claim, we will have what Williams calls a *responsible* claim (2005a, 122). For political purposes, we should regard the voicing of a responsible claim of a loss in liberty as a sufficient reason to assume that there *has been* a loss in liberty.

This is not a metaphysical argument resting on an independent account of the nature of liberty; it is an argument in conceptual ethics, which advocates a certain way of thinking in politics: namely, one on which we *count* responsible claims of a loss in liberty as *reason enough* to assume that there has been a loss liberty; and it is an *argument* rather than the blank assertion of a liberal piety because the conceptual need engendered by the concern for freedom constitutes a *reason* to prefer a conception of liberty along these lines to the one advocated by Dworkin. In leaving no conceptual room for reasonable complaints, on the part of those whose desires are frustrated by rightful political decisions, that a cost in liberty has been incurred, Dworkin forecloses an important form of political argument—a form of argument that, especially in pluralistic and polarized societies in which full and general identification with the rightful activities of the state is bound to be rare, is crucial to the political expression of the concern for freedom.

Thus, a conception of liberty capable of serving the concern for freedom of those who end up on the losing side of a rightful political decision needs to allow for reasonable complaints in liberty grounded in the residual losses incurred by that decision. In other words, Dworkin and Williams agree that not every loss in primitive freedom can be reasonably resented as a loss in liberty, since the concept of liberty, just because it is a political concept, needs to be narrower in scope than the concept of primitive freedom; but Williams insists, against Dworkin, that not every *reasonably* resented loss in liberty has to be *rightfully* resented as such, because the political concept of liberty needs to be broader in scope than the concept of rightful freedom.

Of course, this will cast the net for complaints in liberty that are intelligible input to political debate fairly wide, but if the concept of liberty is to serve the concern for freedom, the net *needs* to be cast wide, because how seriously any of these complaints should be taken is itself a political question, not one to be settled in advance by a definition. The concept's role, insofar as it serves the concern for freedom, is to determine what can go into the funnel of political debate, not what comes out of it. As Williams puts it:

> A construction of liberty on these lines...means that, within certain limits, anyone with a grievance or who is frustrated by others' actions can appropriately complain about restrictions on his liberty. If 'appropriately' means that it is semantically, conceptually, indeed psychologically, intelligible that he should do so, that is right. If it means that it is necessarily useful, helpful, to be taken seriously as a contribution to political debate, and not a waste of everyone's time, it is not right. The point is that these latter considerations are in the broadest sense political considerations, and that is the point of the construction. (2005c, 92)

Williams's preferred way of conceptualizing liberty constrains what losses in primitive freedom merit to be so much as *intelligible as* responsible input to political debate, but it does not by itself determine how much weight that input should be given, or what should come out of the debate—it treats these questions as *political* questions to be settled through political debate, not as questions that philosophers might settle in advance of political debate, at the drop of a definition. That is a further respect in which the conception is thoroughly political.

Dworkin's conception, by contrast, collapses these two steps into one, and, in so doing, entrains a loss in freedom: in particular, a loss in the freedom to contest rightful restrictions on one's freedom through complaints that have a claim on society's attention.[8] The concept of liberty can only serve the concern for freedom in this regard if liberty is conceptualized as something broader than rightful freedom. Instead of serving the concern for freedom that most basically animates the use of the concept of liberty, Dworkin's conception of liberty thus ends up working against the concern for freedom.

At its core, then, Williams's first positive argument for a certain conception of liberty is an argument from the concern with primitive freedom to what a thoroughly political conception of liberty needs to be. The concept fundamentally serves the concern with primitive freedom, focusing that

---

[8] The focus here is on claims in liberty in political debates, but parallel considerations apply also to the *legal* treatment of complaints about restrictions on freedom. Cueni spells this out in an article arguing that due respect can be paid to reasonable claims in liberty even when they are not ultimately found to be rightful thanks to the legal distinction between rights infringements and rights violations; see Cueni (manuscript-b).

concern in the political context. Dworkin's proposed conception fails to serve that concern in one crucial respect: it achieves congruence with the concept of equality at the cost of failing to serve people's concern for freedom when they end up on the losing side of a political decision and their freedom is rightfully restricted. A conception of liberty able to serve people's concern for freedom under those circumstances cannot therefore coincide with the notion of rightful freedom.

10.5 Conceptual Needs on the Winning Side

The second conceptual need that a thoroughly political conception of liberty must meet, according to Williams, arises from the requirement on a shared political system to contain pluralistic and conflicting concerns. We might put this by saying that the pluralism of concerns itself engenders a conceptual need for a conception of liberty that facilitates our living together in a pluralistic society with others whose concerns radically differ from our own.

One notable way in which a conception of liberty can facilitate this is by equipping those on the winning side of a political decision to make sense of, and acknowledge the costs in liberty incurred by, those on the losing side—as opposed to treating their complaints as products of error, ignorance, immaturity, confusion, delusion, or deception. The conception thereby enables what we might call *respect across the aisle*. Whether those on the winning side have the conceptual wherewithal to make sense of the resentment of those on the losing side as reasonable makes a great difference to the character of liberal democratic politics—in the first instance, by affecting what those on the winning side *can say to* those on the losing side. That, Williams insists, is also an important 'form of citizenly address, particularly in a pluralistic society' (2001a, 102).

In effect, Williams proposes to extract, from a pluralist understanding of politics, a sense of what conception of liberty we need. 'The idea of value pluralism', he writes, is no mere 'aestheticism of politics'; it 'tells you how to speak to the people who have to pay, not just in their interests but in their values, for things that have to be done' (2001a, 102). The legal scholar Jamal Greene observes that while the last century may have given us tools to fight political exclusion, 'in this century, we need the tools to build a politics of pluralism' (2021, xxi). The conception of liberty that Williams advocates is just such a tool: it is tailored to the conceptual needs of the politics of pluralism.

In particular, we need a conception of liberty that allows us to make sense of, and, on that basis, to acknowledge and perhaps show remorse, apologize, or make amends for, the costs in liberty incurred by those on the losing side of political decisions. Yet all that Dworkin's tidy equation of liberty with rightful freedom encourages those on the winning side to say to those who feel they have incurred a cost in liberty although their freedom has been rightfully curtailed is that they are mistaken: they may *think* they incurred a cost in liberty, but if only they achieved a clear-headed understanding of the concept of liberty, they would recognize that no such loss was incurred, and their resentment was therefore unreasonable.[9]

Adopting this attitude towards our political opponents' complaints, Williams maintains against Dworkin, is 'objectionable' (2005c, 85). In particular, 'telling these people that they had better wise up and revise their definition of the values involved', as Dworkin's proposed conception invites us to do, 'is not in many cases prudent, or citizenly, or respectful of their experience' (2001a, 102). Note how Williams is drawing on the rest of our conceptual repertoire, and more particularly on the thick normative concepts *prudent*, *citizenly*, and *respectful*, to evaluate the conception of liberty proposed by Dworkin. This illustrates the broadly Neurathian strategy I have been advocating. And each of these thick concepts forms the basis of a distinct objection to Dworkin's proposal.

First, it is not *prudent*, because dismissing their complaints as conceptually confused only makes it harder to secure the consent of those who end up on the losing side of a political decision, and securing losers' consent is vital to the stability and health of a democracy.[10] This is presumably why Williams writes that Dworkin's outlook 'does not encourage a helpful— one might say, healthy—relation to one's opponents' (2005c, 85). What it is unhealthy *for* is democracy: it amplifies resentment, polarization, and ultimately the threat of violent confrontations of just the sort that the political order was meant to sublimate.[11] Cueni (2024b) thus rightly compares this strand in Williams's argument to Chantal Mouffe's (2000, 13)

---

[9] See Williams (2001a, 100; 2005c, 85). In fairness to Dworkin, he does allow that when a right is overridden in virtue of a special emergency, it is occasionally appropriate 'for the state to show remorse, to apologize, and even, when this is feasible, to make amends or compensation' (2001, 121–2). But he is talking about exceptional circumstances, whereas Williams is talking about more quotidian conflicts of liberty and equality.

[10] On losers' consent and its importance to democratic legitimacy and stability, see the essays in Anderson et al. (2005).

[11] On this strand in Williams's political thought, see Williams (2005i, 3; 2005d, 62–3; 2005j, 136–7; 2006l, 12).

insistence on the need for politics to prevent adversaries from turning into enemies.

Once this is understood, it also becomes clear why Williams goes on to note that brushing off one's political opponents as failing to grasp the nature of liberty is not *citizenly*. So far from being a manifestation of civic virtue, i.e. of the character traits and dispositions associated with the successful functioning of the civil order, it is 'hostile to the relations of fellow citizenship' (Williams 2005c, 86), undermining the civil order by threatening to alienate from the political process those who feel they have incurred a cost in liberty as a result of a decision going against them; by noting that Dworkin's view encourages a notably *uncitizenly* form of citizenly address, moreover, Williams is implicitly suggesting that the view falls foul of the Rousseauian tradition he sees it as standing in (2005c, 85; 2005a, 120–1), since it was Rousseau who, more than anyone in modern political theory, revived the ancient ideal of citizenly behaviour.

Third, Williams objects that to dismiss our political opponents' complaints in liberty as conceptually confused is not *respectful of their experience*. We should 'take seriously the idea that if, under certain conditions, people think that there is a cost in liberty, then there is'—this is a condition 'not only of taking seriously the idea of political opposition, but of taking our political opponents themselves seriously' (2005c, 85). And 'what we should take seriously', in particular, 'are their reactions, or at least their deeper reactions, rather than the extent to which we are disposed to share or morally approve of their reactions' (2005c, 85–6). That is to say, we should take seriously the reactive attitudes they continue to have once we have subtracted the superficial reactions due merely to insufficient attention, reflection, or information.

The relation of political opposition is a relation that not only specially calls for respect, but also leaves more space for it.[12] After all, as Williams repeatedly emphasizes, a political decision 'does not in itself announce that the other party was morally wrong or, indeed, wrong at all. What it immediately announces is that *they have lost*' (2005i, 13). That is why regarding someone as a *political* opponent is subtly but crucially different from regarding them as someone one is *morally* at odds with. In a moral disagreement, we treat the other party primarily as someone we have to argue into seeing the moral situation aright, and hence into recognizing that they are wrong. This is what we tend to think of as respectful engagement in a moral disagreement. But in a

---

[12] On the idea that political opposition specially calls for respect, and that legitimate opposition is an achievement worth defending, see Kirshner (2022).

political disagreement, Williams thinks, 'we should not think that what we have to do is simply to argue with those who disagree: treating them as *opponents* can, oddly enough, show more respect for them as political actors' (2005i, 13). In coming to think of those with whom we disagree as political opponents, we foreground not the extent to which *we disapprove* of their reactions, but *their reactions*; not our sense that *they are wrong* to disagree with us, but *the fact that* they disagree with us.

This consideration for the fact of their disagreement and the reactions that underlie it opens up the possibility of recognizing further that they do not necessarily disagree with us merely out of error, but might have come by their political convictions much as we came by ours: through an obscure confluence of sociohistorical and biographical circumstances and forces (Williams 2005i, 12–13). On this basis, we can then recognize that a political decision going against them may come at a real cost to them in terms of their values. This is a precondition—and it is no more than that—of acknowledging what resentment this produces as reasonable, and thus of taking their reactions seriously.

To conceive of their political opponents in this fashion, however, those on the winning side of a political decision need a conception that is, in Williams's words, less 'instructional' and 'patronizing' (2005c, 86) than Dworkin's. They need a conception that enables them to respect those on the losing side *as* people who have suffered costs in liberty. For, as Cueni emphasizes (2024a), respect is characteristically respect *under a description*: we do not just show respect *for* people, but for people *as* people who possess some property, and this requires the conceptual wherewithal to make sense of them as possessing that property. Even to show respect for persons *as* persons already requires not just some concept of a person, but, specifically, a conception on which the fact of being a person itself already entitles one to respect under that description. *A fortiori*, to show respect for persons *as* persons who have incurred a cost in liberty when their freedom has been rightfully curtailed requires a conception of liberty that makes conceptual room for the thought that even a *rightful* restriction on someone's freedom can still *reasonably* be resented as a loss in liberty.

If a certain conception of liberty can help us to make sense of our political opponents' resentment, this is also due to our ability to use concepts in a disengaged way. Besides thinking in terms of the conceptions of political values that we are engaged users of, we also have to be capable of thinking, if only in a disengaged way, in terms of the different conceptions of political values that 'move around society in their variously resentful or hopeful ways' (Williams

2005a, 126). Recognizing that some might reasonably resent the enactment of some policy we are fully identified with ourselves, given how we conceive of our own political values, requires the ability to imaginatively identify with the perspective of those who view things in terms of rival conceptions, and recognize how these conceptions would give them grounds for resentment. This feat of disengaged or vicarious resentment requires what Williams calls 'double-mindedness' (2005a, 125–6). By making disengaged use of their conceptions even while remaining fully engaged users of our own, we can come to discriminate between restrictions they could or could not *reasonably* resent.

As the qualification 'reasonably' registers, however, it makes a difference whether their conceptions really are *authoritative for them*, i.e. whether, in light of their concerns, capacities, and circumstances, they in fact have reasons to think in these terms, or feel resentful merely because they are in the grip of conceptions that they would immediately jettison if only they reflected on how these related to their concerns.

Whether it makes sense *to us* that it should make sense *for them* to think in these terms will thus also inform our judgement as to whether they have a solid basis for reasonable resentment. If only inchoately, our sense of our political opponents' reasons for concept use plays a part in determining how seriously we take the reactive attitudes they form in light of those concepts: if we feel that their resentment is entirely an artefact of their confidence in notions that seems misplaced even by their own lights, in that they would themselves reject those notions upon reflection, we will find it difficult to view their resentment as reasonable; conversely, if we feel that they have good reasons to think as they do, they will seem to us to be on solid ground, and their resentment will at least seem reasonable on their own terms, even if these are terms we do not share. Thus, whether claims in liberty are *responsible* depends not just on whether they are made sincerely and after due consideration, but also on whether they are made on the basis of *responsible conceptions* of political values.

When 'double-minded' reflection on our political opponents' first- and second-order reasons for thinking as they do reveals their conceptions of political values as well as the claims they make on that basis to be responsible, this licenses respect across the aisle: it enables us to take a respectful view of those political opponents as standing on ground as solid as our own, in that they appeal to conceptions that are as authoritative for them as ours are for us. Consequently, when they end up on the losing side of a political decision, it enables us to take their complaints seriously. It makes sense to us that some different way of conceptualizing the situation should make sense to them. We may not agree with them, but we can also see that they are not simply conceptually confused.

Those on the winning side of a rightful political decision thus need the conceptual wherewithal to acknowledge the costs in liberty suffered by those on the losing side: they need a conception of liberty that facilitates a prudent, citizenly, and respectful attitude towards their political opponents. That is part of what is required to address one's political opponents in ways that help secure losers' consent, cultivate healthy relations of fellow citizenship, and foster respect across the aisle. Hence Williams's emphatic conclusion that *'the proposed interpretation of liberty is what we need'* (2005a, 125–6), particularly in order to live together with people who conceptualize other political values differently from us.

The Dworkin–Williams debate thus boils down to the following disagreement: for Dworkin, we have a standing reason to prefer conceptions that do not conflict, and this gives us a reason to use a conception of liberty under which the reasons grounding claims in liberty are exhausted by one's rights. For Williams, on the other hand, the pursuit of conceptual integrity must take a backseat when it threatens to sever the connection to the underlying concern for freedom that most basically animates our use of anything like the concept of liberty, and this is what Dworkin's proposed conception threatens to do when it denies people any reasonable claims in liberty beyond those grounded in rights.[13] In the process of whittling away the aspects of the concept of liberty that bring it into tension with the concept of equality, moreover, Dworkin also ends up shaving off a second valuable feature of the concept of liberty: that it enables those on the losing side of a rightful political decision to make claims in liberty that those on the winning side can acknowledge as reasonable even when they are not backed by rights.

On this needs-based reconstruction of Williams's argument, there are therefore two reasons to prefer a conception of liberty along the lines Williams advocates over Dworkin's tidier conception. First, to serve the concern for freedom in the political sphere, those on the losing side of a rightful political

---

[13] Note that Williams's point is not that Dworkin's preferred conception of liberty is inadequate because it fails to serve the *concern for liberty*. Since the concern for liberty is focused by the concept of liberty, arguing for a particular understanding of the concept of liberty based on the concern for liberty would be circular, a form of self-validation that precisely fails to leverage any common ground with those who, like Dworkin, favour a different conception of liberty. Williams agrees that—in Dworkin's phrase—'part of politics consists in arguing about' (2001b, 255) what precisely political concepts like liberty and equality amount to, and hence what the concern for liberty and the concern for equality should be concerns *for*. Yet Williams accommodates this fact better than Dworkin does, because he argues *from* that fact *to* a certain conception of liberty.

decision need a conception capable of acting as the political sharp end of the concern for primitive freedom, enabling them to express and promote that concern, or else to demand compensation for the frustration of that concern. This calls for a conception of liberty under which the reasons grounding claims in liberty are not exhausted by one's rights, but allow for reasonable complaints in liberty grounded in the residual losses in liberty one has incurred as a result of rightful state action. And once we are conceptually sensitive to the residual losses produced by conflicting political values, we shall also be better equipped to understand how these residual losses can be important engines of political change.[14]

Second, those on the winning side need a conception that equips them to make sense of, and acknowledge the costs in liberty incurred by, those on the losing side if they are to secure losers' consent, cultivate healthy relations of fellow citizenship, and foster respect across the aisle. This need can also only be met if the conception of liberty does not limit reasonable claims in liberty to those that can be grounded in rights. For both of these reasons, the conception of liberty we need cannot be one that is immunized against conflict in the way Dworkin proposes. By attending to the concerns to which the concepts of liberty and equality should be responsive, we thus recognize that the concepts carry the 'permanent possibility of conflict' because that possibility is 'implicit in the structure of these concepts as values' (Williams 2001a, 95). These values *need* to carry the permanent possibility of conflict if they are to serve the concerns that animate their use. That is why the pursuit of conceptual integrity in this particular case is not merely a lost cause, but an ill-advised one. However tentative the spirit in which Dworkin strives for conceptual integrity, he must in the end be nurturing an illusory hope in entertaining the prospect that our political lives could be shielded from tragic conflicts of values.

For the needs-based approach to conceptual authority, the broader lesson is that even a highly conflictual pluralism of concerns need not be fatal to the prospects of uniformly shared reasons for concept use. Williams's argument draws uniformly shared reasons for concept use out of the observation that politics must contend with differences and conflicts of concerns. Under circumstances of liberal democratic pluralism, only a conception of liberty that is more elastic than the conception of liberty as rightful freedom will allow us

---

[14] I am grateful to Jane Manners for helping me see this last point, which is connected to the idea we encountered in Chapter 4, that recognizing the inherent tensions between our concepts helps us understand our outlook as an inherently dynamic structure whose change over time is at least partly endogenous and reason-driven, and not just a brute imposition from outside.

to understand and respect our political opponents when, in response to some measure enacted because they lost at the ballot box, they insist that they incurred a loss in liberty. The very fact that people's concerns are at variance can therefore itself give us certain reasons for concept use.

10.6 Placing the Demand for Theoretical Virtues

If our concerns are such that we sometimes need incongruent and tension-ridden concepts, however, then they might presumably also be such that we sometimes need tidy and congruent concepts. In other words: if we only manage to properly *place* the demand for theoretical virtues within some need matrix in which it answers to genuine conceptual needs, that pursuit will to that extent be vindicated even on the needs-based approach. The purpose of this final section is to indicate how the needs-based approach can accommodate the Dworkinian intuition about the value of tidy-mindedness in politics.

Once we buy into the idea that tidy-mindedness must be answerable to a *need for* tidiness, the question 'Should we tidy up our conceptual repertoire?' assumes a markedly different shape. It no longer looks like a binary yes-or-no question, because we can have *more* or *less* of a need for tidy, theoretically virtuous concepts; and it no longer appears to be answerable in the absolute, because the extent to which we have a need for tidy concepts can only be determined in relation to a concrete practical context in which the need arises out of a combination of concerns, capacities, and circumstances. Even if it can be shown that tidy-mindedness answers to a real need, therefore, it does not follow that there always is such a need. Rather, the need for theoretically virtuous concepts will be *scalable* and *context-sensitive*—a need that grows out of, and varies with, concept-users' practical situations.[15]

In fact, even Williams, though often regarded as an arch-critic of theory-building in ethics, grants that once we reflect on when and why people might experience a need for more systematic concepts, a legitimate place *can* be found for the aspiration to reduce conceptual conflict by tidying up thought:

---

[15] I draw here on an article I co-authored with Damian Cueni on the practical pressures that give rise to the demand to explicate values in terms of stateable principles, to make them consistent by using some of them to overturn others in systematic ways, and to render them as far as possible discursively justifiable; see Cueni and Queloz (2021). I am also indebted to Cueni's (2024b) account of how Dworkin's position is more charitably construed as reflecting a pressure on the judiciary to speak with one voice.

If...conflict is not a logical affliction of our thought, it must be a mistake to regard a need to eliminate conflict as a purely rational demand.... Rather we should see such needs as there are to reduce conflict and to rationalise our moral thought as having a more social and personal basis. In particular, in a modern complex society functions which are ethically significant are performed by public agencies and, if the society is relatively open, this requires that they be governed by an explicable order which allows those agencies to be answerable. (1981a, 81)

The key idea hinted at here is that tidy-mindedness answers to a need *to hold public agencies accountable.* Williams never quite spells out this line of thought, but by piecing together various remarks and elaborating them into a continuous line of argument, we can narrow the chasm between him and Dworkin and illustrate how the needs-based approach accommodates the Dworkinian aspiration to tidy up thought.

In particular, if that aspiration is understood not as reflecting a categorical demand inherent in rationality itself, but as having a more social basis in the conceptual needs of people in positions of public authority in modern liberal democracies, we may yet be able to find a place for a certain degree of tidy-mindedness in social affairs.

To see how the need to tidy up thought might arise even outside scientific contexts, start with conflicts between people rather than concepts. Whatever exactly their concerns are directed to, people will come into conflict with each other as they seek to meet those concerns: the exercise of one person's primitive freedom is bound eventually to get in the way of other people's exercise of their primitive freedom. Such restrictions on one's freedom by other intentional agents are especially prone to breed resentment, much more so than restrictions by the blind forces of nature: people will stoically accept being locked in a hut by a blizzard, yet grow deeply resentful if locked in by someone else, even though the degree of restriction on one's freedom is the same—as Rousseau notes, we 'endure patiently the necessity of things but not the ill will of others' (1979, 91).[16] To prevent the antisocial sentiment of resentment from dissolving social relations, some sort of impartial or public authority is needed that can resolve these conflicts, determining the priority of conflicting parties' concerns and how far these are to be met.

To be effective, however, that impartial or public authority will need the power to enforce its decisions, and whenever this power to enforce is used

---

[16] See Geuss (2001, 104–5).

coercively, that coercion again risks arousing resentment. Coercion by purely arbitrary assertions of will—even if it is the will of an impartial authority—is still just as much coercion as coercion by other parties. To avoid recreating, at a different level, the very problem of coercion-induced resentment that it was meant to solve, 'the authority needs to *have* authority' (2005c, 94), as Williams puts it: the people on whom the decisions are enforced need to be able to see how this exercise of power differs from sheer coercion by arbitrary assertions of will. To this end, they need some basis on which to distinguish between might and right, in particular by being able to make sense of this exercise of power *as authoritative*. It is the authority of impartial conflict resolvers that ultimately distinguishes their decisions from coercion and allows them to quell rather than breed resentment.

If we now consider how this highly general and underdetermined schema has been elaborated in the modern world, the most significant fact, as Williams points out with a nod to Max Weber's distinction between rational-legal, traditional, and charismatic authority, is that the modern state is 'a formation in which authority is peculiarly vested in discursive argument, rather than in traditional or charismatic leadership' (1996a, 33).[17] This partly reflects the fact that many of the traditional stories that formerly enabled societies to make sense of decision-making as authoritative—stories about divine right, revealed knowledge, or natural hierarchies, for example—no longer carry enough conviction in the modern world; and it partly reflects the sheer size of modern societies, which makes it much harder for personal trust in public decision-makers to be sustained on the required scale: insofar as one is personally acquainted with a public decision-maker, one might trust them not to decide arbitrarily, which would leave them free to resolve conflicts by exercising their judgement and drawing on whatever concepts have force with them, much as people do in their private deliberation. In large-scale societies, however, not everyone can be personally acquainted with every public decision-maker,[18] and those subject to the decisions will consequently want to be able to *ascertain* that the decision-making was an exercise of reasonable judgement rather than an arbitrary assertion of will.

---

[17] Weber (2019, 338–78) distinguishes three *Idealtypen* or pure types of authoritative rule or leadership which in reality are often combined in varying proportions: the rational (or rational-legal) type derives its authority from formal rules and a legally formulated impersonal order; the traditional type derives it from the sanctity of established traditions and customs; and the charismatic type derives it from the special personal qualities or powers of a leader. On Weber's influence on post-World War II Oxford, see Finnis (1985).

[18] On the first point, see Williams (2003, 117–18; 2005c, 95–6; 2009, 200–1); on the second, see Cueni and Queloz (2021).

In large modern societies, and especially in liberal democracies, the concern for primitive freedom thus gives rise to a need to hold public decision-makers to account by *demanding discursive justifications* for their decisions (as opposed to simply trusting them to make the right decisions). Yet this alone still provides little check on arbitrariness if today's declared justifications are permitted to be entirely inconsistent with yesterday's. This helps explain why 'there is a demand of rational consistency and principle in public positions' (Williams 2006h, 164). Non-arbitrariness requires some degree of *systematicity over time*.

In their private deliberation, individuals may be allowed to rely on intuitive and particularized judgement that draw on conflicting concepts and adjudicate conflicts on a case-by-case basis, without explicitly formulating general principles by which to justify each decision. And as long as personal charisma or the effects of tradition ensure that public decision-makers are simply trusted to make non-arbitrary decision, they might get away with similarly untidy modes of thought.

But once those subject to such public power demand accountability, the demand for accountability will drive public decision-making away from this intuitive and unsystematic condition. To be *verifiably* non-arbitrary, decision-making needs to be discursively justified by explicitly stateable general principles, which moreover need to exhibit some degree of systematicity over time, because they need to be consistent and cohere with a series of past decisions and their discursive justifications. Intuitive and unsystematic judgements whose authority rests on personal charisma or tradition thus come under pressure to become verifiably non-arbitrary by assuming a more systematic form.

The demand to give reasons for reasons holds an important place in these dynamics, since one way in which public decision-making will need to be answerable to the public is by having something to say about why the currencies of reasons that guide public decision-making should be accepted—why these reasons should *count as* reasons. As Williams observes, 'some distinction, not further reasoned, can ground agreement in private and less impersonal connections, but may not serve, or may not continue to serve, where a public order demands a public answer' (1981a, 81). So long as public confidence in a concept articulating a currency of reasons is sufficiently strong and communally shared, the use of the concept and its correlative reasons need not be vindicated by a further reason. The reasons *in* concept use are felt to be so convincing that no reasons *for* concept use are required.

But the larger and the more pluralistic societies become, the less it can be taken for granted that such confidence—especially confidence in highly variable thick normative concepts—will be broadly shared. In particular, an increase in society's size and pluralism is likely to bring two developments in its wake.

On the one hand, it is likely to entrain an increasing need for *further rationalization* of the discursive justifications offered: the fewer the concepts that can be assumed to be shared between those doing the justifying and those to whom the justifications are addressed, the more it will be felt that the concepts at work in the justifications are themselves in need of reasons bolstering their authority. That is one important way in which the authority question comes to play a role in modern life. Public decision-making is subjected to a demand for further rationalization that private deliberation is not subjected to in the same way.

On the other hand, greater pluralism encourages a *shift from thicker to thinner* concepts in public discourse: just because thick concepts are richly expressive of a certain social and evaluative perspective, they are only forceful as long as that perspective is shared between justifiers and their addressees, and the greater the variety of perspectives that a society harbours, the more the stock of unquestioningly shared thick concepts shrinks.

Of course, the need for further rationalization does not strictly *entail* a shift from thick to thin—a highly homogeneous community might conceivably share a large stock of thick concepts that allowed that need to be met by drawing on further thick concepts. In a less homogeneous society, however, the need for the further rationalization of discursive justifications *also* drives the thinning of thought.

In particular, the shift to thinner concepts becomes inevitable in public contexts whenever these are the only concepts that all addressees can be expected to live by. There is then a conceptual need for public justifications to abstract away from the peculiarities of distinctive perspectives and draw on thinner concepts, arrived at through reflection on what remains common across different perspectives articulated in terms of different thick concepts.[19] Under the pressure to offer widely intelligible justifications, public decision-makers are driven to retreat from the more parochial components of their conceptual apparatus and fall back on concepts that are more widely shared among their addressees, for instance because they are more formal or

---

[19] On the process of abstraction by which one arrives at thin concepts, see Williams (1985, 162) and Grönert (2016).

procedural concepts. In some cases, such a retreat to more widely shared concepts may even have the added benefit of contributing to shaking off prejudices and biases encoded in certain parochial thick concepts; but there is no guarantee that it will do so—there are notoriously many ways in which such biases can be recreated even within thinner, less manifestly prejudiced frameworks.[20]

Such retreats to more widely shared concepts under pressure to justify one's judgements to a wider audience are familiar also from situations in which professionals need to justify their judgements to an audience of non-professionals. For example, a radiologist looking at a CT scan can distinguish the radiological features of brittle bone disease from the radiological features of child abuse by deploying concepts that are the preserve of specialists; but when pressed to justify her judgement in terms that make sense to non-specialists, she will retreat to concepts that are more widely shared, such as *line, angle, thinning,* or *mosaic pattern.*

Thus, within the needs-based framework, the conceptual need for discursive justifications to be further rationalized in terms of reasons articulated in thinner terms can be seen not as a 'demand of pure rationality', but rather as a need growing out of 'a certain kind of public order' (Williams 1981a, 81). It grows out of the concern to honour a certain ideal of public life in liberal democracies, an ideal that 'requires in principle every decision to be based on grounds that can be discursively explained' (Williams 1985, 20). If public agencies are to be answerable to the *demos,* their decision-making needs to be governed by an explicitly justifiable order that makes sense from a plurality of perspectives.

This need paradigmatically applies to the state's communication with its subjects, but it is not confined to it. It applies equally to public commissions, ethics committees, and public-facing decision-making bodies in private institutions, including hospitals and universities. This reflects another characteristic development of modernity, namely that 'the extent of the public is growing', as Williams puts it: issues of ethical and political significance are increasingly 'governed by regulations that are publicly declared and debated' (2005g, 45). Difficult decisions that used to be left to the judgement of private individuals—think of doctors, who, especially before the rise of the modern hospital, visited patients in their homes, and made whatever hard calls they had to make by themselves, *in foro interno,* or at least within the privacy of those homes—are increasingly being taken within more institutionalized

---

[20] See Cueni and Queloz (2022) for a discussion of various examples.

settings of public concern, and shouldered by decision-making bodies such as hospital ethics committees. As a result, these formerly private decisions are increasingly subjected to the demand for currencies of reasons that facilitate discursive justification in terms that make sense from a plurality of perspectives. And the same demand applies, at a second-order level, to the increasing number of bodies tasked to regulate how such decisions are taken.[21]

These developments affect both the way in which socially significant issues are addressed and our conception of what counts as a rational way of addressing them. When thorny issues are settled through silent personal deliberation on a case-by-case basis, there is a great deal less pressure to think in explicit, determinate, principled, consistent, generally applicable, and widely shared terms than when such issues are adjudicated through formalized committee meetings and public regulations. That is not to say that silent personal deliberation is devoid of any pressure in that direction: there is likely to be a demand for a modest degree of systematization even there.[22] But there is certainly a great deal more pressure to tidy up thought in public deliberation. It is, above all, the conceptual needs of high-quality, widely accessible, transparent, and accountable public deliberation that require the implicit to be made explicit, the vague determinate, the unprincipled principled, the inconsistent consistent, and the parochial general.[23] If the extent of 'the public' is growing, therefore, then so is the pressure on practical thought to approximate a tidy system.

But just how much like a tidy system does thought need to become, on this view? If we understand the demand to systematize—i.e. to rearticulate thought in more theoretically virtuous terms—not, in the first instance, as an unconditional and universal dictate of rationality itself, but as a conceptual need growing out of a concern to render public decision-making accountable, this transforms the binary question 'To systematize or not to systematize?' into a question whose answer will vary, both from one context to another and with regard to the degree of systematization required. Conceptual needs are not standing imperatives that apply regardless of context. Nor are they

---

[21] See the valuable discussion of this development in Harcourt (manuscript), who connects it to reflections by Williams (2005g) and to a discussion on 'the administered world' between Theodor Adorno, Max Horkheimer, and Eugen Kogon (1989).

[22] Attention to the distinctive conceptual needs to which different forms of thought are answerable should thus not make us too quick to follow radical particularists like Jonathan Dancy (2004, 2017) in excising principles from personal deliberation; see Heney (2016, 134–8) for a critique of Dancy along these lines.

[23] Some of the pressures in this direction are emphasized by O'Neill (1987), Page (1996), Zacka (2017), and Prescott-Couch (2021).

binary: they are not simply flicked on or off depending on whether their needfulness conditions are satisfied. They must be thought of in more dynamic terms, as functions of needfulness conditions that are fulfilled to varying degrees in different contexts. In short, conceptual needs are context-sensitive and scalable.

Accordingly, we can derive a *dynamic* understanding of the need to systematize thought from what we might call a *parametric* need matrix that presents the resultant need as a function of the following three parameters *within* its needfulness conditions:[24]

Three Parameters of the Need to Systematize Thought:
[Who] needs to give reasons for [what] in terms that must make sense to [whom]?

The first parameter concerns *who* is subject to the need: is it everyone capable of practical reason, for instance, or merely people in positions of public authority? The second parameter concerns *what* those subject to the need must be able to give reasons for. Do they have to justify any conceivable case in a manner consistent with any other conceivable case, or only the cases that actually arise within a certain society in a manner consistent with the past cases that actually arose in that society? The third parameter concerns *to whom* the discursively articulated reasons for the decisions are addressed and need to be intelligible. Do these reasons have to make sense to anyone capable of practical reason, or can they draw on the shared conceptual resources and concerns of a more local constituency? Of course, the reasons must make sense of the decision to those addressees not just in the minimal sense of rendering it *humanly intelligible*, but in the normative sense of presenting it as *authoritative* for them. Protection rackets *make sense* to us in that they are humanly intelligible. But they do not make sense *as examples of authoritative order*.[25]

In light of this parametric need matrix, the applicability, scope, and strength of the need to systematize can be seen to vary with the values of these three parameters. Consider what form that need would take if all three parameters were dialled up to their maximum. This would mean that *everyone* capable of practical reason would need to be able to decide and justify

---

[24] In this and the following four paragraphs, I elaborate on a line of thought presented in Cueni and Queloz (2021).
[25] This distinction is central to Williams's conception of legitimacy; see Williams (2005i, 10–11).

any conceivable case in a manner consistent with *every other conceivable case*, and in terms that made sense *to anyone* capable of practical reason. The need for systematicity would then be ubiquitous. It would also take an extremely demanding form, pushing concepts-users all the way to a highly systematic and thinned out conceptual framework, for only a highly systematic framework could yield reasons applicable to and consistent with any conceivable case. Moreover, nothing short of highly general considerations and principles articulated in terms of very thin concepts would do, since any more thickly perspectival considerations would be disqualified by the fact that their authority would be too contingent and counterfactually fragile to yield justifications making sense to anyone capable of practical reason. We can perhaps recognize, in this demand that everyone be able to decide and justify any case in terms that make sense to anyone, something of the universalist spirit that animates theories such as Kantianism and utilitarianism.

If we understand the need for systematicity as growing out of a concern to render public decision-making bodies accountable to those whom the decisions affect, by contrast, this suggests a more specific way to set the three parameters. It suggests, first, that those who need to systematize are *people in positions of public authority*; second, that what they need to be able to decide and justify are *the cases that actually arise within that particular society*, and then only in a manner consistent with *past cases that actually arose in that society*; and third, that the decisions need to be justified in terms that have to make sense *to the members of the society at the time*.

If the three parameters are set this way, the need for systematicity mainly arises in the context of public administration or public agencies, and then only in a less demanding form. As a result of keeping both the justifications' scope of application and the circle of their addressees narrowly concrete, less systematization is required, and thicker conceptual resources are available: a justification applicable to as many cases as necessary but as few as possible can remain thicker and more particularized than one that is applicable to any conceivable case; and even within a highly pluralistic society, there is still far more shared confidence in concepts that can provide common currencies for reason-giving than there would be between beings who shared nothing but the faculty of practical reason.

By Dworkin's lights, the prime example of a public decision-making body dedicated to resolving fundamental conflicts of values by discursively setting them out and debating them 'as issues of principle' (Dworkin 1985, 70) is the US Supreme Court. And indeed, the systematizing pursuit of theoretical virtues undeniably has a place here, as Damian Cueni (2024b) shows by explaining Dworkin's advocacy of 'justice for hedgehogs' (2011) in terms of the pressures on the judiciary to speak with one voice.

Yet even the US Supreme Court is not subjected to the need to systematize in a maximally strong form.[26] It only addresses cases that actually arise within US jurisdiction, raise issues of constitutional interpretation, and pass various procedural hurdles; it aims to justify its decisions in terms that cover only as many cases as necessary; and since its discursive justifications are addressed to the citizens of a concrete political community, even the Supreme Court can rely on some measure of contingent agreement among them, even if it is only what Cass Sunstein calls *incompletely theorized agreement*—agreement on the value of some grand abstraction without agreement on how exactly it should be specified or realized, for example, or agreement on what the upshot or outcome should be without agreement on the reasons why it should be the upshot or outcome.[27] Well-functioning legal systems in pluralistic societies tend to exploit such incompletely theorized agreements among citizens by exercising *judicial minimalism*, preferring to articulate their decisions in terms of concepts that are, in Sunstein's terminology, 'shallow rather than deep, and narrow rather than wide' (1996, xii): concepts that skirt around the deeper and more contested theoretical issues and decide the case at hand in a way that predetermines or constrains as few other decisions as possible.[28] As Sunstein shows in *One Case at a Time: Judicial Minimalism on the Supreme Court* (2001), there are many merits to the judicial disposition to keep rulings shallow and narrow instead of digging down to first principles with ramifications for a broad range of cases.

While public decision-making bodies like the Supreme Court do need to resolve fundamental conflicts between value concepts and justify their decisions in terms of explicitly stateable and consistent principles, therefore, that need does not drive them all the way to fully systematized conceptual edifices by which they can adjudicate everything from first principles. They only need to resolve certain conceptual tensions rather than all of them; they only need to resolve them on a case-by-case basis rather than once and for all; they do not need to fall back on universally authoritative concepts, but are free to draw on the local and thick conceptual resources that command allegiance in that jurisdiction at the time; and they need to systematize them only a little, in a way that falls far short of yielding a neatly axiomatized theory.

---

[26] See Cueni and Queloz (2021).   [27] See Sunstein (1996, xi–xii, 35–60).
[28] On judicial minimalism and the contrasts between shallowness and depth on the one hand and narrowness and width on the other, see Sunstein (1996, xii, 44–5, 114–15; 2001).

Nevertheless, this needs-based approach to systematization goes some way towards accommodating the Dworkinian intuition that the values of liberty and equality need to be reconciled. Some people, some of the time, really do need to resolve conflicts of liberty and equality in principled and moderately systematic fashion. When an instance of such a conflict comes before a court, the judge must look for a way to resolve the tension, to systematize the considerations involved, and to discursively justify the decision reached. Hence the allure of picturing the law as a 'seamless web', as one nineteenth-century legal historian famously put it.[29] Even on the needs-based approach, therefore, we are led to acknowledge that when a judge faces a conflict between liberty and equality, the Dworkinian aspiration to resolve the conflict by coming as close as possible to reconciling the two concepts is grounded in a real need.

At the same time, there is a price to be paid for systematizing thought. That is why we should remain mindful of the difference between resolving a tension between two concepts in a particular case and resolving it once and for all, by immunizing our conceptualizations of the relevant values against conflict. Even if our concerns sometimes give rise to the need to systematize thought to some degree, this need must still be balanced against competing needs arising from countervailing concerns—it will not simply override or silence them. The systematization of thought may therefore come at a price even when it serves some of our concerns. And it certainly comes at the expense of the satisfaction of other concerns when it is pursued beyond need.

The fundamental reason for this is that there is an inevitable trade-off between the systematization of thought and the cultivation of its density, texture, and richness. An outlook that is maximally regimented by the requirements of systematicity and realizes a slew of theoretical virtues is not just a particular outlook, but a particularly trimmed and pared-down one. Some degree of systematization may be a practical requirement on public agencies in pluralistic and liberal democratic societies; but extending these demands on administrative forms of reasoning to personal deliberation threatens to flatten and impoverish personal deliberation and experience.

In particular, there is a danger of what C. Thi Nguyen calls *value capture*, where thinner, simpler, more widely accessible, and more aggregable conceptions of value end up displacing thicker, richer, subtler, and more local

---

[29] See Maitland (1898, 13), who primarily applied the image to history, though in a way that implied a similar interconnectedness in the law. Dworkin himself applies the image to the law, though he claims not that the law *is* a seamless web, but that the ideal judge should treat it *as if* it were; see Dworkin (1977, 115–16).

conceptions of value.[30] The simplified conceptualizations may be seductively clear and better tailored to the needs of public administration; but just because of this, they are likely to be less well tailored to the needs of individuals and their private deliberation. And if the thinned-out conceptions tailored to public discourse encroach sufficiently on personal deliberation, individuals risk losing touch with the more complex conceptions of value that sustain their ethical lives—and whose importance in those lives motivated their incorporation into public discourse in the first place.

The worry here is not just that value capture would involve an epistemic loss in the diversity and richness of thought; it is also an ethical worry: that these thinned-out conceptions of value cannot provide enough substance to sustain a worthwhile kind of life.[31] As Williams articulates the point, 'it is precisely the use of "thick" ethical concepts...that contributes to a more substantive type of personal ethical experience' (2005g, 48–9). What he calls the 'intuitive condition', in which we live by a motley of thick concepts that are in various respects vague, indeterminate, or practically incongruent:

> is not only a state which private understanding *can* live with, but a state which it must have as part of its life, if that life is going to have any density or conviction and succeed in being that worthwhile kind of life which human beings lack unless they feel more than they can say, and grasp more than they can explain. (Williams 1981a, 82)

If systematization comes at a cost to the conceptual diversity that gives experience its substance, we should be hesitant to subject all our thought to the systematizing pursuit of theoretical virtues. Bringing the full kaleidoscopic jumble of our concepts to bear on our experience is part of what gives it its multi-layered density and richness.

It also facilitates a form of comprehensiveness—even, as Nietzsche observes, a form of objectivity, because there is a kind of objectivity that does precisely not consist in throwing off whatever is distinctive and parochial about one's perspective until one anaemically inhabits a view from nowhere, but consists, rather, in taking up and being informed by as many different perspectives on a matter as possible: '*the more feelings* we allow to come to expression on a matter, *the more* eyes, different eyes, we can use to view the

---

[30] See Nguyen (2020, 200–3).
[31] See also Cueni and Queloz (2021) and Harcourt (manuscript).

same matter, the more complete will our "concept" of this matter, our "objectivity" be' (1998, III, §12).

Even so, simply rejecting the demand for systematization is, as we saw, no longer an option. The bind we are in is that we are subject to conceptual needs that pull in different directions: we need public thought to take one form, personal thought to take another, and the encroachment of either style of thought on the other entrains a kind of loss.[32]

Once this is recognized, the rationalistic conception of rationality on which rationality inherently requires systematization can itself be recognized as such an encroachment. The conception is encouraged by importing into personal deliberation a demand that has its proper place in public deliberation: the rise of ethics committees, commissions, and panels is not the faithful institutionalization of an antecedent ideal of rationality, but rather what fosters this ideal in the first place. Hence, as Williams notes in an echo of Nietzsche, it is a reversal of cause and effect to view the increasing delegation of decisions of intimate significance to hospital ethics committees and comparable institutional bodies as 'the fulfilment of an Enlightenment dream, the regulation of ultimate questions by the institutional embodiment of systematic ethical reason' (2005g, 46).[33] In reality, it is the conception of practical reason that is being shaped by liberal democratic requirements on public administration, not the other way round.

To recapitulate: modernity combines the growth of public decision-making with the concern that public decision-making be verifiably based on good reasons. This engenders the need for decisions to be discursively justified in principled and consistent terms that are authoritative for those to whom the decision-makers are answerable. But under conditions of pluralism, those addressees differ widely in their thicker, more substantive concepts. As a result, there is a need for public reasoning to take a more systematic and discursively justifiable form than personal reasoning, and to be articulated in thinner terms. This serves the concern to hold public decision-makers accountable. But to the extent that this ideal of public reasoning also influences people's conception of rationality in personal reasoning, it risks

---

[32] Hegelian theorists of 'the virtuous republic' offer examples of attempts to model public administrative reasoning on personal virtue ethics, while direct utilitarianism exemplifies the opposite tendency to model personal on administrative reasoning (Williams 2005g, 50). Harcourt (manuscript), drawing on Adorno, illuminatingly explores some further ways in which administrative reasoning encroaches on personal life as its metrics and standards are internalized by private individuals; and so, coming from a different direction, does Nguyen (2020).

[33] As Williams acknowledges, this is a prime example of what Nietzsche described as one of the four great errors, the '*error of confusing cause and effect*' (2005c, Errors, §1).

entraining a loss of substance in personal thought. The systematization of practical reasoning that has a rightful place in public contexts threatens, when needlessly generalized beyond its proper remit, the conceptual variety and richness that is an essential component of the variety and richness of experience itself.

On the needs-based approach, the way out of this distinctively modern bind, where we face diverging demands in the personal and public sphere, lies in recognizing that we have different conceptual needs in different domains. The most helpful conceptual apparatus is likely to be a *patchwork* of thicker and thinner concepts, of more socio-culturally distinctive and more widely shared concepts.[34]

Given such a conceptual patchwork view, it would be a mistake to think that we first need to choose, say, between the thick concepts of virtues and vices favoured by ancient ethics, the thin deontological concepts favoured by Kantianism, and the equally thin consequentialist notions favoured by utilitarianism; and that once we have chosen one set of concepts, we should deploy that one set, and only that one set, across the board, to govern our personal lives as well as our public and institutional discourse.

There are different practical pressures acting on the way we think in different contexts, and the concepts that serve us best in our personal lives are not necessarily the same as those that serve us best in positions of public authority. We should not aim to find a single, all-purpose set of concepts that we can apply uniformly across different areas of life. And even where we have reason to systematize and move towards concepts at the thinner end of the spectrum, we should do so only to the extent required by the degree of plurality that actually obtains among those to whom the decision-making is answerable. We should aim to think in terms that are as thin and unified as they must be when they must be, but as thick and varied as they can be when they can be.

The Ethics of Conceptualization: Tailoring Thought and Language to Need. Matthieu Queloz, Oxford University Press.
© Matthieu Queloz 2025. DOI: 10.1093/9780198926283.003.0011

---

[34] I read Williams as envisaging something like such a model when he gestures towards the idea of an 'ethical federation' (2005g, 40). See also Bavister-Gould (2013) and van Domselaar (2020) on this idea of an ethical federation.

Conclusion: Tailoring Thought to Need

Philosophy, then, not only has to attend to the reasons our concepts render us sensitive to. It also has to understand, at a metaconceptual level, *why* our concepts advert to those reasons. Our first-order reasons are only as good as our second-order reasons to be sensitive to just these reasons.

By inviting us to find reasons for concept use in conceptual needs apparent even from the autoethnographic stance, the approach presented in this book gives us a new way of looking at concepts. In coming to perceive the dense array of needs our conceptualizations are enmeshed in, we come to see that we have more reasons than we knew to conceptualize the world along certain lines rather than others. It is not simply a matter of mirroring the world's antecedent structure. Nor is it simply a matter of using whatever concepts transparently further the goals, aims, and purposes we choose to pursue. Conceptual needs are something we can have unwittingly and unwillingly, and their relation to our consciously pursued concerns can be complex and puzzling. One really has to *discover* which concepts are in fact needful and why. Only then can one tailor thought to need.

Considering what concepts we now need proves rewarding on several fronts. It allows us to identify the proper place of efforts to tidy up thought; it helps us to adjudicate between competing conceptions of things, even when they are as contested as voluntariness and liberty; and it more generally puts us in a position to decide which parts of our conceptual repertoire to revise, retain, or reject.

What is more, it does all this while reconciling us to the contingency of our concepts: where our thick normative concepts are concerned, certainly, it makes the urge to wring ourselves and our local peculiarities out of our ways of thinking appear misguided. What is distinctive about us and our situation is, in the first instance, not a distortion to be overcome, but what our conceptualizations are primarily answerable to. Which concepts we use may be causally contingent. But once it is recognized that the needs they must meet are similarly subject to causal contingency, the sense of the rational contingency of our conceptual repertoire can be dispelled and replaced by a sense of its necessity given our needs.

The result is a form of conceptual ethics that is as much about extraconceptual reality as it is about concepts. It does not fall into the trap that the linguistic turn rendered so tempting, of conceiving of every problem as a conceptual problem that can be solved by exchanging the conceptual lens through which we perceive it. The needs-based approach gives us the means to recognize that solving a problem merely at the conceptual level is often not to solve it at all, but only to aggravate it by rendering us conceptually blind to the problem and the costs associated with it. Which concepts we use may often be a crucial aspect of a situation; but it is only one aspect of it, and one that needs to be responsive to the other aspects of the situation. Our conceptualizations are answerable to something outside themselves.

Nor is the idea that our otherwise rationally undetermined choices of concepts are constrained at the edges by 'merely pragmatic' considerations arising from limitations of human nature or contingent features of the world we inhabit. When philosophers have paid any heed to 'pragmatic' considerations at all, they have tended to think of them simply as *constraints* on concept choice: constraints that impose outer limits on what our conceptual scheme could possibly be, but otherwise leave it completely undetermined, so that our choice of concepts is ultimately an arbitrary, if bounded, choice.[1]

Within the framework I have developed, by contrast, the kinds of contingent instrumental considerations that normally get brushed aside and consigned to the leftover category of the 'merely pragmatic' are no longer an afterthought, but figure front and centre, differentiating into a rich set of intellectual resources that include, alongside limitations by human nature and constraints by physical laws, the local concerns we identify with, the distinctive elaborations of our capacities and circumstances, and the conceptual needs that result from their combination in a particular context.

On the resulting view, conceptual needs do not merely constrain our choices of concepts. They can positively inform and guide them. As long as they are merely thought of as constraints, considerations of a practical sort can only ever explain why our concepts never seem to stray beyond certain boundaries. But such constraints could not give us reasons to revise the conceptual repertoire we already have, or to introduce new concepts we currently lack. Thinking of practical considerations as constraints therefore itself constrains our thinking, because it leaves out the most interesting ways

---

[1] See e.g. Hirsch (1993, 115–16) and Forster (2004, 67–81; 2017, 271).

in which practical pressures reflecting our own concerns can rationally determine the proper shape of our conceptual apparatus. The present account fills this blind spot. Practical considerations figure in it not just negatively, as constraints *ruling out* the use of certain concepts, but positively, as reasons *for* concept use.

Becoming sensitive to these reasons, and recognizing the need for them, itself requires using a certain concept, namely the concept of a second-order reason. The great benefit of ascending to the metaconceptual level is that it enables us to raise, from within our practices of reason-giving, the question of whether our reason-giving distinctions can themselves be grounded in reasons. Demanding reasons for reasons transforms the reason relations that govern our reasoning into objects of that reasoning: we treat the recognized patterns of correct reasoning that enable us to reason in the first place as themselves standing in need of reasons. This makes it possible to assess and, where necessary, revise our conceptual architecture from within. The concept of a second-order reason thus itself turns out to be one of the more needful concepts in our repertoire. We need to be able to conceive of second-order reasons in order to critically examine which first-order reasons we should be responsive to.

In making the case that such second-order reasons are to be found in our conceptual needs, I have, in effect, been articulating *third-order* reasons: reasons to *count* conceptual needs *as* second-order reasons to heed certain first-order reasons. In the process, I have also advanced third-order reasons *against* counting the alternative considerations cited by foundationalism, ironism, and holism as second-order reasons: the first, when generalized to cover thick normative concepts, has become incredible; the second results in indiscriminate disengagement from our concepts; and the third results in undiscriminating acceptance of them. To escape this trilemma and find more critical leverage by which to discriminate between concepts that merit confidence and concepts that do not, I have argued that the picture of our conceptual apparatus as something harmonious, largely tensionless, and inherently static must be replaced with a kaleidoscopic picture on which our conceptual apparatus is tension-ridden and dynamic; and that the critical leverage of local needs must be harnessed by recognizing that the contingency of our conceptual repertoire extends also to the needs these concepts must meet.

In the case of the most direct rival to the needs-based approach, the tidy-minded pursuit of conceptual authority through the realization of theoretical virtues, the verdict is more nuanced: there is indeed a place for it, but theoretical virtues are not best understood as being themselves what confers authority on a concept—it is rather that our conceptual needs sometimes render theoretically virtuous concepts needful; but equally, our conceptual needs sometimes call for different kinds of concepts, including concepts that are appropriately vague, superficial, or conflictual.

Ultimately, of course, there is only so much that living by needful concepts can, just by itself, achieve. Once it has been settled *that* a concept is the one we have most reason to use, the question remains *how* it should be used: when that concept should steer one's deliberation and when it should take a backseat, for instance; but also how the concept is to be concretely applied to a particular situation; and how the indeterminate and often conflicting demands that the situation, thus conceptualized, makes on us should be further concretized, weighed against each other, and acted on. The network of reason relations encoded by our concepts is one thing; our actual practice of reasoning is another. We cannot simply rely on the virtues, theoretical or practical, of concepts, but must rely on the virtues *of concept-users*—and that means flesh-and-blood human beings, who, for all the good reasons adverted to by the carefully curated currencies of thought at their disposal, retain a mind of their own.

Downstream of conceptual ethics as the reflection on which concepts we have most reason to use, then, lies conceptual ethics as the reflection on how best to use those concepts. The larger task served by conceptual ethics does not end with the specification of the right concepts, just as the task of building a well-functioning state does not end with the specification of the right laws and regulations. Both open out into wider questions of application and implementation. In the end, conceptual ethics can be but a tributary to the deeper waters of ethics and politics, whose currents are unlikely to be redirected merely by adjusting what concepts we look to.

But even if our conceptualizations cannot—and need not—do all the work, they do a great deal of it, and rather more than they are given credit for. By identifying what concepts best meet our needs, we can help ensure that our ways of thinking do the right kind of work, and do it well. Even when we do not control the currents, we can control which stars we navigate by.

The Ethics of Conceptualization: Tailoring Thought and Language to Need. Matthieu Queloz, Oxford University Press.
© Matthieu Queloz 2025. DOI: 10.1093/9780198926283.003.0012

Bibliography

Abend, Gabriel. 2023. *Words and Distinctions for the Common Good: Practical Reason in the Logic of Social Science.* Princeton: Princeton University Press.
Adamson, Peter. 2022. *Don't Think for Yourself: Authority and Belief in Medieval Philosophy.* Notre Dame: University of Notre Dame Press.
Adorno, Theodor W., Max Horkheimer, and Eugen Kogon. 1989. 'Die verwaltete Welt oder: Die Krisis des Individuums'. In *Max Horkheimer, Gesammelte Schriften Bd. 13: Nachgelassene Schriften 1949-72*, 121-42. Frankfurt am Main: Fischer.
Aeschylus. 1966. *The Oresteia*. Translated by Robert Fagles. London: Penguin.
Alanen, Lilli. 2002. 'Descartes on the Will and the Power to Do Otherwise'. In *Emotions and Choice from Boethius to Descartes*. Edited by Henrik Lagerlund and Mikko Yrjönsuuri, 279-98. Dordrecht: Springer.
Alshanetsky, Eli. 2019. *Articulating a Thought*. Oxford: Oxford University Press.
Altham, J. E. J. 1995. 'Reflection and Confidence'. In *World, Mind, and Ethics: Essays on the Ethical Philosophy of Bernard Williams*. Edited by J. E. J. Altham and Ross Harrison, 156-69. Cambridge: Cambridge University Press.
Alvarez, Maria. 2010. *Kinds of Reasons: An Essay in the Philosophy of Action*. Oxford: Oxford University Press.
Alvarez, Maria, and John Hyman. 2019. 'Philosophy of Action 1945-2015'. In *The Cambridge History of Philosophy, 1945-2015*. Edited by Kelly Becker and Iain D. Thomson, 103-14. Cambridge: Cambridge University Press.
Alznauer, Mark. 2023. 'Untrue Concepts in Hegel's Logic'. *Journal of the History of Philosophy* 61 (1): 103-24.
Anderson, Christopher J., André Blais, Shaun Bowler, Todd Donovan, and Ola Listhaug, eds. 2005. *Losers' Consent: Elections and Democratic Legitimacy*. Oxford: Oxford University Press.
Anderson, Elizabeth. 1995. 'Knowledge, Human Interests, and Objectivity in Feminist Epistemology'. *Philosophical Topics* 23 (2): 27-58.
Anderson, Elizabeth. 2001. 'Unstrapping the Straitjacket of "Preference": A Comment on Amartya Sen's Contributions to Philosophy and Economics'. *Economics and Philosophy* 17 (1): 21-38.
Anderson, Elizabeth. 2004. 'Uses of Value Judgments in Science: A General Argument, with Lessons from a Case Study of Feminist Research on Divorce'. *Hypatia* 19 (1): 1-24.
Anscombe, G. E. M. 2005. 'Action, Intention and "Double Effect"'. In *Faith in a Hard Ground: Essays on Religion, Philosophy and Ethics by G. E. M. Anscombe*. Edited by Mary Geach and Luke Gormally, 207-26. Exeter: Imprint Academic.
Anscombe, G. E. M. 2008a. 'On Being in Good Faith'. In *Faith in a Hard Ground: Essays on Religion, Philosophy and Ethics by G. E. M. Anscombe*. Edited by Mary Geach and Luke Gormally, 101-12. Exeter: Imprint Academic.
Anscombe, G. E. M. 2008b. 'Sin: The McGivney Lectures'. In *Faith in a Hard Ground: Essays on Religion, Philosophy and Ethics by G. E. M. Anscombe*. Edited by Mary Geach and Luke Gormally, 117-56. Exeter: Imprint Academic.
Anscombe, G. E. M. 1957. *Intention*. Oxford: Blackwell.
Appiah, Kwame Anthony. 2010. *The Honor Code: How Moral Revolutions Happen*. New York: W. W. Norton.
Appiah, Kwame Anthony. 2017. *As If: Idealization and Ideals*. Cambridge, MA: Harvard University Press.
Arendt, Hannah. 1956. 'Authority in the Twentieth Century'. *Review of Politics* 18 (4): 403-17.

Arendt, Hannah. 1958. 'What Was Authority?'. *NOMOS: American Society for Political and Legal Philosophy* 1: 81–112.
Arendt, Hannah. 1968. 'Truth and Politics'. In *Between Past and Future: Eight Exercises in Political Thought*, 227–64. New York: Viking.
Asgeirsson, Hrafn. 2015. 'On the Instrumental Value of Vagueness in the Law'. *Ethics* 125 (2): 425–48.
Asgeirsson, Hrafn. 2020. *The Nature and Value of Vagueness in the Law*. Oxford: Hart.
Austin, John. 1885. *Lectures on Jurisprudence: Or, The Philosophy of Positive Law*. Edited by Robert Campbell. 5th ed. London: John Murray.
Austin, John Langshaw. 1961. 'A Plea for Excuses'. In *Philosophical Papers*. Edited by J. O. Urmson and G. J. Warnock, 123–52. Oxford: Clarendon Press.
Austin, John Langshaw. 1962. *Sense and Sensibilia*. Edited by G. J. Warnock. Oxford: Oxford University Press.
Austin, Michael. 2010. *Useful Fictions: Evolution, Anxiety, and the Origins of Literature*. Lincoln: University of Nebraska Press.
Babiotti, Paolo. 2021. 'Compression: Nietzsche, Williams, and the Problem of Style'. *European Journal of Philosophy* 29 (4): 937–47.
Bader, Ralf M. 2015. 'Kantian Axiology and the Dualism of Practical Reason'. In *The Oxford Handbook of Value Theory*. Edited by Iwao Hirose and Jonas Olson, 175–202. Oxford: Oxford University Press.
Baillie, James. 2000. *Hume on Morality*. London: Routledge.
Balkin, Jack M. 1998. *Cultural Software: A Theory of Ideology*. New Haven: Yale University Press.
Ball, Derek. 2020. 'Metasemantic Ethics'. *Ratio* 33 (4): 206–19.
Ball, Terence, James Farr, and Russell L. Hanson, eds. 1989. *Political Innovation and Conceptual Change*. New York: Cambridge University Press.
Barber, Nicholas. 2010. *The Constitutional State*. Oxford: Oxford University Press.
Baron, Marcia. 2003. 'Manipulativeness'. *Proceedings and Addresses of the American Philosophical Association* 77 (2): 37–54.
Bavister-Gould, Alex. 2013. 'Bernard Williams: Political Realism and the Limits of Legitimacy'. *European Journal of Philosophy* 21 (4): 593–610.
Baz, Avner. 2017. *The Crisis of Method in Contemporary Analytic Philosophy*. Oxford: Oxford University Press.
Beaver, David I., Bart Geurts, and Kristie Denlinger. 2021. 'Presupposition'. In *The Stanford Encyclopedia of Philosophy*. Edited by Edward N. Zalta. Spring 2021 ed.
Beebe, James R. 2012. 'Social Functions of Knowledge Attributions'. In *Knowledge Ascriptions*. Edited by Jessica Brown and Mikkel Gerken, 220–42. Oxford: Oxford University Press.
Beisbart, Claus, and Georg Brun. 2024. 'Is There a Defensible Conception of Reflective Equilibrium?'. *Synthese* 203 (79): 1–27.
Benedict, Ruth. 1934. *Patterns of Culture*. New York: Penguin.
Bennett, Jonathan. 1976. *Linguistic Behaviour*. Cambridge: Cambridge University Press.
Bennett, Jonathan. 2008. 'Accountability (II)'. In *Free Will and Reactive Attitudes: Perspectives on P. F. Strawson's 'Freedom and Resentment'*. Edited by Michael McKenna and Paul Russell, 47–68. Farnham: Ashgate.
Bennett, Maxwell R., and Peter M. S. Hacker. 2008. *History of Cognitive Neuroscience*. Oxford: Wiley-Blackwell.
Bentham, Jeremy. 1843. *The Works of Jeremy Bentham*, Vol. 2. Edinburgh: William Tait.
Berlin, Isaiah. 2002a. 'The Birth of Greek Individualism: A Turning-Point in the History of Political Thought'. In *Liberty*. Edited by Henry Hardy, 287–321. Oxford: Oxford University Press.
Berlin, Isaiah. 2002b. 'Two Concepts of Liberty'. In *Liberty*. Edited by Henry Hardy, 166–217. Oxford: Oxford University Press.
Berlin, Isaiah. 2013a. 'The Decline of Utopian Ideas in the West'. In *The Crooked Timber of Humanity: Chapters in the History of Ideas*. Edited by Henry Hardy, 21–50. Princeton: Princeton University Press.

Berlin, Isaiah. 2013b. 'European Unity and Its Vicissitudes'. In *The Crooked Timber of Humanity: Chapters in the History of Ideas*. Edited by Henry Hardy, 186–218. Princeton: Princeton University Press.
Berlin, Isaiah. 2013c. 'My Intellectual Path'. In *The Power of Ideas*. Edited by Henry Hardy. 2nd ed., 1–28. Princeton: Princeton University Press.
Berlin, Isaiah. 2013d. 'The Pursuit of the Ideal'. In *The Crooked Timber of Humanity: Chapters in the History of Ideas*. Edited by Henry Hardy, 1–20. Princeton: Princeton University Press.
Berlin, Isaiah. 2014a. 'Helvétius'. In *Freedom and Its Betrayal: Six Enemies of Human Liberty*. Edited by Henry Hardy, 11–27. Princeton: Princeton University Press.
Berlin, Isaiah. 2014b. 'Politics as a Descriptive Science'. In *Political Ideas in the Romantic Age: Their Rise and Influence on Modern Thought*. Edited by Henry Hardy, 21–111. Princeton: Princeton University Press.
Berlin, Isaiah. 2015. *Affirming: Letters 1975–1997*. Edited by Henry Hardy and Mark Pottle. London: Chatto and Windus.
Berlin, Isaiah, and Bernard Williams. 1994. 'Pluralism and Liberalism: A Reply'. *Political Studies* 42 (2): 306–9.
Bermúdez, José Luis. 2021. *Frame It Again: New Tools for Rational Decision-Making*. New York: Cambridge University Press.
Bernays, Edward. 1969. *The Engineering of Consent*. Norman: University of Oklahoma Press.
Berson, Josh. 2021. *The Human Scaffold: How Not to Design Your Way Out of a Climate Crisis*. Oakland, CA: University of California Press.
Besson, Corinne. 2018. 'Norms, Reasons, and Reasoning: A Guide through Lewis Carroll's Regress Argument'. In *The Oxford Handbook of Reasons and Normativity*. Edited by Daniel Star, 504–28. New York: Oxford University Press.
Besson, Corinne. Forthcoming. *Logic, Reasoning, and Carroll's Regress: A Defense of Logical Cognitivism*. Oxford: Oxford University Press.
Bierson, Marshall, and John Schwenkler. 2022. 'What Is the Bearing of Thinking on Doing?'. In *The Anscombean Mind*. Edited by Adrian Haddock and Rachael Wiseman, 312–32. Abingdon: Routledge.
Binmore, Ken. 2005. *Natural Justice*. New York: Oxford University Press.
Binmore, Ken. 2007. *Playing for Real: A Text on Game Theory*. Oxford: Oxford University Press.
Blackburn, Simon. 1986. 'Making Ends Meet'. *Philosophical Books* 27 (4): 193–203.
Blackburn, Simon. 1993. *Essays in Quasi-Realism*. Oxford: Oxford University Press.
Blackburn, Simon. 1998. *Ruling Passions*. Oxford: Oxford University Press.
Blackburn, Simon. 1999. *Think: A Compelling Introduction to Philosophy*. Oxford: Oxford University Press.
Blackburn, Simon. 2005. 'Success Semantics'. In *Ramsey's Legacy*. Edited by Hallvard Lillehammer and D. H. Mellor, 22–36. Oxford: Oxford University Press.
Blackburn, Simon. 2013a. 'Pragmatism in Philosophy: The Hidden Alternative'. *Philosophic Exchange* 41 (1): 2–13.
Blackburn, Simon. 2013b. 'Pragmatism: All or Some?'. In *Expressivism, Pragmatism and Representationalism*. Edited by Huw Price, 67–84. Cambridge: Cambridge University Press.
Blackburn, Simon. 2017. 'Pragmatism: All or Some or All and Some?'. In *The Practical Turn: Pragmatism in Britain in the Long Twentieth Century*. Edited by Cheryl Misak and Huw Price, 61–74. Oxford: Oxford University Press.
Blackburn, Simon. 2019. 'Lonely in Littlemore: Confidence in Ethics and the Limits of Philosophy'. In *Ethics Beyond the Limits: New Essays on Bernard Williams' Ethics and the Limits of Philosophy*. Edited by Sophie-Grace Chappell and Marcel van Ackeren, 27–36. London: Routledge.
Blome-Tillmann, Michael. 2009. 'Contextualism, Subject-Sensitive Invariantism, and the Interaction of "Knowledge"-Ascriptions with Modal and Temporal Operators*'. *Philosophy and Phenomenological Research* 79 (2): 315–31.
Bloor, David. 1983. *Wittgenstein: A Social Theory of Knowledge*. New York: Columbia University Press.

Bloor, David. 1992. 'Left and Right Wittgensteinians'. In *Science as Practice and Culture*. Edited by Andrew Pickering, 266–82. Chicago: University of Chicago Press.
Bloor, David. 1997. *Wittgenstein, Rules and Institutions*. London: Routledge.
Bloor, David. 2000. 'Wittgenstein as a Conservative Thinker'. In *The Sociology of Philosophical Knowledge*. Edited by Martin Kusch, 1–14. Dordrecht: Springer Netherlands.
Bloor, David. 2004. 'Ludwig Wittgenstein and Edmund Burke'. In *Essays on Wittgenstein and Austrian Philosophy: In Honour of J. C. Nyiri*. Edited by Tamás Demeter, 109–34. Amsterdam: Rodopi.
Boghossian, Paul. 2003. 'Blind Reasoning'. *Proceedings of the Aristotelian Society Supplementary Volume* 77 (1): 225–48.
Bowles, Samuel, and Herbert Gintis. 2011. *A Cooperative Species: Human Reciprocity and Its Evolution*. Princeton: Princeton University Press.
Brandom, Robert. 1994. *Making It Explicit. Reasoning, Representing, and Discursive Commitment*. Cambridge, MA: Harvard University Press.
Brandom, Robert. 2000. *Articulating Reasons*. Cambridge, MA: Harvard University Press.
Brandom, Robert. 2001. 'Reason, Expression, and the Philosophic Enterprise'. In *What Is Philosophy?* Edited by C. P. Ragland and Sarah Heidt, 74–95. New Haven: Yale University Press.
Brandom, Robert. 2002a. *Tales of the Mighty Dead: Historical Essays in the Metaphysics of Intentionality*. Cambridge, MA: Harvard University Press.
Brandom, Robert. 2002b. 'When Philosophy Paints Its Blue on Gray: Irony and the Pragmatist Enlightenment'. *boundary* 29 (2): 1–28.
Brandom, Robert. 2004. 'The Pragmatist Enlightenment (and Its Problematic Semantics)'. *European Journal of Philosophy* 12 (1): 1–16.
Brandom, Robert. 2008. *Between Saying and Doing*. Oxford: Oxford University Press.
Brandom, Robert. 2009. *Reason in Philosophy: Animating Ideas*. Cambridge, MA: Belknap Press.
Brandom, Robert. 2011. 'Vocabularies of Pragmatism: Synthesizing Naturalism and Historicism'. In *Perspectives on Pragmatism: Classical, Recent, and Contemporary*, 116–57. Cambridge, MA: Harvard University Press.
Brandom, Robert. 2013. 'Global Anti-representationalism?'. In *Expressivism, Pragmatism and Representationalism*. Edited by Huw Price, 85–111. Cambridge: Cambridge University Press.
Brandom, Robert. 2014. 'A Hegelian Model of Legal Concept Determination: The Normative Fine Structure of the Judges' Chain Novel'. In *Pragmatism, Law, and Language*. Edited by Graham Hubbs and Douglas Lind, 19–39. New York: Taylor and Francis.
Brandom, Robert. 2015a. 'Den Abgrund reflektieren: Vernunft, Genealogie und die Hermeneutik des Edelmuts'. *West End: Neue Zeitschrift für Sozialforschung* 1: 3–26.
Brandom, Robert. 2015b. *From Empiricism to Expressivism: Brandom Reads Sellars*. Cambridge, MA: Harvard University Press.
Brandom, Robert. 2019a. 'Some Strands of Wittgenstein's Normative Pragmatism, and Some Strains of His Semantic Nihilism'. *Disputatio* 8 (9): 1–29.
Brandom, Robert. 2019b. *A Spirit of Trust: A Reading of Hegel's Phenomenology*. Cambridge, MA: Harvard University Press.
Brandom, Robert. 2021. 'Achieving the Enlightenment'. In *Pragmatism as Anti-Authoritarianism*. Edited by Eduardo Mendieta, vii–xxvi. Cambridge, MA: Belknap Press.
Brigandt, Ingo. 2006. *A Theory of Conceptual Advance: Explaining Conceptual Change in Evolutionary, Molecular, and Evolutionary Developmental Biology*. Doctoral Dissertation, University of Pittsburgh, http://d-scholarship.pitt.edu/8849/.
Brigandt, Ingo. 2010. 'The Epistemic Goal of a Concept: Accounting for the Rationality of Semantic Change and Variation'. *Synthese* 177 (1): 19–40.
Brigandt, Ingo. 2011. 'Natural Kinds and Concepts: A Pragmatist and Methodologically Naturalistic Account'. In *Pragmatism, Science and Naturalism*. Edited by Jonathan Knowles and Henrik Rydenfelt, 171–96. Frankfurt a. M.: Peter Lang.
Brigandt, Ingo. 2012. 'The Dynamics of Scientific Concepts: The Relevance of Epistemic Aims and Values'. In *Scientific Concepts and Investigative Practice*. Edited by Uljana Feest and Friedrich Steinle, 75–103. Berlin: De Gruyter.

Brigandt, Ingo. 2013. 'A Critique of David Chalmers' and Frank Jackson's Account of Concepts'. *ProtoSociology* 30: 63–88.
Brigandt, Ingo, and Esther Rosario. 2020. 'Strategic Conceptual Engineering for Epistemic and Social Aims'. In *Conceptual Engineering and Conceptual Ethics*. Edited by Alexis Burgess, Herman Cappelen, and David Plunkett, 100–24. Oxford: Oxford University Press.
Brown, Thomas. 2012. *Inquiry into the Relation of Cause and Effect*. Cambridge: Cambridge University Press.
Brun, Georg. 2014. 'Reflective Equilibrium without Intuitions?'. *Ethical Theory and Moral Practice* 17 (2): 237–52.
Brun, Georg. 2016. 'Explication as a Method of Conceptual Re-engineering'. *Erkenntnis* 81 (6): 1211–41.
Brun, Georg. 2020. 'Conceptual Re-engineering: From Explication to Reflective Equilibrium'. *Synthese* 197 (3): 925–54.
Brun, Georg. 2022. 'Re-engineering Contested Concepts. A Reflective-Equilibrium Approach'. *Synthese* 200 (2): 1–29.
Buchler, Justus. 1955. *Nature and Judgment*. New York: Columbia University Press.
Burge, Tyler. 1979. 'Individualism and the Mental'. *Midwest Studies in Philosophy* 4 (1): 73–122.
Burgess, Alexis, and David Plunkett. 2013a. 'Conceptual Ethics I'. *Philosophy Compass* 8 (12): 1091–1101.
Burgess, Alexis, and David Plunkett. 2013b. 'Conceptual Ethics II'. *Philosophy Compass* 8 (12): 1102–10.
Burgess, Alexis, and David Plunkett. 2020. 'On the Relation between Conceptual Engineering and Conceptual Ethics'. *Ratio* 33 (4): 281–94.
Buss, Sarah. 2005. 'Valuing Autonomy and Respecting Persons: Manipulation, Seduction, and the Basis of Moral Constraints'. *Ethics* 115 (2): 195–235.
Byron, George Gordon, Lord. 2015. *Manfred: An Edition of Byron's Manuscripts and a Collection of Essays*. Edited by Peter Cochran. Cambridge: Cambridge Scholars Publishing.
Camp, Joseph L. 2004. *Confusion: A Study in the Theory of Knowledge*. Cambridge, MA: Harvard University Press.
Campbell, John Keim, Michael O'Rourke, and Matthew H. Slater, eds. 2011. *Carving Nature at Its Joints: Natural Kinds in Metaphysics and Science*. Cambridge, MA: MIT Press.
Candea, Matei. 2010. *Corsican Fragments: Difference, Knowledge and Fieldwork*. Bloomington: Indiana University Press.
Candlish, Stewart, and Nic Damnjanovic. 2013. 'Reasons, Actions, and the Will: The Fall and Rise of Causalism'. In *The Oxford Handbook of the History of Analytic Philosophy*. Edited by Michael Beaney, 689–708. Oxford: Oxford University Press.
Cappelen, Herman. 2013. 'Nonsense and Illusions of Thought'. *Philosophical Perspectives* 27 (1): 22–50.
Cappelen, Herman. 2018. *Fixing Language: An Essay on Conceptual Engineering*. Oxford: Oxford University Press.
Cappelen, Herman. 2020. 'Conceptual Engineering: The Master Argument'. In *Conceptual Engineering and Conceptual Ethics*. Edited by Alexis Burgess, Herman Cappelen and David Plunkett, 132–51. Oxford: Oxford University Press.
Cappelen, Herman. 2023. *The Concept of Democracy: An Essay on Conceptual Amelioration and Abandonment*. Oxford: Oxford University Press.
Cappelen, Herman, and David Plunkett. 2020. 'Introduction: A Guided Tour of Conceptual Engineering and Conceptual Ethics'. In *Conceptual Engineering and Conceptual Ethics*. Edited by Alexis Burgess, Herman Cappelen, and David Plunkett, 1–26. Oxford: Oxford University Press.
Carey, Susan. 1985. *Conceptual Change in Childhood*. Cambridge, MA: MIT Press.
Cargile, James. 1991. 'Real and Nominal Definitions'. In *Definitions and Definability: Philosophical Perspectives*. Edited by J. H. Fetzer, D. Shatz, and G. N. Schlesinger, 21–50. Dordrecht: Springer.
Carnap, Rudolf. 1947. *Meaning and Necessity: A Study in Semantics and Modal Logic*. Chicago: University of Chicago Press.
Carnap, Rudolf. 1950. *Logical Foundations of Probability*. Chicago: University of Chicago Press.
Carnap, Rudolf. 1952. 'Meaning Postulates'. *Philosophical Studies* 3 (5): 65–73.

Carnap, Rudolf. 1962. *Logical Foundations of Probability*. 2nd ed. Chicago: University of Chicago Press.
Carroll, Lewis. 1895. 'What the Tortoise Said to Achilles'. *Mind* IV (14): 278–80.
Carruthers, Peter. 1987. 'Conceptual Pragmatism'. *Synthese* 73 (2): 205–24.
Carus, André. 2007. *Carnap and Twentieth-Century Thought: Explication as Enlightenment*. Cambridge: Cambridge University Press.
Carus, André W. 2017. 'Carnapian Rationality'. *Synthese* 194 (1): 163–84.
Celikates, Robin. 2015. 'Against Manichaeism: The Politics of Forms of Life and the Possibilities of Critique'. *Raisons politiques* 57 (1): 81–96.
Celikates, Robin. 2018. *Critique as Social Practice: Critical Theory and Social Self-Understanding*. London: Rowman and Littlefield.
Chadha-Sridhar, Ira. 2021. 'The Value of Vagueness: A Feminist Analysis'. *Canadian Journal of Law and Jurisprudence* 34 (1): 59–84.
Chalmers, David J. 2002. 'On Sense and Intension'. *Philosophical Perspectives* 16: 135–82.
Chalmers, David J. 2011. 'Verbal Disputes'. *Philosophical Review* 120 (4): 515–66.
Chanan, Michael. 1972. 'Ep. 3: Appearance and Reality'. In *Logic Lane*. United Kingdom: Chanan Films.
Chang, Hasok. 2004. *Inventing Temperature: Measurement and Scientific Progress*. Oxford: Oxford University Press.
Chang, Ruth, ed. 1997. *Incommensurability, Incomparability, and Practical Reason*. Cambridge, MA: Harvard University Press.
Chang, Ruth. 2002. *Making Comparisons Count*. London: Routledge.
Chang, Ruth. 2009. 'Voluntarist Reasons and the Sources of Normativity'. In *Reasons for Action*. Edited by David Sobel and Steven Wall, 243–71. Cambridge: Cambridge University Press.
Chang, Ruth. 2015. 'Value Incomparability and Incommensurability'. In *The Oxford Handbook of Value Theory*. Edited by Iwao Hirose and Jonas Olson, 205–24. Oxford: Oxford University Press.
Chang, Ruth. 2016. 'Comparativism: The Grounds of Rational Choice'. In *Weighing Reasons*. Edited by Errol Lord and Barry Maguire, 213–40. New York: Oxford University Press.
Chappell, Sophie-Grace, ed. 2015. *Intuition, Theory, and Anti-Theory in Ethics*. Oxford: Oxford University Press.
Chappell, Timothy. 2009. 'Ethics beyond Moral Theory'. *Philosophical Investigations* 32 (3): 206–43.
Chesebro, James W. 1985. 'Definition as a Rhetorical Strategy'. *Pennsylvania State Communication Annual* 45 (1): 5–15.
Chihara, Charles. 1979. 'The Semantic Paradoxes: A Diagnostic Investigation'. *Philosophical Review* 88 (4): 590–618.
Christiano, Tom. 2020. 'Authority'. In *The Stanford Encyclopedia of Philosophy*. Edited by Edward N. Zalta. Summer 2020 ed.
Churchland, Patricia. 1986. *Neurophilosophy*. Cambridge, MA: MIT Press.
Clark, Andy. 2013. *Mindware: An Introduction to the Philosophy of Cognitive Science*. New York: Oxford University Press.
Clark, Maudemarie. 2015. 'On the Rejection of Morality: Bernard Williams's Debt to Nietzsche'. In *Nietzsche on Ethics and Politics*, 41–61. Oxford: Oxford University Press.
Clarke-Doane, Justin. 2020. *Morality and Mathematics*. Oxford: Oxford University Press.
Cohen, Jean L. 2012. *Globalization and Sovereignty: Rethinking Legality, Legitimacy, and Constitutionalism*. Cambridge: Cambridge University Press.
Colton, Russ. 2023. 'To Have a Need'. *Ergo* 10 (13): 373–94.
Congdon, Matthew. 2024. *Moral Articulation: On the Development of New Moral Concepts*. New York: Oxford University Press.
Coons, Christian, and Michael Weber. 2014. *Manipulation: Theory and Practice*. New York: Oxford University Press.
Craig, Edward. 1986. 'The Practical Explication of Knowledge'. *Proceedings of the Aristotelian Society* 87: 211–26.

Craig, Edward. 1990. *Knowledge and the State of Nature: An Essay in Conceptual Synthesis.* Oxford: Clarendon Press.
Craig, Edward. 1993. *Was wir wissen können: pragmatische Untersuchungen zum Wissensbegriff. Wittgenstein-Vorlesungen der Universität Bayreuth.* Edited by Wilhelm Vossenkuhl. Frankfurt am Main: Suhrkamp.
Craig, Edward. 2000. 'Response to Lehrer'. *Philosophy and Phenomenological Research* 60 (3): 655–65.
Crisp, Roger. 2017. 'Moral Luck and Equality of Opportunity'. *Proceedings of the Aristotelian Society Supplementary Volume* 91 (1): 1–20.
Cueni, Damian. 2020. *Public Law Analogies in International Legal Theory.* Doctoral Thesis, Rechtswissenschaftliches Institut, University of Zurich.
Cueni, Damian. 2024a. 'Basic Rights and Costs in Political Value: The Expressive Point of the Two-Step Framework'. *International Journal of Constitutional Law.*
Cueni, Damian. 2024b. 'Constructing Liberty and Equality – Political, Not Juridical'. *Jurisprudence* 15 (3): 341–60.
Cueni, Damian. Manuscript-a. 'The Legal Architecture of Freedom: Reconstructing the Two-Step Framework'.
Cueni, Damian. Manuscript-b. 'Revitalizing the Doctrinal Notion of a Basic Rights Infringement'.
Cueni, Damian, and Matthieu Queloz. 2021. 'Whence the Demand for Ethical Theory?'. *American Philosophical Quarterly* 58 (2): 135–46.
Cueni, Damian, and Matthieu Queloz. 2022. 'Theorizing the Normative Significance of Critical Histories for International Law'. *Journal of the History of International Law* 24 (4): 561–87.
Cullity, Garrett. Forthcoming. 'Williams, Berlin, and the Vindication Problem'. In *Bernard Williams on Philosophy and History.* Edited by Marcel van Ackeren and Matthieu Queloz. Oxford: Oxford University Press.
Cummins, Robert. 1996. *Representations, Targets, Attitudes.* Cambridge, MA: MIT Press.
Dancy, Jonathan. 1995. 'In Defense of Thick Concepts'. *Midwest Studies In Philosophy* 20 (1): 263–79.
Dancy, Jonathan. 2000. *Practical Reality.* Oxford: Oxford University Press.
Dancy, Jonathan. 2003. 'What Do Reasons Do?'. In *Metaethics after Moore.* Edited by Terry Horgan and Mark Timmons, 39–59. Oxford: Oxford University Press.
Dancy, Jonathan. 2004. *Ethics without Principles.* Oxford: Clarendon Press.
Dancy, Jonathan. 2017. 'Moral Particularism'. In *The Stanford Encyclopedia of Philosophy.* Edited by Edward N. Zalta. Winter 2017 ed.
Daniels, Norman. 1979. 'Wide Reflective Equilibrium and Theory Acceptance in Ethics'. *Journal of Philosophy* 76 (5): 256–82.
Daniels, Norman. 1996. *Justice and Justification: Reflective Equilibrium in Theory and Practice.* Cambridge: Cambridge University Press.
Daniels, Norman. 2020. 'Reflective Equilibrium'. In *The Stanford Encyclopedia of Philosophy.* Edited by Edward N. Zalta. Summer 2020 ed.
Darden, Lindley. 2006. *Reasoning in Biological Discoveries: Essays on Mechanisms, Interfield Relations, and Anomaly Resolution.* Cambridge: Cambridge: Cambridge University Press.
Darwall, Stephen. 2006. *The Second-Person Standpoint: Morality, Respect, and Accountability.* Cambridge, MA: Harvard University Press.
Darwall, Stephen. 2010. 'Authority and Reasons: Exclusionary and Second-Personal'. *Ethics* 120 (2): 257–78.
Daston, Lorraine. 2022. *Rules: A Short History of What We Live By.* Princeton: Princeton University Press.
Davidson, Donald. 1980. *Essays on Actions and Events.* Oxford: Clarendon Press, Oxford University Press.
Davidson, Donald. 1990. 'The Structure and Content of Truth'. *Journal of Philosophy* 87 (6): 279–328.
Davidson, Donald. 2001. 'Actions, Reasons, and Causes'. In *Essays on Actions and Events*, 3–20. Oxford: Clarendon Press, Oxford University Press.

De Jaegher, Kris. 2003. 'A Game-Theoretic Rationale for Vagueness'. *Linguistics and Philosophy* 26 (5): 637–59.
De Jaegher, Kris, and Robert van Rooij. 2011. 'Strategic Vagueness, and Appropriate Contexts'. In *Language, Games, and Evolution: Trends in Current Research on Language and Game Theory*. Edited by Anton Benz, Christian Ebert, Gerhard Jäger, and Robert van Rooij, 40–59. Berlin: Springer.
De Mesel, Benjamin. 2021. 'Being and Holding Responsible: Reconciling the Disputants through a Meaning-Based Strawsonian Account'. *Philosophical Studies* 179 (6): 1893–1913.
Deigh, John. 2008. *Emotions, Values, and the Law*. Oxford: Oxford University Press.
Delacroix, Sylvie. 2022. *Habitual Ethics?* Oxford: Hart.
Dennett, Daniel Clement. 1989. *The Intentional Stance*. Cambridge, MA: MIT Press.
Descartes, René. 1996. *Oeuvres de Descartes*. Edited by Charles Adam and Paul Tannery. 11 vols. Paris: Vrin. Cited by volume and page number.
Dewey, John. 1938. *Logic: The Theory of Inquiry*. New York: Henry Holt.
Diamond, Cora. 1988. 'Losing Your Concepts'. *Ethics* 98 (2): 255–77.
Diamond, Cora. 2010. 'Henry James, Moral Philosophers, Moralism'. In *A Companion to the Philosophy of Literature*. Edited by Garry L. Hagberg and Walter Jost, 268–84. Oxford: Blackwell.
Diamond, Cora. 2018a. 'Bernard Williams on the Human Prejudice'. *Philosophical Investigations* 41 (4): 379–98.
Diamond, Cora. 2018b. 'Wittgenstein, Mathematics, and Ethics: Resisting the Attractions of Realism'. In *The Cambridge Companion to Wittgenstein*. Edited by Hans Sluga and David G. Stern. 2nd ed., 209–44. Cambridge: Cambridge University Press.
Diamond, Cora. 2021. 'Suspect Notions and the Concept Police'. In *Cora Diamond on Ethics*. Edited by Maria Balaska, 7–30. New York: Palgrave.
Djordjevic, Charles M. 2021. 'When Clarity and Consistency Conflicts with Empirical Adequacy: Conceptual Engineering, Anthropology, and Evans-Pritchard's Ethnography'. *Synthese* 198 (10): 9611–37.
D'Oro, Giuseppina, and Constantine Sandis, eds. 2013. *Reasons and Causes: Causalism and Anti-Causalism in the Philosophy of Action*. New York: Palgrave Macmillan.
Dorsey, Dale. 2016. *The Limits of Moral Authority*. Oxford: Oxford University Press.
Dover, Daniela. 2024. 'Two Kinds of Curiosity'. *Philosophy and Phenomenological Research* 108 (3): 811–32.
Dretske, Fred. 1981. *Knowledge and the Flow of Information*. Cambridge, MA: MIT Press.
Duff, Anthony. 2004. 'Action, the Act Requirement and Criminal Liability'. In *Agency and Action*. Edited by John Hyman and Helen Steward, 69–103. Cambridge: Cambridge University Press.
Duff, Anthony, and Andrew von Hirsch. 1997. 'Responsibility, Retribution and the Voluntary: A Response to Williams'. *Cambridge Law Journal* 56 (1): 103–13.
Dummett, Michael. 1964. 'Bringing about the Past'. *Philosophical Review* 73 (3): 338–59.
Dummett, Michael. 1973. *Frege: Philosophy of Language*. New York: Harper and Row.
Dummett, Michael. 1996. *The Seas of Language*. Oxford: Clarendon Press.
Dunaway, Billy. 2020. *Reality and Morality*. Oxford: Oxford University Press.
Dutilh Novaes, Catarina. 2020a. 'Carnap meets Foucault: Conceptual Engineering and Genealogical Investigations'. *Inquiry*: 1–27.
Dutilh Novaes, Catarina. 2020b. 'Carnapian Explication and Ameliorative Analysis: A Systematic Comparison'. *Synthese* 197 (3): 1001–34.
Dutilh Novaes, Catarina, and Erich Reck. 2017. 'Carnapian Explication, Formalisms as Cognitive Tools, and the Paradox of Adequate Formalization'. *Synthese* 194 (1): 195–215.
Dworkin, Gerald. 1989. *The Theory and Practice of Autonomy*. Cambridge: Cambridge University Press.
Dworkin, Ronald. 1977. *Taking Rights Seriously*. Cambridge, MA: Harvard University Press.
Dworkin, Ronald. 1985. *A Matter of Principle*. Cambridge, MA: Harvard University Press.
Dworkin, Ronald. 1986. *Law's Empire*. Cambridge, MA: Harvard University Press.

Dworkin, Ronald. 1996. 'Objectivity and Truth: You'd Better Believe it'. *Philosophy & Public Affairs* 25 (2): 87–139.
Dworkin, Ronald. 2000. *Sovereign Virtue: The Theory and Practice of Equality*. Cambridge, MA: Harvard University Press.
Dworkin, Ronald. 2001a. 'Do Liberal Values Conflict?'. In *The Legacy of Isaiah Berlin*. Edited by Mark Lilla, Ronald Dworkin, and Robert Silvers, 73–90. New York: New York Review of Books.
Dworkin, Ronald. 2001b. 'Do Values Conflict: A Hedgehog's Approach'. *Arizona Law Review* 43 (2): 251–60.
Dworkin, Ronald. 2006. *Justice in Robes*. Cambridge, MA: Harvard University Press.
Dworkin, Ronald. 2011. *Justice for Hedgehogs*. Cambridge, MA: Harvard University Press.
Dworkin, Ronald, Bernard Williams, Mark Lilla, Thomas Nagel, Richard Wollheim, Frances Kamm, and Steven Lukes. 2001. 'Pluralism'. In *The Legacy of Isaiah Berlin*. Edited by Mark Lilla, Ronald Dworkin, and Robert Silvers, 121–39. New York: New York Review of Books.
Eberhardt, Jennifer L., Philip Attiba Goff, Valerie J. Purdie, and Paul G. Davies. 2004. 'Seeing Black: Race, Crime, and Visual Processing'. *Journal of Personality and Social Psychology* 87 (6): 876–93.
Eco, Umberto. 1984. *Semiotics and the Philosophy of Language*. Bloomington: Indiana University Press.
Edmonds, David. 2020. *The Murder of Professor Schlick: The Rise and Fall of the Vienna Circle*. Princeton: Princeton University Press.
Egré, Paul, and Cathal O'Madagain. 2019. 'Concept Utility'. *The Journal of Philosophy* 116 (10): 525–54.
Eklund, Matti. 2002. 'Inconsistent Languages'. *Philosophy and Phenomenological Research* 64 (2): 251–75.
Eklund, Matti. 2007. 'Meaning-Constitutivity'. *Inquiry* 50 (6): 559–74.
Eklund, Matti. 2017. *Choosing Normative Concepts*. Oxford: Oxford University Press.
Eklund, Matti. 2019. 'Inconsistency and Replacement'. *Inquiry* 62 (4): 387–402.
Eklund, Matti. 2021. 'Conceptual Engineering in Philosophy'. In *The Routledge Handbook of Social and Political Philosophy of Language*. Edited by Rachel Sterken and Justin Khoo. London: Routledge.
El Kassar, Nadja. 2015. *Towards a Theory of Epistemically Significant Perception: How We Relate to the World*. Berlin: De Gruyter.
Elgin, Catherine Z. 1983. *With Reference to Reference*. Indianapolis: Hackett.
Elgin, Catherine Z. 1996. *Considered Judgment*. Princeton: Princeton University Press.
Elgin, Catherine Z. 2017. *True Enough*. Cambridge, MA: MIT Press.
Eliot, George. 1999. *Daniel Deronda*. Edited by John Rignall. London: Everyman.
Elliott-Graves, Alkistis, and Michael Weisberg. 2014. 'Idealization'. *Philosophy Compass* 9 (3): 176–85.
Emilsson, Anton. Manuscript. 'The Unanswered Question of "Freedom and Resentment"'.
Endicott, Timothy. 2000. *Vagueness in Law*. Oxford: Oxford University Press.
Eschenburg, Theodor. 1976. *Über Autorität*. Frankfurt: Suhrkamp.
Feigl, Herbert. 1981a. 'De Principiis Non Disputandum...? On the Meaning and the Limits of Justification'. In *Inquiries and Provocations: Selected Writings 1929–1974*. Edited by Robert S. Cohen, 237–68. Dordrecht: Springer.
Feigl, Herbert. 1981b. 'Validation and Vindication'. In *Inquiries and Provocations: Selected Writings 1929–1974*. Edited by Robert S. Cohen, 378–92. Dordrecht: Springer.
Finnis, John. 1985. 'On "Positivism" and "Legal Rational Authority"'. *Oxford Journal of Legal Studies* 5 (1): 74–90.
Finocchiaro, Peter. 2023. 'Seek the Joints! Avoid the Gruesome! Fidelity as an Epistemic Value'. *Episteme* 20 (2): 393–409.
Fischer, John Martin, and Mark Ravizza. 1998. *Responsibility and Control: A Theory of Moral Responsibility*. Cambridge: Cambridge University Press.
Fodor, Jerry A. 1998. *Concepts: Where Cognitive Science Went Wrong*. Oxford: Clarendon Press.

Fodor, Jerry A. 2003. *Hume Variations*. Oxford: Clarendon Press.
Fodor, Jerry A. 2004. 'Having Concepts: A Brief Refutation of the Twentieth Century'. *Mind and Language* 19 (1): 29–47.
Forrester, Katrina. 2019. *In the Shadow of Justice: Postwar Liberalism and the Remaking of Political Philosophy*. Princeton: Princeton University Press.
Forster, Michael N. 2004. *Wittgenstein on the Arbitrariness of Grammar*. Princeton: Princeton University Press.
Forster, Michael N. 2017. 'The Autonomy of Grammar'. In *A Companion to Wittgenstein*. Edited by Hans-Johann Glock and John Hyman, 269–77. Oxford: Wiley.
Foucault, Michel. 1994. 'La vérité et les formes juridiques'. In *Dits et Ecrits 1954–1988*. Vol. II (1970–5), 538–646. Paris: Gallimard.
Frankfurt, Harry G. 1984. 'Necessity and Desire'. *Philosophy and Phenomenological Research* 45 (1): 1–13.
Frankfurt, Harry G. 2004. *The Reasons of Love*. Princeton: Princeton University Press.
Franklin-Hall, Laura R. 2015. 'Natural Kinds as Categorical Bottlenecks'. *Philosophical Studies* 172 (4): 925–48.
Fredericks, Rachel. 2018. 'Moral Responsibility for Concepts'. *European Journal of Philosophy* 26 (4): 1381–97.
Fredericks, Rachel. 2020. 'Moral Responsibility for Concepts, Continued: Concepts as Abstract Objects'. *European Journal of Philosophy* 28 (4): 1029–43.
Freund, Michael. 2022. 'What Does a Concept Entail?'. In *Logic in Question: Talks from the Annual Sorbonne Logic Workshop (2011–2019)*. Edited by Jean-Yves Béziau, Jean-Pierre Desclés, Amirouche Moktefi, and Anca Christine Pascu, 337–51. Cham: Springer International Publishing.
Fricker, Miranda. 1998. 'Rational Authority and Social Power: Towards a Truly Social Epistemology'. *Proceedings of the Aristotelian Society* 98 (2): 159–77.
Fricker, Miranda. 2000. 'Confidence and Irony'. In *Morality, Reflection, and Ideology*. Edited by Edward Harcourt, 87–112. Oxford: Oxford University Press.
Fricker, Miranda. 2007. *Epistemic Injustice: Power and the Ethics of Knowing*. Oxford: Oxford University Press.
Fricker, Miranda. 2010a. 'Can There Be Institutional Virtues?'. In *Oxford Studies in Epistemology (Special Theme: Social Epistemology)*, Vol. 3. Edited by Tamar Szabo Gendler and John Hawthorne, 235–52. Oxford: Oxford University Press.
Fricker, Miranda. 2010b. 'The Relativism of Blame and Williams's Relativism of Distance'. *Proceedings of the Aristotelian Society Supplementary Volume* 84 (1): 151–77.
Fricker, Miranda. 2010c. 'Scepticism and the Genealogy of Knowledge: Situating Epistemology in Time'. In *Social Epistemology*. Edited by A. Haddock, A. Millar, and D. Pritchard, 51–68. Oxford: Oxford University Press.
Fricker, Miranda. 2012. 'Group Testimony? The Making of a Collective Good Informant'. *Philosophy and Phenomenological Research* 84 (2): 249–76.
Fricker, Miranda. 2013. 'Styles of Moral Relativism: A Critical Family Tree'. In *The Oxford Handbook of the History of Ethics*. Edited by Roger Crisp, 793–817. Oxford: Oxford University Press.
Fricker, Miranda. 2016a. 'Fault and No-Fault Responsibility for Implicit Prejudice: A Space for Epistemic "Agent-Regret"'. In *The Epistemic Life of Groups: Essays in the Epistemology of Collectives*. Edited by Michael S. Brady and Miranda Fricker, 33–50. Oxford: Oxford University Press.
Fricker, Miranda. 2016b. 'What's the Point of Blame? A Paradigm Based Explanation'. *Noûs* 50 (1): 165–83.
Fricker, Miranda. 2019. 'Forgiveness: An Ordered Pluralism'. *Australasian Philosophical Review* 3 (1): 241–60.
Fricker, Miranda. 2020a. 'Bernard Williams as a Philosopher of Ethical Freedom'. *Canadian Journal of Philosophy* 50 (8): 919–33.
Fricker, Miranda. 2020b. 'Institutional Epistemic Vices: The Case of Inferential Inertia'. In *Vice Epistemology*. Edited by Ian James Kidd, Heather Battaly, and Quassim Cassam, 89–107. London: Routledge.

Fricker, Miranda. Forthcoming-a. *Blaming and Forgiving: The Work of Morality*. Oxford: Oxford University Press.
Fricker, Miranda. Forthcoming-b. 'A Project of "Impure" Enquiry: Williams' Historical Self-Consciousness'. In *Bernard Williams on Philosophy and History*. Edited by Marcel van Ackeren and Matthieu Queloz. Oxford: Oxford University Press.
Fricker, Miranda. Manuscript. 'Williams' "Philosophical Anthropology": A Humean and Nietzschean Synergy'.
Friedman, Richard B. 1990. 'On the Concept of Authority in Political Philosophy'. In *Authority*. Edited by Joseph Raz, 56–91. New York: New York University Press.
Friedrich, Carl Joachim. 1958. *Authority*. Cambridge, MA: Harvard University Press.
Friedrich, Carl Joachim. 1971. 'Authority, Reason, and Discretion'. In *Authority and Social Work*. Edited by Shankar A. Yelaja, 17–34. Toronto: University of Toronto Press.
Friedrich, Carl Joachim. 1972. *Tradition and Authority*. London: Pall Mall.
Gaitán, Antonio, and Hugo Viciana. 2018. 'Relativism of Distance—a Step in the Naturalization of Meta-Ethics'. *Ethical Theory and Moral Practice* 21 (2): 311–27.
Galston, William A. 2002. *Liberal Pluralism: The Implications of Value Pluralism for Political Theory and Practice*. Cambridge: Cambridge University Press.
Galston, William A. 2005. *The Practice of Liberal Pluralism*. Cambridge: Cambridge University Press.
Gauker, Christopher. 2011. *Words and Images: An Essay on the Origin of Ideas*. Oxford: Oxford University Press.
Geertz, Clifford. 1973a. 'Ideology as a Cultural System'. In *The Interpretation of Cultures: Selected Essays*, 193–233. New York: Basic Books.
Geertz, Clifford. 1973b. 'Thick Description: Toward an Interpretive Theory of Culture'. In *The Interpretation of Cultures: Selected Essays*, 3–30. New York: Basic Books.
Geertz, Clifford. 1983a. '"From the Native's Point of View": On the Nature of Anthropological Understanding'. In *Local Knowledge: Further Essays in Interpretive Anthropology*, 55–70. New York: Basic Books.
Geertz, Clifford. 1983b. 'Introduction'. In *Local Knowledge: Further Essays in Interpretive Anthropology*, 3–16. New York: Basic Books.
Gellner, Ernest. 1984. 'The Gospel According to Ludwig'. *American Scholar* 53 (2): 243–63.
George, Alexander. 2012. 'Opening the Door to Cloud-Cuckoo-Land: Hempel and Kuhn on Rationality'. *Journal for the History of Analytical Philosophy* 1 (4): 1–17.
Geuss, Raymond. 2001. *History and Illusion in Politics*. Cambridge: Cambridge University Press.
Geuss, Raymond. 2020. *Who Needs a Worldview?* Cambridge, MA: Harvard University Press.
Gibbard, Allan. 1992. 'Morality and Thick Concepts (I): Thick Concepts and Warrant for Feelings'. *Proceedings of the Aristotelian Society Supplementary Volume* 66 (1): 267–83.
Gibbons, Adam F. 2023. 'Bad Language Makes Good Politics'. *Inquiry*, 1–30.
Ginsborg, Hannah. 2018. 'Normativity and Concepts'. In *The Oxford Handbook of Reasons and Normativity*. Edited by Daniel Star, 989–1014. New York: Oxford University Press.
Glasgow, Joshua. 2020. 'Conceptual Revolution'. In *Shifting Concepts: The Philosophy and Psychology of Conceptual Variation*. Edited by Teresa Marques and Åsa Wikforss, 149–66. Oxford: Oxford University Press.
Glasgow, Joshua, Sally Haslanger, Chike Jeffers, and Quayshawn Spencer. 2019. *What Is Race? Four Philosophical Views*. New York: Oxford University Press.
Gleitman, Lila R., and Anna Papafragou. 2012. 'New Perspectives on Language and Thought'. In *The Oxford Handbook of Thinking and Reasoning*. Edited by Keith J. Holyoak and Robert G. Morrison, 543–68. Oxford: Oxford University Press.
Glock, Hans-Johann. 1996. *A Wittgenstein Dictionary*. Oxford: Blackwell.
Glock, Hans-Johann. 2000. 'Animals, Thoughts and Concepts'. *Synthese* 123 (1): 35–64.
Glock, Hans-Johann. 2006. 'Concepts: Representations or Abilities?'. In *Content, Consciousness, and Perception: Essays in Contemporary Philosophy of Mind*. Edited by Ezio Di Nucci and Conor McHugh, 36–61. Cambridge: Cambridge Scholars Press.
Glock, Hans-Johann. 2009a. 'Concepts, Conceptual Schemes and Grammar'. *Philosophia* 37 (4): 653.

Glock, Hans-Johann. 2009b. 'Concepts: Where Subjectivism Goes Wrong'. *Philosophy* 84 (1): 5–29.
Glock, Hans-Johann. 2010a. 'Concepts: Between the Subjective and the Objective'. In *Mind, Method, and Morality: Essays in Honour of Anthony Kenny*. Edited by J. Cottingham and P. M. S. Hacker, 306–29. Oxford: Oxford University Press.
Glock, Hans-Johann. 2010b. 'Wittgenstein on Concepts'. In *Wittgenstein's Philosophical Investigations: A Critical Guide*. Edited by Arif Ahmed, 88–108. Cambridge: Cambridge University Press.
Glock, Hans-Johann. 2014. 'Reasons for Action: Wittgensteinian and Davidsonian Perspectives in Historical, Meta-Philosophical and Philosophical Context'. *Nordic Wittgenstein Review* 3 (1): 7–46.
Glock, Hans-Johann. 2017. 'Impure Conceptual Analysis'. In *The Cambridge Companion to Philosophical Methodology*. Edited by Giuseppina D'Oro and Søren Overgaard, 77–100. Cambridge: Cambridge University Press.
Glock, Hans-Johann. 2020. 'Concepts and Experience: A Non-Representationalist Perspective'. In *Concepts in Thought, Action, and Emotion: New Essays*. Edited by Christoph Demmerling and Dirk Schröder, 21–41. Abingdon: Routledge.
Glock, Hans-Johann, and Eva Schmidt. 2021. 'Pluralism about Practical Reasons and Reason Explanations'. *Philosophical Explorations* 24 (2): 119–36.
Goetze, Trystan S. 2018. *Conceptual Responsibility*. PhD Thesis, University of Sheffield.
Goetze, Trystan S. 2021. 'Conceptual Responsibility'. *Inquiry* 64 (1–2): 20–45.
Goldfarb, Warren. 1997. 'Wittgenstein on Fixity of Meaning'. In *Early Analytic Philosophy: Frege, Russell, Wittgenstein*. Edited by William Walker Tait, 75–89. Chicago and La Salle, IL: Open Court.
Goldie, Peter. 2009. 'Thick Concepts and Emotion'. In *Reading Bernard Williams*. Edited by Daniel Callcut, 94–109. London: Routledge.
Goldman, Alvin I. 1976. 'Discrimination and Perceptual Knowledge'. *Journal of Philosophy* 64 (12): 771–91.
Goodman, Nelson. 1977. *The Structure of Appearance*. 3rd ed. Dordrecht: Springer.
Goodman, Nelson. 1978. *Ways of Worldmaking*. Indianapolis: Hackett.
Goodman, Nelson. 1983. *Fact, Fiction, and Forecast*. 4th ed. Cambridge, MA: Harvard University Press.
Gordon, Adam, René Rohrbeck, and Jan Oliver Schwarz. 2019. 'Escaping the "Faster Horses" Trap: Bridging Strategic Foresight and Design-Based Innovation'. *Technology Innovation Management Review* 9 (8): 30–42.
Gray, John. 2013. *Isaiah Berlin: An Interpretation of His Thought*. Princeton: Princeton University Press.
Green, Leslie. 1988. *The Authority of the State*. Oxford: Clarendon Press.
Green, Matthew James, and Kees van Deemter. 2019. 'The Elusive Benefits of Vagueness: Evidence from Experiments'. In *Vagueness and Rationality in Language Use and Cognition*. Edited by Richard Dietz, 63–86. Cham: Springer.
Greene, Jamal. 2021. *How Rights Went Wrong: Why Our Obsession with Rights Is Tearing America Apart*. Boston: Houghton Mifflin Harcourt.
Greenough, Patrick. 2020. 'Neutralism and Conceptual Engineering'. In *Conceptual Engineering and Conceptual Ethics*. Edited by Alexis Burgess, Herman Cappelen, and David Plunkett, 205–29. Oxford: Oxford University Press.
Greenspan, Patricia. 2003. 'The Problem with Manipulation'. *American Philosophical Quarterly* 40 (2): 155–64.
Grönert, Peter. 2016. *Thick Concepts and Reasons for Actions*. PhD Thesis, Habilitation, University of Leipzig.
Guest, Stephen. 2013. *Ronald Dworkin*. 3rd ed. Stanford: Stanford University Press.
Guignon, Charles B. 2004. *On Being Authentic*. London: Routledge.
Gupta, Anil. 2019. *Conscious Experience: A Logical Inquiry*. Cambridge, MA: Harvard University Press.

Gustafsson, Martin. 2020. 'Wittgenstein on Using Language and Playing Chess: The Breakdown of an Analogy and Its Consequences'. In *The Logical Alien*. Edited by Sofia Miguens, 202–21. Cambridge, MA: Harvard University Press.

Gutzmann, Daniel. 2013. 'Expressives and Beyond: An Introduction to Varieties of Conventional Non-Truth-Conditional Meaning'. In *Beyond Expressives: Explorations in Use-Conditional Meaning*. Edited by Daniel Gutzmann and Hans-Martin Gärtner, 1–58. Leiden: Brill.

Hacker, Peter Michael Stephan. 2013. 'Wittgenstein's Anthropological and Ethnological Approach'. In *Wittgenstein: Comparisons and Context*, 111–27. Oxford: Oxford University Press.

Hall, Edward. 2014. 'Contingency, Confidence, and Liberalism in the Political Thought of Bernard Williams'. *Social Theory and Practice* 40 (4): 545–69.

Hall, Edward. 2017. 'How to Do Realistic Political Theory (and Why You Might Want To)'. *European Journal of Political Theory* 16 (3): 283–303.

Hall, Edward. 2020. *Value, Conflict, and Order: Berlin, Hampshire, Williams, and the Realist Revival in Political Theory*. Chicago: University of Chicago Press.

Hämäläinen, Nora. 2009. 'Is Moral Theory Harmful in Practice?—Relocating Anti-theory in Contemporary Ethics'. *Ethical Theory and Moral Practice* 12 (5): 539–53.

Hampshire, Stuart. 1983. *Morality and Conflict*. Oxford: Blackwell.

Hampton, Jean E. 1998a. 'The Anatomy of a Reason'. In *The Authority of Reason*. Edited by Richard Healey, 44–82. Cambridge: Cambridge University Press.

Hampton, Jean E. 1998b. 'Reasons' Authority'. In *The Authority of Reason*. Edited by Richard Healey, 83–122. Cambridge: Cambridge University Press.

Handelman, Sapir. 2009. *Thought Manipulation: The Use and Abuse of Psychological Trickery*. Santa Barbara: Praeger Publishers.

Hanna, Robert. 2015. *Cognition, Content, and the A Priori: A Study in the Philosophy of Mind and Knowledge*. Oxford: Oxford University Press.

Hannon, Michael. 2013. 'The Practical Origins of Epistemic Contextualism'. *Erkenntnis* 78 (4): 899–919.

Hannon, Michael. 2015. 'The Universal Core of Knowledge'. *Synthese* 192 (3): 769–86.

Hannon, Michael. 2019. *What's the Point of Knowledge? A Function-First Epistemology*. Oxford: Oxford University Press.

Harcourt, Edward. Manuscript. 'Consequentialism, Moralism, and the "Administered World"'.

Hardimon, Michael O. 2017. *Rethinking Race: The Case for Deflationary Realism*. Cambridge, MA: Harvard University Press.

Harman, Gilbert. 1984. 'Logic and Reasoning'. *Synthese* 60 (1): 107–27.

Harré, Rom. 1964. 'Concepts and Criteria'. *Mind* LXXIII (291): 353–63.

Hart, Herbert Lionel Adolphus. 1963. 'Acts of Will and Legal Responsibility'. In *Freedom and the Will*. Edited by David Pears, 38–47. New York: Palgrave.

Hart, Herbert Lionel Adolphus. 2008a. 'Acts of Will and Responsibility'. In *Punishment and Responsibility: Essays in the Philosophy of Law*. 2nd ed., 90–112. Oxford: Oxford University Press.

Hart, Herbert Lionel Adolphus. 2008b. 'Legal Responsibility and Excuses'. In *Punishment and Responsibility: Essays in the Philosophy of Law*. 2nd ed., 28–53. Oxford: Oxford University Press.

Hart, Herbert Lionel Adolphus. 2008c. 'Negligence, Mens Rea, and Criminal Responsibility'. In *Punishment and Responsibility: Essays in the Philosophy of Law*. 2nd ed., 136–57. Oxford: Oxford University Press.

Hart, Herbert Lionel Adolphus. 2008d. 'Prolegomenon to the Principles of Punishment'. In *Punishment and Responsibility: Essays in the Philosophy of Law*. 2nd ed., 1–27. Oxford: Oxford University Press.

Hart, Herbert Lionel Adolphus. 2012. *The Concept of Law*. 3rd ed. Oxford: Oxford University Press.

Hartman, Robert J. 2019. 'Kant Does Not Deny Resultant Moral Luck'. *Midwest Studies in Philosophy* 43 (1): 136–50.

Hasan, Ali, and Richard Fumerton. 2018. 'Foundationalist Theories of Epistemic Justification'. In *The Stanford Encyclopedia of Philosophy*. Edited by Edward N. Zalta. Fall 2018 ed.

Haslanger, Sally. 2012. *Resisting Reality: Social Construction and Social Critique*. Oxford: Oxford University Press.

Haslanger, Sally. 2014. 'Social Meaning and Philosophical Method'. *Proceedings and Addresses of the American Philosophical Association* 88: 16–37.

Haslanger, Sally. 2018. 'Cognition as a Social Skill'. *Australasian Philosophical Review* 2 (4): 5–25.

Haslanger, Sally. 2020a. 'Going On, Not in the Same Way'. In *Conceptual Engineering and Conceptual Ethics*. Edited by Alexis Burgess, Herman Cappelen, and David Plunkett, 230–60. Oxford: Oxford University Press.

Haslanger, Sally. 2020b. 'How Not to Change the Subject'. In *Shifting Concepts: The Philosophy and Psychology of Conceptual Variation*. Edited by Teresa Marques and Åsa Wikforss, 235–59. Oxford: Oxford University Press.

Haslanger, Sally. 2021. *Ideology in Practice: What Does Ideology Do?* Milwaukee, WI: Marquette University Press.

Hayward, Max Khan. 2019. 'Immoral Realism'. *Philosophical Studies* 176 (4): 897–914.

Heal, Jane. 2003. *Mind, Reason, and Imagination: Selected Essays in Philosophy of Mind and Language*. Cambridge: Cambridge University Press.

Heal, Jane. 2007. '"Back to the Rough Ground!" Wittgensteinian Reflections on Rationality and Reason'. *Ratio* 20 (4): 403–21.

Hegel, Georg Wilhelm Friedrich. 1968–. *Gesammelte Werke*. Hamburg: Meiner.

Hegel, Georg Wilhelm Friedrich. 1975. *Aesthetics: Lectures on Fine Art*. Oxford: Oxford University Press.

Heinze, Richard. 1925. 'Auctoritas'. *Hermes* 60 (3): 348–66.

Heller, Mark. 1990. *The Ontology of Physical Objects: Four-Dimensional Hunks of Matter*. Cambridge: Cambridge University Press.

Helmig, Christoph. 2013. *Forms and Concepts: Concept Formation in the Platonic Tradition*. Berlin: De Gruyter.

Heney, Diana B. 2016. *Toward a Pragmatist Metaethics*. New York: Routledge.

Henne, Céline. 2022. *Framed and Framing Inquiry: Development and Defence of John Dewey's Theory of Knowledge*. PhD Thesis, University of Cambridge.

Henne, Céline. 2023. 'Framed and Framing Inquiry: A Pragmatist Proposal'. *Synthese* 201 (2): 60.

Heraclitus. 1981. *The Art and Thought of Heraclitus*. Edited by Charles H. Kahn. Cambridge: Cambridge University Press.

Herman, Edward S., and Noam Chomsky. 1988. *Manufacturing Consent: The Political Economy of the Mass Media*. New York: Pantheon Books.

Herodotus. 1920. *Histories*. Translated by A. D. Godley. Cambridge, MA: Harvard University Press.

Heuer, Ulrike, and Gerald Lang. 2012. *Luck, Value, and Commitment: Themes from the Ethics of Bernard Williams*. Oxford: Oxford University Press.

Heyd, David. 1997. 'Moral And Legal Luck: Kant's Reconciliation with Practical Contingency'. *Annual Review of Law and Ethics* 5: 27–42.

Hippo, Augustine of. 1992. *Confessions*, Vol. 1. Edited by James J. O'Donnell. Oxford: Oxford University Press.

Hirsch, Eli. 1993. *Dividing Reality*. New York: Oxford University Press.

Hirsch, Eli. 2013. 'The Metaphysically Best Language'. *Philosophy and Phenomenological Research* 87 (3): 709–16.

Hlobil, Ulf. 2015. 'Anti-Normativism Evaluated'. *International Journal of Philosophical Studies* 23 (3): 376–95.

Hlobil, Ulf, and Robert Brandom. 2025. *Reasons for Logic, Logic for Reasons: Pragmatics, Semantics, and Conceptual Roles*. New York: Routledge.

Hofstadter, Richard. 2008. *The Paranoid Style in American Politics and Other Essays*. New York: Vintage.

Holbraad, Martin. 2012. *Truth in Motion: The Recursive Anthropology of Cuban Divination*. Chicago: University of Chicago Press.
Hom, Christopher, and Robert May. 2018. 'Pejoratives as Fiction'. In *Bad Words: Philosophical Perspectives on Slurs*. Edited by David Sosa, 108–31. Oxford University Press.
Horkheimer, Max. 1987. *Studien über Autorität und Familie: Forschungsberichte aus dem Institut für Sozialforschung*. Lüneburg: zu Klampen.
Hornsby, Jennifer. 1980. *Actions*. London: Routledge.
Horty, John F. 2012. *Reasons as Defaults*. New York: Oxford University Press.
Hoyningen-Huene, Paul. 2013. *Systematicity: The Nature of Science*. New York: Oxford University Press.
Huddleston, Andrew. 2019. *Nietzsche on the Decadence and Flourishing of Culture*. Oxford: Oxford University Press.
Hume, David. 1998. *An Enquiry Concerning the Principles of Morals*. Edited by Tom L. Beauchamp. Oxford: Clarendon Press.
Hume, David. 2000. *A Treatise of Human Nature*. Edited by David Fate Norton and Mary J. Norton. Oxford: Oxford University Press.
Hyde, Harford Montgomery. 1973. *The Trials of Oscar Wilde*. New York: Dover.
Hyman, John. 2011. 'Action and the Will'. In *The Oxford Handbook of Wittgenstein*. Edited by Oskari Kuusela and Marie McGinn, 451–71. Oxford: Oxford University Press.
Hyman, John. 2015. *Action, Knowledge, and Will*. Oxford: Oxford University Press.
Ichikawa, Jonathan Jenkins. 2017. *Contextualising Knowledge: Epistemology and Semantics*. Oxford: Oxford University Press.
Isaac, Manuel Gustavo. 2023. 'Which Concept of Concept for Conceptual Engineering?'. *Erkenntnis* 88 (5): 2145–69.
Isaac, Manuel Gustavo. 2024. 'Post-Truth Conceptual Engineering'. *Inquiry* 67 (1): 199–214.
Jaeggi, Rahel. 2016. *Critique of Forms of Life*. Cambridge, MA: Harvard University Press.
James, William. 1975–88. *The Works of William James*. Edited by F. H. Burkhard, F. Bowers, and I. K. Skrupskelis. 18 vols. Cambridge, MA: Harvard University Press.
James, William. 1981. *The Principles of Psychology*, Vol. II. Edited by Frederick H. Burkhardt, Fredson Bowers, and Ignas K. Skrupskelis. Cambridge, MA: Harvard University Press.
Jamieson, Dale. 2007. 'When Utilitarians Should Be Virtue Theorists'. *Utilitas* 19 (2): 160–83.
Jamieson, Dale. 2014. *Reason in a Dark Time: Why the Struggle against Climate Change Failed—and What It Means for Our Future*. New York: Oxford University Press.
Jansen, Ludger, and Niko Strobach. 2003. 'The So-Called Materially Valid Inferences and the Logic of Concepts'. In *Foundations of the Formal Sciences II: Applications of Mathematical Logic in Philosophy and Linguistics, Papers of a Conference held in Bonn, November 10–13, 2000*. Edited by Benedikt Löwe, Wolfgang Malzkom, and Thoralf Räsch, 113–18. Dordrecht: Springer Netherlands.
Jayasekera, Marie. 2016. 'Responsibility in Descartes's Theory of Judgment'. *Ergo* 3 (12): 321–47.
Johnston, Mark. 2001. 'The Authority of Affect'. *Philosophy and Phenomenological Research* 63 (1): 181–214.
Jorem, Sigurd. 2021. 'Conceptual Engineering and the Implementation Problem'. *Inquiry* 64 (1–2): 186–211.
Jorem, Sigurd. 2022. 'The Good, the Bad and the Insignificant—Assessing Concept Functions for Conceptual Engineering'. *Synthese* 200 (106): 1–20.
Jorem, Sigurd, and Guido Löhr. 2024. 'Inferentialist Conceptual Engineering'. *Inquiry* 67 (3): 932–53.
Jouvenel, Bertrand de. 1963a. *The Pure Theory of Politics*. New Haven: Yale University Press.
Jouvenel, Bertrand de. 1963b. *Sovereignty: An Inquiry into the Political Good*. Cambridge: Cambridge University Press.
Joyce, Richard. 2006. *The Evolution of Morality*. Cambridge, MA and London: MIT Press.
Kaeslin, Isabel. Manuscript. 'Hermeneutic Attention'.
Kagan, Shelly. 1989. *The Limits of Morality*. Oxford: Oxford University Press.

Kail, Peter J. E. 2011. '"Genealogy" and the Genealogy'. In *Nietzsche's On the Genealogy of Morality: A Critical Guide*. Edited by Simon May, 214–33. Cambridge: Cambridge University Press.
Kant, Immanuel. 1900–. *Kants gesammelte Schriften*. Edited by Preussische Akademie der Wissenschaften (vols. 1–22), Deutsche Akademie der Wissenschaften zu Berlin (vol. 23), and Akademie der Wissenschaften zu Göttingen (from vol. 24). Akademieausgabe. Berlin: De Gruyter.
Kant, Immanuel. 2015. *Critique of Practical Reason*. Translated by Mary Gregor. Cambridge: Cambridge University Press.
Kappel, Klemens. 2010. 'On Saying That Someone Knows: Themes from Craig'. In *Social Epistemology*. Edited by Adrian Haddock, Alan Millar, and Duncan Pritchard, 69–88. Oxford: Oxford University Press.
Keefe, Rosanna. 2000. *Theories of Vagueness*. Cambridge: Cambridge University Press.
Keil, F. C. 1989. *Concepts, Kinds, and Cognitive Development*. Cambridge, MA: MIT Press.
Kelp, Christoph. 2011. 'What's the Point of "Knowledge" Anyway?'. *Episteme* 8 (1): 53–66.
Kenny, Anthony. 2010. 'Concepts, Brains, and Behaviour'. *Grazer Philosophische Studien* 81 (1): 105–13.
Kenny, Anthony John Patrick. 1972. 'Descartes on the Will'. In *Cartesian Studies*. Edited by R. J. Buter, 1–31. Oxford: Blackwell.
Kenny, Anthony John Patrick. 1992. *The Metaphysics of Mind*. Oxford: Oxford University Press.
Kim, Brian, and Matthew McGrath, eds. 2019. *Pragmatic Encroachment in Epistemology*. New York: Routledge.
Kirchin, Simon. 2010. 'The Shapelessness Hypothesis'. *Philosophers' Imprint* 10 (4): 1–28.
Kirshner, Alexander S. 2022. *Legitimate Opposition*. New Haven: Yale University Press.
Kitcher, Philip. 2001. *Science, Truth, and Democracy*. New York: Oxford University Press.
Kitcher, Philip. 2008. 'Carnap and the Caterpillar'. *Philosophical Topics* 36 (1): 111–27.
Kitcher, Philip. 2011. *The Ethical Project*. Cambridge, MA: Harvard University Press.
Kletzer, Christoph, and Massimo Renzo. 2020. 'Authority and Legitimacy'. In *Cambridge Companion to the Philosophy of Law*. Edited by John Tasioulas, 191–207. Cambridge: Cambridge University Press.
Koch, Steffen. 2019. 'Carnapian Explications, Experimental Philosophy, and Fruitful Concepts'. *Inquiry* 62 (6): 700–17.
Koch, Steffen. 2021. 'Engineering What? On Concepts in Conceptual Engineering'. *Synthese* 199 (1): 1955–75.
Kojève, Alexandre. 2014. *The Notion of Authority (A Brief Presentation)*. Translated by Hager Weslati. Edited by François Terré. London: Verso.
Kolodny, Niko, and John Brunero. 2020. 'Instrumental Rationality'. In *The Stanford Encyclopedia of Philosophy*. Edited by Edward N. Zalta. Spring 2020 ed.
Koreň, Ladislav. 2021. *Practices of Reason: Fusing the Inferentialist and Scientific Image*. New York: Routledge.
Korsgaard, Christine. 1996. *The Sources of Normativity*. Cambridge: Cambridge University Press.
Koslicki, Kathrin, and Olivier Massin. 2023. 'A Socratic Essentialist Defense of Non-Verbal Definitional Disputes'. *Ratio* 36 (4): 319–33.
Krebs, Angelika. 1999. *Ethics of Nature: A Map*. Berlin: De Gruyter.
Kripke, Saul A. 1980. *Naming and Necessity*. Cambridge, MA: Harvard University Press.
Kripke, Saul A. 1982. *Wittgenstein on Rules and Private Language*. Cambridge, MA: Harvard University Press.
Krisch, Nico. 2010. *Beyond Constitutionalism: The Pluralist Structure of Postnational Law*. Oxford: Oxford University Press.
Krishnan, Nikhil. 2023. *A Terribly Serious Adventure: Philosophy at Oxford 1900–60*. London: Profile Books.
Krishnan, Nikhil, and Matthieu Queloz. 2023. 'The Shaken Realist: Bernard Williams, the War, and Philosophy as Cultural Critique'. *European Journal of Philosophy* 31 (1): 226–47.
Kuhn, Thomas. 1970. *The Structure of Scientific Revolutions*. Chicago: University of Chicago Press.

Kukla, Rebecca. 2000. 'Myth, Memory and Misrecognition in Sellars' "Empiricism and the Philosophy of Mind"'. *Philosophical Studies* 101 (2–3): 161–211.
Kukla, Rebecca, and Mark Lance. 2009. *'Yo!' and 'Lo!': The Pragmatic Topography of the Space of Reasons*. Cambridge, MA: Harvard University Press.
Kusch, Martin. 2006. *A Sceptical Guide to Meaning and Rules: Defending Kripke's Wittgenstein*. Chesham: Acumen.
Kusch, Martin. 2009. 'Testimony and the Value of Knowledge'. In *Epistemic Value*. Edited by Adrian Haddock, Alan Millar and Duncan Pritchard, 60–94. Oxford: Oxford University Press.
Kusch, Martin. 2011. 'Knowledge and Certainties in the Epistemic State of Nature'. *Episteme* 8 (1): 6–23.
Kusch, Martin. 2013. 'Naturalized Epistemology and the Genealogy of Knowledge'. In *Contemporary Perspectives on Early Modern Philosophy: Nature and Norms in Thought*. Edited by Martin Lenz and Anik Waldow, 87–100. Dordrecht: Springer.
Kusch, Martin. 2015. '"A Branch of Human Natural History": Wittgenstein's Reflections on Metrology'. In *Standardization in Measurement: Philosophical, Historical and Sociological Issues*. Edited by Lara Huber and Oliver Schlaudt, 11–24. London: Pickering and Chatto.
Kyritsis, Dimitrios. 2021. 'Williams and Rawls in Philadelphia'. *Res Publica* 27 (2): 203–18.
La Boétie, Etienne de. 2016. *Discours de la servitude volontaire*. Paris: Flammarion.
Ladd, John. 1957. *The Structure of a Moral Code: A Philosophical Analysis of Ethical Discourse Applied to the Ethics of the Navaho Indians*. Cambridge, MA: Harvard University Press.
Laden, Anthony Simon. 2012. *Reasoning: A Social Picture*. Oxford: Oxford University Press.
Laidlaw, James. 2014. *The Subject of Virtue: An Anthropology of Ethics and Freedom*. Cambridge: Cambridge University Press.
Lane, Melissa. 2018. 'Placing Plato in the History of Liberty'. *History of European Ideas* 44 (6): 702–18.
Lanius, David. 2019. *Strategic Indeterminacy in the Law*. New York: Oxford University Press.
Lanius, David. 2021. 'What Is the Value of Vagueness?'. *Theoria* 87 (3): 752–80.
Laplace, Pierre Simon. 1951. *A Philosophical Essay on Probabilities*. Translated by F. W. Truscott and F. L. Emory. New York: Dover.
Latham, Andrew J., Kristie Miller, and James Norton. 2019. 'Philosophical Methodology and Conceptions of Evil Action'. *Metaphilosophy* 50 (3): 296–315.
Lau, Ting Cho. 2024. 'How to Choose Normative Concepts'. *Analytic Philosophy* 65 (2): 145–61.
Lauener, Henri. 2001. 'Ethik des methodologischen Humanismus: Kritische Bemerkungen zur Relativität von Normen und zum Pluralismus von Systemen der Moral'. *Erkenntnis* 54 (1): 77–103.
Lawlor, Krista. 2013. *Assurance: An Austinian View of Knowledge and Knowledge Claims*. Oxford: Oxford University Press.
Lazar, Seth. 2024. *Connected by Code: How AI Structures, and Governs, the Ways We Relate*. Oxford: Oxford University Press.
Lear, Jonathan. 2011. 'Foreword to the Routledge Classics Edition'. In *Ethics and the Limits of Philosophy*, ix–xiv. London: Routledge.
Leiter, Brian. 2015. *Nietzsche on Morality*. 2nd ed. London: Routledge.
Leiter, Brian. 2019a. 'The Innocence of Becoming: Nietzsche against Guilt'. *Inquiry* 62 (1): 70–92.
Leiter, Brian. 2019b. *Moral Psychology with Nietzsche*. Oxford: Oxford University Press.
Leiter, Brian. 2022. 'Williams's Debt to Nietzsche: Real or Illusory?'. In *Morality and Agency: Themes from Bernard Williams*. Edited by András Szigeti and Matthew Talbert, 17–35. New York: Oxford University Press.
Leitgeb, Hannes, and André W. Carus. 2021. 'Rudolf Carnap'. In *The Stanford Encyclopedia of Philosophy*. Edited by Edward N. Zalta. Summer 2021 ed.
Leuenberger, Muriel. 2021. 'What Is the Point of Being Your True Self? A Genealogy of Essentialist Authenticity'. *Philosophy* 96 (3): 409–31.
Levy, Neil. 2011. *Hard Luck: How Luck Undermines Free Will and Moral Responsibility*. Oxford: Oxford University Press.

Lewis, David. 1973. *Counterfactuals*. Oxford: Blackwell.
Lewis, David. 1983a. 'Languages and Language'. In *Philosophical Papers*, Vol. 1, 163–88. Oxford: Oxford University Press.
Lewis, David. 1983b. 'New Work for a Theory of Universals'. *Australasian Journal of Philosophy* 61 (4): 343–77.
Lewis, David. 1983c. *Philosophical Papers*, Vol, 1. Oxford: Oxford University Press.
Lewis, David. 1984. 'Putnam's Paradox'. *Australasian Journal of Philosophy* 62 (3): 221–36.
Lifschitz, Avi. 2012. *Language and Enlightenment: The Berlin Debates of the Eighteenth Century*. Oxford: Oxford University Press.
Lilla, Mark, Ronald Dworkin, and Robert Silvers. 2001. 'Introduction'. In *The Legacy of Isaiah Berlin*. Edited by Mark Lilla, Ronald Dworkin, and Robert Silvers, ix–xiii. New York: New York Review of Books.
Lindauer, Matthew. 2020. 'Conceptual Engineering as Concept Preservation'. *Ratio* 33 (3): 155–62.
Lindholm, Charles. 2013. 'The Rise of Expressive Authenticity'. *Anthropological Quarterly* 86 (2): 361–95.
Lipscomb, Benjamin J. B. 2021. *The Women Are Up to Something: How Elizabeth Anscombe, Philippa Foot, Mary Midgley, and Iris Murdoch Revolutionized Ethics*. Oxford: Oxford University Press.
Little, Daniel. 2020. 'Philosophy of History'. In *The Stanford Encyclopedia of Philosophy*. Edited by Edward N. Zalta. Winter 2020 ed.
Lloyd, Dan Edward. 1989. *Simple Minds*. Cambridge, MA: MIT Press.
Louden, Robert B. 2007. 'The Critique of the Morality System'. In *Bernard Williams*. Edited by Alan Thomas, 104–34. Cambridge: Cambridge University Press.
Lovibond, Sabina. 2015. 'Ethical Upbringing: From Connivance to Cognition'. In *Essays on Ethics and Feminism*, 128–45. Oxford: Oxford University Press.
Lukes, Steven. 1987. 'Perspectives on Authority'. *Nomos* 29: 59–75.
Łukomska, Agata. 2022. 'Confidence: On the Possibility of Ethical Knowledge'. In *Morality and Agency: Themes from Bernard Williams*. Edited by András Szigeti and Matthew Talbert, 110–31. New York: Oxford University Press.
Lyons, Johnny. 2020. *The Philosophy of Isaiah Berlin*. London: Bloomsbury.
Lyons, Johnny. 2021. *Isaiah Berlin and His Philosophical Contemporaries*. New York: Palgrave.
Machery, Edouard. 2017. *Philosophy Within Its Proper Bounds*. Oxford: Oxford University Press.
MacIntyre, Alasdair C. 1978. *Against the Self-Images of the Age*. Notre Dame: University of Notre Dame Press.
MacIntyre, Alasdair C. 1988. *Whose Justice? Which Rationality?* Notre Dame: University of Notre Dame Press.
MacIntyre, Alasdair C. 2007. *After Virtue: A Study in Moral Theory*. 3rd ed. Notre Dame: University of Notre Dame Press.
MacLeod, Alan, ed. 2019. *Propaganda in the Information Age: Still Manufacturing Consent*. Abingdon: Routledge.
Macnish, Kevin, and Jai Galliott, eds. 2020. *Big Data and Democracy*. Edinburgh: Edinburgh University Press.
Maitland, Frederic William. 1898. 'A Prologue to a History of English Law'. *Law Quarterly Review* 14: 13–33.
Mameli, Matteo. 2001. 'Mindreading, Mindshaping, and Evolution'. *Biology and Philosophy* 16 (5): 595–626.
Mann, Roni. 2021. 'Political Moralism and Constitutional Reasoning: A Reply to Bernard Williams'. *Res Publica* 27 (2): 235–53.
Marconi, Diego. 1997. *Lexical Competence*. Cambridge, MA: MIT Press.
Marcuse, Herbert. 2002. *One-Dimensional Man: Studies in the Ideology of Advanced Industrial Society*. London: Routledge.
Margolis, Eric, and Stephen Laurence. 1999. *Concepts: Core Readings*. Cambridge, MA: MIT Press.

Margolis, Eric, and Stephen Laurence. 2015. *The Conceptual Mind: New Directions in the Study of Concepts*. Cambridge, MA: MIT Press.
Margolis, Eric, and Stephen Laurence. 2019. 'Concepts'. In *The Stanford Encyclopedia of Philosophy*. Edited by Edward N. Zalta.
Marques, Teresa. 2020. 'Amelioration vs Perversion'. In *Shifting Concepts: The Philosophy and Psychology of Conceptual Variation*. Edited by Teresa Marques and Åsa Wikforss, 260–84. Oxford: Oxford University Press.
Marušić, Berislav. 2022. *On the Temporality of Emotions: An Essay on Grief, Anger, and Love*. Oxford: Oxford University Press.
Mashaw, Jerry L. 1983. *Bureaucratic Justice: Managing Social Security Disability Claims*. New Haven: Yale University Press.
Matravers, Matt. 2007. *Responsibility and Justice*. London: Polity.
Matthews, Robert J. 2010. *The Measure of Mind: Propositional Attitudes and their Attribution*. Oxford: Oxford University Press.
McConnell-Ginet, Sally. 2006. 'Why Defining Is Seldom "Just Semantics": Marriage and Marriage'. In *Drawing the Boundaries of Meaning: Neo-Gricean Studies in Pragmatics and Semantics in Honor of Laurence R. Horn*. Edited by Betty J. Birner and Gregory Ward, 217–40. Amsterdam: John Benjamins.
McDowell, John. 1996. *Mind and World*. Cambridge, MA: Harvard University Press.
McDowell, John. 1998a. 'Aesthetic Value, Objectivity, and the Fabric of the World'. In *Mind, Value, and Reality*, 112–30. Cambridge, MA: Harvard University Press.
McDowell, John. 1998b. 'Non-Cognitivism and Rule-Following'. In *Mind, Value, and Reality*, 198–220. Cambridge, MA: Harvard University Press.
McGrath, Matthew. 2015. 'Two Purposes of Knowledge-Attribution and the Contextualism Debate'. In *Epistemic Evaluation: Purposeful Epistemology*. Edited by John Greco and David Henderson, 138–57. Oxford: Oxford University Press.
McPherson, Tristram. 2011. 'Against Quietist Normative Realism'. *Philosophical Studies* 154 (2): 223–40.
McPherson, Tristram. 2018. 'Authoritatively Normative Concepts'. In *Oxford Studies in Metaethics*, Vol. 13. Edited by Russ Shafer-Landau, 253–77. Oxford: Oxford University Press.
McPherson, Tristram. 2020a. 'Deliberative Authority and Representational Determinacy: A Challenge for the Normative Realist'. *Ergo* 6 (45): 1331–58.
McPherson, Tristram. 2020b. *Epistemology and Methodology in Ethics*. Cambridge: Cambridge University Press.
McPherson, Tristram, and David Plunkett. 2020. 'Conceptual Ethics and the Methodology of Normative Inquiry'. In *Conceptual Engineering and Conceptual Ethics*. Edited by Alexis Burgess, Herman Cappelen, and David Plunkett, 274–303. Oxford: Oxford University Press.
McPherson, Tristram, and David Plunkett. 2021. 'Evaluation Turned on Itself: The Vindicatory Circularity Challenge to the Conceptual Ethics of Normativity'. In *Oxford Studies in Metaethics*, Vol. 16. Edited by Russ Shafer-Landau, 207–32. Oxford: Oxford University Press.
Mele, Alfred R. 2017. *Aspects of Agency: Decisions, Abilities, Explanations, and Free Will*. New York: Oxford University Press.
Merrill, Sarah Bishop. 1998. *Defining Personhood: Toward the Ethics of Quality in Clinical Care*. Amsterdam: Rodopi.
Midgley, Mary. 1996. 'Philosophical Plumbing'. In *Utopias, Dolphins and Computers: Problems of Philosophical Plumbing*, 1–12. London: Routledge.
Mill, John Stuart. 1874. *Autobiography*. London: Longmans, Green, Reader, and Dyer.
Mill, John Stuart. 1988. *The Subjection of Women*. Edited by Susan Moller Okin. Indianapolis: Hackett.
Mill, John Stuart. 2003. *On Liberty*. Edited by Mary Warnock. 2nd ed. Oxford: Wiley-Blackwell.
Miller, Alexander, and Crispin Wright, eds. 2002. *Rule-Following and Meaning*. Chesham: Acumen.
Miller, Geoffrey. 2000. *The Mating Mind: How Sexual Choice Shaped Human Nature*. New York: Anchor Books.

Miller, Kristie. 2010. 'On the Concept of Sexual Perversion'. *Philosophical Quarterly* 60 (241): 808–30.
Millikan, Ruth Garrett. 2000. *On Clear and Confused Ideas: An Essay about Substance Concepts.* Cambridge: Cambridge University Press.
Millikan, Ruth Garrett. 2017. *Beyond Concepts: Unicepts, Language, and Natural Information.* Oxford: Oxford University Press.
Mills, Claudia. 1995. 'Politics and Manipulation'. *Social Theory and Practice* 21 (1): 97–112.
Mommsen, Theodor. 1888. *Römisches Staatsrecht.* Leipzig: S. Hirzel.
Montaigne, Michel de. 1967. *Essays.* Paris: Éditions du Seuil.
Moody-Adams, Michele M. 2017. 'Moral Progress and Human Agency'. *Ethical Theory and Moral Practice* 20 (1): 153–68.
Moore, Adrian W. 1991. 'Can Reflection Destroy Knowledge?'. *Ratio* 4 (2): 97–106.
Moore, Adrian W. 1993. 'Ineffability and Reflection: An Outline of the Concept of Knowledge'. *European Journal of Philosophy* 1 (3): 285–308.
Moore, Adrian W. 1997. *Points of View.* Oxford: Oxford University Press.
Moore, Adrian W. 2003. 'Williams on Ethics, Knowledge and Reflection'. *Philosophy* 78: 337–54.
Moore, Adrian W. 2006. 'Bernard Williams: Ethics and the Limits of Philosophy'. In *Central Works of Philosophy,* Vol. 5: *The Twentieth Century: Quine and After.* Edited by John Shand, 207–26. Chesham: Acumen.
Moore, Adrian W. 2012. *The Evolution of Modern Metaphysics: Making Sense of Things.* Cambridge: Cambridge University Press.
Moore, Adrian W. 2019a. 'Apperception and the Unreality of Tense'. In *Language, World, and Limits: Essays in the Philosophy of Language and Metaphysics,* 143–57. Oxford: Oxford University Press.
Moore, Adrian W. 2019b. 'How Significant Is the Use/Mention Distinction?'. In *Language, World, and Limits: Essays in the Philosophy of Language and Metaphysics,* 11–38. Oxford: Oxford University Press.
Moore, Adrian W. 2019c. 'The Metaphysics of Perspective: Tense and Colour'. In *Language, World, and Limits: Essays in the Philosophy of Language and Metaphysics,* 158–64. Oxford: Oxford University Press.
Moore, Adrian W. 2020. 'The Concern with Truth, Sense, et al.—Androcentric or Anthropocentric?'. *Angelaki* 25 (1–2): 126–34.
Moore, Adrian W. 2023a. 'Maxims and Thick Ethical Concepts'. In *The Human A Priori: Essays on How We Make Sense in Philosophy, Ethics, and Mathematics,* 210–25. Oxford: Oxford University Press.
Moore, Adrian W. 2023b. 'Quasi-Realism and Relativism'. In *The Human A Priori: Essays on How We Make Sense in Philosophy, Ethics, and Mathematics,* 226–32. Oxford: Oxford University Press.
Moore, Adrian W. 2024a. 'More on Williams on Ethical Knowledge and Reflection'. *Topoi* 43 (2): 381–86.
Moore, Adrian W. 2024b. 'The Possibility of Absolute Representations'. In *Reading Rödl on Self-Consciousness and Objectivity,* 153–61. Edited by James Conant and Jesse Mulder. London: Routledge.
Moore, Michael S. 2010. *Act and Crime: The Philosophy of Action and Its Implications for Criminal Law.* Oxford: Oxford University Press.
Moran, Richard. 2001. *Authority and Estrangement: An Essay on Self-Knowledge.* Princeton: Princeton University Press.
Moravcsik, Julius. 1976. 'Ancient and Modern Conceptions of Health and Medicine'. *Journal of Medicine and Philosophy: A Forum for Bioethics and Philosophy of Medicine* 1 (4): 337–48.
Morton, Adam. 1980. *Frames of Mind: Constraints on the Common-Sense Conception of the Mental.* Oxford: Clarendon Press.
Mouffe, Chantal. 2000. *The Democratic Paradox.* London: Verso.
Moyn, Samuel. 2010. *The Last Utopia.* Cambridge, MA: Harvard University Press.
Mühlebach, Deborah. 2019. *The Politics of Meaning: A Non-Ideal Approach to Verbal Derogation.* PhD Thesis, University of Basel.

Mühlebach, Deborah. 2021. 'Semantic Contestations and the Meaning of Politically Significant Terms'. *Inquiry* 64 (8): 788–817.
Mühlebach, Deborah. 2022. 'Tackling Verbal Derogation: Linguistic Meaning, Social Meaning, and Constructive Contestation'. In *The Political Turn in Analytic Philosophy: Reflections on Social Injustice and Oppressions*. Edited by D. Bordonaba Plou, V. Fernández Castro, and J. R. Torices Vidal, 175–98. Berlin: De Gruyter.
Mühlebach, Deborah. 2023a. 'Meaning in Derogatory Social Practice'. *Theoria* 89 (4): 495–515.
Mühlebach, Deborah. 2023b. 'A Non-Ideal Approach to Slurs'. *Synthese* 202 (97): 1–25.
Mühlebach, Deborah. Forthcoming. 'Neopragmatist Inferentialism and the Meaning of Derogatory Terms—A Defence'. *Dialectica*.
Mulhall, Stephen. 2021. *The Ascetic Ideal*. Oxford: Oxford University Press.
Müller, Andreas. 2019. 'Reasoning and Normative Beliefs: Not Too Sophisticated'. *Philosophical Explorations* 22 (1): 2–15.
Müller, Andreas. 2020. *Constructing Practical Reasons*. Oxford: Oxford University Press.
Müller, Jan-Werner. 2012. 'Value Pluralism in Twentieth-Century Anglo-American Thought'. In *Modern Pluralism: Anglo-American Debates since 1880*. Edited by Mark Bevir, 81–104. Cambridge: Cambridge University Press.
Müller, Jan-Werner. 2019. 'The Contours of Cold War Liberalism (Berlin's in Particular)'. In *Isaiah Berlin's Cold War Liberalism*. Edited by Jan-Werner Müller, 37–56. New York: Palgrave.
Murata, Daniel Peixoto. 2022a. 'Obligations beyond Morality: A Critique of Ronald Dworkin's View on Legal Normativity'. *Revista Direito Mackenzie* 16 (2): 1–25.
Murata, Daniel Peixoto. 2022b. *Reason, Respect, and the Law: Bernard Williams and Legal Normativity*. PhD Thesis, School of Law, Faculty of Arts and Social Sciences (FASS), University of Surrey.
Murata, Daniel Peixoto. Forthcoming. 'Practical Reasoning as Interpretation: Williamsian Remarks on Dworkin's Methodology'. In *Bernard Williams: From Responsibility to Law and Jurisprudence*. Edited by Veronica Rodriguez-Blanco, Daniel Peixoto Murata, and Julieta Rabanos. Oxford: Hart.
Murdoch, Iris. 1956. 'Vision and Choice in Morality'. *Proceedings of the Aristotelian Society Supplementary Volume* 30: 32–58.
Murdoch, Iris. 1961. 'Against Dryness: A Polemical Sketch'. *Encounter* 16 (1): 16–20.
Murdoch, Iris. 1999. 'Metaphysics and Ethics'. In *Existentialists and Mystics: Writings on Philosophy and Literature*. Edited by Peter Conradi, 59–75. London: Penguin.
Murdoch, Iris. 2013. *The Sovereignty of Good*. London: Routledge.
Nado, Jennifer. 2021. 'Conceptual Engineering, Truth, and Efficacy'. *Synthese* 198 (7): 1507–27.
Nado, Jennifer. 2023a. 'Classification Procedures as the Targets of Conceptual Engineering'. *Philosophy and Phenomenological Research* 106 (1): 136–56.
Nado, Jennifer. 2023b. 'Taking Control: Conceptual Engineering Without (Much) Metasemantics'. *Inquiry* 66 (10): 1974–2000.
Nagel, Thomas. 1986. *The View from Nowhere*. New York: Oxford University Press.
Nagel, Thomas. 2001. 'Pluralism and Coherence'. In *The Legacy of Isaiah Berlin*. Edited by Mark Lilla, Ronald Dworkin, and Robert Silvers, 105–11. New York: New York Review of Books.
Nemitz, Paul. 2018. 'Constitutional Democracy and Technology in the Age of Artificial Intelligence'. *Philosophical Transactions of the Royal Society A: Mathematical, Physical and Engineering Sciences* 376 (2133): 1–14.
Ng, Geraldine. 2019. 'The Irrelativism of Distance'. In *Ethics beyond the Limits: New Essays on Bernard Williams' Ethics and the Limits of Philosophy*. Edited by Sophie-Grace Chappell and Marcel van Ackeren, 148–67. London: Routledge.
Ng, Sai Ying. 2023. 'Relational Normativity: Williams's Thick Ethical Concepts in Confucian Ethical Communities'. *Philosophy East and West* 73 (4): 937–57.
Nguyen, C. Thi. 2020. *Games: Agency as Art*. New York: Oxford University Press.
Nguyen, C. Thi. 2021. 'The Seductions of Clarity'. *Royal Institute of Philosophy Supplement* 89: 227–55.

Nietzsche, Friedrich. 1979. 'On Truth and Lies in a Nonmoral Sense'. In *Philosophy and Truth: Selections from Nietzsche's Notebooks of the Early 1870's*. Edited and translated by Daniel Breazeale, 79-97. Atlantic Highlands: Humanities Press International.
Nietzsche, Friedrich. 1986. *Human, All Too Human*. Translated by R. J. Hollingdale. Edited by Richard Schacht. Cambridge: Cambridge University Press.
Nietzsche, Friedrich. 1998. *On the Genealogy of Morality*. Translated by Maudemarie Clark and Alan J. Swensen. Indianapolis: Hackett.
Nietzsche, Friedrich. 2001. *The Gay Science: With a Prelude in German Rhymes and an Appendix of Songs*. Translated by Josefine Nauckhoff and Adrian Del Caro. Edited by Bernard Williams. Cambridge: Cambridge University Press.
Nietzsche, Friedrich. 2005a. 'Nietzsche contra Wagner'. In *The Anti-Christ, Ecce Homo, Twilight of the Idols, and Other Writings*. Edited by Aaron Ridley and Judith Norman, 263-82. Cambridge: Cambridge University Press.
Nietzsche, Friedrich. 2005b. *Nietzsche: The Anti-Christ, Ecce Homo, Twilight of the Idols: And Other Writings*. Translated by Judith Norman. Cambridge: Cambridge University Press.
Nietzsche, Friedrich. 2005c. *Twilight of the Idols*. Translated by Judith Norman. Edited by Aaron Ridley and Judith Norman. Cambridge: Cambridge University Press.
Nietzsche, Friedrich. 2009a. *Digital Critical Edition of the Complete Works and Letters*. Edited by Paolo D'Iorio. Berlin: De Gruyter. Based on the critical text by G. Colli and M. Montinari. Berlin: De Gruyter. www.nietzschesource.org/eKGWB/.
Nietzsche, Friedrich. 2009b. 'On Truth and Lie in an Extra-Moral Sense'. In *Writings from the Early Notebooks*. Translated by Ladislaus Löb. Edited by Raymond Geuss and Alexander Nehamas, 253-64. Cambridge: Cambridge University Press.
Nimtz, Christian. 2024a. 'Engineering Concepts by Engineering Social Norms: Solving the Implementation Challenge'. *Inquiry* 67 (6): 1716-43.
Nimtz, Christian. 2024b. 'The Power of Social Norms: Why Conceptual Engineers Should Care about Implementation'. *Synthese* 203 (6): 215.
Nisbett, Richard. 2015. *Mindware: Tools for Smart Thinking*. London: Allen Lane.
Nisbett, Richard, and Dov Cohen. 1996. *Culture Of Honor: the Psychology Of Violence In The South*. Boulder: Westview Press.
Noggle, Robert. 1996. 'Manipulative Actions: A Conceptual and Moral Analysis'. *American Philosophical Quarterly* 33 (1): 43-55.
Noggle, Robert. 2022. 'The Ethics of Manipulation'. In *The Stanford Encyclopedia of Philosophy*. Edited by Edward N. Zalta. Summer 2022 ed.
Norris, Andrew. 2009. '"La chaîne des raisons a une fin." Wittgenstein et Oakeshott sur le rationalisme et la pratique'. *Cités: Philosophie, Politique, Histoire* 38: 95-108.
Nozick, Robert. 1981. *Philosophical Explanations*. Cambridge, MA: Harvard University Press.
Nussbaum, Martha C. 1988. 'Non-Relative Virtues: An Aristotelian Approach'. *Midwest Studies in Philosophy* 13 (1): 32-53.
Nussbaum, Martha C. 2000. 'Why Practice Needs Ethical Theory—Particularism, Principle, and Bad Behavior'. In *The Path of the Law and Its Influence: The Legacy of Oliver Wendell Holmes*. Edited by Steven J. Burton, 50-86. Cambridge: Cambridge University Press.
Nussbaum, Martha C. 2001. *The Fragility of Goodness: Luck and Ethics in Greek Tragedy and Philosophy*. Rev. ed. Cambridge: Cambridge University Press.
Nyíri, J. C. 1976. 'Wittgenstein's New Traditionalism'. *Acta Philosophica Fennica* 28: 501-12.
Nyíri, J. C. 1982. 'Wittgenstein's Later Work in Relation to Conservatism'. In *Wittgenstein and His Times*. Edited by Brian McGuinness, 44-68. Chicago: University of Chicago Press.
O'Doherty, Marianne, and Felicitas Schmieder. 2015. 'Introduction: Travels and Mobilities in the Middle Ages: From the Atlantic to the Black Sea'. In *Travels and Mobilities in the Middle Ages: From the Atlantic to the Black Sea*. Edited by Marianne O'Doherty and Felicitas Schmieder, ix-xliii. Turnhout: Brepols.
O'Neill, Onora. 1987. 'Abstraction, Idealization and Ideology in Ethics'. *Royal Institute of Philosophy Lecture Series* 22: 55-69.
O'Shaughnessy, Brian. 1973. 'Trying (as the Mental "Pineal Gland")'. *Journal of Philosophy* 70 (13): 365-86.

O'Shaughnessy, Brian. 2008a. *The Will: A Dual Aspect Theory*, Vol. I. Cambridge: Cambridge University Press.
O'Shaughnessy, Brian. 2008b. *The Will: A Dual Aspect Theory*, Vol. II. Cambridge: Cambridge University Press.
Ober, Josiah. 2022. *The Greeks and the Rational: The Discovery of Practical Reason*. Oakland: University of California Press.
Olsson, Erik. 2017. 'Coherentist Theories of Epistemic Justification'. In *The Stanford Encyclopedia of Philosophy*. Edited by Edward N. Zalta. Spring 2017 ed.
Orwell, George. 2008. 'Politics and the English Language'. In *All Art Is Propaganda: Critical Essays*. Edited by George Packer and Keith Gessen, 270–86. Boston and New York: Mariner.
Owen, David. 2002. 'Criticism and Captivity: On Genealogy and Critical Theory'. *European Journal of Philosophy* 10 (2): 216–30.
Owen, David. 2007. *Nietzsche's Genealogy of Morality*. Stocksfield: Acumen.
Owen, David. 2008. 'Nietzsche's Genealogy Revisited'. *Journal of Nietzsche Studies* 35 (1): 141–54.
Owen, David. 2018. 'Nietzsche's Antichristian Ethics: Renaissance Virtù and the Project of Reevaluation'. In *Nietzsche and The Antichrist: Religion, Politics, and Culture in Late Modernity*. Edited by Daniel Conway, 67–88. London: Bloomsbury Academic.
Owen, David. 2022. 'The *Crisis* in Critique: Justification, Vindication and Confidence'. In *Modernità e critica*, Vol. I. Edited by Raffaele Carbone, 574–91. Napoli: La Città del Sole.
Owen, David. Forthcoming. 'On Vindication in Ethical Life'. *Public Reason*.
Page, Benjamin I. 1996. *Who Deliberates? Mass Media in Modern Democracy*. Chicago: University of Chicago Press.
Paine, Thomas. 1998. *Rights of Man, Common Sense, and Other Political Writings*. New York: Oxford University Press.
Palmeri, Frank. 2016. *State of Nature, Stages of Society: Enlightenment Conjectural History and Modern Social Discourse*. New York: Columbia University Press.
Paul, Elliot Samuel. 2020. 'Cartesian Clarity'. *Philosophers' Imprint* 20 (19): 1–28.
Paul, Laurie Ann. 2012. 'Metaphysics as Modeling: The Handmaiden's Tale'. *Philosophical Studies* 160 (1): 1–29.
Peacocke, Christopher. 1992. *A Study of Concepts*. Cambridge, MA: MIT Press.
Peacocke, Christopher. 1998. 'Implicit Conceptions, Understanding and Rationality'. *Philosophical Issues* 9: 43–88.
Pedersen, Morten Axel. 2011. *Not Quite Shamans: Spirit Worlds and Political Lives in Northern Mongolia*. Ithaca: Cornell University Press.
Peirce, Charles Sanders. 1931. *Collected Papers of Charles Sanders Peirce*. Edited by C. Hartshorne, P. Weiss, and A. Burks. Cambridge, MA: Belknap Press.
Percival, Philip. 1994. 'Absolute Truth'. *Proceedings of the Aristotelian Society* 94 (1): 189–214.
Pereboom, Derk. 2001. *Living without Free Will*. Cambridge: Cambridge University Press.
Peregrin, Jaroslav. 2014. *Inferentialism: Why Rules Matter*. New York: Palgrave Macmillan.
Pérez Carballo, Alejandro. 2020. 'Conceptual Evaluation: Epistemic'. In *Conceptual Engineering and Conceptual Ethics*. Edited by Alexis Burgess, Herman Cappelen, and David Plunkett, 304–32. Oxford: Oxford University Press.
Perry, Stephen. 2005. 'Law and Obligation'. *American Journal of Jurisprudence* 50 (1): 263–95.
Pettit, Philip. 1996. 'Functional Explanation and Virtual Selection'. *British Journal for the Philosophy of Science* 47 (2): 291–302.
Pettit, Philip. 1997. *Republicanism: A Theory of Freedom and Government*. Oxford: Oxford University Press.
Pettit, Philip. 2008. *Made with Words: Hobbes on Language, Mind, and Politics*. Princeton: Princeton University Press.
Pettit, Philip. 2018. *The Birth of Ethics: Reconstructing the Role and Nature of Morality*. Edited by Kinch Hoekstra. Oxford: Oxford University Press.
Pettit, Philip. 2019. 'Social Norms and the Internal Point of View: An Elaboration of Hart's Genealogy of Law'. *Oxford Journal of Legal Studies* 39 (2): 229–58.
Pettit, Philip. Forthcoming. *When Minds Converse: A Social Genealogy of the Human Soul*. Oxford: Oxford University Press.

Pinder, Mark. 2022. 'What Ought a Fruitful Explicatum to Be?'. *Erkenntnis* 87 (2): 913–32.
Pinder, Mark. 2023. 'Scharp on Inconsistent Concepts and Their Engineered Replacements, or: Can We Mend These Broken Things?'. *Inquiry* 66 (5): 863–84.
Pleasants, Nigel. 1999. *Wittgenstein and the Idea of a Critical Social Theory: A Critique of Giddens, Habermas and Bhaskar*. London: Routledge.
Pleasants, Nigel. 2002. 'Towards a Critical Use of Marx and Wittgenstein'. In *Marx and Wittgenstein: Knowledge, Morality and Politics*. Edited by Gavin Kitching and Nigel Pleasants, 160–81. London: Routledge.
Plotica, Luke Philip. 2015. *Michael Oakeshott and the Conversation of Modern Political Thought*. Albany: State University of New York Press.
Plunkett, David. 2015. 'Which Concepts Should We Use? Metalinguistic Negotiations and The Methodology of Philosophy'. *Inquiry* 58 (7–8): 828–74.
Plunkett, David. 2016. 'Conceptual History, Conceptual Ethics, and the Aims of Inquiry: A Framework for Thinking about the Relevance of the History/Genealogy of Concepts to Normative Inquiry'. *Ergo: An Open Access Journal of Philosophy* 3 (2): 27–64.
Plunkett, David. 2020. 'Normative Roles, Conceptual Variance, and Ardent Realism about Normativity'. *Inquiry* 63 (5): 509–34.
Plunkett, David, and Timothy Sundell. 2013a. 'Disagreement and the Semantics of Normative and Evaluative Terms'. *Philosophers' Imprint* 13 (23): 1–37.
Plunkett, David, and Timothy Sundell. 2013b. 'Dworkin's Interpretivism and the Pragmatics of Legal Disputes'. *Legal Theory* 19 (3): 242–281.
Plunkett, David, and Timothy Sundell. 2021. 'Metalinguistic Negotiation and Speaker Error'. *Inquiry* 64 (1–2): 142–67.
Podosky, Paul-Mikhail Catapang. 2021. 'Agency, Power, and Injustice in Metalinguistic Disagreement'. *Philosophical Quarterly* 72 (2): 441–64.
Pollock, John. 1984. *The Foundations of Philosophical Semantics*. Princeton: Princeton University Press.
Prescott-Couch, Alexander. 2015. 'Genealogy and the Structure of Interpretation'. *Journal of Nietzsche Studies* 46 (2): 239–47.
Prescott-Couch, Alexander. 2021. 'Deliberation through Misrepresentation? Inchoate Speech and the Division of Interpretive Labor'. *Journal of Political Philosophy* 29 (4): 496–518.
Prescott-Couch, Alexander. Manuscript. 'Nietzsche and the Significance of Genealogy'.
Price, Huw. 1988. *Facts and the Function of Truth*. Oxford: Blackwell.
Price, Huw. 2003. 'Truth as Convenient Friction'. *Journal of Philosophy* 100 (4): 167–90.
Price, Huw. 2011. *Naturalism without Mirrors*. Oxford: Oxford University Press.
Price, Huw. 2018. 'Carnapian Voluntarism and Global Expressivism: Reply to Carus'. *The Monist* 101 (4): 468–74.
Price, Huw. 2013. 'Naturalism without Representationalism'. In *Expressivism, Pragmatism and Representationalism*. Edited by Huw Price, 3–21. Cambridge: Cambridge University Press.
Price, Huw, and David Macarthur. 2007. 'Pragmatism, Quasi-Realism and the Global Challenge'. In *New Pragmatists*. Edited by Cheryl Misak, 91–120. Oxford: Oxford University Press.
Priest, Graham. 2006. *In Contradiction: A Study of the Transconsistent*. Oxford: Oxford University Press.
Priest, Graham. 2014. 'Contradictory Concepts'. In *Contradictions: Logic, History, Actuality*. Edited by Elena Ficara, 13–26. Berlin: De Gruyter.
Priest, Graham. 2016. 'Logical Disputes and the a priori'. *Logique et Analyse* 236: 347–66.
Pritchard, Duncan. 2007. 'Anti-Luck Epistemology'. *Synthese* 158 (3): 277–97.
Pritchard, Duncan. 2012. 'The Genealogy of the Concept of Knowledge and Anti-Luck Virtue Epistemology'. In *Conceptions of Knowledge*. Edited by Stefan Tolksdorf, 159–78. Berlin: De Gruyter.
Putnam, Hilary. 1973. 'Meaning and Reference'. *Journal of Philosophy* 70 (19): 699–711.
Putnam, Hilary. 1981. *Reason, Truth and History*. Cambridge: Cambridge University Press.
Putnam, Hilary. 1992. *Renewing Philosophy*. Cambridge, MA: Harvard University Press.
Putnam, Hilary. 2001. 'Reply to Bernard Williams' "Philosophy as a Humanistic Discipline"'. *Philosophy* 76 (4): 605–14.

Putnam, Hilary. 2002. *The Collapse of the Fact-Value Distinction and Other Essays*. Cambridge, MA.: Harvard University Press.
Queloz, Matthieu. 2016. 'Wittgenstein on the Chain of Reasons'. *Wittgenstein-Studien* 7 (1): 105–30.
Queloz, Matthieu. 2017a. 'Nietzsche's Pragmatic Genealogy of Justice'. *British Journal for the History of Philosophy* 25 (4): 727–49.
Queloz, Matthieu. 2017b. 'Two Orders of Things: Wittgenstein on Reasons and Causes'. *Philosophy* 92 (3): 369–97.
Queloz, Matthieu. 2018a. 'Davidsonian Causalism and Wittgensteinian Anti-Causalism: A Rapprochement'. *Ergo: An Open Access Journal of Philosophy* 5 (6): 153–72.
Queloz, Matthieu. 2018b. 'Williams's Pragmatic Genealogy and Self-Effacing Functionality'. *Philosophers' Imprint* 18 (17): 1–20.
Queloz, Matthieu. 2019. 'Nietzsches Affirmative Genealogien'. *Deutsche Zeitschrift für Philosophie* 67 (3): 429–39.
Queloz, Matthieu. 2021a. 'Choosing Values? Williams contra Nietzsche'. *Philosophical Quarterly* 71 (2): 286–307.
Queloz, Matthieu. 2021b. 'Nietzsche's English Genealogy of Truthfulness'. *Archiv für Geschichte der Philosophie* 103 (2): 341–63.
Queloz, Matthieu. 2021c. *The Practical Origins of Ideas: Genealogy as Conceptual Reverse-Engineering*. Oxford: Oxford University Press.
Queloz, Matthieu. 2021d. 'The Self-Effacing Functionality of Blame'. *Philosophical Studies* 178 (4): 1361–79.
Queloz, Matthieu. 2022a. 'The Essential Superficiality of the Voluntary and the Moralization of Psychology'. *Philosophical Studies* 179 (5): 1591–1620.
Queloz, Matthieu. 2022b. 'Genealogy, Evaluation, and Engineering'. *The Monist* 105 (4): 435–51.
Queloz, Matthieu. 2022c. 'A Shelter from Luck: The Morality System Reconstructed'. In *Morality and Agency: Themes from Bernard Williams*. Edited by András Szigeti and Matthew Talbert, 182–209. New York: Oxford University Press.
Queloz, Matthieu. 2023. 'Nietzsche's Conceptual Ethics'. *Inquiry* 66 (7): 1335–64.
Queloz, Matthieu. 2024a. 'Internalism from the Ethnographic Stance: From Self-Indulgence to Self-Expression and Corroborative Sense-Making'. *Philosophical Quarterly*: 1–30.
Queloz, Matthieu. 2024b. 'The Dworkin–Williams Debate: Liberty, Conceptual Integrity, and Tragic Conflict in Politics'. *Philosophy and Phenomenological Research* 109 (1): 3–29.
Queloz, Matthieu. Forthcoming. 'Reasons of Love and Conceptual Good-for-Nothings'. In *Themes from Susan Wolf*. Edited by Michael Frauchiger and Markus Stepanians. Berlin: De Gruyter.
Queloz, Matthieu, and Friedemann Bieber. 2022. 'Conceptual Engineering and the Politics of Implementation'. *Pacific Philosophical Quarterly* 103 (3): 670–91.
Queloz, Matthieu, and Damian Cueni. 2019. 'Nietzsche as a Critic of Genealogical Debunking: Making Room for Naturalism Without Subversion'. *The Monist* 102 (3): 277–97.
Queloz, Matthieu, and Damian Cueni. 2021. 'Left Wittgensteinianism'. *European Journal of Philosophy* 29 (4): 758–777.
Queloz, Matthieu, and Nikhil Krishnan. Forthcoming. 'Williams's Debt to Wittgenstein'. In *Bernard Williams on Philosophy and History*. Edited by Marcel van Ackeren and Matthieu Queloz. Oxford: Oxford University Press.
Queloz, Matthieu, and Marcel van Ackeren. 2024. 'Virtue Ethics and the Morality System'. *Topoi* 43 (2): 413–24.
Quine, Willard Van Orman. 1960. 'Carnap and Logical Truth'. *Synthese* 12 (4): 350–74.
Quine, Willard Van Orman. 2013. *Word and Object*. Cambridge, MA: MIT Press.
Radzik, Linda. 2000. 'Incorrigible Norms: Foundationalist Theories of Normative Authority'. *Southern Journal of Philosophy* 38 (4): 633–49.
Rathgeb, Nicole. 2020. *Die Begriffsanalyse im 21. Jahrhundert: Eine Verteidigung gegen zeitgenössische Einwände*. Paderborn: Mentis.
Rawls, John. 1955. 'Two Concepts of Rules'. *Philosophical Review* 64 (1): 3–32.
Rawls, John. 1971. *A Theory of Justice*. Cambridge, MA: Harvard University Press.
Rawls, John. 1993. *Political Liberalism*. New York: Columbia University Press.

Raz, Joseph. 1979. *The Authority of Law: Essays on Law and Morality*. Oxford: Clarendon Press.
Raz, Joseph. 1986. *The Morality of Freedom*. Oxford: Clarendon Press.
Raz, Joseph. 1989. 'Liberating Duties'. *Law and Philosophy* 8 (1): 3–21.
Raz, Joseph. 1995. *Ethics in the Public Domain: Essays in the Morality of Law and Politics*. Rev. ed. Oxford: Clarendon Press.
Raz, Joseph. 1999. *Practical Reason and Norms*. Oxford: Oxford University Press.
Raz, Joseph. 2009. *Between Authority and Interpretation: On the Theory of Law and Practical Reason*. New York: Oxford University Press.
Reader, Soran, ed. 2005. *The Philosophy of Need*. Cambridge: Cambridge University Press.
Reader, Soran. 2007. *Needs and Moral Necessity*. London: Routledge.
Reader, Soran, and Gillian Brock. 2004. 'Needs, Moral Demands and Moral Theory'. *Utilitas* 16 (3): 251–66.
Rechnitzer, Tanja. 2022. *Applying Reflective Equilibrium: Towards the Justification of a Precautionary Principle*. Cham: Springer.
Reck, Erich. 2012. 'Carnapian Explication: A Case Study and Critique'. In *Carnap's Ideal of Explication and Naturalism*. Edited by P. Wagner, 96–116. New York: Palgrave Macmillan.
Reck, Erich. 2024. 'Carnapian Explication: Origins and Shifting Goals'. In *Interpreting Carnap: Critical Essays*. Edited by A. Richardson and A. T. Tuboly. Cambridge: Cambridge University Press.
Rée, Jonathan. 1998. 'Strenuous Unbelief'. *London Review of Books*, October 15, 1998, 7–11.
Reginster, Bernard. 2021. *The Will to Nothingness: An Essay on Nietzsche's On the Genealogy of Morality*. Oxford: Oxford University Press.
Rescher, Nicholas. 1979. *Cognitive Systematization: A Systems Theoretic Approach to a Coherentist Theory of Knowledge*. Oxford: Blackwell.
Rescher, Nicholas. 2005. *Cognitive Harmony: The Role of Systemic Harmony in the Constitution of Knowledge*. Pittsburgh: University of Pittsburgh Press.
Reynolds, Steven L. 2017. *Knowledge as Acceptable Testimony*. Cambridge: Cambridge University Press.
Rice, Allen Thorndike. 1909. *Reminiscences of Abraham Lincoln by Distinguished Men of His Time*. New York: Harper & Brothers Publishers.
Richard, Mark. 2008. *When Truth Gives Out*. New York: Oxford University Press.
Richardson, John. 2020. *Nietzsche's Values*. New York: Oxford University Press.
Rickert, Heinrich. 1896. *Die Grenzen der naturwissenschaftlichen Begriffsbildung*. Tübingen: Mohr.
Ridley, Aaron. 2005. 'Nietzsche and the Re-evaluation of Values'. *Proceedings of the Aristotelian Society* 105 (1): 155–75.
Rieland, Indrek. 2024. 'Meaning Change'. *Analytic Philosophy* 65 (3): 434–51.
Rigby, Kate. 2023. 'Discourses of Nature'. In *The Cambridge History of European Romantic Literature*. Edited by Patrick Vincent, 73–104. Cambridge: Cambridge University Press.
Riggs, Jared. 2021. 'Deflating the Functional Turn in Conceptual Engineering'. *Synthese* 199 (3): 11555–86.
Riley, Jonathan. 2019. 'Liberal Pluralism and Common Decency'. In *Isaiah Berlin's Cold War Liberalism*. Edited by Jan-Werner Müller, 57–92. New York: Palgrave Macmillan.
Rini, Regina. 2019. 'Epoch Relativism and Our Moral Hopelessness'. In *Ethics beyond the Limits: New Essays on Bernard Williams' Ethics and the Limits of Philosophy*. Edited by Sophie-Grace Chappell and Marcel van Ackeren, 168–87. London: Routledge.
Ritschl, Otto. 1906. *System und systematische Methode in der Geschichte des wissenschaftlichen Sprachgebrauchs und der philosophischen Methodologie*. Bonn: C. Georgi.
Roberts, Debbie. 2011. 'Shapelessness and the Thick'. *Ethics* 121 (3): 489–520.
Roberts, Debbie. 2013. 'Thick Concepts'. *Philosophy Compass* 8 (8): 677–88.
Robinson, Richard. 1954. *Definition*. Oxford: Oxford University Press.
Robson, Jon, and Neil Sinclair. 2023. 'Speculative Aesthetic Expressivism'. *British Journal of Aesthetics* 63 (2): 181–97.
Rödl, Sebastian. 2018. *Self-Consciousness and Objectivity: An Introduction to Absolute Idealism*. Cambridge, MA: Harvard University Press.

Rorty, Richard. 1983. 'Postmodernist Bourgeois Liberalism'. *Journal of Philosophy* 80 (10): 583–9.
Rorty, Richard. 1989. *Contingency, Irony, and Solidarity*. Cambridge: Cambridge University Press.
Rorty, Richard. 2007. 'Cultural Politics and the Question of the Existence of God'. In *Philosophy as Cultural Politics*. Cambridge: Cambridge University Press.
Rorty, Richard. 2021. *Pragmatism as Anti-Authoritarianism*. Edited by Eduardo Mendieta. Cambridge, MA: Belknap Press.
Rosen, Gideon. 2022. 'Moral Realism with a Human Face: Objectivity in Ethics and the Limits of Philosophy'. In *Agency, Fate, and Luck: Themes from Bernard Williams*. Edited by Andras Szigeti and Matthew Talbert, 132–57. New York: Oxford University Press.
Rosen, Michael. 1996. *On Voluntary Servitude: False Consciousness and The Theory of Ideology*. Cambridge, MA: Harvard University Press.
Rothstein, Edward. 1998. 'Fresh Debates on the Legacy Of Isaiah Berlin'. *New York Times*, 14 November, 9.
Rouse, Joseph. 2015. *Articulating the World: Conceptual Understanding and the Scientific Image*. Chicago: University of Chicago Press.
Rousseau, Jean-Jacques. 1979. *Emile, or On Education*. Translated by Alan Bloom. New York: Basic Books.
Rowe, M. W. 2023. *J. L. Austin: Philosopher and D-Day Intelligence Officer*. Oxford: Oxford University Press.
Rudy-Hiller, Fernando. 2018. 'The Epistemic Condition for Moral Responsibility'. In *The Stanford Encyclopedia of Philosophy*. Edited by Edward N. Zalta. Fall 2018 ed.
Russell, Bertrand. 1921. *The Analysis of Mind*. London: George Allen and Unwin.
Russell, Paul. 2013. 'Responsibility, Naturalism, and "The Morality System"'. In *Oxford Studies in Agency and Responsibility*, Vol. 1. Edited by David Shoemaker, 184–204. Oxford: Oxford University Press.
Russell, Paul. 2017a. 'Free Will Pessimism'. In *Oxford Studies in Agency and Responsibility*, Vol. 4. Edited by David Shoemaker, 93–120. Oxford: Oxford University Press.
Russell, Paul. 2017b. 'Free Will Pessimism'. In *The Limits of Free Will: Selected Essays*, 243–76. Oxford: Oxford University Press.
Russell, Paul. 2017c. *The Limits of Free Will: Selected Essays*. Oxford: Oxford University Press.
Russell, Paul. 2018. 'Bernard Williams: Ethics from a Human Point of View'. *Times Literary Supplement*, 18 December.
Russell, Paul. 2019. 'Hume's Optimism and Williams's Pessimism: From "Science of Man" to Genealogical Critique'. In *Ethics beyond the Limits: New Essays on Bernard Williams' Ethics and the Limits of Philosophy*. Edited by Sophie-Grace Chappell and Marcel van Ackeren, 37–52. London: Routledge.
Russell, Paul. 2022. 'Free Will and the Tragic Predicament: Making Sense of Williams'. In *Morality and Agency: Themes from Bernard Williams*. Edited by András Szigeti and Matthew Talbert, 161–81. New York: Oxford University Press.
Russell, Paul. 2023. 'Responsibility after "Morality": Strawson's Naturalism and Williams's Genealogy'. In *P. F. Strawson and his Philosophical Legacy*. Edited by A. Bengtson, B. De Mesel, and S. Heyndels, 234–59. Oxford: Oxford University Press.
Ryle, Gilbert. 2009a. *The Concept of Mind*. Edited by Julia Tanney. London: Routledge.
Ryle, Gilbert. 2009b. 'Phenomenology versus "The Concept of Mind"'. In *Critical Essays: Collected Papers*, Vol. I, 186–204. Abingdon: Routledge.
Ryle, Gilbert. 2009c. 'Thinking and Reflecting'. In *Collected Papers*, Vol. 2: *Collected Essays 1929–1968*, 479–93. Abingdon: Routledge.
Ryle, Gilbert. 2009d. 'The Thinking of Thoughts: What is "Le Penseur" Doing?'. In *Collected Papers*, Vol. 2: *Collected Essays 1929–1968*, 494–510. Abingdon: Routledge.
Rysiew, Patrick. 2012. 'Epistemic Scorekeeping'. In *Knowledge Ascriptions*. Edited by Jessica Brown and Mikkel Gerken, 270–94. Oxford: Oxford University Press.
Sagar, Paul. 2017. 'Beyond Sympathy: Smith's Rejection of Hume's Moral Theory'. *British Journal for the History of Philosophy* 25 (4): 681–705.

Sagar, Paul. 2024. *Basic Equality*. Princeton: Princeton University Press.
Sainsbury, R. M., and Michael Tye. 2012. *Seven Puzzles of Thought: An Originalist Theory of Concepts*. Oxford: Oxford University Press.
Sandel, Michael. 1981. *Liberalism and the Limits of Justice*. 2nd ed. Cambridge: Cambridge University Press.
Sandel, Michael. 1996. *Democracy's Discontent*. 2nd ed. Cambridge, MA: Harvard University Press.
Santarelli, Matteo. 2024. 'Improving Concepts, Reshaping Values: Pragmatism and Ameliorative Projects'. *Inquiry* 67 (3): 872–90.
Santelli, Mauro. 2020. 'Redescribing Final Vocabularies: A Rortian Picture of Identity and Selfhood'. *European Journal of Pragmatism and American Philosophy* XII (1): 1–21.
Saunders, Kevin W. 1988. 'Voluntary Acts and the Criminal Law: Justifying Culpability Based on the Existence of Volition'. *University of Pittsburgh Law Review* 49 (2): 443–76.
Sawyer, Sarah. 2018. 'The Importance of Concepts'. *Proceedings of the Aristotelian Society* 118 (2): 127–47.
Sawyer, Sarah. 2020a. 'The Role of Concepts in Fixing Language'. *Canadian Journal of Philosophy* 50 (5): 555–65.
Sawyer, Sarah. 2020b. 'Talk and Thought'. In *Conceptual Engineering and Conceptual Ethics*. Edited by Alexis Burgess, Herman Cappelen, and David Plunkett, 379–95. Oxford: Oxford University Press.
Sawyer, Sarah. 2020c. 'Truth and Objectivity in Conceptual Engineering'. *Inquiry* 63 (9–10): 1001–22.
Scanlon, Thomas M. 1992. 'The Aims and Authority of Moral Theory'. *Oxford Journal of Legal Studies* 12 (1): 1–23.
Scanlon, Thomas M. 1998. *What We Owe to Each Other*. Cambridge, MA: Harvard University Press.
Scanlon, Thomas M. 2003. 'Thickness and Theory'. *Journal of Philosophy* 100 (6): 275–87.
Schaffer, Jonathan. 2004. 'From Contextualism to Contrastivism'. *Philosophical Studies* 119 (1–2): 73–103.
Scharp, Kevin. 2013. *Replacing Truth*. Oxford: Oxford University Press.
Scharp, Kevin. 2020. 'Philosophy as the Study of Defective Concepts'. In *Conceptual Engineering and Conceptual Ethics*. Edited by Alexis Burgess, Herman Cappelen, and David Plunkett, 396–416. Oxford: Oxford University Press.
Scharp, Kevin. 2021. 'Conceptual Engineering for Truth: Aletheic Properties and New Aletheic Concepts'. *Synthese* 198 (Suppl 2): 647–88.
Schauer, Frederick. 1987. 'Authority and Indeterminacy'. *Nomos* 29: 28–38.
Scheffler, Samuel. 1992. *Human Morality*. Oxford: Oxford University Press.
Schiappa, Edward. 2003. *Defining Reality: Definitions and the Politics of Meaning*. Carbondale: Southern Illinois University Press.
Schneck, Ariane Cäcilie. 2019. 'Elisabeth of Bohemia's Neo-Peripatetic Account of the Emotions'. *British Journal for the History of Philosophy* 27 (4): 753–70.
Schneewind, Jerome B. 1998. *The Invention of Autonomy*. Cambridge: Cambridge University Press.
Schroeder, Mark. 2007. *Slaves of the Passions*. Oxford: Oxford University Press.
Schroeder, Mark. 2014. *Explaining the Reasons We Share: Explanation and Expression in Ethics*, Vol. 1. Oxford: Oxford University Press.
Schroeter, Laura, and François Schroeter. 2015. 'Rationalizing Self-Interpretation'. In *The Palgrave Handbook of Philosophical Methods*. Edited by Chris Daly, 419–47. New York: Palgrave Macmillan.
Searle, John. 2010. *Making the Social World: The Structure of Human Civilization*. Oxford: Oxford University Press.
Sederberg, Peter C. 1984. *The Politics of Meaning: Power and Explanation in the Construction of Social Reality*. Tucson: University of Arizona Press.
Sellars, Wilfrid. 1958. 'Counterfactuals, Dispositions, and the Causal Modalities'. In *Minnesota Studies in the Philosophy of Science*, Vol. II. Edited by Herbert Feigl, Michael Scriven, and Grover Maxwell, 225–308. Minneapolis: University of Minnesota Press.

Sellars, Wilfrid. 1997. *Empiricism and the Philosophy of Mind*. Edited by Richard Rorty. Cambridge, MA: Harvard University Press.
Sellars, Wilfrid. 2007. *In the Space of Reasons: Selected Essays of Wilfrid Sellars*. Edited by Kevin Scharp and Robert Brandom. Cambridge, MA: Harvard University Press.
Sen, Amartya, and Bernard Williams. 1982. 'Introduction: Utilitarianism and Beyond'. In *Utilitarianism and Beyond*. Edited by Amartya Sen and Bernard Williams, 1–21. Cambridge: Cambridge University Press.
Shackelford, Todd K. 2005. 'An Evolutionary Psychological Perspective on Cultures of Honor'. *Evolutionary Psychology* 3 (1): 381–91.
Shapin, Steven. 1994. *A Social History of Truth: Civility and Science in Seventeenth-Century England*. Chicago: University of Chicago Press.
Shaw, Ashley. 2023. 'The Necessity of "Need"'. *Ethics* 133 (3): 329–54.
Shea, Nicholas. 2024. *Concepts at the Interface*. Oxford: Oxford University Press.
Sher, George. 2021. *A Wild West of the Mind*. New York: Oxford University Press.
Shields, Matthew. 2021a. 'Conceptual Change and Future Paths for Pragmatism'. *Southern Journal of Philosophy* 59 (3): 405–34.
Shields, Matthew. 2021b. 'Conceptual Domination'. *Synthese* 199 (5): 15043–67.
Shields, Matthew. 2021c. 'On Stipulation'. *European Journal of Philosophy* 29 (4): 1100–14.
Shields, Matthew. 2023. 'Conceptual Engineering, Conceptual Domination, and the Case of Conspiracy Theories'. *Social Epistemology* 37 (4): 1–17.
Shun, Kwong-loi, and David B. Wong, eds. 2004. *Confucian Ethics: A Comparative Study of Self, Autonomy, and Community*. New York: Cambridge University Press.
Sider, Theodore. 2011. *Writing the Book of the World*. Oxford: Oxford University Press.
Simion, Mona. 2018. 'The "Should" in Conceptual Engineering'. *Inquiry* 61 (8): 914–28.
Simion, Mona, and Christoph Kelp. 2020. 'Conceptual Innovation, Function First'. *Noûs* 54 (4): 985–1002.
Sinclair, Neil. 2018. 'Conceptual Role Semantics and the Reference of Moral Concepts'. *European Journal of Philosophy* 26 (1): 95–121.
Sinclair, Neil. 2021. *Practical Expressivism*. Oxford: Oxford University Press.
Skinner, Quentin. 1994. 'Modernity and Disenchantment: Some Historical Reflections'. In *Philosophy in an Age of Pluralism: The Philosophy of Charles Taylor in Question*. Edited by Tully James and Daniel M. Weinstock, 37–48. Cambridge: Cambridge University Press.
Skinner, Quentin. 1997. 'Rhetoric and Conceptual Change'. In *Quentin Skinner's Rhetoric of Conceptual Change*. Edited by Kari Palonen, 60–73. London: SAGE.
Skinner, Quentin. 1998. *Liberty before Liberalism*. Cambridge: Cambridge University Press.
Skinner, Quentin. 2002. *Visions of Politics*, Vol. 2: *Renaissance Virtues*. Cambridge: Cambridge University Press.
Skinner, Quentin. 2009. 'A Genealogy of the Modern State'. In *Proceedings of the British Academy*, Vol. 162, 2008 Lectures. Edited by Ron Johnston, 325–70. Oxford: Oxford University Press.
Skinner, Quentin. 2017. 'Machiavelli and the Misunderstanding of Princely Virtù'. In *Machiavelli on Liberty and Conflict*. Edited by David Johnston, Nadia Urbinati and Camila Vergara, 139–63. Chicago: University of Chicago Press.
Skyrms, Brian. 1996. *Evolution of the Social Contract*. Cambridge: Cambridge University Press.
Skyrms, Brian. 2004. *The Stag Hunt and the Evolution of Social Structure*. Cambridge: Cambridge University Press.
Sliwa, Paulina. 2024. 'Making Sense of Things: Moral Inquiry as Hermeneutical Inquiry'. *Philosophy and Phenomenological Research* 109 (1): 117–37.
Smith, David Livingstone. 2020. *On Inhumanity: Dehumanization and How to Resist It*. New York: Oxford University Press.
Smith, Helen. 2021. 'Clinical AI: Opacity, Accountability, Responsibility and Liability'. *AI and Society* 36 (2): 535–45.
Smith, Michael. 2013. 'On the Nature and Significance of the Distinction between Thick and Thin Ethical Concepts'. In *Thick Concepts*. Edited by Simon Kirchin, 97–120. Oxford: Oxford University Press.

Smith, Sophie. 2021. 'Historicizing Rawls'. *Modern Intellectual History* 18 (4): 906–39.
Smithson, Robert. 2021. 'Conceptual Cartography'. *Inquiry* 64 (1–2): 97–122.
Smyth, Nicholas. 2018. 'Integration and Authority: Rescuing the "One Thought Too Many" Problem'. *Canadian Journal of Philosophy* 48 (6): 812–30.
Smyth, Nicholas. 2019. 'The Inevitability of Inauthenticity: Bernard Williams and Practical Alienation'. In *Ethics beyond the Limits: New Essays on Bernard Williams' Ethics and the Limits of Philosophy*. Edited by Sophie-Grace Chappell and Marcel van Ackeren, 188–208. London: Routledge.
Smyth, Nicholas. 2020. 'Socratic Reductionism in Ethics'. *European Journal of Philosophy* 28 (4): 970–85.
Smyth, Nicholas. 2022. 'Nothing Personal: On the Limits of the Impersonal Temperament in Ethics'. *Journal of Value Inquiry* 56 (1): 67–83.
Snell, Bruno. 1953. *The Discovery of the Mind: The Greek Origins of European Thought*. Translated by T. G. Rosenmeyer. Cambridge, MA: Harvard University Press.
Soames, Scott. 2011. 'The Value of Vagueness'. In *Philosophical Foundations of Language in the Law*. Edited by Andrei Marmor and Scott Soames, 14–30. Oxford: Oxford University Press.
Sober, Elliott. 1984. *The Nature of Selection*. Cambridge, MA: MIT Press.
Sorensen, Roy. 1991. 'Vagueness and the Desiderata for Definition'. In *Definitions and Definability: Philosophical Perspectives*. Edited by J. H. Fetzer, D. Shatz, and G. N. Schlesinger, 71–109. Dordrecht: Springer.
Sorensen, Roy A. 1988. *Blindspots*. New York: Oxford University Press.
Sosa, Ernest. 1999. 'How Must Knowledge Be Modally Related to What Is Known?'. *Philosophical Topics* 26 (1–2): 373–84.
Spencer, Jack. 2016. 'Relativity and Degrees of Relationality'. *Philosophy and Phenomenological Research* 92 (2): 432–59.
Srinivasan, Amia. 2015. 'The Archimedean Urge'. *Philosophical Perspectives* 29 (1): 325–362.
Srinivasan, Amia. 2019. 'Genealogy, Epistemology and Worldmaking'. *Proceedings of the Aristotelian Society* 119 (2): 127–56.
Srinivasan, Amia. Manuscript. *The Contingent World: Genealogy, Epistemology, Politics*.
Stampe, Dennis W. 1987. 'The Authority of Desire'. *Philosophical Review* 96 (3): 335–81.
Steinbeck, John. 2006. *The Grapes of Wrath*. New York: Penguin.
Steinberger, Florian. 2016. 'How Tolerant Can You Be? Carnap on Rationality'. *Philosophy and Phenomenological Research* 92 (3): 645–68.
Stevenson, Charles Leslie. 1938. 'Persuasive Definitions'. *Mind* XLVII (187): 331–350.
Stevenson, Charles Leslie. 1944. *Ethics and Language*. New Haven: Yale University Press.
Stich, Stephen. 1983. *From Folk Psychology to Cognitive Science*. Cambridge, MA: MIT Press.
Stine, Gail C. 1976. 'Skepticism, Relevant Alternatives, and Deductive Closure'. *Philosophical Studies* 29 (4): 249–61.
Strathern, Marilyn. 2004. *Partial Connections*. Walnut Creek, CA: AltaMira Press.
Strawson, Peter Frederick. 1959. *Individuals*. London: Routledge.
Strawson, Peter Frederick. 1966. *The Bounds of Sense: An Essay on Kant's Critique of Pure Reason*. Abingdon: Routledge.
Strawson, Peter Frederick. 2008a. 'Freedom and Resentment'. In *Freedom and Resentment and Other Essays*, 1–28. Abingdon: Routledge.
Strawson, Peter Frederick. 2008b. 'Social Morality and Individual Ideal'. In *Freedom and Resentment and Other Essays*, 29–49. Abingdon: Routledge.
Strawson, Peter Frederick. 2011. *Philosophical Writings*. Oxford: Oxford University Press.
Strevens, Michael. 2008. *Depth: An Account of Scientific Explanation*. Cambridge, MA: Harvard University Press.
Stroud, Sarah. 2019. 'Conceptual Disagreement'. *American Philosophical Quarterly* 56 (1): 15–27.
Stuurman, Siep. 2017. *The Invention of Humanity: Equality and Cultural Difference in World History*. Cambridge, MA: Harvard University Press.
Summers, Lawrence H. 2003. 'The Authority of Ideas'. *Harvard Business Review* 81 (8): 144–144.

Sunstein, Cass R. 1996. *Legal Reasoning and Political Conflict*. New York: Oxford University Press.
Sunstein, Cass R. 2001. *One Case at a Time: Judicial Minimalism on the Supreme Court*. Cambridge, Massachusetts: Harvard University Press.
Sunstein, Cass R. 2016. *The Ethics of Influence: Government in the Age of Behavioral Science*. New York: Cambridge University Press.
Susskind, Jamie. 2018. *Future Politics: Living Together in a World Transformed by Tech*. New York: Oxford University Press.
Tasioulas, John. 1998. 'Relativism, Realism, and Reflection'. *Inquiry* 41 (4): 377–410.
Taylor, Charles. 1985. *Philosophy and the Human Sciences: Philosophical Papers*, Vol. II. Cambridge: Cambridge University Press.
Taylor, Charles. 1989. *Sources of the Self*. Cambridge, MA: Harvard University Press.
Taylor, Craig. 2012. *Moralism: A Study of a Vice*. Durham: Acumen.
Teichmann, Roger. 2021. 'Conceptual Corruption'. In *Cora Diamond on Ethics*. Edited by Maria Balaska, 33–55. New York: Palgrave Macmillan.
Temelini, Michael. 2015. *Wittgenstein and the Study of Politics*. Toronto: University of Toronto Press.
Tersman, Folke. 2018. 'Recent Work on Reflective Equilibrium and Method in Ethics'. *Philosophy Compass* 13 (6): e12493.
Testini, Francesco. 2021. *Crabwalk: Applying Pragmatic Genealogy to Contextualist Political Theory*. PhD Thesis, University of Milan.
Testini, Francesco. 2022. 'Genealogical Solutions to the Problem of Critical Distance: Political Theory, Contextualism and the Case of Punishment in Transitional Scenarios'. *Res Publica* 28 (2): 271–301.
Testini, Francesco. 2024. 'How Far Can Genealogies Affect the Space of Reasons? Vindication, Justification and Excuses'. *Inquiry*: 1–29.
Thomas, Alan. 2006. *Value and Context: The Nature of Moral and Political Knowledge*. Oxford: Clarendon Press.
Thomasson, Amie. 2021. 'Conceptual Engineering: When Do We Need It? How Can We Do It?'. *Inquiry*: 1–26.
Thomasson, Amie. 2025. *Rethinking Metaphysics*. New York: Oxford University Press.
Thomasson, Amie L. 2015. *Ontology Made Easy*. New York: Oxford University Press.
Thomasson, Amie L. 2020a. *Norms and Necessity*. New York: Oxford University Press.
Thomasson, Amie L. 2020b. 'A Pragmatic Method for Normative Conceptual Work'. In *Conceptual Engineering and Conceptual Ethics*. Edited by Alexis Burgess, Herman Cappelen, and David Plunkett, 435–58. Oxford: Oxford University Press.
Thomasson, Amie L. 2024. 'How Should We Think about Linguistic Function?'. *Inquiry* 67 (3): 840–71.
Thompson, Edward Palmer. 1975. *Whigs and Hunters. The Origin of the Black Act*. London: Penguin.
Tiberius, Valerie. 2018. *Well-Being as Value Fulfillment: How We Can Help Each Other to Live Well*. Oxford: Oxford University Press.
Tooley, Michael. 1972. 'Abortion and Infanticide'. *Philosophy & Public Affairs* 2 (1): 37–65.
Tooley, Michael. 1983. *Abortion and Infanticide*. Oxford: Clarendon Press.
Toulmin, Stephen. 1953. *An Examination of the Place of Reason in Ethics*. Cambridge: Cambridge University Press.
Trilling, Lionel. 1972. *Sincerity and Authenticity*. Cambridge, MA: Harvard University Press.
Tuck, Richard. 1979. *Natural Rights Theories: Their Origin and Development*. Cambridge: Cambridge University Press.
Tye, Larry. 1998. *The Father of Spin: Edward L. Bernays and The Birth of Public Relations*. New York: Henry Holt.
Ulaş, Luke. 2020. 'Can Political Realism Be Action-Guiding?'. *Critical Review of International Social and Political Philosophy* 26 (4): 1–26.
van Deemter, Kees. 2010. *Not Exactly: In Praise of Vagueness*. Oxford: Oxford University Press.

van Domselaar, Iris. 2017. 'On Tragic Legal Choices'. *Law and Humanities* 11 (2): 184–204.
van Domselaar, Iris. 2020. 'All Judges on the Couch? On Iris Murdoch and Legal Decision-Making'. In *Virtue, Emotion and Imagination in Law and Legal Reasoning*. Edited by Amalia Amaya and Maksymilian Del Mar, 77–98. London: Bloomsbury.
van Domselaar, Iris. 2022. 'Law's Regret: On Moral Remainders, (In)commensurability and a Virtue-Ethical Approach to Legal Decision-Making'. *Jurisprudence* 13 (2): 220–39.
van Riel, Raphael. 2022. 'Weberian Ideal Type Construction as Concept Replacement'. *European Journal of Philosophy* 30 (4): 1358–77.
Väyrynen, Pekka. 2013. *The Lewd, The Rude, and the Nasty: A Study of Thick Concepts in Ethics*. Oxford: Oxford University Press.
Vecht, Joost Jacob. 2023. 'Open Texture Clarified'. *Inquiry* 66 (6): 1–21.
Véliz, Carissa. 2020. *Privacy is Power: Why and How You Should Take Back Control of Your Data*. London: Bantam Press.
Veluwenkamp, Herman, and Jeroen van den Hoven. 2023. 'Design for Values and Conceptual Engineering'. *Ethics and Information Technology* 25 (1): 1–12.
Virgil. 2007. *Aeneid*. Oxford: Oxford University Press.
Waismann, Friedrich. 1945. 'Verifiability'. *Proceedings of the Aristotelian Society Supplementary Volume* 19: 119–50.
Wakil, Samantha. 2023. 'Experimental Explications for Conceptual Engineering'. *Erkenntnis* 88 (4): 1509–31.
Waller, Bruce N. 2011. *Against Moral Responsibility*. Cambridge, MA: MIT Press.
Walzer, Michael. 1983. *Spheres of Justice*. Oxford: Blackwell.
Walzer, Michael. 1987. *Interpretation and Social Criticism*. Cambridge, MA: Harvard University Press.
Wanderer, Jeremy. 2008. *Robert Brandom*. Montreal: McGill-Queen's University Press.
Weaver, Bryan R., and Kevin Scharp. 2019. *Semantics for Reasons*. Oxford: Oxford University Press.
Weber, Marcel. 2005. *Philosophy of Experimental Biology*. Cambridge: Cambridge University Press.
Weber, Max. 2019. *Economy and Society: A New Translation*. Edited and translated by Keith Tribe. Cambridge, MA: Harvard University Press.
Wedgwood, Ralph. 2007. *The Nature of Normativity*. New York: Oxford University Press.
Wedgwood, Ralph. 2015. 'An Inferentialist Conception of the *A Priori*'. In *Oxford Studies in Epistemology*, Vol. 5. Edited by Tamar Szabo Gendler and John Hawthorne, 295–314. Oxford: Oxford University Press.
Wei, Xintong. 2022. 'A Practice-Based Account of the Truth Norm of Belief'. *Episteme*: 1–21.
Weisberg, Michael. 2007. 'Three Kinds of Idealization'. *Journal of Philosophy* 104 (12): 639–59.
Weisberg, Michael. 2013. *Simulation and Similarity: Using Models to Understand the World*. Oxford: Oxford University Press.
Westerblad, Oscar. 2024. 'Deweyan Conceptual Engineering: Reconstruction, Concepts, and Philosophical Inquiry'. *Inquiry* 67 (3): 985–1008.
Westermarck, Edvard. 1924. *The Origin and Development of the Moral Ideas*. 2nd ed. London: Macmillan.
Wiggins, David. 1990. 'Moral Cognitivism, Moral Relativism and Motivating Moral Beliefs'. *Proceedings of the Aristotelian Society* 91: 61–85.
Wiggins, David. 2002. 'Claims of Need'. In *Needs, Values, Truth*. 3rd ed., 1–57. Oxford: Clarendon Press.
Wiggins, David, and Sira Dermen. 1987. 'Needs, Need, Needing'. *Journal of Medical Ethics* 13: 62–8.
Wille, Katrin. 2018. *Die Praxis des Unterscheidens: historische und systematische Perspektiven*. Freiburg: Karl Alber.
Willerslev, Rane. 2007. *Soul Hunters: Hunting, Animism, and Personhood among the Siberian Yukaghirs*. Berkeley: University of California Press.
Williams, Bernard. 1963. 'Postscript'. In *Freedom and the Will*. Edited by David Pears, 105–37. New York: Palgrave.

Williams, Bernard. 1971. 'Conversation with Bernard Williams: Philosophy and Morals'. In *Modern British Philosophy*. Edited by Bryan Magee, 150–65. New York: St. Martin's Press.
Williams, Bernard. 1973a. 'Deciding to Believe'. In *Problems of the Self*, 136–51. Cambridge: Cambridge University Press.
Williams, Bernard. 1973b. 'Egoism and Altruism'. In *Problems of the Self*, 250–65. Cambridge: Cambridge University Press.
Williams, Bernard. 1973c. 'Ethical Consistency'. In *Problems of the Self*, 166–86. Cambridge: Cambridge University Press.
Williams, Bernard. 1973d. 'The Idea of Equality'. In *Problems of the Self*, 230–49. Cambridge: Cambridge University Press.
Williams, Bernard. 1981a. 'Conflicts of Values'. In *Moral Luck*, 71–82. Cambridge: Cambridge University Press.
Williams, Bernard. 1981b. 'Internal and External Reasons'. In *Moral Luck*, 101–13. Cambridge: Cambridge University Press.
Williams, Bernard. 1981c. 'Moral Luck'. In *Moral Luck*, 20–39. Cambridge: Cambridge University Press.
Williams, Bernard. 1981d. '*Ought* and Moral Obligation'. In *Moral Luck*, 114–23. Cambridge: Cambridge University Press.
Williams, Bernard. 1981e. 'Persons, Character and Morality'. In *Moral Luck*, 1–19. Cambridge: Cambridge University Press.
Williams, Bernard. 1981f. 'Practical Necessity'. In *Moral Luck*, 124–31. Cambridge: Cambridge University Press.
Williams, Bernard. 1981g. 'The Truth in Relativism'. In *Moral Luck*, 132–43. Cambridge: Cambridge University Press.
Williams, Bernard. 1981h. 'Utilitarianism and Moral Self-Indulgence'. In *Moral Luck*, 40–53. Cambridge: Cambridge University Press.
Williams, Bernard. 1982. 'The Spell of Linguistic Philosophy: Dialogue with Bernard Williams'. In *Men of Ideas: Some Creators of Contemporary Philosophy*. Edited by Bryan Magee, 110–24. Oxford: Oxford University Press.
Williams, Bernard. 1984. 'The Scientific and the Ethical'. In *Royal Institute of Philosophy Lecture Series*, Vol. 17. Edited by Stuart C. Brown. 209–28. Cambridge: Cambridge University Press.
Williams, Bernard. 1985. *Ethics and the Limits of Philosophy*. Routledge Classics Edition. London: Routledge.
Williams, Bernard. 1986. 'Reply to Simon Blackburn'. *Philosophical Books* 27 (4): 203–8.
Williams, Bernard. 1993. *Shame and Necessity*. Berkeley: University of California Press.
Williams, Bernard. 1995a. 'Ethics'. In *Philosophy 1: A Guide through the Subject*. Edited by A. C. Grayling, 545–82. Oxford: Oxford University Press.
Williams, Bernard. 1995b. 'Formal and Substantial Individualism'. In *Making Sense of Humanity and Other Philosophical Papers 1982–1993*, 123–34. Cambridge: Cambridge University Press.
Williams, Bernard. 1995c. 'How Free Does the Will Need to Be?'. In *Making Sense of Humanity and Other Philosophical Papers 1982–1993*, 3–21. Cambridge: Cambridge University Press.
Williams, Bernard. 1995d. 'Internal Reasons and the Obscurity of Blame'. In *Making Sense of Humanity and Other Philosophical Papers 1982–1993*, 35–45. Cambridge: Cambridge University Press.
Williams, Bernard. 1995e. 'Moral Luck: A Postscript'. In *Making Sense of Humanity and Other Philosophical Papers 1982–1993*, 241–7. Cambridge: Cambridge University Press.
Williams, Bernard. 1995f. 'Must a Concern for the Environment Be Centred on Human Beings?'. In *Making Sense of Humanity and Other Philosophical Papers 1982–1993*, 233–40. Cambridge: Cambridge University Press.
Williams, Bernard. 1995g. 'Nietzsche's Minimalist Moral Psychology'. In *Making Sense of Humanity and Other Philosophical Papers 1982–1993*, 65–78. Cambridge: Cambridge University Press.
Williams, Bernard. 1995h. 'The Point of View of the Universe: Sidgwick and the Ambitions of Ethics'. In *Making Sense of Humanity and Other Philosophical Papers 1982–1993*, 153–71. Cambridge: Cambridge University Press.

Williams, Bernard. 1995i. 'Professional Morality and Its Dispositions'. In *Making Sense of Humanity and Other Philosophical Papers 1982–1993*, 192–202. Cambridge: Cambridge University Press.

Williams, Bernard. 1995j. 'Replies'. In *World, Mind, and Ethics: Essays on the Ethical Philosophy of Bernard Williams*. Edited by J. E. J. Altham and Ross Harrison, 185–224. Cambridge: Cambridge University Press.

Williams, Bernard. 1995k. 'Saint-Just's Illusion'. In *Making Sense of Humanity and Other Philosophical Papers 1982–1993*, 135–50. Cambridge: Cambridge University Press.

Williams, Bernard. 1995l. 'Truth in Ethics'. *Ratio* 8 (3): 227–42.

Williams, Bernard. 1995m. 'Voluntary Acts and Responsible Agents'. In *Making Sense of Humanity and Other Philosophical Papers 1982–1993*, 22–34. Cambridge: Cambridge University Press.

Williams, Bernard. 1995n. 'What Does Intuitionism Imply?'. In *Making Sense of Humanity and Other Philosophical Papers 1982–1993*, 182–91. Cambridge: Cambridge University Press.

Williams, Bernard. 1995o. 'What Has Philosophy to Learn from Tort Law?'. In *The Philosophical Foundations of Tort Law*. Edited by David G. Owen, 487–98. Oxford: Oxford University Press.

Williams, Bernard. 1995p. 'Who Needs Ethical Knowledge?'. In *Making Sense of Humanity and Other Philosophical Papers 1982–1993*, 203–12. Cambridge: Cambridge University Press.

Williams, Bernard. 1996a. 'Contemporary Philosophy: A Second Look'. In *The Blackwell Companion to Philosophy*. Edited by Nicholas Bunnin and Eric P. Tsui-James, 23–35. Oxford: Blackwell.

Williams, Bernard. 1996b. 'A Fugitive from the Pigeonhole'. Interview by John Davies. *Times Higher Education Supplement*, Issue 1252, 1 November, 15.

Williams, Bernard. 1998. 'Virtues and Vices'. In *Routledge Encyclopedia of Philosophy*. Edited by Edward Craig. London: Routledge.

Williams, Bernard. 1999. 'Seminar with Bernard Williams'. *Ethical Perspectives* 6 (3–4): 243–65.

Williams, Bernard. 2001a. 'Liberalism and Loss'. In *The Legacy of Isaiah Berlin*. Edited by Mark Lilla, Ronald Dworkin, and Robert Silvers, 91–103. New York: New York Review of Books.

Williams, Bernard. 2001b. *Morality: An Introduction to Ethics*. Cambridge: Cambridge University Press.

Williams, Bernard. 2002. *Truth and Truthfulness: An Essay in Genealogy*. Princeton: Princeton University Press.

Williams, Bernard. 2003. 'Relativism, History, and the Existence of Values'. In *The Practice of Value*. Edited by R. Jay Wallace, 106–17. Oxford: Clarendon Press.

Williams, Bernard. 2005a. 'Conflicts of Liberty and Equality'. In *In the Beginning Was the Deed: Realism and Moralism in Political Argument*. Edited by Geoffrey Hawthorne, 115–27. Princeton: Princeton University Press.

Williams, Bernard. 2005b. *Descartes: The Project of Pure Enquiry*. London: Routledge.

Williams, Bernard. 2005c. 'From Freedom to Liberty: The Construction of a Political Value'. In *In the Beginning Was the Deed: Realism and Moralism in Political Argument*. Edited by Geoffrey Hawthorne, 75–96. Princeton: Princeton University Press.

Williams, Bernard. 2005d. 'Human Rights and Relativism'. In *In the Beginning Was the Deed: Realism and Moralism in Political Argument*. Edited by Geoffrey Hawthorne, 62–74. Princeton: Princeton University Press.

Williams, Bernard. 2005e. 'In the Beginning Was the Deed'. In *In the Beginning Was the Deed: Realism and Moralism in Political Argument*. Edited by Geoffrey Hawthorne, 18–28. Princeton: Princeton University Press.

Williams, Bernard. 2005f. 'The Liberalism of Fear'. In *In the Beginning Was the Deed: Realism and Moralism in Political Argument*. Edited by Geoffrey Hawthorne, 52–61. Princeton: Princeton University Press.

Williams, Bernard. 2005g. 'Modernity and the Substance of Ethical Life'. In *In the Beginning Was the Deed: Realism and Moralism in Political Argument*. Edited by Geoffrey Hawthorne, 40–51. Princeton: Princeton University Press.

Williams, Bernard. 2005h. 'Pluralism, Community and Left Wittgensteinianism'. In *In the Beginning Was the Deed: Realism and Moralism in Political Argument*. Edited by Geoffrey Hawthorne, 29–39. Princeton: Princeton University Press.
Williams, Bernard. 2005i. 'Realism and Moralism in Political Theory'. In *In the Beginning Was the Deed: Realism and Moralism in Political Argument*. Edited by Geoffrey Hawthorne, 1–17. Princeton: Princeton University Press.
Williams, Bernard. 2005j. 'Toleration, a Political or Moral Question?'. In *In the Beginning Was the Deed: Realism and Moralism in Political Argument*. Edited by Geoffrey Hawthorne, 128–38. Princeton: Princeton University Press.
Williams, Bernard. 2006a. 'The Actus Reus of Dr. Caligari'. In *Philosophy as a Humanistic Discipline*. Edited by A. W. Moore, 97–108. Princeton: Princeton University Press.
Williams, Bernard. 2006b. 'An Essay on Collingwood'. In *The Sense of the Past: Essays in the History of Philosophy*. Edited by Myles Burnyeat, 341–60. Princeton: Princeton University Press.
Williams, Bernard. 2006c. 'The Human Prejudice'. In *Philosophy as a Humanistic Discipline*. Edited by Adrian W. Moore, 135–54. Princeton: Princeton University Press.
Williams, Bernard. 2006d. 'The Legacy of Greek Philosophy'. In *The Sense of the Past: Essays in the History of Philosophy*. Edited by Myles Burnyeat, 3–48. Princeton: Princeton University Press.
Williams, Bernard. 2006e. 'Moral Responsibility and Political Freedom'. In *Philosophy as a Humanistic Discipline*. Edited by A. W. Moore, 119–25. Princeton: Princeton University Press.
Williams, Bernard. 2006f. 'Pagan Justice and Christian Love'. In *The Sense of the Past: Essays in the History of Philosophy*. Edited by Myles Burnyeat, 71–82. Princeton: Princeton University Press.
Williams, Bernard. 2006g. 'Philosophy as a Humanistic Discipline'. In *Philosophy as a Humanistic Discipline*. Edited by Adrian W. Moore, 180–99. Princeton: Princeton University Press.
Williams, Bernard. 2006h. 'Political Philosophy and the Analytical Tradition'. In *Philosophy as a Humanistic Discipline*. Edited by A. W. Moore, 155–68. Princeton: Princeton University Press.
Williams, Bernard. 2006i. 'The Primacy of Dispositions'. In *Philosophy as a Humanistic Discipline*. Edited by A. W. Moore, 67–75. Princeton: Princeton University Press.
Williams, Bernard. 2006j. 'The Structure of Hare's Theory'. In *Philosophy as a Humanistic Discipline*. Edited by A. W. Moore, 76–85. Princeton: Princeton University Press.
Williams, Bernard. 2006k. 'Subjectivism and Toleration'. In *Philosophy as a Humanistic Discipline*. Edited by Adrian W. Moore, 86–96. Princeton: Princeton University Press.
Williams, Bernard. 2006l. 'Tolerating the Intolerable'. In *Philosophy as a Humanistic Discipline*. Edited by A. W. Moore, 126–34. Princeton: Princeton University Press.
Williams, Bernard. 2006m. 'Values, Reasons, and the Theory of Persuasion'. In *Philosophy as a Humanistic Discipline*. Edited by A. W. Moore, 109–18. Princeton: Princeton University Press.
Williams, Bernard. 2009. 'A Mistrustful Animal'. In *Conversations on Ethics*. Edited by Alex Voorhoeve, 195–214. Oxford: Oxford University Press.
Williams, Bernard. 2010. 'Who Needs Ethical Knowledge?'. *Royal Institute of Philosophy Supplement* 35: 213–22.
Williams, Bernard. 2013. 'Introduction'. In *Concepts and Categories: Philosophical Essays*. Edited by Henry Hardy. 2nd ed., xxix–xxxix. Princeton: Princeton University Press.
Williams, Bernard. 2014a. 'Intellectuals, by Paul Johnson'. In *Essays and Reviews 1959–2002*. Edited by Michael Wood, 288–95. Princeton: Princeton University Press.
Williams, Bernard. 2014b. 'The Last Word, by Thomas Nagel'. In *Essays and Reviews 1959–2002*. Edited by Michael Wood, 371–87. Princeton: Princeton University Press.
Williams, Bernard. 2014c. 'The Logic of Abortion'. In *Essays and Reviews 1959–2002*. Edited by Michael Wood, 146–52. Princeton: Princeton University Press.
Williams, Bernard. 2014d. 'A Matter of Principle, by Ronald Dworkin'. In *Essays and Reviews 1959–2002*. Edited by Michael Wood, 256–61. Princeton: Princeton University Press.

Williams, Bernard. 2014e. 'Realism with a Human Face, by Hilary Putnam'. In *Essays and Reviews 1959–2002*. Edited by Michael Wood, 320–6. Princeton: Princeton University Press.

Williams, Bernard. 2014f. 'Sense and Sensibilia and Philosophical Papers, by J. L. Austin'. In *Essays and Reviews 1959–2002*. Edited by Michael Wood, 40–5. Princeton: Princeton University Press.

Williams, Bernard. 2014g. 'Why Philosophy Needs History'. In *Essays and Reviews 1959–2002*. Edited by Michael Wood, 405–12. Princeton: Princeton University Press.

Williams, Bernard. 2019. 'Left-Wing Wittgenstein'. *Common Knowledge* 25 (1–3): 321–31.

Williams, Bernard. 2021. 'Ethics, A Matter of Style? Introduction to the French Edition'. *Philosophical Inquiries* 9 (2): 269–84.

Williams, Michael. 2010. 'Pragmatism, Minimalism, Expressivism'. *International Journal of Philosophical Studies* 18 (3): 317–30.

Williams, Michael. 2013. 'How Pragmatists Can Be Local Expressivists'. In *Expressivism, Pragmatism and Representationalism*. Edited by Huw Price, 128–44. Cambridge: Cambridge University Press.

Williams, Robert. A. 2012. *Tragedy, Recognition, and the Death of God: Studies in Hegel and Nietzsche*. Oxford: Oxford University Press.

Williamson, Timothy. 2000. *Knowledge and Its Limits*. Oxford: Oxford University Press.

Williamson, Timothy. 2003. 'Understanding and Inference'. *Proceedings of the Aristotelian Society Supplementary Volume* 77 (1): 249–93.

Williamson, Timothy. 2017. 'Model-Building in Philosophy'. In *Philosophy's Future: The Problem of Philosophical Progress*. Edited by Russell Blackford and Damien Broderick, 159–72. Hoboken, NJ: Wiley-Blackwell.

Williamson, Timothy. 2018a. *Doing Philosophy: From Common Curiosity to Logical Reasoning*. Oxford: Oxford University Press.

Williamson, Timothy. 2018b. 'Model-Building as a Philosophical Method'. *Phenomenology and Mind* 15: 16–22.

Williamson, Timothy. 2020. *Philosophical Method: A Very Short Introduction*. Oxford: Oxford University Press.

Wilson, George, and Samuel Shpall. 2012. 'Action'. In *The Stanford Encyclopedia of Philosophy*. Edited by Edward N. Zalta. Winter 2016 ed.

Wilson, John Cook. 1926. *Statement and Inference*. Edited by A. S. L. Farquharson. Oxford: Clarendon Press.

Wilson, Mark. 2006. *Wandering Significance: An Essay on Conceptual Behavior*. Oxford: Clarendon Press.

Winch, Peter. 1958. *The Idea of a Social Science and Its Relation to Philosophy*. London: Routledge.

Wittgenstein, Ludwig. 1958. *The Blue and Brown Books: Preliminary Studies for the Philosophical Investigations*. Oxford: Blackwell.

Wittgenstein, Ludwig. 1966. *Lectures and Conversations on Aesthetics, Psychology and Religious Beliefs: Compiled from Notes Taken by Yorick Smythies, Rush Rhees and James Taylor*. Edited by C. Barrett. Oxford: Blackwell.

Wittgenstein, Ludwig. 1969. *On Certainty*. Edited by G. E. M. Anscombe and G. H. von Wright. Oxford: Blackwell.

Wittgenstein, Ludwig. 1974. *Philosophical Grammar*. Edited by R. Rhees. Oxford: Blackwell.

Wittgenstein, Ludwig. 1975. *Philosophical Remarks*. Translated by Raymond Hargreaves and Roger White. Edited by Rush Rhees. Oxford: Blackwell.

Wittgenstein, Ludwig. 1978. *Remarks on the Foundations of Mathematics*. Edited by G. H. von Wright, R. Rhees, and G. E. M. Anscombe. 3rd ed. Oxford: Blackwell.

Wittgenstein, Ludwig. 1979. *Wittgenstein's Lectures: Cambridge 1932–35. (From the notes of Alice Ambrose and Margaret Macdonald)*. Edited by Alice Ambrose. Oxford: Blackwell.

Wittgenstein, Ludwig. 1981. *Zettel*. Edited by G. E. M. Anscombe and G. H. von Wright. 2nd ed. Oxford: Blackwell.

Wittgenstein, Ludwig. 2000. *Wittgenstein's Nachlass. The Bergen Electronic Edition*. Edited by The Wittgenstein Archives at the University of Bergen. Oxford: Oxford University Press.

Wittgenstein, Ludwig. 2005. *The Big Typescript*. Edited by C. Grant Luckhardt and Maximilian A. E. Aue. Oxford: Blackwell.
Wittgenstein, Ludwig. 2009. *Philosophische Untersuchungen = Philosophical Investigations*. Translated by G. E. M. Anscombe, P. M. S. Hacker, and Joachim Schulte. Edited by P. M. S. Hacker and J. Schulte. Rev. 4th ed. Chichester: Wiley-Blackwell.
Wodak, Daniel. 2019. 'Mere Formalities: Fictional Normativity and Normative Authority'. *Canadian Journal of Philosophy* 49 (6): 828–50.
Wolcher, Louis E. 2008. *Law's Task: The Tragic Circle of Law, Justice and Human Suffering*. Aldershot: Ashgate.
Wolf, Susan. 2010. *Meaning in Life and Why It Matters*. Princeton: Princeton University Press.
Wolf, Susan. 2015a. 'Good-for-Nothings'. In *The Variety of Values: Essays on Morality, Meaning, and Love*, 67–85. New York: Oxford University Press.
Wolf, Susan. 2015b. 'Loving Attention'. In *The Variety of Values: Essays on Morality, Meaning, and Love*, 163–80. New York: Oxford University Press.
Wolf, William Clark. 2020. 'The Authority of Conceptual Analysis in Hegelian Ethical Life'. In *An Ethical Modernity? Hegel's Concept of Ethical Life Today—Its Limits and Potential*. Edited by Tereza Matějčková and Jiří Chotaš, 15–35. Leiden: Brill.
Wollstonecraft, Mary. 2014. *A Vindication of the Rights of Woman*. Edited by Eileen Hunt Botting. New Haven: Yale University Press.
Wong, David B. 1991. 'Is There a Distinction between Reason and Emotion in Mencius?'. *Philosophy East and West* 41 (1): 31–44.
Wong, David B. 2006. *Natural Moralities: A Defense of Pluralistic Relativism*. New York: Oxford University Press.
Wood, A. W. 2010. 'Respect and Recognition'. In *The Routledge Companion to Ethics*. Edited by John Skorupski, 562–72. London: Routledge.
Woodward, James. 2003. *Making Things Happen: A Theory of Causal Explanation*. New York: Oxford University Press.
Wright, Crispin. 1992. *Truth and Objectivity*. Cambridge, MA: Harvard University Press.
Yablo, Stephen. 1993. 'Hop, Skip and Jump: The Agonistic Conception of Truth'. *Philosophical Perspectives* 7 (Language and Logic): 371–96.
Yablo, Stephen. 2006. 'Non-Catastrophic Presupposition Failure'. In *Content and Modality: Themes from the Philosophy of Robert Stalnaker*. Edited by Judith Thomson and Alex Byrne, 164–90. Oxford: Oxford University Press.
Yap, Audrey. 2022. 'Conceptual Engineering and Neurath's Boat: A Return to the Political Roots of Logical Empiricism'. In *The Political Turn in Analytic Philosophy: Reflections on Social Injustice and Oppression*. Edited by David Bordonaba Plou, Víctor Fernández Castro, and José Ramón Torices, 31–52. Berlin: De Gruyter.
Yeager, Daniel Brian. 2006. *J. L. Austin and the Law: Exculpation and the Explication of Responsibility*. Lewisburg: Bucknell University Press.
Zacka, Bernardo. 2017. *When the State Meets the Street: Public Service and Moral Agency*. Cambridge, MA: Harvard University Press.
Zagzebski, Linda Trinkaus. 1996. *The Dilemma of Freedom and Foreknowledge*. Oxford: Oxford University Press.
Zagzebski, Linda. 2015. 'Omniscience and the Arrow of Time'. In *Freedom, Fatalism, and Foreknowledge*. Edited by John Martin Fischer and Patrick Todd, 189–208. New York: Oxford University Press.
Zalta, Edward N. 2001. 'Fregean Senses, Modes of Presentation, and Concepts'. *Philosophical Perspectives* 15: 335–59.
Zawidzki, Tadeusz Wieslaw. 2013. *Mindshaping: A New Framework for Understanding Human Social Cognition*. Cambridge, MA: MIT Press.
Zimmerman, Michael J. 2002. 'Taking Luck Seriously'. *Journal of Philosophy* 99 (11): 553–76.
Zuboff, Shoshana. 2015. 'Big Other: Surveillance Capitalism and the Prospects of an Information Civilization'. *Journal of Information Technology* 30 (1): 75–89.
Zuboff, Shoshana. 2019. *The Age of Surveillance Capitalism: The Fight for a Human Future at the New Frontier of Power*. London: Profile Books.

Index

Since the index has been created to work across multiple formats, indexed terms for which a page range is given (e.g., 52–53, 66–70, etc.) may occasionally appear only on some, but not all of the pages within the range.

adaequatio intellectus ad rem 57 (*see also* worldly structure)
Aeschylus 46–7, 47 n.33
Agamemnon 46–7, 315–16
Anscombe, Gertrude Elizabeth Margaret 222–3, 259, 308–10, 309 n.6, 312 n.12, 315, 324–6, 324 n.27
anti-psychologism 80–3
arbitrariness of grammar 18–19, 127–8, 127 n.20, 281–3
Archimedean urge 123–5
aspectival captivity 89–90
  vs. ideological captivity 89–90
Augustine 272–3
authenticity 22–3, 125–6, 126 n.18, 137, 199, 275
authority 31–4, 273–85
  authority question 31–2
  linguistic expressions of the authority question 43–7
  of use vs. in use 33
  what prompts the authority question 47–53
autoethnographic stance 65–6
Austin, John Langshaw 129 n.22, 131, 131 n.27

Berlin, Isaiah 162 n.35, 173 n.56, 181–9, 185 n.12, 185 n.10, 193, 348
Brandom, Robert 1 n.1, 15, 32–3, 37–8, 41, 87 n.4, 105

Carnap, Rudolf 44 n.30, 81–2, 127–8, 127 n.20, 133, 147–8, 148 n.12, 165, 175–6
carving at the joints. *See* worldly structure
causation 222, 245
circularity 135–8, 258
concepts
  conceptual architecture 35–9, 43
  imprisonment by 10, 13, 18–19, 62–3
  loss of 84–5, 106–7
  nature of 78
  possession of 77–8
  power of 34–43
  vs. reasons 39–40
conceptual ethics. *See* ethics of conceptualization
conceptual needs 20–3, 135–43, 213–23
concerns, definition of 194–6
  critique of 196–200
confidence 85–8
  vindicable 89
  vindicated 89
  vindication vs. justification 2, 89–90
conflicts of values 23, 50–1, 130, 152–64, 182–9, 191–4, 201–5, 343, 360–3, 370–2
consequentialism 263–4, 375
contingency 93, 118–27, 138–43
  causal 93–5
  rational 95

Descartes, René 49–50, 113–14, 123, 123 n.15, 146, 148, 307–8, 330, 330 n.35
Diamond, Cora 34, 40
Dworkin, Ronald 31, 33–4, 47, 133–4, 181–94, 230–1, 235, 346–56, 360–3, 370–1

Eco, Umberto 130
emotions 34, 63–6, 86–8, 199, 330
engaged concept use 61
  vs. disengaged use 61
  vs. disengaged non-use 66
ergonomics, conceptual 247–8
ethics of conceptualization 21–2
  definition 14, 76–80
  vs. conceptual ethics 14
  vs. morality of conceptualization 299
ethnographic stance 63
existence claims 53–9
expressive character of concepts 199, 223–30

foundationalism 113–18
  counterfactual 120–1
framing inquiry 51
framing effects 7–10

Frankfurt, Harry 216–18, 296–7, 297 n.46
free will 304, 307–11, 318, 332–42 (*see also* voluntariness)
Frege, Gottlob 55, 75–6, 76 n.20, 79 n.29, 80, 205, 205 n.37
Freud, Sigmund 49–50
Fricker, Miranda 10, 86, 98 n.17, 140–3

Geertz, Clifford 2 n.2, 3 n.4, 62–3, 65
genealogy 235–6
gerrymandering, conceptual 23, 48–9, 144, 147, 164, 239–40
Goodman, Nelson 36 n.15, 57, 175–6
Grotius, Hugo 17
grue 57, 175–6

Hart, Herbert Lionel Adolphus 187–8, 206 n.41, 320 n.20, 321–3, 321 n.21, 323 n.23, 325
hermeneutical injustice 10
Hobbes, Thomas 17, 49–50, 308 n.2
holism 18–19, 69, 127–36, 221, 260, 378
honour, concept of 252–4
Horkheimer, Max 31–2

ideological 173–4, 195–6, 211, 224, 274, 274 n.20, 318
ideology critique. *See* ideological
inferentialism 5, 38 n.20, 41, 119 n.8
inferential consequences 4–6
instrumentalism 264–7
irony 118–22

James, William 57 n.58, 145, 308–9

Kant, Immanuel 1 n.1, 16–17, 16 n.30, 24–5, 33 n.7, 140–1, 170, 172, 174, 188–9, 282, 299–300, 334–5, 339–40, 369–70, 375
knowledge
  needs-based appraisal of the concept of 241–8
  destruction of knowledge by reflection 100–6
  metaconceptual knowledge 108–10, 278–9
  non-relational conception of metaconceptual knowledge 109
  relational conception of metaconceptual knowledge 110
  under concepts 100–7
Korsgaard, Christine 16 n.30, 53–4

legitimacy. *See* authority
liberty 11–12, 182–93, 202–3, 235, 343, 346–72
La Boétie, Étienne de 318
Lovibond, Sabina 51–4, 52 n.42
luck, moral 16 n.27, 169–70, 188–9, 321, 327–41

Marcuse, Herbert 206–8
metalinguistic negotiation 45
Mill, John Stuart 42, 53 n.46, 94, 307–8
Montaigne, Michel de 71
morality system 25 n.40, 70, 311 n.11, 329 n.33
Murdoch, Iris 3 n.4, 6, 8, 10, 35–6, 43, 53 n.47, 106–7, 107 n.26, 298, 302, 328

Nagel, Thomas 67, 163 n.38, 177–8
natural kind 21, 79, 117 n.7, 147, 190 n.22, 239, 294–5 (*see also* worldly structure)
need matrix 22, 231–48, 369–72
  parametric 369
needs, conceptual 214–19
  vs. goals 22
Nietzsche, Friedrich 4–5, 13, 24–5, 39, 47, 121, 130, 132–5, 162–4, 186–7, 213–14, 223, 226, 229–30, 339, 339 n.44, 341–2, 373–4
non-foundationalism 122–7
normativity of concepts 32–4, 82–3, 152–4
  (*see also* authority in use)

Orwell, George 145, 205, 207

Pascal, Blaise 123
Peirce, Charles Sanders 47
perspective 122–7 (*see also* contingency)
Pettit, Philip 11–12, 140–3, 235–6
Plato 16 n.27, 17–18, 47, 49–50, 115, 328, 334
pluralism about values 184–6
pragmatic encroachment 286
progress 42–3, 54, 85, 106–7, 175, 298, 302
Pufendorf, Samuel von 17

Raz, Joseph 10–11, 283–5
Rorty, Richard 118–22, 281 n.28
Rousseau, Jean-Jacques 357, 363
Russell, Bertrand 53–5, 55 n.55, 131, 308–9
Ryle, Gilbert 40, 75–6, 308–9
rationalism 16–17, 172–8, 258–9, 282–3, 374
reasons for concept use 2–3, 13, 256–62, 267–9
reflective equilibrium 175–8
relativism 64, 71–3, 75, 84, 97–100, 278–81
  of distance 97–9
  vs. relationalism 276–7

second-order reasons. *See* reasons for concept use
Sellars, Wilfrid 4–5, 15–16, 81, 271 n.17
Sider, Theodore 4, 57–8, 58 n.60, 115, 277
Skinner, Quentin 11–12, 15–16, 94–5, 235–6
Spinoza, Baruch 47
Stoicism 93 n.9, 113–14, 176–7, 188–9, 189 n.19, 330, 331 n.38, 339, 363

Strawson, Peter Frederick 55, 67, 136, 140–1, 185–6, 220, 266, 311 n.9
superficiality, conceptual 23, 26–7, 56, 149–52, 307–42, 378–9
systematicity 172–3, 175–8, 365, 369–72

tensions, conceptual 50–1, 128, 134, 143–4, 152–64, 194, 204, 371 (*see also* conflicts of values)
thick concepts 3–4, 34–43, 60–2, 71, 79, 92, 101–9, 115–19, 124–30, 139, 170–8, 193–202, 224–5, 269–82, 284, 288, 294–5, 325–6, 356, 366–75

utilitarianism 50, 170, 172, 174–5, 188–9, 285, 287–99, 369–70, 374 n.32, 375

vagueness, value of 205–8
voluntariness 304, 307–42
  definition of 325

voluntarism 18–19, 127–9, 127 n.20, 281–3
  (*see also* arbitrariness of grammar)

Wilde, Oscar 52–4, 104–5
Williams, Bernard 3–4, 17–18, 25, 36, 43, 50–1, 63–5, 70, 77, 85, 97–110, 119–20, 123–5, 139, 145, 170–4, 181–96, 199–200, 219, 235, 270, 277–8, 299, 302, 310–11, 314–20, 324–9, 333, 337–40, 346–68, 373–4
Wittgenstein, Ludwig 10, 12–15, 35 n.11, 45–7, 57–8, 64, 73 n.18, 116 n.5, 127–30, 127 n.20, 128 n.21, 133, 153–4, 157, 200, 205, 222–3, 258, 267, 292, 308–9
Wolf, Susan 297, 300–4
worldly structure 21–2, 57–9, 115–18, 277
  (*see also* natural kind)
wrong kind of reason worry,
  epistemological version 292–5
  deontological version 295–300